MASSES IN FLIGHT

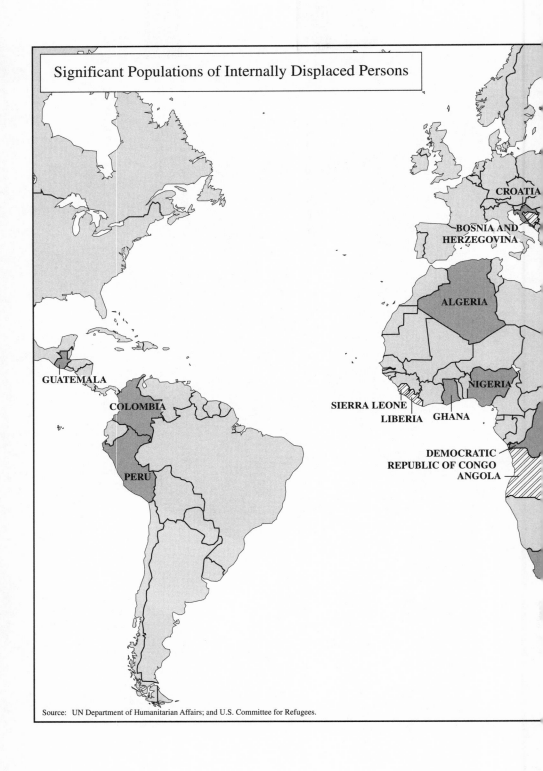

Significant Populations of Internally Displaced Persons

CROATIA

BOSNIA AND HERZEGOVINA

ALGERIA

GUATEMALA

NIGERIA

COLOMBIA

SIERRA LEONE

LIBERIA   GHANA

PERU

DEMOCRATIC
REPUBLIC OF CONGO
ANGOLA

Source: UN Department of Humanitarian Affairs; and U.S. Committee for Refugees.

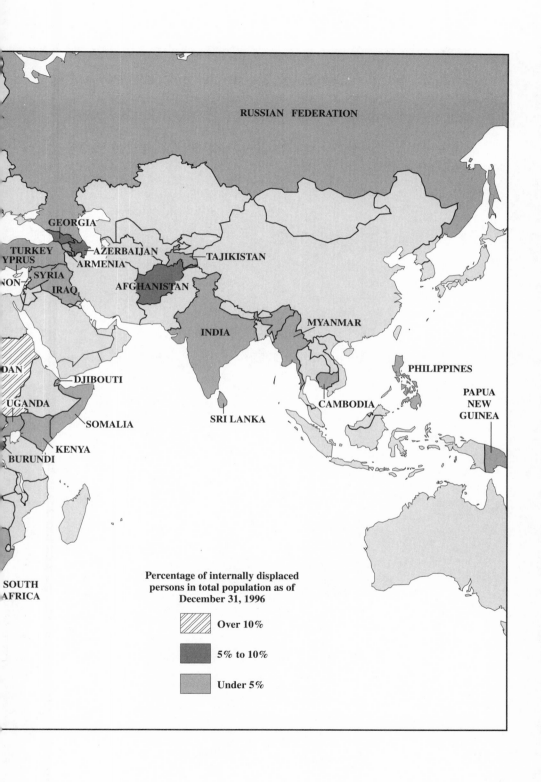

RUSSIAN FEDERATION

GEORGIA
TURKEY
YPRUS · AZERBAIJAN
ARMENIA · TAJIKISTAN
NON · SYRIA
IRAQ · AFGHANISTAN

MYANMAR
INDIA

PHILIPPINES

DAN · DJIBOUTI

UGANDA · PAPUA
NEW
GUINEA
SOMALIA · SRI LANKA · CAMBODIA

KENYA
BURUNDI

SOUTH
AFRICA

Percentage of internally displaced
persons in total population as of
December 31, 1996

Over 10%

5% to 10%

Under 5%

MASSES IN FLIGHT

The Global Crisis of
Internal Displacement

ROBERTA COHEN AND FRANCIS M. DENG

BROOKINGS INSTITUTION PRESS
Washington, D.C.

Copyright © 1998
The Brookings Institution
1775 Massachusetts Avenue, N.W., Washington, D.C. 20036

Library of Congress Cataloging-in-Publication data:

Cohen, Roberta
    Masses in flight : the global crisis of internal displacement /
Roberta Cohen and Francis M. Deng.
        p.   cm.
    Includes bibliographical references and index.
    ISBN 0-8157-1512-9 (cloth : alk. paper)
    ISBN 0-8157-1511-0 (pbk. : alk. paper)
    1. Refugees.   2. Migration, Internal.   3. Forced migration.   4.
Humanitarian assistance.   I. Deng, Francis Mading, 1938–   II. Title.
HV640 .C614   1998
304.8—ddc21   98-8939
                                                                        CIP

9 8 7 6 5 4 3 2 1

The paper used in this publication meets the minimum requirements of the American
National Standard for Information Sciences—Permanence of Paper for Printed Library
Materials, ANSI Z39.48—1984.

Set in Times Roman

Composition by Harlowe Typography Inc.
Cottage City, Maryland

Printed by R. R. Donnelley & Sons Co.
Harrisonburg, Virginia

Foreword

SINCE THE END of the cold war, increasing numbers of persons in Africa, Asia, Europe, and Latin America have been forced to leave their homes as a result of armed conflicts, internal strife, and systematic violations of human rights. Unlike refugees, who cross a border and have access to an established system of international protection and assistance, internally displaced persons remain within their own countries, without legal or institutional bases for receiving protection from the international community. For this very reason, internal displacement poses a challenge to the international community to develop norms, institutions, and operational strategies for preventing such dislocation, addressing its consequences, and finding durable solutions.

The international community's recognition of the magnitude of the crisis and the urgent need for action led the secretary-general of the United Nations, at the request of the Commission on Human Rights, to appoint a representative on internally displaced persons in 1992. The assignment was given to Francis M. Deng, senior fellow in the Foreign Policy Studies program of the Brookings Institution and former Sudanese diplomat. The idea for this study emerged from discussions between former Secretary-General Boutros Boutros-Ghali and the representative. The secretary-general asked Deng, apart from the normal requirements of his mandate, to conduct, in partnership with independent research institutions, an in-depth examination of the problem of internal displacement and develop a comprehensive global strategy for providing effective protection, assistance, and reintegration and development support for the internally displaced.

In response to this request, the Brookings Institution developed a collaborative project with the Refugee Policy Group (RPG), an independent center for policy research and analysis concerning refugee and related humanitarian emergency issues. Roberta Cohen, senior adviser to RPG and guest scholar at the Brookings Institution, joined the project as associate and then co-director.

Two studies have emerged from the project: the present volume and an edited volume of case studies, *The Forsaken People: Case Studies of the Internally Displaced*, prepared by leading experts and academics. Their findings, although published separately, have been infused in the current text.

The authors of this volume come to their subject from different, but complementary, backgrounds. Francis Deng, who directs the Africa project at the Brookings Institution, has had a distinguished diplomatic career. Before leaving the Sudanese diplomatic service in 1983, he served as ambassador to Canada, the Scandinavian countries, and the United States and as minister of state for foreign affairs. Among other activities, he is currently acting chairman of the Africa Leadership Forum, substituting for the founding chairman, General Olusegun Obasanjo, former head of state of Nigeria, who remains a political prisoner in his country. Roberta Cohen has held senior positions on human rights in nongovernmental organizations (NGOs) and in the U.S. government, where she served as deputy assistant secretary of state and senior adviser to the U.S. delegation to the United Nations. She has also served as consultant to international organizations and NGOs on humanitarian and refugee issues and played a major role in bringing the subject of internal displacement onto the agenda of the Commission on Human Rights.

Leading UN agencies and departments, including the Department of Humanitarian Affairs, the UN High Commissioner for Refugees, the UN Development Programme, and the Office of the High Commissioner for Human Rights, endorsed the undertaking of this project, and their staffs provided important information and materials for the work. Current UN Secretary-General Kofi Annan expresses his support for the project in the preface to this study. Regional organizations, in particular the Organization of African Unity, the Inter-American Commission on Human Rights of the Organization of American States, and the Organization for Security and Cooperation in Europe, provided encouragement and information for this study.

Because of the complex nature of internal displacement and the inter-disciplinary approaches required to address the problem, the study also relied upon and benefited enormously from the contributions of a wide range of nongovernmental organizations and research and academic institutions. The U.S. Committee for Refugees developed statistical information for the study and contributed substantially to the global overview of the problem. The Refugee Policy Group contributed to the analysis of institutional mechanisms and arrangements for addressing the protection, assistance, and development needs of internally displaced persons. The American Society of International Law, the Ludwig Boltzmann Institute of Human Rights of the University of Vienna, the International Human Rights Law Group, the Washington College of Law of American University, and the University of Bern contributed resources and efforts to the development of a legal framework for the internally displaced. The International Committee of the Red Cross, the UN High Commissioner for Refugees, and other UN agencies and NGOs also contributed to the legal analysis. The Norwegian Refugee Council organized the research work on NGOs. World Bank staff assisted with reintegration and development strategies.

In particular, the authors wish to express appreciation to the following individuals for their direct and active involvement in the preparation of different parts of the study: Tom Argent, Jacques Cuenod, Jean-François Durieux, Jeff Drumtra, Bill Frelick, Dennis Gallagher, Robert Kogod Goldman, Virginia Hamilton, Daniel Helle, Steven Holtzman, Walter Kälin, David A. Korn, Curtis Lambrecht, Jean-Philippe Lavoyer, Terrence Lyons, Jennifer McLean, Cecile Meijer, Erin Mooney, Trygve Nordby, Manfred Nowak, Toni Pfanner, Hiram Ruiz, Maria Stavropoulou, and Roger Winter. They are particularly grateful to John D. Steinbruner, former director of the Foreign Policy Studies program, who encouraged the development of the study, and to the current director, Richard N. Haass, for his support of the study and his valuable comments.

The authors are also grateful for the information, advice, or support provided by Michael Amitay, Dee Dee Angegaw, Hrair Balian, David Bassiouni, Pierre Bertrand, Jan Borgen, Philippe Boullé, Paul Brandrup, Rachel Brett, Claude Bruderlein, Ulrike von Buchwald, Edward Cain, Antonio Augusto Cancado Trindade, Burgess Carr, Bertrand Coppens, Jeff Crisp, Lance Clark, Alvaro De Soto, Manuel Da Silva, Juergen Dedring, Otto Denes, Adama Dieng, Janelle Diller, Alan Doss, Quazi

Shaukat Fareed, Nigel Fisher, Carlo Flue, Ann Forrester, Leonardo Franco, Felice Gaer, Pierce Garety, Thomas Greene, Martin Griffiths, Iain Guest, Steven Hansch, Sigrid Higgins, William Hyde, Bernd Kass, Zdzislaw Kedzia, Randolph Kent, Charlotte Ku, Hanne Lund Madsen, Ian Martin, Georges Mautner-Markoff, Peter McDermott, Gay McDougall, Dennis McNamara, Sergio Vieira de Mello, Larry Minear, Michel Moussalli, Ngung Mpotsch, Charles LaMunière, Binaifer Nowrojee, Liliana Obregón, Philip O'Brien, Herbert Okun, David Padilla, Amir Pasic, Diane Paul, Richard Perruchoud, Soren Jessen Petersen, John Rogge, Sharon Rusu, Peter Schatzer, Annette Scheckler, Erika Schlager, Colin Scott, H. L. Seneviratne, Khalid Shibib, Harald Siem, John Stremlau, Astri Suhrke, Serge Telle, Hans Thoolen, Edward Tsui, Bhim Udas, Michel Veuthey, Gerald Walzer, Thomas Weiss, Tim Wichert, and Cristina Zeledon.

Expert research assistance was provided by Peter Bach, Frederik Holst, Curtis Lambrecht, Jennifer McLean, Rochus Pronk, Heidi Worley, and Ellen Zeisler. Editing was done by Venka Macintyre. David Hammond proofread the pages, and Julia Petrakis provided the index.

Because of the unusual nature, diversity, and remoteness of the sources in the research conducted outside Brookings, the manuscript has not been subjected to the verification procedures established for research publications of the Brookings Institution. Nonetheless, the authors have made a concerted effort to provide citations where they are needed and to ensure that they are as accurate and complete as possible.

Finally, Brookings gratefully acknowledges the financial support of the project's funders. They not only made the study possible but supported the authors' concurrent efforts to strengthen international and regional arrangements for the internally displaced. Since the project's inception, we have received generous support from the Office of the UN Secretary-General, the Ford Foundation, the McKnight Foundation, the Rockefeller Brothers Fund, and the governments of Austria, the Netherlands, Norway, and Sweden.

The views expressed in this book are those of the authors and should not be ascribed to the people or organizations whose assistance is acknowledged above, or to the trustees, officers, and other staff members of the Brookings Institution.

Michael H. Armacost
President

March 1998
Washington, D.C.

Contents

Preface, by Kofi Annan   xix

1. Introduction   1

2. Global Overview   15
   Framing a Definition   16
   Causes of Internal Displacement   19
   Impact of Displacement   23
   Internally Displaced Persons as a Special Category   26
   Why Internally Displaced Persons Do Not Become Refugees   29
   Statistics on Internally Displaced Persons   31
   When Does Displacement End?   35
   Regional Dynamics   39
   Conclusion   71

3. Legal Framework   73
   Applicable Law in Recognized Situations   77
   Protection against Forced Displacement   85
   Protecting the Particular Needs of Internally Displaced
     Persons   92
   International Provision of Humanitarian Assistance   113
   Conclusion   122

4. Institutional Arrangements   126
   Mandates and Capacities of Operational Organizations   128
   Coordination by the Emergency Relief Coordinator   143
   UN Human Rights System   151

Representative of the Secretary-General on Internally Displaced
   Persons   *156*
Gaps in the International System   *159*
Options for Institutional Reform   *168*
Steps to Improve the Current System   *172*
Conclusion   *184*

5. The Role of Nongovernmental Organizations   187
Selection of NGOs   *189*
Mandates and Policies on Internally Displaced Persons   *189*
Definitional Issues   *191*
Scope of Assistance Activities and the Need for Coordination   *191*
Improving NGO Practices   *193*
Protection and Human Rights Concerns   *195*
Promoting Durable Solutions   *207*
Conclusion   *209*

6. Regional Responses   213
Africa: Grappling with Sovereignty   *214*
Europe: Preventive Diplomacy   *223*
The Americas: Institutional Innovations   *228*
The Middle East: A Narrow Focus   *232*
Asia: Organizational Vacuum   *234*
Conclusion   *236*

7. Strategies and Recommendations   239
Preventive Strategies   *240*
Protection Integrated with Assistance   *254*
Enforcement Measures When Human Rights Abuses Are Gross
   and Systematic   *280*
Solutions   *284*
Conclusion   *303*

Appendix: Proposed Guiding Principles on Internal
            Displacement   305

Notes   317

Index   401

Acronyms

ASEAN	Association of Southeast Asian Nations
CAP	consolidated appeals process (UN)
CCPR	Covenant on Civil and Political Rights
CDR	Centre for Documentation on Refugees
CEDAW	Convention on the Elimination of Discrimination against Women
CESCR	Covenant on Economic, Social and Cultural Rights
CIREFCA	International Conference on Central American Refugees
CIS	Commonwealth of Independent States
CONDEG	National Council of the Displaced in Guatemala
CPDIA	Permanent Consultation on Internal Displacement in the Americas
CPRs	Popular Communities of Resistance (Guatemala)
CRC	Convention on the Rights of the Child
CSCE	Conference on Security and Cooperation in Europe (replaced by OSCE)
DHA	Department of Humanitarian Affairs (UN, replaced by OCHA)
DMTs	disaster management teams (UN)
ECHA	Executive Committee on Humanitarian Affairs (UN)
ECOSOC	United Nations Economic and Social Council
ECOMOG	Economic Community of West Africa Monitoring Group
ECOWAS	Economic Community of West African States

ERC	Emergency Relief Coordinator (UN)
EU	European Union
EXCOM	Executive Committee of the High Commissioner's Programme (UNHCR)
HEWS	humanitarian early warning system, managed by OCHA
HRFOR	Human Rights Field Operation in Rwanda (UN)
IASC	Inter-Agency Standing Committee (UN)
ICJ	International Commission of Jurists
ICRC	International Committee of the Red Cross
ICVA	International Council of Voluntary Agencies
IDPs	internally displaced persons
IFRC	International Federation of Red Cross and Red Crescent Societies
IGAD	Inter-Governmental Authority on Development
IIDH	Inter-American Institute of Human Rights
ILO	International Labor Organization
IMF	International Monetary Fund
InterAction	American Council for Voluntary International Action
IOM	International Organization for Migration
JNA	Yugoslav People's Army
JRS	Jesuit Refugee Service
LAS	League of Arab States
LTTE	Liberation Tigers of Tamil Eelam (Sri Lanka)
LWF	Lutheran World Federation
MSF	Médecins sans Frontières
NATO	North Atlantic Treaty Organization
NGO	nongovernmental organization
NRC	Norwegian Refugee Council
OAS	Organization of American States
OAU	Organization of African Unity
OCHA	Office for the Coordination of Humanitarian Affairs (UN)
ODIHR	Office for Democratic Institutions and Human Rights (OSCE)
OECD	Organization for Economic Cooperation and Development
OSCE	Organization for Security and Cooperation in Europe
PAR	Proyecto de Apoyo a la Republación (Peru)

PARINAC	Partnership in Action (UNHCR program)
PKK	Kurdish Workers Party (Turkey)
PRODERE	UN Development Program for Displaced Persons, Refugees, and Returnees in Central America
QIPs	quick-impact projects
RPG	Refugee Policy Group
SAARC	South Asian Association for Regional Cooperation
SADC	Southern African Development Community
SARRED	Conference on the Plight of Refugees, Returnees, and Displaced Persons in Southern Africa
SLORC	State Law and Order Restoration Council (Myanmar)
UNAMIR	United Nations Assistance Mission for Rwanda
UNDP	United Nations Development Programme
UNEP	United Nations Environment Programme
UNHCR	United Nations High Commissioner for Refugees
UNICEF	United Nations Children's Fund
UNIFEM	United Nations Development Fund for Women
UNOMIG	United Nations Observer Mission in Georgia
UNOMIL	United Nations Observer Mission in Liberia
UNPROFOR	United Nations Protection Force (former Yugoslavia)
UNRWA	United Nations Relief and Works Agency
UNV	United Nations Volunteers
USCR	U.S. Committee for Refugees
WCC	World Council of Churches
WEU	West European Union
WFP	World Food Programme
WHO	World Health Organization

Preface

INTERNAL DISPLACEMENT has emerged as one of the great human tragedies of our time. It has also created an unprecedented challenge for the international community: to find ways to respond to what is essentially an internal crisis. The severity of the problem, both in intensity and scope, is obvious from the numbers of the displaced, now estimated at between 20 million and 25 million, and the fact that virtually no region of the world is spared from this epidemic. This study by Francis Deng and Roberta Cohen is one of the first in-depth looks at a problem of great concern to the international community.

Internal displacement is particularly tragic because of the physical, social, and psychological dangers and indignities to which it exposes innocent people. The usual causes of the most problematic type of displacement are themselves traumatic: violent conflicts, systematic violations of human rights, forced dislocation, and other man-made and natural disasters in which discrimination on a variety of grounds features conspicuously. Whether the victims are forced into camps, choose to hide away in uncharted territory, or merge into communities that are often equally ravaged, internal displacement nearly always has a devastating effect on families, cultures, jobs, education, and the security of a stable society. Above all, it denies innocent people access to food, shelter, and medicine and exposes them to all manner of violence. If left unaddressed, internal displacement not only causes internal instability but may spill across borders and upset external and regional stability. There is therefore a compelling need for the international community to strengthen its support for national efforts to assist and protect displaced populations.

Since the issue of internal displacement was first brought to the attention of the United Nations nearly a decade ago, the international community has been seeking ways to organize itself to meet this challenge. The International Committee of the Red Cross has long had a mandate in this area. And many other organizations, intergovernmental and nongovernmental, have broadened their mandates or scope of activities to cover the internally displaced. A number of governments have become more responsive by acknowledging that protecting and assisting affected populations under their control is their primary responsibility, and when they cannot discharge that responsibility for lack of capacity, they are becoming less reluctant to seek assistance from the international community.

As the representative of the secretary-general on internally displaced persons, Francis Deng has focused his attention on developing appropriate normative and institutional frameworks for the international protection and assistance of these populations. To this end, he has undertaken country missions to enter into dialogue with the governments and other authorities concerned. He has played a catalytic role in raising awareness of the problem and in promoting international support for the plight of internally displaced populations worldwide.

The present study offers proposals for filling the gaps in existing legal norms for the internally displaced. It rightly emphasizes that protection should be central to the international response and that assistance should be provided in a comprehensive way that brings together the humanitarian, human rights, and development components of the United Nations. It also demonstrates the importance of seeking political solutions to the conflicts and eliminating conditions that cause displacement. To judge from my own experience with peacekeeping operations, the United Nations is increasingly called upon to adopt a comprehensive approach aimed not only at keeping the peace but also at protecting civilian populations, monitoring human rights violations, facilitating the delivery of needed humanitarian assistance, and promoting lasting solutions that include reintegration, development, and transitions to democracy. Implementing these multidimensional mandates is clearly a challenge for the United Nations, which it cannot hope to meet without the full understanding and support of the governments concerned.

While the recommendations made in this study are those of the authors alone, I am confident that it will prove a valuable contribution to the formulation of specific measures for addressing the problem of internal displacement, particularly in the areas of protection, humanitarian assistance, and development. The resolution of these issues remains of the utmost importance, not only for the countries concerned but also for the international community. The challenge is indeed a formidable one. But it is also one to which the international community and the United Nations can respond effectively if they develop the necessary capability and wherever possible take preventive action to avert future tragedies.

Kofi Annan
Secretary-General of the United Nations

CHAPTER ONE

Introduction

We are clearly witnessing what is probably an irresistible shift in public attitudes towards the belief that the defense of the oppressed in the name of morality should prevail over frontiers and legal documents.
—Former UN Secretary-General Javier Perez de Cuellar, 1991

SINCE THE LATE 1980s a challenging issue has emerged on the international agenda: the global crisis of internal displacement. Between twenty and twenty-five million persons have been forced from their homes by armed conflicts, internal strife, systematic violations of human rights, and other causes traditionally associated with refuge across international borders. But unlike refugees, the internally displaced remain within the borders of their own countries, dispossessed by their governments and other controlling authorities and forced into a life of destitution and indignity. Their plight poses a challenge of humanitarian, political, and strategic dimensions. In some cases the degree of displacement may be so high that one can speak of whole societies becoming displaced. As the country falls into disarray, whether in part or in entirety, surrounding countries are affected as well. They may be forced to bear the brunt of refugee flows and cope with substantial political and economic disruptions. Violence and instability often spread through entire regions. These circumstances plead for regional and international responses, not only because of humanitarian and human rights concerns but also because of the collective interest in regional stability and global peace and security.

1

Of the world's populations at risk, internally displaced persons tend to be among the most desperate. They may be forcibly resettled on political or ethnic grounds or find themselves trapped in the midst of conflicts and in the direct path of armed attack and physical violence. On the run and without documents, they are easy targets for roundups, arbitrary detention, forced conscription, and sexual assaults. Uprooted from their homes and deprived of their resource base, many suffer from profound physical and psychological trauma. They are more often deprived of shelter, food, and health services than other members of the population. The U.S. Centers for Disease Control reports that death rates among the internally displaced have been as much as sixty times higher than those of nondisplaced within the same country. In fact, the highest mortality rates ever recorded during humanitarian emergencies have involved internally displaced persons.[1]

Their predicament, and the challenge it poses to the international community, is no less acute than the refugee crisis that confronted Europe in the aftermath of the Second World War. At that time, those displaced *outside* their countries became the focus of attention. A complex network of institutions, laws, and agreements came into being designed to protect persons who were forced to seek asylum on the territory of a foreign state. Humanitarian concerns, as well as reasons of practical political, economic, and strategic interest, made it imperative to establish a system of international protection and assistance for refugees. The position of United Nations High Commissioner for Refugees (UNHCR) was created in 1951, and a UN convention was adopted to protect persons forced from their homes owing to a well-founded fear of being persecuted, and to seek permanent solutions to their plight.[2] In the years that followed, the refugee concept, based on individualized persecution, was broadened in Africa and Latin America to include persons forced from their homes by generalized violence, internal conflicts, foreign aggression and occupation, and events that seriously disrupted public order.[3]

Those who were forced from their homes for the same reasons as refugees but who remained under the jurisdiction of their own governments were excluded from international protections: their own governments were expected to provide for their well-being and security. When they failed to do so, or deliberately subjected the displaced to starvation and other abuses, governments managed to keep the international community at bay by invoking their sovereignty and insisting on noninterference in the internal affairs of states. Needless to say, some international organizations and nongovernmental organizations did seek to assist the internally displaced. Notable among them were the International Committee of the Red Cross (ICRC), whose mandate is to protect civilians in armed conflict, and UNHCR to a limited extent.[4] But, by and large, it was not until the late 1980s that the problem of internal displacement finally came onto the international agenda.

Several factors contributed to its becoming a subject of international concern. One was the growing number of internally displaced persons. A first counting in 1982 found 1.2 million in eleven countries. By 1986 the total had risen to an estimated 11.5 million to 14 million, with twenty countries affected. By 1997 more than 20 million were reported in thirty-five to forty countries.[5] The main reason for this increase was internal conflict, which became far more prevalent than interstate wars in the post–cold war era.[6] In 1993 and 1994 alone, internal conflicts worldwide forced an estimated 10,000 persons a day to flee their homes and either cross borders or become displaced inside their own countries.[7]

International preoccupation with preventing refugee flows has also brought increased attention to the internally displaced. The political advantage that motivated many states to accept refugees during the cold war gave way in the early 1990s to a desire to limit their entry. Not only Western governments but those in other parts of the world became less willing to receive large numbers of refugees. This spurred greater interest in protecting and assisting persons displaced within their own countries as a means of discouraging them from seeking asylum abroad. The fact that, as of the mid-1990s, the number of internally displaced persons receiving attention had surpassed the 13.2 million refugees of concern to UNHCR reflected, in part, this reversal of attitudes.[8]

The telecommunications revolution also has helped bring the issue to public attention. In 1984 and 1985 the media broadcast the plight of hundreds of thousands of starving Ethiopians searching for food and tens of thousands forcibly displaced on political grounds. The result was an outpouring of international aid despite the Ethiopian government's efforts to minimize the extent of the crisis. At about the same time, masses of people in the Sudan were reported fleeing from drought and related famine or starving in their areas of residence, while the government denied that an emergency existed. Ultimately, media attention combined with pressure by the international community compelled the government to acknowledge the problem and allow the international community to provide the needed assistance. Similarly, in 1991 televised images of hundreds of thousands of displaced Kurds trapped in the mountains of Iraq and fleeing government attacks mobilized world attention and helped bring about international intervention.

Another important factor in bringing displacement to the fore was the ending of the cold war. When the superpowers were engaged in proxy wars, as in Afghanistan, Angola, and El Salvador, the internal displacement produced by these struggles received little or no attention. Whatever political advantage may have existed lay in supporting refugees of these conflicts, such as Afghans who fled to Pakistan after the Soviet invasion. It was only when these geopolitical struggles began to wane that the plight of those caught within their own borders by civil wars and other forms of internal strife came into full view and were recognized as requiring international humanitarian attention.

The cold war's end facilitated access to countries no longer "protected" by one superpower or another. There also came to be growing acceptance of the idea that events taking place within a state are a legitimate subject of international concern. The international human rights movement had long championed the view that human rights violations transcend frontiers and that when governments fail to meet their obligations under the UN Charter, they should be held accountable by the international community.[9] Humanitarian organizations also began to insist that when governments denied access to populations at risk, the international community should find ways of providing assistance. The Sudan was a case in point. At first, international organizations and voluntary agencies basically stood by while a quarter of a million people in war-torn Sudan died for lack of food and emergency supplies.[10] But in 1989 the United Nations took a more determined approach. Through hard diplomatic bargaining, it persuaded the government and the rebel forces to accept Operation Lifeline Sudan, a program that allowed the international community to provide desperately needed relief to displaced and other persons throughout that country.[11]

This growing willingness to intervene in exceptional circumstances, if need be without the consent of the government, rests on the view that some manner of international involvement becomes essential in a humanitarian crisis caused by a government's failure to fulfill its responsibilities to its citizens. This was clearly reflected in the precedent-setting intervention on behalf of the internally displaced in Iraq following the 1991 Gulf War. There the Security Council justified intervention on the grounds that massive flows of refugees were a threat to international peace and security. Subsequent Security Council resolutions on Somalia, Bosnia, and Rwanda have also authorized the use of force to facilitate the delivery of relief to civilian populations, and in the latter two cases, to provide protection to internally displaced and other affected populations.[12]

The displacement issue has become more prominent also because of the realization that peace and reconstruction in war-torn societies depend in part on the effective reintegration of displaced persons. Many of the countries devastated by civil strife during the cold war—Mozambique, Angola, Afghanistan, Cambodia, El Salvador, among others—had anywhere from one-third to one-half of their population uprooted. It thus became impossible to design development plans without taking into account the situation of returning refugees and internally displaced persons.[13] The reintegration of uprooted persons took center stage at two major international conferences: the 1988 Conference on the Plight of Refugees, Returnees, and Displaced Persons in Southern Africa (SARRED); and the May 1989 International Conference on Central American Refugees (CIREFCA).

Increased attention to the problem of internal displacement, however, has not made it more tractable. Unlike wars between nations, civil wars, particularly when they divide countries along racial, ethnic, linguistic, or religious lines, do not resolve themselves easily or neatly. Often they recur and may persist for long periods because they leave deep wounds within the society. Many conflicts that produce mass displacement are between governments and minorities or among different ethnic groups. Often, they are incited or exploited by political leaders seeking to gain or consolidate power. Competition for scarce economic resources, resulting in disparities among different groups and the marginalization of some, also has been a significant factor contributing to the civil strife bringing about displacement. In the Sudan, the country with the largest number of internally displaced persons, a power struggle between the Arabized Islamic north and the black African south has forcibly displaced more than four million persons, mostly from the south, who are subject to "appalling" conditions.[14] In Turkey, the country with the second largest number of internally displaced persons, an estimated two million Kurds have been forcibly evacuated from their homes as part of a government counterinsurgency campaign reportedly accompanied by severe human rights abuses.[15] Most of the displaced Kurds are said to be crowded into shantytowns on the outskirts of the major cities, many without access to proper sanitation, health care, or educational facilities for the young, and without stable employment prospects.[16]

Wars within states often reflect a crisis of national identity in a society that occurs when a state becomes monopolized by and identified with the dominant group or groups to the exclusion or marginalization of others, who are thereby denied the protection and assistance that a state owes its citizens. The displaced are perceived as the "enemy," either through their association with an insurgent group, an opposing political or ideological tendency, or more generally with an ethnic, cultural, religious or social group considered inferior, threatening, or simply, "other." The cleavages generated between the affected population and the government or controlling authorities force the displaced into a vacuum of responsibility, which often makes international involvement necessary.

Internal conflicts that disintegrate into, or are caused by, warlordism are equally problematic. The belligerents accept almost no ground rules of battle and show almost no respect for the personnel and equipment of humanitarian agencies. If anything, they appear willing "to use humanitarian access, life-saving assistance, and even civilians themselves as weapons in their political-military struggles."[17] In fact, their targets are often civilians, who reportedly account for 90 percent of the casualties in internal wars.[18] Conflicts rooted in racial, ethnic, or religious issues frequently make displacement a weapon and sometimes even their goal.

Access to internally displaced populations may be further complicated by the different manifestations of displacement. In some countries internally displaced persons cluster in camps or settlements, which may be reachable to outside assistance. In other countries they may disperse so as to avoid identification, which makes access more difficult. Or they may merge into local communities, where gaining access to them may require the development of special community-based approaches.

How to deal with governments that are unwilling to provide for the security and well-being of their displaced populations remains a daunting challenge. When persons are internally displaced by natural and manmade disasters, such as drought or nuclear accidents, governments are usually more willing—if not always able—to provide assistance in cooperation with the international community. But when persons are displaced by conflict or political causes, governments are often less willing to protect and assist their internally displaced populations. Even those that invite international assistance may be suspicious of efforts that reach out to all sides in a conflict. More problematic, however, are governments that deliberately bar or try to obstruct humanitarian assistance, which they often see as strengthening their opponents and undermining their own authority, especially if administered in insurgent areas. Some may not want to admit that insurgent groups control parts of their territory or that the central government is unable to provide for all of its citizens. Or they may want to conceal the extent to which their own policies or actions have contributed to war and mass displacement. Frequently they justify their obstruction on grounds of defending their national sovereignty.

For all of the foregoing reasons, it has become essential to develop a broadly recognized framework of normative standards and institutional arrangements to guide the actions both of governments and of international humanitarian and development agencies in dealing with crises of internal displacement. The major objective of this study is to advance that goal. The study emphasizes that the concept of sovereignty cannot be dissociated from responsibility: that is to say, a state should not be able to claim the prerogatives of sovereignty unless it carries out its internationally recognized responsibilities to its citizens, which consist of providing them with protection and life-supporting assistance. Failure to do so would legitimize the involvement of the international community in such protection and assistance. States unable to meet the urgent life-saving needs of their citizens would be expressly required to accept offers of humanitarian assistance. When states whose populations are at risk deliberately obstruct or outright refuse access, they should expect calibrated actions that range from diplomatic demarches to political pressures, sanctions, or, as a last resort, military intervention.

To mitigate the international legal vacuum that prevails in instances of internal displacement, the study advocates international acceptance of a set of guiding principles developed by a team of international lawyers, under the direction of the representative of the secretary-general on internally displaced persons. These principles (see the appendix) bring together in one document the various legal norms applicable to the internally displaced and offer remedies for the significant gaps and gray areas identified in the norms. Although the principles do not have the force of law, they set standards that should put both governments and insurgent groups on notice that their conduct is open to scrutiny and will be measured against specific standards. They reflect the needs of the displaced, their corresponding rights, and the duties and obligations of states and other controlling authorities. And they provide the international community with a basis for legitimate action. In time it is hoped that they will lead to the development of a legally binding instrument for protecting and assisting victims of internal displacement and safeguarding them against unlawful displacement. A first step in this direction would be for the appropriate organs of the United Nations to give authority to the principles by formally acknowledging them and recommending that they be observed.

A related issue that has yet to be resolved is to what extent the international community should be considered to have an obligation to come to the aid of internally displaced populations. Since the late 1980s enormous progress has been made in meeting the challenges posed by humanitarian emergencies. An array of UN agencies, humanitarian organizations, and nongovernmental organizations (NGOs) have come forward to provide protection, assistance, and development aid when governments have been unable or unwilling to meet their responsibilities. In particular, the UN High Commissioner for Refugees, the World Food Programme (WFP), and the International Committee of the Red Cross have expanded their areas of operation to respond to the needs of the internally displaced. In addition, the United Nations Children's Fund (UNICEF), the United Nations Development Programme (UNDP), the World Health Organization (WHO), and the International Organization for Migration (IOM) have enlarged their involvement with internally displaced populations, as has the Office of the UN High Commissioner for Human Rights. In addition, the office of the Emergency Relief Coordinator has undertaken steps to strengthen coordination. A large number of NGOs work alongside these organizations.

None of these organizations, however, has a global mandate to protect and assist the internally displaced. Their action is ad hoc. As various agencies pick and choose the situations in which they wish to become involved, many internally displaced persons may be neglected. Collaborative endeavors aimed at remedying this defect thus far have tended to be poorly coordinated, plagued by inordinate delays, and have accorded too little attention to the protection of the physical security and human rights of those displaced. Furthermore, reintegration and development support have received insufficient consideration. There has also been reluctance to undertake preventive measures against the conditions that lead to mass displacement.

Clearly, far more decisive international action is needed to protect and assist the millions who are displaced in their own countries. The options examined in this study range from creating a new agency to deal with problems of internal displacement to assigning responsibility to an existing agency, or strengthening and better coordinating existing collaborative relationships.

Although a new agency might be attractive in theory, the idea is unlikely to win political support, resources would be difficult to garner, and a new agency would duplicate existing capacities. A more persuasive alternative would be to enlarge the mandate of an existing agency, such as UNHCR, which has already developed special expertise in working with internally displaced populations. While UNHCR has indeed expanded its competence to deal with situations of internal displacement, it is not yet ready to shoulder the entire responsibility. Proposals that it move beyond refugees have met with resistance both from within and outside the agency.

Of necessity, then, the choice at present is to make more effective use of existing mandates and capacities through a collaborative effort under the emergency relief coordinator (ERC) at headquarters and the resident/humanitarian coordinators in the field. Indeed, this is the option endorsed by the UN secretary-general in his 1997 reform program. Since past efforts in this direction have only met the needs of the internally displaced in varying degrees or largely neglected them, this study recommends a more targeted approach: in each serious emergency, the principal responsibility for the internally displaced should be assigned to one operational agency backed by an effective interagency coordinating mechanism; or the agency itself could be authorized to perform the coordination. A system of this sort would ensure a definite locus of responsibility for the internally displaced in any given situation. It would encourage the various agencies to carve out specific areas of expertise in situations of internal displacement so as to establish an effective division of labor, encompassing not only the provision of material assistance to the displaced but also their need for physical security, protection of human rights, and reintegration and development support.

To date, the international community has focused largely on providing humanitarian relief to displaced populations while giving lower priority to other important considerations. Humanitarian assistance is far more effective, however, when it is part of a larger strategy. Neglecting the political context in which humanitarian supplies are delivered may serve to strengthen warring factions and make relief into a substitute for the political action needed to prevent and resolve the crises. Attention to protection and human rights is also critical. Internally displaced persons have regularly pointed out that security is as important to them as food. Providing food and supplies without attending to protection can undermine assistance programs and even lead to situations in which the victims become the "well-fed dead." Furthermore, programs that fail to deliver relief in the context of development only encourage dependency and generate unviable solutions. Too often the broader context in which displacement takes place is ignored because the actions required are said to be too difficult or too costly. Even so, no strategy can be effective without addressing the broader dimensions of the problem.

The concept of protection proposed in this study goes beyond the provision of food, medicine, and shelter to include measures that ensure respect for the physical safety and human rights of the affected population. Although ICRC and to a lesser extent UNHCR engage in protection activities, these organizations are not always on the scene of humanitarian emergencies. UN human rights bodies, which up to now have not been present in most such instances, will clearly have to play a greater role. Humanitarian and development agencies, whether intergovernmental or nongovernmental, will also have to lend a hand. Many have been reluctant to become involved in protection issues for fear of having their access restricted, or for lack of experience and expertise in these issues. Nonetheless, they can take certain steps to promote protection: they can use their aid as leverage, build closer working relationships with human rights bodies, and coordinate their policies and actions on behalf of the displaced.

In recent years military intervention has taken place in several cases of internal displacement. Although in general these operations have been credited with preventing starvation, in the matter of safeguarding the physical safety of the persons at risk their record has been mixed. Whatever the problems and difficulties associated with intervention, greater priority needs to be given to protection strategies and to steps to prevent genocide and other crimes against humanity that lead to mass murder and displacement. The emphasis should be on encouraging judicious action in the face of compelling warning signs and on ensuring that the forces charged with protecting the displaced have the equipment, resources, training, and mandates to do so.

Ultimately, however, military measures are likely to provide little more than momentary solutions unless steps are also taken to address the underlying causes of the crises. Only through a broader commitment to the peaceful management and mediation of disputes can conflict and internal displacement ultimately be resolved. Humanitarian organizations can contribute to the achievement of this goal by insisting that efforts be made to resolve conflicts and by using assistance to promote that end, or at least not to impede it.

Regional organizations have an important role to play in helping to resolve conflicts, avert their spread, and ensure that situations of internal displacement are addressed. Because the consequences of conflicts can be dramatic at the regional level, it is essential for the Organization of African Unity (OAU), the Organization of American States (OAS), the Organization for Security and Cooperation in Europe (OSCE), and subregional groups to develop their capacities to become the first line of defense in their areas. Such groups must forge effective partnerships with international organizations, especially in developing policies and programs regarding internal displacement.

Overall, a graduated response is needed, one that places primary responsibility with the local community, then the national government, the region, and ultimately the international community. For such a system to be put in place, it is essential to strengthen local institutions and indigenous NGOs. Too often they are bypassed in the rush by outsiders "to get things done" efficiently. Yet it is the actors at the local level who can play a decisive role in restoring communal links, reunifying families, developing support structures for unaccompanied children, and bolstering the capacities of displaced communities to care for themselves, and who will have to take over when the outsiders depart.

At the same time, capacities at the national level must be in a position to respond to an emergency. National structures need to be developed to deal with displacement. In a number of countries, where they already exist, they could be made more effective if supported and monitored.

Since displacement reflects profound problems within a society, solutions must address the root causes of the conflicts. They must include measures to strengthen democratic institutions and the protection of human rights, in particular the rights of minorities and other ethnic and indigenous communities. They must include safeguards for NGOs, whose members are often under attack, yet whose work with the displaced is vital. Solutions must also address land and property issues and the economic disparities at the heart of many conflicts.

The repair of physical infrastructure and a massive injection of investment capital turned out to be an effective means of reconstructing the highly developed economies of Western Europe after the Second World War, but today's conflicts require a different strategy. Since they are mainly internal in nature, take place largely in developing countries, and may go on for decades, international development and financial institutions cannot afford to wait until conflicts end to become involved. They need to become engaged early on, while societies are still in conflict, so as to influence the outcome and help lay the foundation for a transition out of conflict. By taking advantage of windows of opportunity during conflicts and by investing in displaced populations, they can help stabilize situations and make reintegration more favorable.[19]

Furthermore, international development and financial institutions have a role to play in the prevention of conflicts through programs to redress the economic inequities underlying conflict. In postconflict reconstruction they can shape how displaced populations become reintegrated and how societies make the overall transition from war to sustainable peace. Indeed, the success of postconflict reconstruction and development may in large part depend on international development and financial institutions working alongside political, peacekeeping, humanitarian assistance, and human rights agencies. The establishment of a global reconstruction fund would be an important step toward strengthening their capability.[20]

Developing an effective international system for the internally displaced will affect the lives of millions of people whose need for protection and assistance is immense, compelling, and urgent but for whom the normative principles, institutional arrangements, and enforcement mechanisms remain grossly inadequate. Human rights and humanitarian precepts alone should provide sufficient justification for international efforts to prevent mass starvation and death or to combat flagrant and massive violations against populations who have no recourse but to turn to the international community for help. But there are also compelling political and strategic reasons for supporting international and regional involvement, for civil wars and violence rarely remain confined within borders. The world has become too connected to ignore the plight of millions of persons uprooted within their own countries. This volume provides a comprehensive base of information about these populations. It suggests strategies and offers recommendations for mitigating their plight. The authors hope that it will contribute to the creation of a more effective international system for addressing the post–cold war era's global crisis of internal displacement.

CHAPTER TWO

Global Overview

Over the past decade, the number of internally displaced people in the world has grown substantially but they are largely beyond the regular mechanisms of the international community. Statistics and information about their conditions are sorely needed so that strategies can be developed to protect and assist them.
—Roger P. Winter
Director, U.S. Committee for Refugees, 1997

INTERNALLY DISPLACED PERSONS are the largest "at-risk" population in the world. Yet the international community has had difficulty defining who they are and gathering information about them. Until recently, no office either within or outside the United Nations systematically collected data about their numbers worldwide, the causes and manifestations of their displacement, their access to basic services, their protection needs, the capacity and willingness of their governments to address their problems, and the response of the international community.[1]

This chapter, which is based on data compiled by the U.S. Committee for Refugees (USCR), represents the first attempt at providing a global and regional overview of internal displacement. It defines the internally displaced, examines the causes of displacement and its impact, and presents statistics on the plight of displaced populations. It ends with a region-by-region survey.

15

Framing a Definition

The two distinctive features of internal displacement are that movement is coerced or involuntary and that the populations affected remain within their national borders. The most widely used working definition of internally displaced persons, presented in a 1992 report of the secretary-general of the United Nations, identifies them as "persons who have been forced to flee their homes suddenly or unexpectedly in large numbers, as a result of armed conflict, internal strife, systematic violations of human rights or natural or man-made disasters, and who are within the territory of their own country."[2] The definition includes the major causes of displacement, which are drawn in part from the broad refugee definitions used in Africa and Latin America. Persons fleeing armed conflict, internal strife, and systematic violations of human rights would, if they were to cross a border, qualify as refugees both under the Organization of African Unity Convention and the Cartagena Declaration, and, arguably, in many cases, under the narrower definition of the Refugee Convention.[3]

Persons uprooted by natural disasters would not, however, qualify as refugees. They are included in the definition because in some natural disasters governments respond by discriminating against or neglecting certain groups on political or ethnic grounds, or by violating their human rights in other ways. When drought and famine ravaged Ethiopia in the mid-1980s, its government forcibly relocated hundreds of thousands of Tigreans it regarded as political opponents, under the pretext of responding to a natural disaster.[4] During the same period, the Sudan suffered a drought-related famine in the western and eastern parts of the country that the government was reticent to recognize until forced by international pressure to declare a state of emergency and request international assistance.[5] In other countries as well, people have been displaced because of a combination of natural disasters and racial, social, and political factors. Including natural disasters in the definition highlights the fact that persons subject to disasters may need special protection.

Man-made disasters, such as nuclear or chemical accidents, are included for the same reason. Although the persons displaced by such disasters usually receive assistance from their governments and the international community, in some instances they may require international protection because of persecution, neglect, and systematic violation of their human rights. Under similar circumstances, those displaced by development projects might also require protection. Where a dam is under construction, say, and a sizable population is forcibly displaced without adequate resettlement, compensation, or respect for human rights, it could qualify as a man-made disaster, and the displaced populations could merit attention under the definition.[6]

Some development agencies have proposed expanding the definition to encompass those who migrate because of extreme poverty or other economic problems. To be sure, persons forced from their homes because of economic injustice and marginalization tantamount to systematic violation of their economic rights would come under the definition. But in most cases of economic migration, the element of coercion is not so clear, and development programs generated by national and international agencies would be the most appropriate means of addressing their problems.[7] What distinguishes the internally displaced and makes them of concern to the international community is the coercion that impels their movement, the human rights abuse they suffer as a result of their displacement, and the lack of protection for them within their own countries.

The 1992 definition overlooks two important factors, however: the time and the numbers involved. If the term "internally displaced" refers only to those forced to leave their homes "suddenly or unexpectedly," or "in large numbers," many serious cases of internal displacement will be excluded. A case in point can be found in Colombia, where the displaced often flee in small numbers in order to make themselves less conspicuous, or in Iraq, where the government organized the uprooting of the Kurds over a considerable period in the late 1970s, 1980s, and early 1990s. The term "forced to flee" is also too narrow. Bosnian Muslims did not flee; they were expelled from their homes on ethnic and religious grounds. Countless numbers in Myanmar (Burma), Iraq, and Ethiopia also did not flee; they were *forcibly moved* by their governments for political and ethnic reasons. There are also cases in which persons feel "obliged" to leave because of impending conflict or other disturbance.

The representative of the secretary-general on internally displaced persons, together with a team of international lawyers, has been seeking to refine the United Nation's working definition to meet some of the foregoing objections. The definition they have arrived at eliminates the requirements relating to time and numbers and explicitly includes persons who have been expelled from or obliged to leave their homes. It maintains explicit reference to those displaced by natural and man-made disasters on the understanding that those cases in which discrimination and persecution are major elements would be the subject of special concern to the international community. It does not include those who migrate voluntarily, but it broadens the text sufficiently so as not to exclude future groups that might need special attention. The modified version therefore defines the internally displaced as persons or groups of persons "who have been forced or obliged to flee or to leave their homes or places of habitual residence, in particular, as a result of, or in order to avoid the effects of, armed conflict, situations of generalized violence, violations of human rights or natural or human-made disasters, and who have not crossed an internationally recognized state border."

This definition is the broadest one in use at the international and regional level.[8] By contrast, the one employed by UNHCR is limited to persons in "refugee-like" situations who have fled their homes because of "persecution, situations of general violence or massive violations of human rights and do not enjoy the full protection of their own government."[9] Likewise, the Permanent Consultation on Internal Displacement in the Americas (CPDIA) uses a definition that pertains only to persons who, were they to cross a border, would be refugees.[10]

Many nongovernmental organizations (see chapter 5) have warned against limiting the definition to persons who would be refugees on the grounds that it "may not accurately depict the variety of the root causes of displacement, which also include socioeconomic conflicts, drug trafficking, development projects [and] natural disasters."[11] The UN definition as modified above recognizes that the reasons for displacement are often complex and interrelated and that persons uprooted by natural disasters and also by development projects may be persecuted and discriminated against, and thus be of special concern as internally displaced persons. The modified definition tries to strike a balance between too narrow a framework that risks excluding people and one so broad that it could prove operationally unmanageable.

It should be borne in mind that "internal displacement" is a descriptive term that can be applied to a broad range of situations. Not all such situations will necessarily be of concern to the international community. If the needs of the internally displaced are met effectively by their own governments, the international community need not become involved, unless at the government's request. On the other hand, if the plight of a displaced population is compounded by persecution, discrimination, or neglect, then the need for international protection and assistance becomes pronounced. These are the cases for which the representative of the secretary-general on internally displaced persons has a specific responsibility.

Causes of Internal Displacement

Because internal displacement did not become noticeable until after the cold war, it is often viewed as a post–cold war phenomenon. The fact of the matter is that some of the major cases of internal displacement over the past two decades are related to conflicts that either took place during the cold war or were significantly affected by cold war policies.

In the four decades of their struggle, the United States and the Soviet Union contributed to the development and intensification of internal conflicts in Africa, Asia, and Latin America. The two superpowers enlisted client governments and political or opposition movements in their "cause," supplying them with arms, often directly, sometimes through proxies, and usually in large quantities. This enabled the clients to establish control over a state, or to pursue a war against an insurgency or against an opposing state. Many of the major instances of internal displacement during the 1970s and 1980s took place in regions and states that were the locus of cold war proxy wars: Ethiopia and Somalia in the late 1970s; and Afghanistan, Angola, Mozambique, El Salvador, and Guatemala in the 1980s.

In Ethiopia, Soviet arms enabled the government of Mengistu Haile Mariam to wage war for more than a decade (1978–91) in an ultimately vain effort to suppress Eritrea's drive for independence and beat down a powerful Tigrean insurgency. In the course of those struggles hundreds of thousands were forcibly displaced. The civil war in Mozambique, in which the Soviet Union and its allies supplied the government while South Africa supported the Renamo insurgency, uprooted at least 5.7 million of the country's 16 million people. The war in Angola, in which the Soviet bloc armed the government and the United States the insurgency, at one time or another displaced more than 2 million.

Millions were also displaced in the struggle in Afghanistan between Soviet invaders and the Afghan resistance armed by the United States and others. In Cambodia, cold war–supplied weaponry fueled a devastating civil war (a sequel to the Vietnam War) in which most of Cambodia's population was uprooted and some two million were killed. In Latin America, hundreds of thousands were displaced in the civil wars in El Salvador, Guatemala, and Nicaragua, for which the United States and the Soviet bloc furnished the bulk of the weaponry.

The ending of the cold war markedly contributed to the decline of civil conflict and the initiation of healing processes that enabled large numbers of displaced persons to return to their homes or to resettle in Ethiopia and Eritrea, Mozambique, Cambodia, and El Salvador. Elsewhere, however, the ending of the cold war had the opposite effect. In Liberia and Somalia, U.S. arms deliveries during the cold war helped maintain in power the abusive regimes of Samuel Doe and Siad Barre. When toward the end of the cold war U.S. support waned and Doe and Siad Barre fell, the arsenals previously amassed provided much of the weaponry for the ethnic and clan warfare that broke out. Interestingly, the nations in Africa that experienced the most extreme violence and the highest levels of displacement were those that were most closely aligned with and received the highest levels of aid from the two cold war protagonists.

During the cold war, Soviet power and the communist system kept a tight lid on nationalist aspirations and ethnic rivalries in Eastern Europe and Central Asia. With the demise of the Soviet Union, fierce struggles over political and territorial ascendency erupted in the Caucasus and parts of Central Asia, and internal rivalries destroyed the former Yugoslavia. The significant point about all the conflicts mentioned above is that they had underlying tensions of a political, ethnic, linguistic, or religious nature. They may have been exacerbated and exploited by cold war politics and arms supplies, but they were anchored in serious problems within the societies and their governance. In Central America, for example, the vast disparities in wealth, land ownership, and access to power were at the root of conflicts that became geopolitical.

Indeed, many major outbreaks of internal conflict developed entirely independently of the cold war and were unaffected, or affected only incidentally, by it. The recurrent wars and mass displacement in the Sudan, for instance, can be traced to the efforts of successive northern governments to impose an Arab and Islamic system on the South. The conflict in Sri Lanka is a direct outcome of the Sinhalese government's long history of discrimination and abuse against the Tamil minority. And the efforts at suppressing Kurdish nationalism in Iraq and Turkey have been at the root of government campaigns and massive forced displacement of the Kurds.

The U.S. Committee for Refugees considers "conflict between a government and a minority" to be one of the principal causes of internal displacement. Minorities caught in these situations feel dispossessed and abandoned by the national authorities and seek to reverse power imbalances or gain some form of political and cultural autonomy. They may foment civil war to achieve their goals, while their governments seek to perpetuate control over the group, fearing claims to self-determination and disruption of the state. By repressing minorities, however, refusing to see them as legitimate members of the nation and preventing truly multiethnic societies from developing, governments often strengthen the very separatist movements they fear.

Some three thousand ethnic groups exist in the world today, and most do not have their own nation-states.[12] Nor do they necessarily identify with or feel loyal to the state in which they live. The more than fifty states of Africa are home to no fewer than a thousand distinct ethnic groups. Given the arbitrary way in which the borders of Africa's nations were drawn, it is easy to understand why ethnicity may be more of a unifying concept than the nation-state. The Middle East, too, has been a scene of conflict, between Israelis and Arabs, Kurds and Arabs, Kurds and Turks, and between competing Moslem sects. In South Asia the Sinhalese and Tamil are pitted against each other, as are Hindus and Moslems and Hindus and Sikhs. In China, Tibetans and other non-Han peoples have been asserting their national identity, while in the former Soviet Union a large number of ethnic and national groups are seeking greater autonomy or have won their independence.

The point must be made, however, that it is seldom mere differences of identity based on ethnic or religious grounds that generate conflict, but the consequences of those differences when it comes to sharing power and distributing the nation's resources and opportunities. According to some analysts, the upsurge in ethnic-based violence since the end of the cold war is due less to frictions growing out of ethnicity, language, or religion than to the manipulation of these differences by government authorities for political or military purposes.[13] In their view, ethnic conflict is deliberately fomented by governments or opposition leaders or groups that play on existing communal tensions to entrench their own power, forcibly acquire territory, or advance a political agenda. To be sure, there are cases of conflict in which political leaders have deliberately manipulated ethnic differences. But the fact that leaders are able to exploit ethnic difference raises a presumption that there may be genuine group concerns. If ethnic differences did not entail shared grievances or causes, they would not be easily exploitable by self-motivated political

leaders. It is therefore essential to acknowledge and address the underlying causes of ethnic animosity.

Most of the conflicts that lead to mass displacement have a strong
ethnic component. Besides internal conflicts between a government and
an ethnic minority, there are interstate conflicts (such as that between
Armenia and Azerbaijan) in which two different ethnic groups attempt
to extend or defend their territorial reach. Even in conflict situations in
which ethnicity may not be apparent, it is often a factor. Politically motivated insurgency, on the face of it, may be a reaction to what is perceived
as bad governance or the inequities of the distribution of wealth. Probing
beneath the surface, however, often reveals that participation in the
power process or economic life of the country is influenced, if not determined, by racial, ethnic, cultural, or religious considerations. In Guatemala, the insurgent group's principal motivation may have been political
but the insurgents drew their support from a particular ethnic group,
which also made up the underclass of the country. Similarly, the config-
uration of the actors on both sides of the conflict in El Salvador shows
that those in power were overwhelmingly of European (Spanish) origin,
whereas the poor peasantry, who were the ones most affected by internal
displacement, were overwhelmingly indigenous.

Tajikistan, too, is often presented as a case of ideological competition
between those committed to the continuation of the Soviet Marxist political and economic system and those seeking a more open democratic
government, with an Islamic orientation. In reality, the conflict involves
rivalries that correlate to ethnic and regional differences, the roots of
which go back to, and even precede, Soviet rule.[14] Moreover, conflicts
between warring groups in collapsed states often divide along clan or
ethnic lines, as in Somalia and Afghanistan.[15]

At times, the level of human rights abuse in a country is so severe or
pervasive that it is the principal cause of displacement. Such abuse often
stems from factors of identity such as race, ethnicity, language, religion,
or culture. The genocide in Rwanda, where hundreds of thousands of
Tutsis were murdered, also forcibly displaced at least 1 million persons.
The former apartheid regime in South Africa forcibly moved hundreds
of thousands of blacks into bantustans. And in Myanmar (Burma), the
State Law and Order Restoration Council (SLORC) has forcibly relocated ethnic minorities and political opponents and created a displaced
population estimated at between 500,000 and 1 million.[16]

Of course, internal displacement can rarely be neatly categorized as having only one distinct cause. Usually there are multiple, overlapping, and interrelated reasons explaining displacement. What is important about the discussion of causes is that it helps one gain a better understanding of the tensions and conflicts that lead to displacement and of the ways of preventing and addressing it. If a preponderant number of situations of internal displacement are related to external political developments such as the cold war or its end, then internal displacement could decline as the world gradually adjusts to a new post–cold war equilibrium. On the other hand, if deep-rooted issues of collective identity are at the base of many conflicts, then the number of internally displaced persons might rise as the demand grows for local or regional autonomy and independence. In the past it was often assumed that religious and ethnic loyalties would fade when countries became more secular and economically developed. This assumption was central to Marxist thought and popular among Western liberals, but it has proved untrue in many instances, in particular in the former Soviet Union and Yugoslavia. Even in Western Europe and Canada, where the democratic nation-state is generally believed to have erased regional and linguistic differences, separatism has gained ground, albeit without violent upheaval. Thus the hope remains that the spread of democracy and respect for human rights may yet show the way toward the easing of crises of national identity and internal displacement.[17]

Impact of Displacement

Many think of displacement as a temporary problem that disappears upon the return home or resettlement of the displaced. On the contrary, it is often a long-term phenomenon that disrupts the lives of not only the individuals and families concerned but also of whole communities and societies. Of the countries that have experienced major conflicts since 1980, thirty have had more than 10 percent of their population dislocated, and ten countries have had more than 40 percent displaced.[18] In such cases, one can hardly speak of the displaced as "vulnerable groups."

The impact of large-scale displacement extends well beyond the numbers counted as being displaced. Those left behind must continue their lives in the vacuum created by the departure of the displaced, while those in areas to which the displaced have moved find their lives altered by major new population inflows. Through the "multiplier effect" of displacement on home communities as well as on the areas where the displaced find refuge, the true impact of displacement rises as much as threefold above the number of those actually displaced.[19]

Entire communities or even entire regions may be depopulated, as was the case in parts of Mozambique and Azerbaijan, or large segments of communities may leave, as happened on the central plateau of Angola. Young men, combatants, and their families, and certain ethnic or linguistic groups may depart. Often, it is the elderly and the very young who are left behind to tend to agricultural land and retain a claim on property. However, departure patterns differ within countries and within regions of the same country. In Bosnia, whole communities were forcibly expelled from their homes in "ethnic cleansing" campaigns while others left their communities to flee the war. Each of these patterns has a particular impact on the home communities.

With departures from rural areas, the human resources needed to maintain adequate levels of cultivation dwindle. In irrigated areas, canals fall into disrepair and cannot be easily rehabilitated. A decade of such neglect in southwestern Afghanistan caused extensive, perhaps irreparable, damage to patterns of cultivation there. In these circumstances, preparing land for cultivation becomes increasingly difficult. Furthermore, crops that demand constant attention, as does coffee, will suffer ill effects for years to come (plants will deteriorate and the quality of harvests will decline) if they are abandoned for even a single season.

Homes, buildings, and infrastructure may also suffer enormous damage. Sometimes it is the direct consequence of the conflict, but often the problem is that those who remain behind are unable to carry out the necessary maintenance. Cycles of repair are disrupted, and after several rainy seasons, neglect can lead to irreversible destruction, especially of homes made of mud and sun-dried brick.

In addition, displacement has a considerable impact on community organization. When populations disappear for more than a year or two, leadership patterns, mechanisms for resolving disputes, and property rights in home areas change drastically, especially in an atmosphere of lawlessness: individuals may encroach on the land of those who are absent and combatant groups may formally or informally distribute "vacant" land to supporters. When the occupants are persons whose own property has been destroyed, the issue of property rights becomes even more complex. Most of the countries that experience internal conflict have sparse land records and even these are often destroyed during the conflict. Questions of land tenure thus become difficult to resolve by traditional methods, especially when the communities that established these methods have fragmented or their system of leadership has been delegitimized and the officeholders killed. Returning populations find property rights to be a confusing and widespread problem, particularly in regard to the double occupancy of housing.

Yet another cause for concern is the environmental impact of displacement. When the displaced flee to rural areas, they may do irreparable damage to ecosystems, especially if they have no other options but to strip surrounding forests and grasslands to satisfy their need for housing and fuel. In Rwanda, the damage done to Akagera National Park by internally displaced persons and returning refugees will have long-term economic consequences. The temporary settlement of internally displaced persons in 1994–95 within the Nyungwi and Gishweti forests in the western part of the country has damaged those protected areas as well.

Major urban centers, too, suffer serious consequences because of displacement. Urban populations may double or triple and overload social services, water supplies, and sanitation facilities and thereby hasten the deterioration of the urban infrastructure, already weakened by conflict. Frequently, state services to the country as a whole become strained or even disrupted. Displacement thus "has ripple effects throughout entire societies," going far beyond the need for humanitarian assistance to those displaced.[20]

The flights themselves are often chaotic. Resources are squandered in the search for security. Families are separated. The physical constitution of the elderly and the young is often irreparably damaged in the first weeks of the move. Any accumulated family savings are likely to be quickly exhausted. Movable property is often sold. Farm animals are lost or sold. The lack of food, clean water, and proper sanitation, along with the outbreak of disease and shock usually causes a significant increase in the mortality rate. Those who are fortunate enough to receive food aid may become dependent on that aid and subsequently have difficulty reintegrating.

Displacement may also lead to the widespread "de-skilling" of the displaced population. Craftspersons often lose or sell their tools or find no use for their skills in new areas, particularly where the markets available for their products are limited. Although farmers do not lose their skills, the longer they have limited or no access to land, the better the chances that their children will lose all links to the land. When agricultural activity disappears from the lives of the displaced, the fabric of rural society is affected: "Patterns of cooperation and social organization become dormant. Subtle rules of behavior, checks and balances, drawn from customary patterns of usage of community resources disappear."[21]

Displacement alters the structure and size of households and changes family patterns and gender roles. Productive older males often become separated from the household in their search for work or recruitment into the military. The number of female-headed households increases significantly. Yet for most women who become sole supporters of their families, the economic opportunities are limited and discriminatory practices are widespread.[22]

The effects of displacement on children and their development have been well documented. Most notable are the problems caused by the lack of shelter, warmth, proper food, and health care; the separation from their families; and the serious lack of protection. Educational opportunities are also in short supply. Only a small percentage of refugee children worldwide attend school.[23] The numbers for internally displaced are presumed to be similar or higher.[24] When displacement endures for a long period, it can produce an entire generation of uneducated children, many of whom may have become combatants, witnessed atrocities against their families, or have themselves committed atrocities against others. The problems they face are immense, especially if they have grown up apart from their families and adult discipline, and have been combatants most of their lives.[25]

It is often impossible to return to previous patterns of community life or socioeconomic frameworks after mass displacement. The codes of social behavior and social institutions that held society together no longer exist. With this collective breakdown of social relationships, confidence in the institutions of the society disappears and postconflict reintegration and development become far more complicated than the mere rebuilding of the physical infrastructure.

Internally Displaced Persons as a Special Category

That internally displaced persons are subject to serious abuse and have special and distinct needs is indisputable. Questions have nonetheless arisen about whether the internally displaced should be identified as a special category. Should they be distinguished from nondisplaced war-affected populations, for example, inasmuch as both groups appear to have the same needs? Would singling out one group discriminate against others equally in need and cause inequity and conflict? Is it not more appropriate to address "situations" and not concentrate on categories of persons, so that all those in need receive attention whether or not they are displaced?[26] The International Committee of the Red Cross, for one, provides assistance and protection to all civilian victims of armed conflict, whether or not they are displaced. Other agencies also favor what they call the "needs approach," or targeting assistance on the basis of need, not individual circumstance. Moreover, several of the case studies in the companion volume to this book point out that when returning refugees, demobilized soldiers, war-affected civilians, and internally displaced persons are intermingled, it may be unwise to distinguish between categories.[27]

There need be no conflict, however, between situational approaches and acknowledging the special needs of the groups involved. The purpose of identifying the internally displaced is not to confer on them a privileged status but to ensure that in a given situation their unique needs are addressed along with those of others. Although situational approaches are said to give greater scope for responding to the problems of all groups, all too often the needs of the internally displaced are largely ignored. It is indisputable, for instance, that considerable discrepancy exists in the way the international community perceives and treats refugees (or returning refugees) and internally displaced persons, even when they face similar problems and sometimes are in virtually the same circumstances. International resources are generally not distributed in a manner sufficiently equitable to enable internally displaced persons to receive protection, assistance, and reintegration support commensurate with their needs. Examples of the discrepancy in treatment between refugees (or returning refugees) and internally displaced persons have been found in Burundi, Armenia, Angola, Mozambique, and Cambodia.[28] Furthermore, internally displaced persons received scant attention in the 1997 crisis in the former Zaire (Democratic Republic of the Congo). And in Rwanda, the United Nations found that the nutritional status of the internally displaced was substantially worse than that of the general population.[29] Focusing attention on a vulnerable group is therefore a way to enhance assistance and protection for them.

Of course, there are cases in which the needs of the internally displaced may be indistinguishable from those of others around them. In the heat of conflict, many persons may find themselves without food or medicines and under attack. In Liberia, where most of the population has been displaced at one time or another, distinctions are difficult to draw. Moreover, when internally displaced persons are intermingled in urban settings, it may be difficult to distinguish their needs from those of other disadvantaged persons. Some may even choose to make themselves indistinguishable as a means of protection.

Nonetheless, even in these situations a closer look may reveal differences that should be taken into account. Around Khartoum, for example, the problems of displaced southern Sudanese who are subjected to round-ups, forcible relocation, and other restrictive practices differ greatly from those of others in the city. The same can be said of the internally displaced in Sarajevo during the war in Bosnia: crowded into centers, they were resented by the local community because they came from rural areas and were uneducated and poorly dressed. Furthermore, the local authorities were attempting to send them back to unsafe areas. Unique problems arose elsewhere as well: in El Salvador and Guatemala, many internally displaced, unlike others, lost their official documents, which undermined their protection; in Sri Lanka and Burundi, their access to land was limited, which made them more dependent on food assistance than others in the local population; in Tajikistan and Rwanda, those returning to their homes faced security problems and disputes over land and thus needed increased protection; and in Colombia, many who had taken refuge in urban slums needed legal recognition, which they came forward to request when the government expressed its readiness to acknowledge their situation.

The United Nations Development Programme has found it effective to consider the internally displaced "a distinct target group" when they live in camps, specific areas, or shantytowns around towns or cities. Only after they return or resettle in communities does it advocate that programming for their reintegration begin to focus on the wider community.[30] Even then, care must be taken not to inadvertently overlook the needs of special groups, as has sometimes happened in such successful programs as the ones that emanated from the International Conference on Central American Refugees (CIREFCA) and the UN Development Program for Displaced Persons, Refugees, and Returnees in Central America (PRODERE).[31] In addition, the internally displaced often face protection problems upon their return and reintegration.[32] Thus, although comprehensive programs are essential and most practical, special attention must also be paid, during return and reintegration, to the distinct problems of vulnerable groups.

The Oslo Declaration and Plan of Action, which synthesized the proposals of hundreds of NGOs and UNHCR, recognized the value of identifying the internally displaced as a specific group.[33] By doing so, the international community would find it easier to call upon governments to assume their responsibility for these populations or to press for international action on their behalf. Humanitarian organizations would also be motivated to integrate into their agendas programs on displacement that they otherwise might overlook.

Why Internally Displaced Persons Do Not Become Refugees

Internally displaced persons and refugees often flee their homes for the same reasons. In some cases—for example, in Cuba, Vietnam, and Tibet—the vast majority of those who flee seek protection and assistance in neighboring countries.[34] In others—as in Colombia, Peru, Turkey, Lebanon, Ghana, and India's Kashmir—the vast majority become internally displaced.[35] In still others—such as the Sudan, Afghanistan, Bosnia and Herzegovina, and Rwanda—the fleeing population becomes a mix of refugees and internally displaced persons (see table 2-1).

Beginning in the mid-1990s, more uprooted people became internally displaced than refugees, even though they could expect more protection and assistance as refugees under the aegis of UNHCR.[36] This trend can be attributed to a number of factors.

To begin with, the distance to frontiers or topographical obstacles, such as mountains and rivers, can be significant factors in preventing flight across borders. Furthermore, many uprooted people seek places of relative safety in familiar surroundings in which they can live and work among groups sharing the same culture, language, and religion. Rural people, in particular, who may not have traveled far from their areas of origin may find the prospect of seeking shelter or employment in a foreign country intimidating and decide to remain despite continuing conflict or human rights abuses. Also, some may decide to flee to an area of their country that is under the control of a group—be it the government or an insurgent force—with which they sympathize and from which they might expect protection.

Increasingly, however, the absence of alternatives is influencing the decision to remain displaced. The growing inclination of the international

Table 2-1. *Top Ten Countries Producing Both Internally Displaced Persons and Refugees, Ranked from Largest to Smallest Totals, 1995*

Country	Number of internally displaced	Number of refugees	Total
Sudan	4,000,000	448,100	4,448,100
Afghanistan	500,000	2,328,400	2,828,400
Bosnia/Herzegovina	1,300,000	905,500	2,205,500
Rwanda	500,000	1,545,000	2,045,000
Turkey	2,000,000	15,000	2,015,000
Angola	1,500,000	313,000	1,813,000
Liberia	1,000,000	725,000	1,725,000
Iraq	1,000,000	622,900	1,622,900
Sierra Leone	1,000,000	363,000	1,363,000
Azerbaijan	670,000	390,000	1,060,000

Source: U.S. Committee for Refugees, *World Refugee Survey 1996.*

community is to prevent refugee flows and restrict refugee admissions. Although the right to seek and enjoy asylum from persecution in other countries is enshrined in international human rights law, large numbers of persons are finding borders closed to them. A striking example is that of the Iraqi Kurds. In early 1991, in the aftermath of the Persian Gulf War, more than a quarter of a million Kurds who had resisted the Saddam Hussein regime fled to the Turkish border in the face of advancing Iraqi troops. Despite their desperate condition, Turkey refused them entry. Under the authority of UN Security Council Resolution 688, the U.S.-led coalition carved out a "security zone" for the Kurds in northern Iraq. Bosnians also met restrictions from neighboring and other countries, which, at the height of the conflict, kept an estimated 1.3 million Bosnians internally displaced.[37] And tens of thousands of Afghans had to remain internally displaced when Pakistan in 1994 denied entry to those fleeing the bombardment of their capital.

Some countries have denied asylum because they say "safe havens" already exist to provide shelter and protection for internally displaced persons. European governments, for example, have denied asylum to Tamils fleeing from Sri Lanka on the grounds that the "open relief centers" created by UNHCR are acceptable alternatives.[38] The safe havens in Bosnia also afforded neighboring governments an excuse to deny entry to Bosnians. As inhospitality to asylum seekers grows, with increasing numbers of countries finding it too costly, burdensome, or destabilizing to admit refugees, the numbers of those displaced within their home countries may continue to rise in proportion to refugees.

Statistics on Internally Displaced Persons

By all accounts, the number of internally displaced persons has increased dramatically during the past quarter century. Estimates reached 25 million to 30 million by the end of 1994 (if one includes natural disasters) and fluctuated between 20 million and 25 million thereafter. The USCR, whose statistics on internal displacement are usually the starting point for any discussion on the subject, acknowledges that information on such populations is "fragmentary" and that its figures are "estimates."[39] Moreover, it does not count persons displaced by natural or man-made disasters unless they are also victims of human rights abuse or persecution. For the USCR, the internally displaced are those who would be "refugees" if they were to cross an international border.[40] The USCR is also known to be conservative in arriving at estimates. Nonetheless, its published data point to an overall upward trend in internally displaced populations. According to the USCR, at the end of 1985 there were at least 9.5 million internally displaced persons.[41] By 1994, the worldwide total reportedly reached nearly 25 million; by 1996 estimates declined to about 20 million, although the USCR believed the total number to be "undoubtedly higher."[42] The decrease after 1995 is largely due to the fact that civil wars ended in a number of countries, among them Mozambique and some states in Central America, and that 3.5 million South Africans were subtracted from the total given the political changes in their country.

Figure 2-1 and table 2-2 show the overall upward trend in internal displacement since 1985 and the countries with significant internally displaced populations in 1995 and 1996, as calculated from USCR data. Since initial reported estimates are often prone to exaggeration, the USCR bases its calculations on its own on-site investigations and knowledge of country conditions. In addition, it uses specially developed criteria: the source of the report; the segment of the population referred to; the nature of the displacement; the preflight population of the affected area; the potential for misrepresentation; the magnitude of flight during previous, similar episodes; seasonal migration patterns; and the method of data collection. The USCR has found the principal obstacles to acquiring accurate statistics to be uncertainty about the reliability of the source, lack of access, reluctance to be identified, mobility, inadequate methodology, and the tendency not to separate other migrants from the displaced.

Figure 2-1. *Reported Estimates of Global Displaced Populations from World Refugee Survey, 1985–96*[a]

Number of internally displaced persons (in millions)

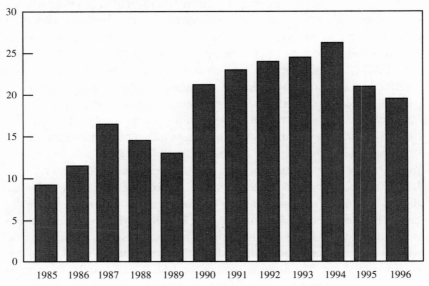

Source: U.S. Committee for Refugees, *World Refugee Survey, 1996.*
a. Does not include persons displaced by natural and man-made disasters.

RELIABILITY OF SOURCES. Estimates of the number of internally displaced persons come from a wide variety of sources: local or national governments, insurgent groups, UN agencies, local and international NGOs, religious institutions, and foreign military offices involved in humanitarian interventions. All have varying objectives. Governments, insurgent groups, or other interested players may understate or overstate the size of displaced populations for political or other reasons. A government in conflict with a rebel movement may understate the magnitude of displacement to play down the severity of the challenge to its authority, or if it has caused significant displacement, to limit criticism of its policies. Governments and insurgent groups also may overstate the size of uprooted populations to entice donors to provide increased humanitarian aid, which may benefit not only the uprooted but also the combatants.

Of course, not all erroneous reports are the result of active disinformation campaigns by governments or insurgent groups. As with refugee

Table 2-2. *Estimates of Internally Displaced Persons, 1995 and 1996*

Country	1995	Country	1996
Sudan	4,000,000	Sudan	4,000,000
Turkey	2,000,000	Turkey	500,000–2,000,000
Angola	1,500,000	Afghanistan	1,200,000
Bosnia and Herzegovina	1,300,000	Angola	1,200,000
Iraq	1,000,000	Bosnia and Herzegovina	1,000,000
Liberia	1,000,000	Myanmar (Burma)	500,000–1,000,000
Sierra Leone	1,000,000	Liberia	1,000,000
Myanmar (Burma)	500,000–1,000,000	Iraq	900,000
Sri Lanka	850,000	Sri Lanka	900,000
Azerbaijan	670,000	Sierra Leone	800,000
Colombia	600,000	Colombia[b]	600,000
Afghanistan	500,000	Azerbaijan	550,000
Mozambique	500,000	South Africa[a]	500,000
Rwanda	500,000	Lebanon	450,000
South Africa[a]	500,000	Peru	420,000
Peru	480,000	Burundi	400,000
Lebanon	400,000	Russian Federation	400,000
Burundi	300,000	Zaire (Congo)	400,000
Somalia	300,000	Georgia	285,000
Syria	300,000	Cyprus	265,000
Georgia	280,000	India	250,000
Cyprus	265,000	Somalia	250,000
India	250,000	Guatemala	200,000
Russian Federation	250,000	Croatia	185,000
Croatia	240,000	Syria	125,000
Zaire	225,000	Kenya	100,000
Kenya	210,000	Philippines	93,000
Guatemala	200,000	Papua New Guinea	70,000
Ghana	150,000	Uganda[b]	70,000
Armenia	70,000	Armenia	50,000
Philippines	60,000	Tajikistan	50,000
Cambodia	55,000	Cambodia	32,000
Tajikistan	17,000	Nigeria	30,000
Mali	10,000	Djibouti	25,000
Algeria	n.a.	Ghana	20,000
Nigeria	n.a.	Algeria[b]	10,000
Uganda	n.a.	Mozambique	n.a.
		Rwanda	n.a.

Source: U.S. Committee for Refugees, *World Refugee Survey*, 1996 and 1997.
n.a. Not available.
  a. The South Africans in the total are for the most part displaced because of violence in Kwa-Zulu Natal. Excluded from the total are the millions of black South Africans who lack land or adequate housing as a result of past apartheid policies, many of whom have integrated into other areas and may no longer consider themselves displaced (see the text, "When Does Displacement End?").
  b. The figure may be much higher.

flights, the size of a rapidly arriving, often traumatized population is difficult to estimate even under ideal circumstances, with access to and cooperation from the authorities.

UN agencies, particularly UNHCR, can be turned to for estimates, but in some instances they count the internally displaced together with other populations in need. Thus overall figures of uprooted persons may include not only the internally displaced but refugees and the local population. Other parties that can provide reliable estimates include local church groups and NGOs, which work most closely with the displaced.

LACK OF ACCESS. Information on displaced populations is particularly difficult to obtain in the midst of an armed conflict, which makes access impossible or dangerous, or when a government or insurgent group makes a concerted effort to block access by outside observers. At various points, conflicts in Afghanistan, Angola, Chechnya, Liberia, and Sierra Leone have prevented outside observers from entering conflict zones to assess the number and needs of the internally displaced. In other settings, governments or rebel groups have blocked access in order to shield from view poor humanitarian conditions or human rights abuses.

In recent years, the governments of Iraq, Myanmar (Burma), the Russian Federation, the Sudan, Turkey, and Sri Lanka, among others, have actively prevented observers and humanitarian aid workers from entering zones of displacement. For some five years, the only consistently reported estimate of the number of displaced persons in Myanmar (Burma) has been in the range of 500,000 to 1 million. The estimate is inexact and other estimates are unavailable because the government has refused to permit outside observers to gauge the extent of displacement.[43]

RELUCTANCE TO BE IDENTIFIED. Some internally displaced persons may have sufficient resources—often in the form of family or friends—in the area of refuge to allow them to forgo registration. Others may decide not to draw attention to themselves for fear of inviting further violence or persecution. For a long time, internally displaced Colombians and Peruvians, many of them rural farmers who sought safety in urban centers, feared that the military or insurgent groups would target them again. Internally displaced persons in Haiti also chose to hide, preferring anonymity to acknowledgment. In Burundi, while displaced Tutsis clustered in camps protected by the Tutsi-dominated army, displaced Hutus dispersed into the hills in order to hide from the army.

MOBILITY. Even if the displaced do not fear being identified as such, their fears for their safety may lead them to move from place to place so frequently that it is difficult to identify and count them. According to a report of the International Organization for Migration, of all the population groups on the move in Angola, "the internally displaced are by far the hardest to keep track of. They move spontaneously and quietly, slipping out of the towns and centers where they have been taking refuge and dispersing to rural areas."[44]

METHODOLOGY. Most estimates of internally displaced populations are broad approximations. Only in a few cases are displaced persons counted individually, usually in connection with food distributions. This connection, however, between being registered for a benefit and being internally displaced can be inaccurate. There may be overregistration and inflated counts. Furthermore, local persons may find it in their interest to gain access to assistance rations and may displace themselves to the areas where assistance is given.[45]

SEPARATING OTHER MIGRANTS FROM THE DISPLACED. With few notable exceptions, the largest displaced populations are to be found in developing countries in which rural-to-urban migration is a common survival strategy. Single men or entire families may migrate to cities in search of work, education, or lifestyles not available in their rural areas of origin. Often, the growth of primary cities in war-torn countries is put forward as evidence that massive internal displacement exists. In reality, even in war-torn countries, not all migration can be attributed to the kinds of actions that cause internal displacement.

The rapid growth of Freetown, Sierra Leone (where the population has reportedly doubled during the five years of conflict in that country), and numerous cities in southeastern Turkey, though partly an outcome of flight from unsafe conditions, is due also to the same rural-to-urban migration seen in relatively stable countries throughout much of the world. Such migration makes it difficult to distinguish the "voluntarily uprooted" from the forcibly displaced.

When Does Displacement End?

No consensus exists on when to stop counting someone as displaced. In the case of refugees, UNHCR has guidelines in determining when it is safe for them to return home. It facilitates the voluntary return process, may play a role helping returnees to reintegrate, and may even monitor their security for a period of time. If UNHCR determines that a particular group no longer needs protection as refugees but that group is reluctant to return home, UNHCR can apply the Refugee Convention's "cessation clause" and end the group's status as refugees, leaving host governments in charge of the persons involved.[46]

No organization has a mandate to make such a determination for internally displaced persons, or to facilitate their return. Nonetheless, there has probably been enough experience of displacement ending, or of displaced populations no longer being considered displaced, that it is possible to map out some of the major considerations in determining when displacement ends.

A common assumption is that internal displacement ends when the displaced voluntarily return home and the situation causing the displacement has ceased to exist. But is the return home the all-important criterion? In some cases, the displaced may have integrated economically and socially into another area and may not choose to return home. They may no longer feel secure in their home areas even though the government or international agencies and NGOs assisting the displaced believe they could safely return. Or they may be unable to return because their land and homes have been occupied by others.

In Peru, for example, 120,000 internally displaced persons have returned home as conflict between the military and Shining Path guerrillas in Peru has diminished. But most of the other internally displaced have remained in the cities and towns to which they fled. Some say that it is not entirely safe to return, others that assistance to returnees is too meager for them to survive, and still others that they have adapted to life in the city. Since some of those who remain away from their homes may yet return, all of those who have not returned tend to be classified as displaced. But if their condition continued to improve, some sort of determination would be needed to establish whether they are still displaced and in need of protection and assistance.

In Guatemala, many people who became displaced from their highland homes in the early 1980s settled in the capital or other cities. Some of those willing to risk returning home found their land occupied by other displaced persons; they also found that the government had created "model villages" on their lands and settled other peasants there. Some who have attempted to reclaim their land have met strong, even violent opposition from the new occupants. This raises the question of whether those who have returned but who are unable to survive in their home areas should still be considered displaced.

In the view of some observers, displacement ends when returnees have both security and the means to reestablish themselves in their areas of origin. Otherwise, they may have to leave again, which would mean continuing displacement.[47] In Angola, groups of internally displaced persons voluntarily transported back to their home areas found that they could not remain there because all the infrastructure had been destroyed.[48] Therefore the mere act of return did not end their internal displacement.

Although a 1992 peace accord made it possible for hundreds of thousands of displaced Mozambicans to return home, a variety of factors prevented many others from doing so, notably the two million or so land mines planted during the conflict on land that had been unoccupied for years. Mozambique's land tenure laws also threatened to complicate the resettlement of returning refugees and internally displaced families. Although the cause of displacement no longer existed, members of both these groups decided not to return. The question is, should they still be considered internally displaced because they have not returned? Or should they not be classified as such since their displacement is no longer due to conflict and persecution, but rather to socioeconomic factors, and since they enjoy the protection of their government?

Although the duration of internal displacement is not necessarily the best indication of whether displacement has become permanent, a population may be less likely to return the longer it has been away from its original home. After Turkey invaded Cyprus in 1974 and set up a Turkish administration on part of the island, about 200,000 Greek and 65,000 Turkish Cypriots became displaced. These groups have now been displaced for more than twenty-three years. Most have permanently resettled in their new environments. Although many may never return home, others maintain that they still want to do so, but cannot. Yet they, too, may be economically and socially integrated in their new homes.

In compiling its annual statistics on refugees and internally displaced persons, the USCR takes the position that internal displacement ends both when the person returns home or resettles locally, or when the conditions that caused the displacement have improved to the point that it should be possible to return home. The USCR has invoked its version of a "cessation clause for displacement" in Nicaragua (1992), El Salvador

(1993), Eritrea (1994), Ethiopia (1995), and South Africa (1995, for those displaced because of apartheid). As a result, it has removed about five million people from its list of internally displaced persons, even though many of those in question probably have not returned home.

The USCR includes internally displaced persons in Cyprus in its statistics because the United Nations continues to be involved, the issue lacks final resolution, and even though they have been resettled for more than twenty years in their current locations, many of the displaced still wish to return home. The USCR also counted 500,000 internally displaced persons in Mozambique in 1995, for although the conflict there was at an end, many displaced persons who planned to return home were prevented from doing so.

Basically, the USCR determines the status of internally displaced persons on a case-by-case basis. In the absence of clear guidelines on when displacement ends, this would appear the most prudent course to take. The complexity of the decision is illustrated by the USCR's discussion of the case of South Africa.

The number of internally displaced South Africans is a politically sensitive issue. A series of apartheid laws passed from 1948 to 1982 forcibly removed millions of blacks from their land. Under apartheid statutes dating back to the South African Land Act of 1913, about 87 percent of all agricultural land was reserved for whites, even though they made up only 13 percent of the population. An estimated 3.5 million people were displaced between 1960 and 1980 alone.[49]

The majority of people uprooted by years of apartheid, however, appear to have no realistic prospects of reclaiming their ancestors' land or gaining new land because of the government's limited resources and competing societal needs. Many families displaced from their property during apartheid have reintegrated into other areas and may no longer consider themselves displaced, despite their poverty. Those who have moved from rural areas to the townships, for example, are unlikely to reclaim land that their ancestors once farmed. They are said to have lost the sense of where they came from and to have urbanized.

In 1994–95 the government began organizing a threefold land reform program consisting of land redistribution, land restitution, and land tenure reform. The Land Claims Court created under the Restitution of Land Rights Act of 1994 received about 5,000 claims by the end of 1995. The claims are only for private property and do not include claims from those who were forcibly removed from one government property to another, which explains in part why the number is so low. South Africans have until May 1998 to submit their claims.

Population displacement was a particularly urgent problem in Kwa-Zulu Natal Province, where political violence and apartheid left about 500,000 persons internally displaced.[50] An estimated 5,000 to 10,000 additional people became displaced in Kwa-Zulu Natal Province in 1995 as a result of political violence between the Inkatha Freedom Party and the African National Congress.

Although the land problems of millions of South Africans have not been resolved, in 1996 the USCR reduced the number of internally displaced persons from 4 million to 500,000 people. The latter estimate was based on the number of internally displaced resulting from recent violence or from formal appeals filed for restitution of land. In a sense, this was an artificial, "book-keeping" adjustment, because the USCR could have revised the figure downward at any time since the change in South Africa's government. However, the decision was finally made after discussions with many people in South Africa (government officials, NGOs, and others) indicated that listing such a large number of internally displaced persons—many of whom had been "displaced" for generations— did not quite capture the problem in South Africa. The listing, moreover, raised expectations that a solution would be forthcoming, something that the government would not be able to deliver. Some of those surveyed in South Africa said that the internally displaced figure used previously may have been too high because some people had been counted twice or may have left the country. Moreover, since the end of apartheid, it could be argued that the displacement of many is now a land and economics issue and that in some cases people who had never been "displaced" are living in worse conditions than those who had been displaced generations ago.

Regional Dynamics

Regional trends, taken together, provide a global picture of internal displacement. The regional trends discussed in this section are constructed from USCR facts and figures on displacement in the four major continents and its analysis of the efforts of governments, the international community, and the displaced themselves to address the problem.[51] The points of primary interest are the number of displaced, causes of displacement, location of the displaced, demographic characteristics, living conditions, protection problems, and the response at the national, regional, and international levels.

Africa: The Greatest Challenge

Half of the world's internally displaced persons—more than 9 million—are to be found in Africa. In 1995 significant displaced populations could be found in at least fourteen countries. Four—Angola, Liberia, Sierra Leone, and the Sudan—each counted a million or more displaced persons (the Sudan was in the lead with 4 million). Three—Mozambique, Rwanda, and South Africa—each had about a half million displaced. Four states—Burundi, Kenya, Somalia, and the Democratic Republic of the Congo (at the time, Zaire) counted 200,000 to 400,000 internally displaced. Smaller, but significant, numbers of persons were displaced in Ghana, Uganda, Nigeria, and Algeria.

But although displacement has grown in some countries, it has declined in others. More than 3 million Mozambicans who were internally displaced as recently as 1993 had returned to their homes or were permanently resettled by the end of 1996. During 1993–96, displaced Angolans declined by a half million or more, and displaced Somalis declined by 400,000. In recent years, the number of displaced Ethiopians has declined by an estimated 200,000.

Most of the countries affected by internal displacement in Africa have suffered from acute problems associated with nation building: crises of national identity and unity, ineffective government authority and control, limited capacity for economic productivity and resource distribution and, above all, tensions between centralized political and economic forces and the demands of various constituencies for autonomy and equitable participation in political and economic life. In most cases, the immediate cause of displacement was civil war or armed insurgency, which forced large numbers from their homes—as in Angola, Burundi, Liberia, Sierra Leone, Somalia, the Sudan, and Uganda. When civil war deteriorated into anarchy and the country suffered near total collapse, as in Liberia, the majority of the population became internally displaced. Egregious human rights abuses, such as the genocide in Rwanda and the white minority regime's forced resettlement of blacks in South Africa, also uprooted large numbers.

Ethnic strife, in some cases manipulated by governments, has contributed heavily to displacement, notably in South Africa, Kenya, Ethiopia,

Congo (Zaire), and Ghana. Often, the objective is to expel certain ethnic groups from their lands while enriching others who have been politically supportive. Investigations in Kenya have shown the complicity of authorities in provoking and sustaining population displacement of certain ethnic groups during the 1990s for political purposes.[52] Forms of "ethnic cleansing" have also been practiced in Burundi, where hundreds of thousands of Hutu civilians have been uprooted in recent years, and "ethnic cleansing" operations have been conducted by the army in sections of the capital, Bujumbura. In Congo (Zaire), government officials instigated "ethnic cleansing" in the southern Shaba region in 1993, while authorities in the eastern part of the country acquiesced and at times assisted in the "ethnic cleansing" of Tutsis in 1995–96.[53] Tutsi retaliation against the government gained momentum and became transformed into the movement that succeeded in overthrowing the Mobutu government in 1997.

Refugee repatriation is another common source of internal displacement in Africa, because many of the returning refugees' villages and towns of origin have been destroyed by war. Following the sudden return of hundreds of thousands of Rwandan refugees from Congo (Zaire) in 1996, many returnees became internally displaced, either because they feared returning to their villages of origin, where they thought they might face reprisal, or because their homes and lands had been occupied by others. In Ethiopia, demobilization following the war with Eritrea became a source of displacement. In Mozambique, a residual population of internally displaced persons remained uprooted in 1996 owing to problems with resettlement assistance, concerns about land mines, or ambivalence about their true "home," even though the civil war ended in 1992.

In at least half of the fourteen African countries with large displaced populations, uprooted families have gravitated to capital cities for protection and assistance. In many cases, however, the internally displaced establish spontaneous settlements or camps. In 1996 the majority of persons displaced by Angola's civil war were living in or near major towns and cities in government-controlled areas. A smaller but still significant number—probably several hundred thousand—lived in camplike settlements in rebel-controlled rural areas. About one-third of the estimated 4 million persons displaced in the Sudan remained in the south in encampments or on their own while nearly half fled to the capital, Khartoum, in the north, where they now live amid the sprawling urban population or in a series of camps or satellite "towns." In Liberia, as many as three-quarters of a million displaced fled to the capital, Monrovia, whose population nearly tripled in size during the civil war. Smaller but significant numbers of Liberians have fled to the country's secondary urban centers.

The flight to major urban centers in Africa has created tremendous pressures on social services, water, and sanitation. In Luanda, Angola, "the pressure of tripling the population overloaded facilities [and] hastened the deterioration of urban infrastructure already near the point of collapse."[54] Camps and settlements have also done damage to rural areas, subjecting them to "unusual patterns of land use and ecological pressures," because of "short-sighted survival strategies."[55] Whatever the form of displacement, its massive nature in Africa has been causing "irreparable damage to ecosystems and overloading urban infrastructure at a time when maintenance capability is at its lowest."[56]

A large proportion of the internally displaced are known to be women and children, as is the case among refugee populations. In African countries beset by armed conflict, many of the displaced women become heads of households because "the men are fighting, have chosen to stay behind to protect their land, have been killed or have gone to cities or left the country to avoid recruitment in the military or to seek employment."[57] Demographic studies of Burundi's displaced population found that a disproportionate number were widows and their children. Many countries also report large numbers of unaccompanied minors who have been separated from their families or whose families have died.[58]

Displacement in some countries is so pervasive that it affects all the main ethnic groups. A case in point is Liberia. So is Burundi, where the Hutu accounted for perhaps two-thirds of the uprooted population, and Tutsi made up the remaining one third. In other countries, those displaced are primarily the ethnic groups subjected to discrimination. In the Sudan, a large proportion of the displaced are Dinkas and Nuers; in Kenya, most of the displaced are Kikuyus and other non-Kalenjin groups. In Congo (Zaire), families that had voluntarily migrated from Kasai to the Shaba region throughout the twentieth century became targets of violence in 1993 and thus were forced to "return" to Kasai, even though many had lived in Shaba for generations. The displaced included large numbers of educated, skilled, white-collar workers.[59]

According to UN studies, ten of the African countries with significant displaced populations are among the thirty poorest countries in the world. Conditions for those who become displaced are abysmal beyond description. Displaced families who are fortunate enough to live with friends or family commonly reside thirty persons or more in a single home, sharing a few small rooms. Others live in abandoned buildings typically lacking windows, doors, or basic amenities. Other displaced Africans dwell in makeshift huts covered, if fortunate, by plastic sheeting supplied by relief agencies. Some have access to farming, some do not. Medical care is usually minimal, if it exists at all. According to health experts, the internally displaced in Mozambique suffered in greater degree than the general population from malnutrition, skin disease, respiratory infections, diarrhea, and malaria, as well as occasional outbreaks of cholera and measles.[60] Their living conditions, particularly the overcrowding and poor sanitation in shantytowns around cities, tended to exacerbate these health problems.

In Liberia, although displaced families have streamed into the capital, finding shelter in bombed-out offices and apartment buildings or crowded shacks where sanitation is often poor, extensive malnutrition has been rare. By contrast, neighboring Sierra Leone reported child malnutrition rates as high as 70 percent among displaced persons in 1995, a period in which the country's armed insurgency made relief deliveries impossible in many areas. During 1995 reports of a "starvation zone" also surfaced in several eastern towns that contained at least a quarter million displaced persons. In late 1995 a cholera epidemic swept through much of the country, particularly in areas of displacement.

In the Sudan, the nearly two million displaced in and around Khartoum inhabit shantytowns and government-designated sites up to thirty miles outside the city, isolated from employment opportunities and often deprived of basic services available in the city. Some persons displaced in the south inhabit camps where food and medical services are occasionally available, while others inhabit remote encampments that are inaccessible to relief supplies and hence suffer high rates of malnutrition and, at times, famine.

Humanitarian relief workers and Africans themselves have observed that living conditions and services in official refugee camps are better in some ways than conditions in the refugees' home areas. For internally displaced Africans, however, living conditions are consistently worse and almost always more arduous than any conditions they might have previously experienced in normal times.

Protection problems, in particular, are severe. Widespread atrocities, ranging from simple banditry to large-scale massacres, have been committed against displaced populations. Liberian camps for displaced persons have been the scenes of numerous massacres throughout the war by all armed factions. The most notorious massacre occurred in mid-1993, when some 550 displaced persons were slaughtered at a camp known as Harbel, outside Monrovia.[61] In the Sudan, uprooted persons have been deliberately bombed by government planes, attacked on the ground by government soldiers and government-backed militias, and ambushed by rebel troops. A government military offensive in late 1994 and early 1995 forced some 60,000 occupants of a displaced persons camp to flee again.[62] In Rwanda, in 1995, government troops fired on displaced Hutus in camps (some of whom were armed, may have participated in the earlier genocide, and were urging others not to return home). The Kibeho massacre, in which several thousand were killed, became the largest known mass killing of the internally displaced in a camp setting (for a fuller discussion, see chapters 4 and 7).

Dangers faced by displaced women and children throughout Africa bear special mention. Many of the women are victims of sexual violence, intimidation, and local inheritance laws that discriminate against widows attempting to retain family property after the death of their husbands.[63] In Liberia, more than 600 women, the majority of them believed to be displaced, were raped in the town of Buchanan in the first half of 1995.[64] Displaced children suffer the same risks encountered by other African children in war-affected areas, but much more. In Liberia and the Sudan, uprooted children have regularly been subjected to military conscription. Perhaps the most extreme abuses against children occurred in Mozambique during the 1980s, when rebel troops in particular forced children to serve as soldiers, porters, sexual partners, and human shields.[65]

As the foregoing remarks suggest, governments and rebel forces are directly implicated in the abuse of the internally displaced in Africa, though not all African governments deal harshly with displaced populations. In Ghana, the government imposed curfews and confiscated weapons in an effort to stem the violence in the north responsible for displacement. In Mozambique, the government has shown genuine concern for the humanitarian needs of the displaced and has encouraged the international community to help them reintegrate. In Rwanda, the country's relatively new government has designated permanent resettlement areas for displaced persons who cannot return to their homes, although as of mid-1996 the policy had produced minimal results.

But even if favorably disposed toward their displaced populations, few African governments have the resources to deal with the problem in its entirety. The overwhelming majority of displaced populations in Africa must rely on international humanitarian agencies and NGOs for emergency aid, protection, and reintegration assistance. Unlike the often systematic relief provided to refugees, however, the assistance displaced populations in Africa receive from UN agencies and NGOs is of an ad hoc nature; as a result, some pockets of displaced populations receive regular aid, whereas others receive little or none.

International attention did focus on Angola and Mozambique in the first half of the 1990s in support of return and reintegration. The United Nation's deployment of peacekeeping troops in these countries played a role in encouraging millions of uprooted Mozambicans to return home, although in Angola, the return process has been impeded by the security situation. In early 1996, UN agencies issued an appeal for $187 million for Angola to fund a range of activities, in part aimed at supporting 700,000 displaced persons and helping 200,000 of them to return home. IOM became involved in transporting displaced persons, UNICEF prepositioned basic relief and survival items in home areas, and a UN humanitarian assistance coordination unit inside Angola established a special group to handle technical matters related to the return home of displaced families, including the deactivation of land mines.

A similar range of UN agencies has operated in Mozambique, partly coordinated on the ground by the UN office for humanitarian assistance coordination. UNHCR emerged in 1993 as the main UN operating agency, largely because of its responsibilities toward the 1.7 million refugees who gradually repatriated during 1993–95. Using food supplied by the World Food Programme, UNHCR distributions to returning refugees at times targeted internally displaced persons going home. During the worst years of Mozambique's war, however, internally displaced populations outside Maputo received minimal UN assistance, partly because of the security concerns of relief workers and partly because no single UN agency had primary responsibility for assisting the internally displaced.

During internal conflicts, ICRC and international NGOs often manage to gain better access to displaced populations than do UN agencies. At times, this was the case in Mozambique, Liberia, Sierra Leone, and Somalia. In Somalia, UN operations in 1995 and early 1996 were hampered by security concerns and financial shortfalls, whereas ICRC was able to provide food, seeds, and fishing equipment to displaced families and undertook efforts at protection. Before 1996 security concerns also limited UN operations in Sierra Leone, although during 1995 the WFP was able to provide food assistance to some 300,000 beneficiaries, most of them displaced. UNICEF implemented programs in health, nutrition, basic education, and water and sanitation. And UNHCR provided limited assistance to internally displaced persons when they were mixed with returning refugees. But overall, UN programs in Sierra Leone have been extremely limited, with NGOs providing most food and nonfood items, operating clinics, and extending agricultural assistance. In 1996, as security conditions improved, UN agencies issued an interagency appeal for $57 million to step up assistance efforts, with much of the money targeted to help displaced persons and refugees return home.

In the Sudan, the United Nations has played a significant role in reaching internally displaced populations through Operation Lifeline Sudan (OLS). As earlier mentioned, it was negotiated with the government and rebel forces in 1989 and enabled the United Nations and voluntary agencies to provide food, medicines, and needed relief to substantial numbers of displaced persons throughout the country. In recent years, however, the Sudanese government has effectively managed to obstruct aid deliveries to the internally displaced in government-controlled areas in the north and in the Nuba mountains, and the United Nations has been sharply criticized for not effectively challenging this.[66]

In many African countries, indigenous NGOs are able to play some role, although most such organizations are small and can offer only limited assistance to the internally displaced. Sometimes they are linked to, or perceived to be linked to, local political groups or to combatants, which makes their role less effective. But at times, they may be the only source of assistance and protection for the internally displaced, especially in conflict situations. Local NGOs have played a substantial role in Sierra Leone: local Red Cross and church groups have been major distributors of food supplied by the WFP; the Council of Churches has operated several camps for uprooted families; the Methodist Church has administered camps, clinics, and feeding stations in western areas of the country; and the local YMCA operated a loan program for women and small education programs. A large number of indigenous churches and NGOs have flourished in Liberia as well.[67] And local church groups have been instrumental in providing assistance in Kenya, while human rights organizations have investigated the causes of displacement.

At times, local groups have found that the involvement of UN agencies and international NGOs undercuts rather than reinforces their operations with the internally displaced. In Kenya, local groups working with the displaced claimed that the UNDP "ignored and marginalized NGO advice," tried to do everything itself, and did not provide NGOs "with protection from government criticism for the work they were doing."[68] In the view of one church group, the United Nations "should have tapped into existing structures which the NGO community in Kenya had already set up. Instead, they came in and centralized their program through the local government administration structures and completely marginalized the NGOs."[69] When the UN withdrew, local efforts nearly collapsed.

Regional organizations in Africa have not yet begun to play a role among the internally displaced other than in Liberia, where the Economic Community of West African States (ECOWAS) sent a military force (see chapter 6). The difficulty for Africa is that, being the poorest continent, it has the fewest resources to deal with its crises of internal displacement and the least prospect of receiving outside assistance commensurate with the magnitude of its problems. The pervasive crisis of national identity created by the artificial borders of the colonial state can be expected to continue to give rise to ethnic and racial strife within and between states. Intense competition for power and scarce economic resources will also remain at the core of many crises. Although some of Africa's conflicts were compounded by the cold war and stopped when U.S.-Soviet rivalry ended, others intensified with the removal of superpower control mechanisms, causing states to collapse. The great challenge for Africans will be to find the means and the methods to cope with crises of internal displacement through their own national capacities and those of regional and subregional organizations, albeit with a helping hand from the international community.

Europe: Waves of Ethnic Dislocation

For the first time since the end of the Second World War, Europe has become home to large numbers of internally displaced persons and refugees. At the end of 1996, the continent had close to five million internally displaced persons, roughly double the number of its refugees and nearly as many as in Asia. Apart from Turkey and Cyprus, which have the longest history of internal displacement in the region, Eastern Europe and the Caucasus are the main centers of internally displaced populations, as a direct result of the breakdown of the former Soviet Union and the former Yugoslavia. In 1996 significant displaced populations existed in seven countries (in order of gravity): Turkey, Bosnia and Herzegovina, Azerbaijan, the Russian Federation, Georgia, Cyprus, and Croatia. Throughout Europe, the predominant cause of internal displacement was ethnic-related conflict.

Turkey has up to 2 million internally displaced persons, uprooted because of the conflict between the government and the Kurdish Workers Party (PKK) that began in 1984. According to the USCR, "although PKK threats and attacks have caused some of the displacement, during the past two years, much of the displacement was caused by the government's deliberate and systematic campaign to depopulate villages" thought to provide support for the PKK.[70] Some 2,000 Kurdish villages have been destroyed or damaged since 1992. Estimates of the number of displaced vary widely. Turkey's minister for human rights, in a statement made in 1994, put the figure at 2 million; other Turkish authorities have reported much lower figures or have denied that any displacement has occurred.[71] Kurdish sources, on the other hand, say the figure is as high as 3 million.

As in the case of Turkey, it is difficult to estimate the number of internally displaced in Chechnya in the Russian Federation. In part, this is due to the actual fluctuations in the number of persons displaced at any one time, as massive displacements caused by periods of intense fighting are often followed by a quick return after the fighting subsides. This was the case in December 1994, when Russian government forces invaded Chechnya and the number of displaced swelled to about 450,000, but then most returned after the fighting subsided. However, with vast destruction of population centers—Grozny was 70 percent destroyed at the end of December 1994—many were not able to return to their original homes.

Also within the Russian Federation, an estimated 50,000 persons from the Prigorodnyi region of North Ossetia were displaced because of ethnic conflict between Ossetians and Ingush. Although both ethnic groups were displaced at the height of the fighting in 1992, most of the estimated 9,000 displaced Ossetians have since returned to their home areas, which are under Ossetian control. The displaced Ingush, on the other hand, fear being attacked by Ossetians if they return, a fear substantiated by the shooting and stoning of Ossetians who have attempted to go home.[72]

In the first phase of the breakup of Yugoslavia, the situation was in some respects comparable to that in Russia and Chechnya. The central organs of the state, including the Yugoslav People's Army (JNA), were dominated by Serbs (just as the USSR was dominated by Russians). When Croatia and Slovenia declared their independence, the central state power was intent on maintaining the territorial and political status quo as well as protecting the Serbs in areas where secession would transform them from the dominant ethnic group to an ethnic minority.

In Croatia and Bosnia and Herzegovina both types of "ethnic cleansing" occurred—ethnically pure communities were created while rival groups were expelled from valued territories. Serb nationalists in both Croatia and Bosnia sought to create ethnically homogeneous Serb communities in areas that previously had been ethnically mixed. Consequently, "ethnic cleansing" often occurred village by village, house by house, forcing out Muslims and Croats and tilting the demographic balance decidedly toward the Serbs. Also, because concentrations of ethnic Serb communities were often somewhat isolated, another goal of "ethnic cleansing" was to create contiguous territories connecting these various concentrations. In the process, Serb power was also exercised to seek other territory of perceived strategic importance.

As the war progressed, both the Croats and, to a much lesser extent, the Muslims engaged in "ethnic cleansing" as well. The Croatian offensive in the Krajina in August 1995 swept between 150,000 and 200,000 Serbs out of the area; of this number, 60,000 remained internally displaced in the Serb-controlled UN-protected areas (Sector East) in eastern Slavonia. In 1996 most of the 40,000 to 50,000 ethnic Serbs living in the suburbs surrounding Sarajevo left when control of the area was transferred to the Croat-Muslim Federation; most moved to the "Republika Srpska" carved out of eastern and northern Bosnia. Although some pressure to leave was exerted by Muslim elements, nationalist Serbs took the lead in coercing their coethnics to leave the area.

"Ethnic cleansing" has also been evident in the internal displacement occurring in the North Caucasus and Transcaucasus regions. Such practices have also been reported in Azerbaijan. However, the repression of Armenians in cities such as Sumgait and Baku did not result in their internal displacement, but rather in their flight to Armenia or Russia. Most Armenian refugees had fled or been expelled from Azerbaijan by 1990, as had most ethnic Azerbaijanis from Armenia. Internal displacement occurred in and around the Armenian-occupied enclave of

Nagorno-Karabakh, forcing Azerbaijanis into government-controlled areas. After some two years of see-saw battles, the Armenians of Nagorno-Karabakh succeeded in 1992 in pushing out all Azerbaijanis, who constituted about one-quarter of Nagorno-Karabakh's population before the conflict began, making the area purely Armenian in ethnic composition. In 1992 and 1993 the Armenians began expanding their territorial hold, pushing out in all directions from Nagorno-Karabakh and displacing hundreds of thousands of Azerbaijanis from areas that had had negligible Armenian populations before the war.

The location of displaced persons in Europe is closely linked to their ethnic identity. In Cyprus, for example, the island became partitioned along ethnic lines. The first forced displacements occurred between 1963 and 1970, during which time about 20,000 Turkish Cypriots fled threats and violence, congregating in forty-two ethnic enclaves. After the Turkish invasion in 1974, some 50,000 to 60,000 Turkish Cypriots fled north, including most of the people who had previously been displaced. At the same time, some 180,000 to 200,000 Greeks fled south in an uncoordinated exodus.[73] Today, some 200,000 Greek Cypriots and 65,000 Turkish Cypriots are still displaced, although they left their homes in 1974.

In most cases in Europe (but with notable exceptions, such as Turkey), persons are displaced out of areas in which they were part of an ethnic minority into areas in which they belong to the majority group. This is the pattern of displacement not only in Cyprus but also in the Russian Federation, Azerbaijan, Bosnia and Herzegovina, Croatia, and Georgia.

Usually, persons who were displaced for the short term owing to flare-ups in fighting remained close to home, often congregating in collective centers hastily thrown together, or staying with friends or relatives. Such was the case with the Chechens who managed to flee the shelling and bombing of population centers, either by seeking shelter in rural areas within Chechnya itself, or by fleeing to neighboring Ingushetia and Dagestan, autonomous republics, like Chechnya, within the Russian Federation. Of those displaced within Chechnya, the majority were estimated to be in the southern part of the republic, which was under the control of the secessionists. Reception facilities in Ingushetia and throughout the Northern Caucasus were close to the breaking point by the end of 1995. As a result, most of the persons displaced by the war in Chechnya in the early months of 1996 found shelter with relatives, friends, or host families. Russians displaced from Chechnya were more likely to gravitate to areas where Russians form the ethnic majority, particularly to Stavropol

Kray, northwest of Chechnya. Those without family connections were often directed to reception centers in other parts of Russia, including the Volga region, the Urals, and Siberia.

Many Georgians from Abkhazia initially fled on foot across the Georgian range in poor weather conditions. After they were evacuated from the mountains and provided with emergency supplies such as food and blankets, the displaced were brought to various cities and towns in which Georgians are in the majority.[74] About 72,000 moved to Zugdidi, a city very close to Abkhazia, where most were taken in by local families. Others there were living in poor conditions in collective centers, without heat. Some of the displaced Georgians from Abkhazia moved to Kutaisi, where they lived in schoolhouses and hotels. Those who moved to the capital, Tbilisi, were provided with basics, such as heat and electricity, which reportedly caused resentment among Tbilisi's permanent residents.[75]

In Turkey, the general pattern of displacement in Europe, which finds minorities moving to majority areas, is reversed. Displaced Kurds have crowded into cities of southeastern and central Turkey, such as Diyarbakir and Batman, which have more than doubled in population as a result of the influx of displaced persons;[76] substantial numbers have also migrated to Ankara, Istanbul and Izmir.

The displaced in Europe are ethnic groups, and most are women and children. In Chechnya, women and children are estimated to make up more than 95 percent of displaced civilians, as virtually all adult males have taken up arms. Similarly, in Bosnia and Croatia, collective centers for the displaced are overwhelmingly populated by women, children, the infirm, and the elderly, since men of military age have been inducted into armed forces. In Azerbaijan, 42 percent of the beneficiaries are children under fifteen years of age, 31 percent are women, and 15 percent are elderly.

Internal displacement often exacerbates urban-rural tensions. In Cyprus, for example, most of the displaced Greeks were of rural background, but agricultural land was not available in the south.[77] When they moved into urban areas, they had difficulty adjusting to new livelihoods. There was less rural-to-urban movement among displaced Turkish Cypriots because much more agricultural land was available to them: as a result of the Turkish invasion, 18 percent of the island's population gained 37 percent of the land, and some of the richest agricultural land at that.

In Azerbaijan, the displaced from inside Nagorno-Karabakh were mountain people involved in herding, and they had to adapt to life in cities and on plains. The large number from outside Nagorno-Karabakh were displaced from a farming region. Because the strain on the cities of Baku and Sumgait had been so great from earlier waves of rural displaced people, the authorities set up roadblocks in 1993 to prevent the newest wave of displaced persons from entering the municipal areas.

Clearly, it is difficult to generalize about living conditions for internally displaced persons in Europe. Not only does each situation go through its own phases, but conditions vary from country to country, depending on general living standards, climate, topography, numbers of persons affected, severity of the war or conflict, and the extent to which humanitarian aid is obstructed. There is, however, usually an initial phase of internal displacement in which newly displaced persons lack shelter and other basic necessities. In Chechnya and Azerbaijan, it was not uncommon to see groups of displaced persons camped out on the sides of roads, constructing makeshift shelters using sticks, blankets, and vehicles. Such emergency phases usually pass quickly, and European internally displaced persons are generally able to gain access to humanitarian assistance, including temporary shelter either in tents or in collective centers.

Still, for a good number of people living conditions have remained barely tolerable even after the emergency phase has passed, as is the case in Azerbaijan. In 1995 more than 92,000 people were still living in tents and prefabricated shelters; 60,000 were living in mud huts and other makeshift dwellings; 50,000 in sanatoriums, rest houses, and hotels; 40,000 in hostels; and 10,000 in railroad cars. Others were still living in communal buildings such as schools and dormitories. Social services were minimal. More than 30 percent of internally displaced children in Azerbaijan had no access to schools. About 70 percent were estimated to be unemployed.[78]

However, most internally displaced persons in Europe do not live in camps but rather find relatives or friends who are willing to share their homes. Usually, the displaced persons are cut off from their means of livelihood and become dependent on charity (usually private, sometimes international, but seldom national) for their sustenance. In Georgia, the government assistance plan distinguishes between displaced persons living in private homes and those in government-provided accommodations. For the former, the government provides assistance at twice the minimum wage. In cases of internally displaced persons in rural areas, the government also endeavors to provide temporary allotments of land. Persons living in government housing receive monthly assistance equivalent to one-third of the minimum wage, plus rationed bread.[79]

In Russia, more than 90 percent of the persons displaced by the war in Chechnya in the early months of 1995 found shelter with relatives, friends, or host families. However, conditions were poor and assistance meager. Those displaced persons who were unable to find accommodations with host families, relatives, or friends were encouraged by the Federal Migration Service to go to reception centers in other parts of Russia, including the Volga region, the Urals, and Siberia. But for displaced persons from the Caucasus, the long journey to these locations and the bleak prospect of life in a rudimentary accommodation center made this an unattractive option. Conditions in collective centers were crude, especially in Ingushetia and throughout the Northern Caucasus after a major influx of displaced persons from Chechnya in early 1995. In Nazran, Ingushetia, a camp consisting solely of train cars became the temporary home of nearly a thousand displaced persons from Chechnya, each car holding about fifty persons. In Stavropol Kray, where many displaced ethnic Russians from Chechnya fled, about 94 percent of all registered forced migrants did not have adequate housing.[80]

European governments are usually willing to assist persons belonging to the same ethnic group as the dominant one in the government: for example, ethnic Russians in Russia, ethnic Georgians in Georgia, ethnic Azerbaijanis in Azerbaijan, or Bosnian Muslims in government-controlled parts of Bosnia. Others sometimes find themselves badly neglected.

Turkey is a case in point. The government views displaced Kurds as potentially sympathetic to PKK insurgents and has not demonstrated a willingness to assist them. Although it announced two assistance programs—a "Central Villages" project in 1994 and a "Return to Villages" project in 1995—neither project was ever implemented.[81] A July 1995 report to the U.S. Congress from the Department of State called Turkish government programs on behalf of the internally displaced "very inadequate": "Few displaced villagers have been compensated, and there seems to be an ad hoc quality to most compensations."[82] Furthermore, there was no provision in the Turkish government's 1995 budget for assistance to the displaced. Substantial numbers who crowded into shantytowns outside major cities reportedly have no access to proper sanitation, health care, or educational facilities for the young, and no stable employment prospects.[83]

In the Russian Federation, the flow of about 130,000 internally displaced Chechens in January 1995 created a severe strain on the autonomous republic of Ingushetia.[84] The president of Ingushetia complained bitterly of the lack of assistance from Moscow to deal with the displaced population, which as a result of the war in Chechnya almost equaled the republic's permanent population. This gave Ingushetia one of the highest ratios of displaced persons to permanent population in the world. In Stavropol, however, where most of the displaced from Chechnya were ethnic Russians, the migration service did have a budget ($5 million for 1995), although it was inadequate to meet the assistance needs of the estimated 100,000 forced migrants.[85]

In cases where displaced persons belong to the state's ethnic majority, governments are more likely to stretch their resources to accommodate displaced persons, who also receive support from the majority ethnic communities. In Croatia, the government established an Office for Displaced Persons and Refugees to direct and coordinate an ambitious assistance program for displaced persons, making space available during the emergency phase in hotels, hostels, barracks, and gymnasiums, and seeking longer-term accommodation in private homes. Another example of preferential treatment is to be found in Azerbaijan. The government, anxious to help the Azerbaijanis displaced from Nagorno-Karabakh and the surrounding areas, created a State Committee for Refugees and Internally Displaced Persons, as well as a Department on Refugees and Internally Displaced Persons, and provided an allowance equal to the minimum monthly salary.[86]

Internally displaced persons in Europe have often faced severe and continuing threats to their lives after having fled their homes. Displaced persons who congregated in many of the UN-protected "safe areas" in Bosnia found their food and medicine shipments blocked and their members subjected to direct attack. The most tragic and well-publicized event occurred in July 1995 when the Srebrenica "safe area" fell and more than 5,000 Muslim men and boys, separated from their families by Bosnian Serb forces, "disappeared," with only about 4,000 out of 12,000 to 15,000 reaching government lines. In Chechnya in December 1995, internally displaced persons fleeing its second largest city, Gudermes, were attacked by Russian military helicopters as they fled along the three main routes leaving the city.[87] The Russian government's hostility toward displaced persons and at-risk civilians from Chechnya was also evident in the refusal of the Russian military to allow ICRC and other humanitarian organizations to provide humanitarian assistance for long periods or to monitor conditions in Grozny, Gudermes, and other locations.[88]

The role of the United Nations, particularly that of UNHCR, on behalf of internally displaced persons in Europe has been complex, varied, and controversial. Although the UN presence has made humanitarian assistance available to internally displaced persons, it has not had a demonstrated impact in preventing the displacement of civilians from their homes in the midst of ethnic conflict. Nor has it shown itself able to provide effective protection for the displaced at critical periods. Moreover, its presence has unintentionally given neighboring states a pretext to deny would-be refugees avenues of escape, causing them to remain internally displaced.

In Bosnia, the mandate and role of UNHCR underwent a dramatic transformation, from that of an agency whose sole purpose was to secure asylum for refugees and prevent their involuntary return to persecution into an organization that also provided humanitarian assistance during conflict to internally displaced persons and other at-risk populations.[89] UNHCR was designated the lead UN humanitarian agency in Bosnia. It was less than successful in negotiating political solutions to the problems confronting displaced persons, but it played a key role in sustaining besieged populations and maintained a useful coordinating role not only for UN agencies but also for its NGO implementing partners (for a more detailed discussion of the role of the United Nations, see chapters 4 and 7).

In Georgia, the United Nations was instrumental in forging the April 1994 Quadripartite Agreement on Voluntary Return of Refugees and Displaced Persons to Abkhazia and in subsequent negotiations to implement its return provisions, which affected 280,000 internally displaced persons. UNHCR's work was closely coordinated with that of the UN Observer Mission in Georgia (UNOMIG), a presence intended to attenuate conditions causing persons to flee and to ameliorate conditions preventing their return. Unfortunately, the mediating role of the United Nations could be no more effective than the willingness of the parties to the conflict to resolve their differences. In Georgia, Abkhaz authorities interfered with the return of internally displaced persons, rendering the Quadripartite Agreement an empty promise.[90]

Elsewhere, the United Nations and international NGOs have been less active on behalf of internally displaced persons. In Turkey, in particular, they have not sought to challenge the government's resistance to international involvement with its internally displaced populations.

The formerly communist countries producing the largest numbers of internally displaced persons have little or no tradition of national or local NGO involvement in humanitarian affairs. Rather, the activities associated in the West with NGOs were organized and controlled by the state. Efforts to develop and train local NGOs in refugee and migration issues has been undertaken by international NGOs, most notably the European Council on Refugees and Exiles and the Open Society Institute. Not surprisingly, the most well-developed local NGO presence can be found on the Greek Cypriot side of Cyprus, where local NGOs have had many years to organize themselves and to become active. The displaced Greek Cypriots themselves have created the Pan-Cyprien Refugee Committee, an umbrella organization that counts all displaced as its members and works on their behalf.[91]

The Organization for Security and Cooperation in Europe has responded to internal displacement mainly with efforts at conflict resolution, but it has also begun to encourage the discussion of issues relating to forced migration and has initiated activities in the field for the internally displaced (a full discussion of the OSCE's role and potential can be found in chapter 6). In Europe as a whole (except in Turkey), large-scale internal displacement has for the most part been the consequence of the collapse of communist regimes. Authoritarian communism was the glue that held diverse and sometimes mutually antagonistic ethnic communities together, all the while denying them their rights. In some respects, countries in post-communist Europe may be suffering a national identity crisis not unlike that faced by African countries. The test of emerging democracies will be their ability to create pluralistic frameworks in which different ethnic and minority groups can coexist and be accepted as part of the national identity.

Asia: A Patchwork of Displacement

Although internal displacement is not widespread in Asia, it is a serious problem in a number of countries. Altogether, Asia has some 5 million internally displaced persons. Most are located in a patchwork of eight countries in western, central, southern, and southeastern Asia, respectively: Lebanon and Iraq; Tajikistan and Afghanistan; India and Sri Lanka; and Myanmar (Burma) and Cambodia. In East Asia, significant displacement occurs only in the Philippines.

In western Asia the largest uprooted population consists of Palestinians (more than 3.5 million) living on the West Bank, Gaza Strip, and neighboring countries. They are recognized as refugees, however, not internally displaced persons, and are assisted by a UN agency created specifically for them: the United Nations Relief and Works Agency for Palestine Refugees in the Near East (UNRWA).[92]

In Lebanon, the number of displaced persons has dropped by about half since the end of the civil war in 1990. Although estimates have always varied, from a high of about 1 million at the height of the civil war, the number remaining of chronically displaced in Lebanon was approximately 450,000 in 1996. In northern Iraq, about 650,000 persons are displaced out of a total population of about 3.1 million. Of that number, about 420,000 Kurds displaced from homes within the Kurdish-controlled north have not been able to return. Another 230,000 displaced persons in northern Iraq, mostly Kurds, originate in government-controlled areas. In 1996 new groups of Kurds were becoming displaced in northern Iraq as a result of factional fighting between rival Kurdish forces. In southern Iraq the number of persons displaced to, from, and within the marshlands (the region between the Tigris and Euphrates rivers) is nearly impossible to determine because the Iraqi regime denies the United Nations and relief agencies access to the area. Estimates of the number of the displaced and the at-risk populations range from 40,000 to 1,000,000, with 200,000 probably being a fair guess, subject to periodic fluctuations.

In central Asia, Tajikistan's plunge into civil war following independence and the breakup of the Soviet Union caused more than 520,000 Tajiks to become displaced, while some 60,000 Tajik refugees fled to Afghanistan. With a reduction in the fighting, most of the internally displaced returned home in 1993, but renewed conflict in 1996 caused further displacement; and some 20,000 Tajik refugees remained in Afghanistan.[93]

South Asia has the largest internally displaced population in Asia, nearly 2.4 million, as a result of conflicts in Afghanistan, Sri Lanka, and India. Millions of Afghans became uprooted, both as refugees and internally displaced persons, during the years of Soviet occupation and the Mujahedin's war against the Soviet-backed government. Many of the refugees and displaced returned home after the Mujahedin defeated the government. However, a number of them, as well as many Afghans who had remained in place during the "Soviet years," became internally displaced when fighting broke out between the various Mujahedin factions. According to USCR estimates, the displaced numbered some 500,000 at the end of 1995. Intense fighting in 1996, when the militant Islamic Taliban militia clashed with traditional Mujahedin warlords and seized control of Jalalabad and Kabul, resulted in additional large-scale displacement.

Some 250,000 are displaced in India as a result of the conflict in Kashmir state between the Indian authorities and Pakistan-backed Muslim separatists. Since the early 1980s Sri Lanka has experienced waves of internal displacement, which by late 1995 left it with 725,000 displaced persons, mostly Tamils. A government offensive that resulted in the capture of the Liberation Tigers of Tamil Eelam's (LTTE) main base in Jaffna, Sri Lanka's second largest city, displaced hundreds of thousands more. Most of the newly displaced returned to their homes within a few months. However, another government offensive in July 1996 displaced another 200,000 persons, most of whom were still displaced as of late 1996.

In Southeast Asia, estimates for Myanmar (Burma) and Cambodia are particularly hard to come by. The government of Myanmar (Burma) strictly controls outside monitoring, so the number of internally displaced persons in this country, thought to be in the range of 500,000 to 1 million, is only a rough guess. Displacement in Cambodia totals about 55,000 persons, but it is often a temporary phenomenon that fluctuates with the periodic fighting between government forces and the Khmer Rouge.

In the Philippines, most displacement is again temporary and often hidden. Between 1972 and 1984, more than 5.7 million were displaced in conflicts between the armed forces and leftist and Muslim insurgent groups. In recent years, the number of displaced persons has sharply diminished, but at any given point the total may be deceptively low whereas the cumulative total for the year may be high. In 1995, some 60,000 persons were displaced; in 1996, approximately 93,000.[94]

Civil wars have been the main cause of internal displacement in Asia, sometimes fomented or exacerbated by foreign intervention. Their causes range from political struggles to ethnic strife, with religion sometimes playing a prominent role.

The civil war in Lebanon, which began in 1975, stemmed from a volatile mix of Lebanese Christian and Muslim political rivalries, together with the presence of a large Palestinian refugee population that at times usurped the authority of the state, all stirred into conflagration by Syrian and Israeli intervention. During the course of the war, ethnic and religious conflict was the main cause of displacement, although during the final phase, in the early 1990s, fighting within the different groups caused the most serious displacement.[95]

In India, displacement stems mainly from the conflict between India and Pakistan over Kashmir, a dispute that goes back to 1947 when India insisted on holding onto predominantly Muslim Kashmir. The majority of the displaced are Hindus. Ethnicity and religion have also been major elements in the separatist struggle of the Tamils in Sri Lanka. The civil war that erupted in Tajikistan following the breakup of the Soviet Union has pitted groups against each other along clan and regional lines, although politics and religious differences have played an important part.

In Asia the displaced live in cities, in displaced persons camps (some camps have grown into cities in their own right), or throughout the countryside, either in the homes of local people or out in the open. In Lebanon, where the government has tracked the location and origins of the internally displaced, 52.7 percent of the displaced are located in the Mount Lebanon area. Beirut houses the next largest number of displaced, with 20.18 percent of the total. South Lebanon, where Israeli attacks in response to shelling and infiltrations into northern Israel have caused short periods of displacement, accounts for 15.76 percent.

In Iraq, internally displaced Kurds are almost all located in the northern "protected zone." Since large numbers of villages in mountainous border areas were destroyed and have not been reconstructed, many of the displaced are living in the larger towns and cities, such as Erbil, Sulaymania, and Dahok. In southern Iraq, displaced Shiites who did not cross into Iran are believed to have sought shelter mainly in the area's major cities.

In Afghanistan, much of the displacement in 1995 was concentrated around the two largest cities, Kabul and Jalalabad. In Kabul, thousands fled the city even as thousands of others returned, so the numbers have fluctuated. Outside Jalalabad, two camps accommodated some 135,000 persons. Tens, perhaps hundreds, of thousands of other displaced persons were living in Jalalabad and other cities, or were scattered throughout Afghanistan. In India, many of the displaced remained in or near Kashmir, while others moved to a camp for displaced persons near New Delhi. Most of the displaced in Sri Lanka are housed in camps.

Displaced populations in India, Iraq, Lebanon, Sri Lanka, and Afghanistan include both rural and urban people. In Myanmar (Burma), the displaced are mostly rural people who live primarily in the border

areas. In Cambodia, the displaced are also mostly rural, primarily farmers and residents of small towns or villages. The displaced in Lebanon
come from every group, and both rural people and urbanites have been
affected. In rural settings, hundreds of thousands of Christians were
displaced from the Chouf Mountains, which came under Druze control
during the course of the civil war. But hundreds of thousands of others
were displaced from and within Beirut and other cities.

Ethnic and religious groups constitute a large proportion of the internally displaced in Asia. Although the overwhelming majority of the displaced in northern Iraq are Kurds, some are also Turkomans, another
ethnic group at times residing uneasily with their Kurdish neighbors. In
southern Iraq, the displaced are almost all Shiite Muslims who have
opposed the Baath regime or have been identified as suspect. A vast
majority of internally displaced Sri Lankans are ethnic Tamils, including
a large number of urban dwellers. Most of the displaced of Myanmar
(Burma) are members of ethnic (and sometimes religious) minority
groups, including the Karen, Karenni, Mon, and Tavoyan. The military
has used these minority groups as forced labor in major construction
projects such as roads, railroads, and canals, and as porters for the
military.

As in Africa and Europe, women (particularly widows) constitute a
large proportion of internally displaced persons in Asia. Among the Iraqi
displaced were a disproportionate number of women and female-headed
households. During the Anfal campaign, Kurdish men and boys were
rounded up and executed on a regular basis, and in many areas, virtually
all males who were captured by government forces disappeared.[96] In
Afghanistan, nearly one million men are estimated to have been killed
or disabled in the civil war, leaving tens of thousands of widows, thousands of young girls who have lost intended spouses, and other thousands
whose husbands have become disabled.[97] Among the displaced in Sri
Lanka are substantial numbers of widows. The Sri Lankan government
provides financial compensation to women who become widowed or lose
grown sons who might have supported them. However, the cumbersome
application process keeps many women from applying for, or receiving,
grants.

Whether living in camps, with friends and relatives, or in makeshift
shelters out in the open, the displaced of Asia are among the most
destitute and vulnerable within each of their societies. In Lebanon, the
poorest of the homeless, called Muhajjaran, mass along the riverbanks

of the Awwali and Zahrani rivers in makeshift shelters in unsanitary conditions. Those who have found shelter with friends and family fare better, though they often live in overcrowded conditions. In Iraq, living conditions in general have been harsh since the Gulf War, but appear to be worse for displaced persons. On a visit to Basra in southern Iraq in December 1995, staff of the UN coordinator for Iraq found that "internally displaced families were squatting in schools and other public buildings . . . in extremely poor health and sanitation conditions and without sufficient food."[98]

In Tajikistan, some of the internally displaced took shelter in public buildings or private homes until they were expelled by the government and forced onto trains that returned them to their home areas.[99] More than 135,000 displaced Afghans live in the vast displaced persons' camps in Jalalabad, including Sar Shari camp, which was home to some 107,000 people at the end of 1995. In Kabul, tens of thousands of displaced residents of the city live in empty buildings, both public and private. Many are also crowded into their relatives' or friends' houses or apartments.

Asian governments have differed significantly in their responses to internal displacement. At one extreme are the governments of Iraq and Myanmar (Burma), which are directly responsible for causing displacement and whose implacable hostility prevents displaced people from returning to their homes. At the other end of the spectrum, the governments in Lebanon and Sri Lanka have sought to accommodate displaced persons or to assist in their return and reintegration. The Lebanese government has even created a Ministry of Displaced Persons. Somewhere in between are Cambodia, India, and Tajikistan, whose governments seem either incapable of, or uninterested in, offering much in the way of assistance or protection to the internally displaced, although unlike the others, India has barred outside assistance to the Kashmiri displaced.

The Sri Lankan government, though partly responsible for internal displacement through its role in the conflict, assumes responsibility for assisting the displaced in both government and rebel-held areas. It provides them with relief through its emergency reconstruction and rehabilitation program, which is implemented by the Ministry of Reconstruction, Rehabilitation, and Social Welfare. The government maintains some five hundred camps, or "welfare centers" for more than a quarter of a million internally displaced persons but does not provide as much assistance as it promises and at times has restricted shipments of needed medical supplies to displaced Tamils in the north. In the case of the Philippines, various national and local government agencies have been set up to assist the displaced but the government does not always provide them with the requisite resources.[100]

In Asia, as elsewhere, there has been considerable inconsistency in how internally displaced persons are protected by the international community. Following the January-February 1991 Gulf War and the attempted flight of some two million Kurds, the international community undertook its most ambitious protection effort ever on behalf of an internally displaced population. Under Operation Provide Comfort, U.S., British, and French ground forces were initially sent into northern Iraq to force Saddam Hussein's army back, southward, and permit the displaced Kurdish population to return. Coalition forces, however, withdrew from northern Iraq in mid-June 1991. Since then the military protection offered by the international community has been limited to air patrols from a base in Turkey. This has left the Kurdish region vulnerable to skirmishes and shelling by Iraqi government forces, which have displaced civilians living near the confrontation line separating the zones. In addition, Turkey periodically has crossed the border and has bombed and ransacked Kurdish villages in an effort to root out Turkish Kurdish rebels pursuing an insurgency against the Turkish government.

The international community's inability to protect or assist the displaced in Myanmar (Burma) is as clear an example as any in the world that international action is necessarily limited in the absence of an international system to protect the displaced. For years, the international community has stood passively on the sidelines as human rights abuses and the number of internally displaced persons have increased. Although governments and international organizations have criticized the government for its actions, and although in 1997 the United States and the European Union imposed partial economic sanctions, it has never made any attempt to extend any kind of protection or assistance to the displaced. The government of Myanmar (Burma) claims not to be opposed to outside help, but it insists on implementing international assistance itself, which discourages many international organizations and NGOs from becoming involved.

India has also successfully kept the international community at bay. Few in the international community, including some familiar with human rights issues in India, are aware of the displaced or their situation. Consequently, there is little if any international pressure on India to take any positive action on behalf of the displaced.

In the case of Iraq, government resistance did not prevent international involvement. Security Council Resolution 688 of April 5, 1991, demanded that Iraq "allow immediate access to international humanitarian organizations to all those in need of assistance in all parts of Iraq." On April 18, Iraq signed a memorandum of agreement with the United Nations allowing UN humanitarian agencies to operate on Iraqi territory and provide humanitarian assistance to the displaced. At the outset, this effort involved thirty bilateral donors and more than fifty international NGOs, and employed about 20,000 personnel and 200 aircraft.[101] Between October and December 1991, the international community embarked on a massive winterization project in northern Iraq to rehabilitate housing, performing reconstruction work in 1,500 of the 4,000 destroyed villages. Since mid-1996, when Masoud Barzani's Kurdistan Democratic Party called Saddam Hussein's army to his assistance in its struggle with the rival Patriotic Union of Kurdistan, international humanitarian operations in northern Iraq have been suspended, and local personnel who worked with international NGOs in the relief effort evacuated. These developments have put the future of the Kurdish safe haven very much in doubt.

In the case of Lebanon, the danger to international staff limited international involvement. As the civil war in Lebanon escalated and the numbers of internally displaced and their needs increased, fewer and fewer international humanitarian agencies remained to provide assistance. Their personnel came under direct threat, and they were no longer able to function without endangering themselves. In late 1988, long after most international NGOs had left, even ICRC withdrew because of the danger to its personnel. Since the end of the civil war, however, international aid has slowly resumed, as has reconstruction.

The situation in Afghanistan is more complex. During the cold war and the Soviet occupation, the international community, including NGOs, gave massive assistance to the Afghan refugees in Pakistan (though not to those in Iran). After the fall of the Najibullah regime in 1992 and the return of a majority of Afghan refugees, donor interest by and large waned. To be sure, many international organizations and NGOs turned their attention to assisting internally displaced persons and returning refugees, but the overall support for the internally displaced has not matched the kind of support and interest shown to Afghan refugees fleeing communist aggression. Moreover, the takeover by the Taliban, with its discriminatory policies against women, has further complicated international assistance.

Without a regional organization in Asia that covers all countries, the potential for regional discussion and action on internal displacement is weak (see chapter 6). Unlike the refugees in Asia, the internally displaced have not been particularly active in organizing political or self-help groups. Consequently, the displaced do not have a clear or effective voice in matters concerning them. Often, they follow the dictates of their political leaders in determining when or if to attempt to return to their homes. Many Afghans who worked with international NGOs while in exile in Pakistan did go on to create Afghan-led NGOs, although not necessarily to help the displaced. In Sri Lanka, Tamils have formed a number of NGOs to assist the displaced both in government-held areas and LTTE-controlled areas. In the latter, the Tamil Rehabilitation Organization, the lead agency implementing assistance programs for the displaced, considers itself an NGO, but some observers view it as a relief arm of the LTTE.

The fact that Asia is the continent with the smallest percentage of internally displaced persons in relation to the overall population is no reason for complacency. Where displacement problems do exist, they are severe. Moreover, as the most heavily populated continent, and one with a great diversity of ethnic and religious identities, Asia has the potential to generate large flows of refugees and internally displaced persons. Should this happen, it will be at a distinct disadvantage without regional mechanisms for dealing with such problems.

Latin America: Rising to the Challenge

Greater progress in dealing with the crisis of internal displacement has been made in Latin America—particularly in Central America—than perhaps any other region. Much of what has been accomplished must be attributed to the settlement of the civil war in El Salvador (which at its height is believed to have caused the displacement of up to one million persons), the resolution of cold war–related tensions both within Nicaragua and between that country's government and its neighbors, and to the ousting of the military regime in Haiti, under which some 300,000 had become displaced. But credit must also be given to governments, regional bodies, local NGOs and the displaced themselves. These last two, in particular, have made extraordinary efforts, going beyond anything seen elsewhere.

Today, serious problems of internal displacement persist in only three countries in Latin America—Guatemala, Colombia, and Peru—which taken together account for one to two million displaced. In all three, civil war has been the predominant cause of displacement.

The origins of the civil war in Guatemala between the government and insurgent groups, mainly impoverished Mayan peasants, date back several decades. Human rights abuses against these groups, perpetrated by the army backed by large landholders, caused large-scale flight. During the worst period of violence between 1979 and 1983, soldiers reportedly burned more than 440 villages.[102] Estimates of the number of displaced at the end of 1995, as the civil war was drawing to a close, ranged from 200,000 to 1.5 million (the latter figure was reported by CONDEG, the National Council of the Displaced in Guatemala).[103]

Colombia's displacement problems date back to the mid-1970s, when armed insurgencies spread throughout the country and government forces responded, often brutally. More recently, the growth of drug cartels has contributed to the problem. The "triple alliance" of the security forces, drug cartels, and wealthy landowners, who finance and control paramilitary groups, is responsible for most of the displacement. At the same time, insurgent forces are now also contributing to the violence for they depend on extortion, kidnapping, and drug profits to support themselves. More than 600,000 Colombians remained internally displaced at the end of 1995, following a year in which paramilitary groups expanded their areas of operation and stepped up a nationally coordinated offensive against those they deemed subversive.[104]

More than 600,000 Peruvians fled their Andean villages in the 1980s following a violent insurgency and equally violent counterinsurgency. By 1994 the extreme leftist Shining Path insurgents had been substantially weakened, primarily through the efforts of civil defense patrols formed by Peru's rural villagers, with government support. The insurgents remained strong in the Amazon jungle region, however. In response to the reduced violence, between 120,000 and 250,000 internally displaced people returned home during 1994 and 1995.[105]

Most of Latin America's internally displaced are poor, rural, indigenous people; some are not Spanish-speaking groups. The men are often targeted for recruitment or tortured and killed for suspected links with insurgent groups, with the result that women and children form the majority of the displaced. In Guatemala, the displaced are primarily indigenous Mayans. This group represents 60 percent of Guatemala's population, and its members have a distinctive dialect, appearance, and culture.

The vast majority of the internally displaced in Colombia are peasants, members of the organized left, civic leaders, trade unionists, farmers, banana workers, and indigenous leaders, and their wives and children. In Peru the internally displaced are mainly Quechua-speaking peasants of the southern Andes. Some are artisans, shopkeepers, and professionals from small towns, who fled the persecution of the military, which suspected them of being insurgents. Many of the displaced are young, prime targets for Shining Path recruitment. A smaller proportion are the Ashaninkas of Peru's Amazonia, who, starting in the mid-1980s, were forced by Shining Path guerrillas to join them or be killed. Thousands fled the area, abandoning their farms. In 1996 it was reported that up to 3,000 might still remain with the Shining Path, unable to flee.[106]

With regard to living conditions, those displaced in Guatemala have sought shelter in and around the capital, Guatemala City, on the plantations of the south coast, and in the departments of Quiche and Petén. Tens of thousands live in shantytowns in and around the capital, without clean water or health facilities. Unemployment and malnutrition are high and earnings are low. Those along the south coast work on the plantations for low wages and live in poor conditions. In Quiche and Petén, thousands of internally displaced persons have formed alternative villages called Communities of Population in Resistance (CPRs). Some 17,000 displaced live in CPR-Sierra in the mountains of Quiche, while some 1,000 live in CPR-Petén. The CPR-Ixcan, also in Quiche, used to have some 2,500 members who have now found permanent housing. An unknown number of displaced live elsewhere in the country, often in hiding.[107]

Many of the displaced in Colombia also live in shantytowns or in the poorest areas of Bogotá, the country's capital. Military offensives by the government, insurgent forces, and particularly the paramilitary groups in Colombia throughout 1995 forced some 15,000 Colombians to flee from the municipalities of Necoclí, Arboletes, Turbo, and Apartado. Most went to Monteria, the departmental capital.[108]

Most of the displaced in Peru left rural villages in the southern Andes for urban slums. More than 120,000 live in the shantytowns of Lima, the capital. During the earlier stages of displacement, military authorities encouraged, or forced, the peasants in some areas to resettle in military-supervised camps, which served as fortified encampments to repel Shining Path attacks and as a ready source of reserve troops for military-led incursions. In 1984 the Peruvian navy created nine such military camps to house some 1,500 displaced people.[109] The Ashaninkas of Peru's Amazonia congregated in the early 1990s in six centers, defended by Ashaninka civil defense patrols.[110]

More recently, with greater attention focused on the displaced and better security, living conditions have improved for some, and they have been able to buy plots of land and build modest homes. Many of Peru's rural displaced are able to travel to and from farms to cultivate their land. Some of those living in Lima have greater access to services such as running water and electricity. But the majority of the displaced in Peru are still the "poorest of the poor," occupying land illegally, living in flimsy huts without infrastructure, unable to find work.

In recent years, Latin American governments have begun to pay at least pro forma attention to the displaced and have taken some steps toward providing relief. Peru has established a governmental agency, the Proyecto de Apoyo a la Repoblación (PAR), to assist the displaced. The PAR provides development assistance to some 50,000 returnees in 579 returnee communities in four Peruvian departments. However, internally displaced people say that PAR's help is often inappropriate, uneven, or poorly planned. They and local NGOs also complain that the government does not have any programs for those planning to integrate in the cities and not return home.[111] The government claims it does not have the resources to implement separate programs of assistance for both groups, although more recently it has expressed willingness to consider assisting those who remain in the cities. Without such assistance, advocates for the displaced say, these people are likely to fade into Peru's tragic underclass, the most marginal of that nation's dispossessed.

The Colombian government did not formally recognize the plight of the displaced until it set up a fund for them in 1992, which budgeted $1.5 million for research and aid to victims of violence. In 1994 President Ernesto Samper acknowledged the seriousness of the displacement problem and the need for the government to investigate and take responsibility for it. However, even though the government has established a network of organizations and institutions, including nongovernmental groups, to assist the victims of forced migration, administrative obstacles and limited resources have impeded implementation.[112]

Theoretically, structures exist in Guatemala for the benefit of internally displaced persons. In June 1994 the government and four insurgent groups signed an accord for the resettlement of persons uprooted by the armed conflict. It was scheduled to go into effect following a peace agreement, signed on December 29, 1996. Government plans for the internally displaced, however, still remain to be implemented. A National Commission to Aid Repatriates, Refugees, and Displaced Persons has been created, but it is reportedly concentrating on returning refugees, while officials at the national land agency, INTA, are reportedly reticent about supporting internally displaced persons' claims to land or giving them low-interest credit for new land.[113]

In Latin America, many of the internally displaced are viewed with suspicion by government security forces and insurgent groups. As a result, the displaced continue to be persecuted in their places of "refuge." Throughout the region, there are displaced people who have lost or destroyed their identification documents, have found great difficulty in obtaining replacements, and have suffered loss of legal rights as a result.

In Peru, many displaced face the threat of requisición: arrest because of outstanding warrants for suspected terrorist ties. Although some displaced persons voluntarily joined insurgent forces or took part in attacks, many were forced to do so. They now face summary trials and prison terms.[114] In Guatemala, the displaced have been persecuted because of their status; in the Ixil region, the army forced displaced persons either to live in "model villages" and join defense patrols against insurgent groups or to be considered subversive. The number of attacks on Colombia's internally displaced is said to be increasing, as they continue to be persecuted by paramilitaries, government forces, and drug cartels, with the government doing little to protect them.[115]

Although the representative of the UN secretary-general on internally displaced persons visited Colombia in 1994 and Peru in 1995, UN agencies and other international humanitarian organizations have extended only minimal assistance for internal displacement problems in those two countries. By mid-1996, the only bilateral aid the Peruvian government was receiving for displaced persons was $8 million from the U.S. Agency for International Development. UNDP spent $100,000 to study the needs of the displaced and returnees, and IOM spent $80,000 on a program to assist in the return and reintegration of 250 displaced persons.[116] Far greater levels of assistance are crucial now that the level of violence is decreasing, and families are beginning to return home. A greater international presence is also needed in Colombia to help protect and assist the displaced and deter further displacement.

The United Nations has taken a far more active role in Central America, in large part because the conflicts in this region produced refugees. Hence UNHCR became involved in protection, assistance, and the return process. In 1989, in response to peace initiatives in Central America, UNHCR, together with the governments of Central America, convened the International Conference on Central American Refugees. The plan of action agreed to by the conference committed these governments to far-reaching humanitarian and development programs for displaced persons and refugees and committed international donors to channel funds in support of programs for the displaced and exiled. CIREFCA projects have been credited with facilitating the reintegration of displaced persons and refugees who returned to their homes in El Salvador and Nicaragua, although it is also reported that internally displaced persons received less attention than other populations of concern in the overall process.[117]

In recent years regional bodies and local NGOs have begun playing an important role in dealing with internal displacement. By 1995 Peru had a proliferation of NGOs covering a wide spectrum of activities, from health and nutrition to legal assistance and community development. Increasingly, Peruvian religious groups and NGOs have coordinated their activities for the displaced, shared information, and put greater emphasis on public awareness and outreach.[118] In Colombia, the Catholic Church and other local groups have played an important role in assisting the displaced parish by parish, but their staff members often face danger from paramilitary groups.[119]

The Permanent Consultation on Internal Displacement in the Americas, which was created in 1992, has brought together both NGOs and UN agencies to seek solutions to internal displacement in the Americas. It is one of the most innovative regional bodies established for this purpose. The Inter-American Commission on Human Rights of the Organization of American States has also been active in addressing displacement (for details of the role of the OAS and the CPDIA, see chapter 6).

But it is the initiative taken by the displaced themselves that particularly distinguishes Latin America from other regions. Internally displaced persons there have been more active than those in any other continent in organizing politically for their rights, and in creating self-help groups in lieu of aid from the outside.

Internally displaced Peruvians have achieved a high level of organization. In the past few years, displaced persons' associations have sprung up in all major areas of displacement. Among the largest are ASFADEL,

the Interprovincial Association of Displaced Persons, and Jatary Ayllu
(Quechua for "Rise up People"). Significant numbers of displaced have
joined these groups and are speaking out for their protection and rights.
NGOs working in Peru have noted that the willingness of these groups
to speak up and negotiate with the state "is a fundamentally important
development that could be significant in the creation of a lasting
peace."[120] In contrast, donors have concentrated on providing funds
through NGO implementing partners, rather than directly to the displaced persons groups themselves.

In 1989 Guatemalan displaced people created the National Council of
the Displaced in Guatemala (CONDEG) to represent the displaced,
revive their cultural customs, and recover their lost identification documents. However, persons working with human rights NGOs in Guatemala, including many of CONDEG's members, have suffered persecution
for their work.[121] Other organizations, such as the Communities of Population in Resistance of the Sierra and Ixcan regions, have demanded
government recognition as civilian groups and have worked with international NGOs and the Catholic Church to secure humanitarian assistance. Like CONDEG, they have been persecuted by the government,
which alleges that they protect insurgents.

The displaced in Colombia have also been fighting for their rights and
protesting the violence against them through peaceful marches, strikes,
and the occupation of public buildings. They have organized groups such
as the National Association of the Displaced to advocate for the forcibly
displaced communities. They have even used the act of fleeing to press
for change. In January 1995, for example, 2,500 peasants left the department of Meta in a mass exodus to El Castillo municipality and demanded
that the government intervene directly to stop abuses committed against
them by a paramilitary group.[122]

For the most part, displacement in Latin America is the result of
violent conflicts and human rights violations connected with ethnic identity configurations marked by inequitable land distribution, the exclusion
of indigenous peoples from governance and the modern economy, and,
in the particular case of Colombia, rampant violence. In the late 1980s
and early 1990s international and regional involvement played a key role
in helping to resolve the humanitarian problems caused by civil wars in
Central America. Currently, however, Latin America receives less outside help in dealing with problems of internal displacement than any other
region of the world. In each of the three countries still battling serious

displacement problems—Guatemala, Colombia, and Peru—NGOs and the displaced themselves have been promoting solutions, but greater participation by international agencies would strengthen their hand and encourage the governments concerned to carry out promised programs. Definitive solutions are unlikely to be achieved until the underlying causes of displacement are more energetically addressed.

Conclusion

As this overview makes clear, countries with histories of arbitrary rule, underdevelopment, mistreatment of ethnic, clan, or tribal groups, or with serious rivalries among these groups, have been fertile ground for conflict and mass displacement. External influences, such as the cold war, have also contributed substantially. In some cases, displacement is not just a result but the objective of the conflict: "ethnic cleansing" has hardly been confined to the former Yugoslavia; it has been practiced widely in the former Soviet Union, the Middle East, and in parts of Africa, in most cases manipulated by political leaders to achieve political and military ends.

Although displacement may manifest itself differently in different countries and regions, most displaced populations find themselves marginalized within the society and without responsible authorities to turn to. Often they become the most disadvantaged members of the population and find themselves destitute, vulnerable, and subject to severe protection problems, whether in Africa, Asia, Europe, or Latin America. While large numbers can be found in unofficial camps or settlements, or crowded in with relatives, the majority seem to flee to urban centers, whose public services quickly become overwhelmed by the needs of the inflowing population.

Government responses to crises of internal displacement have been notoriously weak, and there are few national institutions to deal with the problem. In many cases, the governments themselves are a part of the problem and have even caused it; in others, they simply do not have the resources to meet the needs of those displaced. In still others, governments have set up offices and implemented assistance programs, but only with a view to helping displaced persons who belong to the same ethnic group as the one in power. Nonetheless, some governments have moved to establish agencies for the displaced and to set up relief centers to protect and assist all their needy displaced populations, without discrimination. This trend should be applauded and encouraged by the international community. Indeed, encouraging governments to strengthen their national capacities was one of the purposes of the 1996 regional conference on displacement in the Commonwealth of Independent States (CIS). Its program of action specifically invited international organizations to offer technical cooperation to the governments of the former Soviet Union in order to help them strengthen national institutions.

Efforts by indigenous nongovernmental organizations to help the internally displaced are among the more promising signs at the national level. But some regions have little or no tradition of NGOs, and governments have often persecuted NGO staff for their work with the displaced. Of particular note, especially in Latin America, are the efforts of the displaced themselves to set up self-help groups and organizations to defend their rights. Regional organizations, although often weak, have nonetheless begun to recognize the existence of the problem, and to seek ways and means of addressing it; some have even undertaken field operations on behalf of the displaced.

Both national and regional efforts bear emphasis because of the ad hoc nature of international assistance. In some cases, international efforts are deliberately thwarted by governments and insurgent groups; in others, the limited mandates and resources of the organizations themselves have restricted their involvement, even though the displaced are huddled together, accessible, and clearly at risk. Without doubt, the international community needs to exercise greater assertiveness and creativity in order to gain access to internally displaced populations. There is also a great need for principles that could serve as a yardstick for governments and insurgent forces in dealing with the internally displaced and that would determine the circumstances necessitating humanitarian intervention. The chapters that follow discuss and propose legal standards for the internally displaced and better institutional arrangements. These are the critical next steps in developing an effective framework and comprehensive strategies for the protection and assistance of persons internally displaced.

CHAPTER THREE

Legal Framework

I believe the [U.N.] Commission [on Human Rights] in its work to strengthen the protection of the internally displaced must seek to bring about a convergence of refugee law, international human rights law and international humanitarian law. . . . [E]ach has a useful contribution to make to the protection of the internally displaced. . . . It is only through such convergence that the lacuna in the law can be addressed.
 —Sadako Ogata, UN High Commissioner for Refugees,
February 9, 1994

THE QUESTION OF HOW internally displaced persons are protected under international law against human rights violations is not merely one of academic interest. Displacement in and of itself may contradict basic human rights guarantees. Even when people are forced to leave their homes for legitimate reasons, displacement generally entails multiple

The legal analysis in this chapter was prepared by Walter Kälin and Robert Kogod Goldman. Kälin is professor of constitutional and international law and former dean of the School of Law of the University of Bern, Switzerland; Goldman is Louis C. James Professor of Law at the Washington College of Law of American University and co-director of its Center for Human Rights and Humanitarian Law. The analysis is based on and draws from a study entitled *Compilation and Analysis of Legal Norms*, which was submitted by the representative of the UN secretary-general on internally displaced persons to the Commission on Human Rights in 1996 as UN Document E/CN.4/1996/52/Add.2. The study was prepared by a team of experts that included Walter Kälin, Robert Kogod Goldman, Manfred Nowak, Janelle M. Diller, Otto Linher, and Cecile E. M. Meijer. The Kälin-Goldman chapter also draws on a sequel to the *Compilation and Analysis*, prepared by Maria Stavropoulou, and submitted by the representative of the secretary-general on internally displaced persons to the commission in 1998.

human rights violations. In many cases, it breaks up the immediate family. It cuts off important social and cultural community ties; terminates stable employment relationships; precludes or forecloses formal educational opportunities; deprives infants, expectant mothers, and the sick of access to food, adequate shelter, or vital health services; and makes the displaced population especially vulnerable to acts of violence, such as attacks on camps, disappearances, or rape.

Because governments frequently cause or tolerate internal displacement and are unwilling or unable to guarantee basic rights and meet the needs of their internally displaced citizens, it is important to ascertain whether international law provides adequate protection for these persons. Internally displaced persons do not forfeit their inherent rights because they are displaced; they can invoke human rights and humanitarian law to protect their rights. At the same time, existing international law does not contain guarantees that explicitly mention internally displaced persons. It is often difficult for governments, international organizations, NGOs, and the internally displaced themselves to determine clearly which guarantees are applicable in a specific situation.

The analysis offered in this chapter seeks to clarify these issues. It examines international human rights law, humanitarian law, and, by analogy, refugee law. It considers the extent to which each meets the basic needs of the internally displaced, and it demonstrates that while existing law provides substantial coverage for the internally displaced, there are significant areas in which the law fails to provide sufficient protection. Some weaknesses relate to the need for an expressed right not to be unlawfully displaced, to have access to protection and assistance during displacement, and to enjoy a secure return and reintegration. There are also gaps in legal protection relating to personal documentation for the internally displaced or restitution or compensation for property lost during displacement. And although there is a general norm for freedom of movement, there is no explicit right to find refuge in a safe part of the country nor an explicit guarantee against the forcible return of internally displaced persons to places of danger.

The law also has inherent shortcomings. First, in some situations of tensions and disturbances short of armed conflict, humanitarian law is not applicable, and human rights law may be restricted or derogated from; as a result, protections that are critical for the well-being or survival of the internally displaced are diminished. Second, international human rights law generally binds only states, not nonstate actors, such as insurgent groups, under whose authority large numbers of internally displaced persons reside. Third, some states have not ratified key human rights treaties or the Geneva Conventions and their Additional Protocols and therefore are not formally bound by their provisions unless they are reflective of customary law. And fourth, although some principles of refugee law may be applicable by analogy, the strong and effective protection accorded refugees under the 1951 Refugee Convention cannot apply directly to internally displaced persons, even though their conditions are similar.

The question is, do these findings amount to a compelling case for the development of a body of principles specifically applicable to the internally displaced? Existing norms, some say, provide adequate coverage. The development of new standards, they argue, would merely detract from efforts to implement what exists and could even undercut existing standards and the extensive coverage they provide. Some also contend that a normative framework specifically tailored to the needs of the internally displaced would discriminate against other groups.

The purpose of developing a normative framework for the internally displaced, however, is to reinforce and strengthen existing protections. By restating norms in one coherent document, it becomes possible to consolidate those that otherwise would be too dispersed and diffuse to be adequate or effective. Restatement also would ensure that real gaps and gray areas in the law are addressed. The analysis in this chapter identifies many areas in which the law provides insufficient protection for internally displaced persons owing to inexplicit articulation or normative gaps. Even critics have come to acknowledge that coverage may need to be expanded to provide more effective protection for the internally displaced. On the basis of the findings in this chapter, the International Committee of the Red Cross has endorsed the preparation of guiding principles for the internally displaced.[1] And the Office of the UN High Commissioner for Refugees has taken the significant step of developing a manual on internally displaced persons for its field staff, on the basis of the legal analysis herein. [2]

Precedents abound in international law for special protections for disadvantaged groups, whether refugees, minorities, indigenous populations, the disabled, women, or children. The purpose in compiling a body of principles tailored to the needs of the internally displaced would not be to discriminate against others but to ensure that, in a given situation, internally displaced persons, like others, are protected and that their unique needs are acknowledged and addressed. Guiding principles would increase international awareness of the needs of internally displaced persons and would give humanitarian and human rights bodies a document to turn to when advocating on behalf of the internally displaced. By offering an authoritative statement of the rights of the internally displaced in one document, guiding principles can also help governments develop national laws for the protection of internally displaced persons.

The appendix to this volume presents a body of principles developed by a team of international lawyers under the direction of the representative of the secretary-general on internally displaced persons. These principles apply to both governments and insurgent groups and pertain to all phases of displacement: they include the norms applicable before internal displacement occurs (that is, protection against arbitrary displacement), those that apply in actual situations of displacement, and those that apply to the postconflict period.

Momentum is now growing for the consolidation of norms specifically applicable to the internally displaced. Both the United Nations General Assembly and the Commission on Human Rights have requested that the representative of the secretary-general develop a normative "framework" for the protection of the displaced, and in 1997 the commission adopted a resolution to take note of the development of guiding principles. This is a significant step because guiding principles, as a nonbinding instrument, could help create the moral and political climate needed to improve protection and assistance for the internally displaced; eventually, they might attain the force of customary international law and lead to the development of a binding legal instrument.

In the remainder of this chapter, Walter Kälin and Robert Kogod Goldman lay out the factors of prime consideration in formulating such principles: the type of law applicable in different situations (tensions, disturbances and disasters, noninternational armed conflict, and interstate armed conflict) recognized by international law; the extent to which persons are protected against forced displacement; and the basic needs of internally displaced persons and how these are protected under international law, with particular reference to nondiscrimination, violence, detention, subsistence needs, personal identification and documentation, freedom of movement, property, family unity, and education. It examines whether a right to humanitarian assistance exists, and whether the international community has a right or even duty to intervene when governments are unwilling or unable to provide for the basic welfare and security of their populations. In the conclusion it identifies the gaps in the legal protection of internally displaced persons and recommends the development of guiding principles to safeguard these populations.

Applicable Law in Recognized Situations

As outlined in chapter 2, internally displaced persons have a multitude of needs. These include needs for equality and nondiscrimination; life and personal security; needs to maintain personal liberty; subsistence needs; movement-related needs; the need for personal identification, documentation, and registration; property-related needs; the need to maintain family and community values; and the need to build self-reliance. These needs require legal protection in three situations recognized by international law, namely, (1) situations of tensions and disturbances, or disasters in which human rights law is applicable; (2) situations of noninternational armed conflicts governed by the central principles of international humanitarian law, that is, the law of armed conflict, and by many human rights guarantees; and (3) situations of interstate armed conflict in which the detailed provisions of humanitarian law become primarily operative, although many important human rights guarantees remain applicable. These three recognized situations cover most cases of internal displacement and thus provide a useful analytical framework.

Situations of Tensions and Disturbances, or Disasters

Two important points to consider in this category of situations are the applicability of human rights law and possible restrictions on, or suspension of, rights.

APPLICABILITY OF HUMAN RIGHTS. Many internally displaced persons live in situations of internal tensions and disturbances, or disasters. The terms "internal tensions" and "disturbances" refer to situations that fall short of armed conflict but involve the use of force, including repressive measures by government agents to maintain or restore public order. Examples of tensions and disturbances include riots, such as demonstrations without a concerted plan from the outset; isolated sporadic acts of violence, as opposed to military operations carried out by armed forces or armed groups; and violent ethnic conflicts not amounting to hostilities.

A situation of serious internal tension characteristically involves specific types of human rights violations, such as large-scale arrests and other measures restricting personal freedom, administrative detention and assigned residence, large numbers of political prisoners, and probably ill-treatment or inhuman conditions of detention.[3] Disasters may be natural or human-made in their origins. Examples include droughts, floods, earthquakes, typhoons, nuclear disasters, and famine.

Human rights law, rather than humanitarian law, guides governmental conduct in the treatment of persons displaced in situations of tensions and disturbances or by disaster.[4] Humanitarian law is inapplicable because internal tensions and disturbances do not amount to armed conflict.[5]

Since existing human rights standards are phrased in rather general terms, they do not provide individuals with explicit protection against being internally displaced or the consequences of displacement. However, just as the freedom from forced or involuntary disappearance was initially recognized as inherent in the right to life, an individual right against forced displacement arguably inheres in the freedom of movement and residence set forth, inter alia, in Article 13 of the Universal Declaration of Human Rights and Article 12 of the Covenant on Civil and Political Rights.[6] This right, like most others, is not absolute and thus may be lawfully restricted or temporarily suspended under certain circumstances. Under a genuine peacetime democracy, however, large-scale internal displacement would rarely be officially executed, except in natural disasters. Such displacement should therefore be viewed as a barometer of something gone terribly wrong within a country. In fact, displacement is largely a by-product of violent conflict and/or serious breakdown of democratic institutions, or, in the case of nondemocratic regimes, of official policy.

Once individuals become displaced, they should, in theory, continue to enjoy the same human rights as the rest of the population. In practice, however, this is rarely the case: displacement, by its very nature, generally entails the deprivation of many rights.

Arguably, a government that is responsible for or condones the large-scale internal displacement of its own citizens (without legitimate reasons related to armed hostilities, as explained later in the chapter), violates its obligations under the Charter of the United Nations. Specifically, under Articles 55 and 56 of the charter, all member states of the United Nations are obliged to "promote universal respect for, and observance of, human rights and fundamental freedoms for all." These clauses are the foundation of the international law of human rights, and their oblig-atory character has been authoritatively confirmed by the World Court.[7] While these articles do not specify or define "human rights and funda-mental freedoms," the Universal Declaration of Human Rights is widely recognized today as an authoritative interpretation of a member state's obligations under the charter.[8]

If a state is also a party to one or more of the universal and/or regional human rights treaties, such as the 1966 Covenants on Economic, Social and Cultural Rights (CESCR) and on Civil and Political Rights (CCPR),[9] the American, African, or European human rights conventions,[10] or the Convention on the Rights of the Child (CRC),[11] it has thereby assumed a solemn duty[12] vis-à-vis other states parties and to its own citizens to respect and ensure the rights guaranteed in these instruments. The government of a state party to these conventions[13] that, as a matter of policy and without a valid cause, deliberately brings about the internal displacement of its citizens or does not adequately protect or even openly disregards their needs would violate many fundamental human rights guarantees.

LIMITATIONS AND DEROGATIONS. Although in principle human rights guarantees are applicable in situations of tensions, disturbances, and disasters, internally displaced persons may face specific problems arising from restrictions imposed on those rights. Most human rights treaties contain limitations clauses that permit governments to lawfully restrict the free exercise of many rights during situations falling short of armed conflict in order to protect public safety or public health and morals, to restore order, and to protect the fundamental rights and freedoms of others.[14] Thus, for example, a government could impose a curfew within a riot-torn area without violating the right to freedom of movement. Likewise, restrictions on otherwise guaranteed human rights may be jus-tifiable in times of disaster. It must be stressed, however, that most human rights treaties permit such limitations only to the extent that they are prescribed by law and are really "necessary in a democratic society." Therefore the mere existence of civil disorder, falling short of armed conflict, should never justify an official policy of forcibly relocating or expelling some or all of a civilian population from affected areas.

Some human rights treaties also contain derogation clauses that permit states to derogate from, that is, to suspend, certain specified rights under narrowly circumscribed situations. Article 4(1) of the CCPR, for exam-ple, permits a state party to temporarily suspend certain guarantees "in time of public emergency which threatens the life of the nation and the existence of which is officially proclaimed." Such derogations, according to the same provision, must be limited "to the extent strictly required by the exigencies of the situation" and shall "not involve discrimination solely on the ground of race, colour, sex, language, religion or social origin."[15] Although situations of tensions and disturbances, as well as disasters, could justify restrictions on certain human rights, they rarely, if ever, threaten the existence of the state and therefore do not constitute the kind of genuine public emergency that would permit a state to derogate guaranteed rights. It should be noted that states rarely invoke derogation clauses. Even if they do, they have to respect the list of rights that cannot be suspended, even in times of emergency. Among these nonderogable guarantees are the right to life, the prohibition of torture and cruel and inhuman or degrading treatment and punishment, the prohibition of slavery, and the prohibition of retroactive application of penal law.[16]

Situations of Noninternational Armed Conflict

Some points of legal concern in cases of internal (that is, noninternational) armed conflict are the applicability of Article 3 common to the four 1949 Geneva Conventions and Additional Protocol II and their interrelationship with human rights law.

HUMAN RIGHTS AND HUMANITARIAN LAW. One of the principal causes of displacement of civilian populations worldwide is internal armed conflicts. Indeed, it is during such hostilities that the basic human rights of the displaced are generally most imperiled and least protected. During situations of noninternational armed conflict, some of the humanitarian law guarantees become applicable together with human rights law, which, however, is increasingly subject to restrictions and, in extreme cases, even derogations.

International humanitarian law, which is designed to apply in situations of armed conflict, contains rules restricting the means and methods of combat in order to spare the civilian population from the effects of hostilities. Inasmuch as human rights and humanitarian law share a common purpose of protecting human life and dignity, the two converge to a large extent in situations of purely internal conflict and thus reinforce each other.

Whereas human rights law generally limits the abusive practices of only one party to the conflict, namely, the government and its agents, humanitarian law is, to a certain extent, binding upon dissident forces as well.[17] Since only states are proper parties to human rights treaties, it is usually the governments of states that are internationally responsible for human rights violations under those treaties. Comparable abuses committed by private actors, such as rebels or other dissident groups, are not the subject matter of admissible complaints before monitoring bodies established under existing human rights conventions unless private acts are instigated, encouraged, or at least acquiesced in by the government concerned; otherwise, they are typically labeled as infractions of a country's domestic laws. However, the notion that nongovernmental actors should be internationally responsible for human rights abuses has gained ground in recent years. To the extent that certain internationally recognized crimes are coextensive with proscriptions under human rights treaties or fall under the jurisdiction of international tribunals, private actors may incur individual penal responsibility for the commission of such crimes, including, inter alia, genocide and torture.[18]

COMMON ARTICLE 3. The principal source of humanitarian law governing all internal, that is, noninternational, armed conflicts is Article 3 common to the four 1949 Geneva Conventions.[19] It should be noted that common Article 3 simply refers to, but does not actually define, "an armed conflict of a non-international character." As confirmed by state practice, it is applicable to low-intensity, open, armed confrontations between relatively organized armed forces or armed groups occurring exclusively within the territory of a particular state. As just mentioned, common Article 3 typically applies to armed strife between governmental armed forces and organized armed insurgents. It also applies to cases in which two or more armed factions within a country confront one another *without* the involvement of governmental forces when, for example, the established government has dissolved or is too weak to intervene.

The nonderogable provisions of common Article 3 are essentially pure human rights law.[20] They prohibit without exception specific acts, including violence to life and person (in particular, murder of all kinds); mutilation, cruel treatment, and torture; hostage taking; and outrages against personal dignity, particularly, humiliating and degrading treatment. Common Article 3 also mandates that the wounded and sick be collected and cared for.

Unlike human rights law, which generally restrains violations inflicted by a government and its agents, the obligatory provisions of common Article 3 expressly bind both parties to the conflict, that is, government and insurgent forces. Moreover, the obligation to apply common Article 3 is absolute for both parties and independent of the obligation of the other party. Accordingly, individual civilians, including those forcibly or voluntarily displaced by virtue of the hostilities, are entitled to common Article 3's absolute guarantees when they are captured by or subjected to the power of either government or dissident forces. Moreover, the warring parties must accord civilians these protections even if they had fought for the opposing party or indirectly participated in hostilities by providing either party with food or other logistical support. Under these circumstances, if these civilians die as a result of summary execution or torture inflicted by a party to the conflict, their deaths are tantamount to homicide. In addition, both common Article 3, inferentially, and customary law,[21] expressly, prohibit direct attacks upon displaced persons and other civilians living in combat zones or areas controlled by the enemy. Deaths resulting from such illicit attacks are also properly classified as homicides.

ADDITIONAL PROTOCOL II. Apart from common Article 3 and customary law, the 1977 Protocol Additional to the Geneva Conventions of 1949, and Relating to the Protection of Victims of Non-International Armed Conflicts (Protocol II)[22] contains other detailed rules applicable to the displaced and other persons affected by hostilities. This instrument's threshold of application is both different from and clearly above that of common Article 3.[23] Indeed, under the objective conditions that must be satisfied to trigger its application, the situation must be one of civil war essentially comparable to a state of belligerency under customary international law.

Significantly, Protocol II develops and supplements the provisions of common Article 3 without modifying that article's existing conditions of application. Thus Protocol II applies cumulatively and simultaneously with common Article 3. Although the protocol, as such, is only directly applicable to hostilities within the territory of a State Party to that instrument, its provisions are, by no means, irrelevant to purely common Article 3 armed conflicts. Since Protocol II incorporates, clarifies, and strengthens common Article 3's customary law rules, it is reasonable to argue that its provisions should also be regarded as declaratory of customary law and thus applied by the parties to *all* internal armed conflicts.

For example, Article 13 of Protocol II expressly accords civilians general protection against direct attacks and inferentially protects them and civilian objects from indiscriminate or disproportionate attacks. By prohibiting starvation of civilians as a method of warfare, Article 14 enjoins a practice all too frequently used by government and/or insurgent forces worldwide.

The nonderogable fundamental guarantees of humane treatment set forth in Article 4 of the protocol are also relevant to the internally displaced and other victims of internal hostilities. This article, which elaborates common Article 3's minimum rules, absolutely prohibits the following acts, among others, under all circumstances: collective and corporal punishment; acts of terrorism, rape, and other kinds of indecent assault; pillage; and threats by the warring parties to commit any of these acts. It also contains special rules for the protection of children, often the most vulnerable group among the displaced. In addition to "the care and aid they require," Article 4(3) imposes an affirmative duty on *all* parties to a conflict to ensure that children "shall receive an education, including religious and moral education," in keeping with the wishes of their parents or those responsible for their care, and that "all appropriate steps shall be taken to facilitate the reunion of families temporarily separated."

The warring parties are similarly required, if necessary, and whenever possible, with parental or comparable consent, "to remove children temporarily from an area in which hostilities are taking place to a safer area within the country and to ensure that they are accompanied by persons responsible for their safety and well-being." Further, children under the age of fifteen may not be recruited by either side, nor allowed to take part in the hostilities.[24]

Situations of Interstate Armed Conflict

Interstate (that is, international) armed conflict, represents a third situation creating internal displacement that receives distinct treatment under international law. Human rights law, in principle, remains applicable during such conflicts, and it becomes especially important to protect internally displaced persons against their own government where humanitarian law may not afford protection. However, because of the nature of an interstate conflict, human rights guarantees may become subject to restrictions or even derogations unless they belong to the nonderogable rights that must be respected under all circumstances.

Humanitarian law, notably the 1949 Geneva Conventions and the 1977 Additional Protocol I, as well as the customary laws of war, becomes fully operative for states parties in interstate hostilities that consist of a declared war, or, in its absence, any conflict between two or more states leading to the intervention of armed forces, including occupation.[25] Many norms, especially those regarding the protection of the civilian population, may be invoked by internally displaced persons. However, most provisions relevant for civilians in international armed conflicts were designed for nonnationals of the state that effectively holds the power in the respective territory. In this regard, Article 4 of the Fourth Geneva Convention provides that "persons protected by the Convention are those who, at a given moment and in any manner whatsoever, find themselves, in case of a conflict or occupation, in the hands of a Party to the conflict or Occupying Power of which they are not nationals." Most provisions of the Geneva Conventions, therefore, are not applicable to persons displaced to an area controlled by their own government. Among the norms that only protect against the authorities of a foreign state (normally an occupying power) are many of those provisions that address the needs of displaced persons in the most comprehensive way.[26]

Significantly, some provisions contained in Part II of the Fourth Geneva Convention have broader applicability as they "cover the whole of the populations of the countries in conflict" (Article 13), including internally displaced persons in the territory controlled by their own government. Among these are provisions for hospital and safety zones and localities (Article 14); neutralized zones (Article 15); the protection of the wounded, sick, infirm, and expectant mothers, including provisions concerning hospitals and transports (Articles 16, 18–22); the "endeavour to conclude local agreements for the removal from besieged or encircled areas, of wounded, sick, infirm, and aged persons, children and maternity cases; the passage of ministers of all religions, medical personnel and medical equipment on their way to such areas" (Article 17). Other provisions pertain to child welfare (Article 24), the exchange of family news (Article 25), and inquiries made by members of dispersed families (Article 26). All these norms may be of particular relevance for the displaced.

With respect to the personal scope of application, Protocol I refers to civilians in general and does not distinguish between nationalities, but it does concentrate on the inoffensive character and noncombatant status of the persons to be spared.[27] Therefore, though not specifically designed for this purpose, almost the whole of Part IV of Protocol I is applicable to internally displaced persons in international conflicts. In this context, the following provisions are particularly important: the prohibition of direct and indiscriminate attacks against civilians (Article 51), the prohibition of starvation of civilians (Article 54, paragraph 1), the protection of nondefended localities (Article 59) and demilitarized zones (Article 60), the provision of relief to the civilian population (Articles 69–71), the reunion of dispersed families (Article 74), the general fundamental guarantees applicable to everyone (Article 75), and the protection of women (Article 76) and children (Articles 77–78). It should be noted, however, that not all states have ratified Protocol I. Hence many internally displaced persons cannot benefit from these guarantees.

Nonapplicability of Refugee Law

Refugee law[28] is not directly applicable to the situation of internally displaced persons as international law defines refugees as persons who have fled across international borders. However, despite the fact that internally displaced persons usually remain in their own countries, they are often forced to leave their homes and thus find themselves in refugee-like situations. Consequently, refugee law, by analogy, can be useful in proposing rules and establishing guidelines to protect the needs of the internally displaced. UNHCR documents, such as the Guidelines on the Protection of Refugee Women and the Guidelines on Protection and Care of Refugee Children,[29] might also inspire standards-setting for internally displaced persons.[30] Such analogies cannot be made, however, where refugee law is limited to provisions granting refugees not more than equal treatment with aliens in the country of refuge.[31] Inasmuch as most internally displaced persons are, in fact, citizens of the country in question, analogous applications of refugee law in such cases would lower their rights in an unacceptable way.

Protection against Forced Displacement

Few express international legal norms protect people against individual or collective eviction and displacement or transfer from one region to another within their own country.[32] When aggregated, however, these norms point to a general rule: that forced displacement may not be effected in a discriminatory way or arbitrarily imposed.

Prohibition of Religious and Racial Discrimination

A particularly serious type of forced movement is that which subjects individuals and groups to actions intended to remove them from their area of habitual residence on grounds such as race, color, religion, culture, descent, or national or ethnic origin. One extreme example of this is apartheid. In recent years the forced movement of persons has become the objective of a number of policies of ethnic separation, homogenization, or "ethnic cleansing."

Despite the absence of explicit legal provisions regarding such actions, they are clearly prohibited under international law, particularly under Article 26 of the CCPR,[33] the Convention on the Elimination of All Forms of Racial Discrimination, and the International Convention on the Suppression and Punishment of the Crime of Apartheid. "Ethnic cleansing" is never permissible: the Committee on the Elimination of Racial Discrimination in its concluding observations on the report of the Republic of Bosnia and Herzegovina, condemned "ethnic cleansing" because it constitutes "a grave violation of all basic principles underlying the International Convention on the Elimination of All Forms of Racial Discrimination."[34]

Not every forcible movement, however, is discriminatory. If it is based on reasonable and objective criteria, and not targeted at any specific group or person on invidious discriminatory grounds, it may not be prohibited. The decisive question is whether a specific distinction between persons or groups of persons who find themselves in a comparable situation is based on unreasonable and subjective criteria. The principle of proportionality is also relevant here. Internal transfers of whole populations or internal displacement of large numbers of persons may be prima facie discriminatory.[35]

Freedom of Movement and Choice of Residence

Forced displacement is the denial of the exercise of freedom of movement and choice of residence since it deprives a person of the choice of moving or not and of choosing where to reside. Under existing law, therefore, protection against individual or collective internal transfers is inferred, among other things, from the right to freedom of movement and choice of residence. This freedom is expressly recognized as a human right in Article 13(1) of the Universal Declaration and is similarly guaranteed in Article 12(1) of the CCPR, which guarantees that "everyone lawfully within the territory of a State shall, within that territory, have the right to liberty of movement and freedom to choose his residence." Similar guarantees are contained in regional instruments.[36]

Most universal and regional human rights instruments permit states to place restrictions on freedom of residence and movement during situations of tensions and disturbances, or during disasters. These restrictions may permit certain limited forced movement of persons or their settlement in other areas. At the same time, Article 12(3) of the CCPR provides that freedom of movement and choice of residence "shall not be subject to any restrictions except those which are provided by law, are necessary to protect national security, public order (*ordre public*), public health or morals or the rights and freedoms of others, and are consistent with the other rights recognized in the present Covenant." Thus the application of such restrictions must be prescribed by law, be based on one of the enumerated grounds justifying limitations, respond to a pressing public or social need, pursue a legitimate aim, and be proportionate to that aim.[37] The decisive criterion for evaluating whether this standard has been observed is the principle of proportionality in the given case. Every interference thus requires a precise balancing between the right to freedom of movement and those interests to be protected by the interference.[38] Finally, restrictions on rights in the covenant are always exceptions and therefore may not become the rule.[39]

The permissible reasons for interference under Article 12(3) of the CCPR are "national security," "public order (*ordre public*)," "public health," "public morals," and the "rights and freedoms of others." National security is endangered only in grave cases of political or military threat to the entire nation; in such situations it may be necessary for persons to be temporarily relocated. Permissible restrictions on freedom of internal movement and residence on the ground of public order (*ordre public*) could exceptionally justify displacement in certain development and infrastructure projects where the interests of general welfare are clearly overriding. The "public health" exception might include relocation away from areas in which acute health dangers exist (for example, areas contaminated as a result of a catastrophe). Finally, restrictions on freedom of movement and residence imposed in the interest of "the rights and freedoms of others" may justify evictions to respect private property. However, states parties are obligated to ensure that interference in favor of private owners is proportional.[40] Any interference must be reasonable and objective and nondiscriminatory.[41]

The question of coerced displacement as it relates to freedom of movement is addressed in a number of initiatives of the United Nations. The Sub-Commission on Prevention of Discrimination and Protection of Minorities, in a noteworthy resolution adopted at its forty-sixth session, entitled "The Right to Freedom of Movement," affirmed "the right of persons to remain in their own homes, on their own lands and in their own countries."[42]

The Draft Code of Crimes against the Peace and Security of Mankind, in the text adopted at the second reading in 1996, in Article 18, entitled "Crimes against humanity," lists five manifestations of practices constituting crimes, when committed in a systematic manner or on a large scale, one of them being "forcible transfer of population."[43]

Protection from Interference with One's Home

Individuals are further protected from arbitrary displacement by provisions relating to privacy. Article 17 of the CCPR provides, among other things, that "no one shall be subjected to arbitrary or unlawful interference with his . . . home."[44] The protection of "home" relates not only to dwellings but also to all types of residential property regardless of legal title or nature of use.[45] An invasion of this sphere without the consent of the individual represents interference, as does any activity, such as forced relocation, that deprives individuals of their "home" altogether.[46]

Any interference will be "unlawful" if it contravenes the national or international legal system. In addition, it will be "arbitrary" if it contains elements of injustice, unpredictability, and unreasonableness.[47] In evaluating whether interference with privacy by a state enforcement organ represents a violation of Article 17, it must be determined whether, in addition to conforming with national law, the specific act of enforcement had a purpose that is legitimate on the basis of the Covenant in its entirety, whether it was predictable in accordance with the rule of law, and whether it was reasonable (proportional) in relation to the purpose to be achieved.[48] A decision to make use of such authorized interference must be made only by the authority designated under the law and on a case-by-case basis.

Right to Housing

The right to housing also provides protection against arbitrary displacement. In addressing this right under Article 11(1) of the CESCR, the Committee on Economic, Social and Cultural Rights stated that "instances of forced eviction are *prima facie* incompatible with the requirements of the Covenant and can only be justified in the most exceptional circumstances, and in accordance with the relevant principles of international law."[49] Limitations on the right to housing must comply with the requirements of Article 4 of the CESCR, namely, that these limitations must be determined by law and be applied only insofar as this may be compatible with the nature of the right and be imposed solely for the purpose of promoting the general welfare in a democratic society. Evictions also may not contravene the basic principle of procedural due process. Therefore, in the case of collective evictions, a certain amount of arbitrariness may be presumed to exist. Furthermore, Article I(b) of the 1968 Convention on the Non-Applicability of Statutory Limitations to War Crimes and Crimes against Humanity defines "eviction by armed attack" as a crime against humanity, whether committed in peace or in war.

Prohibition of Genocide

Certain forms of forced removal, particularly in the context of "ethnic cleansing" or extreme suppression of ethnic or indigenous people (for example, in the case of apartheid), may amount to genocide. Genocide constitutes an especially grave form of violation of the right to life.[50] Article I of the Genocide Convention recognizes genocide committed at any time to be an international crime.

Prohibition of Forced Movement in Emergencies, Including Situations of Armed Conflict

Under human rights law, the right to freedom of movement and the protection of privacy are stipulated to be derogable. Accordingly, population movements may be undertaken during genuine public emergencies, such as armed conflicts, severe communal or ethnic violence, and natural or human-made disasters. Such movements, however, must be "strictly required by the exigencies of the situation"[51] and must not be inconsistent with other state obligations under international law or involve invidious discrimination.[52] Even in emergencies, therefore, forced movement must not violate nonderogable human rights.

Relevant principles of protection that relate to forced relocation in the circumstances of derogation, as applied by the Inter-American Commission on Human Rights in the Miskito case, may be deduced as follows: first, official proclamation of a state of emergency has to be communicated effectively to avoid terror and confusion when it involves relocation; second, relocation should be proportionate to the danger, degree, and duration of a state of emergency; and third, relocation must last only for the duration of an emergency.[53] Consequently, there is a right of return of a displaced population to their original land, if they so desire, following the termination of an emergency situation.[54]

During armed conflicts, international humanitarian law also protects persons from being arbitrarily displaced.[55] In the case of noninternational armed conflicts, Article 17 of Protocol II, entitled "Prohibition of Forced Movement of Civilians," stipulates that "the displacement of the civilian population shall not be ordered for reasons related to the conflict unless the security of the civilians involved or imperative military reasons so demand." This wording makes clear that Article 17 prohibits, as a general rule, the forced movement or displacement of civilians during internal hostilities. The forced displacement of civilians is prohibited unless the party to the conflict were to show that the security of the population or a meticulous assessment of the military circumstances so demands. Clearly, imperative military reasons cannot be justified by political motives, such as the movement of population in order to exercise more effective control over a dissident ethnic group.[56] Accordingly, the burden is squarely on the party initiating such action to justify it under the narrow exceptions to this rule.

In the case of interstate armed conflicts, Article 49 of the Fourth Geneva Convention elaborates on the movement of protected persons in situations of occupation.[57] Paragraph 1 of this article prohibits, regardless of motive, the individual or mass forcible transfer of such persons. Paragraph 2 of Article 49 states: "Nevertheless, the Occupying Power may undertake total or partial evacuation of a given area if the security of the population or imperative military reasons so demand." Furthermore, "such evacuations may not involve the displacement of protected persons outside the bounds of the occupied territory except when for material reasons it is impossible to avoid such displacement." Thus, as a rule, people must be evacuated to reception centers inside the territory. Finally, protected persons who have been evacuated are to be brought back to their homes as soon as the hostilities in the area of origin have ended.

Article 51 (7) of Protocol I (which applies in situations of interstate armed conflict) protects civilians from being forced to leave their residence in order to disrupt the movement of combatants or to shield military objectives from attack. However, paragraph 7 does not prohibit measures "to restrict the movement of civilians so as to avoid their interference with military movement, nor does it prohibit ordering their evacuation if their security or imperative military reasons so demand."[58] In fact, Article 58 of Protocol I provides that "without prejudice to Article 49 of the Fourth Convention," the parties shall "endeavour to remove the civilian population, individual civilians and civilian objects under their control from the vicinity of military objectives." Measures for evacuating children are found in Article 78 (1) of Protocol I. This article sets forth requirements for parents or others to consent to evacuation and detailed procedures for identifying children to be evacuated in a manner that should facilitate their return to their families and country.

Article 147 of the Fourth Geneva Convention provides in part that the unlawful transfer or confinement of protected persons constitutes a grave breach of the convention and shall entail individual criminal responsibility.[59] There is a broad consensus that the key provisions of the four Geneva Conventions and the two additional Protocols have acquired the status of rules of general or customary international law binding on all states.[60]

Law Relating to Indigenous Peoples

Legal protections against removal from the home and environment have been specifically adopted in International Labor Organization (ILO) Convention No. 169 concerning Indigenous and Tribal Peoples in Independent Countries. Article 16 (1) of the convention provides that indigenous people "shall not be removed from the lands which they occupy." If "the relocation of these peoples is considered necessary as an exceptional measure, such relocation shall take place only with their free and informed consent" or, if such "consent cannot be obtained . . . only following appropriate procedures established by national laws and regulations, including public inquiries where appropriate, which provide the opportunity for effective representation of the peoples concerned" (paragraph 2). According to paragraph 3 of the same provision, indigenous peoples "have the right to return to their traditional lands, as soon as the grounds for relocation cease to exist."

The Sub-Commission on Prevention of Discrimination and Protection of Minorities, in its draft United Nations Declaration on the Rights of Indigenous Peoples, also acknowledged that "indigenous peoples shall not be forcibly removed from their lands or territories. No relocation shall take place without the free and informed consent of the indigenous peoples concerned and after agreement on just and fair compensation and, where possible, with the option of return."[61]

Concluding Comment

An express prohibition of arbitrary displacement is contained in international humanitarian law and in the law relating to indigenous peoples. In human rights law, by contrast, this prohibition is only implicit in various provisions, most particularly freedom of movement and choice of residence, freedom from arbitrary interference with one's home, and the right to housing. These rights, however, do not provide adequate and comprehensive coverage for all instances of arbitrary displacement, as they do not spell out the circumstances under which displacement is permissible. In addition, they are subject to restrictions and derogation.

Nevertheless, an analysis of relevant provisions demonstrates that displacement of persons should not be discriminatory and may be undertaken exceptionally and only in the specific circumstances provided for in international law, with due regard for the principles of necessity and proportionality. Displacement should last no longer than absolutely required by the exigencies of the situation. Displacement that is caused by or can be reasonably expected to result in genocide, "ethnic cleansing," apartheid, and other systematic forms of discrimination, torture, or inhuman and degrading treatment is absolutely prohibited and under international law might entail individual criminal responsibility of the perpetrators.

Protecting the Particular Needs of Internally Displaced Persons

As mentioned earlier, the internally displaced have a multitude of needs, ranging from equality before the law to a means of subsistence.[62]

Nondiscrimination

The concepts of equality before the law, equal protection of the law, and nondiscrimination form a cornerstone of international human rights law and have therefore been included in the Charter of the United Nations.[63] Freedom from discriminatory acts or omissions of others is essential for the protection of internally displaced persons who, because of their situation, are likely to be disadvantaged. They often live in alien surroundings, deprived of their security, property, and social status and thus are particularly exposed and vulnerable to discriminatory treatment. Specific grounds on which discrimination is prohibited in many human rights and humanitarian law treaties include race, color, sex, language, religion, political or other opinion, national or social origin, property, birth, or "other status."[64] The term "other status" in these instruments can be interpreted broadly to include nationality and disability,[65] as well as youth and old age.[66] The term "other status" also appears to include prohibited discrimination against internally displaced persons, which is based on grounds of their being displaced; however, this conclusion has yet to be rendered by an authoritative body.

The prohibitions of discrimination play a particularly important role in internal and interstate armed conflicts. Obligations, explicitly recognized in the humanitarian law instruments, to treat all persons not taking active part in the hostilities, including those hors de combat, humanely and with respect for their person, honor, and convictions and to apply all guarantees of humanitarian law without any adverse distinction are especially beneficial for the displaced.[67]

One aspect of nondiscrimination relevant for internally displaced persons is the right of equal access to employment opportunities. This right is frequently denied to the displaced, especially to women. Humanitarian law offers little protection in this regard.[68] In human rights law, Article 6 of the CESCR recognizes the right to work and stipulates that states parties shall take positive steps to achieve the full realization of this right.[69] Article 7 of the CESCR recognizes the right of everyone to the enjoyment of just and favorable conditions of work, which include, inter alia, fair wages and equal remuneration, as well as safe and healthy working conditions. The special needs of women are addressed in Article 11 of the Convention on the Elimination of Discrimination against Women (CEDAW), which guarantees women equal rights with men in the field of employment, including the same employment opportunities, equal remuneration, and equal treatment where the work is of equal value. Article 13 of the convention calls on states to eliminate discrimination against women in other areas of economic and social life in order to ensure, among other rights, the right to family benefits. Of relevance to economic activities generally is Article 15, which stipulates that women are equal with men before the law and that they, in particular, shall be accorded "equal rights to conclude contracts and to administer property." In this regard, the Executive Committee of UNHCR has recognized the particular need to "provide all refugee women and girls with effective and equitable access to basic services, including . . . education and skills training, and to make wage-earning opportunities available to them."[70]

Violence

This section examines violence perpetrated against displaced persons from three perspectives: the phenomenon in general, gender-specific attacks, and the use of land mines.

VIOLENCE IN GENERAL. The personal safety of internally displaced persons is often at risk, particularly when they are in transit to camps and after they arrive there. In several countries, such persons have been the victims of individual and mass killings, including genocide and extrajudicial executions. Internally displaced persons feel the effects of hostilities as well, especially from direct and indiscriminate attacks and acts of terrorism. Of course, internally displaced persons can invoke all guarantees of human rights and humanitarian law against such acts of violence. These include the nonderogable guarantees of the right to life, notably the prohibitions of arbitrary and summary executions, and, in situations of armed conflict, of indiscriminate attacks on the civilian population;[71] the prohibitions of genocide[72] and torture or cruel, inhuman, and degrading treatment or punishment;[73] and the prohibition of enforced disappearances.[74] The fact that internally displaced persons, like many others, often suffer from such acts of violence is not due to a lack of legal protection, but rather to a disregard of these guarantees.

Significantly, there is a gap in the legal protection of important needs of internally displaced persons in situations of tensions and disturbances and during internal armed conflicts. During interstate armed conflicts, authorities are obliged to search for persons missing or dead as a consequence of violence (Article 16 of the Fourth Convention and Articles 32–

34 of Protocol I). Equivalent guarantees are lacking in the law regulating situations of tensions and disturbances, and disasters, or of internal armed conflict.

GENDER-SPECIFIC VIOLENCE. Prevalent forms of gender-specific violence[75] against and among internally displaced persons, particularly women, include rape and other sexual attacks and general physical attacks. Increased spousal battering and marital rape often reflect the stress that displacement inflicts on the family unit. Incidences of sexual abuse of children, especially girls, reportedly occur at higher rates among those children separated from their families.

As emphasized by the CEDAW Committee[76] and explicitly recognized in the Inter-American Convention on Violence against Women,[77] violence against women breaches multiple rights guaranteed under general international law and under human rights treaties. Gender-specific violence is rooted in gender discrimination. Such discrimination is prohibited by well-established principles of international law that prohibit not only violence directed against women on the basis of their gender but also violence that affects women disproportionately.[78] Failure to protect women against violence impairs or nullifies the enjoyment of the rights to liberty, security, and integrity of person, as well as, in some instances, the right to life.[79] Gender-specific violence of such a nature also violates the rights to be free from torture or cruel, inhuman, or degrading treatment.[80] The former as well as the present UN Special Rapporteur on Torture and other UN special rapporteurs have categorized rape by state agents as torture.[81] In interpreting the CCPR, the Human Rights Committee has stressed that the prohibition against torture and cruel, inhuman, or degrading treatment and punishment in Article 7 "relates not only to acts that cause physical pain but also to acts that cause mental suffering to the victim."[82] A fair interpretation of the reference to both physical and mental pain could accommodate a wide range of gender-specific violence and threats thereof. In addition, such forms of gender-specific violence implicate the right to the highest attainable standard of physical and mental health recognized in Article 25 of the Universal Declaration, and in Article 12 of the CESCR.[83]

There is a growing consensus that it is the responsibility of states to eliminate violence against women. That includes both preventing and redressing such violence. The UN Declaration on Violence against Women calls on states to "adopt measures directed towards the elimination of violence against [such] women who are especially vulnerable to violence," a category that encompasses displaced women.[84] These measures are especially important as many acts of gender-specific violence, including domestic violence, are carried out by private individuals. Although a state is not directly liable for the wrongs of nonstate actors, states parties to the CCPR, the American Convention, and the European Convention have assumed an affirmative duty to ensure treaty rights to all, without distinction as to gender.[85] Accordingly, acts by private actors that violate rights to personal integrity give rise to state responsibility under those treaties where the state has failed to establish adequate legal mechanisms to prevent, punish, and redress such acts.[86] In addition, states parties to the Women's Convention assume obligations to work toward eliminating discrimination against women "by any person, organization or enterprise"[87] and eliminating "prejudices and . . . all other practices which are based on the idea of the inferiority or the superiority of either of the sexes or on stereotyped roles for men and women."[88]

Internally displaced persons, particularly women, have frequently been coerced into providing sexual favors in return for essential food, shelter, security, documentation, or other forms of assistance. Exploitation of prostitution is also common, especially in situations where prostitution offers the only means of economic support.[89] Its victims suffer physical and psychological trauma, and many have also become infected with sexually transmitted diseases, including HIV/AIDS.[90] Under the CEDAW, states parties are obligated to take measures to protect women engaged in prostitution or who are subject to sexual exploitation and report on their effectiveness.

Thus present international law in principle affords adequate protection from gender-specific violence against and among internally displaced persons in times of tensions and disturbances. The same is true in situations of armed conflict in which many of the above-mentioned rights continue to apply because of their nonderogable nature. The detailed provisions of humanitarian law afford protection as well. During all armed conflicts, adverse distinctions based on sex are prohibited[91] as are "outrages upon personal dignity" and violence to life and person, in particular . . . mutilation, cruel treatment and torture."[92] These prohibitions encompass many forms of gender-specific violence, as well as the more specific prohibition of rape, enforced prostitution, and any form of indecent assault.[93] Rape of civilians has been recognized as a crime for which military or civilian persons may be subject to universal jurisdiction.[94]

LAND MINES. Antipersonnel land mines pose two significant dangers, particularly to civilians (including internally displaced persons), both during and after the conclusion of hostilities. First, a party to the conflict might place land mines in an area populated by displaced civilians. Second, land mines constitute a continuing threat to noncombatants even after the end of the conflict if they are not removed or do not self-destruct but instead remain active and in place after their military purpose has ceased. Such mines are "blind" weapons and their use is indiscriminate in terms of time and victims. Experience has shown that these indiscriminate weapons present a special danger to internally displaced persons, especially while they are on the run in unfamiliar terrain, relocating to camps, leaving camps for some reason, returning to places of residence, or moving to safe havens.

Protection against land mines is still insufficient. The principal source of international law governing the use of land mines and comparable explosive devices, the Land Mines Protocol annexed to the Weapons Convention,[95] is applicable to international armed conflict and a limited class of wars of national liberation.[96] Arguably, as an expression of customary law, it is also applicable to other armed conflicts.[97] However, the protocol only limits but does not prohibit the use of antipersonnel land mines and, as experience in many parts of the world shows, it has not been able to remove the dangers for the civilian population, including internally displaced persons. This weakness can only be redressed by a far-reaching prohibition of the use of land mines.[98]

Detention

The personal liberty of internally displaced persons is often at risk both during flight and upon relocation in camps. Aside from the risks of being taken hostage, forcibly recruited, or abducted into slavery-like practices, the internally displaced often face internment in a compound or camp with no freedom to leave.[99] In some circumstances, alleged misconduct inside a camp can subject an individual to administrative segregation in a separate cell or building within or outside the camp. In many such cases the accused is not informed of the charges or duration of the disciplinary period, and is not given an opportunity to challenge the legality of the detention. At times, internally displaced individuals are considered to be part of the political opposition or counterinsurgency simply because they are on the run, have left their homes, or have been detained by warring forces in a situation of armed conflict.

In situations of tensions and disturbances, the right to be free from arbitrary arrest or detention is recognized under Article 9 of the Universal Declaration and Article 9(1) of the CCPR. The latter article provides that "everyone has the right to liberty and security of person. No one shall be subjected to arbitrary arrest or detention. No one shall be deprived of his liberty except on such grounds and in accordance with such procedures as are established by law."[100]

The right to one's liberty may be restricted on limited grounds[101] and is derogable under those human rights conventions that contain derogation clauses. Nonetheless, the term "arbitrary arrest or detention" has consistently been interpreted broadly as arrest or detention that is not in accordance with domestic law or is lawful on the domestic level but in violation of international standards respecting liberty and security of the person.[102] These international standards include, inter alia, safeguards such as the right to be informed, at the time of the arrest, of the reasons for the arrest and to be promptly informed of the charges; the right to be brought promptly before a judge; the right to trial within a reasonable time or to release; the right to take proceedings before a court to have the lawfulness of the detention reviewed; and the right to compensation in the case of an unlawful arrest or detention.[103]

The question of whether detention in closed camps is permissible is especially relevant for internally displaced persons. Although there are no precedents on this issue, the act of holding someone in a closed camp constitutes detention under Article 9(1) of the CCPR. The Human Rights Committee has stressed "that paragraph one is applicable to all deprivations of liberty, whether in criminal cases or in other cases such as, for example, mental illness, vagrancy, drug addiction, educational purpose, immigration control, etc."[104] Under Article 9(1) of the CCPR, detention in a closed camp is only permissible if it is imposed "on such grounds and in accordance with such procedures as are established" by domestic legislation. Without a legal basis, then, internally displaced persons cannot be confined to a closed camp. In addition, such detention must not be "arbitrary," meaning that it has to be reasonable and necessary in all circumstances.[105] Thus, while certain restrictions of the liberty of internally displaced persons in the interest of their own security or for imperative public necessity purposes are admissible in exceptional cases, these restrictions should be kept as minimal as possible. Often, measures such as checkpoints or curfews will be sufficient.

Regional law on this subject might be more restrictive. Article 5(1), letters (a)–(f) of the European Convention consists of an exhaustive list of grounds for lawful detention. None of these provisions, however, allows for the detention of someone because he or she is displaced. Letter (f) covers detention aimed at the prevention of illegal immigration or at the preparation of deportation or extradition. While asylum-seekers and even refugees may be detained under letter (f), the detention of internally displaced persons would be unlawful as such persons are most often nationals of the country concerned that will not expel or extradite them.

Problems arise in situations of noninternational armed conflict because the right to one's liberty might be derogated during such conflict if the life of the nation is threatened.[106] It is difficult, however, to imagine cases in which the arbitrary detention of internally displaced persons is really "required by the exigencies of the situation."[107] Still, domestic law might allow for far-reaching limitations of personal liberty in such situations. Humanitarian law applicable to noninternational armed conflicts contains no standards concerning when persons may be detained, interned or otherwise deprived of liberty and how such deprivations of liberty will be reviewed by a court. Other than the general protections, common Article 3 does not provide any special protection for persons whose liberty has been restricted. Article 5 of Protocol II provides a regime for the treatment of persons who are "deprived of their liberty for reasons related to the hostilities" and thus implicitly even allows for the internment or detention of internally displaced persons without limiting the preconditions of such conditions. Here there is a clear gap in the legal protection of the internally displaced.

During interstate armed conflict, the situation is not much better. The Fourth Convention provides that aliens who are protected civilians may be interned or placed in assigned housing only if the security of the detaining power absolutely requires such a step.[108] The Fourth Convention also contains a complete regime for the treatment of internees.[109] These provisions, however, do not protect against the deprivation of liberty by one's own government. More comprehensive protection is provided by Article 75(3) of Protocol I, requiring that persons arrested, detained, or interned be promptly informed of the reasons for the measures and be released as soon as the circumstances justifying the detention have ceased to exist, unless the detention is for a penal offense. At the same time, these guarantees apply only for those "arrested, detained or interned for actions related to the armed conflict" and thus do not cover those among the internally displaced persons who are detained for other reasons.

Subsistence Needs

Subsistence needs can be divided in two main categories: food, water, clothing, and shelter; and health and sanitation.

FOOD, WATER, CLOTHING, AND SHELTER. Without doubt, the protection of subsistence needs is one of the most important human rights issues for many of the displaced. Whether resettled in temporary camps or still in transit, internally displaced persons in many cases suffer from a lack of sufficient food, water, housing, and clothing. Article 11 of the CESCR recognizes "the right of everyone to an adequate standard of living for himself and his family, including adequate food, clothing and housing."[110] Similarly, Article 27 of the Convention on the Rights of the Child grants every child the right "to a standard of living adequate for the child's physical, mental, spiritual, moral and social development." Furthermore, states parties to that instrument "in accordance with national conditions and within their means, shall take appropriate measures to assist parents and others responsible for the child to implement this right and shall in case of need provide material assistance and support programmes, particularly with regard to nutrition, clothing and housing" (paragraph 3).

The Committee on Economic, Social and Cultural Rights has made clear in its general comments interpreting states' obligations under the CESCR that states parties bear a "minimum core obligation to ensure the satisfaction of, at the very least, minimum essential levels of each of the rights."[111] The committee has stated that a "State Party in which any significant number of individuals is deprived of essential foodstuffs, of essential primary health care, of basic shelter and housing, or of the most basic forms of education is, *prima facie,* failing to discharge its obligations under the Covenant" unless it can "demonstrate that every effort has been made to use all resources that are at its disposition in an effort to satisfy, as a matter of priority, those minimum obligations."[112] The committee has further commented that in order for a state party to attribute its failure to carry out these obligations to a lack of available resources, it must demonstrate that it has made a maximum effort to use all the resources at its disposal to satisfy the essential needs listed.[113] Such resources include not only those within a state, but also "those available from the international community through international cooperation and assistance."[114] This statement has been interpreted as signifying that all states must provide, at a minimum, subsistence needs to the population under all circumstances.[115]

In times of noninternational armed conflicts, the "minimum core obligation to ensure the satisfaction of, at the very least, minimum essential levels" of social rights continues to bind states and to protect internally displaced persons.[116] Furthermore, common Article 3 provides for the humane treatment of all persons, including internally displaced persons, who do not or no longer take an active part in the hostilities. Although there is no specific prohibition regarding the deprivation of food and water mentioned, the corresponding subsistence rights, to the extent that they are necessary for survival, should be regarded as inherent in this guarantee of humane treatment. Protocol II contains detailed rules applicable to the displaced and other persons affected by hostilities. Article 14 prohibits not only starvation of a civilian population as a method of combat, but also the attack, destruction, removal, or rendering useless of those objects that are "indispensable to the survival of the civilian population, such as foodstuffs, agricultural areas for the production of foodstuffs, crops, livestock, drinking water, installations and supplies and irrigation works."

Similar provisions apply in times of interstate armed conflict. Article 54(1) of Protocol I prohibits starvation of a civilian population as a method of warfare. Article 54(2) protects objects that are indispensable to the survival of the civilian population by prohibiting attacks, destruction, removal, or the rendering useless of such objects when these actions are taken for the *specific purpose* of denying their sustenance value to a civilian population. However, this provision does not prohibit the incidental suffering or collateral effects on a civilian population of an otherwise lawful military operation.[117] Article 55 of the Fourth Geneva Convention charges the occupying power with the duty of ensuring the food supplies of the population, which would include internally displaced persons. It specifically states that the occupier should provide for the necessary foodstuffs, if the resources of the occupied territory are insufficient. Article 55 also prohibits the occupier from requisitioning food, even when destined for the sole use of its occupying forces, without taking into account the needs of the civilian population. In addition, Article

69(1) of Protocol I obliges the occupying power to ensure the provision of clothing, bedding, means of shelter, and other supplies essential for the survival of the civilian population.

HEALTH AND SANITATION. One very serious consequence of internal displacement is exhaustion and illness. Those among the displaced population who are most in need of urgent or regular medical care are frequently denied such assistance. This group includes the wounded and sick, as well as infants, expectant mothers, and the elderly. Medical problems arise not only during the process of displacement, at which time health care is hardly available, but also in camps where access to health services is limited, not to mention a variety of other circumstances. During hostilities, it is not unusual for internally displaced persons to become sick or wounded when caught in crossfire or subjected to indiscriminate weapons. Such persons require urgent, and often long-term, medical care and treatment.

The right to medical care and necessary social services is set forth in Article 25(1) of the Universal Declaration as part of the right to an adequate standard of living. Article 12 of the CESCR is dedicated to the realization of "the right of everyone to the enjoyment of the highest attainable standard of physical and mental health." Paragraph 2 of that provision elaborates on the commitment by states to take steps to fully realize this right and includes, inter alia, "(c) the prevention, treatment and control of epidemic, endemic, occupational or other diseases [and]; (d) the creation of conditions which assure to all medical service and medical attention in case of sickness."[118] The Committee on Economic, Social and Cultural Rights has stated that the deprivation of any significant number of persons "of essential primary health care" constitutes a violation of the covenant unless the state concerned can demonstrate "that every effort has been made to use all resources that are at its disposition."[119]

During situations of noninternational armed conflict, common Article 3 requires the parties to internal armed conflicts to treat humanely all persons who do not or no longer actively participate in the hostilities. It further obliges the contending parties to collect and care for the wounded and sick without condition. Thus wounded and sick displaced persons who fall under the control of a party to the conflict are entitled to medical care, whether or not they previously committed hostile acts. Protocol II elaborates on the common Article 3 duty by providing in Article 7 that all "wounded, sick and shipwrecked, whether or not they have taken part in the armed conflict, shall be respected and protected." Paragraph 2 of Article 7 specifically requires that the wounded and sick, in all circumstances, "be treated humanely and . . . receive, to the fullest extent practicable and with the least possible delay, the medical care and attention required by their condition." Moreover, the parties cannot make a distinction in the rendition of medical care on any grounds other than medical ones. Persons, including the internally displaced, who are wounded, sick or shipwrecked during hostilities governed by Protocol II must thus be accorded Article 7's nonderogable guarantees. Inasmuch as Article 7 of Protocol II merely clarifies and elaborates on the preexisting duty in common Article 3 to provide the wounded and sick with medical care, it should be regarded as customary law and, as such, be respected and applied by the parties to all internal armed conflict.

For interstate armed conflicts, Article 10 of Protocol I reiterates, in substantially similar terms, Article 7 of Protocol II. The Fourth Convention contains many detailed provisions on health-related aspects. Among them, Article 55 provides that the occupying power has a duty to ensure medical supplies to the population and, if the occupied territory's own resources are insufficient, the occupying power should provide for the necessary medical articles. In addition, Article 56 proclaims the occupying power's duty to ensure and maintain medical and hospital facilities and services, public health, and hygiene. Article 16 of the Fourth Convention covers not only civilians in occupied territories but the whole of the population of belligerent countries; it requires that the wounded and sick, the infirm, and expectant mothers, "shall be the object of particular protection and respect." Paragraph 2 of this article mandates that, as far as military considerations allow, "each Party to the conflict shall facilitate the steps taken to search for the . . . wounded, to assist . . . persons exposed to grave danger, and to protect them against pillage and ill-treatment." Article 17 states that parties to a conflict shall endeavor to conclude local agreements for the evacuation from besieged or encircled areas of the wounded, sick, infirm, aged persons, children and maternity cases. Finally, Articles 18 and 19 of the same Convention protect civilian hospitals from attack.[120]

Personal Identification and Documentation

Internal displacement often results in the loss of personal papers and documentation. It also makes proper registration of events such as births and deaths extremely difficult, if not impossible. Although registration in camps and relocation sites is often required for purposes of documentation and to facilitate family reunification, many internally displaced persons dislike being identified as displaced because they fear that such labeling has discriminatory effects. As a result, displaced persons often lack the legal protections and privileges extended to those who hold identifying documents. Although human rights law acknowledges the right of everyone to be recognized as a person before the law, a right to documentation and registration is not guaranteed as such.[121] Significantly, however, Article 16 of the Convention on the Elimination of Discrimination against Women requires the registration of marriages, and various other instruments recognize the obligations of states to register children immediately after birth and to protect their right to a name from the moment of birth.[122] Article 8 of the convention is also noteworthy as it requires states parties to "undertake to respect the right of the child to preserve his or her identity, including nationality, name and family relations as recognized by law without unlawful interference."

Whereas the fundamental importance of protecting the right to juridical personality in times of national emergency is affirmed by Article 4(2) of the CCPR and Article 27(2) of the American Convention, which declare the right nonderogable, a right to appropriate documentation for internally displaced persons in situations of noninternational armed conflict is not expressly recognized in international humanitarian law. During interstate armed conflicts, protected persons can invoke a series of provisions regarding several aspects of documentation and registration, but these do not apply to relations with one's own government.[123] One has to conclude, therefore, that present international law does not adequately protect the needs of internally displaced persons for personal identification, documentation and registration.

Protection of Movement-Related Needs

Freedom of residence and movement is expressly recognized as a basic human right in Article 13(1) of the Universal Declaration. This freedom is similarly guaranteed in Article 12(1) of the CCPR, which states that "everyone lawfully within the territory of a State shall, within that territory, have the right to liberty of movement and freedom to choose his residence." Comparable guarantees are embodied in regional instruments.[124] Because they not only allow free movement but also guarantee free choice of residence, they contain a right to remain and thus a right not to be displaced. Despite the fact that this right can be limited if the restrictions "are provided by law, [and] are necessary to protect national security, public order (*ordre public*), public health or morals or the rights and freedoms of others," it provides important safeguards for the internally displaced. The requirement of necessity in the limitation clause calls for a narrow interpretation of this clause.

In situations of noninternational armed conflict, Article 17 of Protocol II is relevant for the protection against displacement. Section 2 of this article stipulates that "civilians shall not be compelled to leave their own territory for reasons connected with the conflict." Section 1 effectively prohibits the warring parties from ordering the displacement of the civilian population for reasons related to the conflict, "*unless* the security of the civilians involved or imperative military reasons so demand" (emphasis added). Moreover, in the event of such displacement, the responsible party must take "all possible measures . . . in order that the civilian population may be received under satisfactory conditions of shelter, hygiene, health, safety and nutrition." The negative phraseology of Article 17 clearly evinces an intention to prohibit, as a general rule, the forced movement or displacement of civilians during internal hostilities. Accordingly, the burden is squarely on the party initiating such action to justify it under the narrow exceptions to this rule. Article 17 would, therefore, prohibit a deliberate policy, such as that effected in Guatemala during the 1980s, of forcibly moving most or all of the civilian population from a certain area and resettling it in "strategic hamlets" as part of a counterinsurgency strategy designed to deny dissident forces a perceived social base or logistical support.

A right to find refuge in a safe part of the country is inherent in freedom of movement, although it has not yet been recognized explicitly. Most universal and regional human rights instruments, however, permit states to place restrictions on freedom of residence and movement during situations of tensions and disturbances, or during disasters. Furthermore, derogations of the right are permitted in times of public emergency. These factors considerably reduce the protection afforded by human rights law, and it is here that the more elaborate guarantees of international humanitarian law regarding the movement of displaced persons come into play.[125]

As for the return of displaced persons, it must be recognized that those who have become victims of displacement need to be guaranteed the right to return voluntarily to their place of former habitual residence.

There is no general rule that affirms the right of internally displaced persons to return to their original place of residence or to move to another safe place of their choice. However, such a right in principle can be deduced from freedom of movement and the right to choose one's residence. In the case of the former Yugoslavia, this has been recognized in the Dayton Agreement which states in Article 1(1), of Annex 7 that not only all refugees but also all "displaced persons have the right freely to return to their homes of origin."[126] Therefore the contracting parties are obliged to "create in their territories the political, economic, and social conditions conducive to the voluntary return . . . of refugees and displaced persons." In more general terms, ILO Convention No. 169 concerning Indigenous and Tribal Peoples states explicitly that "whenever possible, these peoples shall have the right to return to their traditional lands, as soon as the grounds for relocation cease to exist" (Article 16, para. 3). It is also noteworthy that, at least in one case, the UN Security Council "affirm[ed] the right of refugees and displaced persons to return to their homes."[127] In a similar vein, the Sub-Commission on the Prevention of Discrimination and Protection of Minorities affirmed "the right of refugees and displaced persons to return, in safety and dignity, to their country of origin and/or within it, to their place of origin or choice."[128]

No human rights or humanitarian law instrument expressly provides internally displaced persons with legal protection against being forcibly returned to places with unsafe conditions. It is true that in the area of refugee law, Article 33(1) of the Refugee Convention establishes the principle of *non-refoulement,* which prohibits a refugee from being returned to a country where he or she has good reason to fear persecution. Similarly, the application of this guarantee is clearly restricted to persons who have left their own country. Another approach to the question of forced return to situations of danger can be found in the law relating to the nonderogable prohibition of torture and cruel or inhuman treatment. Thus Article 3(1) of the Convention against Torture (CAT) provides that "no State Party shall expel, return (*'refouler'*) or extradite a person to another State where there are substantial grounds for believing that he would be in danger of being subjected to torture."

Regarding Article 7 of the CCPR, which prohibits torture and cruel, inhuman, or degrading treatment, the Human Rights Committee has stated, in a similar vein, that "States Parties must not expose individuals to the danger of torture or cruel, inhuman or degrading treatment or punishment upon return to another country by way of their extradition, expulsion or refoulement."[129] The committee has also decided that forcible return is prohibited if the individual concerned risks, in the country to which he or she is returned, a violation of the right to life.[130]

This jurisprudence, which is inspired by the case law of the European Court on Human Rights regarding the prohibition of inhuman treatment (Article 3, European Human Rights Convention), only concerns forcible return across international frontiers and thus is not directly applicable to internally displaced persons. However, it might become relevant for such persons because it regards the act of handing an individual over to his or her torturer, murderer, or executioner as a violation of the obligation to protect individuals against torture and unlawful deprivations of life. Thus the European Court on Human Rights has stated that in cases of inhuman return, "there is no question of adjudicating on or establishing the responsibility of the receiving country, whether under general international law, under the convention, or otherwise. In so far as any liability under the convention is or may be incurred, it is liability incurred by the extraditing Contracting State by reason of its having taken action which has as a direct consequence the exposure of an individual to proscribed ill-treatment."[131]

According to the court, these arguments apply not only to extradition cases but also to cases of deportation.[132] For the reasons just set forth, they are also valid with regard to the forcible return of internally displaced persons to areas where they must face serious risks of torture and cruel or inhuman treatment or of violations of their right to life. If it is the responsibility of states not to make torture or summary or arbitrary executions possible by handing persons over to the actual perpetrators of such human rights violations, then there is no reason why a state's responsibility is not similar, if not greater, when the forcible return takes place within the same country. The same reasoning can also be deduced, by analogy, from Article 33 of the 1951 Refugee Convention.

Property

Internally displaced persons regularly lose much of their property when displaced. Because of their vulnerability, such persons need protection for the property taken with them or acquired during displacement. The destruction or theft of crops and livestock, the bombing or burning of shelters and confiscation or forcible occupation of private homes by military or paramilitary forces are among the experiences faced by internally displaced persons, especially in situations of armed conflict. When internally displaced persons return to their homes, they may find their properties occupied by other people. Therefore they need restitution of the property or compensation for its loss.

The legal protection of property in situations of tensions and disturbances is weak. Although Article 17 of the Universal Declaration grants everyone the right to own property, alone or in association with others, and prohibits arbitrary deprivation of such property, no comparable right has been included in the CCPR or the CESCR. Nevertheless, the regional human rights conventions guarantee the right to property. However, this right may be limited in the public interest.[133]

Humanitarian law explicitly prohibits wanton destruction of property[134] and pillage,[135] a ban that protects the personal property of displaced persons (located in the camps and/or left in the homes from which they have fled) from theft and vandalism. Additional protection against the destruction of property belonging to displaced persons can be derived, at least during internal armed conflicts, from Article 14 of Protocol II. This article prohibits the attack, destruction, removal, or rendering useless of those objects considered indispensable to the survival of the civilian population, such as "foodstuffs, agricultural areas for the production of foodstuffs, crops, livestock, drinking water installations and supplies and irrigation works."

The possibility that internally displaced persons will find their properties occupied by other people upon return to their homes is frequently an obstacle to return. It also raises questions concerning the right to restitution of property lost as a consequence of displacement or compensation for its loss. Although such a right is not explicitly recognized in international law, there is a certain trend in international practice to accept such a guarantee. The Inter-American Commission on Human Rights has recommended payment of just compensation to returning internally displaced persons for the loss of their property, including homes, crops, livestock and other belongings.[136] In the case of Iraqi-occupied Kuwait, the UN Security Council decided "to create a Fund to pay compensation for claims" of those damaged by Iraq's occupation of Kuwait.[137] Victims of human rights violations have been recognized as eligible for compensation.[138] Furthermore, the rules of the International Criminal Tribunal for the former Yugoslavia allow the tribunal, in conjunction with a judgment of conviction, to award the restitution of property or its proceeds to victims, even property in the hands of third parties not otherwise connected with the crime.[139] Finally, Annex 7 to the Dayton Peace Agreement explicitly provides refugees and displaced persons in Article 1(1) with "the right to have restored to them property of which they were deprived during the course of hostilities . . . and to be compensated for any property that cannot be restored to them." Recognition by the international community of a right of internally displaced persons to restitution of lost property and compensation for its loss, on the basis of these precedents, would be of utmost importance for internally displaced persons.[140]

Family Unity

During any stage of internal displacement, it is important for internally displaced families to remain together. The same is true for communities that are culturally considered to be extended families. If these internally displaced persons are nonetheless dispersed and separated, they must be able to reunite as quickly as possible. Although everyone suffers from the pain of involuntary separation, children are particularly vulnerable in those situations.

International law recognizes that the family is a fundamental unit of society requiring special protection. For example, Article 16(3) of the Universal Declaration and Article 23(1) of the CCPR declare that the family is "the natural and fundamental group unit of society and is entitled to protection by society and the State." State Parties to the CESCR likewise recognize the primacy of the family, to which the widest possible protection and assistance should be granted, particularly where dependent children are present (Article 10(1) of the CESCR).[141] Because of a child's vulnerability and dependence on parents and family, children enjoy special protection, both in universal[142] and in special human rights treaties. In this respect, the World Conference on Human Rights has stated: "National and international mechanisms and programmes should be strengthened for the defense and protection of children, in particular . . . displaced children, . . . children in armed conflict, as well as children victims of famine and drought and other emergencies."[143] In this regard, the Convention on the Rights of the Child is particularly specific. Of paramount importance for displaced families are the provisions on children separated from their parents.

Under Article 8 of the Convention on the Rights of the Child, State Parties undertake to respect the child's right to maintain family relations, requiring the state party to provide appropriate assistance and protection in the case of unlawful deprivation of such relations. With regard to a child's separation from his or her parent(s), Article 9(4) (first sentence) provides that "where such separation results from any action initiated by a State Party, such as the detention, imprisonment, exile, deportation or death . . . of one or both parents or of the child, that State Party shall, upon request, provide the parents, the child or, if appropriate, another member of the family with the essential information concerning the whereabouts of the absent member(s) of the family unless the provision of the information would be detrimental to the well-being of the child." Family reunification is addressed in Articles 10 and 22. However, these articles deal only with cases in which children and their parents reside in different countries and, therefore, do not normally apply to internally displaced persons.

Despite this gap in legal protection, the international community has recognized the special protection needs of children separated from their parents during displacement. The participating states to the World Summit on Children stressed "the special needs of children who are separated from their families."[144] In the Plan of Action adopted at the Summit, the participants stated that "every effort should be made to prevent the separation of children from their families. Whenever children are separated . . . arrangements should be made for appropriate alternative family care or institutional placement. . . . Extended families, relatives and community institutions should be given support to help to meet the special needs of . . . displaced . . . children."[145] In addition, various conclusions adopted by the Executive Committee of UNHCR concerning family unity and family reunification of refugees might also serve as guidelines for the internally displaced.[146] UNHCR Policy on Refugee Children incorporates as "fundamental" the "principle of international law [that it is] the primary responsibility of parents or legal guardians to care for children." Along with the best interests of the child, family unity is a guiding principle for decisionmaking involving refugee children.[147] UNHCR Guidelines for action by the agency and states are based in part on the principle that "the single best way to promote the psychosocial well-being of children is to support their families."[148] Special attention has focused on the needs of children during evacuation to ensure adequate registration and documentation in order to enhance the possibility of reuniting such children with their families,[149] and on the needs of unaccompanied children or those separated from their families.[150]

During times of armed conflict, the legal protection provided for separated families is better than in times of tensions and disturbances. In noninternational armed conflicts, Article 4(3) of Protocol II provides that children shall be provided the care and aid they require. This article also requires that all appropriate steps be taken to facilitate the reunion of families temporarily separated (Article 4(3)(b)). Finally, paragraph 3(e) of the same article requires that, if necessary, measures be taken to remove children "temporarily from the area in which hostilities are taking place to a safer area within the country." Such removal must be temporary, within the country, with the consent of the parent or guardian if possible, and the children must be allowed to travel with persons responsible for their safety and well-being.

The set of norms applicable in situations of interstate armed conflict is more elaborate. Among the many provisions designed to protect families, the following are especially relevant for families who are separated by displacement: Article 24 of the Fourth Convention, located in Part II thereof, which applies to all members of the population, including a state party's own nationals, requires parties to the conflict to take measures to protect and identify children under the age of fifteen who are orphaned or separated from their families as a result of the hostilities. In order to facilitate reestablishing contacts between family members, and, when, if possible, reuniting them, Article 26 of the Fourth Geneva Convention requires each party to the conflict to facilitate inquiries made by members of families who are dispersed because of the hostilities. Likewise, each party to the conflict must encourage the work of organizations engaged in this task. In addition, Article 74 of Protocol I, which develops Article 26 of the Fourth Convention, requires the high contracting parties and the parties to the conflict to "facilitate in every possible way the reunion of families dispersed as a result of armed conflicts" and to "encourage in particular the work of the humanitarian organizations engaged in this task." Since Article 74 of Protocol I reaffirms and develops an article found in Part II of the Fourth Convention, it applies to the whole population, including a party's own nationals.[151]

Education

Education is essential to developing a person's sense of identity and human dignity. Nevertheless, internally displaced persons, particularly children, often are deprived of education, either because there are insufficient educational facilities, or none at all, in the area to which they have temporarily relocated, or because alternative learning settings are lacking. Also, parents of displaced children may be unable to pay required school fees, to afford school uniforms or clothing in general (including shoes), or find that it is simply too dangerous for the children to travel to school. Moreover, internally displaced adults may need specialized education, particularly when they have lost their sources of income and livelihood. Such adult education should or could include survival skills training, job skills training, leadership training, and training in conflict resolution.

Human rights and humanitarian law recognize that children have a right to receive at least a basic education even in times of tensions and disturbances or armed conflict. The right to education is recognized by guarantees of Article 13 of the CESCR and Articles 28 and 29 of the Convention on the Rights of the Child, as well as by regional instruments.[152] Whereas common Article 3 is silent on the education of children during internal armed conflicts, Article 4(3)(a) of Protocol II states that children shall be provided with the care and aid they need and, in particular, that they shall receive "an education, including religious and moral education, in keeping with the wishes of their parents, or in the absence of parents, of those responsible for their care." Article 24 of the Fourth Geneva Convention, which is applicable to the whole population in a belligerent country, requires states to take the necessary measures "to ensure that children under fifteen, who are orphaned or are separated from their families as a result of the war, are not left to their own resources, and that . . . the exercise of . . . their education [is] facilitated in all circumstances. Their education shall, as far as possible, be entrusted to persons of a similar cultural tradition."[153]

Thus the right to education can be invoked by internally displaced persons in all situations. Problems arise, however, from the fact that the displaced may have specific educational needs. Here, analogous application of some standards developed by UNHCR's Executive Committee for refugees might be helpful. The committee has stressed the high "priority to the education of all refugee children, ensuring equal access for girls, [and] giving due regard to the curriculum of the country of origin." It has also urged UNHCR "to identify educational requirements in the early stages of an emergency so that prompt attention may be given to such needs."[154] Of particular concern are measures to ensure equal opportunity for refugee girls as for boys, equal access of refugee women to adult education, and skills training to ensure that they are able to support themselves and their families.[155]

International Provision of Humanitarian Assistance

Some points of concern in the international provisions of humanitarian assistance are access to such assistance and the safety of relief workers and organizations.

Access to Assistance

Access to humanitarian assistance in different kinds of situations depends on the governing legal regime, including relevant Security Council actions.

HUMAN RIGHTS AND HUMANITARIAN LAW. One of the most acute needs of internally displaced persons is safe access to those essentials that are indispensable to their survival and to a minimum standard of living. Thus the possibility to seek and receive humanitarian assistance is, itself, a crucial aspect of protection for internally displaced persons.

It is primarily the responsibility of the states to provide humanitarian assistance to their internally displaced persons. Therefore the government of a state that acts in good faith will attempt to protect and provide life-sustaining assistance to its internally displaced citizens, and, if the magnitude of the problem exceeds its relief capabilities, it will call on the international community to perform these humanitarian functions. In such a case, it may invoke Article 1(3) of the Charter of the United Nations, which obliges member states of the United Nations to cooperate "in solving international problems of an economic, social, cultural, or humanitarian character, and in promoting and encouraging respect for human rights and for fundamental freedoms for all."[156]

If, however, a government is unable or unwilling to provide these services and does not request, or rejects, an offer of humanitarian relief by competent external organizations, a question arises as to whether internally displaced persons have a right under international law to request and receive assistance from the international community and/or international humanitarian and relief organizations.

SITUATIONS OF TENSIONS, DISTURBANCES, AND DISASTERS. In situations of tensions, disturbances, and disasters, the right of internally displaced persons to request and receive assistance from their government and the duty of their government to provide assistance necessarily flows from the essential nature of the international law of human rights. Internally displaced persons may seek and receive protection and life-sustaining assistance from their government as a necessary implication of states' recognition of the right to life, which requires that states adopt positive measures, when necessary, to protect that right.[157] In the area of subsistence rights, a state party to the CESCR has additional obligations to "take steps, individually and through international assistance and co-operation . . . to the maximum of its available resources, with a view to achieving progressively the full realization of [the treaty's] rights" (Article 2(1)). Thus the maximum of a state party's available resources includes both "the resources existing within a State and those available from the international community through international cooperation and assistance."[158] Under Article 11 of the CESCR, states parties also recognize the "essential importance of international co-operation based on free consent" for the realization of "the right . . . to an adequate standard of living, . . . including adequate food, clothing and housing."[159] In this regard, the committee has emphasized "that in accordance with Articles 55 and 56 of the Charter of the United Nations, with well-established principles of international law, and with the provisions of the Covenant itself, international cooperation for . . . the realization of economic, social and cultural rights is an obligation of all States."[160] Thus it can be argued that states parties to the CESCR have a duty to at least refrain from unreasonably denying offers of international assistance in cases of imminent humanitarian problems seriously affecting the subsistence needs of internally displaced persons and, perhaps, an obligation to accept reasonable offers.

The international community, however, has been cautious about recognizing a duty of a state to accept offers of humanitarian assistance. In various resolutions, the General Assembly has reaffirmed the primary responsibility of states to assist the victims of natural disasters and similar emergencies that occur within their territory.[161] In addition, in Resolutions 43/131 and 45/100, the General Assembly has declared that the abandonment of the victims of such situations without humanitarian assistance "constitutes a threat to human life and an offence to human dignity."[162] These resolutions invite states to facilitate the work of international and nongovernmental organizations in implementing humanitarian assistance, in particular, by supplying food, medicines, and health care.[163] They implicitly recognize the right, under international law, of international organizations and nongovernmental organizations to offer humanitarian assistance to other states in case of disaster or similar emergency, and they support the view that such offers do not constitute unlawful interference in the internal affairs of these states. However, these resolutions also reaffirm that the right of external actors to provide such assistance to victims in other states depends on the consent of these states. Thus the Guiding Principles in the annex to General Assembly Resolution 46/182, while declaring the importance of humanitarian assistance, state that "the sovereignty, territorial integrity and national unity of States must be fully respected in accordance with the Charter of the United Nations. In this context, humanitarian assistance should be provided with the consent of the affected country and in principle on the basis of an appeal by the affected country."[164]

This principle is confirmed in the context of ICRC activities. During situations of tensions and disturbances, ICRC is empowered by the statutes of the International Red Cross and Red Crescent Movement with a right of initiative to offer its services to assist the victims of such situations, including displaced persons, but a government is not obliged to accept ICRC's offer of services and thus may legitimately deny ICRC access to the country.[165]

SITUATIONS OF ARMED CONFLICT. The law regarding situations of non-international armed conflict is similar. Common Article 3, which is applicable to all internal hostilities, expressly states that "an impartial humanitarian body, such as the International Committee of the Red Cross, may offer its services to the Parties to the conflict"[166] but the parties to the conflict, most particularly the established government, have no express legal obligation to accept the offer.[167] The same is true for Article 18 of Protocol II. Paragraph 1 extends the right to offer services to "relief societies located in the territory of the High Contracting Party, such as Red Cross (Red Crescent, Red Lion and Sun)."[168] Paragraph 2 of the same provision stresses that if "the civilian population is suffering undue hardship owing to a lack of the supplies essential for its survival," relief actions of a purely humanitarian character "shall be undertaken subject to the consent of the High Contracting Party concerned." The words "shall be undertaken" indicate, however, that this provision effectively limits a party's discretion to withhold its consent thereto. It has been noted, in this regard, that the party may refuse relief actions "only for valid reasons, not for arbitrary and capricious ones."[169] Since Article 18 does not stipulate how the High Contracting Party must manifest its consent to relief operations, it clearly may be made expressly and publicly, or, presumably, by way of "private assurances or an attitude which can in good faith be construed as acquiescence."[170]

During interstate armed conflicts, the Fourth Geneva Convention and Protocol I apply. These instruments contain detailed provisions for relief actions on behalf of the civilian populations in both occupied and non-occupied territories during interstate hostilities. Various other provisions in the Fourth Convention deal with collective or individual relief to civilians during situations of occupation and internment.[171] Among the most important provisions is Article 23 of the Fourth Convention, which applies to all internally displaced civilians whether or not they are protected persons under the convention. This article requires each contracting party to "allow the free passage of all consignments of medical and hospital stores and objects necessary for religious worship intended only for civilians of another High Contracting Party, even if the latter is its adversary. It shall likewise permit the free passage of all consignments of essential foodstuffs, clothing and tonics intended for children under fifteen, expectant mothers and maternity cases." Article 70 of Protocol I, which has been referred to as the "new general regulation for relief in non-occupied territories," is less restrictive than Article 23 of the Fourth Convention.[172] It removes several key deficiencies found in this article, principally by broadening the categories of relief supplies[173] and effectively eliminating the restrictive conditions on the passage of relief stipulated therein.[174] The basic new rule for relief actions is stated in the first paragraph of Article 70 as follows:

> If the civilian population of any territory under the control of a Party to the conflict, other than occupied territory, is not adequately provided with the supplies mentioned in Article 69, relief actions which are humanitarian and impartial in character and conducted without any adverse distinction shall be undertaken, subject to the agreement of the Parties concerned in such relief actions. Offers of such relief shall not be regarded as interference in the armed conflict or as unfriendly acts. In the distribution of relief consignments, priority shall be given to those persons, such as children, expectant mothers, maternity cases and nursing mothers, who, under the Fourth Convention or under this Protocol, are to be accorded privileged treatment or special protection.

The second paragraph of Article 70 of Protocol I provides that each contracting party and the parties to the conflict "shall allow and facilitate rapid and unimpeded passage of all relief consignments, equipment and personnel provided in accordance with this Section, even if such assistance is destined for the civilian population of the adverse Party." With regard to potential donor states, this provision, as it embodies the basic principle of humanity, has been interpreted as "creating a duty on those States in a position to do so to make every reasonable effort to contribute to such relief actions, to undertake such actions where appropriate and to allow and facilitate actions which private organizations of that country are prepared to undertake."[175] The party whose civilians are the object of such relief actions cannot arbitrarily refuse to accept that relief.[176] Moreover, Article 70(3) of Protocol I allows transit states to impose conditions on the transit of relief consignments through their territory,[177] but prohibits them from diverting such consignments from the purpose for which they are intended or delaying their forwarding, "except in cases of urgent necessity in the interest of the civilian population concerned" (paragraph 3(c)). In addition, Article 70(4) of Protocol I requires the parties to the conflict to "protect relief consignments and facilitate their rapid distribution." Furthermore, the fifth paragraph of Article 70 requires that all relevant parties must encourage and facilitate "effective international co-ordination of the relief actions referred to in paragraph 1."

During an occupation, the Fourth Convention places primary responsibility on the occupying power to meet the basic needs of the civilian population. Specifically, Article 55 of that instrument states: "To the fullest extent of the means available to it, the Occupying Power has the duty of ensuring the food and medical supplies of the population; it should, in particular, bring in the necessary foodstuffs, medical stores and other articles if the resources of the occupied territory are inadequate."[178] In the event that all or part of the civilian population in an occupied territory is inadequately supplied, Article 59 of the Fourth Convention declares that the occupying power "shall agree to relief schemes on behalf of the said population, and shall facilitate them by all the means at its disposal." Such operations for the provision of food, medical supplies, and clothing may be undertaken by states or impartial humanitarian organizations such as ICRC (paragraph 2). Furthermore, contracting parties must allow free passage to these shipments (but may subject them to searches and regulations as to times and routes, among other things), and they must guarantee their protection (paragraphs 3 and 4).[179] While Article 61, paragraphs 1 and 2, provide for the distribution and exemption from taxation of relief consignments, paragraph 3 states that "all Contracting Parties shall endeavour to permit the transit and transport, free of charge, of such relief consignments on their way to occupied territories." In addition, Article 69(2) of Protocol I requires that relief actions "shall be implemented without delay."

In cases of interstate armed conflicts, Article 10 of the Fourth Geneva Convention allows ICRC and any other impartial humanitarian organization to undertake protection and assistance to civilians, including internally displaced persons, provided the parties to the conflict have consented. Article 81 of Protocol I effectively broadens the provisions of the Geneva Conventions by requiring the warring parties to grant ICRC all facilities within their power to enable ICRC to carry out the humanitarian functions assigned to it by the 1949 Geneva Conventions and the protocol in order to ensure protection and assistance to the victims of conflicts. Article 81 additionally states that ICRC "may also carry out any other humanitarian activities in favour of these victims, subject to the consent of the Parties to the conflict concerned."

RELEVANT SECURITY COUNCIL ACTIONS. Whether states have an obligation to allow the activities of international humanitarian organizations within their territory and whether the international community has a right to provide humanitarian protection and assistance without the consent of the government concerned are questions of ongoing study and debate within the United Nations, as well as among states, relief providers, and others concerned with the plight of internally displaced persons. In recent years, the UN Security Council has made several key decisions relating to humanitarian assistance and protection on the basis of its authority under the Charter of the United Nations. Pursuant to Article 39 of Chapter VII, the Security Council is empowered to determine the existence of "any threat to the peace, breach of the peace or act of aggression" and to make recommendations or decide "what measures shall be taken . . . to maintain or restore international peace and security." Many of these resolutions refer to situations in which internal displacement took place.

In Resolution 688 (1991), the Security Council insisted, for the first time, that a state (Iraq) "allow immediate access by international humanitarian organizations to all those in need of assistance . . . and . . . make available all necessary facilities for their operations."[180] Since then, the Security Council has repeatedly reaffirmed the sovereignty, territorial integrity, and political independence of states with humanitarian problems but at the same time has insisted on or called for "immediate" or "unimpeded" access by international humanitarian organizations to all those in need of assistance, including internally displaced persons.[181]

In the case of Somalia, the Security Council, in Resolution 794, elaborated on the right to seek and the duty to provide international humanitarian relief in the context of disintegration of governmental authority by, inter alia, responding to "the urgent calls from Somalia for the international community to take measures to ensure the delivery of humanitarian assistance."[182] The Security Council determined that "the magnitude of the human tragedy caused by the conflict in Somalia, further exacerbated by the obstacles to the distribution of humanitarian assistance, constitutes a threat to international peace and security."[183] Acting under Chapter VII of the Charter of the United Nations, the Security Council authorized the secretary-general and UN member states "to use all necessary means to establish as soon as possible a secure environment for humanitarian relief operations in Somalia."[184]

Resolution 929 (1994) concerning the situation in Rwanda is of direct relevance for internally displaced persons. Here, the Security Council recognized "that the current situation in Rwanda constitutes a unique case which demands an urgent response by the international community," and welcomed in paragraph 2 the offer of member states to cooperate with the secretary-general "in order to achieve the objectives of the United Nations in Rwanda through the establishment of a temporary operation . . . aimed at contributing, in an impartial way, to the security and protection of displaced persons, refugees and civilians at risk in Rwanda." Therefore, the Security Council, "acting under Chapter VII of the Charter of the United Nations, authorize[d] . . . the Member States cooperating with the Secretary-General to conduct the operation referred to in paragraph 2 above using all necessary means to achieve the humanitarian objectives" as they had been set out previously in Resolution 925.[185] These objectives were as follows: "Contribute to the Security and protection of displaced persons, refugees and civilians at risk in Rwanda, including through the establishment and maintenance, where feasible, of secure humanitarian areas; and . . . provide security and support for the distribution of relief supplies and humanitarian relief operations."[186] Furthermore, in Somalia as well as in Rwanda, the Security Council included in the mandate of UN peace-keeping troops the task of providing assistance and protection to internally displaced persons.[187]

Two conclusions can be drawn from this recent practice of the Security Council. First, in situations of noninternational[188] or interstate armed conflict threatening peace and security in a region, states are obliged to grant UN agencies and international humanitarian organizations access to civilians, including internally displaced persons in need of humanitarian relief when the state concerned is unable or unwilling to provide such assistance. Second, violations of this obligation do not entitle other states or international humanitarian organizations to intervene and distribute relief against the will of the country concerned, except in a very serious humanitarian crisis that in itself contributes to a threat to international peace and security.[189] Under those circumstances, the Security Council, on the basis of Chapter VII of the UN Charter, can authorize states to use "all necessary means," including armed force, to give international humanitarian organizations access to persons in need, including internally displaced persons. Thus, on the one hand, if the Security Council so orders, there is a clear obligation of states to permit humanitarian assistance and protection to their civilian and internally displaced population if they, themselves, are unable or unwilling to provide such aid.[190] On the other hand, outside of exceptional cases involving a threat to international peace and security, there is no right to force a state to accept receipt of this aid if it has been refused or denied.

Safety for Relief Workers and Organizations

The effective provision of assistance to internally displaced persons often depends on the safety of relief workers and their organizations. First and foremost, relief personnel, their means of transportation, and relief supplies must be safe from attack. These workers also must be able to assist and protect the internally displaced without hindrance or other unwarranted interferences. Medical and religious personnel, as well as their units, transports, and facilities must also receive protection if they are to carry out their specialized assistance.

Although attacks and threats of violence against relief workers have occurred during tensions and disturbances and disasters, such acts are not commonplace. In these situations, relief personnel derive legal protection against such acts by state agents directly from human rights law. In addition, the Convention on the Safety of United Nations and Associated Personnel may come into play.[191] It applies to UN and associated personnel deployed within a UN operation, except those operations in which UN personnel are engaged as combatants in an enforcement action under Chapter VII of the Charter of the United Nations.[192]

The Convention on the Safety of United Nations and Associated Personnel also applies in situations of noninternational armed conflict. In addition, medical and religious personnel and their transports are protected, to a certain extent, by Articles 9 to 12 of Protocol II. In contrast, neither common Article 3 nor Protocol II contains provisions expressly requiring the parties to the conflict to respect and protect relief personnel and other non-UN field personnel engaged in fact-finding and monitoring activities related to relief efforts. The protection of these workers from attack and other acts of violence must therefore be based on their status as civilians and the neutral and impartial nature of their humanitarian enterprise. The act of providing traditional relief to the victims of internal hostilities cannot be regarded in any way as hostile or harmful to any party to the conflict. Thus the humanitarian activities of relief workers cannot entail forfeiture of their immunity from direct attack or justify their trial and punishment by any belligerent. Attacks against such persons would flagrantly violate common Article 3's injunction of acts of violence against persons taking no active part in the hostilities.

Like the law applicable to internal hostilities, the Fourth Geneva Convention has no provisions rendering general protection for relief personnel, their transports, and supplies during interstate armed conflicts. Their protection from direct attack during interstate wars necessarily derives from their civilian status and impartial humanitarian activities or from the Convention on the Safety of United Nations and Associated Personnel. By providing that relief "personnel shall be respected and protected," Article 71(2) of Protocol I explicitly protects such personnel, but not their transports and relief supplies. However, regarding medical personnel and their transports, humanitarian law contains detailed provisions ensuring their protection.[193] Under Article 85 of Protocol I, grave breaches of the Geneva Conventions are also considered grave breaches of the protocol if the prohibited acts are committed against medical personnel, medical units and transports, or religious personnel who are under the control of the opposing party and are protected by Protocol I.

Thus, where the Convention on the Safety of United Nations and Associated Personnel does not apply, humanitarian law offers adequate protection to relief workers and field personnel of nongovernmental organizations. Humanitarian law, however, does not at present extend protection to their transports and relief supplies.

Conclusion

Does the abundance of applicable norms permit the conclusion that internally displaced persons are sufficiently protected? Is more legal prescription needed, or simply better implementation of existing law? The representative of the secretary-general on internally displaced persons, in the *Compilation and Analysis of Legal Norms* submitted to the UN Commission on Human Rights in 1996, concludes that although existing law covers many aspects of particular relevance to internally displaced persons, there remain areas in which the law fails to provide sufficient protection for them.[194] Situations where legal protection is totally absent are few. However, there are several significant categories of insufficient protection for internally displaced persons.[195]

—*Normative gaps* are areas in which international law does not provide any protection for the legitimate needs of internally displaced persons. They are few, but they do exist. One clear example is the absence of a right to restitution of property lost as a consequence of displacement during internal or international armed conflict or to compensation for its loss.

—*Applicability gaps* are numerous. They exist where there is a legal norm that is not applicable in all circumstances. For example, because human rights law is usually binding on state actors only, internally displaced persons lack sufficient protection in situations of tensions and disturbances if violations are perpetrated by nonstate actors. Another case of insufficient protection occurs in situations that both fall below the threshold of the application of humanitarian law and allow for the restriction or even derogation of human rights guarantees. In the rare instance of a genuine emergency that does not reach the level of an armed conflict, internally displaced persons may be left with only minimal legal protection because a state may derogate from certain human rights obligations that are key to life-essential protection but that at the same time are derogable. Finally, there are no clear safeguards against arbitrary detention in situations of noninternational armed conflict because respective guarantees are lacking in humanitarian law, and human rights law might be derogable owing to the seriousness of a civil war.

—*Consensus gaps* are less serious in a strictly legal view, but they may cause numerous problems in practice. This kind of gap can be found where a general norm exists but a corollary, more specific right has not yet been articulated and formally recognized that would ensure implementation of the general norm in areas of particular need to internally displaced persons. One example is the prohibition of return to situations of imminent danger. Such a prohibition can be deduced from the prohibition of inhuman treatment. It has been recognized that it is inhuman to send a person to a country in which he or she will face torture, death, or another very serious violation of human rights.[196] As all the case law refers to return across international frontiers, a prohibition of inhuman return of internally displaced persons to dangerous areas within their own country needs to be articulated in order to ensure that such persons will get protection. Another example can be found in the area of nondiscrimination, where conventions prohibit, inter alia, discrimination on the basis of "other status" of the person concerned. Although this could be interpreted to include the status of being displaced, it has not yet been stated as such by an authoritative body. A last example is provided by the prohibition of arbitrary detention, which, as such, is clearly recognized. In both domestic and international practice, however, the preconditions for lawful detention of internally displaced persons in closed camps are unclear. A clarification of these preconditions would help to protect the legitimate rights of internally displaced persons, particularly if they were drafted in a restrictive manner.

—*Ratification gaps* are still numerous. They result in a vacuum of legal protection for internally displaced persons in states that have not ratified key human rights treaties and/or the Additional Protocols to the Geneva Conventions.

Looking at substantive law, the *Compilation and Analysis* concludes that with respect to the right to life, the prohibition of torture, the prohibition of hostage taking, the prohibition of contemporary forms of slavery, subsistence rights, and many aspects of religious rights, present international law seems to sufficiently protect most of the specific needs of internally displaced persons. If these rights are violated frequently, the reason does not lie in inadequate legal protection, but rather in the unwillingness of states and/or of dissident forces in noninternational conflicts to observe binding obligations.

There are, nonetheless, serious gaps in the law. As noted earlier, there are numerous areas in which a general norm exists but a corollary, more specific right relevant for the protection of particular needs of internally displaced persons has not been articulated. In addition, there are some clear gaps in present international law. While it is not possible to discuss all these cases in detail here, it is important to note that the following actions are among those of the highest priority:[197]

—State that the notion of "other status" prohibiting discrimination includes the status of internally displaced persons.

—Establish a clear prohibition on the deployment and use of land mines and like devices by any party to an armed conflict of any kind.[198]

—Draw up specific measures for the protection of internally displaced women against gender-specific violence.

—Clarify and restrict the preconditions for lawful detention of internally displaced persons in closed camps.

—Emphasize that internally displaced persons may never be used as human "shields" in armed conflicts of any kind by any of the parties to the conflict.

—Address the special needs of internally displaced women in the areas of reproductive and psychological health care, as well as the special needs of disabled persons in camps for the displaced.

—Specify that internally displaced persons are entitled to go to a safe place inside or outside of their country in all situations or to return voluntarily and in safety to their place of residence. They also need a specific guarantee against forced return to places dangerous to their safety and/or health.

—Recognize specific duties of states or nongovernmental actors to meet the specific needs of internally displaced persons for personal identification, documentation, and registration.

—Address the special needs of internally displaced persons, particularly of internally displaced women, to seek equal opportunity for employment and other economic activities.

—Create a right to restitution of property lost as a consequence of displacement or to compensation for it in situations of armed conflict, whether internal or international.

—Recognize a duty of states to accept offers of assistance and relief by humanitarian organizations; and protect field representatives of nongovernmental organizations and relief workers, as well as their transports and relief supplies.

Where the analysis shows that the needs of internally displaced persons are insufficiently protected by existing international law, it would be desirable to restate general principles of protection in more specific detail and to address gray areas and gaps in the law through the formulation of a body of principles.

The proposed draft principles appended to this study are desirable for another reason as well: the rights of internally displaced persons are often disregarded or even violated simply because of a lack of awareness. As the *Compilation and Analysis* shows, existing international law protects internally displaced persons in a manner that is too complicated and in many respects incomplete. A body of principles that restates and reinforces the essential rights of internally displaced persons would provide authoritative guidance to and thus would facilitate the work of humanitarian organizations that undertake relief actions and perform other necessary services for these persons.

CHAPTER FOUR

Institutional Arrangements

It is inadmissible that persons who are able to cross a border benefit from the rules of international law while those who have not been able to leave their country and may be just a few hundred meters away should remain without protection.
    —Former UN Secretary-General Boutros Boutros-Ghali,
                                                    January 9, 1996

IN RECENT YEARS a broad range of humanitarian, human rights, and development organizations have begun to provide protection, assistance, and reintegration and development support to internally displaced populations. However, in the absence of strong coordination among these agencies or clear institutional responsibility for the internally displaced, the response has been highly uneven.

This chapter reviews options for strengthening and better coordinating institutional capacities and arrangements within the UN system. It examines the mandates and capacities of existing agencies, identifies the gaps in the international system, and proposes ways in which the institutional arrangements might be improved.

Since the late 1980s, the United Nations has taken steps to enhance its capacity to respond to situations of internal displacement. Following two international conferences on uprooted populations in 1988 and 1989

This chapter draws many basic concepts from an earlier published report authored by Roberta Cohen and Jacques Cuenod, *Improving Institutional Arrangements for the Internally Displaced,* Brookings Institution-Refugee Policy Group Project on Internal Displacement, October 1995.

(see chapter 1), the General Assembly in 1990 assigned to resident coordinators the function of coordinating assistance to internally displaced
persons in the field. The following year, it created the post of emergency
relief coordinator (the ERC) to promote a more rapid and coherent
response to emergency solutions. That same year, with concerns over
human rights and protection mounting, the Commission on Human
Rights requested that the secretary-general prepare an analytical report
on internally displaced persons. And in 1992, at the request of the commission, the secretary-general appointed a representative on internally
displaced persons to focus attention on the human rights dimension of
the problem and to identify ways and means of improving protection and
assistance for the internally displaced. Also in 1992, the United Nations
created the Inter-Agency Standing Committee (the IASC), chaired by
the ERC and composed of the heads of the major UN humanitarian and
development agencies, to strengthen coordination in emergency situations. The IASC created a task force on internally displaced persons,
which operated until 1997, and it designated the ERC "reference point"
for requests for assistance and protection in actual or developing situations of internal displacement. In his 1997 UN reform program, the secretary-general reaffirmed the role of the ERC as being responsible for
"ensuring" that "protection and assistance for internally displaced persons" are addressed.

Taken together, these initiatives represent an important progression
toward developing mechanisms and policies within the UN system to be
applied to situations of internal displacement. Nonetheless, this global
problem is still being addressed in a basically ad hoc manner. Coordination is weak and a comprehensive approach that integrates assistance,
protection, and reintegration and development support has yet to be put
in place.

Situations of internal displacement can be divided into two broad
categories: relatively "simple" situations that do not involve problems of
consent or extensive protection issues and where displacement is for the
most part temporary and geographically confined, as in the case of a
natural disaster; and "complex" situations in which a political emergency
or state collapse may require political, military, humanitarian, and human rights intervention to address both protection and assistance.[1] In the
first instance, the delivery of material aid to internally displaced persons
and others affected is generally a logistical and technical challenge that
the government is usually able to meet with external aid. In complex

situations, however, which constitute most situations of internal displacement, the international community often has difficulty in gaining access to deliver assistance because of civil conflict or noncooperation on the part of governments or insurgent groups.

Protecting the physical safety and human rights of the internally displaced in such circumstances is an especially formidable challenge. Few organizations have the mandate, expertise, or capability to address protection problems. Nor is there any consensus on the role that human rights organizations, humanitarian and development agencies, or peacekeeping operations should play in providing protection.

Difficulties also surround return and reintegration. In some cases, internally displaced persons are forcibly compelled to return to home areas that are not safe. In other cases, they may return to find their homes and land occupied by others, their personal security threatened, and no means of sustaining themselves. In response, international agencies have begun to facilitate and monitor returns, with the cooperation, or at least the tacit consent, of the government. They also have become increasingly involved in providing reintegration and development support, although far more attention and resources continue to go into the emergency phase than into developing capacities and skills to ensure that relief is linked to longer-term solutions.

Mandates and Capacities of Operational Organizations

Seven principal operational organizations play a role with internally displaced persons: the UN High Commissioner for Refugees, the International Committee of the Red Cross, the United Nations Development Programme, the World Food Programme, the United Nations Children's Fund, the World Health Organization, and the International Organization for Migration.[2] Their capacities vary widely, with no one among them having the ability to meet all the needs of the displaced. Some organizations focus on assistance, others on protection and assistance, still others on reintegration and development support, while one has special expertise in transport.

United Nations High Commissioner for Refugees

Of all the UN agencies, UNHCR plays the broadest role in addressing the problems of the internally displaced: it offers protection, assistance, and initial support for reintegration. Although UNHCR's statute does not include internally displaced persons, the organization has increasingly become involved in the situations they face at the request of the secretary-general or the General Assembly, and with the consent of the state concerned.[3]

In 1993 the General Assembly recognized that UNHCR's activities could be extended to internally displaced persons when both refugees and internally displaced persons are so intertwined that it would be practically impossible or inappropriate to assist one group and not the other.[4] This can happen when refugees and the internally displaced are returning to the same area, or when external and internal displacement stem from the same causes and advantages exist in having one operation deal with both groups; or when helping internally displaced persons remain in safety in their own country could prevent a refugee flow.

Application of these criteria has been largely at the organization's discretion, with the result that UNHCR has played a prominent role in assisting and protecting internally displaced populations in some countries (for example, the former Yugoslavia and Tajikistan) but not in others. In some cases it has been involved only if the displaced are mixed with returning refugees (as in Guatemala, Sierra Leone, and Angola), and in several (for example, Cambodia, Peru, the Sudan, and Congo [Zaire]), it has played no role at all, although it could do so by interpreting its criteria more broadly. At the end of 1996 UNHCR deemed 4.85 million internally displaced persons to be "of concern" to the organization. This figure amounts to less than 25 percent of the total number worldwide.[5]

Owing to the similarity between the needs of refugees and internally displaced persons, UNHCR has been able to apply its expertise to the internally displaced. Often, however, there are differences that necessitate new approaches.[6] When UNHCR provides international protection to refugees, it defends refugees' legal right to asylum and *non-refoulement* and seeks to give refugees who lawfully reside on the territory of a foreign state a status as close to that of its nationals as possible. Such international protection is achieved by governmental accession to international treaties on refugees. No specific legal instrument of this nature applies to the internally displaced; protecting them has meant trying to defend their physical safety and human rights under international humanitarian and human rights law, legal instruments with which UNHCR staff are not generally familiar.[7]

The two groups also differ in the conditions surrounding their return. In the case of refugees, UNHCR has a statutory responsibility to promote their voluntary return. This may involve monitoring their return to their final destination in their country of origin and providing initial assistance with reintegration. In the case of internally displaced persons, UNHCR has no statutory responsibility. It has nonetheless helped substantial numbers return and reintegrate in accordance with specific mandates given to the High Commissioner.[8]

The assumption of greater responsibility with regard to internally displaced persons has raised concerns at UNHCR that involvement in countries of origin will change the character of the agency and detract from its primary responsibility of protecting and assisting refugees. For example, when UNHCR assumed responsibility for internally displaced persons and war victims in the former Yugoslavia, this endeavor tied up more than half of its $1.5 billion budget.[9] If UNHCR were to take on greater responsibility for persons in countries of origin, it is argued that it could become overstretched and far exceed its capabilities. Other concerns relate to the difficulty of protecting and assisting persons in situations of internal conflict, the high risk to staff, and most repeatedly, the tensions that arise between protecting people in their countries of origin and simultaneously defending their right to leave their country and seek asylum from persecution.

In the former Yugoslavia, UNHCR has been criticized for paying too little attention to gaining asylum and resettlement for victims of violations while at the same time failing to effectively provide in-country protection.[10] Although UNHCR has repeatedly stated that protection for internally displaced persons cannot be at the expense of the organization's basic commitment to asylum, leading NGOs have pointed to a "conflict of interest" in UNHCR's speaking for both.[11] Governments reluctant to receive refugees also have used UNHCR's in-country protection activities as a pretext for refusing to grant asylum.[12]

As UNHCR continues its involvement with the internally displaced, it will have to deal with this problem as well as with the tensions that arise between seeking to provide protection and assistance to both refugees and internally displaced persons in the same country. When countries that house refugees also produce internally displaced populations of their own, UNHCR has found that it can be difficult to address the problems of both groups. In the Sudan, UNHCR has taken the position that its involvement with refugee programs precludes it from protecting and assisting the internally displaced. It fears a "negative reaction from the Sudanese Government" with respect to refugees were it to undertake an active role in protecting internally displaced populations.[13]

International Committee of the Red Cross

Of all the institutions dealing with the internally displaced, ICRC has the most well-developed protection capability. It also has the clearest mandate to protect and assist victims of internal conflict, a substantial number of whom are internally displaced. An independent non-UN organization, ICRC has overall statutory responsibility for promoting and ensuring respect for the four Geneva Conventions (1949) and Additional Protocols (1977) in both international and noninternational armed conflicts. ICRC's staff worldwide numbers about 7,000, its budget is about $600 million, and it has permanent delegations in more than sixty countries.

In recent years, ICRC has concentrated on building its capacity to protect and assist civilians caught in internal conflicts and has allocated more than 80 percent of its field budget to this purpose. It also has offered its services to governments to protect and assist the civilian victims of "internal strife" (that is, lesser conflict situations) to which the Geneva Conventions and Protocols do not apply. It accomplishes this by exercising its right of initiative under the statutes of the International Red Cross and Red Crescent Movement.[14]

ICRC makes no distinction between protection and assistance activities. Although UN humanitarian and development agencies often contend that protection responsibilities will jeopardize their assistance role, ICRC has gained the acceptance of both governments and insurgent forces in carrying out joint protection and assistance activities. One of ICRC's organizational strengths is that its representatives extend protection on both sides in conflict situations and seek to reach those whom other humanitarian organizations cannot reach because of hazardous conditions or political obstacles. Its willingness to deploy delegates in areas of danger was particularly evident in Somalia in 1990–91 when the United Nations absented itself and ICRC assumed the main responsibility for delivering relief to the Somali people, including large numbers of internally displaced persons. ICRC's responsibility, moreover, is to the victims of conflict whereas that of the United Nation is primarily to governments. And unlike UNHCR and other UN agencies, ICRC never delegates its work in the field beyond the Red Cross and Red Crescent Movement, which enables it to ensure that its operations meet ICRC standards.

ICRC's protection and assistance cover a broad range of activities: monitoring the implementation of the Geneva Conventions and Protocols among civilian populations, making representations to governments and nonstate actors when violations occur, gaining access to and securing the release of detainees, evacuating civilians from situations of danger, creating protected areas, establishing tracing networks, facilitating arrangements for the creation of humanitarian space and cease-fires, and providing material assistance needed for survival. ICRC activities in Rwanda and Chechnya greatly benefited internally displaced persons in the area of both protection and assistance.[15]

ICRC's independence sometimes complicates its ability to work with other agencies in the field. Although its mandate necessarily limits the extent to which it can involve itself in UN affairs, the enormity of humanitarian emergencies makes collaborative work essential. Thus in recent years it has sought ways of working more closely with other humanitarian agencies in situations of armed conflict. UN staff, however, when undertaking protection functions in countries of origin have not always been aware of, or felt bound to comply with, ICRC's rules and procedures.[16] And because UN operations are not always perceived as neutral, ICRC at times has sought to distance itself from the United Nations so as not to compromise its role as an impartial and independent intermediary.[17] Despite these obstacles, collaboration and a division of labor between ICRC and UNHCR have often been accomplished in the field with regard to internally displaced persons.

One aspect of ICRC policy that is viewed with reserve by some human rights organizations is its practice of keeping violations of humanitarian law confidential. This policy, they argue, does not always strengthen protection. They also point out that ICRC usually addresses its public appeals to "all sides" in a conflict. In recent conflicts, however, notably in the former Yugoslavia and Rwanda, ICRC's public statements have exposed the egregious violations of particular sides. Nonetheless, ICRC generally exercises restraint in the face of serious abuse, and in respect of the principle of confidentiality does not transmit information to war crimes tribunals, as human rights bodies do.

Although this policy of confidentiality often gains the organization greater access than other groups, its reach is still limited. Not all states have ratified the Geneva Conventions and Protocols.[18] And even the many states that have ratified them do not always give ICRC entry or admit that a noninternational armed conflict is taking place on their territory. ICRC has not been allowed to assist internally displaced populations in Guatemala and Turkey, for example, even though conflicts in those countries have produced substantial numbers of internally displaced persons. Moreover, ICRC may be precluded from involvement when internal displacement is unrelated to warfare.

United Nations Development Programme

As a rule, UNDP resident representatives act both as the senior UNDP official in a country and as the resident coordinator of the entire UN system. In 1990, as noted earlier, the General Assembly assigned the UN resident coordinator "the function of coordinating assistance to the internally displaced, in close cooperation with Governments, local representatives of donor countries and the United Nations agencies in the field."[19] This step has aroused some resistance. Within UNDP, some have questioned whether senior officials should be involved with issues other than development. Nevertheless, the proliferation of internal conflicts, the increasing number of collapsed and reemerging states, and famine and drought have forced UNDP to rethink its traditional patterns of response. Since the mid-1980s UNDP resident representatives have been called upon to assume key roles in coordinating emergency response. Moreover, UNDP officials in the field have had to deal with the adverse effects of such situations on economic development.

Institutional tensions have also arisen. As development officials, resident representatives report to UNDP, whereas in their capacity as resident coordinators of emergency assistance, they report to the office of the ERC. This dual arrangement is problematic especially since UNDP "manages" the resident coordinator system and has created an emergency division of its own to lend support to resident coordinators.[20]

Another serious problem is that resident representatives generally have no expertise in emergency work. To remedy this, training has been introduced under a disaster management training program, administered jointly by UNDP and the office of the ERC. A move has also been made to broaden the choice so that an individual other than the resident representative can be selected as coordinator in a complex emergency situation. A humanitarian coordinator can now be appointed by the ERC, after consulting with UNDP and the heads of other UN agencies, and most have come from agencies other than UNDP.

The net effect of these efforts over the past several years has been greater acceptance by UNDP that some of its key officials will have to be substantially involved with humanitarian emergencies and play an important role with the internally displaced. UNDP officials, however, still tend to see internally displaced persons as part of a larger population affected by wars, failed states, droughts, and famines. They tend not to emphasize the organization's relationship to this group, which requires not only material assistance but also protection from exposure to human rights abuse. Indeed, most resident coordinators do not consider human rights and protection activities to be compatible with their responsibilities as resident representatives of UNDP, in which position they work closely with governments on development programs. Despite the fact that protection is an integral part of coordinating assistance, their great concern is that by becoming involved with protection issues they may exceed their mandate or even create grounds for expulsion. As a result, many resident coordinators are less than forthright with governments about protection problems confronting the internally displaced, while others have echoed the government's view that internal displacement is not a problem in their country and hence does not require international attention.[21]

At present, resident coordinators receive no training in how to address the protection problems of internally displaced persons. Nor do they have reporting responsibilities in this area. In 1995 resident representatives/coordinators were requested by UNDP to provide information about internal displacement to the representative of the secretary-general on internally displaced persons. But this did not develop into a continuing reporting requirement. The establishment of such a requirement—with reports directed to the representative and the ERC—would help focus attention on protection and other problems confronting the internally displaced.[22]

Greater efforts also need to be made to bridge the gap between UNDP's long-term development role in a country and its assistance to internally displaced persons on an emergency basis. In 1990 UNDP endorsed the view that relief and development work should be more closely linked and that UNDP staff should become more fully engaged in the early phases of an emergency. The UNDP office dealing with emergencies now focuses more attention on bridging the gap between relief and development; and UNDP representatives have become more inclined to initiate programs that take into account displaced populations.[23]

UNDP has also been playing a pioneering role in area-based development, which seeks to ensure that in the aftermath of conflict, areas of return can effectively absorb displaced persons and returning refugees while sustaining the local population. In fact, UNDP sees its development work in the resettlement phase as one of its main roles with regard to the internally displaced, and it has undertaken reintegration programs in Bosnia and Herzegovina, Cambodia, Central America, Mozambique, and the Horn of Africa.[24]

In 1995 UNDP set aside 5 percent of its core resources, or $50 million, for development activities in countries in emergency situations.[25] The bulk of the funding, specifically $35 million, is to be used by the resident representative/coordinator to facilitate the resettlement of internally displaced persons and other uprooted populations, with a small portion going to design reconstruction plans in countries without functioning governments, to build up national preventive capabilities ($10 million), and to strengthen the ability of resident representatives/coordinators to coordinate emergency assistance ($5 million).

This new funding should strengthen UNDP's ability to respond in a more timely and systematic manner to emergencies and to play a more substantial role in assisting internally displaced persons. To do so effectively, resident representatives/coordinators will have to strengthen their advocacy role. They will need to persuade governments to integrate uprooted populations in their national development plans, challenge governments that try to manipulate and obstruct programs for the displaced, and ensure that development programs do not serve to strengthen and legitimize governments that cause mass displacement.[26] Working with uprooted populations will require a broader and more varied approach than UNDP's traditional one of working closely with governments on development programs.

World Food Programme

WFP, which handles one-quarter of the world's food aid, is the single largest provider of food commodities to the internally displaced. About 35 percent of the 57 million persons WFP assists are internally displaced persons, who now constitute WFP's largest category of beneficiaries. In

1995 the agency's allocation of 2.8 million tons of food worldwide covered 14 million internally displaced persons.[27]

Nonetheless, because neither WFP nor any other agency is specifically mandated to ensure that sufficient food is made available to the internally displaced, their needs can easily be overlooked. In Sierra Leone and the Sudan, WFP assistance programs to internally displaced populations were being terminated despite acute malnutrition reported among those populations.[28] And in northern Burundi, a UN interagency body found that WFP had cut off food distribution to internally displaced populations because of food shortages but that refugees in those same areas continued to be served.[29] Problems have also arisen in the distribution systems set up through governments and NGOs. The UN special rapporteur on violence against women has noted "discriminatory practices in the distribution of food and other supplies" to refugee and internally displaced women.[30] One UN expert group also found that decisions about food distribution were generally made "in consultation with the male leaders" in camp situations, and that this practice gave rise to "inappropriate" food distribution procedures for refugee and displaced women.[31]

These and other problems have led WFP to become directly involved in monitoring food distribution in a number of countries.[32] In 1995 its executive director, Catherine Bertini, specifically requested country staff to report instances in which displaced women and children were not being adequately covered by food aid relief distribution lists.[33] In 1996 WFP took an important step toward upgrading attention to internally displaced persons when it asserted that one of its major functions in emergencies is to "monitor and report on food distributions to the internally displaced."[34] WFP has also sought to encourage other UN agencies, such as UNHCR, to increase their oversight of food distribution systems.[35] It further committed itself to the "full involvement of women in planning and managing relief assistance" and to the distribution of relief food "direct to households, especially women."[36]

To improve the timeliness and quality of its emergency response, WFP has created rapid-response teams, stockpiled food and equipment, and strengthened its emergency collaboration with UN agencies, in particular UNHCR and UNICEF, and with NGOs. It has played a major role in meeting the needs of the internally displaced in the former Yugoslavia, the CIS, Somalia, and the Great Lakes region. And it has played the lead role in responding to the needs of the internally displaced in Angola, Cambodia, Liberia, Mozambique, and Sierra Leone.

Although protection concerns per se fall outside WFP's mandate, WFP does negotiate access and safe passage for its food and personnel with governments and rebel forces in order to reach internally displaced persons at risk.[37] When governments or rebel forces have obstructed the delivery of food to internally displaced populations, as in the Sudan and Liberia, WFP has lodged protests, but basically it has turned to others to intercede, most notably the ERC or the Office of the Secretary-General. This has on occasion opened it up to the criticism that it is not assertive enough in ensuring the distribution of food to internally displaced and other needy populations.[38] Strengthened collaboration with organizations such as ICRC and with NGOs should help improve attention to protection issues.

WFP's mandate also extends to providing food aid in support of return, reintegration, and postconflict rehabilitation. In such cases, food is provided on a food-for-work basis to generate employment and stimulate economic and social reconstruction. WFP-supported rehabilitation activities in Afghanistan, Mozambique, Cambodia, and Somalia pay special attention to reintegrating internally displaced persons and returning refugees while targeting entire communities. The strengthening of local capacities and mechanisms to cope with future crises is also an important part of WFP efforts.

Although in the past WFP's primary focus was development assistance, today refugee and emergency work count for as much as 70 percent of its $1.8 billion budget.[39] The declining availability of resources for development assistance combined with the need to divert resources to emergency operations and the difficulty of undertaking development projects in countries affected by internal conflict have all markedly reduced the amount of assistance for development projects. This shift away from development also undermines emergency operations because lower levels of WFP development assistance in different countries reduce the amount of food from which supplies can be borrowed during emergencies.

United Nations Children's Fund

UNICEF has become involved with internally displaced persons through its efforts to provide services to women and children in the areas of health care, nutrition, education, water, and sanitation. Although it views itself primarily as a development organization, emergency situations now account for 25 to 28 percent of its activities.[40]

Initially, UNICEF was dismissive of identifying the internally displaced as a category of persons in need. Staff members argued that singling out the internally displaced from the larger affected population would discriminate against others equally in need and cause inequity and conflict. Like other development-oriented organizations, it emphasized approaches that benefited entire communities and strengthened local capacities.[41]

UNICEF's growing involvement in emergency situations has, however, stimulated the development of policies and programs for the internally displaced. A 1995 memorandum of understanding with UNHCR, for example, specifically references refugees, returnees, and the internally displaced and gives UNICEF responsibility for "unaccompanied children" within countries of origin. In its recent statements and position papers, UNICEF has acknowledged that many internally displaced children "are amongst the most seriously unprotected of all children" and has committed itself to promoting "the rights of displaced children and women to survival, protection and development."[42]

At the same time, there remains a great deal of ambivalence within the organization about the extent to which it should become involved in what it calls "loud emergencies," or those caused by violence and famine, as opposed to focusing primarily on the "silent" ones associated with poverty and underdevelopment. UNICEF's Executive Board has nonetheless encouraged the organization to strengthen its capacity to respond to emergency situations.[43] In recent years UNICEF has created rapid-response teams, stockpiled essential supplies, and established standby arrangements with NGOs.[44]

UNICEF has also adopted a policy on the protection of children in "especially difficult circumstances" and has been in the forefront of negotiations with all sides in conflict situations to gain access to children in need. It secured agreement for relief corridors in Operation Lifeline Sudan and has mounted cross-border operations that have enabled it to reach children behind both government and insurgent lines in other conflicts. UNICEF has nonetheless been criticized for not giving enough priority to human rights and protection issues, such as forcible conscription, sexual violence, the right of beleaguered populations to humanitarian access, and the physical and psychological trauma resulting from exposure to conflict and violence.[45]

Some staff members contend that the UN Convention on the Rights of the Child gives UNICEF increased authority in the area of child protection that should help strengthen its advocacy role. Others are afraid of shifting the emphasis from development to advocating human rights. However, under the impetus of its executive director, Carol Bellamy, UNICEF has begun to pay greater attention to the serious protection problems faced by women and children in emergency situations. In southern Sudan, UNICEF officials have made representations on the forcible conscription of children, and in Burundi UNICEF has been helping to trace the families of unaccompanied children.[46] In 1995 UNICEF served as secretariat to a series of regional consultations organized by Graça Machel for her study on the impact of armed conflict on children. It then announced an "antiwar agenda" that calls for measures to protect women and girls from sexual violence, raise the minimum age for military recruitment from fifteen years to eighteen, set up protective "zones of peace" for children, ban the production of antipersonnel land mines, and address the psychosocial rehabilitation of war-damaged children.[47]

Expanding its emergency and protection work will necessitate broader training for staff in advocacy skills, human rights and humanitarian standards, negotiation techniques, and in the rehabilitation of children and women exposed to conflict and violence. But basically, UNICEF will have to carve out specific areas of responsibility for itself with regard to internally displaced children. Some have suggested that UNICEF provide protection and assistance to children in camps; others have suggested that UNICEF focus on children in urban centers; still others have proposed that UNICEF assist internally displaced children at "acute risk," such as seriously traumatized children, child combatants, and unaccompanied children.[48] UNICEF's Executive Board in 1996 called for greater collaboration with UNHCR in the case of internally displaced children and for an extension of UNICEF child care and protection activities to those children.[49] The extent and way in which UNICEF carries out this role will have a significant impact, given the agency's budget of $1 billion, its offices in seventy-six countries, and its staff of 7,500, 80 percent of whom are in the field.

World Health Organization

WHO's involvement in situations of internal displacement is guided by its constitution, which authorizes it, at the request of governments or the United Nations, to furnish aid in emergencies, act as the directing and coordinating authority on international health work, and provide health services and facilities to special groups. In recent years these groups have been interpreted to include internally displaced persons and refugees.[50]

In an effort to address emergencies more effectively, WHO in 1993 reorganized its Division of Emergency and Humanitarian Action. The division's responsibilities include dispatching emergency teams to the field to assess the health needs of affected populations, providing technical guidance to governments in dealing with emergencies, coordinating emergency response, and training national staff in emergency preparedness.

WHO's Executive Board and the World Health Assembly have approved the agency's assuming a more active role in emergencies, including carrying out limited operational activities.[51] In Rwanda, WHO joined international efforts to aid refugees, internally displaced persons and the local population. Its emergency work has also benefited internally displaced populations in the former Yugoslavia, Afghanistan, Tajikistan, and Iraq.

At the same time, only about 5 percent of WHO's biennial budget of $1 billion is spent on emergency programs, although extrabudgetary funds are also raised.[52] The organization is further constrained by the view that its primary role in emergencies is to provide technical assistance. It does not seek to engage in the "hands-on operational emergency response of other United Nations agencies," which deploy large numbers of staff in the field.[53] Its emphasis is on providing advice with a view to strengthening local capacities and setting up health projects that will benefit entire communities, including the displaced, over the longer term.[54]

The extent to which such programs offer adequate solutions to the problem of internal displacement may be questioned. Development-based approaches to health problems are essential, especially in the post-conflict period, but health care per se is also an essential concern when large numbers are at risk. Death rates among internally displaced populations are among the highest of all groups in humanitarian emergencies, and they are often caused by inattention to clean water, sanitation, and immunizations. In Somalia in the early 1990s, for example, most deaths were attributed not to starvation but to insufficient attention to public health.[55] Clearly there is scope for expanding WHO's activities in emergency situations beyond providing advice to governments and UN agencies. Of necessity this should include working in areas not controlled by governments, in situations where health services are disrupted and governmental authority has broken down.

A more assertive stance is also needed to obtain access to populations in need. In 1995 WHO announced that it would assume a more active role in defense of the victims of armed conflict. At the same time, the World Health Assembly called for stronger WHO "advocacy" for the protection of noncombatants, health personnel, and infrastructure in conflict situations.[56] As a result, WHO has been undertaking more vigorous intercessions for "ease of access to and the provision of necessary health assistance to internally displaced persons," particularly those injured by land mines and collective violence, and for the better protection of health personnel.[57]

Strengthening WHO's capacity to respond to situations involving the internally displaced will require it to give greater priority to emergency operations, engage in more vigorous advocacy on behalf of the affected populations, directly engage in field operations, and establish closer working relationships with NGOs.

International Organization for Migration

The main objective of IOM, a non-UN, intergovernmental institution, is to help ensure the orderly movement of persons in need of migration assistance, whether displaced persons, refugees, or nationals. For IOM, the internally displaced fall within the broader category of "displaced persons" that the organization's mandate covers. In fact, its constitution is unique in providing a mandate for "displaced persons" that is interpreted to encompass both those who migrate internally and internationally.

IOM's migration assistance covers activities such as organizing transport, evacuations, and returns; providing temporary shelter and other material relief; providing early warning and rapid analysis of migratory flows; developing national population information systems and censuses; and providing expert advice to governments on migration policies and laws. In addition, cooperation agreements between IOM and numerous member and observer states provide for migration assistance and protection to internally displaced persons.[58]

In recent years, IOM has begun to play a substantial role in seeking to ensure that those transported to return and resettlement areas are able to sustain themselves. In Mozambique, it has moved more than

100,000 internally displaced persons and returnees to their places of origin or choice and provided reintegration assistance, in collaboration with UN agencies and NGOs. In Angola, IOM has begun to assist with the return and reintegration of 600,000 internally displaced persons. Although not a UN agency, IOM has been increasingly operating "as a member of the team" in the emergency response network under UN auspices.[59]

IOM considers protection and assistance to be closely linked and contends that by moving displaced persons out of danger and meeting their basic assistance needs, it is providing de facto protection. It also believes that the presence of an international organization may serve as a form of protection. In carrying out its activities, IOM considers itself bound by a number of constitutional safeguards and guiding principles. For example, when it provides transport assistance, it insists upon the free and voluntary movement of persons. It also seeks to ensure that persons moved by the organization are given the opportunity to reestablish their lives in dignity and self-respect. It further works to ensure that the human rights of internally displaced persons are respected in all its programs.[60]

Nonetheless, its activities raise protection and ethical concerns that need to be addressed both by IOM and by other organizations that engage in such work. Organizing the registration of internally displaced persons, for example, raises concerns about whether effective safeguards have been developed against potential government abuse for purposes of repression. Centralized census-taking and the development of population information systems, although needed for statistical purposes, raise similar concerns. Transporting internally displaced persons can raise serious protection issues, particularly whether the movements are voluntary, whether transport could be perceived as complicity in forced relocations, and whether conditions are sufficiently safe to warrant return.

IOM itself acknowledges that "it is sometimes difficult to evaluate whether a decision to leave a country is voluntary or not, given the pressures or incentives that might play a preponderant role in the decision-making process."[61] Increased collaborative monitoring with human rights bodies could help IOM ensure that attention is given to protection problems during the return and reintegration process. Similarly, increased safeguards may be needed for activities such as the registration of internally displaced persons, centralized census-taking, and the development of population information systems.

Coordination by the Emergency Relief Coordinator

The growing need to coordinate UN humanitarian assistance led the General Assembly in 1991 to create the post of emergency relief coordinator (the ERC) at the under-secretary-general level.[62] A UN report earlier that year had pointed out the delays and lack of preparedness inherent in the existing ad hoc system and the difficulties UN agencies were having in deciding how "to reach a clear division of responsibilities, to work out a unitary plan of action and to get the Secretary-General to launch a joint appeal."[63] In 1992 the secretary-general created the Department of Humanitarian Affairs (DHA) to assist the ERC. In 1997 DHA was replaced by a smaller more streamlined office, renamed the Office for the Coordination of Humanitarian Affairs (OCHA).[64]

It is the responsibility of the ERC to develop policy and advocate for humanitarian causes within the UN system, coordinate emergency response, and give counsel to the secretary-general, particularly when humanitarian issues are before the Security Council. The ERC is charged with determining which humanitarian emergencies are complex and will require coordination by the UN, assigning responsibility to agencies in the field, mobilizing contributions for emergency response through a consolidated appeals process, allocating funds from a central emergency revolving fund, and ensuring that emergency relief operations are conceived and implemented in such a way that rehabilitation and reconstruction stem naturally from these operations.

One of the main vehicles for the ERC's coordinating role on both policy issues and operational response is the Inter-Agency Standing Committee. Composed of the heads of the major UN humanitarian and development organizations, it is chaired by the ERC.[65] Also chaired by the ERC since mid-1997 is a smaller body, the Executive Committee on Humanitarian Affairs (ECHA), which the secretary-general created in 1997, composed of the heads of humanitarian and development agencies and of the UN departments on peacekeeping and political affairs.[66] As noted above, the ERC retains a direct link in the field through resident and humanitarian coordinators who report to the ERC when dealing with humanitarian issues such as internal displacement.

In December 1994 the IASC designated the ERC the "reference point" for internally displaced persons. The ERC was chosen because the post already had a coordinating mechanism at its disposal both at headquarters and in the field. Specifically, the ERC was asked to receive "requests for assistance and protection in actual or developing situations of internal displacement that might require coordinated international response."[67] In 1997 the secretary-general reaffirmed the ERC's role with regard to the internally displaced and defined the function as one of ensuring that "protection and assistance" for internally displaced persons are addressed.[68]

To date, however, the ERC has not decided what the operational and policy content of a role with the internally displaced should be. Under DHA, insufficient priority was given to the issue of internal displacement. In some countries, such as Azerbaijan and Georgia, where emergency assistance was coordinated by DHA, substantial numbers of internally displaced persons were helped.[69] In Sierra Leone, Liberia, and many other countries, however, there were large gaps in the assistance and protection extended to internally displaced persons. Nor did DHA seek to monitor global displacement worldwide; it was slow in developing an information system on internally displaced persons; and it was hesitant to assign responsibilities to other agencies or to advocate on behalf of the internally displaced in the field. At meetings of the IASC and its working group, issues of internal displacement were rarely given in-depth or systematic attention with follow-up actions planned. Moreover, the IASC task force on internally displaced persons, which DHA chaired, proved extremely cautious in its approach and did not have outreach or impact on the field.

Several factors complicated DHA's efforts to shape an effective role for the ERC as reference point for the internally displaced. Since its successor, OCHA, could face some of the same problems, it is important to review them. One was constantly changing leadership. From 1992 to 1997 three emergency relief coordinators (Jan Eliasson, Peter Hansen, and Yasushi Akashi) were appointed, none of whom had sufficient time to follow the issue of internal displacement in depth and decide how it should be addressed. DHA staff, in the absence of direction, refrained from stepping out front on the issue. No unified view ever emerged. Some senior staff questioned the purpose of focusing on one category of persons in an emergency, while others considered that the needs of the internally displaced merited special interagency attention.

Poor coordination within DHA, exacerbated by bureaucratic rivalries and the department's division between New York and Geneva, further complicated matters. DHA headquarters in New York and its task force on internally displaced persons in Geneva were often at odds. Senior staff in New York questioned the task force's authority to deal with country situations, on the grounds that it lacked operational capacity, viewed the problem of displacement too narrowly, and could undercut and complicate DHA's own initiatives. In one case, DHA New York had the situation in a particular country withdrawn from the agenda of the task force.

DHA also faced resistance from other agencies. It had minimal authority to direct the activities of the UN agencies it was supposed to coordinate, which, unlike DHA, are large operational organizations with extensive funding and staff. The ERC does not outrank the heads of the other agencies and to date has not been able to exercise the kind of leadership needed.

DHA's caution about dealing with protection issues was still another problem. The General Assembly resolution establishing the ERC specified only that assistance should be coordinated, and DHA's mandate gave it no protection responsibilities per se. As a rule, therefore, its staff did not pay attention to such concerns. They defined the needs of the internally displaced in emergency relief terms rather than in terms of protection. This was evident at the IASC and working group meetings, which focused primarily on assistance. It was also evident in most needs assessment missions sent out in emergencies. The staff generally had expertise in food aid, water supply, health and sanitation, as well as shelter, but not in how to deal with the personal security and human rights of the affected population.

DHA and the office replacing it, however, cannot effectively coordinate emergency assistance or negotiate access to emergency areas without taking into account the integral link between humanitarian assistance and protection. In delegating responsibility when emergencies occur, it must be aware of the degree to which UN and other agencies are capable of providing protection and the degree to which their capacities must be strengthened. Moreover, as a reference point for internally displaced persons, the ERC cannot meet its responsibilities without dealing with protection problems.

In recognition of the need to forge a more integrated approach, it was decided in 1994 that the high commissioner for human rights and the representative of the secretary-general on internally displaced persons would be invited to meetings of the IASC and its sub-bodies when issues relating to their mandates were discussed.[70] It was not until 1997, however, that both were made standing members. Despite this welcome move to strengthen the links between providing humanitarian assistance and protecting human rights, protection has not yet received the attention it deserves within the interagency framework chaired by the ERC. The consolidated appeals process (CAP) rarely includes funding for protection and human rights activities.[71] In the case of Rwanda, the CAP did make explicit provision for the Human Rights Field Operation; and in the former Yugoslavia, the CAP process also included funding for human rights monitoring and protection measures for refugees and displaced persons. But in other countries with massive and serious human rights violations, this has not been the case. In Liberia and Angola, for example, the CAP made no provision for human rights monitoring or protection.

IASC did recommend in 1997 that the ERC's role with regard to the internally displaced include global advocacy on both assistance and protection. The secretary-general's 1997 reform program also called on the ERC to ensure that both protection and assistance for internally displaced persons are addressed. The IASC in addition recommended that the ERC's role in respect to the internally displaced should be to help to mobilize resources and identify gaps; assign responsibilities, including camp management; develop information systems; and provide support to the field, which would include negotiating access.[72]

The ERC has all the mandate it needs to assume a more authoritative stance with regard to the internally displaced. The role it plays in fostering a more comprehensive approach to problems of internal displacement will be seen as the test of its readiness to assume leadership within the United Nations system in addressing complex emergencies.

Inter-Agency Task Force on Internally Displaced Persons

The task force created by the IASC in 1992 was discontinued in the fall of 1997. Chaired by DHA, it was composed of representatives of the major UN humanitarian and development agencies, the representative of the secretary-general on internally displaced persons, the Office of the UN High Commissioner for Human Rights, IOM, the Red Cross Movement, and NGO umbrella groups. In its early years, it played an important role in shaping UN policy on internal displacement. It was, for example, the originator of the idea that the ERC should serve as reference point on internally displaced persons within the UN system. It also recommended that the high commissioner for human rights and the rep-

resentative of the secretary-general on internally displaced persons be invited to meetings of the IASC and its sub-bodies to strengthen the links between humanitarian assistance and human rights.[73]

In 1995 the task force's terms of reference were expanded, and it was authorized to review specific situations of internal displacement, analyze assistance and protection needs, examine the capacities of national and international institutions to deal with these situations, and decide on "the most appropriate division of work." It also was requested to recommend practical measures to prevent internal displacement, look into generic problems, and seek durable solutions.[74] The broadness of the mandate turned out to be one reason for the task force's undoing. No priorities were ever set by the task force or its convener. Nor was it given the authority to carry out an effective review of specific situations of internal displacement or to decide on a division of labor in the field. Although the ERC in 1995 described Afghanistan as a "forgotten" emergency and Sierra Leone as a "neglected" emergency, no effort was made to examine the situations in these countries and evaluate whether UN operations should be expanded.[75] Furthermore, neither the Sudan nor Turkey came before the task force in any sustained way, although these countries house the largest numbers of internally displaced persons.

Some have attributed the task force's lack of effective action on country situations to DHA's caution in the face of the divergent views and approaches of member agencies. On a number of occasions, however, the members themselves proposed or supported specific actions on country situations only to have them watered down or ignored.[76] One promising initiative allowed to falter was the holding of special meetings on difficult country situations. Although the convener announced in 1996 that special interagency meetings would be held on Myanmar (Burma), the Sudan, and Peru, none materialized.

DHA's caution basically reflected its ambivalence about whether the task force should become a strong interagency entity. As already noted, some DHA senior staff did not consider the task force the best mechanism for dealing with actual problems of internal displacement, did not collaborate effectively with its Geneva convener, and feared the task force would antagonize the governments with which DHA had to deal. Task force member agencies also contributed to diminishing the body's effectiveness. When it was proposed that the task force organize missions to the field to monitor situations, some members objected, and the proposal was rejected. Thus a field mission to Angola, to ascertain whether protection issues were being adequately addressed, was aborted when the agencies involved opposed outside monitoring of their work.[77] The mission could have proved a valuable means of making the task force's work relevant to actual situations in the field.

When the task force was discontinued in 1997, it aptly described itself as having "a huge although as yet not fully realized potential."[78] In its place, the IASC working group designated itself as the forum for consultations on matters concerning internally displaced persons.

Coordination in the Field

In the field, disaster management teams (DMTs), headed by resident coordinators, are responsible for coordinating humanitarian assistance to internally displaced persons and ensuring that rehabilitation and development activities are undertaken in coordination with relief efforts. The DMTs are generally composed of UN operational agencies, as well as IOM and ICRC, and sometimes include NGOs.

Resident coordinators do not always set up DMTs, however; and even when they are formed, they do not always meet regularly. In a number of countries, they have been found to exist in name only and to engage minimally in disaster management planning. Moreover, their role in coordinating assistance for the internally displaced has not always been exemplary. In some countries, little coordination has been found among the UN and other bodies involved in providing assistance to the internally displaced.[79] According to the inter-agency task force on internally displaced persons:

> Whereas there are notable examples of Resident Representatives/Coordinators who have taken important initiatives to deal with the situation of IDPs in their country, there exist nevertheless a common understanding that this in-country coordination system of the UN, based on the Disaster Management Teams, has often not been fully utilized to provide adequate support to IDPs. . . . The existing inter-agency coordination structure at the country level must be further enhanced.[80]

Strengthening in-country coordination for internally displaced persons will require greater direction and input to the field from the ERC and UNDP to ensure that DMTs or comparable mechanisms are formed, meet regularly, and have the necessary staff support to operate effectively. Part of the problem, as already noted, is that resident representatives/coordinators are development specialists who do not have the necessary experience in the coordination of emergency relief. The different agencies, moreover, often resist coordination even though they acknowledge the need for it. "Everybody agrees to coordination but nobody wants to be coordinated," wrote one resident coordinator to headquarters.[81]

In an effort to deal with these problems, UNDP has made an express "commitment" to "ensure that the Resident Coordinator in place in complex and other emergencies has the training and experience to serve well as the UN's Humanitarian Coordinator."[82] It also has authorized special discretionary funds to enable resident coordinators to offer something concrete in support of coordination. UNDP also plans special training in internal displacement in the emergency training provided to resident coordinators.

In response to this encouragement, some resident coordinators have taken steps to create interagency mechanisms within the DMTs to deal specifically with internally displaced persons. In Somalia, in 1995, the resident coordinator created an interagency "IDP task force" to encourage agencies to share information and develop a joint plan for responding to the emergency and longer-term needs of the internally displaced.[83] In Sri Lanka, the resident coordinator established an emergency task force in 1995 to improve emergency preparedness and contingency planning for affected populations, including the internally displaced. Nonetheless, in-country mechanisms on internal displacement do not exist in most countries and resident representatives/coordinators have not always given high priority to the problem. Moreover, in countries where governments do not invite or accept assistance in dealing with the internally displaced, resident representatives/coordinators have given little attention to the internally displaced.[84]

When persons other than the resident coordinator are sent out to coordinate assistance in emergencies or to represent the UN system, serious institutional problems have arisen. In some countries, ambiguities and overlap have been reported between humanitarian coordinators sent out by DHA and resident coordinators.[85] In such cases, more effective operational lines need to be drawn so that only one individual is considered responsible for coordinating the UN's humanitarian response. In his end-of-mission report, the humanitarian coordinator in Rwanda recommended that when humanitarian coordinators are designated, all humanitarian activities should go through them.[86] The Inter-Agency Standing Committee sought to resolve the problem by deciding in 1997 that in those emergencies requiring a humanitarian coordinator, every effort would be made to designate the same person as both humanitarian and resident coordinator.

Problems have also emerged when the secretary-general has designated a special representative in a country. In such situations, it is important that the resident or humanitarian coordinator and the DMT seek to ensure that the actions of different agencies are coordinated in support of the objectives of that official.[87] In Rwanda, UN agencies on several occasions undercut the special representative's initiatives by rushing ahead with aid deliveries without reference to the overall political and human rights objectives being pursued. At the same time, the resident or humanitarian coordinator must seek to ensure that humanitarian action is not eroded by the political decisions of the special representative. In Liberia, the special representative opposed cross-border feeding operations to help internally displaced persons because such operations would have had to take place in rebel areas and might have jeopardized the peace process.[88] Clearly a balance needs to be struck so that the political objectives of the special representative do not erode humanitarian aid but that the relief provided by humanitarian agencies does not become a vehicle for prolonging conflict and undercutting political goals.[89]

To coordinate assistance and represent the UN system, attention must be paid to protection. The goal should be to develop a common UN approach in response to serious violations of human rights and humanitarian law so that governments and insurgent groups are made aware that they are dealing with a united front and cannot play one UN agency off against another.[90] To this end, resident coordinators should promote respect for the international human rights and humanitarian standards that bind the UN system as a whole. However, resident coordinators do not generally consider protection and human rights concerns to fall within their mandates and do not generally play a strong advocacy role for the internally displaced. One DHA official has recommended that training materials be prepared for resident coordinators that set forth protection responsibilities.[91] A move in this direction was made recently when the DMT training program invited collaboration from the UN high commissioner for human rights to ensure that human rights and protection issues would be integrated in the training provided.

Resident coordinators also need to strengthen their relationships with UN forces stationed in the country, which often play an important role in facilitating the delivery of relief and in providing protection. The experience in Rwanda, in which UN peacekeeping forces did not consult closely enough with the humanitarian coordinator, has given rise to suggestions for improved coordination.[92]

DHA's responsibility to ensure "a smooth transition from relief to rehabilitation and development" was also supposed to be reflected in the work of the DMTs.[93] From the outset of an emergency, the DMT is expected to bring into play the expertise of development-oriented organizations and promote interagency partnerships to address recovery situations. This has often proved difficult because rehabilitation requirements do not always fit strict development criteria. Nonetheless, mobilization of the necessary financial and technical resources, including those from international financial institutions, needs to be undertaken to ensure that UN support addresses the rehabilitation and development needs flowing from emergencies. The new funding authorized by UNDP for resident coordinators in postconflict situations should facilitate this effort.

UN Human Rights System

Unlike the UN's humanitarian and development agencies, the UN's human rights system does not have offices and representatives throughout the world, has not traditionally been involved with humanitarian emergencies, and has very limited resources at its disposal. Because many governments are extremely sensitive to criticism on human rights grounds, UN human rights capacities have been deliberately kept weak. Nonetheless, the UN human rights system has been increasingly called upon in recent years to shoulder some of the human rights and protection responsibilities emanating from emergency situations. The UN High Commissioner for Refugees in particular has called for the increased involvement of UN human rights bodies in field operations and for the development of joint strategies for monitoring the basic human rights and physical safety of the internally displaced.[94] In response to these and other requests, the UN human rights system has begun to take steps to develop more rapid and meaningful responses to emergency situations.

Commission on Human Rights

As the UN's principal human rights body, the Commission on Human Rights, which is composed of fifty-three governments, has taken innovative steps to address human rights and humanitarian emergencies of which internally displaced persons are a part. Faced with the challenge of developing rapid responses to emergency situations, the Economic and Social Council (ECOSOC) empowered the commission in 1990 to convene exceptional sessions when an urgent human rights situation arises and a majority agrees.[95] As a result, in addition to its annual meeting, the commission called two emergency sessions on the former Yugoslavia (1992) and one on Rwanda (1994). In both cases, it appointed special rapporteurs to prepare reports on the human rights situation and for the first time authorized the deployment of human rights staff to the field.

In 1992, as mentioned earlier, the commission took the significant step of requesting that the secretary-general designate a special representative on internally displaced persons, and it asked the representative to evaluate existing legal protections and institutional machinery for the internally displaced and to make recommendations for their improvement (the representative's role and activities are discussed later in this section). In 1996 it expressed support for the *Compilation and Analysis of Legal Norms* presented by the representative (see chapter 3) and called upon the representative to develop an "appropriate framework" of protection based on the compilation.[96] Although it did not explicitly call for the preparation of a legal instrument, it took note in 1997 of the "guiding principles" on internally displaced persons being drafted under the direction of the representative.[97]

In its resolutions, the commission has begun to draw attention to problems of forcible displacement and to the obstruction of humanitarian assistance in different countries. It has publicly called upon the governments of the Sudan and other countries to permit deliveries of aid and has urged the international community to increase assistance to displaced persons in Burundi.[98] It also has requested that all its rapporteurs, working groups and experts include information and recommendations on internal displacement in their reports.[99] As a result, the special rapporteurs on the Sudan, Congo (Zaire), and Myanmar (Burma) have published extensive information on internally displaced persons and made recommendations to these governments to improve conditions. Commission reports on the relationship between human rights and mass exoduses have also included information on internal displacement.

Finally, the commission has begun to seek greater field presence to ensure protection for the internally displaced. In Rwanda, in 1994 and 1995, 130 human rights field staff were deployed to facilitate the return of internally displaced persons and refugees to their homes in addition to performing the more traditional human rights functions of monitoring and reporting.[100] Although the commission is in a position to authorize the deployment of human rights field staff to other locations as well, political and financial considerations have impeded such action.[101] When UNHCR, for example, requested the deployment of human rights field staff to Tajikistan to protect internally displaced persons and refugees returning to their homes, the UN human rights system did not have the capacity or resources to undertake the job.

The commission's capacity for action is also weakened by the fact that its rules set no standards for membership. In consequence, governments notorious for egregious violations of human rights, including forcible displacement, often seek and obtain membership, with the express purpose of impeding action by the commission against themselves or other blatant violators.

Office of the High Commissioner for Human Rights

The appointment by the secretary-general of the high commissioner for human rights in 1994, at the request of the General Assembly, marked the culmination of a thirty-year advocacy effort by NGOs and governments, intended to bring greater leadership and cohesion to the UN human rights program. With the rank of under-secretary-general, the high commissioner was given a broad mandate for prevention and for the promotion and protection of human rights and was placed in charge of the Centre for Human Rights, the arm of the Secretariat that carries out the UN's human rights program.[102] In 1997 the center was merged into the Office of the High Commissioner.

The first high commissioner, José Ayala Lasso, gave priority to strengthening the ability of the center and the commission to react rapidly to human rights emergencies.[103] However, he encountered considerable obstacles in trying to achieve this. In the case of Rwanda, he played a major role in seeing that an emergency session of the commission was called, but the commission did not actually convene its meeting until *after* the genocide. The center, moreover, took months to deploy 130 field staff to Rwanda; many of the staff members selected were reported to be unqualified and to have been given inadequate training, and there were inordinate delays in receipt of communications equipment.[104] The high commissioner himself described the operation as a "logistical failure." [105]

It is generally acknowledged that the Office of the High Commissioner does not yet have the expertise, procedures, and resources needed to organize rapidly a full-scale field operation in an emergency situation. Because of the shortcomings in the Rwanda mission, some have concluded that it should not try to mount such operations.[106] It is more persuasively argued, however, that the office should be reinforced so as to have the capacity to play a meaningful role in humanitarian emergencies. Ayala Lasso did strengthen the center's rapid response mechanisms by developing an emergency roster of human rights experts who could be sent into the field on short notice and by strengthening logistical capacity to rapidly provide material and communications support for field missions. The center also began to work more closely with other UN departments and agencies, as well as regional organizations and NGOs, which have experience in field operations, so that it could rely upon them for logistical and other needed skills.[107]

Clearly, however, the successor Office of the High Commissioner will need to undergo radical transformation to become successful at organizing and overseeing field operations. Its staff, totaling more than 150, has traditionally focused on doing legal research, preparing reports, and servicing the Commission on Human Rights and other UN human rights bodies. Expertise in field work, in servicing on-site operations and in providing on-the-ground protection is largely lacking. The office thus far has no emergency unit; nor does it have a revolving fund for emergency operations. As a UN internal evaluation concluded, these deficiencies made the center "inadequate as a basis for effective and timely response to serious incidents of violations of human rights."[108]

Ayala Lasso, in a report to the General Assembly in 1995, underscored the need to give greater attention to human rights protection for internally displaced persons. He declared that his office was ready to contribute to protection efforts, which would include expanding human rights presence in the field, dispatching field officers to ascertain and monitor protection needs, and providing training in dealing with internally displaced populations.[109] Subsequent to this report, the high commissioner opened a human rights office in Abkhazia, Georgia, to contribute to the safe return of refugees and internally displaced persons through improvement of the human rights situation.[110]

The high commissioner also expressed his intention to become more engaged in the area of prevention of situations that cause mass exodus.[111] In an effort to avert displacement, he introduced human rights field presence in a number of countries to prevent or limit violations and interethnic violence. Such presence has been small, as in Burundi where only twelve experts have been stationed to date.[112] Nonetheless, this initiative marks the beginning of an operational effort to try to deter abuse, avert displacement, and encourage returns of the displaced.[113]

Another important initiative the high commissioner can rely on to benefit the internally displaced is the advisory services and technical assistance program, which works with governments to strengthen national institutions and laws in the furtherance of human rights. In 1996 the commission specifically requested that attention be given to the internally displaced in this program.[114] In Rwanda a project has been undertaken to address property disputes in an effort to facilitate the return of displaced persons; projects are needed in other countries as well with problems of internal displacement.[115]

Limited resources and staff, however, seriously constrain the high commissioner's initiatives. Although shortage of funds is an endemic problem in the United Nations, human rights bodies are especially starved. Funding for the Office of the High Commissioner represents little more than 1.5 percent of the UN's regular budget, or about $24 million, a sum grossly insufficient to keep pace with the many new human rights responsibilities arising from humanitarian emergencies. Although the high commissioner has been able to supplement this budget with voluntary contributions, the absence of a regular budget for field operations has turned monitoring missions, such as the ones in Rwanda and the former Yugoslavia, into largely hand-to-mouth operations. Limited funding has also prohibited the office from taking on additional field operations or deploying preventive missions.

The new high commissioner, Mary Robinson, who was appointed in the fall of 1997, has expressed her intention to further strengthen the operational capacity of her office in emergency situations.[116] The high commissioner's role in developing diplomatic dialogue with governments could be an important means of promoting protection for internally displaced persons. In this role, the high commissioner could reinforce the initiatives of the secretary-general's representative on internally displaced persons by following up with governments on their treatment of displaced populations and by supporting the representative's efforts to gain access to affected areas.

Human rights organizations characterized Ayala Lasso's discussions with governments as "cautious" or "passive" in the face of serious human rights violations.[117] Although he did issue a public statement condemning the killings of internally displaced persons by the government of Rwanda, it was the special rapporteur of the Commission on Human Rights who came forward publicly in the former Yugoslavia to protest the failure of UN forces to defend the "safe areas" and protect internally displaced populations from abuse.[118] One of the challenges facing the new high commissioner is to ensure that the recommendations made by representatives and rapporteurs of the commission are carried out, and to be willing to engage in vigorous private and public diplomacy to accomplish that.

Representative of the Secretary-General on Internally Displaced Persons

The representative of the secretary-general is the only position within the UN system with a mandate from the Commission on Human Rights and the secretary-general to focus exclusively on the problem of internal displacement and to address both protection and assistance. As earlier noted, Francis M. Deng, a former Sudanese diplomat, was designated the representative in 1992 and given a broad mandate by the commission that encompassed both human rights and humanitarian concerns. The representative was authorized to monitor displacement worldwide, undertake fact-finding missions, establish dialogues with governments, coordinate with humanitarian and human rights bodies, make proposals for increased legal and institutional protection, and publish reports for action by the commission, the General Assembly, international organizations, and NGOs. In 1993 the commission extended Deng's mandate for two years and in 1995 for another three years, with the request that he continue to identify "ways and means for improved protection for and assistance to internally displaced persons."[119]

Since his appointment, the representative has visited twelve countries experiencing serious problems of internal displacement.[120] He has published reports on the country situations and made recommendations to governments and international agencies for improving the treatment of the displaced. He has engaged in dialogues with government officials and heads of human rights and humanitarian and development agencies on protection, assistance, and development strategies. He has raised national and international awareness of the plight of the displaced and in a number of instances has stimulated improvements in their condition.

In addition, he has promoted the development of a legal framework for the internally displaced (see chapter 3). In 1996 he submitted to the United Nations the first comprehensive compilation and analysis of legal norms applicable to the internally displaced; and in 1998 he presented an analysis of the extent to which international law provides protection against arbitrary displacement. Working with a group of international legal experts, he has developed guiding principles for the internally displaced that include protection against arbitrary displacement, protection for those already displaced, and protection for returning displaced persons (see the appendix).[121]

He has also made suggestions for improving institutional arrangements. In response, a wide range of humanitarian, development, and human rights bodies have undertaken specific measures geared toward the internally displaced. The Inter-Agency Standing Committee has adopted recommendations made by the representative. Regional organizations and NGOs as well have expanded their activities.[122]

In large part, the position of the representative has evolved into one of catalyst within the UN system, raising awareness of the human rights and protection problems of the internally displaced and stimulating improvements at the institutional level, in the area of legal protection, and on the ground. Until his appointment, there was no systematic UN effort to report on and monitor the protection needs of internally displaced persons. No international official was charged with raising their protection problems with governments, other than on an ad hoc basis. Nor was any official charged with raising the problems of the displaced with international humanitarian and development agencies.

The representative's role, however, has perforce been limited. The position is a voluntary one, expected to be carried out on a part-time basis. The office has no operational authority and limited staff support. The resources placed at the representative's disposal do not enable him to undertake systematic monitoring of situations of internal displacement or frequent visits to countries with serious problems of internal displacement. In his reports, the representative has pointed out that "no established procedure or mechanism exists . . . to monitor situations in the countries visited and to ensure that the points agreed upon are carried out; nor are there resources for follow-up visits."[123] Unless "institutional responsibility" is established, he has warned:

> the faith of displaced populations in the United Nations system will be undermined. It clearly could become counterproductive for the Represen-

tative to pay visits to the displaced, hear moving accounts of their needs, intercede with governments and international agencies, only not to be heard from again. Continued monitoring of these situations is essential to sustain the momentum of the visits and to ensure active collaboration between the government and United Nations agencies on the ground.[124]

The representative needs greater support from other UN departments and agencies in following up on cases of internal displacement. When humanitarian organizations have a presence in countries visited by the representative, they do not necessarily monitor the extent to which the recommendations made by the representative are carried out. In part with the aim of rectifying this, a letter of understanding was concluded in 1996 between the ERC and the representative, stipulating that they would cooperate in monitoring situations of internal displacement and that interagency bodies chaired by the ERC would lend support to the follow-up to the representative's visits.[125] This agreement has not yet been effectively implemented.

The representative faces other challenges as well. Like other representatives and rapporteurs of the Commission on Human Rights, the representative has to find effective ways of dealing with governments that have serious problems of internal displacement but seek to avoid scrutiny. At present, governments that wish to evade the attention associated with a fact-finding mission can do so with impunity, leaving countries with more cooperative governments to become the focus of the representative's attention.[126] Here the UN secretary-general and the high commissioner for human rights could lend increased support.

The representative's relationship to nonstate actors also needs clarification and strengthening. The representative has been authorized to enter into dialogues with governments but has not been given explicit authority to establish direct contacts with insurgent forces even though substantial numbers of internally displaced persons are often found in areas outside of government control. In a report to the secretary-general, the representative pointed out that direct contact with insurgent authorities under compelling and appropriate humanitarian conditions should be recognized as an indispensable aspect of the mandate.[127]

The representative has successfully managed to mobilize support from outside the United Nations—particularly from academic, legal, and NGO constituencies and from governments—in support of his activities. However, the United Nations itself will have to assume a greater part of the burden and place at his disposal more substantial human and material resources if the representative is to carry out his mandate effectively.

Gaps in the International System

When one reviews the large number of humanitarian, human rights, and development organizations that are now involved with the internally displaced, it becomes clear that capacities exist for dealing with internal displacement but that they are frequently not extensive enough or sufficiently honed to address the problem effectively. Some organizations need increased capacity to deal with emergencies; others need more training and experience in working with uprooted populations; still others require expertise in protection work.

At the same time, international organizations have shown themselves remarkably flexible in responding to situations of internal displacement. Some (such as UNHCR) have used their good offices to undertake activities on behalf of the internally displaced at the request of the UN secretary-general or General Assembly. Others (for example, ICRC, UNICEF) have extended coverage to internally displaced persons when they fall within a broader category of concern, such as the victims of armed conflict, or women or children in need. Still others (for example, WHO, IOM) have broadly interpreted their own constitutions to encompass internally displaced persons. They have also developed expertise and innovative skills to reach and deal with persons displaced within the borders of their own countries.

Nonetheless, the international response system is far from adequate. It is too selective, organizations working on behalf of the internally displaced are poorly coordinated, protection and human rights concerns are sorely neglected, and reintegration and development support receive insufficient attention.

Selectivity

Currently, no UN agency can be relied upon to respond to internal displacement in a predictable manner. Nor is there any international accountability when an agency denies coverage to internally displaced populations. The late James Grant, then head of UNICEF, captured the situation well:

> The world has established a minimum safety net for refugees. Whenever people are forced into exile—whether they are a thousand or fifty thousand—experience shows that refugees can expect UNHCR to be on the scene in a matter of days or on the outside, a matter of weeks. Camps are quickly set up to provide shelter, food, and a package of basic services. . . . This is not yet the case with respect to internally displaced populations.[128]

Instead, different agencies pick and choose the situations in which they will become involved, depending on their mandates, resources, and interests. As a result, coverage is often limited and inconsistent. At the end of 1996, for example, UNHCR deemed that 4.85 million internally displaced persons required the organization's attention. This was only a fraction of those estimated to be in need of protection and assistance. Of these, only 1 million were to be found in Africa, even though Africa, the continent most ravaged by conflicts and displacement, is estimated to have at least 9 million internally displaced persons. Among those excluded from consideration were the 4 million internally displaced persons in the Sudan, UNHCR contending that any involvement with them would conflict with its protection for refugees in that country.[129] UNHCR also declined to become involved with internally displaced persons in Uganda, whose government in 1996 requested the organization's involvement.

Also in 1996 UNICEF decided not to assume responsibility for internally displaced persons in camps in Burundi, despite their substandard conditions. Its reluctance was based on the fear that involvement with Tutsi women and children (68 percent of those in the camps) could arouse animosities among the Hutu population outside.[130] In Congo (Zaire) in 1996 and 1997, internally displaced persons received little attention from any agency. Many UN agencies are present in Colombia, but few had anything to do with internally displaced persons until 1998, when UNHCR assumed a technical assistance role. A visit by the representative of the secretary-general in 1994 did spur UNDP and a few of the other UN agencies to look into increasing their involvement, but by and large the main assistance to the internally displaced was the limited amount provided by NGOs and the Catholic Church.[131]

Often, UN agencies are reluctant to become involved when doing so could place them in direct conflict with governments they want to cooperate with. In the Sudan, for example, WHO avoided addressing health problems in the southern part of the country because the area was not under government control.[132] Other UN agencies have been criticized for having "failed to challenge the Sudanese government's virtual blockade of the people of the Nuba Mountains" and its obstruction of the delivery of relief supplies to displaced and other war-affected populations.[133] And in countries whose governments do not acknowledge that the problem of internal displacement exists (for example, Myanmar [Burma]), or refuse international involvement (for example, Turkey and India), UN humanitarian and development organizations have tended to avoid involvement with the internally displaced, and in some cases have even failed to monitor or collect information on these populations.[134]

The absence of reliable international funding for the internally displaced also encourages international organizations to take a selective, case-by-case approach to this group. Unlike the funding for refugees, no overall funding exists for situations of internal displacement. Moreover, funding for humanitarian emergencies, of which the internally displaced are a part, is apparently declining.[135] In 1995, only 28 percent of the funds requested in consolidated appeals for the emergency in Angola came through, and this shortfall made it more difficult for international organizations to undertake projects for the internally displaced.[136] In 1996 less than half the needed amount was made available for Afghanistan.[137] In the Rwanda crisis, most donor funding supported relief work in refugee camps outside Rwanda; only a small fraction went to assistance and development needs within Rwanda, including the needs of the internally displaced.[138]

Ineffective Coordination

No effective central point exists within the international system that routinely and rapidly assigns responsibility in situations of internal displacement. Agencies tend to go their own way and are not likely to become aware of the gaps that need to be addressed. WFP, for example, has pointed out that nonfood items such as fuel and stoves are not regularly delivered to the internally displaced, which means that the commodities they receive cannot always be transformed into edible food.[139] However, agencies are not always inclined to subordinate their priorities to an overall plan. Duplication also becomes a problem.[140] Moreover, the presence of so many agencies, donor organizations, and NGOs in an emergency often represents a serious drain on the limited resources of postconflict states.[141]

In 1995 IASC authorized its task force on internally displaced persons to review all serious situations of internal displacement and recommend the best division of labor among UN agencies. However, the task force made no recommendations to the standing committee about specific situations in which UN agencies might become more involved, such as Sierra Leone, which reportedly had at least one million internally displaced persons in dire straits. Nor was attention paid to the situation in the Great Lakes region, where a well-funded and well-coordinated assistance operation for refugees existed side by side with an underfunded and ill-coordinated response to the problems of the internally displaced.[142] When it comes to situations of internal displacement, little leadership has been shown in addressing internal displacement, notwithstanding the ERC's appointment as reference point for the internally displaced.

Moreover, resident and humanitarian coordinators in the field have often proved unable to coordinate activities effectively on behalf of the internally displaced and have not always alerted the UN system to situations of internal displacement that need to be addressed. Some have found that the backing needed from headquarters is not forthcoming. According to the humanitarian coordinator in Rwanda, "the absence of an effective UN system-wide approach to IDPs" was demonstrated in the response to the Rwanda crisis. Despite efforts at coordination, the mechanism established suffered from "lack of priority to IDP issues in agency headquarters."[143] Coordination remains more of a concept than an effective reality, concluded one recent study.[144] A "hollow core" is how an evaluation report characterized the structure of coordination within the UN system.[145]

Inadequate Protection

In many situations, security is as important a priority as food, but protection of physical safety often takes second place to the provision of food, medical care, and shelter. Internally displaced persons in Bosnia received humanitarian relief from the United Nations but were not afforded much protection, and in Zepa and Srebrenica, they were abandoned. The case study on the former Yugoslavia finds that "UN personnel acted as if the most, and sometimes the only, essential undertaking was the delivery of relief goods. . . . The world organization downplayed such tasks as protecting fundamental rights, gathering information about war crimes, and assertively and routinely investigating alleged abuses."[146] Similarly, little attention was paid to the physical safety of the internally displaced in

Rwanda. One of the largest massacres of internally displaced persons in a camp situation took place in Kibeho in 1995, where the relief operation was effectively coordinated by the United Nations, but where attention to protection was minimal. In Angola in 1996, NGOs reported that the UN agencies engaged in reconstruction and development were paying scant attention to the protection problems of internally displaced persons.[147]

Inattention to protection can, of course, undermine relief operations and jeopardize returns and reintegration. The Inter-Agency Standing Committee has acknowledged the importance of addressing both "protection and relief needs in urgent situations of internal displacement."[148] So have its individual members.[149] These concerns, however, have not been translated into operational policies. Interagency missions sent out to assess emergency situations still do not routinely include persons with expertise in dealing with the human rights and physical safety of affected populations. The team sent by DHA to Rwanda did not include a human rights expert, even though protection problems were paramount.[150] In Angola and Liberia, WFP became the lead UN agency because food and logistics were deemed the most critical needs. Protection problems, although equally severe, received less attention.

Government resistance is a major factor limiting international involvement with protection. But an equally important reason is that international human rights bodies are not yet fully operational and there is little consensus among other UN agencies as to what they should do about identifying, monitoring, and addressing the human rights and protection problems of internally displaced persons. To date, UN human rights bodies have played only a minimal role in protecting the physical security and human rights of such persons. As earlier noted, they are constrained by limited resources and the lack of field experience. In Rwanda, the United Nations did manage to send in 130 human rights field staff, but the government had requested 300, and those sent arrived after months of delay. In Burundi, despite the deteriorating situation, only 5 could be dispatched in 1996, even though the request was made in 1995 and the target was 35. In Tajikistan in 1995, UNHCR requested human rights field staff, but none was sent. In most emergency situations, there is no human rights field presence.

If UN human rights bodies are too weak to participate effectively, many humanitarian and development agencies do not consider defending physical safety and fundamental human rights their central concern or function. Interviews with senior staff in these agencies invariably reveal profound reservations, and sometimes even outright opposition, to association with protection concerns. Such concerns, in their view, are "political" and could jeopardize their agencies' impartiality, neutrality, and ability to provide humanitarian relief. In the main, they recommend that UN human rights bodies or humanitarian agencies, such as UNHCR and ICRC, should deal with such concerns.

Nonetheless, most humanitarian and development agencies do engage in some protection activities in the course of their assistance work. After all, the delivery of food, medicine, and shelter constitutes de facto protection by preserving lives and physical safety. Humanitarian and development agencies also become involved in protection in negotiating access to the internally displaced. Their mere presence may provide an additional form of protection. In some cases, it can deter or at least mitigate abuse, providing, as UNHCR has observed, "some measure of confidence, security, and relief . . . to victims of conflict or human rights violations." [151]

Humanitarian and development agencies are also in a position to engage in advocacy for the physical security and human rights of the internally displaced, particularly when they have gained the confidence of governments or nonstate actors within the framework of providing assistance. But it is at this point that humanitarian and development agencies usually draw the line. Tensions, they argue, can arise between assistance and protection roles, and their first priority must be assistance. In the view of WFP,

> Whilst WFP is fully supportive of the need to ensure protection services for internally displaced persons, it must be accepted that if, on occasion, negotiations are protracted, the provision of emergency food aid may precede the finalization of protection arrangements. Such action should not be seen as undermining negotiations on protection . . . but merely WFP fulfilling its primary mandate, the alleviation of hunger among the poor and needy. [152]

Others, however, maintain that protection should never be given a secondary position. ICRC argues that "humanitarian agencies cannot restrict their role to that of mere suppliers of medical and food aid. They must back up their emergency operations in the field with representations regarding the conduct and policies which lead to famine and violations of fundamental human rights." Although intercessions can be "diplomatically sensitive and politically risky or downright costly," they constitute "the indispensable protective aspect of any relief operation, without which no lasting improvement in the condition of conflict victims can be assured." [153]

UNHCR also stands out as an exception. For it, as for ICRC, humanitarian action is not only about the delivery of relief but also about ensuring the basic human rights and security of the victims. [154] Still, even here there can be problems. UNHCR generally defines its role with the internally displaced more in terms of assistance than protection. In the case of Chechnya, UNHCR was less than outspoken about protection concerns, presumably out of fear of jeopardizing its assistance role. [155] In the former Yugoslavia, UNHCR also paid less attention to protection than to assistance concerns. [156] Moreover, UNHCR and ICRC are not present in all situations of internal displacement. As noted earlier, only 4.85 million internally displaced persons have been determined to be of concern to UNHCR. ICRC's involvement with the internally displaced is limited essentially to wartime situations, but governments often refuse to acknowledge that a noninternational armed conflict is taking place on their territory, and some of the worst offenders refuse to allow ICRC entry.

The human rights and protection gap will remain wide as long as human rights field staff are absent from most humanitarian emergencies and humanitarian and development agencies do not concern themselves with physical safety. Affected most heavily are women and children, as they constitute the vast majority of the internally displaced. The lack of protection for women has been heavily exposed in Bosnia and Rwanda, but substantial numbers elsewhere have been subjected to sexual violence and physical attack as well. An interagency UN mission to Liberia in 1993 found that many internally displaced women had suffered rape and psychological and physical trauma and were infected with sexually transmitted diseases. [157] Yet this appears to be the only instance of a joint UN mission to a country to investigate the plight of internally displaced women. [158] On the whole, interagency meetings under the IASC have not addressed the protection problems facing internally displaced women. A multidonor evaluation of emergency assistance to Rwanda in 1996 found "little" being done to address the "distinctive needs" of the main victims of violence: "widows, rape victims and the disabled." Such negligence, it pointed out, thwarted reintegration. [159]

As a rule, UN agencies do not perform gender evaluations of emergency programs. [160] The UN Development Fund for Women (UNIFEM) and UNICEF have found that although women are an especially vulnerable segment of the internally displaced population, "the incorporation of gender perspectives in response to disasters and emergencies is markedly under-developed." They found that for some operational agencies, the idea of integrating gender considerations into their programs is "an irrelevance, or at best an optional extra, to be bolted on if there is time, rather than being seen as central to planning and implementation of the relief responses." [161]

The protection of displaced children has suffered widespread neglect as well. Graça Machel's report described the "perilous circumstances" of internally displaced children, many of whom are prey to forcible recruitment and sexual violence and have been separated from, or have lost, their parents. According to Machel, one of the biggest challenges is how to transcend the notion that only human rights groups monitor and report on violations. "Much broader participation" is required by humanitarian and development organizations and peacekeeping forces. Without such involvement, the international community will remain deprived of vital information and be unable to protect children adequately. [162]

Insufficient Reintegration and Development Support

As earlier noted, internally displaced persons may return, or be forcibly returned, to areas without due attention to their safety or ability to reintegrate. Neglect of these considerations can jeopardize the entire reconciliation and reintegration process in a country. As a result, humanitarian relief agencies have increasingly become involved in monitoring returns and providing reintegration assistance. In Tajikistan, for example, UNHCR closely monitored conditions in areas of return and worked with local authorities to increase physical security for the displaced, reconstruct houses, and help returnees reclaim their homes. In Mozambique, UNHCR and other agencies have provided reintegration support that has benefited internally displaced persons.

However, many such people are ill-prepared for return and reintegration. In emergency situations, humanitarian activities focus primarily on meeting short-term needs. Education, training, and income-generating activities are rarely available to internally displaced persons; nor are sufficient efforts made to enable them to find land for farming to reduce their dependency on food aid. [163] IOM found that the great majority of the internally displaced in Angola were unable to participate fully in the reconstruction of the Angolan economy owing to the lack of land, tools, and resources. [164]

The much discussed concept of the "continuum from relief to development" depends for its implementation on links between humanitarian assistance provided on a short-term basis and the longer-term reconstruction and development of affected areas. UNHCR's quick-impact projects (QIPs), for example, are increasingly being introduced in areas of return to try to bridge the gap between relief and development. These innovative projects restore roads, schools, and health facilities and provide income-earning opportunities for returning refugees, internally displaced persons, and local residents alike. Income-generating QIPs, however, need to be tied in with development efforts to ensure their sustainability. But UNDP as well as other development agencies have not always been prepared to step in and incorporate these projects into their development schemes.[165] Without such coordination—as UNHCR found in Tajikistan, Cambodia, Nicaragua, and other countries—reintegration projects will not be able to sustain themselves.

Successful reintegration generally depends on development aid to increase the absorptive capacity of return areas. Development agencies, however, seldom have adequate funds for the rehabilitation and development of such areas. For the most part, their resources are expected to be allocated in cooperation with governments and used for regular development purposes. In many cases, governments prefer to use the limited development funds available to them for the benefit of nationals who are not displaced, rather than for the reintegration of uprooted populations.[166]

When rehabilitation and development projects are designed and funded to benefit both the local population and uprooted persons, however, governments are often more responsive. In the Horn of Africa, Cambodia, Central America, and Mozambique, humanitarian relief and development agencies have been providing extensive assistance to community-based projects that help internally displaced populations while simultaneously stimulating the recovery and reconstruction of entire communities.

Nonetheless, donors tend to treat relief and development as separate exercises and to compartmentalize funds for each. This has made it difficult to find funding for rehabilitation purposes, which often fall between the two. The secretary-general's decision in 1997 to include rehabilitation and recovery requirements in emergency funding appeals should help erode some of this division. However, development agencies still are hampered by the lack of rapid and flexible procedures for disbursing rehabilitation funds. Instead they use many of the same procedures for emergencies as they do for regular development projects, which can take several years. In Rwanda, the long delays in the arrival of reconstruction funds served to undermine the reintegration of internally displaced and other uprooted populations and to jeopardize the peace-building process.[167]

The recent creation by UNDP of a $50 million fund for emergency situations should help provide greater flexibility in disbursing rehabilitation funds in postemergency situations. But the amount is small and the extent to which the funds will address the problems of reintegrating internally displaced persons is unclear. The World Bank, whose involvement in postconflict reconstruction is essential, has recently established an $8 million fund to finance preparatory work in postconflict countries. But since the fund does not specifically target the internally displaced, the scope of Bank involvement with reintegration and development programs for uprooted populations remains uncertain.

In general, donors are more willing to allocate resources to emergency and disaster relief than to support the reconstruction and development of areas where internally displaced persons, refugees and returnees should be integrated.[168] Yet the return or resettlement of such populations and their reintegration are critical to reconstruction and to the process of reconciliation in war-torn societies. Moreover, if the process takes into account the inequities and schisms that led to breakdown in the first place, it can help prevent renewed conflict and displacement.

Options for Institutional Reform

In recent years members of the international community, both within and outside the United Nations, have debated how to improve the international response to emergency situations. These discussions have produced several ideas for addressing the problem of internal displacement more effectively. Among the options are whether to create a new agency with responsibility for the internally displaced, assign the responsibility to an existing agency, or strengthen collaborative arrangements among agencies whose mandates and activities relate to the internally displaced.

Create a New Agency

Often it is argued that since refugees have a special organization to address their problems, a parallel agency should be created with broad authority to protect and assist the internally displaced. The obvious appeal of a new agency is that both governments and the internally displaced would have a single operational entity to turn to.

Even if the political will existed to create such an agency, there are many persuasive arguments against it. To begin with, it would duplicate the many existing resources and capacities that have already become involved with the internally displaced, especially at a time when the UN system is under considerable pressure to eliminate duplication and cut back on staff. A new agency might even inhibit existing agencies from extending their services, thereby weakening rather than strengthening the international response.

The cost of a new institution would be substantial, and under present circumstances it would be difficult to include in the regular UN budget. There is also a concern that it would foster dependency by encouraging governments to call upon the new agency to address problems that should fall within their own purview.

A new agency for the internally displaced is certain to arouse considerable opposition from governments that believe the problem belongs within the domestic jurisdiction of states. Whereas existing agencies already present in many countries can become involved with internally displaced persons in the course of their regular work, and often without drawing too much attention to their activities, a new agency that concentrated exclusively on the internally displaced would have to request permission to enter a country and could easily be excluded. This could make it more difficult for other agencies to become involved with internally displaced persons, who could then end up with less protection and assistance than before.

A new agency not only for internally displaced persons but for all populations affected by emergency situations might meet this objection. Some leading experts have proposed that a new agency be created to deal with all casualties of war.[169] Thus far, such proposals have failed to garner support. When the United States suggested that the emergency functions of existing UN agencies be consolidated into a single new agency to deal with emergencies, the proposal had to be withdrawn.[170] Neither the political will nor the resources exist at present to support a new agency.

Assign Responsibility to an Existing Agency

An alternative would be to enlarge the mandate of an existing agency to include protection and assistance for the internally displaced. Whereas a new agency would have to start from scratch, existing agencies already have extensive experience and support.

Within the UN system, UNHCR is the institution best equipped legally and operationally to deal with the internally displaced. The similarities between working with refugees and internally displaced persons are evident, and over the years UNHCR has developed special expertise in working with internally displaced populations. UNHCR's involvement would also help resolve the problems of inequity that often arise between the level of attention given to refugees and to internally displaced persons in the same country. It would further encourage service providers to treat refugees and internally displaced persons "as two sides of one problem" in regional situations.[171]

Yet when the Netherlands proposed in 1993 that the United Nations replace its present ad hoc arrangement for responding to situations of internal displacement with "the assignment of a general competence to UNHCR," neither UNHCR nor its Executive Committee endorsed the idea.[172] The "magnitude of the problem," the high commissioner observed, "far exceeds the capacity and resources of any single agency. It calls for a comprehensive and concerted effort of the United Nations and other humanitarian organizations."[173] The matter was discussed again in 1994 by the Sub-Committee of the Whole on International Protection, an adjunct of the Executive Committee of the High Commissioner's Programme (EXCOM). At that meeting, the high commissioner clearly defined the extent and conditions under which UNHCR is prepared to undertake activities on behalf of internally displaced persons—when specifically requested by the United Nations or when refugees and internally displaced persons are intermingled or it could prevent a refugee flow— and stated that the organization's role would essentially be limited to those criteria.[174] In 1997, before the secretary-general's announcement of UN reforms, UNHCR was again queried about assuming responsibility for internally displaced persons, in the course of being asked to take over the ERC's responsibilities. Although it considered itself able to assume responsibility for many humanitarian assistance functions, it concluded that responsibility for the internally displaced would require additional consultations and a joint effort.[175]

Nonetheless, UNHCR has clearly begun to shift its focus from refugees to persons in need of protection in countries of origin. "We have shifted from a bias towards exile to a focus on the country of origin," the high commissioner told EXCOM in 1995.[176] Of the 27.4 million persons of concern to UNHCR, "almost half" were to be found in their own countries (a combination of war victims, internally displaced persons, and returnees). In the former Yugoslavia, 85 percent of UNHCR's budget was earmarked for nonrefugees; and in Bosnia and Herzegovina, "virtually no UNHCR beneficiary was legally a refugee." [177] Although UNHCR clearly fears that assuming responsibility for the internally displaced will change the character of the organization and overwhelm its staff and resources, it has been inching toward the assumption of greater responsibility for persons in their country of origin. It appears to be moving cautiously, developing its expertise in individual cases of internal displacement, and all the while delaying the larger decision of whether it should assume responsibility for all or most situations of internal displacement. Its greater involvement, however, remains a viable option.

UNICEF has also been suggested as a possible candidate for assuming overall responsibility for the internally displaced. Though not made formally, the proposal was based on the fact that the majority of internally displaced persons are women and children and thus fall naturally within UNICEF's mandate. [178] The organization is highly decentralized, which would allow for rapid action, and it already operates on both sides of conflict zones. Moreover, its international popularity would make it difficult for governments and insurgent groups to criticize its actions.

To make the transition, however, UNICEF would have to completely reorient its priorities. It is structured primarily as a development agency, whose primary concern is to establish water systems, improve medical facilities, and provide vaccinations, inoculations, and oral rehydration salts to children. In countries facing an emergency, it can be found working on development projects in one part of the country without addressing the emergency needs of internally displaced children in another. Unlike UNHCR, it does not have broad expertise in providing protection and assistance to uprooted populations. Nor does it wish to interpret its mandate to go beyond children. It has not sought to establish criteria for its involvement with the internally displaced, let alone assume responsibility for them.

Strengthen Collaborative Arrangements

In the absence of a single organization within the UN system responsible for the internally displaced, the remaining option is to strengthen existing collaborative relationships. As has been shown earlier, a multitude of UN agencies have come forward to address the needs of the internally displaced and are actively exploring and developing new approaches to increasing protection, assistance, and reintegration and development support for this population. Strengthening and better coordinating their efforts could prove a promising prospect for addressing situations of internal displacement if substantial improvements are made. The UN secretary-general essentially endorsed this option in the reform program he introduced in 1997 when he made the ERC responsible for ensuring that the protection and assistance needs of internally displaced persons are addressed.

Steps to Improve the Current System

A number of steps can be taken within the existing system to promote greater responsibility and predictability in addressing situations of internal displacement.

Assign Principal Responsibility to One Operational Agency in Each Acute Emergency

The principal responsibility for monitoring the protection and assistance needs of the internally displaced could be assigned to *one* operational agency in each emergency. This agency would increase awareness of their plight and mobilize support for them. In situations where there exists a "lead agency" (one responsible for monitoring and addressing the needs of all vulnerable groups), it would be an especially suitable candidate.

In the case studies on which this analysis is based, it was found that when one agency is assigned principal responsibility for the internally displaced, as in Tajikistan and the former Yugoslavia, greater attention is paid to their needs. When no one agency is so designated, as in Liberia, Burundi, and Rwanda, internally displaced persons fail to receive adequate attention. Coordination mechanisms alone have generally been ineffective in ensuring that protection and assistance are provided to internally displaced persons.[179]

If only one organization is assigned, some argue, it may have to "bear the political opprobrium of the authorities."[180] But when one organization has the *principal* responsibility, it will need to work with other agencies to take advantage of the expertise they can provide. In Tajikistan, for example, UNHCR served as lead agency for the internally displaced and refugees but shared its responsibilities with ICRC, UNICEF, and WFP. When the emergency was over, it turned to UNDP and international financial institutions for reintegration and development support. When a principal agency is named, the resident/humanitarian coordinator should make sure that it receives the support of other agencies, for they could easily use the designation as an excuse for not becoming involved. In the absence of a resident/humanitarian coordinator, the principal agency itself would assume the coordination function.

The most effective principal agency would be one that is operational and capable of addressing some of the protection, assistance, and initial rehabilitation needs itself. Of the existing agencies, UNHCR appears to be the most appropriate. A recent UNHCR evaluation report recommended that when solutions for the internally displaced are inextricably linked with refugee returns, UNHCR in cooperation with the ERC be "assigned the authority and the leadership role to coordinate operations" on both sides of the border for the internally displaced and refugees.[181] Other UN agencies, such as UNICEF, could also serve; so could WFP, but it would have to go beyond its regular activities and ensure that protection concerns are addressed.

The principal organization for internally displaced persons, however, need not always be a UN agency. Major humanitarian organizations might also be considered. Since 1995 IOM has been serving as lead agency in the provision of assistance to internally displaced persons in Somalia. ICRC became the de facto lead in Chechnya, where it was the only organization allowed in during the height of the conflict, and it worked closely with UNHCR, which stood by in adjacent areas. It also played a prominent role in Somalia. Although ICRC's policy of maintaining strict independence would not allow it to accept a formal conferral of responsibility by the United Nations, and UN agencies would also find it problematic to follow the lead of an outside agency, ICRC has nonetheless become more willing to work together with other agencies, and the United Nations has come to rely on it and others in an increasing number of situations. This should encourage the international community to explore ways in which ICRC, IOM, and even major NGOs could assume wider responsibility in situations of internal displacement.

Although no one model will work in all situations, designating one operational agency as the focal point for the internally displaced should help direct more attention and care toward these populations. As WFP aptly observed: "Although the current system [of coordination] functions, it could be improved by designating an operational lead agency for each situation" of internal displacement.[182]

Strengthen Coordination

The central point from which to allocate responsibility for ensuring that the protection, assistance, and reintegration and development needs of the internally displaced are addressed is the ERC, as chair of the Inter-Agency Standing Committee. But the ERC will need to assume more of a leadership role with the internally displaced. In particular, he or she will need to initiate a division of labor, deciding upon the principal agency to serve as the focal point for the internally displaced and ensuring that other agencies play a role in an agreed-upon cooperative arrangement. Otherwise, as was discovered in Tajikistan when UNHCR left, gaps may develop that will not be easy to fill.[183]

At the same time, individual agencies should be encouraged to boost their capacities and develop specific areas of expertise with regard to the internally displaced so that their response is automatic. When internally displaced persons are congregated in camps and settlements, for example, UNHCR, UNICEF, and WFP should be expected to play a role, given their expertise. Moreover, when large numbers of internally displaced children are at risk, UNICEF should be expected to come forward and play a dominant role. As already noted, some have suggested that UNHCR assume responsibility for the internally displaced when refugee flows and internal displacement are produced by the same cause and where comprehensive strategies are needed to deal with both groups.

In 1996 a memorandum of understanding was signed between UNHCR and UNICEF, under which UNICEF agreed to assume responsibility for protecting, assisting, and tracing unaccompanied children in their countries of origin. This was the first time UNICEF explicitly agreed to assume a particular responsibility with regard to internally displaced children. Additional agreements should be signed by UNHCR, UNICEF, WFP, and other agencies to delineate responsibilities and make responses more predictable.[184]

Having organizations themselves carve out specific areas of expertise would not only increase predictability but also facilitate the work of resident/humanitarian coordinators. As representatives of the UN system in the field, they should be expected to create in-country task forces on internally displaced persons to promote and maintain appropriate divisions of work. They should also promote the cause of the displaced in their discussions with governments and other appropriate authorities.

In addition, the ERC and in-country mechanisms should explore ways to mobilize donor support for less well known or publicized emergencies. Too much attention is paid to high-profile crises. Whereas funds were readily available to meet humanitarian needs in the former Yugoslavia, other pressing situations were largely ignored, especially in Africa.[185] Also, funds in regional emergencies have often been channeled to refugee programs, to the neglect of the internally displaced, as occurred in the Great Lakes region of Africa.[186] In all situations, coordinating mechanisms should seek to ensure that resources are used in a balanced and equitable way.

Finally, the ERC and IASC should make every effort to shield humanitarian organizations from being used as substitutes for political action. Humanitarian relief in the absence of political solutions has been blamed for prolonging conflicts, strengthening the warring factions, and even empowering militant, genocidal forces. This was said to be the case in the Rwandan crisis and also in the former Yugoslavia. In the latter case, the international community and UN political and military bodies accepted the overrunning of two "safe areas" in Bosnia in July 1995 but expected humanitarian agencies to continue to deliver relief and human rights bodies to continue to document atrocities.[187] In the Sudan, no serious effort has been made to deal with the underlying causes of the conflict, with the result that the fighting has continued and the international community has been left to care for the civilian population.[188] As a forum for developing humanitarian strategies, the IASC, through the ERC, should convey the concerns of humanitarian organizations to the political and peacekeeping parts of the United Nations and press them vigorously to try to resolve crises that are causing or exacerbating mass displacement. Humanitarian organizations could become far more vocal "in demanding political action to resolve inherently political crises," as the case study on Rwanda points out.[189]

Establish a Locus of Responsibility in the IASC

To assist the ERC and IASC in their coordinating roles, the IASC's working group will need to monitor all situations of internal displacement, provide advice on the extent to which the needs of displaced persons are being met, and identify situations in which there are serious gaps in the international response. Working closely with the representative of the secretary-general on internally displaced persons and resident/ humanitarian coordinators in the field, it should bring neglected situations to the IASC's attention.

The working group should also help formulate policy on critical issues. In particular, it should discuss the synergy between protection and assistance and the role resident/humanitarian coordinators could play in improving protection. It should consider ways to strengthen the relationship between UN agencies and the representative of the secretary-general, to ensure, above all, that the representative's recommendations in different countries are carried out. It should discuss the policy issues that arise from resettlement programs, as was the case when the government of Myanmar (Burma) in 1996 asked WHO to assist in resettling tens of thousands of villagers. The question of whether an agency should get involved in a program in which coercion might be an element should be aired by the working group.[190] So should cases in which governments are known to be manipulating UN programs for the displaced.

Strategies also need to be developed to cope with situations in which governments obstruct or refuse access to the international community. Information needs to be collected on these situations, analyses made, and recommendations developed for the IASC on the best means of providing support to the internally displaced. Although UN organizations are generally expected to respond to situations of internal displacement at the request of governments, an interagency forum on internal displacement should be able to look at all situations and not just those that governments want them to examine. In cases where state authority has collapsed or is only gradually reasserting itself, joint strategies are needed for dealing with insurgent forces that often challenge the basic tenets of international protection.

Integrate Protection and Assistance More Effectively

The provision of relief must be part of a larger and more integrated approach that includes the protection of physical safety and human rights. As Secretary-General Kofi Annan has observed, "Where security is present, humanitarian aid reaches those who need it. . . . Where security is absent, humanitarian aid is blocked, violence increases, political stability is weakened, and the situation is exacerbated."[191] The relationship of protection to assistance needs to be fully acknowledged and greater co-ordination forged between UN humanitarian and human rights bodies.

In the first instance, in each and every complex emergency involving the internally displaced, interagency discussions should be held under the umbrella of the IASC on how best to integrate protection and assistance through the joint actions of humanitarian and human rights bodies. The IASC might use the list of protection tasks drawn up by its former task force on internally displaced persons as a yardstick for determining the extent to which member agencies are able to perform these tasks. The list includes negotiating with governments and insurgent forces to pro-mote humanitarian action, raising concerns about the safety and security of the internally displaced, securing safe zones, and ensuring respect for basic human rights.[192]

Interagency needs assessments missions dispatched to different coun-tries at the outset of an emergency should routinely include persons with expertise in protection and human rights. Whether a lead agency is in charge or whether there is an interagency coordinated response, human rights and protection needs should be addressed, as well as those relating to food, health, water, and sanitation; and funds should be raised to cover both sets of needs. Human rights and protection needs should also be addressed during the return and reintegration phase. Whether in Liberia or other countries, it is important to recognize that reintegration assistance cannot be provided effectively without considering issues of human rights and protection, including the continued purchase and use of arms and land mines by warring factions.

UNHCR's director of international protection has urged that in every situation of internal displacement, "leadership on protection matters be clearly established from the outset of the operation."[193] Failure to do so can lead to disasters such as the one that occurred in Kibeho, Rwanda, in 1995, when several thousand internally displaced Hutus sheltered in camps were massacred by the Rwandan army in full view of UN peace-keepers and the staff of international humanitarian relief organizations. No one organization—neither UNHCR nor the human rights field op-eration—had been given a role in protecting the internally displaced in the camps.[194] Only the United Nations Assistance Mission for Rwanda (UNAMIR), a military force, had a mandate explicitly authorizing it to provide protection. But its numbers in the camps were small, and it interpreted its mandate in such a way as to absolve it of responsibility for the protection of the internally displaced from violence committed by government forces. A UN internal evaluation of the incident concluded that protection responsibilities should be assigned clearly in situations of internal displacement and leadership on protection matters clearly established.[195]

UNHCR has repeatedly called for the increased involvement of human rights bodies in field operations. Yet in the former Yugoslavia and Tajikistan it was UNHCR protection officers, not human rights field staff, who became involved in trying to protect the internally displaced. An experienced and well-trained corps of UN human rights protection officers is needed, one that could be activated in situations of internal displacement to work together with humanitarian and development organizations. A corps of protection officers could serve in safe areas and camps. It could play a role in the return of internally displaced persons to their homes or to new areas of relocation. It could provide advice on when conditions are sufficiently safe to warrant return, could monitor and assist in the actual returns, and could help to make areas of return more secure. The international community has long accepted the field protection activities that humanitarian organizations such as UNHCR and ICRC provide. Similar acceptance should be extended to the protection activities of human rights bodies.

Some governments are likely to complain that a human rights protection corps would violate their sovereignty and might deny it entry. The record shows, however, that many governments are willing to accept human rights field staff, but because the UN human rights system is unable to deploy them, they are not used. The Centre for Human Rights, for example, has been unable, because of lack of resources, to send in the requisite number of field staff needed to enhance protection in Burundi, Rwanda, Tajikistan, and the former Yugoslavia.[196] Furthermore, no human rights field staff have been involved in the return process in Angola. In Kenya, a human rights component was omitted from a UNDP return program, with the result that some of the internally displaced were forcibly relocated by the government.[197]

Until the UN human rights system is able to play an effective role, humanitarian and development agencies should themselves assume greater responsibility for protecting the internally displaced. Humanitarian agencies working in the field are often the first to identify protection problems. They should develop procedures for the prompt, efficient, and objective reporting of violations and for channeling the information through the resident/humanitarian coordinator to the UN human rights system and the ERC. They should further explore the extent to which they can promote greater physical safety for the internally displaced through their assistance programs and through advocacy. It bears repeating in this regard that governments are often more inclined to deal with humanitarian and development agencies because they fund activities the governments generally consider desirable and usually regard as neutral.[198] Such organizations can maximize the impact of their aid deliveries by negotiating guarantees for physical protection. They can also integrate human rights and protection concerns into return and reintegration programs.

One way to build closer working relationships between humanitarian and human rights bodies is to draw up actual agreements on protection, such as the one signed in 1995 between UNHCR and the Human Rights Field Operation in Rwanda (HRFOR).[199] This agreement defined the respective responsibilities of both organizations with regard to protecting the physical security and integrity of returning refugees and internally displaced persons and provided for joint action in case of protection problems. It could serve as a model for other interagency protection arrangements.

Increased cooperation between humanitarian and development agencies and the representative of the secretary-general on internally displaced persons would be another means of promoting protection. His visits to countries and dialogues about protection problems offer a forum for highlighting the needs of the internally displaced, and in particular, can prove valuable when humanitarian agencies are constrained from raising issues. According to the letter of understanding signed between the ERC and the representative, the office of the ERC may request the representative to visit particular countries in order to bring greater attention to protection problems. Similar arrangements could be made with other humanitarian organizations. At the same time, protection should be made a part of the mandates of resident/humanitarian coordinators so that they can regularly press the case of the displaced for the entire UN system.

Better training in protection problems needs to be provided to the staff of humanitarian and development agencies and to those in human rights field operations. Training should include instruction on how to identify human rights protection problems, how to report them, and what officers to alert at headquarters and in the field when displaced persons are endangered. It also should provide instruction in the practical measures for enhancing physical safety in the field. The training should include the distinctive protection needs of women and children and demonstrate that the way international assistance programs are planned and implemented has direct bearing on the protection of these groups. To this end, UNHCR guidelines for the protection of refugee women and children and its guidelines against sexual violence should be applied to the internally displaced and made an integral part of training programs. The field experience of ICRC, UNHCR, and NGOs should be incorporated into the training.

Closer relationships also need to be forged by humanitarian and human rights organizations with UN peacekeeping units. Although increasingly called upon to play protection roles in emergency situations, peacekeeping units generally have little or no knowledge of human rights or humanitarian or refugee concerns; are not always obliged to report on human rights abuses; and have little experience in providing protection to civilians in armed conflict situations.[200] Secretary-General Annan has acknowledged that peacekeeping units must be able to address massive abuses of human rights.[201] However, the United Nations still does not offer standard training in human rights to its peacekeeping forces.[202] The units are supposed to be trained by their own governments, but most have no programs in the protection of civilians.[203] As a result, opportunities have been missed for protecting displaced populations. Of course, the failure of UN forces to protect displaced persons in Zepa and Srebrenica, and in Kibeho, Rwanda, were not solely a matter of a deficiency in training; the political will was lacking for the troops to defend persons at risk. But this does not mean it is any less important for the United Nations to ensure that its peacekeepers are trained and capable of assuming the protection functions to which they are assigned.

Specifically, the United Nations must see that its peacekeepers are instructed in human rights and humanitarian standards and in the practical measures needed to protect the physical security of displaced persons. When given a specific protection role, they should have a clear understanding of what that means and be afforded the staff and equipment to make their role effective. To this end, humanitarian and human rights bodies should work assiduously to integrate protection concerns into all the political and peacekeeping operations of the United Nations.[204] The importance the new secretary-general attaches to protection issues should augur well for their integration into the UN's humanitarian and peacekeeping operations.

Strengthen the Position of the Representative of the Secretary-General

The catalytic role played by the representative, particularly in the area of protection, has been recognized by the international community and NGOs. The fact that the representative's position is voluntary and part-time, however, imposes major limitations on his ability to carry out his mandate effectively. Some have therefore suggested that arrangements be made to enable the representative to devote more time to the work of the mandate.[205] He could then increase his visits to different countries, undertake follow-up activities, and accelerate his efforts to promote a normative, institutional, and informational framework for dealing with internal displacement. He would be in a position to respond more fully when he is called upon by governments, intergovernmental bodies, NGOs, and displaced communities to carry out significant protection and assistance functions. He would be able to play a more active role in integrating internal displacement into interagency decisionmaking.

Broader staff support for the representative could be provided with minimum additional cost by working within existing structures. For example, the different human rights, humanitarian, and development bodies associated with the mandate could each contribute a staff member, who would operate from his or her respective institutional base. This system of focal points would increase attention to internal displacement within their respective institutions by helping to integrate the issue into day-to-day decisionmaking. At present, the Centre for Human Rights is the only UN office that formally provides staff support to the representative, even though his functions span humanitarian, development, and prevention issues. A senior staff member within the office of the ERC could oversee the network of focal points in close cooperation with the representative.

In making these changes, it will be important to avoid undercutting the strength the representative now derives from being largely independent. His autonomy has enabled him to set forth his findings freely, work closely with experts and institutes outside the United Nations, and bring innovative ideas to his mandate without requiring "clearances" from the UN system. It has also been possible to solicit institutional support from governments, foundations, NGOs, and research institutions outside the United Nations.

Even if the position were made full-time, it need not be within the UN system. It could be supported outside the United Nations, as is the current position, but it could be given the needed staff support from relevant UN bodies, as already described. Whether it is within the UN system or outside, the important point is that the representative's capacity to act on situations of internal displacement would be strengthened and that he would receive a boost in his role of advocating protection, raising consciousness of displacement problems, and mobilizing effective international responses. Unless and until the UN system is more effectively able to address situations of internal displacement, a strong and concerted effort by the representative will remain essential.

Integrate Relief and Development More Effectively

Because emergency assistance and protection are only the first stages of response in dealing with internal displacement, it is essential that humanitarian and development agencies, in cooperation with international financial institutions, put in place strategies and programs for longer-term solutions. To begin with, it is important that humanitarian agencies base their relief programs on the survival mechanisms and capabilities of the communities concerned so as to avoid creating a dependency syndrome. Tajikistan offers a good example of what can happen when international assistance is not sufficiently directed toward building capabilities for self-reliant rehabilitation. Many of the reintegration projects have had to be redesigned and dependency remains high.[206]

Close coordination between emergency assistance and development aid is also needed. While humanitarian relief agencies are still engaged in providing assistance and protection, development agencies should be drawing up plans to increase the coping capacity of affected areas so that they can effectively absorb uprooted populations. As succinctly stated in a UNHCR paper, "The notion of a continuum, in which UNHCR initiates relief and rehabilitation activities, before 'handing over' to development organizations, is not a useful basis for strategic planning. Sustainable reintegration and recovery requires simultaneous rather than sequential activities."[207] Humanitarian relief and development agencies should develop plans for rehabilitation together. The "traditional dichotomy between relief and development funding and operations" should be abandoned.[208]

Flexible mechanisms need to be created for funding rehabilitation in emergency situations. While humanitarian agencies have contingency funds that they can use in emergencies, development agencies have only limited funds readily available to plan the development work required to increase the absorptive capacity of hosting areas. One way to resolve this problem would be for development agencies to have a "rehabilitation fund" to be used at the discretion of the head of the agency in the same way that humanitarian agencies have "emergency funds." The fund could be used for rehabilitation, reconstruction, and development projects to benefit the whole population of designated areas, irrespective of whether they are internally displaced persons, local residents, returnees, or refugees. This is not a new idea. A UN report issued in 1991 recommended that a feasibility study be conducted to determine where such a fund would be likely to work; the number of refugees, returnees, and internally displaced persons involved; the appropriate level of the fund; the mechanisms and procedures required for its administration; and the attitude of the donor community.[209] It is to be hoped that UNDP's new fund for emergency situations will help provide greater flexibility in disbursing rehabilitation funds in postconflict emergency situations.

The Rwanda case study recommends that special representatives of the secretary-general in different countries have access to "quick-action trust funds" to enable them to respond rapidly to immediate recovery requirements.[210] In Rwanda, it points out, resources were urgently needed to rebuild the justice system, recreate the police force, stabilize the military and build prisons—all of which could have facilitated the return of internally displaced persons and refugees to their homes. Such programs did not fit into the conventional development category, however, and funds were slow in coming. A trust fund at the discretion of the special representative could have helped to fund projects that fell outside the traditional mandates of both humanitarian relief and development agencies.

The case study further recommends that when UN member states are assessed for peacekeeping, the assessments also include emergency recovery activities. In this way, the assets of the peacekeepers themselves would be used to rebuild infrastructure, demobilize soldiers, and create a police force. It observes that "had peacekeeping capacity been used alongside the resources of the humanitarian and development agencies, the potential to move more quickly into essential infrastructural and social rehabilitation would have been in place." [211] Peacekeeping activities would thus become an integral part of the overall effort to respond to the legitimate assistance and infrastructural needs of a society traumatized by conflict.

Both UNHCR and UNDP staff recognize that their operational partnership in reintegration situations should be improved. [212] Quick-impact projects, for example, would have a far better chance of succeeding if they were jointly planned and designed by the two agencies. When this is not feasible, UNHCR might consider making a commitment of two to three years to these projects rather than hastily departing; or it might weigh handing them over to appropriate NGOs and local authorities.

In Ethiopia, UNHCR and UNDP effectively introduced a "cross-mandate" approach that pooled the resources and expertise of relief and development agencies to meet the varied needs of both affected populations and entire areas. [213] In Central America, the UN Development Program for Displaced Persons, Refugees and Returnees (PRODERE) brought together in institutional collaboration relief and development agencies over a five-year period to promote and facilitate the reintegration of more than two million uprooted persons. A human rights component was also built into the process. [214] Approaches such as these should be carefully studied with a view to replicating them in other situations.

Regional processes such as CIREFCA might also be attempted in other areas to encourage governments, NGOs, and relief and development agencies to work together in integrating uprooted persons into national development plans. More recently, the Regional Conference on Assistance to Refugees, Returnees and Displaced Persons in the Great Lakes Region of Africa underscored the importance of developing integrated programs to deal with the relief and development needs of uprooted populations. However, the absence of peace in the area and the failure to develop an effective political framework has to a large extent jeopardized this process.

Conclusion

In one way or another, most major humanitarian, human rights, and development agencies now deal extensively with emergency situations involving internal displacement. Nonetheless, a substantial number of the world's internally displaced populations are not adequately reached through these efforts, which remain by and large ad hoc.

The most pressing gaps in the current system are the unpredictability of responses to crises involving internal displacement, inadequate attention to physical and human rights protection, ineffective coordination, and the weakness of reintegration and development support. Possible remedies for these deficiencies range from creating a new agency to assigning the responsibility to an existing one, to strengthening existing capacities and better coordinating the various actors. For reasons already explained, it seems unlikely that a new institution will be created. Assigning responsibility to an existing organization such as UNHCR could be an effective solution if it were assured the support of other agencies with skills needed to deal with the different phases of internal displacement, and if it received full back-up support from the UN system. But there are also steps that can be taken to strengthen the current collaborative system to improve the international response.

These steps will require dynamic leadership on the part of the ERC and his office. In particular, we have recommended that in each serious situation of internal displacement, the principal responsibility for the internally displaced be assigned to one operational agency. At the same time, there should be an effective interagency coordinating mechanism that will ensure that other agencies carve out specific areas of expertise so that a division of labor can be established in support of the focal point. It is unconscionable that internally displaced persons in camps and settlements still cannot expect predictable responses from the international community while refugees in similar situations almost automatically receive protection and assistance. This failing can be remedied only if agencies begin to commit themselves to particular tasks they can be expected to carry out in situations of internal displacement and agree to broaden their responsibilities in the field.

The UN human rights system must also become far more engaged. Together with humanitarian and development bodies and the political and peacekeeping departments, more effective protection systems must be forged and measures undertaken to prevent further conflict and displacement. In each emergency, leadership on protection matters needs to be established and a united front presented by the United Nations to governments and insurgent groups that challenge the basic tenets of international protection. In responding to reintegration and recovery needs, development agencies need far more flexible mechanisms and a broader conception of development to cover the restoration of judicial systems and the promotion and protection of human rights. A comprehensive approach that brings together the different parts of the United Nations will create a more effective system. It must build upon existing capacities but include major reforms.

CHAPTER FIVE

The Role of Nongovernmental Organizations

International NGOs will continue to bear the brunt of operations [to reach the victims of conflict]. While many new local NGOs will spring up and some of the existing ones may expand and become more professional, most will find it difficult to work in conflicts because their governments can pressure their staffs to comply with government policies. . . . International NGOs, supported by donors, can better stand up to repressive governments.
—Frederick C. Cuny, President, Intertect, 1992

NONGOVERNMENTAL ORGANIZATIONS have become a critical component of international humanitarian operations. Since the end of the cold war, NGOs have emerged as major actors in the fields of humanitarian relief, development, human rights advocacy, and most important, internal displacement.[1] Sometimes they are the only ones on the ground working to protect and assist the displaced populations.

NGOs have been successful because of their flexibility, speed, and moral courage. As former Secretary-General Boutros-Ghali has observed, "NGOs were more important in Somalia than the agencies of the United Nations. When the agencies of the United Nations were afraid of the situation, the NGOs were already on the ground."[2] As their credibility and expertise have grown, the aid that governments and the public channel through NGOs, especially the international ones, has also increased to the point where some surpass UN agencies in their relief operations.[3] NGOs are now the second largest source of relief and development assistance after bilateral governmental donors.[4] They are also the main implementing partners of UN agencies in emergency situations, directly delivering humanitarian assistance, setting up water and sanitation systems, offering a modicum of protection, and providing reintegration and development support. By voicing their concerns through the media and playing advocacy roles with governments and intergovernmental organizations, international NGOs have become an important political force.

Some twenty international NGOs in the United States and twenty in Europe are sufficiently involved in complex emergencies to have a substantial impact on the ground.[5] Of these, "perhaps ten U.S. and another ten European NGOs receive seventy-five percent of all the public funds spent by NGOs in complex emergencies."[6] The annual budgets of some of the major international NGOs are now close to the $500 million mark.[7] In third world countries with ineffective or nonfunctioning governments, international NGOs have sometimes assumed responsibility for running vital public institutions and services.

But as NGOs have become more involved in internal conflicts and situations of internal displacement, their weaknesses and shortcomings have also become evident.[8] Their activities are frequently uncoordinated. They may espouse broad humanitarian principles, but the services of some may target one religious or ethnic group over another. NGO assistance may also inadvertently prolong conflicts by permitting belligerents to continue fighting while their civilian populations are cared for by the international community. Moreover, their increasing dependence on governmental funding may compromise their independence and freedom of action.

Because they have emerged as one of the critical participants in international humanitarian response, we asked the Norwegian Refugee Council to investigate how a broad cross section of international NGOs addresses the assistance, protection, and development needs of internally displaced persons. This chapter, which is based primarily on the NRC report, examines the policy orientation of a number of prominent international NGOs with regard to internally displaced persons, identifies the major obstacles and problems they have encountered, and makes recommendations for improving their role, particularly with regard to protection.[9]

Selection of NGOs

Thirteen organizations were selected for the NRC study on the basis of their experience with internally displaced persons.[10] They reflect a wide range of mandates, structures, traditions, and sizes and have developed expertise in one or more of the following areas: emergency relief, protection and human rights matters, rehabilitation and development, and the prevention and resolution of conflicts.

Ten of the NGOs deliver services directly to the internally displaced: CARE USA, Caritas Internationalis, International Federation of Red Cross and Red Crescent Societies (IFRC), International Islamic Relief Organization, Jesuit Refugee Service (JRS), Lutheran World Federation (LWF), Médecins sans Frontières (MSF), OXFAM, World Council of Churches (WCC), and World Vision. Two, Human Rights Watch and World Wide Fund for Nature International, focus on changing and informing the policies and practices of governments and intergovernmental organizations; and one, International Alert, specializes in conflict prevention.

Their organizational structures vary, but there is an increasing trend among all to work more closely with local groups. Some operate from an international headquarters with a network of small field offices at their disposal. While policy is set by the headquarters, programs are implemented in collaboration with local staff and local NGOs.[11] Others constitute an international umbrella organization with independent constituent members at the regional and national level, with decisionmaking power channeled through governing bodies.[12] Still others are national organizations that belong to an international group but have their own field presence and local staff and coordinate their work through an international office or directly among themselves.[13] Many have established liaison offices in Brussels, Geneva, New York, and Washington so as to be close to donor governments, intergovernmental organization headquarters, and political decisionmaking.

Mandates and Policies on Internally Displaced Persons

For the most part, the mandates and charters of the NGOs delivering services do not specifically direct them to help or target the internally displaced. As one NGO spokesperson put it, "It is important to say that neither we nor any other NGO . . . has any formal 'mandate' to work with IDPs. To the extent that we are doing so, it is on the basis of an interpretation of our charitable objectives; but in formal (legal) terms we have no such mandate but are self-appointed."[14]

Nonetheless, NGO programs have increasingly begun to encompass the internally displaced either as people in need of humanitarian assistance or as victims of conflict, human rights abuses, or environmental degradation. The numbers, need, and lack of institutional responsibility for the internally displaced have largely propelled NGOs into this arena. Nearly half of the NGOs interviewed said they actively seek to respond to crises of internal displacement. As OXFAM put it, "Refugees are almost automatically assisted. . . . Too often, IDPs are not."[15] Some NGOs include the internally displaced in a larger category of persons, which WCC has labeled "uprooted people" and takes to include both refugees and the internally displaced.[16] Together with Caritas Internationalis and LWF, it has issued "a call to action" appealing to all member churches to respond to the problems of the forcibly displaced.[17] Human Rights Watch, too, has adopted a policy on forced relocations, and it has designated staff members to serve as focal points for refugees and internally displaced persons in its geographic divisions of Africa, Asia, and the Americas. IFRC has also adopted policy statements on refugees and internally displaced persons as part of a larger category of persons in need.

For other NGOs, their involvement in situations of internal displacement depends on the inability or unwillingness of the national authorities to respond. MSF, for example, launches missions "in areas where either war, massive population movements, famine, or natural disasters have led to a situation where outside assistance is considered necessary."[18] Still other NGOs become involved in situations that might not normally be of great concern to the international community. For example, LWF has programs for internally displaced persons in Mauritania that seek "to limit environmental degradation and slow the exodus of the rural population toward urban centers" through development activities at the community and village level.[19] For Human Rights Watch, involvement depends on whether the persons are "the target of human rights abuse." This includes persons displaced by natural disasters if the government has denied them assistance as "a result of discrimination or hostility toward the IDPs because of ethnicity, race, politics, religion, class."[20]

Definitional Issues

In the absence of an internationally accepted global definition of internally displaced persons, some NGOs have constructed and employed their own definitions for the purposes of their programs. In Peru, MSF staff found it useful to define internally displaced persons as those displaced by violence within the past five years. Most others adhere to the UN working definition or to the one put forward by the Permanent Consultation on Internal Displacement in the Americas (see chapter 2).

Some NGOs use definitions that do not differentiate between internally displaced persons and refugees. LWF, for one, targets those who have been "uprooted as a result of natural disaster, civil conflicts, ethnic strife, economic deprivation and other injustices," thereby placing refugees, internally displaced persons, and economic migrants within the same category.[21] Others focus on persons in need, irrespective of whether they are internally displaced.

Nonetheless, many NGOs consider a definition of the internally displaced valuable to help focus their attention on such populations, especially when organizational priorities are set and resources are mobilized.[22] All of those surveyed emphasized that internal displacement could easily fall outside their purview, given the problem of mandates and limited funds for emergencies.

Those who favor a definition insist on its being broad enough to account for specific regional and local conditions. Like the Oslo Declaration and Plan of Action, which emerged from the partnership in action (PARINAC) consultations between UNHCR and several hundred NGOs, they point to the utility of a "flexible" definition.[23]

Scope of Assistance Activities and the Need for Coordination

NGOs, like intergovernmental organizations, divide crises involving the internally displaced into phases that range from initial emergency to rehabilitation to development. For each phase, NGOs have planning horizons that range from six months for emergency programs to five years for development-oriented assistance.

Most of the NGOs surveyed considered the provision of emergency assistance their main priority. But a frequent concern of the NGOs was that their assistance would create dependency. As a result, many have developed standing arrangements with partner organizations that specialize in development. They have also sought to involve more beneficiaries in the design and implementation of assistance programs and to train local personnel to provide assistance. Many realize that the failure to utilize and strengthen local capacities increases the vulnerability of beneficiary populations. They now see their assistance programs within a broader framework of reintegration and development. As one explained: "We are concerned about perpetuating displacement or even causing it by making assistance available." [24]

When working with the internally displaced, most NGOs concentrate on providing food and health services. But many can be relied upon to provide broader services. Some include the provision of water and sanitation and social and community services in their packages. Nearly half the NGOs surveyed provide shelter for the internally displaced and about half provide income-generation projects. Many provide special services for women, children, the elderly, the disabled and those with chronic health problems. Several have developed special psychosocial support services to meet the needs of persons traumatized by conflict or human rights abuses. Other specialized services include legal counseling and training and dialogue for the resolution and prevention of conflict. The policy-oriented NGOs have developed expertise in areas such as early warning, environmental conservation, and human rights advocacy.

The majority of the NGOs reported that they usually provide assistance in more than one sector. At the same time, many have not developed the capacity to identify or respond to needs that fall outside their traditional areas of involvement. One consequence is that the needs of internally displaced persons that go beyond their areas of expertise may fail to be assessed or addressed in situations of poor coordination. As one NGO remarked: "Everyone is doing bits and pieces without focusing attention on their whole range of needs." [25]

Better coordination was one of the main recommendations NGOs made for improving assistance activities for internally displaced persons. In a given emergency, as many as 100 to 200 NGOs may come into a country in a matter of weeks. In Rwanda, nearly 200 mostly foreign NGOs were operating in the country, and in Angola there were more than 100. Uncoordinated action has been found to lead to inadequate geographical and sectoral coverage, duplication, competition, and ineffective use of resources.[26] One former UN official spoke of "the potential for chaos" that such relief floods create.[27]

NGOs generally look to the United Nations and the host government to organize coordination, since they are considered more institutionally capable. NGOs have found, however, as has this study (see chapter 4), that UN coordination mechanisms in situations of internal displacement are often weak. Most felt that the United Nations should designate an operational focal point to coordinate protection, assistance and reintegration support for the internally displaced. Some felt that it should assign greater authority and resources to an existing agency, such as UNHCR, to ensure that the needs of the internally displaced are addressed.

At the same time, NGOs have begun to try to coordinate their own activities more effectively. Unlike UN agencies, however, NGOs are completely separate entities without organizational ties, joint funding appeals, or a set of common standards by which they are bound. Efforts to improve coordination have been undertaken by NGO umbrella groups such as the International Council of Voluntary Agencies (ICVA) and the American Council for Voluntary International Action (InterAction), which has developed a field coordination protocol for NGOs.[28] Such groups have sought to develop joint NGO positions to maximize impact on governments and intergovernmental bodies.

In the field, NGOs sometimes select a "focal point" to coordinate on their behalf and act as liaison with the UN. They did so in Mozambique, where an NGO umbrella organization was set up, and in Afghanistan.[29] In Rwanda, Save the Children Fund-US became the focal point and assisted the NGO community with information, registration, and coordination with the United Nations. This in turn enhanced the UN's ability to provide grants to NGOs for projects on internally displaced persons.[30] NGOs have also sought to develop common standards and rules of behavior to guide their operations in the field.

Improving NGO Practices

Some NGOs have been criticized for carrying out political agendas, proselytizing, favoring certain groups over others, prolonging wars, showing insensitivity to local customs, paying insufficient attention to the role of women, and creating dependency among populations.[31] Unilateral actions by individual agencies have been found to jeopardize the credibility and effectiveness of the entire NGO community.

To guard against such actions, a code of conduct was developed in 1994 by the International Red Cross and Red Crescent Movement and NGOs in Disaster Relief.[32] Its purpose is to standardize the behavior of agencies engaged in delivering relief. More than one hundred NGOs have pledged adherence to it thus far. The code commits its subscribers to provide assistance on the basis of need, irrespective of the political or religious views of the recipients. It also affirms that assistance should not be driven "by the need to dispose of donor commodity surpluses, nor by the political interest of any particular donor." It promises that in providing assistance, NGOs will involve the beneficiaries, support the role of women, and strengthen local capacities, and that NGOs will "avoid competing" for media coverage in situations where such coverage may work to the detriment of the service being provided the beneficiaries.

In Liberia, NGOs, intergovernmental bodies, and donor agencies also drew up joint "principles and protocols for operation."[33] These principles specifically prohibited NGO acceptance of "conditions" to gain access to beleaguered populations, such as paying bribes to authorities or providing other advantages. They also asserted that "a much stronger front" for negotiating and maintaining access to populations would be created "if all agencies apply the same principles," and that the responsibility of NGOs is to work in "all" areas of a country rather than focus on those areas the government or United Nations might prefer. At the same time, the joint statement called on NGOs to ask questions about whether the humanitarian assistance they are providing "benefits the factions and as a consequence prolongs the fighting."

Reflected in the principles were the difficult dilemmas NGOs face in trying to reach people in need. If an NGO upholds its standards and refuses conditions, for example, it may be denied access, but if it compromises, its concessions may become the first of many.[34] Moreover, if it withdraws aid because it has become an instrument of conflict, this may prove harmful to displaced persons at risk. That NGOs should be aware of the political consequences of the assistance they provide is strongly reflected in the statement. Also reflected is the view that joint NGO action commands more authority and has a better chance of ensuring that assistance is delivered in accordance with humanitarian norms.

Concerns about the politicization of humanitarian aid are particularly relevant when it comes to providing assistance to internally displaced persons. As Human Rights Watch has observed, the "displaced are often convenient bait . . . to attract international relief supplies that could then be diverted for military uses."[35] In Rwanda, Hutu militants and *genocidaires* were able to support their activities through the food aid provided to camps of internally displaced persons.[36] In Ethiopia, Somalia, and the Sudan, humanitarian assistance also has been found to reinforce conditions creating conflict.[37] This has led some humanitarian experts to propose "new paradigms" for emergencies in which priority is given to pressing authorities to assume maximum responsibility for their own citizens while empowering communities to take care of their needs themselves.[38] Although these solutions are theoretically compelling, substantial international assistance will doubtless remain the only way of saving lives in many instances. Rather, NGOs and other humanitarian agencies need to identify inventive ways of minimizing the danger of doing harm through their assistance. They need to seek means of providing aid in a way that undercuts aid diversions and together take tougher stances toward governments and insurgent groups that abuse assistance.[39] And in concert, they need to insist on more effective responses by the international community; in particular, civilians and combatants need to be separated in camp situations and conditions placed on aid when necessary. The Refugee Policy Group considers "the capacity to separate civilians from the military" to be a "key ingredient" in depoliticizing aid.[40] The efforts it identifies to separate noncombatants from combatants range from establishing displaced persons camps that do not accept belligerents to "peace havens" in which the combatants refrain from operating so that assistance can be provided. NGO codes of conduct are also an important means of drawing attention to the broader political framework in which aid is provided and help reduce the chances of NGO participation in actions that reinforce conflicts. There will of course be times when basic humanitarian standards are so undermined that NGOs may have little choice but to withdraw, as would be the case when they find that they risk more lives by acquiescing to conditions imposed by faction leaders or host authorities than by withdrawing from the operation.[41]

Protection and Human Rights Concerns

Another contentious issue confronting operational NGOs is whether they should limit themselves to the provision of humanitarian assistance or also bear some responsibility in ensuring that the physical protection and fundamental human rights of the beneficiaries are respected. IFRC framed the question in these terms: "Keeping someone alive ensures their most basic human right, but should humanitarian agencies do no more than feed the hungry? If aid workers police human rights, will this hamper their ability to work with all those in need?"[42]

Traditionally, NGOs have taken the position that humanitarian agencies "should not take sides in hostilities or engage at any time in controversies of a political, racial, religious, or ideological nature."[43] Neutrality has been seen to be the best way to ensure the right to receive and to offer humanitarian assistance. Human rights advocacy has been viewed as possibly undermining the principle of neutrality and leading to expulsion and denial of access to populations that critically need assistance.[44]

A more recent view, however, is that those who witness violations of human rights and humanitarian law cannot remain silent: "a silent witness to an abuse is necessarily a complicit witness."[45] Silence, moreover, may encourage parties to a conflict to manipulate aid and undermine the human rights of the beneficiaries.

In MSF's view, the operational decisions of humanitarian organizations must be "clearly guided by human rights considerations"; otherwise, they will make "unacceptable compromises" in providing assistance and may also ignore protection concerns.[46] But the dilemma for humanitarian organizations of acting as advocates for human rights concerns while at the same time claiming to be neutral is a real one. As one NGO representative observed: "If human rights testimony is not neutral, can humanitarian intervention remain or claim to be impartial? . . . We are asked to deal with the root causes of humanitarian emergencies. How can we deal with root causes without taking very political positions, without advocating against human rights abuses, breaking the silence that the UN and many NGOs insist is necessary for them to continue their work in conflict zones?"[47]

Nonetheless, the growing realization that the political and human rights context of an emergency affects humanitarian action has led some NGOs to explore the possibility of removing the principle of neutrality from their mandates and replacing it with the principle of "nonpartisanship," or impartiality. Thus if one side in a conflict were committing serious violations of human rights and humanitarian law, the NGO would not have to be neutral, only impartial in its delivery of assistance. Alternatively, some have suggested that the principle of neutrality need not preclude taking positions or acting on human rights violations. Remaining neutral in a conflict need not be incompatible with impartially assessing human rights conditions and communicating the information.[48] Moreover, assessing violations on all sides of a conflict accords with neutrality.

Current Policies of NGOs on Protection

None of the NGOs surveyed felt that they must totally divorce the protection of human rights from the humanitarian assistance they provide. The majority considered that their assistance activities in fact protected human rights. The main point of contention was the extent to which they should become involved in activities such as collecting and forwarding human rights information, interceding with government officials, and publicly condemning violations. Only a few of the operational NGOs had engaged in these kinds of activity.

Although no NGO has a formal mandate to protect civilians (ICRC belongs to a separate category; see chapter 4), two have policies that in effect constitute protection roles. MSF, for example, has a policy of "temoignage," or witnessing, which includes establishing presence near people in danger, reporting on their condition, and engaging in public condemnation when there are massive and repeated violations of human rights and humanitarian law.[49] The policy explicitly includes internally displaced persons insofar as it prescribes advocacy for civilian populations that are forcibly relocated in violation of humanitarian law.

WCC's policy on uprooted people also calls for a wide range of protection activities for internally displaced persons and others who are uprooted, including advocacy, the provision of sanctuary and legal aid, conflict resolution activities, and the monitoring of returns. Although not an operational organization, Human Rights Watch has established a policy on forced relocation that has direct relevance to the protection of internally displaced persons. It regularly documents violations against displaced persons and through its reports brings these to international attention. Other NGOs have been developing protection policies, in particular JRS and International Alert.

A major complaint of the NGOs was the lack of an international instrument that explicitly identifies the protection needs of the internally displaced. Many, as a result, support the initiative of the representative of the secretary-general to establish guiding principles.[50]

Forms of Protection

The NGO survey yielded four broad categories of protection, ranging from least to most active: protection that results from presence and the provision of assistance; protection from community building efforts; protection as a result of advocacy work; and direct intervention to protect physical safety.

PROTECTION THROUGH ASSISTANCE AND PRESENCE. Some NGOs defined the provision of assistance as a form of protection. Since assistance provides life-saving and life-sustaining aid, it "protects" the internally displaced from illness and starvation and secures fundamental human rights such as the right to life, the right to medical care, and the right to shelter. Also, the way assistance is provided can enhance the security of internally displaced persons. Some NGOs, for example, have promoted protection by providing fuel to women so that they do not have to walk into dangerous territory to gather firewood; or they have furnished adequate lighting in camps and settlements to promote safety at night. This kind of preventive protection has for its source UNHCR's guidelines on the protection of refugee women and children, which NGOs are beginning to apply to internally displaced populations.[51]

The presence of NGOs also affords a degree of protection to the internally displaced. "We usually offer protection just by being there, as outsiders," said one NGO. National authorities, NGOs report, are often hesitant to commit serious human rights violations in the presence of nonnationals. At the same time, NGOs admit that presence may offer only "incidental protection," especially in the midst of conflict. To be most effective, presence has to be combined with some form of action or at least a readiness to report violations.

The "way aid workers behave" is critical to the security of internally displaced persons.[52] The code of conduct for the International Red Cross Movement and NGOs seeks to strengthen their accountability to beneficiaries and promote the application of ethical and moral standards in humanitarian operations. Among the key elements it has identified to enhance security are open and continuous dialogue with the beneficiary community; the involvement of the beneficiary and host communities in the relief operation; commitment to a long-term agenda to increase trust; and a clear humanitarian agenda that is separate from political and military issues.

PROTECTION THROUGH COMMUNITY BUILDING. Many NGOs engage local government officials and local communities in seeking solutions to problems of protection. WCC has directed its member churches to strengthen relations with refugee and migration ministries.[53] International Alert has identified four ways in which NGOs can increase protection: by helping governments revise national legislation and practices that may jeopardize the security of the internally displaced; by supporting local NGOs working with the internally displaced; by supporting national reconciliation efforts; and by helping governments to create viable mechanisms to cope with crisis situations.[54]

NGOs have also encouraged local communities to mount collective efforts. In Guatemala, WCC, through a local implementing partner, has been involved in a campaign to promote legal protection and recognition for internally displaced persons. Another NGO has established a neighbor warning system that watches routes and fields at night in Peru. World Vision observes that "a growing awareness and increasing sense of confidence and dignity result from community development enabling the poor themselves to recognize unjust conditions and to begin working for change."[55]

Communities have also been encouraged to increase multiethnic programs to encourage contact and trust among different groups. WCC, for example, promotes the integration of displaced populations into local communities by encouraging its member churches to examine and challenge negative portrayals of the displaced. It also encourages church bodies to bring the issue of displacement to national and local policy-making bodies and to build alliances with trade unions and other community-based groups committed to addressing issues of human rights and justice.[56]

PROTECTION THROUGH ADVOCACY. Most of the NGOs that participated in the study reported that they engaged in advocacy work on behalf of the internally displaced. This meant raising issues, either publicly or privately, in order to improve the basic living conditions, security and human rights of the displaced.

Some limited their advocacy to publicizing information about their own operations in order to increase public awareness about the plight of populations they were assisting and raise funds for their programs. Others sought to promote more effective international policies and programs by publishing reports on specific situations and condemning violations against the internally displaced.[57] Several directed their advocacy toward the United Nations, particularly the Commission on Human Rights.[58] Others have played an active role in alerting UNHCR's Executive Committee to the plight of the internally displaced and have brought situations of internal displacement to UN interagency bodies.[59]

What is particularly important is that several NGOs have assumed a watchdog role with regard to UN operations to make sure that they serve the needs of the internally displaced. MSF, for example, has conducted surveys of the health and nutritional situation of internally displaced populations to highlight the discrepancy between the needs of these populations and the actions of UN agencies. In Sierra Leone, it found severe malnutrition among the internally displaced at the time that WFP was terminating its assistance programs. It used its nutritional surveys of the camps to help turn the situation around.

NGOs have also challenged UN agencies for allowing governments to manipulate programs intended to enhance the security and welfare of the internally displaced. In Kenya, Human Rights Watch found UNDP to be "damaging its credibility" by agreeing to be an implementing partner in a resettlement program for internally displaced persons in which "blatant human rights violations are taking place, such as brutality against displaced persons, forced relocations and dispersal of camps."[60] In the Sudan, NGOs also criticized UN agencies for allowing the government to manipulate Operation Lifeline Sudan, to the detriment of internally displaced persons.[61] NGOs have been vocal as well when UN operations appear to be compromising the security of civilians, as was the case in the safe havens in the former Yugoslavia, or when humanitarian aid is the sole response to situations in which human rights are flagrantly violated and political solutions are sorely needed.[62] According to MSF: "The international community at large, and western governments in particular, have to accept that it is not the role of humanitarian organisations to provide the solutions to a problem. Our role is to help the people in danger. . . . We should not accept our actions being used as a political fig-leaf."[63]

Several of the NGOs surveyed utilize human rights standards as the basis for advocating better treatment for internally displaced persons. In such cases, the NGO may bring information on violations of human rights and humanitarian law to the attention of governments. Or it may provide the information to donor governments and to UN agencies to prompt their intervention. Or it may provide information to international criminal tribunals for purposes of prosecution, or to the media.

These activities are primarily undertaken by human rights NGOs. Humanitarian organizations[64] generally look to human rights groups for advocacy because the latter are not operational and do not have to face the problem of expulsion. Nonetheless, some humanitarian organizations, such as MSF, have been bold in speaking out about violations against internally displaced persons.[65] The price has sometimes been high. In 1984, in retaliation for its public protests against the forcible relocation of Tigreans in Ethiopia, MSF was expelled from the country and its aid programs withdrawn. But its actions also brought forced relocations to international attention and helped stem the practice. In most situations, however, MSF's actions have shown "that it is possible to speak out against abuse and also maintain a field presence." [66]

Other humanitarian NGOs, such as IFRC, do not, as a matter of policy, speak out about human rights violations. When IFRC staff witness abuses in the field, they may interfere, in an ad hoc, informal, and quiet way with governments or may share information with ICRC. In IFRC's view, its national societies do not have the possibility of speaking out because they "have to live in those countries where both humanitarian and human rights issues may be contentious. For them, the luxury of making an advocacy statement and then being expelled or voluntarily leaving a country may not exist."

Recently human rights and humanitarian organizations have begun to discuss how to strengthen cooperation in emergency situations involving the internally displaced. A review of the proceedings of one major conference reveals many NGOs were deeply concerned that they might jeopardize their missions by becoming too involved in human rights monitoring and reporting.[67] Yet the very fact of the meeting demonstrated a readiness to work together to increase protection for displaced populations by sharing resources, knowledge, and expertise in a more organized way.

PROTECTION THROUGH DIRECT ACTION. Providing protection on the ground is a skill in which most NGOs are not trained or experienced. Some staff members consider it too dangerous unless it is done under the auspices of UN operations whereas others may become engaged on an ad hoc basis. Some have become directly engaged in hiding or helping to evacuate internally displaced persons. An implementing partner of WCC helped internally displaced persons flee from their home areas in a Latin American country that was beset by violence. Similarly, in the former Yugoslavia, MSF set up medical facilities along evacuation routes to provide assistance to internally displaced persons in flight. NGOs have also helped the internally displaced to move and settle in safer parts of their countries, and church groups have set up refuge centers for the displaced. Because the protection efforts of UNHCR and ICRC have been overwhelmed by recent crises, "the increased participation of relief and human rights NGOs in protection activities on the ground is arguably not only necessary, but critical." [68]

Strategies for Improving Protection

Humanitarian NGOs surveyed in this study frequently asked how they could work more effectively to improve protection for internally displaced persons. Because of their field presence, they often became aware of protection problems before anyone else. Their staffs were also larger and had greater access to financial resources than human rights groups. Their charters and mandates, moreover, contained standards and values drawn from international human rights and humanitarian law that presented an opportunity for them to assess their operations in the light of the principles they espoused and seek ways to better integrate such concerns into their organization's programs. From the information that the NGOs themselves have provided, several suggestions emerge that can facilitate the work of NGOs in dealing with protection concerns.

DESIGN ASSISTANCE PROGRAMS TO PROMOTE PROTECTION. NGOs have found that the design of an assistance program can affect the security of the beneficiaries. As earlier noted, assistance programs that pay attention to the layout of camps, the placement of lighting, and other practical measures can go a long way toward enhancing security. UNHCR's guidelines on the protection of refugee women and children should therefore be routinely applied in situations of internal displacement. In addition, assistance programs need to be designed to address the psychosocial needs of the internally displaced, given the psychological and physical trauma they may have experienced.

ENGAGE BENEFICIARIES IN PROTECTION. In many instances, human rights discourse and humanitarian intervention fail to engage beneficiaries in the process. To empower internally displaced persons and enhance their protection, they should be active participants in protection programs, and information should be provided to them on human rights and humanitarian standards and relevant domestic mechanisms that they might utilize. Programs developed to protect internally displaced women against sexual violence or that provide legal counseling and representation should be designed in close consultation with the women concerned. Information and training should also be provided to members of the surrounding community and to local officials to acquaint them with their obligations.

INCREASE PRESENCE WHEN PROTECTION PROBLEMS ARISE. When protection problems first appear, additional NGO field staff should be sent out in an effort to prevent abuses. Too often, monitoring occurs after situations have gotten out of hand. In particular, human rights NGOs, which are generally not operational, should consider establishing a field presence to monitor, report, and work together with humanitarian NGOs in developing protection strategies. In some situations, their staff could act as assistants to humanitarian organizations working with the internally displaced or serve as members of mobile teams accompanying refugees or displaced people on the move. Despite the obstacles, steps can be taken to provide better protection, especially through increased on-the-ground presence and through closer cooperation between humanitarian and human rights NGOs.[69]

COMMUNICATE INFORMATION TO THOSE WHO CAN ACT UPON IT. More and more NGOs seem to be urging humanitarian NGOs to communicate information on human rights violations against internally displaced and other affected populations to human rights organizations and others who can act upon it. As the NRC has observed, "Sharing and maintaining an accurate and unbiased flow of information is a prerequisite to providing displaced populations with effective protection."[70] "Silence," on the other hand, "is the best friend of human rights violations. As long as they are not exposed and opposed they continue unchallenged."[71] Failure to transmit information that could be critical for the security and well-being of displaced populations would be "unconscionable," in the view of the executive director of the Refugee Policy Group.[72]

By forwarding information, humanitarian NGOs act as intermediaries. This allows them to avoid the repercussions associated with stronger actions while drawing upon the expertise of those who specialize in human rights and protection. Nonetheless, the sharing of information can be a delicate undertaking in countries whose governments refuse to accept the criticisms leveled at their humanitarian or human rights record by agencies operating in the country. Human Rights Watch, for example, relies heavily on humanitarian organizations for information about internally displaced persons and "for advice, logistics, and locating particular victims and witnesses." But it has been careful not to attribute its information to these organizations because doing so could in certain circumstances jeopardize the security of NGO staff and the continuation of their programs.[73]

Information should be shared early on when human rights problems are easier to address. Some humanitarian NGOs have a threshold below which they do not act (that is, massive and repeated violations). As a result, not enough attention may be paid to the earlier stages of violations, during which preventive action can be taken more effectively.

BETTER COORDINATE PROTECTION ACTIVITIES. The Oslo Declaration and Plan of Action calls for the establishment of "coordinating mechanisms for the implementation of protection activities."[74] While coordination mechanisms in the area of assistance and development are often established, protection is rarely coordinated or even discussed.

Several coordination arrangements are possible in the protection area. As suggested in chapter 4, in-country task forces composed of UN agencies and NGOs could be created that focus not only on assistance but also on protection. Such mechanisms could seek to anticipate protection problems, explore ways to avert them, and seek to overcome constraints. Protocols could be developed to harmonize action on protection in particular situations. The protocol developed by NGOs, UN agencies and ICRC in Liberia set forth principles of action to protect and assist civilian populations, including the displaced.[75]

Joint policy statements could go a long way toward enhancing protection. While one vocal NGO can be easily singled out by a government for expulsion, it is much harder and more costly for a government to take punitive measures against all NGOs. By terminating NGO programs, a government could erode popular support and influence donors and UN agencies to take action in protest. NGO umbrella groups could play an important role in promoting joint positions and defending NGOs that undertake protection activities and as a result are threatened with harassment or expulsion.

The most effective method of coordination would be to divide substantive responsibility between humanitarian and human rights NGOs in a given emergency. An increasing number of NGOs are recognizing that shared responsibility is essential and that the distinctions traditionally drawn between human rights and humanitarian work are often artificial.[76] Consequently, a common platform of action is becoming more visible. MSF's 1996 conference for humanitarian and human rights organizations was a pioneering effort to develop a framework for cooperation in conflict situations.[77] In the declaration it adopted, a common aim was to increase respect for human rights and humanitarian law and to call for "complementary and mutually reenforcing" methods of working together.[78]

NGOs can also strengthen protection by coordinating more of their activities with those of donor governments and UN agencies, whose intercessions may prove critical to gaining access to the internally displaced. UNHCR, in particular, through the PARINAC process, has sought to improve its working relations with NGOs to enhance protection for both internally displaced persons and refugees.

SUPPORT COMMUNITY-BASED PROTECTION. Civil society and community structures can be an important source of protection for internally displaced persons. Indeed, country studies compiled by the representative of the secretary-general on internally displaced persons indicate that a major source of vulnerability for internally displaced persons is the fact that they are separated from their communities.[79] "Practical protection," UNHCR has observed, "is provided first of all by and through the local community, through a complex social network including family, clan, village or tribe."[80] Therefore activities that encourage the restoration of communal links or promote the integration of internally displaced persons into the surrounding community can contribute to their security. Conflict prevention, conflict resolution, and the facilitation of reconciliation all fall within the scope of such activities.[81]

Several of the NGOs surveyed have undertaken measures to engage the local community and the government in the protection of internally displaced persons. These have included promoting social relations among different cultural, ethnic, religious groups; facilitating conflict resolution and reconciliation; supporting local NGOs in extending assistance and protection to internally displaced persons; urging the government to respect the rights of internally displaced persons; and invoking national laws, when they exist, to extend protection to the internally displaced.

ENSURE THAT PROGRAMS ARE CONSISTENT WITH HUMAN RIGHTS. In accordance with the International Red Cross Movement code of conduct, NGOs should regularly evaluate the impact of their interventions and ensure that the immediate and long-term consequences are consistent with the human rights of the beneficiaries and surrounding communities. Assessments should be made of whether the humanitarian assistance is lending legitimacy to a repressive regime or insurgent group, the extent to which the assistance is reaching the intended beneficiaries, and whether the operation reinforces discriminatory or harmful practices, particularly against women. Providers of humanitarian assistance have to take into account the broader political and human rights context in which the aid is delivered.

ESTABLISH TRAINING PROGRAMS FOR OPERATIONAL STAFF. Both humanitarian and human rights NGOs have acknowledged that their staffs need better training in protection issues. Humanitarian NGOs should have a better understanding of human rights issues and the capacity to react to human rights violations within the boundaries of their organizations' mandates. They should be given training in human rights and humanitarian law and in the guiding principles on internal displacement appended to this volume. The *Compilation and Analysis of Legal Norms* on which the principles are largely based should also be part of the training. UNHCR has already developed a manual for its field staff based on the *Compilation and Analysis*. The training should further cover how to collect and report on protection problems concerning the internally displaced and how to bring such information to those who can act upon it. It should include practical measures for enhancing physical safety, especially for women and children.

For their part, human rights organizations would benefit from training in humanitarian standards and operations. Too often internal displacement is viewed as a "humanitarian" issue outside their traditional areas of concern.[82] Focusing almost exclusively on civil and political rights, they often fail to see that violations of the right to adequate shelter, food, or health care may also be human rights problems falling within their sphere of action. As human rights NGOs become more operational, they will need training in response to humanitarian emergencies and in the practical measures to increase protection on the ground.

To promote training, OXFAM is developing a human rights manual for its field staff, and UNHCR together with several NGOs has been putting together a protection guide for staff working with refugees and internally displaced persons. The Office of the UN High Commissioner for Human Rights and UNHCR could play a valuable role by organizing training courses for NGOs.

Promoting Durable Solutions

The NGOs surveyed generally emphasized the need to be cautious in promoting too rapid "solutions" for internally displaced persons. Wherever peace remains fragile, internally displaced persons must have time to question whether they can return in safety and dignity. It takes time to address the root causes of displacement through the resolution of tensions and laying the groundwork for sustainable development. International organizations and governments, in their view, tend to promote hasty solutions in order to exit quickly.

The Oslo Declaration and Plan of Action specifically called upon UNHCR and NGOs to cooperate in the formulation and implementation of assistance programs to enable the internally displaced to reintegrate. Of the surveyed NGOs, the tasks they were ready to assume included monitoring conditions in areas to which internally displaced persons were returning or relocating; providing reintegration assistance; promoting reconciliation among communities; encouraging local and national governments to reassert their protective role; and pressing UN agencies and relevant governments to become engaged in addressing the problems of the displaced.

When the capacity of the government to perform its functions is weak or nonexistent, international and local NGOs have been known to provide a significant portion of the services needed in the reconstruction phase. This has created a number of problems, however; most notably it has made a number of countries dependent on outside sources, especially when conflicts endure and NGO services expand beyond emergency assistance. As one expert described it, "NGOs provide services quickly and flexibly. At the same time, they help to create a de facto decentralization of authority that can complicate the design of national sectoral strategies and can frustrate the attempts of postconflict state leaders to consolidate their power." [83]

Because no one international agency has a clear mandate for addressing the return and reintegration of internally displaced persons, NGOs find their own role unclear. In particular, NGOs feel that UNHCR's ad hoc mandate for internally displaced persons does not provide it with sufficient authority to address critical needs in the reintegration phase. UNDP, which is becoming increasingly involved, does not have a history of providing assistance through NGOs.

Another constraint identified by NGOs to their involvement in rehabilitation and development programs is donor reluctance to fund programs for the reintegration of the internally displaced. Donor support for internally displaced persons is generally more generous in the emergency phase than in long-term development. OXFAM, for example, observed that when internally displaced persons return home, they "may get far less assistance to reintegrate than refugees, though their needs are the same." Donors' budgets, it felt, "do not adequately recognize the longer-term recovery assistance required by people who have been displaced from their homes."

In some instances, NGOs have been able to divert funds from other programs or draw on donations from private sources to undertake reintegration programs. Local NGOs without alternative sources of funding are at a greater disadvantage. Yet their capacities are the ones most needed for durable solutions. As IFRC has aptly observed, these are "the very people all international humanitarian agencies agree are a crucial factor in effective disaster relief, both as today's local partners and as tomorrow's lead agencies in nationally-run disaster response." [84]

The Need for Closer Ties between International and Local NGOs

All the NGOs surveyed favored stronger partnerships between international and local NGOs. Local groups, they pointed out, have roots in the local culture, interact closely with local authorities, can sometimes gain access quicker than other players, and have needed information about internally displaced populations. They can also carry out community-based reconciliation and reintegration projects. Bolstering their efforts was considered essential because they are the ones that will have to carry on after the departure of UN agencies and international NGOs.

Nonetheless, building local capacities has sometimes proved hard to carry out in practice and is not a primary function for many NGOs. In emergency situations, international NGOs try to do the job as rapidly and efficiently as possible and may find that working with local partners slows up their efforts. Whereas in some countries local NGOs are capable and active, in others they may be administratively weak, technically inexperienced, and lacking in financial management capability.[85] In the former Soviet Union, which had no NGO tradition, newly formed local groups have shown their inexperience in working with internally displaced persons and refugees.[86]

It would, however, defeat the very purpose of international NGOs if they were regularly to bypass local groups, thereby undermining the development of local capacities. The funneling of international assistance to international NGOs has tended to dwarf local groups and sometimes create parallel structures. In Kenya, the bypassing of the NGO community produced disastrous results (see chapter 2). Donors and international organizations have as a result been increasingly encouraging international NGOs to involve local partners and include them in reintegration activities. The UN conference organized for the CIS countries specifically called upon international and local NGOs to cooperate, "given the nascent character of non-governmental organizations in the CIS countries."[87]

International and local NGOs will soon be cooperating closely in the development of a worldwide information system on internal displacement. In 1996 the NRC announced plans to produce a global survey of internally displaced persons and to establish an information database. To accomplish this, the NRC will have to establish networks of information that will bring together in close cooperation local and international NGOs. This in turn should increase protection for local groups, which are often harassed by their governments for working on behalf of the displaced. It should also focus attention on forgotten situations, where the operations of UN agencies and international NGOs are minimal or nonexistent, and it should provide early warning of new situations. Ultimately, the development of a worldwide constituency for displaced populations would be the goal.

Conclusion

NGOs have emerged as key players in the humanitarian response system, but substantial work needs to be done to realize their potential fully in providing relief, protection, and development assistance. First and foremost, their partnerships with UN agencies in the field need to be strengthened. As one NGO emphasized, "We would like to be treated as a partner who knows and understands the situation in the field, and is accordingly better aware of the needs of the IDPs." [88] Although UN agencies have come to rely more on NGOs, especially in implementing programs in the field, they have not fully engaged NGOs in the actual development of policies and operational decisions affecting the internally displaced.

This is particularly true in the area of protection. The role that NGOs should play in enhancing physical security for the internally displaced is still one that needs to be clarified. Too often UN agencies and humanitarian NGOs confuse material assistance with providing protection. The two are not the same, however. The provision of material aid does not automatically ensure physical safety.

Human rights and humanitarian NGOs would do well to divide labor in ways that focus on protection as well as assistance. This will require human rights NGOs to increase their presence in the field and humanitarian NGOs to recognize that protection problems are not extraneous to their mandates. Moreover, the assistance provided by NGOs must be seen within the political and human rights context in which humanitarian programs operate so that assistance does not help strengthen the forces responsible for internal displacement.

Better coordination with the United Nations is high on the NGO list as a method of improving international response to situations of internal displacement. Many NGOs recommend that a UN focal point or lead agency is the best means of unifying the international community and gaining the support of governments, local authorities, and armed factions. A recognized UN lead, according to the NRC study, "helps to maintain a common direction" in situations where diverse groups "assume different objectives and working methods." [89]

A worrying dilemma NGOs must face as funds from governments and intergovernmental organizations consume larger portions of their budgets is how to remain true to their own principles as they enlarge their operations. Although NGOs are quick to insist that it is their priorities that prevail over those of the donors, where they go, and the extent to which they become involved is heavily influenced by the resources available. NGOs are supposed to act where humanitarian need is greatest. Yet in Afghanistan, NGOs had difficulty maintaining their operations when the

United States departed and funding declined.[90] In Azerbaijan, where the United States has restricted aid to NGOs, fewer NGOs work with the internally displaced than in Armenia, where there are ten times fewer internally displaced persons.[91]

Too great a dependence on governmental and intergovernmental support could also threaten the NGO role as critic and watchdog. As former UN Secretary-General Boutros-Ghali observed, NGOs are needed to "embarrass governments and international secretariats to do their job." [92] It would jeopardize their role as principal advocates for the internally displaced if they were to become complacent about carrying out this function. NGOs are the most credible means of holding UN agencies and donors accountable for their roles in emergency situations. When UN partners "collude" with governments and undermine the protection and welfare of the internally displaced, it is NGOs who are needed to restore the balance. NGOs are also needed to take a lead in situations of internal displacement where donors show little interest and which receive little attention from the United Nations.

NGOs also need to scrutinize their own conduct. More and more NGOs have been drawing up codes of conduct and protocols to ensure that their own actions in the field on behalf of internally displaced and other affected populations correspond with humanitarian and human rights principles. Greater professionalism of conduct has come to be expected now that their role has expanded.

Perhaps the main constraints to NGO operations in situations of internal displacement are threats to the safety of their field staff.[93] When UN agencies are present in an emergency, NGO staff security is generally enhanced, but that does not mean that UN agencies automatically extend protection to NGOs. A UN convention on the safety of UN and associated personnel applies only to humanitarian workers with a contractual link with the United Nations.[94] One PARINAC recommendation is that UN security measures be extended to "all" NGOs in a field operation.[95] The IASC working group has similarly recommended that NGO personnel be "offered security protection along with staff working directly with the UN."[96] The international humanitarian and political communities, however, have not paid sufficient attention to this problem. As a minimum, the United Nations should provide the NGOs with security briefings, training, and communications equipment, especially when the latter are bolstering UN operations or substituting for UN presence in different locations.

For NGOs, being able to rely on the support mechanisms of the United Nations is important when undertaking their assistance tasks. At the same time, better coordination is needed among the NGOs themselves. Coordinating under the UN umbrella is not enough. Solidarity among the NGOs could also be a source of protection for them. One of their most significant joint aims should be to collaborate with local NGOs to build national capacities for addressing situations of internal displacement and to extend protection to these groups.

CHAPTER SIX

Regional Responses

We in the OAU are concerned that the problem of displaced persons has not attracted the requisite attention of the international community. We are concerned about the silent millions of displaced persons whose suffering is no different from those of the refugees and who seem to have attracted the least attention of the international community.
—Salim Ahmed Salim, Secretary-General,
Organization of African Unity, October 16, 1995

THE CONSEQUENCES of internal conflicts, strife, or massive human rights violations at the regional level are often dramatic. Neighboring countries must bear the brunt of refugee flows and cope with serious political and economic disruptions as a result of dissension next door. Despite the impact, capacities at the regional level are nowhere strong enough to prevent such situations, let alone resolve them or help those displaced by the disruptions. Governments generally look to international organizations for support, but in a number of significant situations, there has been little or no UN response. Such was the case in Liberia, Rwanda, and Somalia during critical periods. In other instances, the international response has been slow in coming owing to limited resources, ineffective emergency systems, or an unwillingness to become involved.

Because the burden of addressing emergencies cannot rest on the shoulders of the United Nations system alone, regional institutions are increasingly being expected to assume some of the responsibility in their own geographic areas. The knowledge and access they have in their regions make them likely candidates to become the first line of defense, the first to alert the international community to potential problems and the first to seek to avert and resolve crises. There is also considerable scope for their cooperation with international organizations, particularly in preventing situations of internal displacement and protecting its victims.

At present, regional initiatives remain at a rudimentary stage of development. Regional bodies such as the Organization of African Unity, the Organization of American States, the Organization for Security and Cooperation in Europe, as well as the League of Arab States (LAS), and the Association of Southeast Asian Nations (ASEAN) are not accustomed to dealing with humanitarian emergencies and the massive displacement they cause. Many are simply not equipped with the political structures and resources to do so, while some are reluctant to interfere in what they deem the internal affairs of states. Almost all lack experience and expertise in addressing emergencies. Political rivalries within regional organizations also limit their effectiveness. Nonetheless, regional organizations are beginning, in varying degrees, to devote some attention to conflict prevention and to the problem of mass displacement. Clearly, they have an important role to play in cooperation with the international community. This chapter evaluates their potential contribution and suggests how their actions might be made more effective.

Africa: Grappling with Sovereignty

Between 1969 and 1994 Africa's refugee population grew from 700,000 to more than 7 million; during the same period the number of internally displaced persons soared, to between 10 million and 15 million.[1] This alarming increase prompted the OAU to affirm in 1994 that internal displacement is "one of the most tragic humanitarian and human rights crises in Africa today."[2]

The OAU has nonetheless been cautious in its approach to this problem. Because one of its founding purposes was to promote respect for the sovereignty of African states, its members have been reluctant to take actions that can be construed as interfering in domestic affairs. Still, the limitations that these restrictions impose have become increasingly evident as massive killings, genocide and deliberate starvation have overcome countries and spilled over borders. Noninterference in internal affairs, observed OAU Secretary-General Salim Ahmed Salim, has been carried to "absurd proportions" in Africa.[3] He has called on the organization to take the lead in promoting protection and assistance for internally displaced persons in cooperation with humanitarian and human rights organizations. He has advocated greater OAU involvement in the prevention of conflicts that give rise to mass displacement and in the strengthening of national and regional capacities.[4]

Conflict Prevention and the Need for an African Military Capacity

The OAU summit of 1990 took the unprecedented step of authorizing the organization to address all types of conflicts in Africa, including conflicts *within* states. A mechanism for conflict prevention, management, and resolution was set up in 1993 together with a conflict prevention center.[5] Among its main objectives are to anticipate and defuse conflicts that give rise to mass displacement and to encourage the return of refugees and displaced persons.

The OAU's conflict prevention machinery has already met with some success, albeit modest. In 1993 the OAU mechanism brokered an agreement in Congo (Brazzaville) between rival political groups, which reportedly had the effect of easing tensions and averting a situation that had the potential to trigger internal displacement. The OAU also sponsored the 1993 Arusha Accords on Rwanda, deployed an observer mission in Burundi, and organized sanctions when the military overthrew the elected government of Burundi.[6] To play a larger role, however, such as preventing potential genocide in Burundi or tackling long-standing civil wars like the one in the Sudan, the countries of the OAU will need far greater political resolve, new initiatives, and strengthened capacities, including military backup.

To date, the OAU has not gone beyond dispatching small numbers of military observers in situations of severe tension. In 1992 it discussed the possibility of creating an OAU peacekeeping force to back up the conflict prevention mechanism but quickly realized that it did not have the capacity to do so and would have to look to the United Nations.[7] After the Rwandan genocide and the UN's failure to take action, the idea of building an African military force to prevent civil wars and deter genocide resurfaced. This time it was raised by Western governments.[8] The United States in particular proposed that an African force be created to protect civilians, including the displaced, in internal conflict situations.[9]

Several objections, however, have been raised to the idea of an all-African military force.[10] Even so, several African states have made known their willingness to provide units, and the OAU secretary-general has not ruled out the possibility of such a force in the future.[11] Basically, it has become clear that Africa will have to bear a larger share of the burden of its own conflicts than has been the case thus far since international action may not always be forthcoming. In Burundi, for example, no states outside of Africa offered to send troops for a potential military force.[12] Moreover, when countries outside Africa have intervened in its disputes, African interests have not always been served. The ultimate failure of international responses to emergencies in Somalia and Rwanda have served as lessons for the continent. As OAU Secretary-General Salim has warned, unless the OAU can "intervene swiftly" in its own internal conflicts, it cannot be sure that situations will be addressed or that those who act will do so "in accordance with African interests."[13]

James Gustave Speth, administrator of the United Nations Development Programme, has urged the international community to contribute $400 million a year to the OAU Peace Fund. This, he points out, would constitute a mere 10 percent of the $3 billion to 4 billion already being spent by the international community on the resolution of conflicts in Africa.[14] In particular, the OAU needs to be able to deploy an extensive field presence in areas of potential conflict. When large-scale violence breaks out, an African force would be in the position to protect civilians and make humanitarian aid possible.

A Call for Action

Thus far the OAU has sponsored a number of meetings to make its members more aware of the problem of internal displacement. In 1994 its Commission on Human and Peoples' Rights held a seminar on the protection of African refugees and internally displaced persons; and that same year, together with UNHCR, the OAU organized a regional symposium on refugees and forced population displacements in Africa. The meetings recommended greater OAU involvement in addressing internal displacement and in formulating a plan of action that would tackle the root causes of displacement and forge stronger linkages between OAU conflict resolution activities and those on behalf of refugees and internally displaced persons.[15] In 1995 a regional conference on the legal status of

refugee and internally displaced women in Africa called for stronger legal protections for uprooted women.[16]

It remains, however, for these recommendations to be translated into operational policies and programs. There is as yet no OAU policy on internal displacement, nor any body within the OAU specifically assigned to deal with the problem. The OAU's principal policymaking body on refugees, the Commission of Twenty on Refugees, a governmental body, has not yet become involved in any sustained or meaningful way with the issue.[17] If the commission were to consider enlarging its agenda and acknowledging that the nature of displacement has changed in Africa, it could then begin to pay regular visits to countries with serious problems of internal displacement, monitor conditions, and provide advice to governments on how to deal with the problem. Joint strategies could be developed with international organizations for increasing protection and facilitating returns.

One promising sign is that the commission's recent reports have begun to emphasize that Africa needs to assume responsibility for its displacement problems. They now also include statistics on internally displaced populations.[18] In 1994, for the first time, commission members, in the course of a visit to Liberia to monitor the refugee situation, looked at the internally displaced and made recommendations to the authorities about their condition.[19] And in 1996 the OAU cosponsored with UNHCR a regional conference to seek solutions to the massive displacement crisis in Rwanda and Burundi and to mobilize resources in support of the countries in the region.[20] At the same time, the commission has sought to avoid exposing situations in which governments have failed to protect and assist their internally displaced populations, as in the Sudan.[21] In short, it has not yet given sustained attention or high priority to the crisis of internal displacement in Africa.

Nor has the OAU Bureau for Refugees, Displaced Persons, and Humanitarian Affairs, which services the commission, expanded its efforts to encompass the internally displaced.[22] Although the bureau's name was changed in 1992 to include displaced persons, its resources and its operations have remained essentially the same. Its main activity is education, training, and more recently, income-generating activities for a limited number of refugees. In the case of the internally displaced, it has no specific programs, and in the area of protection, it does little, whether for refugees or internally displaced persons.[23]

Given the magnitude of the displacement crisis in Africa, a logical step would be for the bureau to develop a plan of action for the internally displaced. One of its five professional staff members could be designated to serve as a focal point on this question, and a special unit could be set up within the Bureau to monitor conditions in close cooperation with the OAU's Women and Children's Unit.[24] In an evaluation undertaken in 1995, the New York-based Lawyers Committee for Human Rights recommended that the bureau reestablish a network of correspondents in different countries to keep it apprised of local conditions in different countries.[25]

The Bureau has not yet expanded its role for several reasons. The first concerns its mandate. The bureau is expected to promote implementation of the OAU Convention on Refugees, but there is no comparable instrument or formal commitment in the case of the internally displaced. The second is limited resources. The bureau's budget is less than $500,000 a year, which barely allows it to support its refugee programs. The third is the culture of caution at the OAU, which prevents the bureau from being assertive in dealing with problems, even though its director is outspoken in acknowledging that the OAU should be able to address the issue.[26]

Given the close links between displacement and violations of human rights, it would be advantageous for the commission to undertake joint strategies with the African Commission on Human and Peoples' Rights. The eleven-member commission, Africa's main human rights body, which sits in Banjul, organized the seminar on refugees and internally displaced persons and is planning a second one. It also adopted a resolution calling on African countries to take measures to alleviate the plight of refugees and internally displaced persons.[27] The commission has the power to request governments, as part of their reporting obligations under the African Charter on Human and Peoples' Rights, to provide information on their laws and practices with regard to the internally displaced. On the basis of this information, it could prepare observations on government responses, and its chair could press governments to take remedial actions in the protection area. Together with the Commission of Twenty on Refugees, it also could undertake missions to countries with serious problems of internal displacement. The two bodies could then issue reports with recommendations for governments and other actors and could hold press conferences on particularly egregious cases. Should governments deny entry to these missions, reports could still be filed and hearings held.

The appointment of a special rapporteur on internal displacement could also be considered. So, too, could emergency procedures that would enable the commission to take action on urgent situations in between its two regular sessions a year.[28] Article 58 of the African Charter empowers the commission to refer to the OAU Assembly "special cases which reveal the existence of a series of serious or massive violations." By means of this article, the commission could alert the assembly to internal displacement situations requiring protection.[29] If the commission is to become relevant to human rights emergencies, it will have to see itself as a body that can take initiatives and not just one that responds to requests from the OAU Assembly. Some of the proposals it is now developing take this more proactive stand.[30]

The African Centre for Democracy and Human Rights Studies, an independent research body established in Banjul in 1989 to promote the work of the commission, could make an important contribution by adopting internal displacement as one of its research priorities. Although the center's research to date has not been extensive, it has published several papers and it has set up a documentation office. Its reconstitution in 1995 with new staff offers a promise of reinvigorated activities.

An OAU policy calling for the integration of internal displacement into the organization's work could go a long way toward encouraging its different commissions and bureaus to undertake the activities outlined above. Given the statements of the OAU secretary-general on the subject, this should not be difficult to achieve.

Resources will also be needed. The OAU's annual budget is only about $30 million and member states are often in arrears in their contributions. As a result, there are numerous delays in undertaking programs. To help alleviate this problem, the OAU Peace Fund, which is supposed to receive 5 percent of the OAU budget, has been allowed to accept, and has solicited, voluntary contributions from outside Africa.[31] Other OAU bureaus, however, have not been permitted to do this. The bureau for refugees and displaced persons, for example, remains confined to the annual 2 percent allocation it receives from the OAU budget. Were it to be authorized to solicit funds directly from governments and foundations, it would have a better chance of undertaking more meaningful programs for refugees and internally displaced persons.[32] The search for funds outside Africa to enable Africans to better address their own conflicts and emergencies will undoubtedly step up as member states become less inhibited about addressing conditions in other states or about becoming involved in internal crises. This trend is also reflected at the subregional level.

Subregional Organizations

African subregional organizations have begun to assume a role in averting and resolving conflicts, and to some extent in promoting assistance, protection, and development for the internally displaced.

THE ECONOMIC COMMUNITY OF WEST AFRICAN STATES (ECOWAS). ECOWAS, through its military organization the Economic Community of West Africa Monitoring Group (ECOMOG), offers a prime example of this. ECOWAS was established in 1975 for the declared purpose of bringing about closer economic cooperation among its sixteen subregional member states. As its executive secretary pointed out, however, "it is futile to talk about economic integration unless the environment in which you pursue such integration is peaceful and secure."[33] In 1978 ECOWAS member states signed a protocol on nonaggression, and in 1981 a military element was added through the ECOWAS defense protocol, which empowers the organization to initiate collective intervention in internal conflicts within member states, to interpose peacekeeping forces between warring parties, and to engage in mediation.[34]

Drawing on this authority as well as on more general principles of humanitarian assistance, in August 1990 ECOWAS dispatched a 3,000-person military observer group to Monrovia, following the outbreak of civil war in Liberia. Known as ECOMOG, it was composed mainly of Nigerian troops, and the intervention itself was seen by many as an effort by Nigeria to establish its primacy in the West African region.[35] Its first action was to secure Monrovia and surrounding areas from threatened seizure by the forces of the insurgent leader, Charles Taylor. Later, strengthened to 16,000, ECOMOG went on the offensive in an unsuccessful attempt to push Taylor out of Liberia.

In their treatment of displaced persons and civilians, ECOMOG soldiers are reported to have engaged in rampant looting and at times in assaults, including rape, against members of the local population.[36] During the ECOMOG offensive against Taylor, its warplanes are said to have bombed and strafed civilian targets, including hospitals and supply depots.[37] Nonetheless, observers have repeatedly testified, as does the case study on Liberia, that ECOMOG played an important role in protecting the population in its zone of occupation and in establishing a modicum of security, first in Monrovia and later more broadly. As one put it, "It [ECOMOG] reduced hostilities and atrocities and, by establishing order in greater Monrovia, set up a safe haven for thousands of [displaced] Liberians. By securing the port and airport it also assisted relief operations."[38] Another commented: "One of its most important accomplishments . . . was that ECOMOG stopped the slaughter of Krahn and Mandingo people in Monrovia. . . . One would be hard pressed to visit Monrovia without hearing, time and again, 'Thank God for ECOMOG. . . . ECOMOG was our savior, it was a salvation. ECOMOG saved the population of Monrovia.'"[39]

ECOMOG played no direct role in providing assistance to the internally displaced, or to others, but its presence made possible the return to Monrovia of UN and other humanitarian agency personnel in the fall of 1990, after their evacuation earlier that year, and the resumption of their programs. According to UN and NGO sources, it was in the ECOMOG-controlled area that the emergency needs of the local population were best being met.[40]

Until the breakdown of the peace agreement in 1996—when ECOMOG failed to contain renewed fighting—the ECOWAS intervention in Liberia offered an example, albeit imperfect, of a subregional group assuming responsibility for the protection of a population affected by civil conflict.[41] It has also been argued, however, that the intervention prolonged the conflict by not allowing Taylor to prevail, all the more so since the peace agreement that was finally accepted permitted Taylor to become Liberia's head of state. This viewpoint relies for its validation on hindsight, and on the supposition that a victory by Taylor would not have entailed the slaughter of many of those who found sanctuary behind ECOMOG's shield in Monrovia. The large-scale atrocities committed by Taylor's forces against civilian populations make it difficult to believe that lives would have been saved without ECOMOG's intervention.

The specific lesson to be drawn from ECOWAS's action in Liberia is that such intervention needs close oversight, both at the regional and the international levels. The OAU played no effective monitoring role in the ECOWAS intervention in Liberia.[42] The United Nations established a monitoring presence only belatedly, in the form of a small UN observer mission (UNOMIL), which, however, failed to exercise serious oversight authority or seek to prevent abuses by ECOMOG troops.[43]

Actions such as that carried out by ECOWAS in Liberia would benefit from coordination in advance with the OAU and the United Nations, which could be specifically authorized to monitor the performance of the intervening force. Military forces would also benefit from training programs in human rights and humanitarian law, particularly norms for the treatment of civilians and displaced persons. Oversight would further seek to ensure that relief operations intended for civilians on all sides of a conflict would not be held hostage to political or strategic objectives, as occurred in Liberia (see chapter 4).[44]

SOUTHERN AFRICAN DEVELOPMENT COMMUNITY (SADC). Another subregional group, SADC, has also played a role in preventing and resolving conflict that may have helped avert displacement in a number of cases and enable substantial numbers of refugees and internally displaced persons to return to their homes.[45] Although primarily concerned with the integration of southern African economies, in Mozambique, SADC is credited with having persuaded the Mozambique National Resistance (Renamo) to remain in the 1994 elections, a move that helped end the conflict and allowed the displaced to return home.[46] In Lesotho, SADC pressured the military to restore elected government in 1994, thereby preventing a crisis that could have led to violence and displacement.[47] SADC's efforts have also contributed to the resolution of conflicts in Zimbabwe and in Angola, as a result of which hundreds of thousands of refugees and internally displaced persons have been able to return home.[48] In 1996 it formally created an "organ on politics, defense and security" that directly concerns itself with resolving the internal security problems of member states.[49]

SADC is also considering becoming more directly engaged in programs to reintegrate former combatants, with support from the European Union. However, SADC projects have not yet sought to reintegrate internally displaced populations, on the grounds that this is a national, not a regional, problem. Thus far, only natural disasters, such as drought, are viewed as regional problems. In such cases, SADC sets up regional task forces and cooperates with international humanitarian agencies in averting famine and coordinating relief.[50]

INTER-GOVERNMENTAL AUTHORITY ON DEVELOPMENT (IGAD). Yet another subregional body, IGAD, has become involved in conflict resolution efforts. Headquartered in Djibouti and composed mainly of the governments of the Horn, it has worked since 1993 to promote an end to the civil war in the Sudan by sponsoring talks between that country and its neighbors.[51] Although the process has not yet produced tangible results, it is critical to the prospects for peace in the Horn and consequently to bringing an end to the massive internal and external displacement that has taken place there.

IGAD is also considering expanding its role to support the recovery and rehabilitation needs of displaced populations. Although its basic role has been to help member states overcome the effects of drought and other natural disasters, more recently it has expressed willingness to collaborate with UN development programs in their efforts to reintegrate uprooted populations.[52]

Europe: Preventive Diplomacy

The Organization for Security and Cooperation in Europe, previously known as the Conference on Security and Cooperation in Europe (CSCE), is the most suitable European institution to deal with Europe's extensive problems of internal displacement.[53] The OSCE has a broad membership: it includes all the countries in Eastern and Western Europe as well as Turkey, the central Asian republics of the former Soviet Union, the United States, and Canada, a total of fifty-five states. Its mandate is flexible, encompassing a broad range of political, security, economic, social, and human rights concerns, which it seeks to address in an integrated fashion. Since the end of the cold war it has evolved from an East-West discussion forum into an operational institution that works to prevent, manage and resolve conflicts within states. Its preventive approach has the potential to defuse tensions and avert mass displacement, which is particularly important in a region with many multiethnic countries where the potential for conflict is high.

The OSCE's preventive diplomacy tools include the regular dispatch of missions to troubled areas to mediate disputes.[54] The OSCE also deploys missions of "long duration" in an effort to ease local tensions, encourage dialogue and reconciliation among communities, and promote the development of democratic institutions.[55]

A particularly innovative creation is that of High Commissioner on National Minorities, who was appointed in 1992 to prevent ethnic and minority conflict "at the earliest possible stage." The high commissioner undertakes on-site visits, engages in preventive diplomacy and mediation, and may issue "early warning" alerts to the OSCE's political bodies. The high commissioner has already proved effective in a number of cases.[56]

In the area of human rights, the OSCE's Office for Democratic Institutions and Human Rights (ODIHR) promotes democracy and human rights through assisting with the drafting of constitutions and laws, monitoring elections, and the convening of biennial meetings to review compliance with "human dimension" commitments, inclusive of migration.[57]

The OSCE considers conflict prevention and resolution an important means of averting mass displacement, but its main concern to date has been to reduce the number of refugees seeking asylum in other European states. Its 1992 Summit Declaration, for example, noted "the importance of preventing situations that may result in mass flows of refugees."[58] Other OSCE meetings have also concentrated on refugees and those displaced externally, largely avoiding the subject of internal displacement.[59]

Need for Policy on Internal Displacement

The OSCE's interest in preventing refugee flows should logically lead it to address the plight of the internally displaced, since protecting the internally displaced would help avert their exodus to other countries. However, it has not yet developed a specific policy or program for internally displaced persons or examined the obligations of states in this regard. It has nonetheless found itself involved with the problem. It was one of the cosponsors of the 1996 UNHCR/IOM conference on refugees, displaced persons, and other forms of involuntary displacement in the CIS and neighboring states.[60] The Conference Programme of Action specifically highlighted the plight of internally displaced persons and the responsibility of governments, in cooperation with the international community, to address their protection, assistance, and reintegration needs. It also called for steps to prevent situations leading to sudden and massive displacement and designated the OSCE as one of the organizations to monitor the program's implementation.

OSCE fact-finding missions have also had to contend with the problems of the internally displaced. A 1996 mission to Chechnya made recommendations about the distribution of humanitarian aid to internally displaced persons and other affected populations.[61] A 1993 mission to Nagorno-Karabakh included a visit to a camp of internally displaced persons. And OSCE long-term missions have become directly involved

on the ground with the protection of the internally displaced. In Tajikistan in 1995, the OSCE took over from UNHCR the role of monitoring
the safety and human rights of internally displaced persons returning to
their home areas.[62] In the case of Bosnia and Herzegovina, the OSCE
dispatched several hundred staff members to monitor human rights conditions under the Dayton accords, including freedom of movement and
the right of displaced persons to repossess their property or receive
compensation.[63]

The large scale of the problem in a number of European countries,
however, makes it imperative to give it more systematic attention. Turkey
has the largest number of internally displaced persons in the European
region, and international humanitarian organizations have been barred
from providing assistance. Yet not much concern has been voiced about
this violation of its humanitarian commitments.[64] The chair-in-office and
OSCE's Permanent Council have not been seized by the issue. No OSCE
fact-finding mission has been sent to the country or "long duration"
mission proposed to monitor the conditions of displaced Kurds and to
promote solutions. And because of the limitations of his mandate, or his
interpretation of it, the High Commissioner on National Minorities has
not become engaged by it.[65] By failing to act upon the Turkish situation,
the OSCE ignores one of the most pernicious cases in Europe and could
undermine its standing on other issues of internal displacement.

Although the OSCE operates on the basis of consensus, which is
considered one of its strengths, in recent years, it has begun to experiment with nonconsensual processes in order to deal with obstructionist
governments. In 1992 the Council of Ministers decided that where there
are "clear, gross and uncorrected violations of relevant CSCE commitments," action could be taken by the council or the Committee of Senior
Officials "in the absence of the consent of the State concerned." This
"consensus-minus-one" decision, however, has been used only once: in
the case of the Federal Republic of Yugoslavia.[66]

There are other nonconsensual decisionmaking processes within the
OSCE framework as well, most notably the human dimension mechanism.[67] Under this mechanism, governments may initiate bilateral dialogues and good-offices missions with a violating government, or they
may air the issue multilaterally, or in extreme cases may undertake mandatory missions, with the support of a requisite number of states.[68] In
the case of Turkey, the Nordic and other states did initiate the process
but were not prepared to invoke the mechanism formally when Turkey

made it clear that it would not give its consent to a mission, and other states refrained from exerting political pressure on Turkey to permit OSCE involvement. Turkey, nonetheless, did allow entry to a delegation of OSCE's Parliamentary Assembly, whose report, although cautious, made reference to the evacuation and destruction of Kurdish villages and the displacement of tens of thousands of Kurds.[69] The report did not, however, call for any follow-up activities; nor did it address the actual conditions and needs of those Kurds internally displaced by the conflict or recommend that Turkey allow entry to international organizations.

Strengthening OSCE's Capacity

The OSCE could take several steps to strengthen its ability to deal with internal displacement. One would be to define internal displacement as a "human dimension" issue of direct concern to the organization. It could then formulate a policy on internal displacement and conduct a review to determine whether governments are in compliance with it. An ODIHR seminar specifically on internal displacement would also help develop the policy and define a specific OSCE role.

A second step would be to develop an information base on the subject within the OSCE framework. The organization would then be in a position to call attention to problems of internal displacement within the European region and promote solutions, in cooperation with international organizations. OSCE long-term missions stationed in different countries would be expected to integrate the issue of internal displacement into their activities and promote the development of national institutions, laws, and policies to help protect, assist, and reintegrate the internally displaced.

The OSCE might also consider developing a cadre of trained professionals to deploy in areas of displacement. In Tajikistan and Bosnia, the OSCE's ability to fulfill monitoring and protection functions has been reportedly hampered by its lack of expertise.[70] The integrity of the monitoring process also needs to be strengthened. In Bosnia, the OSCE easily succumbed to political pressure and certified that free and fair elections could be held even though conditions on the ground did not appear to warrant the return of displaced persons to their homes.[71]

The most important issue, however, is the organization's ability to develop a strong and influential voice to hold participating states accountable to their commitments. In the case of Chechnya, the OSCE's Permanent Council was regularly preoccupied with Russia's disproportionate use of force and its obstruction of humanitarian assistance; and despite considerable stonewalling by the Russian Federation, a small OSCE mission was finally established in Grozny.[72] Overall, however, as both Chechnya and Turkey demonstrate, participating states have been reluctant to exercise strong leverage with those that violate their OSCE commitments.[73]

Clearly, initiatives are needed to deal with governments whose policies directly lead to mass displacement. One way to strengthen the OSCE's role would be to give it the power of enforcement. The OSCE's 1992 summit authorized it to request organizations such as NATO and the West European Union (WEU) "to support it in carrying out peacekeeping activities."[74] Such activities were broadly defined to include not only the supervision of cease-fires but the maintenance of law and order, the provision of humanitarian and medical aid, and assistance to refugees. NATO has affirmed its willingness to support enhancement of the operational capabilities of the OSCE.[75] The WEU, for its part, plans to create a military force that could be sent on humanitarian missions and play a role in European crises in which NATO might be unwilling or unable to act.[76] If it does so, OSCE cooperation with the WEU could increase the OSCE's effectiveness in preventing or dealing with emergencies involving internal displacement.

Thus far, the OSCE has been cautious about developing a peacekeeping or preventive deployment capability. Although agreement was reached in principle in 1994 on establishing a peacekeeping force in the Caucasus, no force has as yet been created.[77] Nonetheless in certain cases, European governments have shown themselves willing to back OSCE preventive diplomacy with military force. In Albania in 1997, a European "multinational protection force" under OSCE auspices was deployed to facilitate the delivery of humanitarian assistance and help build a secure environment for a potential political solution.[78] Although OSCE resources are not extensive (its 1996 budget was an estimated $32 million), its participating states are prosperous, industrialized countries, and it can turn to long-established European military and political organizations for support.

Other European Regional Organizations

The OSCE might also find it fruitful to collaborate with European organizations engaged in integrating the economic, social, and human rights policies and standards of different European states. The European Union (formerly the European Economic Community) in recent years has become involved in extending humanitarian aid in emergency situations, mediating political disputes, and contributing monitors to UN human rights and humanitarian operations in the field.[79] The OSCE would do well to seek out the European Union's expertise and support, particularly for its monitoring missions that involve the displaced. By coordinating its activities with those of the EU, it would also be able to put pressure on states that cause mass displacement. Acceptance into the EU is an important objective for many countries. Membership, however, is conditioned on democratic practices and respect for human rights, which gives the EU powerful leverage over states' behavior.[80]

Cooperation with the Council of Europe would also be important for furthering protection for internally displaced persons.[81] The Parliamentary Assembly of the Council has been particularly outspoken in reports and resolutions about the forcible displacement of Kurds in Turkey and the indiscriminate and disproportionate targeting of civilians in Chechnya. Moreover, the council's "judicial" arm, composed of the European Commission of Human Rights and the Court of Human Rights, acts on individual cases and since 1991 has been deluged with close to 800 complaints, mostly from ethnic Kurds and directed against the government of Turkey.[82]

The growing dilemma for the council is whether to expand its membership and admit governments with poor human rights records.[83] The council was after all set up to deal essentially with the human rights violations of democratic governments. It is now finding itself challenged by one of its longer-standing members, Turkey, which has been harassing those who bring cases before the European Commission, and by newer members such as Russia.[84] The council may have to develop stronger measures in the case of governments that systematically flout its standards.

The Americas: Institutional Innovations

The Organization of American States, the hemisphere's regionwide political institution, has made the defense of democracy one of its main objectives in recent years.[85] This has helped reduce the potential for massive displacement in the Americas. In the cases of Haiti, Guatemala, and Paraguay, the OAS took strong steps to reverse actual or potential threats to the democratic process.[86]

The OAS General Assembly has nonetheless acknowledged that despite the advance of democracy in the hemisphere, "large numbers of internally displaced persons continue to require special attention" and that it is important to identify the causes of the problem as well as innovative solutions.[87] In 1995 it underscored the need to undertake "programs of assistance and human rights protection for internally displaced persons."[88] And in 1996 it suggested the "possible convocation" of a regional meeting to develop "quick-acting mechanisms" to address the needs of refugees and displaced persons in a timely fashion.[89]

The OAS, however, has not followed through with concrete steps to deal with internal displacement. In 1993 the OAS Inter-American Commission on Human Rights requested that the assembly appoint a working group to elaborate a program to address the needs of internally displaced persons and refugees. In particular, it called for the establishment of emergency measures to address the human rights aspects of internal displacement; the preparation of a code of conduct that would obligate governments to protect the internally displaced; and an early warning system to identify potential or emerging situations of displacement. It also recommended that internally displaced and other uprooted persons be included on the agenda of international development institutions.[90]

Beyond implementing these steps, the OAS could take other steps as well. It could urge governments—especially those of Colombia, Peru, and Guatemala—to establish more effective national institutions and remedies for the internally displaced, and it could monitor the performance of these institutions and provide technical assistance, if needed. It also could promote conflict resolution activities designed to prevent and help resolve displacement. In Guatemala, for example, the OAS has introduced a pilot project that provides conflict resolution training to groups, including the displaced, in rural areas.[91] One leading expert has suggested that the OAS call upon its member states to seek out and bring to trial state agents and nongovernmental actors who by their actions cause displacement or violate the rights of those who are internally displaced.[92]

Inter-American Commission on Human Rights

Spearheading action on internal displacement within the OAS is the Inter-American Commission on Human Rights, which is composed of seven independent legal experts. Since its founding in 1959, the commission has developed into an effective and autonomous body for investigating and disclosing human rights abuses in OAS member states and recommending remedial action. Its country reports have included proposals to governments with regard to forcible displacement.[93] In making its recommendations to the General Assembly in 1993, it underscored the need for more permanent mechanisms "for monitoring and supervising the situation of the internally displaced."[94]

To create a more systematic framework for addressing the problem of internal displacement, the commission decided in February 1996 to appoint a special rapporteur on internally displaced persons. The decision was made "in recognition of the grave situation of internally displaced persons in several countries of the Hemisphere" and following a meeting with the representative of the UN secretary-general on internally displaced persons.[95] The position, however, is a voluntary one with limited human and material resources available to it. Reports by rapporteurs, moreover, have not always received sustained or serious attention by the OAS. Nonetheless, it is the first institutional position at the regional level to deal with internal displacement and should raise the visibility of the problem and help stimulate solutions.

In support of the rapporteur, the commission could consider adopting an emergency procedure so that when a severe case of internal displacement develops, an emergency mission could be sent and an urgent action report issued. Deploying staff in the field could also help prevent violations and increase protection for the displaced. To date, the commission has not yet developed an operational capacity for human rights protection.

Furthermore, the commission could make known to displaced populations how to bring cases before it for decision. The commission could also bring questions of internal displacement before the Inter-American Human Rights Court, which has broad jurisdiction and an important advisory opinion role. It could ask the court to determine whether a government has violated the American Convention on Human Rights in cases of internal displacement or it could ask the court to issue an advisory opinion, for example, on the extent to which insurgent forces are obligated under international law to respect the rights of the internally displaced.

Joint initiatives could be undertaken and strategies developed with international bodies, in particular the representative of the UN secretary-general who has paid visits to three countries in the Americas and issued reports on their displacement problems. Unfortunately, the commission's role is constrained by its enormous workload of individual human rights cases. Moreover, its human and material resources are limited; it receives less than 2 percent of the OAS overall budget (of more than $100 million) even though human rights and democracy are considered major OAS objectives. However, the commission has made a commitment in appointing a rapporteur on internally displaced persons and has emphasized "the need to include the protection of refugees, repatriates, and internally displaced persons within the mandate of the regional human rights mechanisms."[96] It remains for the OAS to make good on this promise.

Permanent Consultation on Internal Displacement in the Americas

Outside the OAS structure, but functioning in collaboration with commission members, is a unique, innovative hemispheric initiative launched to address the problem of internal displacement. It is called the Permanent Consultation on Internal Displacement in the Americas, the Spanish equivalent of which is abbreviated as CPDIA.

CPDIA was created in 1992 by the Inter-American Institute of Human Rights (IIDH) to coordinate efforts with regard to internally displaced persons.[97] It is composed of representatives from intergovernmental organizations such as UNHCR, UNDP, UNICEF, WFP, IOM, the Inter-American Commission on Human Rights, and IIDH; NGOs such as the World Council of Churches and the Refugee Policy Group; independent experts; and an observer from ICRC. Its functions are to serve as a clearinghouse of information on internally displaced persons; to analyze specific country situations and make recommendations for solutions; to provide technical assistance to governments and organizations working with the displaced; to establish a legal framework; and to promote respect for the human rights of displaced populations through meetings, forums, and educational and training programs.[98]

To date, CPDIA has drafted a body of legal principles that have proved valuable to the United Nations in developing guiding principles for the internally displaced. It has undertaken two on-site missions to Colombia and one to Guatemala at the invitation or support of the government, and it has developed recommendations for improving the situation of internally displaced persons in those countries.[99] It has also provided support for grass roots projects for the displaced.[100]

CPDIA's unique strength lies in its broad membership. Its UN agency members enhance its influence with governments; yet because agency representatives serve in their private capacities, CPDIA is not subject to the kinds of political constraints that UN agencies are. At the same time, it is forced to rely on IIDH for staff and resources, but IIDH cannot always make these readily available. Also, because of its quasi-governmental status, IIDH is at times unwilling to exert pressure on governments when they violate human rights.[101] To ensure that it remains a consistent, dynamic, and ongoing program, CPDIA should try to develop into a more autonomous body replete with staff and resources of its own, but closely collaborating with IIDH. In 1996 both UNHCR and UNICEF made contributions to CPDIA's work, an encouraging sign, and CPDIA began to take steps to develop its own resource base.

CPDIA also will have to decide to what extent its work can be made public. At present, its reports are presented to governments privately, which has its advantages in certain situations. But if it is to become an effective clearinghouse of information on internal displacement, it will have to find ways of disseminating its information, especially when governments prove obstructive. At a minimum, CPDIA should consider publishing certain basic information about the numbers, needs, and problems of internally displaced populations and should make this available in languages other than Spanish.

CPDIA would also benefit from stronger institutional links with the representative of the UN secretary-general on internally displaced persons and with the new rapporteur on internally displaced persons of the Inter-American Commission on Human Rights. CPDIA could serve as an early warning system for both, calling to their attention information and problems in different countries. It could also monitor the extent to which their recommendations have been implemented in different countries. In addition, joint on-site missions could be planned or at least coordinated so that they complement each other.[102] CPDIA stands out as a unique example of a regional solution for internal displacement that deserves the support of regional and international bodies.

The Middle East: A Narrow Focus

This region, unlike Africa, Europe, and the Americas, has no all-encompassing regional organization. The League of Arab States, based in Cairo and comprising twenty-two members, comes closest to fulfilling the regional function, but it excludes Iran and Israel and spills over into a large swath of North Africa. Since the late 1940s, the LAS has concentrated its attention on the needs of externally and internally displaced Palestinians.[103] When it comes to cases of other internally displaced persons—notably in the Sudan, Somalia, and Iraq—it has invoked national sovereignty to preclude involvement.

Nothing in the LAS constitution prohibits it from addressing the problem of internal displacement. Rather, its efforts in this direction have been constrained by its political proclivities, limited resources, and reluctance to support the causes of non-Arabs. Nonetheless, voices have been raised in the Arab world to urge the LAS to undertake broader activities on behalf of internally displaced persons and refugees. The "Cairo Declaration on the Protection of Refugees and Displaced Persons in the Arab World," issued by a group of Arab experts in 1992, called upon Arab governments to provide the secretariat of the League of Arab States with information and statistical data on the condition of refugees and displaced persons in their countries and on the national laws, regulations, and decrees in force relating to these groups. It also emphasized the need to provide special protection for women and children, who constitute the largest category of refugees and displaced persons.[104] A second conference in Tripoli, Lebanon, in 1995, the "Regional Seminar on Internal Displacement of Populations in Arab Countries, Human Rights and Humanitarian Law," recommended that each Arab state in the region create institutions to deal with internal displacement and that when a problem of internal displacement arises, the state should cooperate with and give access to international humanitarian organizations. It further called on countries of the region, together with international and regional organizations, to create a data base of information on displacement. Finally, it called on Arab states to draft instruments for the protection and assistance of displaced persons in the region.[105]

The LAS has not yet acted on these recommendations. While its Department of Palestine Affairs oversees a well-established structure of councils and committees that address the issue of displaced Palestinians, the LAS leaves to the attention of the international community the needs of other displaced persons in the region, whether displaced Kurds in Iraq or non-Arab southern Sudanese. LAS officials claim that it would violate national sovereignty if it were to deal with internal displacement.[106] They also point out that Arab governments prefer to provide assistance on a bilateral basis. Nonetheless, the LAS did attempt to help out in Somalia, although it was reportedly rebuffed by local factions.[107]

One step the LAS could take would be to help Arab governments establish national institutions to deal with internal displacement. It could also collect information, monitor conditions, and develop a plan of action for dealing with internal displacement in its region. The organization has departments and agencies whose present activities could be of direct relevance to internally displaced persons. For example, its social affairs department is already geared to dealing with issues related to women, children, health, and the environment. Equally helpful could be its educational, cultural, and scientific organization; its human rights bodies; and its fund for economic and social development. In these and other ways, the organization could overcome the self-imposed restrictions that impede it from addressing the needs of internally displaced populations so it could begin to assume broader responsibility within its region.

Asia: Organizational Vacuum

Although the largest and most populous of the world's regions, Asia has no overarching regional structure. For more than ten years, the United Nations has convened workshops and seminars to try to encourage it to develop regional human rights structures, pointing to models in Africa, Europe, and the Americas that it could follow.[108] Private organizations have done likewise.[109] However, no regional body on human rights comparable to the African Commission, European Commission, or Inter-American Commission has emerged.

Widely divergent political, economic, and social systems as well as ideological differences have made it impossible for the countries of the region to agree on such a body. To complicate matters, China, the region's largest and potentially most powerful state, has opposed the introduction into Asia of human rights models from other regions.[110] Most Asian governments consider it too early to create a regional mechanism and instead endorse an evolutionary approach. Human rights organizations do so as well because they fear that the creation of machinery now might formalize a standard for Asia that would be contrary to that of the rest of the world and would undermine the work of Asian NGOs.[111]

The only working regional grouping within Asia is a subregional organization, the Association of Southeast Asian Nations (ASEAN), with its headquarters in Jakarta.[112] Its main purpose is to promote regional stability and economic and social cooperation. To this end it has discussed refugee issues, in particular mass exoduses from Indochina, but its main interest has been to curtail such flows and repatriate nonrefugees. Internal displacement has not figured in its agenda, and it is unlikely to do so in the near future, for ASEAN has scrupulously avoided taking positions on "internal" conditions within member states. In fact, several ASEAN governments have taken the lead in international conferences in arguing that action on issues within the domestic sphere of states constitutes an infringement of state sovereignty.[113] Furthermore, ASEAN does not as a rule engage in the prevention or resolution of internal conflicts. Although it did participate in the negotiations leading to the settlement of Cambodia's civil war and played a strong role in opposing Vietnam's invasion of Cambodia, it does not consider insurgency or civil conflict to be within its orbit.[114]

However, nothing within ASEAN's mandate precludes it from undertaking initiatives to prevent or resolve internal conflicts or to discuss internal displacement.[115] It could, for example, form a working group on humanitarian issues to address the subject of internal displacement, just as it formed a working group on Indochinese refugees. It could also raise the issue of internal displacement on a regional or even global basis at its annual postministerial conferences, where ASEAN foreign ministers meet with "dialogue partners" from other Asian countries and the West to discuss regional security matters.[116] The issue of refugees has come up at these meetings. Given the substantial number of internally displaced persons in Asia, particularly in Afghanistan, Cambodia, India, Myanmar (Burma), the Philippines, and Sri Lanka, the demonstration of political will to raise the problem would be a long overdue development.

Another subregional organization, the South Asian Association for Regional Cooperation (SAARC), founded in 1985, also seeks to promote economic and social cooperation.[117] Through its programs in rural development, health, and education, and for women and children, it could extend support to internally displaced populations. But its members' emphasis on noninterference in internal affairs has discouraged it from becoming involved in the issue. Thus the need for political and humanitarian solutions to the Kashmir dispute, a source of internal displacement in India, has not been addressed by the organization. Its interest in reducing natural disasters in the region has not been paralleled by any comparable initiatives with regard to man-made disasters.[118]

The absence of a regional intergovernmental structure inclusive of all Asia has not discouraged NGOs from forming regional groupings to promote and protect human rights.[119] These organizations should be encouraged to include the issue of internal displacement on their agendas and to mobilize support for addressing the problem within the region.

Conclusion

If internal displacement is to be dealt with effectively, greater capacity for such endeavors will need to be developed at the regional level and a division of labor worked out with international organizations. Ideally, under a system of shared responsibilities regional organizations would be the first to monitor potentially dangerous situations that threaten mass displacement. They would also be the first to intercede politically to avert a crisis and to alert the international community when there is insufficient regional capacity to deal with the problem. In the event of a full-blown conflict and large-scale displacement, regional bodies would collaborate with international organizations to ensure that humanitarian assistance and protection are provided. When military intervention is decided upon, regional bodies would be the preferred instrument, but their action would be sanctioned and monitored by the United Nations to ensure that it accords with the human rights and humanitarian principles in the Charter of the United Nations.[120] Once the crisis is past, support for recovery and reintegration would become part of a regional framework, when appropriate.

No such system exists, however. Few regional institutions have the requisite capacities to play a role of such magnitude. They are still struggling to develop responses to humanitarian emergencies. Nonetheless, over the past five years most regional bodies have begun to take a more aggressive approach. In particular, attitudes have changed with regard to traditional notions of sovereignty and the principle of nonintervention in member states. Although respect for the sovereignty and integrity of member states remains critical to regional systems, the importance of heading off conflicts, reaching people in need, and holding governments accountable when they violate regional and international standards have gained increasing recognition.

The OAU in particular has articulated a stronger role for itself. Secretary-General Salim has called for swift OAU intervention in Africa's internal conflicts and has advocated preemptive involvement by the OAU "in situations where tensions evolve to such a pitch that it becomes apparent that a conflict is in the making."[121] Similarly, the OAS has become more activist in its approach to maintaining democratic regimes in the Western Hemisphere, as demonstrated by its role in Haiti and Paraguay. In Europe, the OSCE has been exploring avenues of decision-making beyond the strictly consensual. In 1992 the organization was empowered to take steps, without the consent of the state concerned, in the event of clear, gross, and uncorrected violations of human rights commitments. This is the first time a regional (or international) organization has articulated a justifiable defense, based on human rights and humanitarian norms, for overriding state sovereignty. All these steps mark the beginning of a framework in which the humanitarian and human rights interests of internally displaced persons can be given more effective consideration.

The direct link between conflict prevention and averting mass displacement has become another new tenet of regional bodies. Both the OAU and the OSCE have pointed out that the special conflict prevention machinery they have set up should help stem displacement. When such efforts fail, the stationing of regional staff in the field to defuse tensions and protect the internally displaced has thus far been tried only in Europe. In Tajikistan, for example, OSCE field officers have brought to the attention of the authorities instances of harassment of internally displaced persons and have taken up individual cases of illegal house occupation to facilitate the return and reintegration of the displaced. In Bosnia, the OSCE as well as the European Commission Monitoring Mission and the Council of Europe have been playing critical operational roles in the peace-building phase.

Most regional organizations, however, have no operational capabilities or enforcement powers of their own. Some have begun to strengthen their links to other bodies or governments that do have the needed resources and forces. The OAU has sought support from the United Nations and donor governments to bolster its conflict prevention efforts, and it has been considering the possibility of an African force to facilitate the delivery of relief and to protect civilians in internal conflict situations. The OSCE has been exploring the possibility of developing closer ties with the WEU and NATO in emergency situations. In the former Yugoslavia, the OSCE's role in the return and reintegration of displaced persons has been carried out under the NATO umbrella. In Albania, OSCE preventive efforts were backed by a European multinational protection force, authorized by the United Nations.

Indeed, the United Nations has warmly welcomed the involvement of regional organizations in conflict prevention and peacekeeping activities.[122] But the regional role has to be more effectively supported and monitored to ensure that international standards are complied with, that powerful regional states do not subvert the undertaking, and that military forces receive training in how to deal with civilian populations.[123] The extent to which regional organizations and the United Nations can increase their cooperation should be closely examined.[124] One means of promoting closer cooperation between regional and international bodies would be for the UN secretary-general, and other senior UN officials such as the under-secretary-general for humanitarian affairs and the high commissioner for human rights, to meet with the heads of regional organizations and discuss emergency response. The jointly organized regional conferences on population displacement, held both in the CIS and in the Great Lakes region of Africa, should give impetus to this effort. They have achieved broad agreement on preventive and development strategies for addressing displacement, although more effective implementation and follow-up mechanisms, as well as increased resources, are needed to ensure that the provisions of the agreements are carried out. In the case of Asia, where no overall regional body exists, attention needs to be paid to developing mechanisms and approaches for dealing with internal displacement. At a minimum, the UN Economic and Social Commission for Asia and the Pacific could be assigned a role; and UN workshops in Asia on the regional promotion of human rights could explore ways of promoting regional protection for the internally displaced.

The dynamics of population displacement require the involvement not only of the affected countries but of those that surround them. Regional efforts, if supported and strengthened, can provide a framework for the prevention and resolution of displacement problems and also for reconstruction and peace-building in postconflict situations. In the Americas, displacement issues have been met with particularly innovative responses. The CIREFCA process to help reintegrate displaced persons, the appointment of a rapporteur on internally displaced persons within the OAS framework, and the creation of the Permanent Consultation on Internal Displacement in the Americas could all serve as models for other regions. So could the operational role played by the OSCE.

CHAPTER SEVEN

Strategies and Recommendations

In these times of unrestrained brutality, the number of victims claimed by war, wanton violence and hatred is incalculable. Many of these people have been displaced within their own countries. . . . [These] tragedies . . . which have forced hundreds of thousands of people to flee their home, underscore the need to come up with effective means of curbing these mass population movements and facilitating the return of displaced persons.
—Jean de Courten, Director of Operations,
International Committee of the Red Cross

EFFECTIVE STRATEGIES for dealing with internal displacement must involve a broad range of players, beginning with the displaced populations themselves, their surrounding communities, the authorities under which they reside, and the local groups working with them. They must then be reinforced by capacities at the national, regional, and international levels.

There must also be a comprehensive approach. As already noted, too much of the debate surrounding internal displacement has concentrated

The authors express appreciation to Erin Mooney for her research and assistance in compiling the prevention and protection portions of this chapter; to Curtis W. Lambrecht for his research into protection issues; and to Steven Holtzman for his contribution to the development strategies. The papers they prepared for this study are cited in the chapter.

on the delivery of emergency relief. Strategies to address mass displacement need to encompass prevention, protection, and political and economic solutions as well. They need to go beyond the mere fact of the existence of conflicts and human rights violations to their potential roots in identity crises within a nation, the denial of democratic liberties, and the deprivations of poverty and severe underdevelopment. The remedies designed should not only be a response to emergency needs but should seek to prevent the conditions that caused the problem. The search for lasting solutions in turn becomes a form of prevention against recurrence.

Preventive Strategies

It is precisely in the area of prevention that responses are weakest at all levels. As one observer has pointed out, "While humanitarian assistance has become a multi-billion dollar enterprise, there has been little investment in conflict prevention or postconflict stabilization."[1] The emphasis in the preventive strategies outlined here falls on effective information and early warning systems, good governance, a strengthened civil society, and humanitarian intervention prior to mass displacement.

Improved Early Warning

The initial ingredient of any preventive strategy is an effective early warning system, one that combines early alert with early action. In most cases, the international community has shown itself to be willing to come to the aid of the displaced only after problems have reached an advanced stage. What is needed is a system that sounds the alarm and advocates for the necessary political and humanitarian actions to avert displacement.

In 1991 the General Assembly of the United Nations called on the emergency relief coordinator to develop an early warning system for humanitarian emergencies.[2] Interagency consultations on early warning of mass displacement met throughout 1993 and 1994 under the auspices of DHA and produced a list of possible "hot spots," but no suggested course of action.[3] At the same time, the consultation did recommend that advanced technology and information systems be introduced to enhance the UN system's capacity for collecting, processing, and analyzing early warning information. The office of the ERC has since developed a database as part of its humanitarian early warning system (HEWS), which is capable of generating data on more than a hundred countries. But more needs to be done if early warning is to be effective. The consultation will have to develop plans for timely action and press for follow-up by the Office of the Secretary-General and the UN departments and agencies capable of averting crises.

Another important step would be to integrate human rights bodies into the early warning system.[4] Rapporteurs of the Commission on Human Rights often have access to early warning information. Almost a year before the genocide in Rwanda in April–May 1994, the special rapporteur on extrajudicial, summary, or arbitrary executions warned that preparations were being made for genocidal massacres and recommended swift and decisive measures to stave off the impending humanitarian crisis.[5] However, his report was not placed on the agenda of the early warning consultation or drawn to the attention of other parts of the United Nations.

Situations of this sort could be avoided in the future if the high commissioner for human rights were empowered, through the secretary-general, to bring reports of impending large-scale displacement and massive human rights violations to the attention of the Security Council, with recommendations for international response. In 1995 the commissioner was specifically asked by the Commission on Human Rights to address situations that cause or threaten to cause mass exodus.[6]

Broadening the membership of the UN's early warning system to include relevant NGOs and research bodies is also essential. Some UN staff fear that this would breach the confidentiality of UN information, but the inclusion of NGOs and research bodies would ensure that early warning information goes beyond the circumspect desks of bureaucrats and that valuable expert information from NGOs is taken into account. After all, NGOs are the ones most familiar with the situation on the ground and often are privy to information about possible human rights violations and displacement available through community-level systems.[7] In Rwanda, Tutsi villages developed a simple civil defense system of nocturnal lookouts to warn local residents of impending incursions and other threats to their physical security.[8] The international community could tap into such systems so that the messages of the affected population could be heard and acted upon. Telecommunications and business firms could play a role by providing the necessary technical assistance and equipment to set up a system of early warning for threatened communities.[9] Above all, NGOs could help draw international attention to dire situations through their use of the media.

An early warning system should also have close links with regional bodies. An evaluation of the failure of early warning in the Rwanda crisis concluded that effective capacity should exist at the regional level since UN deliberations might be too far removed from the situation.[10] The importance of early warning has been recognized by the OSCE, which created the post of High Commissioner on National Minorities with an explicit mandate to engage in early warning of minority tensions threatening to erupt into armed conflict (see chapter 6). The CIS conference on refugees and displaced persons, sponsored by the OSCE, UNHCR, and IOM, recommended that national networks and special subregional migration centers be established for early warning,[11] and the Inter-American Commission on Human Rights in 1993 also has proposed an early warning system for the OAS, but it has yet to be set up. In Africa, the international joint evaluation of the Rwanda experience found that the OAU possessed "virtually no capacity at all for early warning data collection and policy analysis."[12]

Early warning systems have been particularly effective in forecasting and averting famine and responding to other consequences of natural disasters.[13] Progress in forecasting and averting humanitarian crises stemming from internal conflicts and gross violations of human rights has been slower. In Macedonia, early warning combined with early action led to the preventive deployment of UN peacekeeping troops and an OSCE observer mission for the purpose of preserving peace there.[14] For the most part, however, the link between early warning and early action, so critical to prevention, has been absent at both the international and regional levels. The secretary-general's 1997 recommendation that the UN's early warning consultation be resumed should provide an opportunity to strengthen the UN's capacity for preventive action.[15]

Information Systems on Internal Displacement

No early warning system can operate effectively without accurate information about pending and current situations of internal displacement. In 1996 the ERC affirmed that an information system on internally displaced persons would be established within DHA and be linked to HEWS, but no follow-up action took place.[16] In 1997 the ERC again agreed to develop an information system, although this time it said it would "promote" the establishment of a system "in consultation with external institutions," in particular NGOs.[17] The ERC remains a logical candidate to oversee an information system on internal displacement because it has been designated the reference point for the internally displaced and can count on resident/humanitarian coordinators to provide it information.

Should the ERC's office prove unable to develop a system, another candidate would be UNHCR's Centre for Documentation on Refugees (CDR), which is already experienced in collecting data on the subject of displacement and has amassed considerable information about internally displaced populations in the course of its research on refugees. UNHCR's increasing involvement in situations of internal displacement provides a persuasive argument for expanding CDR's role and exploring cost-sharing arrangements with other UN agencies. At the same time, it would have to enlarge its information base, since at present it does not actively seek information on internal displacement but simply collates whatever it receives, and its collection does not include what is outside the public domain.

The Office of the High Commissioner for Human Rights is also an option, owing to its role in servicing the mandate of the representative of the secretary-general and its reports on situations that cause or threaten to cause mass exoduses. Its field operations, although limited, and its network of rapporteurs provide important sources of information on pending and current situations of internal displacement. However, its method of organizing information strictly for meetings of UN human rights bodies would have to be altered. This could be accomplished by adding a corps of country or regional specialists and expanding the office's information-gathering function.

NGOs also need to establish an information center. The distinct advantage of an NGO center is that it would be free from the constraints to which intergovernmental bodies are subject and could rely on data provided by nongovernmental sources. One particularly promising initiative is the Norwegian Refugee Council's global survey on internally displaced persons, to be published in 1998. The NRC also expects to publish information on current trends and concerns regarding this population, develop a database in cooperation with the ERC, and maintain a web-site for up-to-date information on the internally displaced.

Needless to say, a global information system would provide statistics not merely on the numbers and location of persons affected, but also on the extent to which national, regional, and international efforts are addressing their needs. It should help in the development of containment strategies as well as promote solutions. It could also publicize ideas and programs that have proved effective in different parts of the world, so as to promote their replication. The Permanent Consultation on Internal Displacement in the Americas (CPDIA) has become a clearinghouse of information at the regional level, but its reports and recommendations are not widely known outside the Americas. A worldwide information system on the internally displaced could bring together information about programs from different sources and in the process help create a global constituency on behalf of the internally displaced. This could enhance both prevention and protection.

An information system's value also lies in helping the states concerned to act in a timely and effective manner. In this sense, it should be viewed as an instrument of good governance, alerting the state to take measures to address the conditions causing displacement.

Good Governance

Since internal displacement is due in large part to internal conflicts, communal violence, and systematic violations of human rights, there is need for states to institutionalize effective systems of managing conflicts to prevent them from escalating into destructive violence. This means regulating relations among diverse racial, ethnic, cultural, and religious groups to avoid violent confrontation; ensuring participatory democracy and respect for fundamental rights; managing the economy responsibly to generate growth and promote a broadly based distribution of national resources; and last, but not least, adhering to the norms of regional and international cooperation. When governments fail to discharge these responsibilities to a reasonable level of satisfaction for their citizens, either because of a fundamental lack of capacity or because of lack of political will, governance deteriorates and makes it difficult to prevent displacement.[18]

Given that human rights are at the heart of the social order, protecting them is the best means of preventing conflict and displacement. "Human rights" encompasses the entire spectrum of universal norms, ranging from civil and political rights, to economic, social, and cultural rights, to minority rights that recognize the inherent dignity and equality of all human beings regardless of their race, ethnicity, religion, culture, nationality, political opinion, social origin, or gender. Inequities and injustices in the enjoyment of rights inevitably foster the type of conflicts that threaten the violent collapse of society.[19]

Internally displaced persons are often members of racial, ethnic, or religious minorities, marginalized by a system of inequitable and discriminatory governance. Although democracy is rooted in the will of the majority, it is supposed to create an equitable system for all identity groups, which means recognizing and implementing standards respecting the rights of minorities. Regional and international organizations have become a crucial factor in trying to persuade states to exercise greater responsibility in this regard. In recent years, they have adopted standards to serve as a guide for national legislation and practice. In 1992 the United Nations adopted the Declaration on the Rights of Persons Belonging to National or Ethnic, Religious, or Linguistic Minorities. Although nonbinding in character, it is the first universal instrument directed at the protection of minorities.[20] At the regional level, legally binding treaties and other instruments have been adopted within the framework of the Council of Europe and the OSCE to increase protection for national minorities.[21]

Present international and regional mechanisms for resolving conflicts with minorities, though still rudimentary in nature, show considerable potential.[22] Through the efforts of the Council of Europe and the OSCE, Europe now has a well-developed system of monitoring mechanisms for minority protection that is beginning to produce some good results. The OSCE's High Commissioner on National Minorities, for example, has successfully prevented several disputes from escalating (see chapter 6). No other region has comparable machinery, although there is now discussion of initiating a "Helsinki process" in Africa.[23]

At the international level, the UN Sub-Commission for the Prevention of Discrimination and the Protection of Minorities established a working group in 1995 to develop strategies for protecting minorities. These should certainly include conciliation and mediation procedures and a calibrated program of action when dialogue does not achieve results. Where group identities correspond to geographical areas, as in Chechnya, southern Sudan, and Iraq, another strategy would be to propose a significant degree of autonomy, through a federal or confederal devolution of power.[24] It has also been proposed that mediators be trained both within states and in the United Nations to help them respond to conflicts involving national, ethnic, religious, and linguistic groups.[25]

The Convention on the Prevention and Punishment of the Crime of Genocide commits states "to prevent" those "acts committed with intent to destroy, in whole or in part, a national, ethnical, racial or religious group."[26] Unfortunately, the political will to prevent or halt brutal forms of violence against ethnic groups has in most cases not been forthcoming. Considering that one of the main aims of the founders of the United Nations in 1945 was to prevent genocide against minority groups of the kind that occurred in Europe during the Second World War, one of the high priorities of this body, and of regional organizations, should be to strengthen the procedures for containing and resolving conflicts involving minorities, and to promote activities that can prevent the kinds of conflicts that produce such crimes against humanity.

Effective National Institutions

Conflict management requires not only the setting of standards for good governance but effective and responsible national institutions to ensure the realization of these standards. It has been observed that "building the institutional capacity for civil society . . . to negotiate and mediate differences and potential incompatibilities within itself and also with the government, is the sine qua non of a successful system of governance."[27] Effective institutions include an independent judiciary, an uncorrupted civil service and parliament, a police force and a military respectful of human rights, free-functioning nongovernmental organizations, and independent news media. Indeed, no degree of economic development can compensate for the internal instability wrought by the absence of such institutions.

The international community has a role to play in strengthening weak or poorly developed institutions. The impact national institutions can have on helping to avert displacement is considerable. Of the regional organizations, the OSCE has been especially active in helping to establish and strengthen national institutions in Europe. Its Office for Democratic Institutions and Human Rights (ODIHR) has conducted training programs for ombudsmen in several countries and has brought together human rights experts and representatives of international organizations to exchange views on the role of national human rights committees and ombudsmen in preventing and resolving conflicts.[28]

Support from the OSCE, UNHCR, and IOM has enabled the newly independent former Soviet republics to initiate a process of subregional consultation in a direct effort to prevent displacement. The CIS Conference on Refugees and Displaced Persons, held in Geneva in May 1996, was convened specifically for the purpose of preventing further displacement in a region where the problem is already acute.[29] Its program of action calls for the development of national institutions and laws to ensure good governance and avert displacement. Although the program is nonbinding, it provides a useful framework for both preventing and addressing displacement in the region.[30]

Strengthening the independence of the judiciary and conducting human rights training for judges and law enforcement and other officials are also essential. Without an effective judicial system to redress violations, the conditions that cause displacement are given free rein to persist and can impede the return and reintegration of uprooted populations.[31] In Tajikistan, international assistance provided in the drafting of legislation on property rights and the protection of minorities has facilitated returns and helped avert further displacement. A strengthened judicial system is also needed to resolve the land and property disputes emanating from displacement. In Guatemala, a strengthened legal system could help address the problems internally displaced persons face with regard to land, housing, official papers, employment, and protection from harassment, and thereby discourage further displacement.

An independent media can also contribute to averting displacement by exposing human rights violations and raising awareness of problems before they escalate into crises. Here, too, international and regional organizations and NGOs have been playing important roles. The OSCE, for example, has convened regional conferences and meetings among government and media representatives to emphasize the media's role in transitions to democracy. NGOs such as Freedom House and Article 19 have sponsored training seminars for members of the media in Eastern Europe and Africa to promote the development of independent media.

As emphasized throughout this volume, international and local NGOs have a critical role to play in strengthening national institutions. Alongside regional and international organizations and particularly in their absence, they can contribute to the development of viable mechanisms for national prevention and preparedness.[32]

A Functioning Civil Society: Strong NGOs

The array of nongovernmental actors who make up civil society play a critical role in mediating between the state and the community at large. By strengthening civil society at the grass roots level, communities gain the stability needed to guard against social unrest and its consequences, including displacement.[33] Empowered populations that face discrimination are spurred to organize and work for change. NGO workshops, such as those held in Cambodia and El Salvador that provide training in monitoring techniques and networking skills, are instrumental in this regard. So, too, are NGO seminars, of the kind held in Colombia and Peru, that focus specifically on empowering displaced populations.[34]

The need to strengthen local NGOs is essential. They are the first to become aware of situations of poor governance that threaten displacement, and often they are the best judges of how to prevent them. Yet local NGOs typically lack resources and expertise. In some parts of the world, most notably the former Soviet Union, the local NGO network is barely in its infancy. In other parts of the world, local NGOs come under attack by governments and military factions precisely because of their efforts on behalf of human rights and displaced persons.

International and regional conferences have been building a strong case for strengthening the role of local NGOs, encouraging the formation of local and regional networks, and promoting partnerships between those at the international and local levels.[35] The Open Society Institute has been especially active in lending support to fledgling groups in the former Soviet Union, particularly those seeking to assist and protect refugees and displaced persons.[36] The sharing of information, resources, and expertise among international and local NGOs can lead to a more efficient division of labor. Moreover, contact with outside groups stands to bring much-needed protection to local NGOs. The partnerships currently being forged by the Norwegian Refugee Council with local groups to develop its global survey on internally displaced persons are expected to bolster those monitoring displacement problems in different countries.

Among regional organizations, the OSCE, through its NGO liaison adviser in ODIHR, has played a catalytic role in the formation of NGO networks. With a database of more than one thousand NGOs in the region, it has facilitated the formation of networks whose members have been convened for training programs on subjects including displacement, minority issues, and conflict resolution.[37] The OSCE's efforts to strengthen the capacity of NGOs provide a model for other regional organizations.

At the international level, the high commissioner for human rights, as part of the United Nations decade for human rights education (1995–2004), is committed to building and strengthening human rights education programs among NGOs, professional associations, and community leaders as an essential element of prevention.[38] ICRC has been educating NGOs and civilian populations in the humanitarian standards that should apply in armed conflict situations. All such programs provide an opportunity to discuss the problem of internal displacement and the need to contain it.

Given the high incidence of conflict along ethnic, racial, or religious lines, programs fostering trust and understanding among communities of competing identity are important ways to manage conflict. Several of the NGOs surveyed in this study sponsor programs (such as International Alert) that promote better relations among different ethnic, cultural, and religious groups. Regional organizations have been taking a similar tack. The OAS, for example, has sponsored a pilot project in Guatemala to provide training in conflict resolution to displaced persons and other affected groups in rural areas. And the OSCE High Commissioner for National Minorities is specifically mandated to work with local communities and NGOs to prevent the escalation of minority conflicts.

A Right Not to Be Arbitrarily Displaced

Even countries with a relatively strong civil society need to protect against arbitrary displacement. Yet most intergovernmental and nongovernmental actors still focus on responding to displacement rather than on strengthening protection against unlawful displacement. One means to broaden this scope is to promote a right not to be arbitrarily displaced.

As chapter 3 points out, international humanitarian law and the law relating to indigenous peoples expressly prohibit arbitrary displacement.[39] In human rights law, by contrast, this prohibition is only implicit in certain provisions, particularly in those regarding freedom of movement and choice of residence, freedom from arbitrary interference with one's home, and the right to housing. However, these rights fail to provide adequate coverage for all instances of arbitrary displacement and do not spell out the circumstances under which displacement is permissible and where there are restrictions and derogation. They do, nonetheless, point to a general rule according to which forced displacement may not be discriminatory or imposed without due process. Displacement that is caused by, or that can be reasonably expected to result in genocide, "ethnic cleansing," apartheid, and other systematic forms of discrimination, torture, and inhuman and degrading treatment, is absolutely prohibited and may entail individual criminal responsibility under international law.

The guiding principles appended to this study hold that many situations of displacement could be avoided or at least minimized if competent authorities would respect and ensure respect for their existing obligations under international law. A right to be protected against arbitrary displacement from one's home or place of habitual residence is explicitly defined and detailed in the principles. They specify the grounds and conditions by which displacement is impermissible and the minimum procedural guarantees to be complied with, should displacement occur. Displacement, they make clear, shall not be carried out in a manner that violates the rights to life, dignity, liberty, or the security of those affected. Finally, the guiding principles note that states have a particular obligation to provide protection against displacement to indigenous peoples, minorities, peasants, pastoralists, and other groups with a special dependency on and attachment to their lands.

The development of norms concerning the prevention of displacement should serve as a reminder of a responsibility on the part not only of the controlling authorities but also of the international community not to create the conditions causing displacement. International financial institutions, for example, have begun to pay greater attention to the displacement caused by development projects and to take this into account when deciding upon projects to support. The guiding principles consider displacement caused by large-scale development projects as arbitrary when it is not justified by compelling and overriding public interests. For cases in which displacement is unavoidable, both the World Bank and the Organization for Economic Cooperation and Development (OECD) have formulated guidelines specifying requirements (including community participation, conditions of resettlement, and provision for compensation) to ensure that it occurs in a manner in keeping with international law.[40] The articulation of a right not to be arbitrarily displaced should raise awareness of the need to protect against unlawful displacement and provide a basis for preventive actions. If an international criminal court is created, it could reinforce this right by issuing judgments against unlawful displacement.

Strengthening Regional and International Capacities to Prevent Conflict

When national efforts at conflict prevention fail, regional and international organizations must develop their own contingency plans for prevention. In this connection, it is important to emphasize sovereignty's dual function: internally, the state has an obligation to fulfill the responsibilities of good and legitimate governance; externally, it must be responsive to international scrutiny and involvement. The management of conflict at the regional and international levels, then, is fundamental to the notion of sovereignty as responsibility. As UN Secretary-General Boutros-Ghali observed in the Agenda for Peace in 1992, "The time of absolute and exclusive sovereignty . . . has passed"; it has become necessary "to find a balance between the needs of good internal governance and the requirements of an ever more interdependent world."[41]

Regional organizations have a significant, though still unrealized, potential for preventing conflict (see chapter 6). Initiatives in this direction, such as the OAU's Mechanism for Conflict Prevention, Management, and Resolution, which has among its aims anticipating and defusing conflicts that cause displacement, merit strong support. The OAU secretary-general has emphasized the importance of the organization's being able to prevent conflicts from escalating into mass displacement. In Europe, the OSCE is the first organization to have articulated a justification, based on human rights and humanitarian principles, for intervening in the internal affairs of its member states. The OSCE is also unique among regional organizations for deploying field staff with the aim of defusing tensions as a conflict prevention strategy. Equally direct in its approach, the OAS has focused, as in Paraguay, Guatemala, and Haiti, on sustaining democratic regimes in order to stave off a recurrence of conflict and massive human rights violations.

Even so, regional organizations have a long way to go before they will be able to avert such extreme problems as genocide or tackle intractable civil conflicts. The intent, expressed in the Agenda for Peace, to place greater reliance on regional and subregional organizations for conflict prevention and management is far from being realized. To be successful, the ability of regional organizations to undertake political initiatives must be strengthened, and they must be endowed with enforcement powers. Most regional bodies do not yet possess enforcement capability except on an ad hoc basis. The OAU-sponsored regional conference on refugees, returnees, and displaced persons in the Great Lakes region, for example, called for the reinforcement of OAU military and civilian observers in Burundi in an effort to reduce further displacement.[42] Yet proposals for the creation of an African force with preventive and protection responsibilities have still not gained broad consensus.

An enforcement capability already exists at the subregional level in West Africa, where ECOWAS has a mandate to intervene militarily in internal armed conflict within member states, to deploy peacekeeping forces, and to engage in mediation. While the activation of this mandate with the dispatch of troops to Liberia in 1990 offers an example of a subregional group assuming responsibility for the protection of civilians caught in internal conflict, it also highlights the need for regional bodies and the United Nations to monitor such action in order that it comply with international standards and to safeguard against hegemonic ambitions.

The OSCE has supported developing its peacekeeping and preventive deployment capability, authorizing for the first time the establishment of a peacekeeping force in 1994 for Nagorno-Karabakh. Since no such OSCE force has come into being, however, the OSCE must rely on other organizations in the region that possess or are developing a military capability—namely, NATO and the West European Union—to lend force to its decisions and strengthen its leverage in negotiations.

Regional organizations have not always received sufficient cooperation and support from the United Nations. With greater UN support in Rwanda, for example, the OAU could have played a more significant role in resolving the conflict and "could have made a major difference to the genocidal outcome."[43] Indeed, the failure of actors at all levels—international, regional, and subregional—to suppress genocide in Rwanda, underlines the need to strengthen and activate more readily the peacekeeping and enforcement capacity of intergovernmental bodies in a mutually reinforcing manner. The international community should support the development and first use of rapid deployment capabilities by regional and subregional organizations while establishing a rapid reaction force of its own to act as both a deterrent and an operational enforcement mechanism when regional efforts of conflict prevention are insufficient or absent.

Although the overriding purpose of the United Nations is to prevent war, its main areas of activity—humanitarian assistance and peacekeeping—usually have focused on the consequences of conflict, not its causes. To complicate the matter, the nature of conflict is changing, from the interstate wars that the United Nations was designed to address to the civil conflicts prevalent today, some of which do not even involve a state party at all. Though the United Nations has become more willing to intervene in internal conflicts, the organization has paid little or no attention to prevention. An exception, already mentioned, was the Security Council's preventive deployment of a UN peacekeeping force in Macedonia in 1993 with the aim, successful to date, of safeguarding against an extension of the Yugoslav conflict to this volatile area of the Balkans. But when the secretary-general in 1995 called for the deployment of an international force to avert mass killings in Burundi, he received no response because states considered they had too few interests at stake to warrant the costs and risks of intervention. Nor did the international community see fit to try to stop the genocide in Rwanda a year earlier, in 1994.

When it comes to preventing or stopping genocide or crimes against humanity, justification for intervention exists in law, but in practice states have been reluctant to create an international force to avert human rights violations of magnitude in other states. There has even been reticence to deploy human rights field staff in preventive efforts. The high commissioner for human rights, for example, deployed staff in Burundi to reduce interethnic violence, but this preventive presence (numbering 12 to date) has been too small to handle the task at hand. A more appropriate human rights field presence would be on the scale of the 130-member mission in Rwanda. Such a mission would cost per annum the same amount as a single day of the UN military force for Rwanda.[44]

Arguments of cost-effectiveness should strengthen support for prevention. The $200 million estimated annual cost of the proposed UN rapid reaction force for preventing conflict pales by comparison with the more than $1 billion spent by the international community on aid in Rwanda alone following its failure to act in a timely manner to prevent the genocide there.[45] Sadako Ogata, the high commissioner for refugees, has applauded the proposal to create an early and rapid UN deployment capability, noting that it "would prevent escalation, would save money, and, what is more important would save lives."[46] Moreover, international burden-sharing would reduce the risks of having one or two nations alone putting their own soldiers at risk in faraway lands. Neighboring states would also be less likely to intervene injudiciously.

Though the secretary-general's initial recommendation for such a force in the 1992 Agenda for Peace failed to generate sufficient support, recent events attest to its continued relevance. The secretary-general's special representative in Somalia concluded that "much of the catastrophe that has unfolded could have been avoided" had the United Nations intervened earlier and more effectively in Somalia.[47] Aid agencies in Somalia in 1992 also argued that the deployment of armed UN forces "may actually decrease the likelihood of conflict."[48] In the case of Rwanda, the former UN commander has concluded that the "international community missed a golden opportunity to resolve the crisis because it reacted too late to the burgeoning refugee situation and much too late to stop the ongoing genocide."[49] Had UNAMIR received an appropriate mandate and had its troop strength been reinforced rather than reduced to all but 270 troops when the mass killings began in the spring of 1994, it could have become an effective deterrent force.[50]

Of course, in promoting efforts to prevent displacement and protect persons within their countries of origin, it is important to ensure that these are not misinterpreted to mean preventing refugee flight. When the United Nations worked to mitigate the conditions forcing people into flight in the former Yugoslavia, asylum states used those efforts as an excuse to deny entry to those wishing to flee.[51] According to UNHCR, the concept of prevention "can be used in the constructive sense of removing the underlying causes of forced migratory movements. But it can also mean building barriers to stop the victims of persecution from entering another country."[52] Safeguarding against this risk, however, does not mean that preventive strategies should be abandoned, only that they should reinforce rather than undermine the traditional notion of protection through asylum.[53] The internally displaced are after all potential refugees; their right to seek asylum needs to be safeguarded when they cannot find safety in their own countries.

Protection Integrated with Assistance

As UN Secretary-General Kofi Annan has rightly pointed out, providing humanitarian assistance in today's crisis zones demands not only an efficient relief delivery system but a means of ensuring that vulnerable populations will survive in a hostile environment.[54] Whether in Bosnia, Iraq, or Rwanda, security is as critical a concern as food. If anything, protection is "a prerequisite for the efficacy of assistance" in such circumstances.[55] Feeding and assisting displaced people "so that they can survive to be caught in the cross-fire of conflict and acts of ethnic cleansing" can hardly be considered effective humanitarian action.[56] As a non-Serb threatened with expulsion from Banja Luka explained to UNHCR: "We do not need food, we are not starving to death. We are being persecuted and we prefer to be hungry for a week than not to sleep every night, in fear of being beaten, raped, or killed."[57] At the time, the international community had effectively addressed the risk of starvation in the former Yugoslavia. But as one observer wryly commented, the international community's response could be considered a success only insofar as it "allowed Bosnians to die on a full stomach."[58]

Some have compared the international response system to a tripod, with relief, development, and protection constituting each of the legs: while the relief and development legs are more or less at full length, the protection leg is short, and thus the whole apparatus is wobbly.[59] The only way to correct this imbalance is to extend the third leg. To begin the process, the meaning of protection needs to be clarified.

Clarifying Protection as a Concept

The great difficulty in protecting the internally displaced is that there is no legal instrument that stipulates what protection should mean in their case. By contrast, UNHCR has a clear understanding that "international protection" for refugees means defending their legal right to asylum and non-refoulement. Furthermore, it seeks to give refugees who lawfully reside on the territory of a foreign state a status as close to that of its nationals as possible.[60] Thus refugee protection also means defending the rights, security, and welfare of refugees, particularly their "personal security" against acts of violence and mistreatment.[61] Indeed, refugee protection involves an unrestricted human rights competence to ensure respect for refugees' human dignity and integrity.[62] Because refugees are outside of their national territory and lack the protection of their government, international law substitutes its own protection for that which the country of origin cannot or will not provide.[63]

Although refugee law cannot apply directly to internally displaced persons, a concept of protection can be derived from relevant or analogous legal standards contained in refugee, humanitarian, and human rights law and from the activities of UNHCR and other organizations in providing protection to the internally displaced. UNHCR's interpretation of personal security for refugees has in fact come to be applied on an ad hoc basis to internally displaced persons. In a 1994 note to its Executive Committee, UNHCR described the "protection activities" its staff had been called upon to perform in defense of the internally displaced. These included monitoring the treatment of threatened minority groups, intervening with the authorities to request protective action, investigating and prosecuting specific cases, providing assistance and protection in temporary relief centers, and helping governments provide personal documentation. In situations of armed conflict or massive violations of human rights, UNHCR activities consisted of helping civilians secure safe passage through front lines, relocating and evacuating civilians from conflict areas, assisting besieged populations unable or unwilling to move from their homes, intervening with local authorities to prevent the involuntary return of the internally displaced to areas of danger, alerting governments and the public to human rights abuses, and promoting the right of the internally displaced to return voluntarily to their homes. UNHCR also participated in mediation and reconciliation efforts between returning displaced persons and local residents.[64] The internally displaced thus benefited from protection activities adapted from the refugee experience, but also going beyond it, they have benefited from the application of humanitarian law.

Like refugee protection, protection under international humanitarian law entails safeguarding personal security. Although the term "protection" per se is not defined in the Geneva Conventions and Protocols, for ICRC, the custodian of international humanitarian law, protection means "preserving victims of conflict who are in the hands of an adverse authority from the dangers, sufferings and abuses of power to which they may be exposed, defending them and giving them support."[65] Both common Article 3 to the Geneva Conventions and Protocol II relating to the protection of victims of noninternational armed conflicts stipulate the protections the civilian population is to enjoy (see chapter 3). In situations of armed conflict, ICRC undertakes a wide range of activities to protect civilians, including internally displaced persons. It makes representations to governments and nonstate actors when violations of humanitarian law occur, evacuates civilians from situations of danger, creates protected areas, establishes tracing networks, provides material assistance needed for survival, and facilitates arrangements for the creation of humanitarian space and cease-fires.

Both UNHCR and ICRC find that translating protection into direct actions in the field "frequently depends on non-legal skills and initiatives."[66] Legal remedies alone would involve processes too lengthy to address the immediate protection concerns of persons at risk. Furthermore, they could become virtually irrelevant in complex emergencies when the state structures upholding the rule of law have collapsed or are unable to operate free of political or military interference.[67] Operational agencies, sometimes backed up by military force, are therefore needed to provide protection to affected populations.

Protection for the internally displaced can thus be said to mean measures that ensure respect for the fundamental human rights of the displaced, particularly their safety and dignity. These measures go beyond providing material assistance to encompass defending the personal security and fundamental rights of the displaced.

Guiding Principles

When intergovernmental and nongovernmental organizations decide to provide protection to the internally displaced, they base their activities on a myriad of provisions in human rights and humanitarian law, and, by analogy, refugee law. No specific instrument on the internally displaced exists to guide them. A normative framework specifically tailored to the needs of the internally displaced should therefore be an important component of any strategy for protection.

As the analysis of legal norms in chapter 3 points out, substantial gray areas and gaps exist in the law as it applies to internally displaced persons; this situation calls for a body of principles that would restate general principles of protection, make key provisions more explicit, and address clear gaps in the law; and it would be desirable, as NGOs have insisted, to consolidate into one "compact and usable document" existing norms that at present are dispersed in many different instruments.[68] UNHCR, ICRC, and other humanitarian agencies have also testified to the value of having principles specific to the internally displaced, while the United Nations General Assembly and Commission on Human Rights have called for a normative framework to enhance protection for internally displaced persons.

The body of principles developed under the direction of the representative of the secretary-general and appended to this volume consolidates into one document the relevant norms applicable to the internally displaced. It is the first attempt to define protection for the internally displaced in terms of protection against displacement, during displacement, and during return and reintegration. The principles apply both to governments and insurgent forces, are nonderogable, and are applicable in all circumstances. Although not a binding instrument, the principles could contribute, over time, to the creation of a moral and political climate in which they might eventually attain the force of customary law.

Even more important than their eventual legal status, however, is their value in providing a yardstick for monitoring the treatment of the internally displaced. They can be expected to strengthen the advocacy work of humanitarian, human rights, and development organizations on behalf of the internally displaced. UNHCR has already taken the step of developing a manual for its field staff on the basis of the legal analysis on which the principles are based.[69] These principles can also be of use to governments in drafting laws to protect the internally displaced.

The representative of the secretary-general will introduce the guiding principles to the Commission on Human Rights in 1998. Wide acceptance and dissemination of the principles would encourage their use by relevant actors at all levels. Most significantly, they could prove an important means of encouraging affected populations themselves to mobilize and develop strategies to increase protection at the local level.

Community-Based Protection

Internally displaced persons, like any group of civilians under threat, will instinctively devise their own strategies for addressing their immediate needs. As earlier noted, even before displacement takes place, populations at risk tend to form community-level systems that forewarn other members of their group of impending displacement.

Local coping mechanisms are particularly important in the absence of an effective government. In Somalia in the early 1990s, under the most dangerous conditions, local citizens created their own organizations to provide educational and health services, employment, and development opportunities and to mediate disputes. Clan elders, civic leaders, health professionals, and women's groups, among others, sought to salvage what remained of civil society and provide a modicum of protection and assistance to displaced and other populations. When international assistance was provided, however, it did not adequately take into account and build upon these local efforts.[70]

If humanitarian assistance is to be effective, it must be based on the recognition that "the delivery of aid directly interacts with the recipients' own physical, social, and psychological capacities and must be designed to support and build on these."[71] Otherwise, the capacities inherent among beneficiary populations will go to waste and they will only become more vulnerable.[72] Indeed, self-help has been shown to have an immediate protective effect in reducing the violence in displaced persons camps and their individual homes caused by feelings of frustration and dependency.[73]

Given that the local community represents the most fundamental source of protection, activities that encourage the restoration of communal links or that support the reintegration of internally displaced persons into new communities can enhance their security. Efforts to reunify families, create support structures for unaccompanied children, and enable displaced persons to remain with or rejoin members of their clan, tribe, or village should receive high priority in emergency situations. Over the longer term, activities facilitating conflict resolution and reconciliation at the local level among different cultural, ethnic, and religious groups can contribute to the security of internally displaced persons as well as to their eventual return to their areas of origin or their integration into areas of resettlement.

Equally important is the sense of community internally displaced persons experience in creating their own organizations. In Peru, Colombia, and Guatemala, such groups are active in speaking out for the protection of their rights. In the former Yugoslavia, internally displaced persons from Srebrenica have issued repeated joint demands for information on the fate of the more than 5,000 men reported "missing" when Bosnian Serb forces overran this "safe area" in 1995. In Georgia, internally displaced persons from the secessionist region of Abkhazia regularly stage demonstrations to protest the obstructions impeding their return, which they consider to violate agreements signed by the authorities.[74] The field staff of UN and regional monitoring missions and of international NGOs should support such community efforts. In particular, they might be visibly present at demonstrations in order to discourage potential abuses.[75]

It is essential to consider the views of the internally displaced in designing and implementing programs for them because they know better than anyone else how to meet their protection and assistance needs. In UNHCR's experience, involving the beneficiaries "in solving their own problems is the best way to ensure that the problem is solved in the most satisfactory manner."[76] Community participation, moreover, can help to ensure that programs do not unintentionally reinforce repressive authorities or perpetuate discriminatory practices, particularly against women.[77]

As protectors and providers for their families, women play a central role in reducing the vulnerability of entire communities to the effects of displacement.[78] Their participation in the design of protection strategies therefore is essential to ensuring that not only their own needs but those of the affected populations as a whole are adequately addressed. Too often, displaced women's capacities are ignored in the structures set up in camps and settlements. In Burundi, for instance, internally displaced women were found to play no role at all in camp decisionmaking. When the representative of the secretary-general on internally displaced persons asked to meet with the spokespersons of a camp housing several thousand women and twenty-five men, only men came forward to discuss the problems of the camp.[79] Such practices undermine protection. UNDP and other relief and development agencies have strongly endorsed women's involvement and have recommended that the organizations formed by internally displaced women be strengthened since these groups are often the most effective means of identifying the needs and capabilities of the displaced populations and of organizing programs to assist them.[80]

National Protective Mechanisms

As noted earlier, UN programs and those of regional organizations and NGOs to develop and strengthen national institutions in support of democratization and human rights have benefited the internally displaced. In Cambodia, internationally assisted efforts to clarify the wording of the constitution and to extend citizenship to ethnic Vietnamese encouraged the return of forcibly displaced communities. In Guatemala, Liberia, and the former Yugoslavia, international monitoring of elections helped create respect for the voting rights of internally displaced persons and made an important contribution to peace-building and societal reconstruction.[81]

A more direct response to situations of internal displacement is also needed at the national level. With increased capacity for responding to emergencies, states themselves could address humanitarian crises instead of immediately having to appeal to the international community for assistance. The UNDP and other international organizations have been particularly active in lending support to national preparedness efforts. Even so, few countries have national institutions or offices that directly or indirectly relate to the problem of internal displacement.

Of course, the mere existence of an office for internally displaced persons does not necessarily denote a national framework that is responsive to their plight.[82] Structures set up in Guatemala and Kenya to deal with the internally displaced have worked better in theory than in practice.[83] Or, the attention paid to the internally displaced may be uneven: in Peru, in keeping with the government's objective of reversing mass migration to urban centers, it provides support mainly to returnees, while neglecting the needs of those who have chosen to resettle.[84]

Sometimes, the political interests of the government benefit the displaced. These interests tend to be heightened in cases of ethnic conflict when, as in Croatia, Cyprus, Azerbaijan, and Georgia, the authorities prove exceptionally anxious to assist displaced members of the ethnic group corresponding with the majority or even official national identity (see chapter 2). But strong motivation for the establishment of national structures does not always translate into effective institutions. In Azerbaijan, the government has been discouraging the displaced from resettling in an effort to promote their return to Nagorno-Karabakh, now overrun by Armenia. Moreover, as the experience in Colombia attests, initially promising steps may be thwarted by a volatile political climate.[85]

Sri Lanka, by contrast, provides a good example of government support not only for establishing national institutions but, equally important, for ensuring that this machinery functions effectively. The representative of the secretary-general on internally displaced persons found in 1993 that the government assumed "full responsibility" for providing relief to its internally displaced population.[86] It does so through the Emergency Reconstruction and Rehabilitation Program implemented by the Ministry of Reconstruction, Rehabilitation, and Social Welfare which maintains hundreds of camps and "welfare centers" serving more than a quarter million internally displaced persons. Admittedly, resource constraints and aid diversions have sometimes prevented the program from providing as much assistance as it promises, and the government has also been known to restrict shipments to displaced Tamils.[87] In fact, in recent years, there appears to be a gradual subordination to military priorities of the government's commitment to the displaced.[88] On the whole, however, the government is assuming responsibility for providing protection and assistance to the internally displaced in both government-held and rebel-controlled areas.[89]

Lebanon's Ministry of Displaced Persons also reportedly operates effectively.[90] Elsewhere, the fledgling efforts on the part of governments to assume their responsibilities for the internally displaced require outside assistance. Exemplary in this regard is the program of action adopted by the 1996 CIS regional conference, which encourages governments to establish high-level migration agencies to "develop policy and co-ordinate all relevant governmental bodies" but also calls for international support of this process.[91] Specifically, international organizations are invited to develop technical cooperation programs "aimed to assist the CIS Governments in strengthening their organizational structures and management capacity and in developing their information systems."[92] The case of Georgia exemplifies ways in which international organizations, donor governments, and NGOs might help strengthen national capacities. The international community helped create the Coordination Bureau for International Humanitarian Aid, which coordinates all international and NGO assistance programs for the internally displaced and other needy groups. In 1996, international organizations agreed to assist the government in developing a unified migration management system to address, among other problems, the return and reintegration of internally displaced persons from Abkhazia.[93]

International organizations have a role to play not only in supporting national institutions but in monitoring their effectiveness. UNHCR, IOM, and the OSCE under the CIS process have assumed this role and have been working with governments in this region to promote implementation. In other areas, the country visits of the representative of the secretary-general on internally displaced persons have provided an opportunity to analyze whether national institutions represent genuine efforts on behalf of the internally displaced. In his discussions with governments, the representative regularly encourages the creation or strengthening of national institutions for the protection and assistance of internally displaced and other affected populations. NGOs have also been instrumental in this regard. The U.S. Committee for Refugees, Human Rights Watch, and the Open Society Institute have evaluated national responses to displacement and made recommendations for their improvement.

Needless to say, such strategies have the best prospects of success in states that have the political will to address the plight of the internally displaced. They will do less well in countries such as Turkey, Myanmar (Burma), and the Sudan, where, ethnic, cultural, or religious groups falling outside the official identity framework may be purposely denied the protection and assistance of the state. In other cases, state structures and the traditional system of social administration and leadership at all levels may have collapsed, leaving no national framework through which to address the needs of the displaced. Such circumstances call for other protection strategies.

International Arrangements to Increase Protection

At present, the international institutional framework has no effective locus of responsibility for internally displaced persons, leaving many without protection and assistance. Of the various options discussed in chapter 4, two are especially persuasive. The first is to assign responsibility for most internally displaced persons to an existing UN agency, preferably UNHCR, since it has the necessary protection and assistance skills. A second option would be to designate an operational focal point for the internally displaced in each complex emergency. The focal point would be expected to monitor the situation of the internally displaced; develop strategies for ensuring that their protection, assistance, and reintegration and development needs are met; and directly address some of these needs itself. Again, UNHCR would be a most suitable candidate, but UNICEF and WFP could also act as focal points, and when appropriate, humanitarian organizations outside the United Nations, such as ICRC or IOM, could do so. Resident/humanitarian coordinators, or the focal point itself, would be expected to mobilize the support of other relevant agencies so that they could contribute their expertise.

The ERC and the Inter-Agency Standing Committee, for their part, should assess whether assistance, protection, and reintegration and development activities are well integrated on behalf of the displaced in each complex emergency. Even in the event that one agency was assigned principal responsibility for the internally displaced, the IASC would have to ensure that other agencies played strong supporting roles and that problems were not being neglected (either because governments did not acknowledge the problem or request assistance, or because donors failed to respond effectively). In short, under ERC leadership, the IASC should become an effective forum for dealing with problems of internal displacement.

IASC leadership is also needed to press for political action to resolve the crises that are causing or exacerbating mass displacement. As one of UNHCR's special envoys to the former Yugoslavia reflected in 1994: "We felt more and more that we were used as a palliative, an alibi, an excuse to cover the lack of political will to confront the reality of the war in Bosnia with the necessary political and, perhaps, military means."[94] The case of Bosnia clearly illustrates the dangers of relying on humanitarian action to the point that it becomes a substitute for political action and more direct and concerted protection measures. To the extent that the IASC can become an effective spokesperson for the humanitarian, human rights, and development communities, the greater the chances that efforts will be made by the international community to resolve the underlying causes of conflict and displacement. The strengthening of the mandate of the representative of the secretary-general on internally displaced persons, now a full member of the IASC, would also help further protection considerably.

Protection through Presence

Protection, as earlier noted, means taking measures to ensure respect for the basic human rights of the displaced, particularly their safety and dignity. Consequently, for UNHCR, "protection through presence" has become one of its key strategies:

> As structures break down, as central authority is challenged, as borders change, international presence in the country of origin is becoming an essential feature of our preventive strategy. Through international humanitarian presence, some measure of security and relief can be provided to victims of conflict or human rights violations who may otherwise feel compelled to cross borders or be unable to return home. In this sense, there is a close connection between presence, prevention, and the pursuit of solutions.[95]

This view has come to be shared by humanitarian actors, human rights bodies, and peacekeepers alike.[96]

To be sure, presence can enhance protection, especially in areas where the government and the insurgent forces cooperate. As the case study on

Sri Lanka points out, in certain areas, "UNHCR presence was a restraining influence on the action of the combatant parties."[97] In many other cases, however, presence in and of itself, rarely assures protection. The presence of expatriates "watching and listening" may deter some human rights violations, but when these are committed as part of systematic campaigns, mere presence is an ineffective protection strategy.[98] If presence is accompanied by silent or tacit acceptance of violations, it might even encourage them. Rather, the value of presence is it provides the potential for developing more direct strategies to ensure protection.

Many of the field-based protection strategies that have been devised—such as accompaniment, protective custody, neighborhood patrols, protection watches, safe houses, interventions with the authorities, and evacuations of life-threatening cases—fall within the domain of those humanitarian actors, such as UNHCR and ICRC, that have a protection mandate. However, other humanitarian agencies and NGOs having an earlier and more extensive presence on the ground also must seek to maximize the utility of their presence for protective purposes. Even if they restrict themselves to providing relief or development assistance, their programs should be designed in ways that integrate protection concerns. Moreover, when serious, life-threatening protection problems arise, they should, at the very least, communicate this information to those in a better position to respond to the situation. In short, presence should prompt international protection, not preclude it.[99]

An Operational Human Rights Role

If they are to provide more protection on the ground, human rights bodies must expand their traditional role of monitoring, reporting, and advocacy through various practical measures in the field. In the former Yugoslavia in 1993, collecting, verifying, and assessing information on human rights violations for the special rapporteur sometimes generated positive changes in human rights practices.[100] But the mandate did not go far enough, given the egregious violations of human rights being perpetrated: "It is not possible to limit the mandate to the preparation of reports. . . . The mandate should lead to prompt and concrete measures benefiting populations which are suffering and whose rights are being violated."[101] Indeed, a mere reporting role without backup becomes "primarily a highly sophisticated and well-documented 'bookkeeping' of horrors."[102]

Under their mandate, the UN human rights field staff deployed to Rwanda in 1994 were to try to redress existing human rights problems as well as prevent anticipated violations.[103] In addition, they were charged with facilitating the return of internally displaced persons and refugees by helping to create conditions of safety in areas of return. As mentioned earlier, this was the first time that a UN human rights mandate specifically addressed the protection needs of internally displaced persons.

Despite a host of logistical and other difficulties, the hundred or more field staff sent to Rwanda by the Centre for Human Rights helped, albeit unevenly, to improve protection for returning internally displaced persons and refugees. Of course, the massacre at the Kibeho camp in April 1995 tragically underlined the need for a human rights presence, not only in the communes but also in camp situations and settlements. Overall, however, the Rwanda deployment has shown that field staff with a mandate for more than mere monitoring and reporting can be of service in protecting internally displaced persons.

El Salvador provides further such evidence. The 100 UN human rights monitors who were deployed to deter abuses and build a climate of confidence even before a peace accord was signed had good coverage of the country and enjoyed unimpeded access. The moral authority of the United Nations combined with the high-level grass roots organization among Salvadorans themselves further contributed to the mission's effectiveness in decreasing human rights abuses in the country.[104]

Human rights field staff could also serve in designated safe areas and camps for the internally displaced, intercede with local authorities when protection problems arise, develop protection strategies in cooperation with humanitarian organizations, and alert appropriate UN bodies to protection problems they cannot resolve themselves. In addition, they could play an active role in monitoring and protecting the return and resettlement of internally displaced persons. According to the senior UNHCR protection officer in the former Yugoslavia, the "lack of early on-the-spot involvement of international human rights bodies" was "one of the major deficiencies" in the UN's response to that situation.[105]

Since overall UN human rights field presence is limited, regional counterparts have at times compensated for their absence. The OSCE and, to a lesser extent, the European Union, have begun to deploy their own on-site human rights field staff. Members of the European Community Monitoring Mission (ECMM) deployed to the former Yugoslavia provided a valuable source of information for the UN special rapporteur, as well as a modicum of security to populations under threat. This was particularly important in areas to which UN human rights field staff were denied access.[106] Moreover, in the reconstituted Federal Republic of Yugoslavia, to which UN human rights bodies were also regularly denied access, the OSCE was able to establish several long-term missions for the dual purposes of monitoring and seeking to redress violations. A local NGO attests that these missions had a significant protective effect, not only by means of their presence in the volatile areas of Kosovo, Vojvodina, and Sandzak, but also in reportedly resolving a number of the protection cases that they took up with the authorities.[107] The success of the missions, however, was short-lived for in less than a year they were expelled by the government, which ignored the repeated demands of both the OSCE and the United Nations for their reinstatement.[108] The experience has not deterred the OSCE from undertaking on-site human rights monitoring and protection roles elsewhere, as in Tajikistan, but it does highlight one of the main problems inherent in human rights field operations.

International human rights NGOs also are beginning to take more of an operational approach to protection by establishing a long-term presence in the field. Exemplary in this regard is the field office established by Human Rights Watch in Bosnia and Herzegovina. Where conditions of safety allow, other human rights NGOs might consider following suit, especially in situations where the absence of any other human rights field presence leaves threatened populations with no expert advocates to bring their plight to the attention of the authorities and to the international community. Another strategy is to second human rights experts to humanitarian organizations, as MSF/Netherlands did with the attachment of two members of the International Human Rights Law Group to its mission in Rwanda.[109] In some situations, NGO field staff would be safer under a broader international umbrella that includes humanitarian organizations and peacekeeping forces. Whatever the mode of deployment, their presence in the field is an important element in overall strategies to increase protection for the internally displaced.

Integrating Protection Concerns into Assistance and Development Operations

It has been said that humanitarian action performed "in a contextual vacuum can have inhumane consequences."[110] That is to say, it could lend legitimacy to repressive regimes, harm the welfare of the displaced, sustain the conflict, and create conditions that impede the return and reintegration of uprooted populations. NGOs in particular have expressed concern about perpetuating or even causing displacement by means of assistance and development programs that do not take into account the broader context in which they occur. "Humanitarian aid," the president of Interaction has emphasized, "can have political consequences totally unintended by [those who administer] that aid. NGOs cannot—and should not—ignore the political consequences of their efforts."[111]

The case of Somalia is instructive. The concentration of assistance programs in urban areas drew people from rural areas into urban-based displaced persons camps, where the need for protection inadvertently generated a whole range of other relief requirements. When assistance agencies proved unable to meet these needs, not only did disease replace malnutrition as the greatest threat, but populations were forced to turn to warlords for protection, and in return they had to take up arms, which only intensified the conflict.[112] Similarly, the creation of illusory "safe areas" in Bosnia encouraged populations to flee to areas where, as it would turn out, their lives would possibly be in even greater danger than in the areas from which they had fled.

Considerations of context also are important for development programs, which, without adequate attention to human rights conditions, may actually aggravate the problem in a way that eventually can cause further displacement. As noted earlier, UNDP's operations with internally displaced persons in Kenya serve as a warning that if international involvement on behalf of internally displaced persons is to be to their benefit, it must encompass human rights and protection concerns in all phases.[113]

In a welcome development, the IASC has recognized the necessity of addressing both the protection and the assistance needs of internally displaced persons. In 1997 it recommended that steps be taken "to formulate guidelines for better practices, which will enhance the synergy between assistance and protection of IDPs." It also called upon resident/ humanitarian coordinators to "advocate for the assistance and protection of IDPs."[114]

Advocacy is a particularly important strategy for all actors on the ground. It can take the form of private as well as public initiatives and should be directed to the national and local authorities in the country concerned. Insofar as sharing information on protection issues with the authorities may bring to their attention circumstances of which the authorities were not aware, they should be given the opportunity to take remedial action. In cases where the authorities are themselves undermining the protection of the displaced, the conveyance of outside awareness and concern should seek to create pressure upon the authorities to fulfill their responsibilities. When private advocacy fails, organizations may resort to various forms of public advocacy to attract attention to the failure of the government or insurgent forces to meet basic protection and assistance needs. They may also encourage outside actors to exert pressure.[115]

Although many humanitarian and development organizations are reluctant to do anything that may violate the principle of neutrality on which their assistance operations are based, ignoring the protection problems of the internally displaced may undermine their assistance programs, and the victims may become the so-called well-fed dead.[116]

Like MSF, the UNHCR, ICRC, and NGOs have often observed the principle of neutrality in a way that does not demand turning a blind eye to human rights violations. As UNHCR's special envoy to the former Yugoslavia has explained: "To be silent could be a form of partiality in favour of the criminals. If by neutrality, one means to help all victims without discrimination . . . that is correct. But if neutrality means not to take sides, not even in favour of the victims, that would be a wrong interpretation: we chose to be on the side of the victims."[117] For its part, ICRC generally tends to forgo public advocacy except in the most extreme cases and then only on several conditions, such as major and repeated violations of humanitarian law, the failure of confidential representations with the authorities, the helpfulness of publicity to the victims, and incontrovertible evidence of the violations.[118] By contrast, MSF has been bolder in speaking out about violations against internally displaced persons.

At other times, humanitarian and development organizations may find that vocalizing protection concerns may be unwise. Even so, they can still mobilize others to respond, particularly donors who can lobby the concerned governments to change their policies.[119] In the case of Kenya, UNDP's donors represented a powerful potential ally for raising the human rights and protection issues that UNDP itself proved unwilling to broach.[120] At the same time, UNDP's integration of human rights and protection concerns into the Development Program for Displaced Persons, Refugees, and Returnees in Central America (PRODERE) indicates that at times it is willing and able to engage directly in the promotion and protection of human rights.

To be sure, advocacy, whether private or public, carries risks. It can provoke governments to restrict access or even expel and attack personnel. International agencies and NGOs alike can effectively manage these risks by taking joint stands. Solidarity not only reduces the risks involved for all but it is likely to strengthen the overall impact of the initiative by drawing greater attention to the problem. Faced with a united front, governments and insurgent groups are far more likely to respond positively to the agencies providing the material assistance that they presumably want.

Similarly, threats to withdraw operations will have greater force if issued collectively. A joint press release issued by sixteen NGOs threatening to withdraw unless the dangerous working conditions in refugee camps in Congo (Zaire) and Tanzania were rectified succeeded in bringing about some improvements in the security situation.[121] Collective threats of suspended aid could prove a powerful weapon, but it must be used sparingly, since withdrawal can harm the very people the aid was intended to help.[122]

UN Secretary-General Annan has stated that one of his objectives is to make human rights concerns an integral part of all main UN activities.[123] The institutional strategies proposed in this study suggest integrating the work of the United Nation's humanitarian and human rights organizations in the following ways. First, persons with expertise in human rights and protection could be included in interagency needs assessment missions and interagency discussions could be held under the umbrella of the IASC to determine an appropriate division of labor among UN human rights and humanitarian bodies. Second, UN humanitarian and human rights bodies could develop joint strategies in the field for monitoring the physical safety and basic human rights of the internally displaced. UNHCR's agreement with the high commissioner for human rights in the case of Rwanda is noteworthy in dividing responsibilities for the protection of uprooted populations in that country. Under a memorandum of understanding between UNHCR and UNICEF, the latter agency assumed responsibility for protecting and assisting unaccompanied children in their countries of origin. These and other interagency agreements demonstrate the type of collaboration required to ensure a comprehensive response to protection concerns in situations of internal displacement.

Greater collaboration between humanitarian and development agencies and the representative of the secretary-general on internally displaced persons is also in order. The representative, in his dialogues with governments and in his reports to the United Nations, can raise protection problems that humanitarian and development agencies may feel constrained from discussing themselves. Pursuant to a letter of understanding between the Under-Secretary-General for Humanitarian Affairs and the representative, resident/humanitarian coordinators are now expected to ask the representative to visit countries where there is need to highlight such concerns.[124] By participating more in the work of the IASC, the representative and the high commissioner for human rights should be able to systematically draw the attention of the humanitarian and development agencies to protection concerns.

Efforts to integrate protection and assistance are also beginning among NGOs in the field. As elaborated in chapter 5, humanitarian assistance NGOs can do even more in this respect by identifying the least to most direct means by which they can aid in physical protection. Those unwilling to take steps to provide protection should be expected to communicate information on protection problems to others who are willing to act upon them and to participate, when appropriate, in joint positions. Further coordination in the form of a framework for cooperation among human rights and humanitarian organizations in conflict situations, such as that initiated by MSF in 1996, would ensure that their protection and assistance work occurs in a more complementary and mutually reinforcing manner.

The safety needs of NGO field staff also merit close attention, particularly in areas where law and order have broken down and undisciplined armed factions deliberately target relief groups for the goods they have, or because they perceive them as aiding an adversary. Not only are new NGO strategies needed, especially ones that place more emphasis on joint programs and security training, but UN efforts are also needed, as chapter 5 suggested. The United Nations should include NGOs in briefings and security training, especially when NGOs are supporting UN operations or substituting for UN presence.

Intergovernmental and nongovernmental organizations will in addition require training in the protection needs of internally displaced persons and how best to respond to them. Even for UNHCR staff, who are adept at protecting refugees, working in countries of origin with the internally displaced requires specialized knowledge.[125] To complement UNHCR's manual on legal standards applicable to the internally displaced, training in practical measures could ensure that the norms it outlines are applied in the field. The staff of international organizations should be taught how to report on protection problems, whom to alert both in the field and at headquarters, and what practical measures might enhance protection. The UN Centre for Human Rights in cooperation with UNHCR and, if possible, ICRC, could institute training in both law and practical measures for UN staff and for interested NGOs.

The training should extend as well to international civilian police forces and peacekeepers, since they are increasingly expected to assume responsibilities for protecting the physical security of threatened populations. Reports of UN peacekeepers abusing, even torturing, members of civilian populations underline the need not only for training but for procedures for dealing with abuses by UN personnel.[126]

Protection Strategies for Women and Children

The special protection needs of women and children, who constitute the overwhelming majority of internally displaced populations, have received far too little attention in the operational programs of international and nongovernmental organizations. When women's needs are neglected, the consequences can be felt in entire communities and can pose obstacles to the process of return and reintegration.[127] A series of regional and international conferences have highlighted the plight of displaced women and pointed to the scant attention paid to developing strategies for remedying their problems.[128]

A significant first step toward improving conditions would be to compile gender-specific information as a routine part of assessments done by humanitarian and development agencies. When large-scale protection problems are reported, a special UN fact-finding mission would go out to evaluate the situation more fully and make recommendations. This apparently took place only once in Liberia in 1993, when an interagency mission was dispatched specifically to look into the problems facing internally displaced women and suggest remedial action.[129]

In addition, humanitarian and development organizations working with the internally displaced should be expected to apply the relevant provisions of UNHCR's guidelines on sexual violence and on the protection of refugee women. These guidelines identify numerous preventive measures for protecting displaced women, especially in camps and settlements. The measures cover the design of camps, placement of latrines, lighting, and how far women have to go for firewood. They point out how trading sexual favors for food and supplies can be reduced by designating women as the initial point of control for the distribution of food. They provide for women's active participation in camp administration and decisionmaking and suggest measures to deter abuses, such as giving protection and field staff a more visible presence. They also identify steps to take where women have suffered sexual violence.[130]

Implementing the guidelines and advocating on behalf of displaced women with the competent authorities would be an important way of addressing the needs of internally displaced women. This activity could be undertaken by the UN Development Fund for Women (UNIFEM), UNICEF, or UNHCR, individually or jointly, with the support of the resident/humanitarian coordinator. NGOs also have an important role to play. The Women's Commission on Refugee Women and Children, for example, has expanded the scope of its activities to monitor the extent to which UNHCR guidelines are being applied in the case of internally displaced women. The revision of the guidelines on the protection of refugee women, currently under way at UNHCR, provides the opportunity to formally extend their application to internally displaced women and to include in the guidelines issues of particular concern to the internally displaced, such as access to identity papers and documents and overcoming discrimination in owning and acquiring land.

Camps and settlements, although intended to provide refuge for the displaced, often expose women to new threats to their physical security, especially sexual violence and harassment.[131] In such situations, UN agencies and NGOs should be encouraged to increase the visibility of their field staff or deploy additional staff, particularly female staff in cases where male staff have limited access, where women are in need of counseling and other services, or where testimony needs to be taken about sexual violence. Regular contact with internally displaced women may provide a sense of security and reassurance, encourage the women to speak up, and promote the undertaking of preventive measures by the entire community.

Too often the response to sexual violence against women focuses on assisting victims *after* the attack has taken place rather than trying to prevent the violence.[132] In Bosnia and Herzegovina, the campaigns of mass rape did receive international exposure and condemnation, but the international response often concentrated on compiling evidence for the international criminal tribunal without making any companion efforts to protect against the rapes that continued to occur.[133] Moreover, in Rwanda and Liberia, the world paid little attention to the systematic use of rape, and little was done to try to prevent it.[134]

Of course, it must be recognized that humanitarian and human rights bodies are likely to prove as powerless to stop deliberate mass rape as they are the campaigns of "ethnic cleansing" of which rape can be a part. However, there is still a tendency among some personnel at humanitarian agencies and NGOs to view rape as a regrettable but unavoidable part of conflict situations and make this an excuse for doing little to try to prevent it.[135] Recognition of rape as a criminal offense, together with exposure of such acts in whatever parts of the world they occur, can serve as a preventive measure or at the very least result in punishment for the perpetrators. The extent to which the international criminal tribunals on Rwanda and the former Yugoslavia prosecute rape as a war crime and crime against humanity will be an important test of changing perceptions about sexual violence.

The special protection needs of internally displaced children also tend to be neglected by humanitarian agencies.[136] Here, the IASC, in cooperation with the special representative on children in armed conflict, appointed by the secretary-general in 1997, should assess the extent to which assistance and protection are being provided to internally displaced children in different emergency situations and develop strategies to address their needs.[137] UNICEF should be expected to play the lead role in the field in the protection and assistance of internally displaced children, even in the event that another organization is assigned primary responsibility for the internally displaced. In a welcome move, UNICEF's Executive Board in 1996 committed the organization to "ensur[ing] that its activities in . . . child care and protection are extended to displaced children," but programs to accomplish this have still to be designed.[138]

All other operational agencies should also be expected to undertake both advocacy and practical measures for the protection of internally

displaced children who come within their purview, particularly with regard to preventing sexual violence, forcible recruitment into armed
forces, and the denial of relief and services. Special attention should be
paid to ensuring the survival and protection of unaccompanied children,
many of whom are orphans and require medical attention and psychosocial services.

Although sufficient legal protection for children does exist, most notably in the Convention on the Rights of the Child, these standards need
to be widely known, understood, and implemented by national mechanisms and community structures as well as by the staff of international
and regional organizations, NGOs, and peacekeeping forces.[139] Training
of these various actors should therefore include components on the rights
of children and strategies for promoting and protecting them. Field personnel should establish mechanisms to assess and to report on implementation of the convention in the areas falling within the scope of their
activities. The guiding principles appended to this volume and UNHCR
guidelines on the protection of refugee children should also be widely
disseminated and applied in the case of internally displaced children.

Dealing with Sovereignty as Responsibility

Providing protection, assistance, and development aid to internally
displaced persons requires a new framework for dealing with issues of
sovereignty. Specifically, a more equitable balance is needed between the
principle of nonintervention in internal affairs and the equally compelling
obligation to provide humanitarian assistance and promote observance
of human rights. In an internal document, UNHCR speaks of the need
for a framework of principles to deal with the pressures exerted by governments against humanitarian action.[140] The WFP has suggested a review of "the international community's approach to sovereignty and the
rights of humanitarian intervention in order to provide satisfactory access
to IDPs."[141]

The authors of this volume recommend recasting sovereignty as a
concept of responsibility, that is, as an instrument for ensuring the protection and welfare of all those under a state's jurisdiction. Since there
is no adequate replacement in sight for the system of state sovereignty,
primary responsibility for promoting the security, welfare, and liberty of
populations must remain with the state. At the same time, no state
claiming legitimacy can justifiably quarrel with the commitment to pro-

tect all its citizens against human rights abuse. Effective sovereignty implies a system of law and order that is responsive to the needs of the national population for justice and general welfare. Sovereignty cannot be used as a justification for the mistreatment of populations. Although conceived centuries ago as a monarch's instrument of authoritative control over a given territory and its populations, "monarchical sovereignty" has evolved markedly over time.[142] Demands for democratic values, institutions, and practices have transferred the classic notion of sovereign will and authority to the population at large. Particularly since the mid-twentieth century, increased recognition has been given to the fact that it is the will of the people, invested in the leaders they elect or otherwise accept as their representatives, that entitles authorities to exercise and uphold the sovereignty of a nation.[143]

To be meaningful, sovereignty must include accountability not only to the domestic constituency but to the international community. This assumption is in fact inherent in sovereignty, for the concept implies an international system that imposes responsibilities on the state.[144] Moreover, since the domestic constituency may lack the political power to hold the government accountable, ultimate responsibility falls upon the international community. International human rights and humanitarian law oblige governments to provide for the security and well-being of all those under their jurisdiction. Governments are expected to bring their domestic law and practice into line with established international standards. International scrutiny of governmental practices is an integral part of government accession to international agreements.

Rather than shield governments and regimes from international scrutiny, sovereignty as a concept of responsibility ensures that basic human rights are respected. When governments fail to meet their obligations to beleaguered populations, such as the internally displaced, they are expected to request outside assistance to help them fulfill their responsibilities (see chapter 3). Should they refuse to accept such assistance, the international community can and should assert its concern and step in when the government has failed to discharge its responsibility.

Since 1990, there has been a perceptible shift at the international level toward recognizing that people in need of humanitarian assistance have certain rights and claims on the international community when their governments do not act responsibly or where there is a disintegration of the state. The legal analysis in this volume affirms that the international community has a right, possibly even a duty, to provide humanitarian relief, and in exceptional cases, to do so against the will of the government concerned. UN resolutions have legitimized the establishment of relief corridors and cross-border operations to reach people in need. They also have called for access for the delivery of relief and in some cases have authorized the use of force to ensure the delivery of relief supplies.[145] Whether or not the resolutions have been well implemented, they undeniably point to the emergence of a right to humanitarian assistance and access when states fail to meet the needs of their citizens and large numbers are at risk.

Although international actors, intergovernmental and nongovernmental alike, have a right to offer humanitarian aid, a corollary and general duty on the part of states to accept such offers has not yet been *explicitly* recognized.[146] The Security Council has *implicitly* recognized in several situations a duty on the part of certain states to accept international assistance by "insisting" that they allow "immediate" or "unimpeded" access by humanitarian organizations to internally displaced and other populations in need. But it is only in exceptional situations—when the Security Council determines that there is a threat to international peace and security—that a state can be compelled to accept international assistance. This study argues for the express recognition of the duty of states to accept offers of humanitarian assistance (see chapter 3). The obligation imposed on states by humanitarian and human rights law to refrain from refusing reasonable offers of international assistance makes it difficult to dispute the existence of a duty to accept such offers.

International practice suggests a variety of strategies for gaining access to populations in need. In some instances, obstructionist governments have been persuaded by hard diplomatic bargaining; in other cases, the imposition of economic and political sanctions has achieved results. In situations of civil war, humanitarian agencies such as ICRC, UNICEF, and UNHCR have negotiated directly with insurgent groups in order to reach persons on all sides of the conflict. Although the United Nations is supposed to gain the consent of governments before stepping in to provide assistance, when mass starvation results from government obstructionism or from government disintegration, international intervention has increasingly come to be expected and considered justified.

Tragically, the international community has been slower to act to prevent mass killings or the crime of genocide than it has to head off starvation. As earlier noted, a justification to prevent or stop genocide does exist in international law, but international practice has not yet created the expectation that action will readily be taken. The allied intervention in northern Iraq in 1991, in the wake of a war against Iraq, did provide protection to the Kurdish minority, and UN peacekeepers in a number of situations have made a contribution to preventing outbreaks of violence.[147] But no country was prepared to send forces to Rwanda at the height of the genocide in 1994. In the case of Burundi, the secretary-general proposed an international force to forestall massacres predicted for early 1996. Although the proposal failed to garner support, the reason was not Burundi's sovereignty but rather that the countries capable of fielding such a force considered the cost and risks of the intervention too high.

The establishment of what might be called a right to humanitarian protection has not yet emerged to justify action in all situations. Nor have there been sufficient attempts to provide protection and halt brutal forms of violence against groups of people. In the case of Chechnya, the UN secretary-general and key governments treated the disproportionate Russian military action which led to widespread destruction, killing and displacement in the secessionist republic largely as an "internal matter."[148] In other situations as well, deference to the interests of states over and above concern for the protection of populations is evident. There are governments, such as those of Myanmar (Burma), Turkey, India, and Algeria, that have failed to acknowledge either the existence of situations of internal displacement on their territory or the fact that these may require international attention.

In such cases, it is incumbent upon the United Nations to make its own assessment. Information should be collected on these situations and brought before the IASC, which in turn should develop strategies, together with donors and NGOs, for responding to them. This will not, of course, be easy to achieve, given the United Nation's cautiousness in the face of its member states' sensibilities. But those entrusted with the role of overseeing the coordination of assistance to the internally displaced should be expected to assess *all* situations of internal displacement, in particular those where inadequate protection and assistance is being provided by the governments in question.

Cases in which states deliberately obstruct or outright refuse access by the international community call for the direct involvement of the secretary-general who, together with UN agencies and donors, should insist upon the delivery of supplies to areas in need and access for UN personnel. Resolutions by the General Assembly and, in extreme cases, the Security Council would add significant political force to these demands. UN agencies need to present a strong and united front when governments restrict access to populations or threaten to expel UN humanitarian and development personnel. They must make clear that their presence in a country is indivisible, so that governments have no choice but to carefully calculate the costs involved in restricting international efforts to provide protection and assistance.

Since 1994 the government of the Sudan has sought to manipulate Operation Lifeline Sudan to the extent that OLS no longer has adequate access to internally displaced and other war-affected people in government-controlled areas. In the face of pressure from the government, as the case study on this country points out, the United Nations has done little to address the problems of war-displaced populations in camps outside Khartoum, which has the largest concentration of internally displaced people in the Sudan. Assertive action is recommended by the case study to regain UN control over the OLS program and better address the needs of the internally displaced in government-controlled areas. Specifically, cross-border operations could go deeper into the Sudan, the Inter-Governmental Authority on Development peace talks between north and south and between the rival southern factions could be revived, and if need be, the Security Council could impose sanctions, including an arms embargo, an energy embargo, and a ban on Sudanese exports to diminish the government's ability to finance the war.[149]

Where governments deny entry to UN representatives and rapporteurs, a series of calibrated actions is called for. As mentioned earlier, the representative of the secretary-general on internally displaced persons, like other representatives and rapporteurs, has been denied entry to countries that seek to avoid scrutiny. To address this, the secretary-general and the high commissioner for human rights should be expected, as a matter of course, to undertake a series of steps, ranging from quiet diplomacy to more public exposure, to ensure that the governments concerned extend invitations. Although efforts have been made on an ad hoc basis, it is timely to consider the development of a procedure to enable the United Nations to deal more consistently and effectively with governments that shun its representatives.

In cases where state authority is weak, has collapsed, or is only gradually reasserting itself, joint strategies are also needed to deal with insurgent forces. The tendency of the United Nations to deal only with governments has changed dramatically, but greater flexibility is still needed on the part of many international agencies to negotiate with insurgent forces so as to be able to reach beleaguered populations on all sides of conflict lines. The case studies on the Sudan, Sri Lanka, and Liberia point up the importance of contact with insurgent forces as a means of increasing protection for internally displaced populations.[150]

While international intervention can be expected more regularly than in the past to ensure that populations at risk receive protection and assistance, there is still a long way to go to make this process more consistent and effective. Clearly, humanitarian action needs to be made automatic in cases of mass starvation, impending genocide, or large-scale massacres. Some have called for the development of criteria, both of a political and a humanitarian character, that would justify intervention in such cases; others have called for a rapid reaction force. Both merit attention. In the meantime, the secretary-general has available the option of affirming that the concept of sovereignty can no longer be used as a screen behind which states hide mistreatment of their populations; and UN agencies can become more assertive on behalf of people at risk. Such steps will, it is to be hoped, bring closer the day when the concept of sovereignty as responsibility will have been wholeheartedly embraced by the international community and a readiness exhibited to uphold the provisions in the UN Charter calling for "universal respect for, and observance of, human rights and fundamental freedoms."

Enforcement Measures When Human Rights Abuses Are Gross and Systematic

Protection problems of the magnitude and severity of those in Bosnia, Rwanda, Iraq, or Liberia clearly require outside intervention. As ICRC President Cornelio Sommaruga has correctly pointed out, massacres and genocide "can be effectively combated only through political and if necessary military action."[151] Although recent years have witnessed several military interventions in situations of internal displacement, these operations have not always succeeded in providing extensive protection. While they have generally been credited with preventing starvation, the record has been more problematic when it comes to safeguarding the physical safety of persons at risk.

The problem in part is that UN peacekeeping forces have been placed in situations of ongoing conflict but have not always been given the requisite resources, training, and mandates needed to provide adequate protection. Absent at the international level has been the political will needed to enable the forces to carry out adequate protection. Thus, in Somalia, international forces failed to disarm the local factions when they arrived on the scene, even though they were sent to create a more secure environment.[152] The enforcement operation in Bosnia, meanwhile, provides a lesson on the limits of the use of force "when sustained political will to back such force, and a willingness to accept the responsibilities and consequences arising from such action, do not exist."[153] As one former UN commander described it, there arose a "fantastic gap between the resolutions of the Security Council, the will to execute these resolutions, and the means available to commanders in the field."[154] By contrast, in Iraq, in 1991, the allied coalition operating under Security Council Resolution 688 did create a safe area in the north of the country to protect the Kurdish minority, although in more recent years, the protection provided has diminished.

Safe or protected areas continue to be a primary vehicle for providing protection for internally displaced persons in situations of conflict. It is therefore important to take a closer look at this strategy in order to identify ways that it might be improved in future.

According to the Security Council, safe areas should only be created if there is consent on the part of the parties to the conflict and agreement to respect their inviolability.[155] Although this ideally should be the case, it presumes a shared interest in protecting civilian populations which often is absent. In many contemporary conflicts, civilians are the targets. The six Muslim enclaves designated safe areas in Bosnia and Herzegovina had to be established without the consent of the Serb authorities who considered them obstacles to their campaigns of ethnic cleansing and territorial conquest.[156]

The demilitarization of safe areas is another suggested criterion. In Bosnia, the fact that the safe areas were not fully demilitarized permitted Bosnian government forces to use them to support, and sometimes, launch their military activities, thereby giving Serb forces a rationale for targeting them.[157] As the secretary-general rightly pointed out, "unprovoked attacks launched from safe areas are inconsistent with the whole concept."[158] Similarly in Rwanda, ineffective efforts to disarm Hutu militia in camps for the internally displaced and apprehend those responsible for the genocide resulted in the camps being perceived by the government as a threat to national security.[159] In this latter case in particular, the security of the displaced was undermined by human rights abuses committed by armed groups in the protected areas.

By far the most critical factor for the safety of a protected area is the commitment of international forces to protect the civilians. In Bosnia and Herzegovina, internally displaced persons in the safe areas failed to be protected by the United Nations Protection Force (UNPROFOR), which, on the one hand, was not given adequate capability to accomplish this and, on the other, interpreted its mandate narrowly.

UNPROFOR was authorized by the Security Council to "deter attacks against the safe areas" and "to take the necessary measures, including the use of force," in replying to bombardments against the safe areas or armed incursion into them.[160] Yet, as the secretary-general observed, "UNPROFOR is neither structured nor equipped for combat and has never had sufficient resources, even with air support [from NATO] to defend the safe areas."[161] Moreover, it and others basically interpreted its mandate to mean that it would use force only if its own troops were attacked, in accordance with a clause in the Security Council resolution that spoke of UNPROFOR's "acting in self-defense."[162] This narrow interpretation was used to absolve UNPROFOR of having to defend the safe areas or their populations. Against this background, UN forces basically stood by as the safe area of Srebrenica was overrun and thousands of Muslim men and boys disappeared. It was only after the fall of Srebrenica and Zepa in July 1995 that the international community undertook the type of decisive military action that long had been demanded.

In contrast, the mandate for the protected areas established by French forces and then by the United Nations in Rwanda seemed to be clearer with regard to protecting the displaced. The Security Council authorized a French force, Operation Turquoise, to use "all necessary means" to create a humanitarian zone and to "contribute to the security and protection of displaced persons, refugees and civilians at risk."[163] United Nations Assistance Mission for Rwanda (UNAMIR) troops deployed in conjunction with the withdrawal of Operation Turquoise were authorized "to take action in self-defense against persons or groups who threaten protected sites and populations."[164] But UNAMIR failed to intervene when government forces began forcibly closing camps for internally displaced persons, in which several thousand displaced persons were killed. Its numbers in the camps were insufficient and it interpreted its mandate in such a way as not to include defending internally displaced persons from actions by their own government.[165]

Creating the unwarranted expectation that internally displaced persons will be protected in safe areas and camps not only jeopardizes their security but their ability to seek asylum in outside countries. For example, Bosnians, although facing threats to their lives and personal security in the safe areas, were denied asylum on the grounds that they did not need protection. Neighboring European states in fact supported the establishment of safe areas because of their interest in averting new refugee flows.[166] Similarly in the case of Iraq, it was Turkey's announcement that it would close its borders to Kurdish refugees that led to the creation of the safe haven in northern Iraq.[167]

The protected zone established in 1991 for the threatened Kurdish population in northern Iraq has provided greater protection than in Bosnia, but here too, protection has seriously eroded. While the fear of renewed international military intervention or redoubled sanctions has deterred the Iraqi Government from outright military takeover, the Kurdish region is still vulnerable to skirmishes and shelling by Iraqi government forces and attacks from Turkey and Iran. Moreover, abuses emanating from fighting between Kurdish factions there have been frequent.

The fact that the safe areas in Bosnia, Rwanda, and Iraq have failed to provide full protection for internally displaced and other populations should not occasion the rejection of safe areas as a protection strategy, but rather its refinement. When safe areas are established, they should be demilitarized at the outset. In addition, greater attention will need to be paid to ensuring that the forces charged with protecting them do in fact have the equipment, resources, training and mandates to accomplish this. Human rights and humanitarian agencies have a role to play in evaluating the quality of protection provided in such circumstances and in alerting international opinion when it proves inadequate. The limited knowledge of human rights and humanitarian standards on the part of military forces and the need for integration of such standards into their training and operations call for urgent attention. UNHCR has a particular role to play in defending the right to asylum and publicizing when safe areas are not safe but are being used as a pretext for denying asylum.[168]

The strategy of safe areas as well as military intervention requires oversight. ECOMOG's intervention in Liberia, as noted earlier, provided protection for displaced persons in Monrovia, but at the same time was responsible for abuses against civilians. Under such circumstances, greater international oversight of regional interventions to ensure adherence to international standards is needed. At the international level too, there is need for greater adherence on the part of military forces to concepts of protection and human rights. Ultimately, however, both safe areas and military intervention, while a last resort after preventive measures fail, must be seen only as interim measures and as such, as part of a larger effort to find a solution to conflicts.

Solutions

When displacement is engendered by conflict, safe and viable returns or settlement can only be achieved through the restoration of peace accompanied by rehabilitation and development programs. Such solutions are costly and time-consuming, but without them, there is little or no chance that the underlying causes of the conflict will be addressed, that displacement will be resolved, and that reconciliation, reconstruction, and development will follow.

Resolving Conflicts

The overriding strategy in the international response must be to seek solutions that promote respect for human rights and democratic participation, combined with programs that guarantee economic access and opportunity for the displaced and other affected populations. Humanitarian assistance alone cannot be expected to stabilize dangerous situations or end violations of humanitarian and human rights standards and the internal conflicts they engender. Time and again, organizations involved with the displaced have found that "in the absence of a political resolution of a conflict, humanitarian assistance and international presence cannot by themselves provide effective protection to victims nor prevent further displacement and refugee flight."[169] Concerted political efforts to find long-lasting solutions are essential.

One of the consequences of the strictly palliative response in which major unlawful violence is responded to "not by stopping that violence, but by trying to provide relief" is that humanitarian assistance may go on for decades.[170] The clearest evidence of this is found in the Sudan, the country with one of the longest-running internal conflicts, and the one to which international and regional organizations have responded largely with relief programs for over a decade. In situations such as Cyprus, the former Yugoslavia, and the Caucasus, where forcible displacement constituted a conscious aim rather than a consequence of the conflict, the resolution of both the conflict and the displacement crisis is all the more inextricably linked. In such situations, the failure to reach or implement a political solution translates into a precarious future for the displaced. In the former Yugoslavia, for example, many of the displaced are largely stranded in the face of NATO unwillingness to implement the provisions of the Dayton accords, which provide for their return. In Azerbaijan, the displaced are unlikely to find a sustainable solution as long as the government insists that they return to Nagorno Karabakh, an area over which no political agreement has been reached with Armenia.

The case study on Rwanda recommends a far more vigorous stand by humanitarian organizations in demanding political action to resolve inherently political crises: "Aid organizations need to be more willing to engage and challenge the governments on which they depend for resources. While the humanitarian community cannot abandon those in need . . . it must resist being used as a Potemkin village to protect the sensitivities of those who hold the key to real solutions."[171] To reiterate an earlier suggestion, the IASC should make its voice heard in pressing for the resolution of conflicts when its members are called upon to provide assistance for the displaced generated by those conflicts. Moreover, the assistance provided should be designed in a way to promote peace and the potential for constructive solutions. Although unrealistic and even counterproductive in some circumstances, at times it might be effective to condition aid on the willingness of the parties to search for solutions and work together with regional and international organizations to this end.[172]

Some governments may react adversely when humanitarian and development agencies point out to them that political solutions are the only way to solve the problem of internal displacement.[173] But since addressing the underlying causes of a conflict is essential to preventing further displacement and encouraging the return of those already displaced, the representative of the secretary-general on internally displaced persons and all other entities within the international system should be expected to draw attention to the fact that complex emergencies can only be effectively resolved through conflict resolution and that the parties to the conflict are responsible and must be held accountable for effective conflict management.

Promoting Voluntary Returns or Resettlement

Once conflicts come to an end or at least subside, and returns or resettlement become possible, serious problems can arise when internally displaced persons are compelled to return to unsafe areas or to areas in which they do not wish to reside. Voluntary return to places of origin or resettlement must be a central component of the return and reintegration process.

The guiding principles appended to this study expressly stipulate voluntary returns for the internally displaced, in accordance with international standards on freedom of movement and the right to choose one's residence. Applying the guiding principles would thus mean defending the right of the displaced freely to decide on whether or not they wish to return or whether they prefer to remain in a location where they may have integrated, or to resettle in another area. It should be borne in mind that the displaced may not wish to return to home areas. Or returns may not be possible, such as in Cyprus or the former Yugoslavia, where ethnic groups have been deliberately uprooted, or in Azerbaijan, where displaced populations may risk becoming hostages of politics if they insist that return to Nagorno Karabakh is their only option. Applying the guiding principles would mean providing internally displaced persons with an impartial assessment of the conditions to which they would return so that they are able to make an informed decision about whether or not to return or resettle elsewhere.

The need for the guiding principles is made manifest by the number of cases in which internally displaced persons have been forced to return to unsafe or unsustainable areas or to areas where they do not choose to reside. In the Sudan, as already noted, the displaced have been forcibly moved from Khartoum to outlying areas where they are neither part of the urban community nor in their own natural setting.[174] In other countries, internally displaced persons have been subjected to lesser forms of coercion. In Peru, for instance, assistance is provided predominantly to those internally displaced persons who return to their homes, as part of an overall strategy to induce return.[175] In Sri Lanka, assistance has also been used to promote returns, but the government, to its credit, has adopted Guidelines for the Resettlement of Displaced Persons, which imply that physical coercion is unacceptable and provide that return and resettlement can only take place to areas that are "secure and safe."[176] Of course, there may be situations where the overcrowding of urban areas by displaced persons can become a threat to the provision of health and social services. Promotion of return, nonetheless, has to be undertaken in such a way so as not to impinge upon freedom of movement and choice of residence; great care, moreover, has to be taken to assure that persons are not pressed to return to precarious security conditions and unsustainable living conditions.

By far the most blatant and tragic case of forced return occurred in Rwanda, where the government stated its intention forcibly to close the camps of internally displaced persons. The government had legitimate reasons for wanting to do so, namely to normalize conditions in the country and to deny refuge to criminal elements, but it was also evident that security conditions in areas of return were far from safe and that there were extremely limited resources to deal with the assistance and protection problems of the displaced. Many of the internally displaced as a result refused to move. The forcible closure of the camps by the government in April 1995 and the excessive use of force by the army—in which 4,000 to 8,000 reportedly died—underlines how important it is for an international consensus to develop on the need for voluntary returns that are undertaken in safety and dignity.[177]

UN resolutions, including those on the former Yugoslavia, Azerbaijan, and Georgia, have articulated a right of internally displaced persons and refugees to "return in safety and dignity." But the precise meaning of these terms needs elaboration. The UNHCR Handbook on Voluntary Repatriation defines voluntary return "in safety" as return that must take place under conditions of "legal safety" and "physical security," and under conditions of "material security," which means being able to sustain oneself through access to land or means of livelihood.[178] As to return with dignity, the handbook considers this to include being treated with respect, or not being "manhandled," arbitrarily separated from family members or having conditions placed on returns. Ensuring return in safety and dignity therefore requires strategies that address both protection and reintegration and development concerns.

Providing Protection upon Return

One important means of providing protection to the internally displaced is to have international agencies facilitate and monitor the return process. Even when conflicts causing internal displacement have subsided, and peace agreements are signed, continuing animosities among individuals or groups may jeopardize returns. Indeed, societal tensions actually may heighten in the postconflict phase, especially if the displaced return to find their homes, land and personal property taken by others and no functioning judicial system in place to resolve disputes. Moreover, in countries where severe abuses of human rights and humanitarian law have been committed, there may be unsettled scores in villages and towns throughout the country, and a targeting of persons who return.

Consequently, in recent years humanitarian organizations, human rights field staff, NGOs, and peacekeeping forces have become involved in facilitating and monitoring returns in a number of countries. Their efforts have included attempts to foster reconciliation among different ethnic, religious, and racial communities and to promote the peaceful and equitable resolution of land and property disputes. To address security problems in home areas, UNHCR has physically accompanied returnees home or arranged short trial visits allowing prospective returnees to assess the situation themselves. In Tajikistan, its staff worked with local authorities to increase physical security for returnees and assisted them to reclaim their homes. In Rwanda, UN human rights field staff monitored conditions in areas of return and sought to contribute to the security of return areas. UNAMIR also played a role in increasing security and building confidence among returnees and the local population.

These examples demonstrate that assigning human rights field staff and peacekeeping forces specific duties is an effective strategy of protection during return processes. It was precisely the failure of UNDP to include a human rights monitoring component in its program for the return and reintegration of internally displaced persons in Kenya that was found to undermine the program's effectiveness.[179] It has therefore been suggested that UNDP in future "ensure that human rights and protection components are a central part of its responsibilities in programs it administers for the internally displaced."[180] Returns can only be viable when both basic security and survival needs are met. Noteworthy in this regard is the plan of action of the 1995 Regional Conference on Assistance to Refugees, Returnees and Displaced Persons in the Great Lakes Region of Africa, which called upon the government of Rwanda to cooperate fully with the deployment of human rights field staff in areas of return; and in the case of Burundi, called on the government to grant full access to international observers for the purpose of monitoring returns. While the increased involvement of human rights field staff in the return process should strongly be encouraged, UNHCR could also expand its own role in the return process of internally displaced persons, modeled after its activities in Tajikistan. ICRC should also consider the extent to which it can play an expanded protection role in the context of return and reintegration.

Among the more insidious protection problems internally displaced persons face upon return is land mines, whether in Cambodia, the former Yugoslavia, Georgia, Angola, or Mozambique. In Mozambique alone, mines killed more than 10,000 displaced persons over the course of the return and resettlement program.[181] Mine clearance programs funded by the World Bank can play a significant role in enhancing security in areas of return. For their part, humanitarian and human rights agencies can mount mine-awareness campaigns among returnees, of the kind initiated by ICRC together with other private groups, which contributed to the adoption of a worldwide ban on antipersonnel land mines in 1997.[182] The guiding principles appended to this study specifically prohibit the deployment and use of antipersonnel land mines because of the significant danger they pose to civilians, and to internally displaced persons in particular, during and after the conclusion of hostilities.

Providing longer-term protection means the inclusion in reintegration and development programs of support for the restoration of civil society, of electoral systems, of judicial institutions that can resolve property and land disputes, and of due process procedures to safeguard human rights and ensure that those who have committed crimes against humanity or genocide are apprehended and prosecuted. The integration of human rights and protection concerns into reintegration and development programs is by far one of the most effective means of making returns durable and of preventing a return to hostilities. Most welcome in this regard is the increased recognition given by development agencies to the view that postconflict reconstruction must include both the rebuilding of physical infrastructure and the restoration of a framework of governance inclusive of democratization, social justice and respect for human rights.[183] UNDP's reintegration programs in Central America have largely been considered successful because they included human rights as a central component. At the same time, not all United Nations postconflict reconstruction programs have given sufficient attention to human rights concerns, a goal toward which the new secretary-general has stated his intention to work.[184]

Integrating Relief with Development

A further important action is that the links between relief and development need to be made stronger. Instead of compartmentalizing relief and development, development organizations should engage in relief efforts early on, during the emergency phase of displacement, so that programs may be planned to further longer-term solutions. Since displacement crises may become protracted, it is all the more important to develop the skills and capacities of the displaced during the emergency phase so that over time they become less dependent on their host communities and the international community and can better adapt to return and resettlement. Humanitarian assistance, it has rightly been noted, should not be "an end itself but part of a process leading to the rebuilding of disaster-stricken societies."[185] There is a need to re-focus the provision of humanitarian assistance to displaced populations through a "development lens," viewing it "not as 'charity' but as investment in the maintenance of human and social capital towards an eventual transition to peace and a reintegration of these populations into a peacetime society."[186]

In support of the need for such an approach, the UN's Administrative Coordination Committee is currently in the process of developing a conceptual framework for more effectively integrating relief and development.[187] Its effort hopefully will spawn a more unified approach to effecting smooth transitions from emergency relief to development. As a first step, it will need to refine the concept of the "continuum from relief to development." Rather than a sequential "continuum," consideration needs to be given to a "parallelism" where development planning is integrated into the relief effort.[188] In other words, the provision of emergency assistance to the displaced and the planning of development programs should occur simultaneously and in a mutually reinforcing manner.[189]

Relief programs should be designed to lay the foundation for development, while development-oriented programs should be planned during the emergency phase in order to build self-reliance into rehabilitation programs. Building upon the capacities and skills of displaced persons would facilitate their transition from passive recipients of relief to active participants in the development process. Humanitarian agencies must therefore base their relief programs on the survival mechanisms and capacities of the communities concerned. The case of Tajikistan serves as warning of the consequences of not adequately directing international assistance toward building capacities for self-reliant rehabilitation. Lack of emphasis on developing agricultural production and employment opportunities resulted in large segments of Tajikistan's rural and urban population remaining dependent on the continued delivery of relief more than five years after the civil war had ended.[190]

In recognition of the flaws inherent in the traditional approach to emergency assistance, some humanitarian agencies have begun to incorporate development-oriented initiatives into their operations. Particularly noteworthy in this regard are UNHCR's quick-impact projects (QIPs), discussed in chapter 4.

Development agencies have also begun to become involved with helping to reintegrate uprooted populations, even though this activity is considered a departure from their traditional development work. In Central America the regionwide PRODERE successfully brought together relief and development agencies to facilitate the reintegration of uprooted persons. The cross-mandate approach, used in the Horn of Africa, has also integrated the resources and expertise of relief and development agencies to meet the needs of affected populations in areas of return. Area-based development aid, as earlier noted, which helps rehabilitate and reconstruct entire areas so that they can absorb returnees and also sustain the local population has been particularly effective in reintegrating displaced populations. At the same time, recognizing and targeting the specific needs of the displaced is also necessary within the more comprehensive area-based approach.

UNDP's new $50 million rehabilitation fund for emergency situations represents a welcome attempt by a development agency to meet rehabilitation needs, but the amount is small and the procedures for accessing the funds still not tested. More promising still is the decision by the World Bank to become involved in post conflict reconstruction. Its new "Framework for World Bank Involvement in Post Conflict Reconstruction," endorsed in May 1997, specifically includes the "reintegration of displaced populations" as one of the Bank's new areas of activity in postconflict countries.[191] But the Bank as well as other development institutions have only just begun to play a role in return and reintegration processes. They need strategies to guide their involvement as they expand beyond traditional development activities.

Development Strategies for Dealing with
Conflict-Induced Displacement

The repair of physical infrastructure and a massive injection of investment capital turned out to be the correct strategy for reconstructing the highly developed economies of Western Europe after the Second World War. Today's conflicts, however, according to an analysis by Steven Holtzman, that is the basis for the present section, require a new strategy because they are mainly internal in nature, take place for the most part in developing countries, and may go on for decades.[192] Moreover, in civil wars the gestures made toward peace often prove to be only momentary interruptions of the conflict. In Liberia, for example, thirteen separate peace agreements over a five year period were broken by a resumption of conflict. In Angola, the resumption of conflict in 1992 following a failed peace treaty cost more lives in the two-year extension of hostilities than the entire previous decade of conflict. Lebanon, Uganda, the Sudan, Sri Lanka, and Afghanistan provide only a few examples of cyclical patterns in and out of conflict lasting more than a decade. Unlike most interstate wars, internal wars dissipate only gradually.[193]

This difference is critical to the speed with which reconstruction can occur. Civil wars usually leave in their wake severely fragmented societies in which the divisions caused by the conflict long outlast the actual hostilities and impede the processes of reconstruction and reconciliation for years after the signing of peace accords. The fact that most of today's conflicts constitute total and fratricidal war, pervading all aspects of society and making civilians the principal victims, leaves scars which may take generations to heal. The significant risk that conflict may resume makes for narrow windows of opportunity for postconflict reconstruction and requires that some visible and sustainable sign of economic and political progress occur in a short period of time to spur confidence in a continuation of the process of reconstruction.

The World Bank's new framework for postconflict reconstruction recognizes that since half of the world's low income countries have been directly involved in conflict over the past fifteen years, the Bank, as an institution concerned with development, must acknowledge the impact of conflict on development and become involved with societies still in conflict in order to help lay the foundations for their transition out of conflict.[194]

The Bank's new framework differs also in the strategies it employs. It requires not only the traditional response of rebuilding physical infrastructure but reknitting the very fabric of society.[195] Among the legacies of internal conflicts, apart from damaged infrastructure and loss of life, are reduced productive capacity, an erosion of human and social capital, a decimated government revenue base, and an increase in the number of people in need of social assistance. Markets, distribution networks, and banking and credit systems are disrupted, and decades of cumulative development investment destroyed. There is a collective breakdown of social relationships. Family units are sundered, gender roles are altered, entire communities may become marginalized, and trust in most institutions shattered. In short, internal conflicts break down the very underpinnings of the society in countries which already were poor in infrastructure and human capital to begin with.[196]

Population displacements compound the problem and make efforts at reconstruction more difficult. If, as is often the case, displacement endures for many years, a widespread and chronic "de-skilling" of the displaced population may result, as described in chapter 2. The flight to urban centers often makes the transition back to rural occupations more difficult. The destruction of housing as well as conflicts over land and property pose severe obstacles to return. The disruptive effect of displacement on community organization and leadership patterns often means that traditional methods of dispute resolution are no longer available. Even if the confusion surrounding property rights can be resolved in a way that enables the displaced to return to their property, patterns of land use developed during an extended period of occupation may alter previous arrangements or conflict with the needs of returnees.[197]

Communities both from and to which the displaced flee have been shown to experience dramatic alterations to their economic and social fabric. In the absence of the displaced, communities suffer a significant loss in their consumer and producer populations while the impact of mass influxes on the economic development of host communities can be devastating, with social services disrupted in urban centers, and ecological damage produced in rural areas.[198] Displacement has ripple effects throughout entire societies and requires a response that goes beyond providing emergency and development assistance solely to the populations directly affected. At the same time, it is important to note that the effects of displacement on host communities are not all negative: displaced persons may bring with them skills and, to varying extents, physical and investment capital as well as an entrepreneurial spirit, evident particularly among women who have been known to form cooperatives while displaced.

Development agencies therefore need to take a two-pronged approach: on the one hand, to increase the capacity of communities to cope with the many varied and long-lasting impacts of displacement; and, on the other, to enhance the ability of displaced persons to contribute to the economic and social fabric of the communities to which they flee. The fact that most displacement occurs in situations of armed conflict compounds this dual challenge and requires that it be met by integrating into the vision of development a sensitivity not only to internal displacement but also to conflict. The "development lens" through which to view conflict and its concomitant displacement, moreover, should not limit its focus strictly to the postconflict phase.

PREVENTING CONFLICT. There is a role for development agencies to play in preventing conflicts. Breaking the cycle of conflict requires paying attention to the root causes of conflict, such as inequity of land distribution or competition for scarce resources, as well as recognizing that conflict engenders its own dynamics such as militarization, state fragmentation, displacement and the victimization of particular groups, which provide fuel for future conflict. Addressing the inequities and schisms and creating conditions which either resolve points of contention or effectively manage them are prerequisites to preventing further conflict. To rebuild societies ravaged by conflict, reconstruction efforts need to take account of underlying problems and to help reunify the society, particularly by addressing the "patterns of social behaviour and social institutions which facilitate interactions and exchanges" and serve as "the glue which holds society together."[199]

The World Bank framework paper on postconflict reconstruction identifies four ways in which development investments can contribute to the prevention of conflict.[200] First, development planning should include social assessments which expressly recognize fault lines of social tension and focus in particular on resource distribution within a society, including attention to disparities among geographic regions and social groups. Second, development should take a participatory approach which engages civil society but bears in mind that social organizations through which their investments are distributed can both further as well as frustrate reconstruction efforts. Third, an emphasis on good governance should help introduce greater accountability and transparency into governments' distribution and management of resources and underline their role in providing the predominant legal and political framework for dispute resolution and conflict management. Finally, a frank exploration of the costs of both random and organized violence in undermining socioeconomic activity is needed. The impact of violence and the dissolution of bonds

of trust in a society alter strategies of household accumulation and investment but are as yet little understood. Development programs need
to be drawn up with the goal of reducing violence and preventing displacement. Some nascent attempts at such strategies, supported by
UNDP, the World Bank and other donors, are underway in Colombia,
Algeria, and Macedonia, where programmatic investment in community
organization and massive grassroots employment generation are perceived as possible components of heading off major crises.[201]

DEVELOPMENT-ORIENTED PROGRAMS DURING CONFLICT. The most important reason for development agencies to enter into conflict situations
early on is to initiate the process of planning for an eventual transition
out of conflict. The more preparation which occurs and the more long-
term planning which is possible, the likelier that a sustainable and orderly
reintegration of displaced populations will take place. If development
agencies begin a partnership with relief agencies early in the process,
transitions will be smoother. Interaction with displaced populations will
also lead to a greater understanding of how their needs can be met during
reconstruction.

As pointed out earlier, providing assistance with a development perspective should help minimize the most detrimental aspects of displacement. This would entail the introduction of education and skills-training
programs and income-generating projects and making credit available to
enhance the capacities of the displaced. Such capacity-building programs
would ease the burden placed on host communities as well as prepare
societies for return or reintegration. This approach should prove far more
economical than attempting during reconstruction to retrain a deskilled
society and develop confidence within a population weakened and de-
moralized by years of dependence on international relief.[202]

Bolstering the socioeconomic fabric of communities in conflict areas
could reduce pressures on their members to flee and thereby prevent
further displacement. Decreasing the rate of displacement during a conflict could be accomplished through targeted interventions to enhance the
survival strategies of communities in conflict zones.[203] Quick-impact projects, for example, which have so far been reserved for areas of return,
might be introduced during conflict, especially in "pockets of peace."
They could aim at improving the situation of people who otherwise would
be likely to leave their area of residence and become internally displaced.
Similarly, work could be done to maintain the quality of agriculture in

regions in conflict through provision of seed stock and other inputs. Investing in communities in conflict allows them to continue to function and thus reduces the pressure for them to leave. Note, too, that the stronger the socioeconomic fabric of these areas remains during conflict, the easier it will be for the return of displaced populations when the situation allows. UNIFEM has found that training and income-earning activities can be successfully introduced in war-torn countries even though the requirements for traditional development programs are not in place.[204]

Of course, when development investments are made in the home areas of displaced persons while they are absent, caution will have to be taken to avoid creating dynamics which work against a smooth return of the displaced. As earlier pointed out, those who remain in or resettle in an area from which displacement occurred may occupy the housing and other assets left behind by the displaced or may otherwise alter patterns of land tenure and use. Development investments that reinforce such patterns would make the return of the rightful owners of this property more difficult.[205]

Because the effects of conflict rarely are uniform throughout a country, development investments may be feasible in zones and sectors where active conflict is not occurring and where normal social and economic relations still exist.[206] Such zones will probably experience mass influxes of displaced persons and could benefit from targeted interventions. For instance, to safeguard against ecological damage, experts from the UN Environmental Programme (UNEP) could advise on the placement and design of displaced persons' camps with a view to minimizing their negative effects on the environment. Agronomists, meanwhile, could work with relief agencies to think through the long-term implications of food distribution strategies and their impact on farmers. If the distribution of food grain were to lead to a drop in prices in agricultural commodities, it could have significant implications for the crop patterns of farms both within conflict countries and in neighboring states. Moreover, conflict could lead to shifts in cultivation patterns that could undermine postconflict efforts to return to a market economy.[207]

Most important is that relief and development investments focus on projects that will encourage reintegration and reconstruction. Seeds distributed as part of relief packages should include seeds similar to those used in home areas of the displaced in order to help them retain skills relevant to the areas of expected return. Internally displaced persons who have been provided with seeds from ecosystems similar to those in areas of return have been far better equipped for reintegration. In Azerbaijan, for example, the internally displaced come largely from mountainous areas where grape cultivation is an important part of their economy, whereas in areas to which they were displaced, agricultural production focused on food grains. Skill retention would thus need to take account of their areas of return as well as target the agricultural needs in areas of displacement.[208] Increased interaction between relief and development personnel could produce more effective interventions in this regard.

Another practical yet far-reaching strategy of skill retention concerns the education of internally displaced and refugee children. Maintaining parallel standards of education for all citizens of a country, whether displaced in settlements or not, will facilitate the reintegration of the displaced as well as the reconstruction of the affected society as a whole.[209]

The clearance of land mines is yet another area in which development investments among displaced populations can be targeted toward eventual reintegration. Training the displaced in mine awareness and in mine clearing would not only accelerate progress with this task but make the return to mine-affected areas safer and impart a useful skill that could generate income for displaced persons during reconstruction.[210]

Development institutions may also be able to play a role in efforts to help reduce the destruction of the national patrimony of countries in conflict. In many internal conflicts, "criminalization" of the economies occur where the state has broken down. Liberian factions have stripped forests of tropical wood, while unsustainable patterns of settlement of displaced herders in northern Rwanda may have totally altered the ecosystem in that region, thereby depleting critical resources needed to finance reconstruction.[211]

Although the internally displaced are often difficult to reach, in any number of war situations they are concentrated in accessible areas. They even have been known to recreate their previous communities while in displacement. In Azerbaijan, a community of about 15,000 internally displaced Kurds have resettled together and could be viewed as almost the same community they once were. Indeed, the 500,000 persons estimated to be internally displaced in Azerbaijan are readily accessible. Many of the urban internally displaced in Angola are similarly accessible and in concentrated areas.[212] In short, a sufficient number of situations exist where it is possible to introduce reintegration-focused interventions in areas of displacement. Community associations can be supported, schools and clinics can be built, and teachers and health workers trained on the assumption that they will return together with their communities, thus accelerating the reintegration process.

Investments in displaced populations during a conflict that maintain human and social capital within these populations and within their communities of origin will contribute to making reintegration more favorable.[213]

POSTCONFLICT RECONSTRUCTION. When conditions do indeed allow reintegration and return to occur, development investments supporting these processes should take into account the broader context in which they occur. The very way in which international development investments are made can influence the structure of nascent postconflict states, especially when they represent the majority of funds available to new governments.[214] Thus a centralized provision of development funds through a single international coalition of donors could tend to support the creation of a centralized and hierarchical government structure which risks perpetuating inequities in the distribution of national resources. Conversely, a decentralized approach to development investments could empower local community groups as a check against too great a concentration of power in a postconflict national government but weaken the authority of central ministries. Although sectorally targeted investments may seem logical in cases where certain sectors are less damaged than others, in the case of a postconflict coalition government which distributes control over ministries to various factions of former combatants, this strategy may inadvertently contribute to political and social instability by increasing the power of one party to the conflict over another. At the other extreme, a disorganized provision of development funds risks undermining the unity of a postconflict government, thereby contributing to a chaotic and less successful transition out of conflict.[215]

While the success of postconflict reconstruction and reintegration ultimately lies in the hands of local actors, the cost to the international community of failed postconflict reconstruction, owing either to intractable political issues or missed opportunities, is high. Not only does failure discourage donors from later attempts when conditions again are propitious but, more fundamentally, it undermines confidence within the societies involved, thereby accelerating an exodus of the professionals and businesspeople needed for reconstruction. The collective disposition of societies is a critical element in the transition out of conflict and a determinant of the further outbreak of conflict. Assistance and development programs that aim to strengthen the fabric and confidence of societies therefore make an invaluable contribution to prevention and to postconflict reconstruction.

To improve the chances for a viable reconstruction process, greater coordination is needed between the providers of aid and those concerned with political negotiation so that aid interventions do not inadvertently support the position of one or another combatant.[216] In addition, aid interventions must seek to address the problems that beset the society before the conflict erupted, such as inequities in land distribution, the exodus of trained personnel, or weak infrastructure. If some progress can be made in these areas within the limited window of opportunity in which transitions occur, it could solidify a return to peace and contribute to a more successful transition.[217]

The success of a reconstruction program also depends on the extent to which international financial institutions become involved not only in the implementation of transitions but also in their planning. Encouraging developments in this regard include the World Bank's participation in the preparation of the Dayton accords for Bosnia and its role, along with that of the International Monetary Fund, in helping to formulate the peace accords in Guatemala. The involvement of international financial institutions in the negotiation of peace accords and the design of early transitional initiatives can help ensure that the economic consequences of reconstruction programs are taken into account. Furthermore, the inclusion of the World Bank and the IMF in the peace process can serve to spur investments by bilateral donors and others in financing and otherwise supporting the reconstruction effort.[218]

Because displaced populations often have the most difficult time in adjusting to transitions to peace, both relief and development agencies can help promote their reintegration through efforts to jump-start the economy, provide jobs, and unify the society in ways that support its interest in maintaining peace. Programs to demobilize, retrain, and reintegrate former combatants are important in this connection because significant numbers of displaced families tend to be relatives and dependents of combatants. Demining to clear access routes and land is another key activity to promote the reintegration of the displaced.

Consideration should be given to sequencing reconstruction strategies in a way that complements the effective reintegration of displaced persons. There is already wide recognition among humanitarian assistance and development agencies that reintegration to rural areas should occur in a way that allows returning farmers to make the most efficient use of planning and harvesting periods. Coordination is also needed with regard to demining programs and returns. Moreover, greater thought needs to be given to the timing of reconstruction programs in urban areas. Rapid investments in urban infrastructure in the early days of a transition may influence internally displaced persons who flocked to cities and their outskirts to remain there. This would not only undermine attempts at rural reintegration but could result in an overloading of urban infrastructure. Similarly, if reconstruction strategies give lower priority to investment in regions of high displacement, this could sow the seeds for further conflict as war-affected regions are left behind.[219]

To reiterate, reintegration must also concern itself with the degree to which social organization and leadership patterns in home communities are receptive to and inclusive of returning populations. Here, the work of NGOs and others in developing techniques for dispute resolution are essential. Although still experimental, small-scale interventions in matters such as land disputes and water rights have shown signs of significant success.[220] Much more needs to be done, however, in promoting reconciliation among ethnic groups. To this end, reconstruction efforts must include programs that support the strengthening of judicial systems, pluralistic political frameworks and institutions that safeguard human rights. Although such programs ultimately rely for their success upon the willingness and commitment of local actors to promote their objectives, if effectively introduced and implemented, they should be an important determinant of the success of reintegration efforts.

Another indicator will be the extent to which women are integrated in processes of return and reintegration. For the large numbers of widows and female-headed households among the displaced who become the sole caretakers of their families, skills training and income-generating activities are essential. Because of the breakdown of traditional social welfare systems in many war-torn societies, female-headed households can no longer be expected to be absorbed by their husbands' families. Rather, the greater involvement of development agencies, NGOs and multilateral development banks will be required to help strengthen their capacities for self-sufficiency.[221]

Specifically, women will need to be included more regularly in the large-scale development projects introduced by development agencies in areas hosting refugees and displaced persons. In a number of locations, displaced women have shown themselves adept at working in nontraditional activities such as reforestation and other environmental and reconstruction projects. One means of promoting this would be to design specific components for women in these projects. The World Bank did just that in Pakistan when it organized an overall forestry program that provided for a portion of the seedlings to be grown at home by displaced women.[222]

Another way to increase women's participation is to build support services into large-scale projects responsive to women's needs, such as transportation, child care facilities and labor-saving devices. Special affirmative action measures may also be needed. UNHCR, for example, introduced gender clauses into quick-impact reintegration projects in Nicaragua which stipulated that women workers would receive equal pay with men and that up to fifty percent of the persons involved in the planning and implementation of the projects would be women. Tens of thousands of women as a result were able to receive a much higher share of the wage-earning, income-generating and training opportunities than might otherwise have been the case.[223] Further, the introduction of QIP-FEMs, or QIPs designed specifically for women, can provide returning internally displaced women, refugees and local women with training and employment opportunities in both traditional and nontraditional spheres.[224] UNICEF, UNIFEM, and NGOs have likewise sought to enlarge women's access to training and employment opportunities, but the scope of UN agency and NGO projects is limited.[225] UNIFEM's budget, for example, is only $14 million, with only about $1 million allocated to projects for refugee and internally displaced women.[226] The need for the involvement of development banks is evident if women are to be included in reintegration programs in a manner that is adequate to meet their needs.

The World Bank can play a particularly significant role in empowering uprooted women through credit programs. Uprooted women need far greater access to credit than can possibly be made available by relief agencies on an ad hoc basis. Many uprooted women exhibit promising entrepreneurial spirit and require only a minimum of credit to establish and maintain the type of small businesses that can make the difference between absolute dependency and the ability to become self-supporting or at least to meet the daily subsistence needs of their families. But gender discrimination often affects women's credit opportunities, and in displaced persons' settings, credit programs can rarely be found.[227]

To compensate for this, international financial institutions and development banks should consider orienting more of their funds to supporting small-scale programs of direct benefit to internally displaced women. For instance, a share of the World Bank's new $200 million microcredit program for providing small loans to women should be targeted specifically to the internally displaced.[228] Such microenterprises could prove successful in facilitating the reintegration of returning displaced women into their home communities by helping them acquire skills, experience and resources.[229]

Restrictions on women's ability to own, acquire, manage or dispose of property also impedes reintegration.[230] Widowed women are particularly vulnerable since in some countries, such as Burundi and Rwanda, they are unable to inherit land or other immovable property from either their husbands or parents and, unless they have sons, risk losing their property to their deceased husband's relatives. The representative of the secretary-general on internally displaced persons has recommended to these and other governments that they adopt legal measures to address the problems facing returning displaced women, especially with regard to property and inheritance rights.[231] This suggestion has since been reiterated by the Fourth World Conference on Women as well as by the Addis Ababa Regional Conference on the Legal Status of Refugee and Internally Displaced Women in Africa.[232] Development agencies involved in reintegration efforts need to promote international standards on equal opportunity and make clear that if assistance is expected, steps at the national level will have to be taken in furtherance of this goal.

As long as internally displaced women heads of household lack the means of sustaining themselves and their families, they will continue to require relief long after the emergency has ended and they have returned. Given their large numbers, ensuring that their returns occur in such a way as to enhance their capacities to achieve self-sufficiency will work to the benefit of entire communities.

An expanded role for the World Bank in postconflict reconstruction could prove significant in shaping how displaced populations are reintegrated into their societies and how these societies overall make the transition from war to sustainable peace. There are of course obstacles that the Bank must overcome to translate into effective operational policies its new framework for involvement in postconflict reconstruction. Like other agencies involved in development, the Bank has little experience in working with uprooted populations or in conflict situations requiring a rapid development-oriented response. Some for example have pointed out the Bank's slowness in implementing its stated objective of encouraging the greater participation of civil society in loan projects.[233] Nonetheless, given the Bank's economic resources, its commitment to the reintegration of displaced populations, and its growing involvement in postconflict reconstruction, there is reason for hope that it will be able to address the underlying causes of conflict and shape solutions for their lasting resolution.

One means of developing sufficient and timely resources for the reintegration of displaced populations and for the overall tasks in rebuilding societies emerging from conflict would be the creation of an international trust fund where donors could pool money and provide a united source for reconstruction funding. The creation of such a trust fund would not only provide reliable financing for transitional activities but also contribute to donor coordination, reduce duplication and make it easier for new postconflict governments, which currently must attempt to understand all the varied rules and procedures of multiple donors. A Global Reconstruction Fund could be administered under the umbrella of the World Bank. It could be patterned after the Global Environmental Fund and also benefit from the experience gained from reconstruction trust funds developed in the West Bank and Gaza, Bosnia, and elsewhere.[234]

As this section has shown, development and international financial institutions have a critical role to play, along with political, peacekeeping, and humanitarian assistance agencies, in making postconflict reconstruction and development a success. But they must become involved at an early stage in order to prepare the groundwork for viable development plans and the reintegration of displaced populations. Development agencies also have a role to play in the prevention of conflicts by seeking to remedy the economic inequities underlying conflict. And in introducing development-oriented programs into actual conflict situations, they can help displaced populations make more manageable transitions out of conflict.

Conclusion

In terms of the magnitude of the crisis and the challenge it poses to the international community, today's problem of internal displacement is no less acute or pressing than the post–World War II refugee crisis. Although there are no easy or quick solutions to conflicts caused by oppressive systems of governance, denial of democratic rights and liber-ties, and gross economic inequities, there are nonetheless steps that can be taken. The strategies and recommendations outlined in this chapter focus on preventing the conditions that give rise to displacement, increas-ing international protection once persons are displaced, and promoting lasting and sustainable solutions. They call for a combination of norma-tive, institutional, and practical measures and the engagement of actors at all levels—local, national, regional, and international—with strong leadership by the United Nations and regional organizations in support of these efforts.

While humanitarian imperatives and human rights precepts should be sufficient justification for international involvement, there are additional reasons of practical mutual interest. The world today is far more inter-connected politically and economically than ever before. What happens in one country reverberates regionally and even internationally. Conflicts allowed to fester and go unchecked can produce mass migration and leave deep political and economic scars which ultimately affect the eco-nomic well-being and political security of neighboring states and of the international order as a whole. Harmonious worldwide development can-not be achieved as long as conflict and its devastating consequences are allowed to destroy the fabric of societies. A world in which the privileged among nations ignore the plight of the unfortunate can be neither pros-perous nor safe for anyone.

Guiding Principles on Internal Displacement

Introduction: Scope and Purpose

1. These guiding principles address the specific needs of internally displaced persons worldwide. They identify rights and guarantees relevant to the protection of persons from forced displacement and to their protection and assistance during displacement, as well as during return or resettlement and reintegration.

2. For the purposes of these principles, internally displaced persons are persons or groups of persons who have been forced or obliged to flee or to leave their homes or places of habitual residence, in particular as a result of or in order to avoid the effects of armed conflict, situations of generalized violence, violations of human rights, or natural or human-made disasters, and who have not crossed an internationally recognized state border.

3. These principles reflect and are consistent with international human rights law and international humanitarian law. They provide guidance to
   a. the Representative of the Secretary-General on Internally Displaced Persons in carrying out his mandate;
   b. states when faced with the phenomenon of internal displacement;
   c. all other authorities, groups, and persons in their relations with internally displaced persons; and

d. intergovernmental and nongovernmental organizations when addressing internal displacement.

4. These guiding principles should be disseminated and applied as widely as possible.

Section I: General Principles

Principle 1

1. Internally displaced persons shall enjoy, in full equality, the same rights and freedoms under international and domestic law as do other persons in their country. They shall not be discriminated against in the enjoyment of any rights and freedoms on the ground that they are internally displaced.

2. These principles are without prejudice to individual criminal responsibility under international law, in particular relating to genocide, crimes against humanity, and war crimes.

Principle 2

1. These principles shall be observed by all authorities, groups, and persons irrespective of their legal status and applied without any adverse distinction. The observance of these principles shall not affect the legal status of any authorities, groups, or persons involved.

2. These principles shall not be interpreted as restricting, modifying, or impairing the provisions of any international human rights or international humanitarian law instrument or rights granted to persons under domestic law. In particular, these principles are without prejudice to the right to seek and enjoy asylum in other countries.

Principle 3

1. National authorities have the primary duty and responsibility to provide protection and humanitarian assistance to internally displaced persons within their jurisdiction.

2. Internally displaced persons have the right to request and to receive protection and humanitarian assistance from these authorities. They shall not be persecuted or punished for making such a request.

Principle 4

1. These principles shall be applied without discrimination of any kind, such as race; color; sex; language; religion or belief; political or other opinion; national, ethnic, or social origin; legal or social status; age; disability; property; birth; or on any other similar criteria.

2. Certain internally displaced persons—such as children, especially unaccompanied minors, expectant mothers, mothers with young children, female heads of household, persons with disabilities and elderly persons—shall be entitled to protection and assistance required by their condition and to treatment that takes into account their special needs.

Section II: Principles Relating to Protection from Displacement

Principle 5

All authorities and international actors shall respect and ensure respect for their obligations under international law, including human rights and humanitarian law, in all circumstances, so as to prevent and avoid conditions that might lead to the displacement of persons.

Principle 6

1. Every human being shall have the right to be protected against being arbitrarily displaced from his or her home or place of habitual residence.

2. The prohibition of arbitrary displacement includes displacement
   a. when it is based on policies of apartheid, "ethnic cleansing," or similar practices aimed at or resulting in altering the ethnic, religious, or racial composition of the affected population;
   b. in situations of armed conflict, unless the security of the civilians involved or imperative military reasons so demand;
   c. in cases of large-scale development projects, which are not justified by compelling and overriding public interests;
   d. in cases of disasters, unless the safety and health of those affected requires their evacuation; and
   e. when it is used as a collective punishment.

3. Displacement shall last no longer than required by the circumstances.

Principle 7

1. Prior to any decision requiring the displacement of persons, the authorities concerned shall ensure that all feasible alternatives are explored in order to avoid displacement altogether. Where no alternatives exist, all measures shall be taken to minimize displacement and its adverse effects.

2. The authorities undertaking such displacement shall ensure, to the greatest practicable extent, that proper accommodation is provided to the displaced persons; that such displacements are effected in satisfactory conditions of safety, nutrition, health, and hygiene; and that members of the same family are not separated.

3. If displacement occurs in situations other than during the emergency stages of armed conflicts and disasters, the following guarantees shall be complied with:
   a. a specific decision shall be taken by a state authority empowered by law to order such measures;
   b. adequate measures shall be taken to guarantee those to be displaced full information on the reasons and procedures for their displacement and, where applicable, on compensation and relocation;
   c. the free and informed consent of those to be displaced shall be sought;
   d. the authorities concerned shall endeavor to involve those affected, particularly women, in the planning and management of their relocation;
   e. law enforcement measures, where required, shall be carried out by competent legal authorities; and
   f. the right to an effective remedy, including the review of such decisions by appropriate judicial authorities, shall be respected.

Principle 8

Displacement shall not be carried out in a manner that violates the rights to life, dignity, liberty and security of those affected.

Principle 9

States are under a particular obligation to protect against the displacement of indigenous peoples, minorities, peasants, pastoralists, and other groups with a special dependency on and attachment to their lands.

Section III: Principles Relating to Protection during Displacement

Principle 10

1. Every human being has the inherent right to life which shall be protected by law. No one shall be arbitrarily deprived of his or her life. Internally displaced persons shall be protected in particular against
   a. genocide;
   b. murder;
   c. summary or arbitrary executions; and
   d. enforced disappearances, including abduction or unacknowledged detention, threatening or resulting in death.
Threats and incitement to commit any of the foregoing acts shall be prohibited.

2. Attacks or other acts of violence against internally displaced persons who do not or no longer participate in hostilities are prohibited in all circumstances. Internally displaced persons shall be protected, in particular, against
   a. direct or indiscriminate attacks or other acts of violence, including the creation of areas wherein attacks on civilians are permitted;
   b. starvation as a method of combat;
   c. their use to shield military objectives from attack or to shield, favor, or impede military operations;
   d. attacks against their camps or settlements; and
   e. the use of antipersonnel land mines.

Principle 11

1. Every human being has the right to dignity and physical, mental, and moral integrity.

2. Internally displaced persons, whether or not their liberty has been restricted, shall be protected in particular against

    a. rape, mutilation, torture, cruel, inhuman or degrading treatment or punishment, and other outrages upon personal dignity, such as acts of gender-specific violence, forced prostitution, and any form of indecent assault;

    b. slavery or any contemporary form of slavery, such as sale into marriage, sexual exploitation, or forced labor of children; and

    c. acts of violence intended to spread terror among internally displaced persons.

Threats and incitement to commit any of the foregoing acts shall be prohibited.

Principle 12

1. Every human being has the right to liberty and security of person. No one shall be subjected to arbitrary arrest or detention.

2. To give effect to this right for internally displaced persons, they shall not be interned in or confined to a camp. If in exceptional circumstances such internment or confinement is absolutely necessary, it shall not last longer than required by the circumstances.

3. Internally displaced persons shall be protected from discriminatory arrest and detention as a result of their displacement.

4. In no case shall internally displaced persons be taken hostage.

Principle 13

1. In no circumstances shall displaced children be recruited or be required or permitted to take part in hostilities.

2. Internally displaced persons shall be protected against discriminatory practices of recruitment into any armed forces or groups as a result of their displacement. In particular, any cruel, inhuman, or degrading practices that compel compliance or punish noncompliance with recruitment are prohibited in all circumstances.

Principle 14

1. Every internally displaced person has the right to liberty of movement and freedom to choose his or her residence.

2. In particular, internally displaced persons have the right to move freely in and out of camps or other settlements.

Principle 15

Internally displaced persons have
    a. the right to seek safety in another part of the country;
    b. the right to leave their country;
    c. the right to seek asylum in another country; and
    d. the right to be protected against forcible return to or resettlement in any place where their life, safety, liberty, and/or health would be at risk.

Principle 16

1. All internally displaced persons have the right to know the fate and whereabouts of missing relatives.

2. The authorities concerned shall endeavor to establish the fate and whereabouts of internally displaced persons reported missing, and cooperate with relevant international organizations engaged in this task. They shall inform the next of kin of the progress of the investigation and notify them of any result.

3. The authorities concerned shall endeavor to collect and identify the mortal remains of those deceased, prevent their despoliation or mutilation, and facilitate the return of those remains to the next of kin or dispose of them respectfully.

4. Grave sites of internally displaced persons should be protected and respected in all circumstances. Internally displaced persons should have the right of access to the grave sites of their deceased relatives.

Principle 17

1. Every human being has the right to respect of his or her family life.

2. To give effect to this right for internally displaced persons, family members who wish to remain together shall be allowed to do so.

3. Families that are separated by displacement should be reunited as quickly as possible. All appropriate steps shall be taken to expedite the reunion of such families, particularly when children are involved. The

responsible authorities shall facilitate inquiries made by family members and encourage and cooperate with the work of humanitarian organizations engaged in the task of family reunification.

4. Members of internally displaced families whose personal liberty has been restricted by internment or confinement in camps shall have the right to remain together.

Principle 18

1. All internally displaced persons have the right to an adequate standard of living.

2. At the minimum, regardless of the circumstances, and without discrimination, competent authorities shall provide internally displaced persons with and ensure safe access to
   a. essential food and potable water;
   b. basic shelter and housing;
   c. appropriate clothing; and
   d. essential medical services and sanitation.

3. Special efforts should be made to ensure the full participation of women in the planning and distribution of these basic supplies.

Principle 19

1. All wounded and sick internally displaced persons as well as those with disabilities shall receive, to the fullest extent practicable and with the least possible delay, the medical care and attention they require, without distinction on any grounds other than medical ones. When necessary, internally displaced persons shall have access to psychological and social services.

2. Special attention should be paid to the health needs of women, including access to female health care providers and services, such as reproductive health care, as well as appropriate counseling for victims of sexual and other abuses.

3. Special attention should also be given to the prevention of contagious and infectious diseases, including AIDS, among internally displaced persons.

Principle 20

1. Every human being has the right to recognition everywhere as a person before the law.

2. To give effect to this right for internally displaced persons, the authorities concerned shall issue to them all documents necessary for the enjoyment and exercise of their legal rights, such as passports, personal identification documents, birth certificates, and marriage certificates. In particular, the authorities shall facilitate the issuance of new documents or the replacement of documents lost in the course of displacement, without imposing unreasonable conditions, such as requiring the return to one's area of habitual residence in order to obtain these or other required documents.

3. Women and men shall have equal rights to obtain such necessary documents and shall have the right to have such documentation issued in their own names.

Principle 21

1. No one shall be arbitrarily deprived of property and possessions.

2. The property and possessions of internally displaced persons shall in all circumstances be protected, particularly against the following acts:
   a. pillage;
   b. direct or indiscriminate attacks or other acts of violence;
   c. being used to shield military operations or objectives;
   d. being made the object of reprisal; and
   e. being destroyed or appropriated as a form of collective punishment.

3. Property and possessions left behind by internally displaced persons should be protected against destruction and arbitrary and illegal appropriation, occupation, or use.

Principle 22

1. Internally displaced persons, whether or not they are living in camps, shall not be discriminated against as a result of their displacement in the enjoyment of the following rights:

a. the rights to freedom of thought, conscience, religion or belief, opinion, and expression;
b. the right to seek freely opportunities for employment and to participate in economic activities;
c. the right to associate freely and participate equally in community affairs;
d. the right to vote and to participate in governmental and public affairs, including the right to have access to the means necessary to exercise this right; and
e. the right to communicate in a language they understand.

Principle 23

1. Every human being has the right to education.

2. To give effect to this right for internally displaced persons, the authorities concerned shall ensure that such persons, particularly displaced children, receive education that shall be free and compulsory at the primary level. Education should respect their cultural identity, language, and religion.

3. Special efforts should be made to ensure the full and equal participation of women and girls in educational programs.

4. Education and training facilities shall be made available to internally displaced persons, particularly adolescents and women, whether or not living in camps, as soon as conditions permit.

Section IV: Principles Relating to Humanitarian Assistance

Principle 24

1. All humanitarian assistance shall be carried out in accordance with the principles of humanity and impartiality and without discrimination.

2. Humanitarian assistance to internally displaced persons shall not be diverted, particularly for political or military reasons.

Principle 25

1. The primary duty and responsibility for providing humanitarian assistance to internally displaced persons lies with national authorities.

2. International humanitarian organizations and other appropriate actors have the right to offer their services in support of the internally displaced. Such an offer shall not be regarded as an unfriendly act or an interference in a state's internal affairs and shall be considered in good faith. Consent thereto shall not be arbitrarily withheld, particularly when authorities concerned are unable or unwilling to provide the required humanitarian assistance.

3. All authorities concerned shall grant and facilitate the free passage of humanitarian assistance and grant persons engaged in the provision of such assistance rapid and unimpeded access to the internally displaced.

Principle 26

Persons engaged in humanitarian assistance, their transport, and supplies shall be respected and protected. They shall not be the object of attack or other acts of violence.

Principle 27

1. International humanitarian organizations and other appropriate actors, when providing assistance, should give due regard to the protection needs and human rights of internally displaced persons and take appropriate measures in this regard. In so doing, these organizations and actors should respect relevant international standards and codes of conduct.

2. The preceding paragraph is without prejudice to the protection responsibilities of international organizations mandated for this purpose, whose services may be offered or requested by states.

Section V: Principles Relating to Return, Resettlement, and Reintegration

Principle 28

1. Competent authorities have the primary duty and responsibility to establish conditions, as well as provide the means, that allow internally displaced persons to return voluntarily, in safety, and with dignity, to their homes or places of habitual residence, or to resettle voluntarily in another part of the country. Such authorities shall endeavor to facilitate the reintegration of returned or resettled internally displaced persons.

2. Special efforts should be made to ensure the full participation of internally displaced persons in the planning and management of their return or resettlement and reintegration.

Principle 29

1. Internally displaced persons who have returned to their homes or places of habitual residence or who have resettled in another part of the country shall not be discriminated against as a result of their having been displaced. They shall have the right to participate fully and equally in public affairs at all levels and have equal access to public services.

2. Competent authorities have the duty and responsibility to assist returned and/or resettled internally displaced persons to recover, to the extent possible, their property and possessions that they left behind or were dispossessed of upon their displacement. When recovery of such property and possessions is not possible, competent authorities shall provide or assist these persons in obtaining appropriate compensation or another form of just reparation.

Principle 30

All authorities concerned shall grant and facilitate for international humanitarian organizations and other appropriate actors, in the exercise of their respective mandates, rapid and unimpeded access to internally displaced persons to assist in their return or resettlement and reintegration.

Notes

Chapter One

1. Michael Toole, testimony before the U.S. Senate Subcommittee on Children, Family, Drugs, and Alcoholism, April 3, 1990, cited in Refugee Policy Group, "Internally Displaced Women and Children in Africa," Washington, D.C., February 1992.

2. The Convention Relating to the Status of Refugees defines a refugee as a person who, "owing to a well-founded fear of being persecuted in his country of origin for reasons of race, religion, nationality, membership of a particular social group or political opinion, is outside the country of his nationality and is unable or, owing to such fear, is unwilling to avail himself of the protection of that country."

3. Under the OAU (Organization of African Unity) Convention Governing the Specific Aspects of Refugee Problems in Africa (1969), the term "refugee" encompasses the definition in the 1951 Refugee Convention and "every person who, owing to external aggression, occupation, foreign domination or events seriously disturbing public order in either part or the whole of his country of origin or nationality, is compelled to leave his place of habitual residence in order to seek refuge in another place outside his country of origin or nationality." The Cartagena Declaration on Refugees (1984), which is pertinent to Latin America, defines as refugees persons forced to move "because their lives, safety or freedom have been threatened by generalized violence, foreign aggression, internal conflicts, massive violations of human rights or circumstances which have seriously disturbed public order."

4. The United Nations High Commissioner for Refugees provided assistance in a number of cases at the request of the UN secretary-general or the General Assembly, although it also turned down many requests. See *Refugees: Dynamics*

317

of Displacement: A Report for the Independent Commission on International Humanitarian Issues (London: Zed Books, 1986), pp. 120–22.

5. U.S. Committee for Refugees (USCR), "State of the World's IDPs," paper prepared for Brookings, 1996.

6. From less than ten internal conflicts in 1960, the number rose to about fifty in 1992. See Peter Walker, "Working for Internally Displaced Persons: Prospects for the Future," paper presented at the symposium Internally Displaced Persons, International Committee of the Red Cross, Geneva, October 23–25, 1995, p. 75. See also Boutros Boutros-Ghali, "Beleaguered Are the Peacekeepers," *New York Times,* October 30, 1994, p. 15.

7. Sadako Ogata, UN High Commissioner for Refugees, "Displacement or Development: Bridging the Gap," address to the World Bank/International Monetary Fund, Washington, D.C., June 8, 1994.

8. UNHCR, "UNHCR by Numbers 1997," Geneva, 1997, p. 5.

9. See Roberta Cohen, "Human Rights Protection for Internally Displaced Persons," Refugee Policy Group, Washington, D.C., 1991, p. 19.

10. See, for example, Raymond Bonner, "Famine," *New Yorker,* March 13, 1989; and Millard Burr, "Khartoum's Displaced Persons," U.S. Committee for Refugees, Washington, D.C., 1990.

11. See Francis M. Deng and Larry Minear, *The Challenges of Famine Relief: Emergency Operations in the Sudan* (Brookings, 1992).

12. See Commission on Human Rights, *Compilation and Analysis of Legal Norms,* Report of the Representative of the Secretary-General on Internally Displaced Persons, E/CN.4/1996/52/Add.2 (United Nations, December 5, 1995), pp. 96–98.

13. In Mozambique, more than 25 percent of the population has been displaced inside the country or in neighboring countries; in Afghanistan, about 50 percent of the population was uprooted; and in El Salvador, about one-fifth of the population became internally displaced or fled to Mexico or the United States. See Roberta Cohen, "Refugee and Internally Displaced Women: A Development Perspective," Brookings Institution–Refugee Policy Group Project on Internal Displacement, November 1995, p. 2.

14. Division of International Protection, *UNHCR's Operational Experience with Internally Displaced Persons* (UNHCR, 1994), p. 50.

15. Human Rights Watch, *World Report 1996* (New York, 1995), p. 242.

16. Brookings Institution–Refugee Policy Group Project on Internal Displacement, Case Sheet on Turkey, March 1996.

17. Larry Minear and Thomas Weiss, *Humanitarian Politics* (New York: Foreign Policy Association, 1994).

18. See Médecins sans Frontières, *World in Crisis* (London, 1997), p. 80.

19. See Steven Holtzman, "Conflict-Induced Displacement through a Development Lens," paper prepared for Brookings, May 1997. This paper is discussed in chapters 2 and 7 in this volume.

20. Holtzman, "Conflict-Induced Displacement."

Chapter Two

1. The Norwegian Refugee Council (NRC) will be publishing a global internally displaced persons survey in 1998 and additional papers and reports on this group thereafter; it also plans to develop a data base in cooperation with the United Nations and the U.S. Committee for Refugees (USCR), a nonprofit organization headquartered in Washington, D.C., that provides an annual assessment of conditions affecting refugees, asylum seekers, and internally displaced people.

2. Commission on Human Rights, *Analytical Report of the Secretary-General on Internally Displaced Persons,* E/CN.4/1992/23 (United Nations, February 14, 1992), para. 17.

3. For the definitions contained in the OAU Convention, Cartagena Declaration and Refugee Convention, see chapter 1, notes 2 and 3.

4. David A. Korn, *Ethiopia, the United States and the Soviet Union* (London: Croom Helm, 1986).

5. Francis M. Deng and Larry Minear, *The Challenges of Famine Relief: Emergency Operations in the Sudan* (Brookings, 1992).

6. See, for example, Roberta Cohen, "Woe to Those Displaced by China Dam Project," *New York Times,* January 19, 1996, p. A28.

7. International organizations generally classify persons displaced by economic or developmental factors differently from those internally displaced. Of the world's displaced population, the International Federation of Red Cross and Red Crescent Societies estimates that 141 million are economically displaced, development displaced, environmentally displaced, and urban displaced, while 29.1 million are internally displaced. See Peter Walker, "Working for Internally Displaced Persons: Prospects for the Future," paper presented at the symposium Internally Displaced Persons, International Committee of the Red Cross, Geneva, October 23–25, 1995, p. 77. The U.S. Committee for Refugees, in preparing the statistics on which this chapter is based, excluded persons uprooted by nuclear accidents and development projects and used the term "ecological migrants" to describe persons displaced by environmental accidents and disasters. See USCR, "State of the World's IDPs," paper prepared for Brookings, 1996. For a separate definition of "environmentally displaced persons," see "Environmentally-Induced Population Displacements and Environmental Impacts Resulting from Mass Migrations," Symposium of UNHCR, IOM, and Refugee Policy Group, Geneva, April 21–24, 1996, p. 10. The government of Armenia, it might be noted, considers those displaced by the 1988 earthquake to be "ecological migrants," although some Armenian officials consider them internally displaced. See Thomas Greene, "Case Study on the Caucasus," in Roberta Cohen and Francis Deng, eds., *The Forsaken People: Case Studies of the Internally Displaced* (Brookings, 1998).

8. The International Organization for Migration also uses a broad definition. It uses as a base the UN working definition but excludes the suddenness or magnitude of movements and includes demobilized soldiers and returning refugees. See International Organization for Migration, "Internally Displaced Persons: IOM Policy and Programmes," Geneva, April 1997.

9. UNHCR considers the internally displaced to be "persons who have had to leave their homes for refugee-like reasons and are in a refugee-like situation, but who remain within the border of their own country. They have fled persecution, situations of general violence or massive violations of human rights and do not enjoy the full protection of their own government." See Division of International Protection, *International Legal Standards Applicable to the Protection of Internally Displaced Persons: A Reference Manual for UNHCR Staff* (UNHCR, 1996), p. 2.

10. According to CPDIA's definition, widely used in Latin America by both operational agencies and NGOs, the internally displaced are "those who have been obliged to migrate within national territory, abandoning their places of residence or habitual economic activities because their lives, physical safety or freedom have been harmed or are under threat due to the presence of any of the following situations of human origin: internal armed conflict, internal disturbances or tensions, widespread violence, massive violations of human rights or other circumstances deriving from these situations that may disturb or drastically disturb public order." For a description of CPDIA, see chapter 6.

11. See UNHCR, *Oslo Declaration and Plan of Action,* Recommendation 40, Partnership in Action (PARINAC) (June 1994).

12. Professor Myron Weiner, Director of the Center for International Studies at MIT, in a statement to the Fund for Peace, New York, June 4, 1990. See also Herbert B. Lewis, "Ethnic Loyalties Are on the Rise Globally," *Christian Science Monitor,* December 28, 1992, p. 18.

13. See Human Rights Watch, *Playing the "Communal Card": Communal Violence and Human Rights* (New York, April 1995).

14. Jennifer McLean and Thomas Greene, "Case Study on Tajikistan," in *The Forsaken People.*

15. Recent studies of conflicts in failed states also show that the fighting can dissolve into "resource wars" and a push to establish private fiefdoms of power and profit. See, for example, Dylan Hendrickson, "The Changing Nature of Warfare in the Third World: Some Thoughts on Current Trends and Forced Displacement," paper presented at the UNHCR conference on people of concern, Geneva, November 21–24, 1996; and Lidwien Kapteijns, "Somalia's 'Clans,'" *Christian Science Monitor,* December 18, 1992, p. 19.

16. Because the minorities in Myanmar (Burma) live in areas in which armed opposition groups are active, the government seeks through relocation to eliminate local support for the insurgents. See Commission on Human Rights, *Human Rights and Mass Exoduses,* E/CN.4/1997/42 (United Nations, High Commissioner for Human Rights, December 1996).

17. The rise of Catalan nationalism in Spain, the north-south split in Italy, cultural and linguistic tensions in Canada, friction between French- and Flemish-speaking populations in Belgium, and the division of Czechoslovakia have all taken place with little or no violence. Northern Ireland has proved one of the few exceptions. According to Freedom House, since the end of the cold war there has been a "democratic momentum" and "a continuing expansion of electoral

democracy and the further expansion of free societies." See "1997 Freedom around the World," *Freedom Review*, vol. 28, no. 1 (1997), p. 16.

18. Steven Holtzman, "Conflict-Induced Displacement through a Development Lens," paper prepared for Brookings, May 1997, p. 10. Holtzman is a social scientist employed in the Social Policy and Resettlement Division of the Environment Department at the World Bank. This paper is the basis for the section in this chapter on the impact of displacement.

19. See Holtzman, "Conflict-Induced Displacement," pp. 9–10. See also Holtzman, "Post-Conflict Reconstruction," Environment Department Papers, World Bank, Washington, D.C., 1995; and World Bank, "A Framework for World Bank Involvement in Post Conflict Reconstruction," Washington, D.C., April 25, 1997.

20. Holtzman, "Conflict-Induced Displacement," p. 13.

21. Holtzman, "Conflict-Induced Displacement," p. 11.

22. See Francis M. Deng, *Report on Internally Displaced Persons*, E/CN.4/1995/50 (United Nations, Commission on Human Rights, February 2, 1995), pp. 9–10. See also Roberta Cohen, "Refugee and Internally Displaced Women: A Development Perspective," Brookings Institution–Refugee Policy Group Project on Internal Displacement, November 1995.

23. In 1992, it was estimated that only 36 percent of primary-age refugee children were covered by UNHCR-funded primary schools, the main source of schooling for refugee children. See Cohen, "Refugee and Internally Displaced Women," p. 17. Other estimates indicate that 12 percent of refugee children attend school. See Holtzman, "Conflict-Induced Displacement," p. 17.

24. Internally displaced children are often deprived of education because schools have been destroyed or closed, or because educational facilities do not exist or are insufficient in the areas to which they have relocated. Also, parents of displaced children may be unable to pay required school fees, or it may simply be too dangerous for the children to travel to school. In addition, many displaced children have had to help support their families rather than attend school. In other cases, children may not possess the personal documentation, such as birth certificates, that is necessary to register with schools. Internally displaced children who speak a minority or nonofficial language and are relocated to new areas in which a different language is spoken may experience significant difficulties in understanding teachers. Few children living in displaced camps throughout Africa have access to formal education. See Francis M. Deng, *Report on Internally Displaced Persons*, E/CN.4/1996/52 (United Nations, Commission on Human Rights, February 22, 1996), pp. 19–20. See also USCR, "State of the World's IDPs."

25. Deng, *Report on Internally Displaced Persons*, E/CN.4/1996/52, pp. 18–20.

26. See, for example, Division of International Protection, *UNHCR's Operational Experience with Internally Displaced Persons* (UNHCR, 1994), pp. 68–72; Centre for Documentation and Research, "People of Concern," UNHCR, Geneva, November 21–23, 1996, p. 14; Roberta Cohen, "Protecting the Internally Displaced," in *World Refugee Survey 1996* (Washington, D.C.: U.S. Committee

for Refugees, 1996), p. 24. The USCR reports that several NGOs in African countries prefer the term "vulnerable groups" as an umbrella concept; in this way all those in need are covered whether they are war-affected civilians, returning refugees, demobilized soldiers, or internally displaced persons. See USCR, "State of the World's IDPs."

27. In the case study on the former Yugoslavia, for example, it was found that the most effective way to assist persons in armed conflict situations is to do so on the basis of need, whether or not they have been displaced. See Thomas G. Weiss and Amir Pasic, "Case Study on the Former Yugoslavia," in *The Forsaken People*. Similarly, in Liberia, where the vast majority of the population was displaced, it made little sense to distinguish between those displaced and others equally in need. See Colin Scott, "Case Study on Liberia," in *The Forsaken People*. Moreover, the representative of the secretary-general on internally displaced persons found in Mozambique that targeting assistance to internally displaced persons produced resentment among the local population, which led to the adoption of a community-based approach, although the internally displaced remained the major beneficiaries. See Francis M. Deng, *Profiles in Displacement: Mozambique*, E/CN.4/1997/43/Add.1 (United Nations, Commission on Human Rights, February 1997), paras. 51, 74.

28. On Burundi, see Francis M. Deng, *Profiles in Displacement: Burundi*, E/CN.4/1995/50/Add.2 (United Nations, Commission on Human Rights, November 28, 1994); Deng, *Report on Internally Displaced Persons*, E/CN.4/1995/50. On Armenia, see Greene, "Case Study on the Caucasus." On Angola, see Report of IOM and UN Unit for Humanitarian Assistance, Luanda, 1995. On Mozambique, see Deng, *Profiles in Displacement: Mozambique*, para. 71. On Cambodia, see Francis M. Deng, *Comprehensive Study on the Human Rights Issues Related to Internally Displaced Persons*, E/CN.4/1993/35 (United Nations, Commission on Human Rights, January 21, 1993), pp. 60–61.

29. For Zaire, see Senior Official, United Nations, Department of Humanitarian Affairs, interview, April 1997. For Rwanda, see Department of Humanitarian Affairs, *DHA News*, January/February 1994.

30. United Nations Development Programme, "UNDP and Internally Displaced Persons in 1997," New York, November 1996.

31. Studies have found that internally displaced persons received less attention in the CIREFCA process than did other populations of concern. In some cases, institutional mandates restricted actions: UNDP did not focus on specific population groups, whereas UNHCR focused on the needs of refugees and returning refugees. Moreover, donors did not commit sufficient resources for projects for internally displaced persons. In the PRODERE process, the focus on geographic regions meant that internally displaced persons in regions that were not targeted received little or no protection. See Mary Ann Larkin, "Review of the CIREFCA Process," EVAL/CIREF/14/May 1994, (UNHCR, 1994), pp. 4, 26, 40; Dennis Gallagher and Janelle M. Diller, "CIREFCA: At the Crossroads between Uprooted People and Development in Central America," Commission for the Study of International Migration and Cooperative Economic Development, Washington, D.C., March 1990, p. 22; and Jennifer McLean, "Regional

Approaches to Problems of Internal Displacement," paper prepared for this study, February 19, 1997.

32. In Kenya, for example, the government instigated violence against certain displaced ethnic groups and interfered with a UN program to reintegrate them. See Human Rights Watch/Africa, *Failing the Internally Displaced: The UNDP Displaced Persons Program in Kenya* (New York, June 1997).

33. UNHCR, *Oslo Declaration and Plan of Action,* Recommendation 40.

34. Other examples of forced population movements in the past decade that were almost entirely across borders can be found among Myanmar's (Burma's) Rohingya, Mauritanians, Togolese, Sahrawis, Tuaregs, and Bhutanese. See USCR, "State of the World's IDPs."

35. See, for example, Commission on Human Rights, *Human Rights and Mass Exoduses,* para. 27.

36. U.S. Committee for Refugees (USCR), *World Refugee Survey 1996* (Washington, D.C., 1996), pp. 4–6.

37. USCR, "State of the World's IDPs."

38. USCR, "State of the World's IDPs"; see also Karin Landgren, "Danger: Safe Areas," *Refugees,* no. 103 (January 1996).

39. USCR, *World Refugee Survey 1996,* p. 6. UNHCR collects documentation on internally displaced persons of concern; however, these are but a fraction of the world's internally displaced people. See UNHCR, "Populations of Concern to UNHCR: A Statistical Overview 1994," Geneva, 1994, p. 9.

40. The USCR considers the internally displaced to be "persons who have been forced to abandon their homes as a result of armed conflict, internal strife, or systematic violations of human rights" and are within the borders of their own country.

41. USCR, *World Refugee Survey: 1985 in Review* (Washington, D.C., 1985).

42. USCR, *World Refugee Survey 1997* (Washington, D.C., 1997). The U.S. government also found that the overall number of people in need of emergency humanitarian assistance in 1997 was triple that of the early 1980s; however, the total dropped in 1996 and 1997. See U.S. Mission to the United Nations, "Global Humanitarian Emergencies, 1997," New York, April 1997.

43. USCR, "State of the World's IDPs."

44. Report of IOM and UN Unit for Humanitarian Assistance, Luanda, 1995.

45. In Kenya, for example, agencies monitoring famine among the population regularly found more people listed as "affected by famine" in a given area than were listed as living in that area. See Thomas Greene, "A Global Overview of Internal Displacement," paper prepared for this study, June 6, 1996.

46. When UNHCR does apply the cessation clause, it always recognizes that there may be persons who continue to need international protection because of their specific circumstances, and governments are expected to consider these cases.

47. Cohen, "Protecting the Internally Displaced," p. 23.

48. Cohen, "Protecting the Internally Displaced," p. 23.

49. South African Department of Land Affairs, Green Paper on Land Affairs Policy in South Africa, February 1996.

50. Report by the Regional Peace Committee, South Africa, 1994.

51. Since much of the information comes from USCR's *World Refugee Survey,* 1985 to 1997, individual citations are mostly not given; supplementary sources, however, are cited.

52. See Human Rights Watch/Africa, *Failing the Internally Displaced*; and USCR, *World Refugee Survey 1995,* p. 62, and *World Refugee Survey 1996,* p. 53.

53. Sheldon Yett, "Masisi, Down the Road from Goma: Ethnic Cleansing and Displacement in Eastern Zaire," U.S. Committee for Refugees, Washington, D.C., 1996, p. 6.

54. Holtzman, "Conflict-Induced Displacement," p. 16.

55. Holtzman, "Conflict-Induced Displacement," p. 9.

56. Holtzman, "Conflict-Induced Displacement," p. 10.

57. Refugee Policy Group, "Internally Displaced Persons in Africa: Assistance, Challenges and Opportunities," Washington, D.C., October 1992, p. 17.

58. There were an estimated 200,000 unaccompanied children in Rwanda, Burundi, and the Democratic Republic of the Congo (Zaire). See Deng, *Report on Internally Displaced Persons,* E/CN.4/1995/50, p. 10.

59. U.S. Committee for Refugees, "Inducing the Deluge: Zaire's Internally Displaced People," Washington, D.C., October 1993, p. 3–4.

60. Refugee Policy Group, "Internally Displaced Persons in Africa," pp. 18–21.

61. USCR, *World Refugee Survey 1994,* p. 58.

62. USCR, "State of the World's IDPs."

63. In Burundi and Rwanda, for example, women cannot inherit land from their husbands or their parents. See Deng, *Report on Internally Displaced Persons,* E/CN.4/1995/50, p. 10. See also Deng, *Report on Internally Displaced Persons,* E/CN.4/1996/52, pp. 15–18.

64. USCR, "State of the World's IDPs."

65. See, for example, Refugee Policy Group, "Internally Displaced Persons in Africa," p. 21.

66. See Hiram A. Ruiz, "Case Study on the Sudan," in *The Forsaken People.*

67. In the early years of Liberia's conflict, one local NGO, known as Special Emergency Life Food, recruited more than 1,000 volunteers to distribute food to some 600,000 persons in Monrovia. Some Liberians and non-Liberian relief workers, however, complained that its operations were inefficient and tinged by politics, and that its activities declined in later years.

68. Human Rights Watch/Africa, *Failing the Internally Displaced.*

69. Human Rights Watch/Africa, *Failing the Internally Displaced.*

70. USCR, *World Refugee Survey 1996,* p. 171.

71. See letter from Turkish Embassy, Washington, D.C., to U.S. Committee for Refugees, November 10, 1994; and Human Rights Watch/Helsinki, "Turkey: Turkey's Failed Policy to Aid the Forcibly Displaced in the Southeast," New York, June 1996, p. 3.

72. Human Rights Watch/Helsinki, "The Commonwealth of Independent States: Refugees and Internally Displaced Persons in Armenia, Azerbaijan, Georgia, the Russian Federation, and Tajikistan," New York, May 1996, p. 21.

73. Nurit Kliot and Yoel Mansfeld, "Resettling Displaced People in North and South Cyprus: A Comparison," *Journal of Refugee Studies,* vol. 7, no. 4 (1994), p. 329.

74. UNHCR and CIS Conference Secretariat, *The CIS Conference on Refugees and Migrants,* vol. 2, no. 1 (1996), p. 100.

75. Kathleen Hunt, *Forced Migration: Repatriation in Georgia* (New York: Open Society Institute, 1995), pp. 21–22.

76. Salih Smer, former State Minister for City Planning, *Cumhuriyet,* Istanbul, March 26, 1995, cited in Human Rights Watch/Helsinki, "Turkey," p. 12.

77. Kliot and Mansfeld. "Resettling Displaced People in North and South Cyprus," p. 336.

78. UNHCR and CIS Conference Secretariat, *CIS Conference on Refugees and Migrants,* pp. 39, 96–97.

79. UNHCR and CIS Conference Secretariat, *CIS Conference on Refugees and Migrants,* p. 38.

80. Open Society Institute, "Displaced Persons in Southern Russia," *Forced Migration Monitor,* no. 13 (September 1996), p. 2.

81. Human Rights Watch/Helsinki, "Turkey."

82. Cited in USCR, *World Refugee Survey 1996,* p. 172.

83. Brookings Institution–Refugee Policy Group Project on Internal Displacement, Case Sheet on Turkey, March 1996.

84. Before the outbreak of hostilities in Chechnya, Ingushetia was already hosting an estimated 50,000 displaced persons from the 1992 clash between Ossetians and Ingush in North Ossetia.

85. The money was devoted almost exclusively to housing and did not begin to address other needs. See Open Society Institute, "Displaced Persons in Southern Russia," p. 2.

86. UNHCR and CIS Conference Secretariat, *CIS Conference on Refugees and Migrants,* pp. 33, 37.

87. Human Rights Watch/Helsinki, "The Commonwealth of Independent States," p. 22; and Human Rights Watch/Helsinki, "Caught in the Crossfire: Civilians in Gudermes and Pervomysloye," New York, March 1996, pp. 23–27.

88. Human Rights Watch/Helsinki, "Caught in the Crossfire," p. 28.

89. See Mikhael Barutciski, "The Reinforcement of Non-Admission Policies and the Subversion of UNHCR: Displacement and Internal Assistance in Bosnia-Herzegovina (1992–1994)," *International Journal of Refugee Law,* vol. 8, no. 1–2 (1996), p. 80.

90. Hunt, *Forced Migration,* pp. 19–21.

91. Kliot and Mansfeld. "Resettling Displaced People in North and South Cyprus," p. 340.

92. Palestinians have, nonetheless, become displaced from their land within the West Bank and Gaza by the creation of Israeli settlements and practices such as the demolition of houses.

93. See McLean and Greene, "Case Study on Tajikistan"; USCR, *World*

Refugee Survey 1993 (Washington, D.C., 1993), pp. 100–01; and USCR, *World Refugee Survey 1996,* p. 105.

94. Hiram A. Ruiz, "Internal Displacement in the Philippines," U.S. Committee for Refugees, Washington, D.C., 1997.

95. USCR, *World Refugee Survey 1991,* pp. 99–100.

96. USCR, *World Refugee Survey 1996,* pp. 357–59, 363.

97. Cohen, "Refugee and Internally Displaced Women," p. 22.

98. United Nations Department of Humanitarian Affairs, press advisory, December 8, 1995.

99. The government, in particular, forced those who had sought refuge in Dushanbe, the capital, to return home. See USCR, *World Refugee Survey 1993,* pp. 100–01.

100. Ruiz, "Internal Displacement in the Philippines," p. 7.

101. UNHCR, *State of the World's Refugees* (New York: Penguin Books, 1993), p. 84.

102. Hiram A. Ruiz, "El Retorno: Guatemalans' Risky Repatriation Begins," U.S. Committee for Refugees, Washington, D.C., 1993, p. 6.

103. USCR, *World Refugee Survey 1996,* p. 6.

104. See Liliana Obregón and Maria Stavropoulou, "Case Study on Colombia," in *The Forsaken People;* and Robin Kirk, "Feeding the Tiger: Colombia's Internally Displaced People," U.S. Committee for Refugees, Washington, D.C., 1993.

105. Hiram A. Ruiz, "Go Home/Stay Put: Tough Options for Displaced Peruvians," U.S. Committee for Refugees, Washington, D.C., 1996, p. 1.

106. Ruiz, "Go Home/Stay Put," p. 9

107. Ruiz, "El Retorno," p. 9.

108. USCR, *World Refugee Survey 1996,* p. 6.

109. Robin Kirk, "The Decade of Chaqwa: Peru's Internal Refugees," U.S. Committee for Refugees, Washington, D.C., 1991.

110. Robin Kirk, "To Build Anew: An Update on Peru's Internally Displaced People," U.S. Committee for Refugees, Washington, D.C., 1993.

111. Ruiz, "Go Home/Stay Put," pp. 22, 27.

112. See Obregón and Stavropoulou, "Case Study on Colombia."

113. Ruiz, "El Retorno," p. 17. See also Juliana Lindsey, "Guatemala's Peace Program: Empty Promise or Peace Dividend for the Internally Displaced," unpublished report for the U.S. Committee for Refugees, March 1997.

114. Ruiz, "Go Home/Stay Put," p. 6. According to human rights groups, thousands of innocent Peruvians have been prosecuted under these laws. The appointment of a human rights ombudsman in 1996 has resulted in pardon for about one hundred cases to date.

115. Kirk, "Feeding the Tiger," pp. 11–12.

116. Ruiz, "Go Home/Stay Put," p. 25.

117. Patricia Weiss Fagen, "Peace in Central America: Transition for the Uprooted," in *World Refugee Survey 1993.* See note 31 for the limitations of CIREFCA.

118. Ruiz, "Go Home/Stay Put," p. 24.

119. In 1992, for example, the Peasant Shelter for the displaced in Barrancabermeja had to be closed after a paramilitary group attacked it. See Kirk, "Feeding the Tiger," pp. 11–12.

120. Ruiz, "Go Home/Stay Put," p. 8.

121. Ruiz, "El Retorno," p. 13.

122. USCR, *World Refugee Survey 1996,* p. 86.

Chapter Three (The notes in this chapter comply with law review style.)

1. *See* Statement by the International Committee of the Red Cross [hereafter ICRC], Human Rights, Mass Exodus and Displaced Persons, to the Commission on Human Rights, Geneva, Apr. 2, 1997. After studying the findings in the legal analysis, an ICRC official recommended that more explicit protections for the internally displaced be taken into account when humanitarian law is next reviewed. *See* Jean-Philippe Lavoyer, *Protection under International Humanitarian Law,* in ICRC, INTERNALLY DISPLACED PERSONS 34 (1995).

2. OFFICE OF THE UNITED NATIONS HIGH COMMISSIONER FOR REFUGEES (UNHCR), DIVISION OF INTERNATIONAL PROTECTION, INTERNATIONAL LEGAL STANDARDS APPLICABLE TO THE PROTECTION OF INTERNALLY DISPLACED PERSONS: A REFERENCE MANUAL FOR UNHCR STAFF (1996).

3. *See ICRC Protection and Assistance Activities in Situations Not Covered by International Humanitarian Law,* 262 INT'L REV. OF THE RED CROSS, 9, 13 (1988) (detailing examples of tensions and disturbances).

4. *See* Hans-Peter Gasser, *A Measure of Humanity in Internal Disturbances and Tensions: Proposal for a Code of Conduct,* 262 INT'L REV. OF THE RED CROSS 38, 42 (1988) (providing an overview of existing human rights legislation and offering a new approach to better protect human values in instances of internal disturbances and tensions); Theodor Meron, *Draft Model Declaration in Internal Strife,* 262 INT'L REV. OF THE RED CROSS 59 (1988) (focusing on the general characteristics of internal strife and providing a model declaration).

5. Nevertheless, ICRC is empowered by its own statute with the right to render assistance and protection to the victims of such situations, which would include internally displaced persons. Governments, however, are not legally required to admit ICRC in such situations.

6. As explained later in the chapter, since these instruments not only permit free movement but also guarantee free choice of residence, they contain a right to remain and thus a right not to be displaced.

7. *See* Barcelona Traction, Light & Power Co., Ltd. (New Application) (Belg. v. Spain), 1970 I.C.J. 4 (Feb. 5) (referring to the "basic rights of the human person"); *Legal Consequences for the States of the Continued Presence of South Africa in Namibia (South West Africa) Notwithstanding Security Council Resolution 276,* 1971 I.C.J. 16, 57 (Advisory Opinion of June 21) (stating, in an advisory opinion of the Court, that the "denial [by South Africa] of fundamental human rights is a flagrant violation of the purposes and principles of the Charter").

8. In this regard, Thomas Buergenthal has written: "U.N. practice . . . in-

dicates agreement that governmental policies instituting or tolerating large scale denials of basic human rights violate the U.N. Charter because such measures are incompatible with the obligations to 'promote' human rights." T. BUERGEN-THAL, R. NORRIS, AND D. SHELTON, PROTECTING HUMAN RIGHTS IN THE AMERICAS 29 (2d ed. 1986).

9. International Covenant on Economic, Social and Cultural Rights, *adopted* Dec. 16, 1966, ratified by 133 states on Feb. 15, 1996 (hereafter CESCR). International Covenant on Civil and Political Rights, *adopted* Dec. 16, 1966, ratified by 132 states on Feb. 15, 1996 (hereafter CCPR).

10. American Convention on Human Rights, signed at the Inter-American Specialized Conference on Human Rights, San Jose, Costa Rica, Nov. 22, 1969, ratified by twenty-five states as of Jan. 1, 1995 (hereafter American Convention); Additional Protocol to the American Convention on Human Rights in the Area of Economic, Social and Cultural Rights "Protocol of San Salvador," signed at San Salvador, El Salvador on Nov. 17, 1988, not yet in force (hereafter Protocol of San Salvador); African (Banjul) Charter on Human and Peoples' Rights, adopted by Organization of African Unity at Nairobi, Kenya, on June 27, 1981, ratified by forty-nine states as of Jan. 1, 1995 (hereafter African Charter); European Convention for the Protection of Human Rights and Fundamental Freedoms of 4 Nov. 1950, ratified by thirty states as of Jan. 1, 1995 (hereafter European Convention); European Social Charter of 18 Oct. 1961, ratified by twenty states as of Jan. 1, 1995.

11. Convention on the Rights of the Child, *adopted* by UN General Assembly on Nov. 28, 1989, ratified by 181 states as of Jan. 1, 1996 (hereafter CRC); *see also* Convention on the Elimination of Discrimination Against Women, *adopted* by UN General Assembly on Dec. 18, 1979, ratified by 147 states as of Jan. 1, 1996 (hereafter CEDAW); International Convention on the Elimination of All Forms of Racial Discrimination, done at New York on Jan. 7, 1966, ratified by 145 states as of Jan. 1, 1996 (hereafter CERD); and Convention on the Prevention and Punishment of the Crime of Genocide, *adopted* Dec. 9, 1948, ratified by 116 states as of Jan. 1, 1995 (hereafter Genocide Convention).

12. The duty "to respect" rights under Art. 1(1) of the American Convention, for example, is fulfilled simply by the state's not violating any of the enumerated rights. The obligation "to ensure the free and full enjoyment" of these rights under Art. 1(1) is substantially broader. In its opinion in the Velasquez Rodriguez case, the Inter-American Court stated that this obligation "implies the duty of the State Parties to organize the governmental apparatus, and, in general, all the structures, through which public power is exercised, so that they are capable of judicially ensuring the free and full enjoyment of human rights." Decision of the Inter-American Court of Human Rights, Velasquez Rodriguez case, Judgment of July 29, 1988, Ser. C No. 4. The court also stated that whenever a state organ, agent or public entity violates a right protected by the Convention, the state is internationally responsible not only for the violation of the infringed right, but also for the violation of its duty under Art. 1(1), to respect and ensure that right. It found, further, that by virtue of its dual obligations under Art. 1(1) a state

must "prevent, investigate and punish any violation of" guaranteed rights. Similar reasoning applies to the obligations under the covenants.

13. The Human Rights Committee has stressed that the CCPR obligates states not only to refrain from interference with its guarantees but also requires them to actively protect human rights.

14. *See, e.g.*, CCPR, Arts. 12, 13, 18, 21, 22; CRC, Arts. 10, 14, and 15; African Charter, Art. 11; American Convention, Arts. 12, 13, 15, 16, and 22; European Convention, Arts. 8–11. In this chapter, the terms "restriction" and "restrict" are used interchangeably with the terms "limitation" and "limit," respectively.

15. Similar provisions are contained in Art. 27 of the American Convention and Art. 15 of the European Convention on Human Rights. *See also The Siracusa Principles on the Limitation and Derogation Provisions in the International Covenant on Civil and Political Rights*, 7 Hum. Rts. Q. 237 (1985).

16. *See* Arts. 4(2), CCPR (in which the freedoms of thought, conscience, and religion are included in the list of nonderogable rights); 27(2), American Convention (adding the right to juridical personality, the freedom of conscience and religion, the right of family, the right to a name, the right of the child, the right to nationality, and the right to participate in government); and 15(2), European Convention.

17. *See* the following discussions of Common Art. 3 and Protocol II in this chapter.

18. *See, e.g.*, Arts. IV–VII, Genocide Convention, Arts. 4–9, CAT, and the Statute of the International Tribunal for Rwanda, annexed to S.C. Res. 955, *adopted* Nov. 8, 1994, UN Doc. S/Res/955 (1994). *See also* International Law Commission (ILC), Draft Code of Crimes Against the Peace and Security of Mankind, Part II, in Report of the International Law Commission on the Work of Its Forty-third Session, Apr. 29–July 19, 1991, UN Doc. A/46/10, pp. 243–50. For the customary law status of provisions creating criminal responsibility of individuals in times of internal armed conflict, *see* Appeals Chamber of the International Tribunal for the Prosecution of Persons Responsible for Serious Violations of International Humanitarian Law Committed in the Territory of Former Yugoslavia since 1991, Decision on the Defence Motion for Interlocutory Appeal on Jurisdiction of 2 Oct. 1995, The Prosecutor v. Dusko Tadic, pp. 53–71, *reprinted in* XXXV ILM (1996) at 62–71.

19. Geneva Convention for the Amelioration of the Condition of the Wounded and Sick in Armed Forces in the Field, Aug. 12, 1949; Geneva Convention for the Amelioration of the Condition of Wounded, Sick and Shipwrecked Members of Armed Forces at Sea, Aug. 12, 1949; Geneva Convention relative to the Treatment of Prisoners of War, Aug. 12, 1949; Geneva Convention Relative to the Protection of Civilian Persons in Time of War, Aug. 12, 1949 (hereafter Fourth Geneva Convention). These four Geneva Conventions entered into force on Oct. 21, 1950, and have been ratified by 188 states as of Oct. 1996.

20. Significantly, Art. 3 is the only provision of the four Geneva Conventions that directly applies to internal armed conflicts.

21. Although Art. 3 does not by its terms prohibit attacks against the civilian populations in noninternational armed conflicts, such attacks are prohibited by customary law. United Nations General Assembly Resolution 2444 ("Respect for Human Rights in Armed Conflict"), *adopted* by unanimous vote on Dec. 19, 1969, expressly recognized this customary principle of civilian immunity and its complementary principle requiring the warring parties to distinguish civilians from combatants at all times. The preamble to this resolution clearly states that these fundamental humanitarian law principles apply "in all armed conflicts," meaning both international and internal armed conflicts. Furthermore, ICRC has long regarded these principles as basic rules of the laws of war that apply in all armed conflicts.

22. Protocol Additional to the Geneva Conventions of August 12, 1949, and Relating to the Protection of Victims of Non-International Armed Conflicts (Protocol II), *adopted* June 8, 1977, ratified by 125 states as of Jan. 1, 1995 (hereafter Protocol II).

23. Art. 1, paragraph 1 of Protocol II limits that instrument's application to a noninternational armed conflict that "takes place in the territory of a high Contracting Party between its armed forces and dissident armed forces or other organized armed groups which, under responsible command, exercise such control over a part of its territory as to enable them to carry out sustained and concerted military operations and to implement this Protocol."

24. Another very important provision is Art. 17 (protection against displacement) which will be discussed later in the chapter.

25. Art. 2 common to the four 1949 Geneva Conventions.

26. *See* Part III, Section III of the Fourth Geneva Convention, which includes the particularly important and clear obligation of the occupying power to grant passage to humanitarian operations (Art. 59).

27. ICRC, COMMENTARY ON THE ADDITIONAL PROTOCOLS OF 8 JUNE 1977 TO THE GENEVA CONVENTIONS OF 12 AUGUST 1949, 610, para. 1909 (Yves Sandoz et al. eds., 1986).

28. *See* Convention Relating to the Status of Refugees, July 28, 1951, ratified by 127 states as of Jan. 19, 1996 (hereafter Refugee Convention); Protocol Relating to the Status of Refugees, New York, 31 Jan. 1967, ratified by 127 states as of Jan. 19, 1996 (hereafter Refugee Protocol).

29. UNHCR, UNHCR GUIDELINES ON THE PROTECTION OF REFUGEE WOMEN (1991) (hereafter UNHCR GUIDELINES ON REFUGEE WOMEN); UNHCR, REFUGEE CHILDREN: GUIDELINES ON PROTECTION AND CARE (1994) (hereafter UNHCR GUIDELINES ON REFUGEE CHILDREN).

30. The same is true for certain UNHCR Executive Committee Conclusions that provide guidance for States Parties in implementing their obligations under the Refugee Convention and Protocol.

31. *See* Art. 13 (movable and immovable property); Art. 15 (right of association); Art. 17 (wage-earning employment); Art. 18 (self-employment); Art. 19 (liberal professions); Art. 21 (housing); and Art. 26 (freedom of movement) of the Refugee Convention.

32. This section is based on UN Commission on Human Rights, Compilation

and Analysis of Legal Norms, Part II: Legal Aspects Relating to the Protection against Arbitrary Displacement, Report of the Representative of the Secretary-General, Mr. Francis M. Deng, submitted pursuant to Commission on Human Rights resolution 1997/39 (United Nations 1997).

33. UN Human Rights Committee, General Comment No. 18, *reprinted in* Note by the Secretariat, Compilation of General Comments and General Recommendations Adopted by Human Rights Treaty Bodies, UN Doc. HRI/GEN/1/Rev. 1 (1994) (hereafter HRC General Comments).

34. Report Submitted by Bosnia and Herzegovina Pursuant to a Special Decision Taken by the Committee (CERD/C/247/Add. 1 1993).

35. This point has been convincingly argued with regard to collective expulsions. *See* Jean-Marie Heckaerts, MASS EXPULSION IN MODERN INTERNATIONAL LAW AND PRACTICE 47 (1995).

36. *See* Art. VIII of the American Declaration, Art. 22(1) of the American Convention, Art. 2(1) of the Fourth Protocol to the European Convention, and Art. 12(1) of the African Charter.

37. *The Siracusa Principles on the Limitation and Derogation Provisions in the International Covenant on Civil and Political Rights*, 7 Hum. Rts. Q. 237, para. 10 (1985).

38. MANFRED NOWAK, UNITED NATIONS COVENANT ON CIVIL AND POLITICAL RIGHTS: CCPR COMMENTARY 211 (1993).

39. NOWAK, *supra* note 38, at 211.

40. NOWAK, *supra* note 38, at 216.

41. *See* UN Human Rights Committee, Lovelace case, No. 24/1977.

42. Sub-Commission on Prevention of Discrimination and Protection of Minorities, The Right of Freedom of Movement, Resolution 1994/24 (Aug. 26, 1994).

43. International Law Commission, Draft Code of Crimes Against the Peace and Security of Mankind, UN Doc. A/51/10 (1996).

44. Similar protections are found in Art. IX of the American Declaration, Art. 11 of the American Convention, and Art. 8 of the European Convention.

45. NOWAK, *supra* note 38, at 302.

46. NOWAK, *supra* note 38, at 303.

47. NOWAK, *supra* note 38, at 293.

48. HRC General Comments, *supra* note 33, at No. 16.

49. General Comments of the Committee on Economic, Social and Cultural Rights, No. 4, para. 18, *reprinted in* Note by the Secretariat, Compilation of General Comments and General Recommendations adopted by Human Rights Treaty bodies, UN Doc. HRI/GEN//Rev. 1 (July 29, 1994) (hereafter CESCR General Comments).

50. For a more detailed discussion of the notion of genocide, *see* Compilation and Analysis, Report of the Representative of the Secretary-General, Mr. Francis Deng, submitted pursuant to Commission on Human Rights Resolution 1995/57, E/CN.4/1996/52/Add.2 (1996), paras. 73–74 (hereafter Compilation and Analysis).

51. *See* Art. 4 (1) of the CCPR.

52. *Id.*

53. Report on the Situation of Human Rights of a Segment of the Nicaraguan Population of Miskito Origin, OEA/Ser.L/V/II.62, Doc. 10, rev. 3 (Nov. 29, 1983).

54. *See* Awn Sagawhat Al-Khasawneh, The Human Rights Dimensions of Population Transfer, Including the Implantation of Settlers, UN Doc. E/CN.4/Sub.2/1994/18 (1994).

55. *See also* Compilation and Analysis, paras. 21–23.

56. *See* ICRC, COMMENTARY ON THE ADDITIONAL PROTOCOLS OF 8 JUNE 1977 TO THE GENEVA CONVENTIONS OF 12 AUGUST 1949, at 1473 (1987).

57. "Persons protected by the Convention are those who, at a given moment and in any manner whatsoever, find themselves, in case of a conflict or occupation, in the hands of a Party to the conflict or Occupying Power of which they are not nations." Art. 4 of the Fourth Geneva Convention.

58. BOTHE, PARTSCH AND SOLF, NEW RULES FOR VICTIMS OF ARMED CONFLICTS: COMMENTARY ON THE TWO 1977 PROTOCOLS ADDITIONAL TO THE GENEVA CONVENTIONS OF 1949, at 317 (hereafter NEW RULES).

59. In addition, Art. 85 (4) (a) of Protocol I typifies the wilful "transfer of all or parts of the population of the occupied territory within . . . this territory, in violation of Art. 49 of the Fourth Convention" as a grave breach of the Protocol. The Statute of the International Criminal Tribunal for the Prosecution of Persons Responsible for Serious Violations of International Humanitarian Law Committed in the Territory of the Former Yugoslavia (ICTY), in Art. 2 (entitled Grave Breaches of the Geneva Conventions of 1949) explicitly refers to "unlawful . . . transfer" as a crime over which the Tribunal has competence. The Statute of the International Tribunal for Rwanda (ICTR) in Art. 4 provides that the ICTR will have jurisdiction over serious violations of Common Article 3 of the Geneva Conventions and of Protocol II.

60. *See* Compilation and Analysis, para. 22. *See also* Prosecutor v. Tadic, Case No. IT-94-1-AR72, appeal on jurisdiction, Oct. 2, 1995 in 35 ILM 32, para. 127 (1996).

61. United Nations Sub-Commission on Prevention of Discrimination and Protection of Minorities, Draft Declaration on the Rights of Indigenous Peoples, as adopted by the sub-commission at its forty-sixth session (Resolution 1994/45; E/CN.4/Sub.2/1994/2/Add.1).

62. This section limits the discussion of applicable human rights and humanitarian law to selected guarantees that are of particular relevance to internally displaced persons. For a comprehensive analysis, *see* Compilation and Analysis, paras. 47–358.

63. UN Charter, Arts. 1, 13, 55, 76.

64. *See, e.g.,* CESCR, Arts. 2(2); CCPR, Art. 26; Protocol I, Art. 75(1); and Protocol II, Art. 2(1). Article 3 common to the four 1994 Geneva Conventions speaks about "any other similar criteria."

65. *See* the views of the Human Rights Committee in Communication No. 196/1985 (Gueye et al. v. France), paras. 9.4, 9.5, 10; and CESCR General Comments, *supra* note 49, at No. 5, para. 2.

66. A broad interpretation was intended by the drafters. *See*, e.g., MARC

BOSSUYT, GUIDE TO THE "TRAVAUX PREPARATOIRES" OF THE INTERNATIONAL COVENANT ON CIVIL AND POLITICAL RIGHTS 486 (1987).

67. Common Art. 3(1); Protocol I, Art. 75(1); and Protocol II, Arts. 2(1) and 4(1).

68. *See*, however, Fourth Geneva Convention, Arts. 39–40 and 51–52.

69. These steps include "technical and vocational guidance and training programmes, policies and techniques to achieve steady economic, social and cultural development and full and productive employment under conditions safeguarding fundamental political and economic freedoms to the individual." CESCR, Art. 6(2).

70. UNHCR EXECUTIVE COMMITTEE, CONCLUSION NO. 64 (XLI) REFUGEE WOMEN AND INTERNATIONAL PROTECTION (1990), para. (a)(ix). Programs to improve equal access of refugee women to skills training and income-generating activities are discussed in UNHCR, GUIDELINES ON REFUGEE WOMEN, *supra* note 29 at paras. 111–20 (1991).

71. *See* Compilation and Analysis, paras. 67–88.

72. Genocide Convention, Art. II.

73. *See* Compilation and Analysis, paras. 114–23.

74. *See id.* at paras. 89–101.

75. The term "gender-specific violence" refers to violence against individuals of either sex; the term "gender-based violence" applies to women and girls in particular.

76. General Recommendations Adopted by the Committee for the Elimination of All Forms of Discrimination Against Women, No. 19, para. 7(a), reprinted in Note by the Secretariat, Compilation of General Comments and General Recommendations Adopted by Human Rights Treaty Bodies, UN Doc. HRI/GEN/1/Rev. 1 (July 29, 1994) (hereafter CEDAW General Recommendations), No. 19, para. 7. In particular, the CEDAW Committee referenced the right to equal protection according to humanitarian norms in times of international or internal armed conflict. *Id.*, para. 7(c).

77. Inter-American Convention on the Prevention, Punishment and Eradication of Violence Against Women "Convention of Belem Do Para" (Resolution adopted at the seventh plenary session, held on June 9, 1994), AG/RES. 1257 (XXIV-O/94) (hereafter Inter-American Convention on Violence against Women), Art. 5.

78. CEDAW General Recommendations, *supra* note 76, No. 19, para. 6.

79. International and regional standards specify that violence against women impairs or nullifies the rights to life, liberty, security, and integrity of person. *E.g.*, UN Declaration on the Elimination of Violence against Women, GA Res. 104, adopted without a vote on Dec. 20, 1993, UN GAOR, 48th Sess., Supp. No. 49, at 217, UN Doc. A/48/49 (vol. I) (1994) (hereafter UN Declaration on Violence against Women), Art. 3(a), (life, liberty, and security); CEDAW General Recommendation, *supra* note 76, No. 19, para. 7(a), (d) (life, liberty, and security); Inter-American Convention on Violence against Women, *supra* note 77, Art. 4(a), (b), (c), (e) (life, physical, mental, and moral integrity; personal liberty and security; inherent dignity of person).

80. International and regional standards specify that violence against women impairs or nullifies the right to be free from torture and cruel, inhuman or degrading treatment and punishment. *E.g.*, UN Declaration on Violence against Women, *supra* note 79, Art. 3(h); CEDAW General Recommendations, *supra* note 76, No. 19, para. 7(b); Inter-American Convention on Violence against Women, *supra* note 77, Art. 4(d) (torture only).

81. *See, e.g.*, the 1986 Report of the Special Rapporteur on Torture, UN Doc. E/CN.4/1986/15 (1986), para. 119; Report of the Special Rapporteur on Torture, UN Doc. E/CN.4/1995/34 (1995), paras. 16–19; Report of the Special Rapporteur on the Situation on Human Rights in Myanmar, UN Doc. E/CN.4/1993/37 (1993), paras. 136, 138 (noting "a systematic practice of torture [including rape]") and UN Doc. E/CN.4/1995/65, para. 114 ("Other reported methods of torture include sexual assault and rape"); Report of the Special Rapporteur on the Situation of Human Rights in Occupied Kuwait, *infra* note 104 at paras. 111 (describing rape of female detainees as sexual torture) and 184 (characterizing "rapes committed by members of the Iraqi occupying forces during the exercise of their official functions, especially in the context of house searches or interrogations in detention" as torture and cruel, inhuman, or degrading treatment); Report of the Secretary-General, Rape and Abuse of Women in the Territory of the Former Yugoslavia, UN Doc. E/CN.4/1994/5 (1994); *see also* several reports by the Special Rapporteur on Former Yugoslavia, especially Report on the Situation of Human Rights in the Territory of the Former Yugoslavia, submitted by Mr. Tadeusz Mazowiecki, Special Rapporteur of the Commission on Human Rights, pursuant to Commission Resolution 1992/S-1/1 of Aug. 14, 1992, UN Doc. E/CN.4/1993/50 (1993), paras. 82–89 and Annex II (report of the team of experts on their mission to investigate allegations of rape in the territory of the Former Yugoslavia from Jan. 12 to 23, 1991).

82. Note by the Secretariat, Compilation of General Comments and General Recommendations adopted by Human Rights Treaty Bodies, UN Doc. HRI/GEN/1/Rev.1 (July 29, 1994) (hereafter HRC General Comments), General Comment No. 20, para. 5. However, the Human Rights Committee did not mention rape as a form of torture in its General Comment on Art. 7 of the CCPR.

83. Art. XI of the American Declaration and Art. 11 of the European Social Charter similarly affirm a right to preservation of health. *See also* UN Declaration on Violence against Women, *supra* note 79, Art. 3(f); CEDAW General Recommendations, *supra* note 76, No. 19, para. 7(g).

84. Art. 4(l) of the UN Declaration on Violence against Women, *supra* note 79. The Declaration notes the special vulnerability of refugee women, migrant women, women living in rural or remote communities, destitute women, women in detention, and women in situations of armed conflict. *Id.*, preambular, para. 7. The Inter-American Convention on Violence against Women, *supra* note 77, similarly provides in Art. 9 that "with respect to the adoption of the measures in this Chapter, the States Parties shall take special account of the vulnerability of women to violence by reason of . . . their status as . . . displaced persons."

85. *See* CCPR, Art. 2(1); American Convention, Art. 1(1); and European Convention, Art. 1. These treaty rights include, of course, the rights to life,

liberty, security, and integrity of person, and the right to freedom from torture and ill-treatment.

86. In commenting on violence against women, the CEDAW-Committee has emphasized that "[u]nder general international law and specific human rights covenants, States may also be responsible for private acts if they fail to act with due diligence to prevent violations of rights or to investigate and punish acts of violence, and for providing compensation." CEDAW General Recommendations, *supra* note 76, No. 19, para. 9.

87. CEDAW, Art. 2(e).

88. *Id.* at Art. 5(a).

89. In certain situations, prostitution serves as one of the few forms of economic support for women heads of households separated from male family members either during flight or as a result of violence before displacement. At the root of this phenomenon, there is often a discriminatory allocation to men of essential food, water, and nonfood items.

90. *See, e.g.*, Preliminary Report submitted by the Special Rapporteur on Violence against Women, Its causes and Consequences, UN Doc. E/CN.4/1995/42 (1994), paras. 210–19.

91. On noninternational armed conflicts, see Protocol II, Common Art. 3 and Art. 2(1). On interstate armed conflicts, see Fourth Geneva Convention, Art. 27; and Protocol I, Art. 75(1).

92. Common Art. 3.

93. Protocol I, Arts. 75(2) and 76(1); Protocol II, Art. 4(2); and Fourth Geneva Convention, Art. 27 (limited to protected persons).

94. The ICRC has declared the rape of protected civilians to be encompassed in the grave breach of "willfully causing great suffering or serious injury to body or health" under Art. 147 of the Fourth Geneva Convention (ICRC, Aide-Memoire of Dec. 3, 1992, quoted by Meron, *Rape as a Crime under International Humanitarian Law*, 87 AM. J. INT'L L. 426 (1993). The statutes for the War Crimes Tribunal for Former Yugoslavia (Art. 5) and the Statute of the International Tribunal for Rwanda (Art. 3(g)) also declare rape as punishable.

95. United Nations Conference on Prohibitions or Restrictions of Use of Certain Conventional Weapons Which May Be Deemed to Be Excessively Injurious or to Have Indiscriminate Effects (United Nations Conference on Prohibitions or Restrictions of Use of Certain Conventional Weapons: Final Act, opened for signature Apr. 10, 1981, UN Doc. A/CONF.95/15 (1980), *reprinted in* IXX ILM 1523 (1980) (hereafter Conventional Weapons Convention). The convention and its three protocols entered into force on Dec. 2, 1983, and have been ratified by fifty-four states as of Oct. 22, 1995.

96. *Id.*

97. The third paragraph of the Conventional Weapons Convention's preamble declares that a basic purpose of the convention and its Land Mines Protocol is to give effect to two fundamental customary principles of the laws of war, namely, that the rights of the parties to an armed conflict to adopt methods or means of warfare are not unlimited and the use of weapons, projectiles, or material calculated to cause superfluous injury or unnecessary suffering is prohibited. An-

other customary principle of the laws of war—the protection of the civilian population against the effects of hostilities—is recited in the convention's second preambular paragraph.

98. A review process under the auspices of the United Nations and another under the leadership of Canada are currently under way, but many states are still opposed to a ban on the use of anti-personnel land mines.

99. Regarding protection against these violations, *see* Compilation and Analysis, paras. 157–79.

100. Regarding children, *see* CRC, Art. 37(b), which further provides that "no child shall be deprived of his or her liberty unlawfully or arbitrarily. The arrest, detention or imprisonment of a child shall be in conformity with the law and shall be used only as a measure of last resort and for the shortest appropriate period of time."

101. CCPR, Art. 9(1); CRC, Art. 37(b); American Convention, Art. 7(2); European Convention, Art. 5(1); and African Charter, Art. 6.

102. *See, e.g.*, Report of the Working Group on Arbitrary Detention, UN Doc. E/CN.4/1992/20 (Jan. 21, 1992), para. 10. A broad interpretation of the term "arbitrary" is supported by the 1964 Commission on Human Rights Study of the right of everyone to be free from arbitrary arrest, detention and exile. UN Doc. E/CN.4/826/Rev. 1 (1964), p. 7, para. 27 (1964).

103. *See* CCPR, Art. 9(2) through 9(5). Similar safeguards exist at the regional level in, inter alia, American Convention, Art. 7(4)–(7); American Declaration, Art. XXV; European Convention, Art. 5; and African Charter, Art. 7.

104. HRC General Comments, *supra* note 33, at No. 8, para. 1. In the case of Ngalula Mpandanjila and other former members of parliament in Zaire, the committee was also of the view that house arrest and certain forms of internal banishment constitute deprivation of liberty (Annual Report of the Human Rights Committee, Communication No. 138/1983 [1986], p. 121, para. 10). Under Art. 5 of the European Convention, the European Court of Human Rights considered banishment to a small island (2.5 square kilometers) to be detention as the social contacts of the banished person were restricted to contacts with other inmates and the guards (Guzzardi case II, Judgment of Nov. 6, 1980, Ser. A, No. 39, para. 95). In contrast, banishment to a remote village in the mountains with the obligation to report to the police post in the next town were not considered to amount to detention: (Guzzardi case I, unpublished report of the European Commission on Human Rights of 5 Oct. 1970, Application 7960/77).

105. *See, e.g.*, the committee's view on Communication 305/1988 (van Alphen v. the Netherlands) para. 5.8 (Annual Report of the Human Rights Committee 1990 at 115) and Nowak, *supra* note 38, at 172–73.

106. *See supra* note 15 and accompanying text.

107. CCPR, Art. 4(1), permits derogation from the obligations of the Covenant only "to the extent strictly required by the exigencies of the situation."

108. Art. 42 is located in Section II of Part III of the Fourth Convention, entitled: Aliens in the Territory of a Party to the Conflict.

109. Arts. 79–135.

110. *See also* Universal Declaration, Art. 25(1), CEDAW, Art. 14(2); and CRC, Arts. 24 and 27.

111. CESCR, General Comments, *supra* note 49, at No. 3, para. 10.

112. *Id.*

113. *Id.*

114. *Id.* at para. 13, noting the inclusion of "international assistance and cooperation" in the undertaking of States Parties under Art. 2(1).

115. Robert Robertson, *Measuring State Compliance with the Obligation to Devote the "Maximum Available Resources" to Realizing Economic, Social, and Cultural Rights*, 16 Hum. Rts. Q. 692, 698–701 (1994), citing, inter alia, The Realization of Economic, Social and Cultural Rights: Realization of Economic, Social and Cultural Rights, Second Progress Report Prepared by Danilo Turk, Special Rapporteur, UN Commission on Human Rights, Sub-Commission on Prevention of Discrimination and Protection of Minorities, 43d Sess., Prov. Agenda Item 9, at 18, UN Doc. E/CN.4/Sub.2/1991/17 (1991); Limburg Principles on the Implementation of the International Covenant on Economic, Social and Cultural Rights, UN Commission on Human Rights, 43d Sess., Annex, Prov. Agenda Items 8, 18, at 3, para. 25, UN Doc. E/CN.4/1987/17 (1987). Three levels of state obligations have been identified: (1) the obligation to respect, that is, to avoid depriving individuals of resources; (2) the obligation to protect from deprivation; and (3) the obligation to fulfill the need, essentially to aid the deprived.

116. *See supra* note 111.

117. *See* New Rules, *supra* note 58, at 677. Art. 54(3) contains exceptions to these prohibitions (attacks on supplies of foodstuffs that are intended for the sole use of the enemy's armed forces as long as such supplies are not intended to provide sustenance for prisoners of war or civilians), which, however, have to be narrowly interpreted.

118. *See* CEDAW, Arts. 12 and 14(2); and Convention on the Rights of the Child, Arts. 24(1) and 39, addressing the specific health-related needs of women and children.

119. CESCR, General Comments, *supra* note 65, at No. 3, para. 10.

120. Fourth Geneva Convention, Art. 18, para. 1, states: "Civilian hospitals organized to give care to the wounded and sick, the infirm and maternity cases, may in no circumstances be the object of attack, but shall at all times be respected and protected by the Parties to the conflict."

121. Universal Declaration, Art. 6; CCPR, Art. 16; American Declaration, Art. XVII; American Convention, Art. 3; and African Charter, Art. 5.

122. *E.g.*, CCPR, Art. 24(2); and CRC, Art. 7(1).

123. Fourth Convention, Arts. 50 and 97, Protocol I, Art. 78, regulates documentation of evacuated children.

124. In American Human Rights Declaration, Art. VIII; American Human Rights Convention, Art. 22(1); Fourth Protocol to the European Human Rights Convention, Art. 2(1); and African Charter, Art. 12(1).

125. *See, e.g.*, Protocol II, Art. 4(3)(e) (temporary evacuation of children) and Art. 17 (prohibition of forced movement of civilians) for noninternational

conflicts, and Fourth Geneva Convention, Art. 49 (deportations, transfers, evacuations), as well as Protocol I, Art. 51(7) (prohibition of using civilians as shields) for interstate armed conflicts.

126. Dayton Peace Agreement, *Agreement on Refugees and Displaced Persons*, Annex 7, *reprinted in* XXXV ILM 136 (1996).

127. On the situation in Abkhazia, *see* UN Security Council Resolution 876 (Oct. 19, 1993).

128. Sub-Commission Resolution 1994/24, para. 2, Report of the Sub-Commission on Prevention of Discrimination and Protection of Minorities at its Forty-Sixth Session, Geneva, August 1–26, 1994, UN Doc. E/CN.4/Sub.2/1994/56 (Oct. 28, 1994), at 67.

129. HRC General Comments, *supra* note 33, at No. 20, para. 3. Similar views of the Human Rights Committee in respect of communication No. 469/1991 (Charles Chitat Ng v. Canada), *adopted on* Nov. 5, 1993, para. 14.2.

130. *Id.* at paras. 14.1 and 15.3.

131. Cruz Varas case, Judgment of Mar. 20, 1991, Ser. A, No. 201, para. 69. Similarly, views of the Human Rights Committee in respect of communication No. 469/1991 (Charles Chitat Ng v. Canada), *adopted on* Nov. 5, 1993, para. 16.1.

132. Cruz Varas case, *supra* note 131, at para. 70.

133. American Declaration, Art. XXIII; American Convention, Art. 21; First Protocol to the European Convention, Art. 1; and African Charter, Art. 14.

134. *See, e.g.,* Fourth Geneva Convention, Art. 53. The Fourth Convention, Art. 147, typifies as a grave breach "extensive destruction and appropriation of property, not justified by military necessity and carried out unlawfully and wantonly." Under this provision, destruction of property protected under the convention subjects the perpetrators to prosecution under universal jurisdiction.

135. Common Art. 3, para. 2(g); Regulations Respecting the Laws and Customs of War on Land, Arts. 28 and 47, annex to the 1907 Convention (IV) Respecting the Laws and Customs of War on Land, signed at The Hague, Oct. 18, 1907; Fourth Geneva Convention, Art. 33.

136. Report on the Situation of Human Rights of a Segment of the Nicaraguan Population of Miskito Origin, OEA/Ser.L/V/II.62, doc. 10, rev. 3 (Nov. 29, 1983). *See also* World Bank, Operational Directive on Involuntary Resettlement, Operational Manual, OD 4.30 (June 1990) (providing for compensation for losses at full replacement cost for persons displaced involuntarily as a result of development projects that give rise to severe economic, social, and environmental problems).

137. Resolution 687(1991), para. 16.

138. *See* UN Compensation Commission, Governing Council Decision 1, UN Doc. S/22885, *reprinted in* XXX ILM 1713 (1991), paras. 10–14, and Decision 3, UN Doc. S/24589, *reprinted in* 31 ILM 1028 (1992).

139. Rules of Procedure and Evidence, Art. 105, *adopted* Feb. 11, 1994, by the International Tribunal for the Prosecution of Persons Responsible for Serious Violations of Humanitarian Law Committed in the Territory of the Former Yugoslavia since 1991, UN Doc. IT/32 (Mar. 14, 1994).

140. *See also* Study concerning the right to restitution, compensation and rehabilitation for victims of gross violations of human rights and fundamental freedoms: Final report submitted by Mr. Theo van Boven, Special Rapporteur, UN Doc. E/CN.4/Sub.2/1993/8 (1993).

141. On the regional level, the American Declaration, Art. VI, considers the family to be the basic element of society and grants every individual the right to receive protection therefore. The American Convention, Art. 17(1), reiterates CCPR, Art. 23(1). According to the African Charter, Art. 18(1), the family "shall be the natural unit and basis of society. It shall be protected by the State which shall take care of its physical health and moral needs." Furthermore, the state "shall have the duty to assist the family which is the custodian of morals and traditional values recognized by the community" (para. 2). Finally, the European Social Charter provides a right of the family to social, legal and economic protection.

142. *See, e.g.*, CCPR, Art. 24(1).

143. Vienna Declaration and Programme of Action of the World Conference on Human Rights, held at Vienna, June 14–25, 1993, UN Doc. A/CONF.157/23, pt. 1, para. 21 (July 12, 1993) (emphasis added).

144. World Declaration on the Survival, Protection and Development of Children and Plan of Action for Implementing the World Declaration on the Survival, Protection and Development of Children in the 1990s, *adopted at* New York, Sept. 30, 1990, para. 20(5) (Declaration), in Note by the Secretary-General on the Status of the Convention on the Rights of the Child, annex, UN Doc. E/CN.4/1991/59 (Dec. 12, 1990).

145. *Id.* at para. 19 (Plan of Action).

146. For example, UNHCR EXECUTIVE COMMITTEE CONCLUSION NO. 24 (XXXII), FAMILY REUNIFICATION (1981) (hereafter ExCom CONC. NO. 24) (the principle of the unity of the family and humanitarian reasons requires that "every effort should be made to ensure the reunification of separated refugee families"); EXECUTIVE COMMITTEE CONCLUSION NO. 9 (XXVIII), FAMILY REUNION (1977).

147. UNHCR EXECUTIVE COMMITTEE CONCLUSION NO. 47 (XXXVIII), REFUGEE CHILDREN (1987), para. d (hereafter ExCom CONC. NO. 47).

148. UNHCR GUIDELINES ON REFUGEE CHILDREN, *supra* note 29, at 43. Such support has included measures to protect and assist refugee mothers, trace parents, provide extra help to single or isolated parents, organize parental support networks, and prepare families for reunion. *Id.* at 43–44, 128–29.

149. Report of the Forty-Fifth Session of the Executive Committee of the High Commissioner's Programme (Geneva, Oct. 3–7, 1994), UN Doc. A/AC.96/839 (Oct. 11, 1994), Conc. B2, para. 23(h) (hereafter ExCom 1994 REPORT).

150. Every effort to trace parents or close relatives must be made before resettlement or adoption are considered and, in the interim, physical and emotional support as well as training must be provided. ExCom CONC. NO. 24, *supra* note 146, at para. 7; ExCom CONC. NO. 47, *supra* note 147, at para. I; UNHCR GUIDELINES ON REFUGEE CHILDREN, *supra* note 29, at 130–34, 146–48.

151. NEW RULES, *supra* note 58, at 452.

152. American Declaration, Art. XII; Protocol of San Salvador, Art. 13; First

Protocol to the European Human Rights Convention, Art. 2; and African Charter, Art. 17.

153. Protocol I, Art. 78(2), I similarly requires "the greatest possible continuity" in education for children evacuated under the terms of paragraph 1 of that article.

154. Executive Committee of the High Commissioner's Programme, Executive Committee Conclusion B2, Conclusion on Refugee Children, in ExCom 1994 REPORT, *supra* note 149, at para. 23(c) and (d), at 17-18.

155. UNHCR, GUIDELINES ON REFUGEE WOMEN, *supra* note 29, at 16, 21, and paras. 103-10. In order for women to participate as fully as possible in these programs, due attention must be given to possible cultural barriers inhibiting women's participation in training sessions, as well as their needs for appropriate child care. Furthermore, women should be engaged and consulted in the process of developing and implementing such training programs. *Id.* at 56-57.

156. GA Resolution 131, UN GAOR, 43d Sess., Supp. No. 49, at 207, UN Doc. A/43/49 (1989), *adopted without a vote* Dec. 8, 1988 (hereafter GA Res. 43/131), preambular para. 1 and GA Resolution 100, UN GAOR, 45th Sess., Supp. No. 49A, at 183, UN Doc. A/45/49 (1991), *adopted without a vote* Dec. 14, 1990 (hereafter GA Res. 45/100), preambular para. 2.

157. *See* HRC General Comments, *supra* note 33, at No. 6, para. 5.

158. CESCR General Comments, *supra* note 49, at No. 3, para. 13.

159. Under Art. 22, the Economic and Social Council may bring specific situations where international measures are "likely to contribute to the effective progressive implementation" of the CESCR to the attention of other UN organs, subsidiary organs and specialized agencies. CESCR General Comments, *supra* note 49, at No. 2, para. 3 (1990) (in pertinent part). Art. 23 sets forth the States Parties' agreement that international action include, inter alia, furnishing of technical assistance. Indeed, one objective of State Party reporting is to enable the Committee and other States Parties to "identify the most appropriate means by which the international community might assist States, in accordance with Arts. 22 and 23." CESCR General Comments, *supra* note 49, at No. 1, para. 9 (1989).

160. CESCR, General Comments, *supra* note 49, at No. 3, para. 14.

161. In GA Res. 43/131, which is entitled, "Humanitarian assistance to victims of natural disasters and similar emergency situations," the General Assembly recognized "that it is up to each State first and foremost to take care of the victims of natural disasters and similar emergency situations occurring on its territory" (preambular para. 2). Para. 2 of the resolution reiterates this as follows: "*Reaffirms also* the sovereignty of affected States and their primary role in the initiation, organization, co-ordination and implementation of humanitarian assistance within their respective territories." (GA Res. 43/131, UN GAOR, 43d Sess., Supp. No. 49, at 207, UN Doc. A/43/49 [1989], *adopted without a vote* Dec. 8, 1988 (hereafter GA Res. 43/131). The same language is found in GA Res. 45/100, preambular para. 3 and resolution para. 2. In 1991 the General Assembly adopted resolution 46/182 entitled, "Strengthening of the Coordination of Humanitarian Emergency Assistance of the United Nations." The annex to

this resolution contains, inter alia, guiding principles that state that humanitarian assistance "must be provided in accordance with the principles of humanity, neutrality and impartiality" (para. 2). Para. 4 of the guiding principles states: Each State has the responsibility first and foremost to take care of the victims of natural disasters and other emergencies occurring on its territory. Hence, the affected State has the primary role in the initiation, organization, coordination, and implementation of humanitarian assistance within its territory. Guiding Principles in the annex to GA Resolution 182, UN GAOR, 46th Sess., Supp. No. 49, at 49, 50, UN Doc. A/46/49 (1992), *adopted without a vote* Dec. 19, 1991 (hereafter Annex to GA Res. 46/182).

162. GA Res. 43/131, *supra* note 161, at preambular para. 8, and GA Res. 45/100, *supra* note 161, at preambular para. 6.

163. GA Res. 43/131, *supra* note 161, at para. 4, and GA Res. 45/100, *supra* note 161, at para. 4.

164. Guiding Principles in the Annex to GA Res. 46/182, *supra* note 161, at para. 3. GA Res. 43/131 (*supra* note 161) and GA Res. 45/100 (*supra* note 161) likewise urge states close to disaster or emergency areas to facilitate the transit of humanitarian assistance (paras. 6 and 7, respectively).

165. ICRC, *Twenty-fifth International Conference of the Red Cross* (Geneva, Oct. 1986), Art. 5(3), *reproduced in* INTERNATIONAL COMMITTEE OF THE RED CROSS AND THE LEAGUE OF THE RED CROSS AND RED CRESCENT SOCIETIES, COMPENDIUM OF REFERENCE TEXTS ON THE INTERNATIONAL RED CROSS AND RED CRESCENT MOVEMENT (1990).

166. Over the years, ICRC has developed a particular expertise and operational capability to assist and protect victims of internal armed conflicts. The broad range of "traditional" activities or functions it normally undertakes for these victims includes emergency medical assistance to wounded and sick civilians; providing emergency food, drinkable water, and other essential supplies to the civilian population; protection of civilians; visits to detainees; searches for missing persons; and efforts to reestablish contact between family members separated by the conflict. These activities are extended to internally displaced civilians, if ICRC has access to such persons.

167. Governments, especially, have occasionally refused to do so.

168. The authors of one authoritative commentary on the protocols write: "If the article is to have any meaning (and it should be interpreted in this way), the party to which the service is offered must at least give sympathetic consideration to the offer" (NEW RULES, *supra* note 58, at 695). The NEW RULES submit that these duties imply "an *obligation to accept offers* made under Art. 18, para. 1 if the party itself is unable or unwilling to take the necessary measures through its own agents" (emphasis added).

169. NEW RULES, *supra* note 58, at 696. According to the wording of Art. 18(2), only the consent of the "High Contracting Party concerned," that is, the established government, is required for relief actions, not that of rebel forces "even if the relief action takes place in an area under their control."

170. NEW RULES, *supra* note 58, at 697.

171. Internees are allowed to receive relief packages, individually or collec-

tively, under Art. 108 of the Fourth Convention, but the number of such consignments, which may contain, inter alia, food, clothing, medical supplies, and devotional, educational, or recreational books or objects, may be restricted on grounds of military necessity. In the case of transfer of the internee, mail and packages must be forwarded to him or her without delay (Fourth Convention, Art. 128, para. 3). Art. 109 of this treaty as well as its Annex II (Draft Regulations Concerning Collective Relief) provide for the distribution and receipt of collective relief for internees.

172. NEW RULES, *supra* note 58, at 432.

173. Art. 70 incorporates by reference the following supplies mentioned in Protocol I, Art. 69: "clothing, bedding, means of shelter, other supplies essential to the survival of the civilian population . . . and objects necessary for religious worship."

174. *See* NEW RULES, *supra* note 58, at 429.

175. NEW RULES, *supra* note 58, at 433. Regarding the kind of organization that can undertake relief actions, the NEW RULES state that "in principle, it could be anybody, . . . a private individual, a national relief society, the League of Red Cross Societies, the ICRC, a non-governmental international organization [or] a governmental international organization."

176. Such an agreement under Protocol I, Art. 70, "has to be granted as a matter of principle, but . . . it can be refused for valid and compelling reasons," such as imperative considerations of military necessity. NEW RULES, *supra* note 58, at 434.

177. NEW RULES, *supra* note 58, at 436.

178. Protocol I, Art. 69, applicable to occupied territories, simply expands the list of goods that the occupying power is obliged to supply the civilian population.

179. The Fourth Convention, Art. 60, makes clear that the provision of such humanitarian relief "shall in no way relieve the Occupying Power of any of its responsibilities under Arts. 55 . . . and 59." It also enjoins the occupying power from diverting relief shipments from the intended purposes, except "in cases of urgent necessity, in the interests of the population of the occupied territory and with the consent of the Protecting Power."

180. Security Council Resolution 688 of Apr. 5, 1991, UN Doc. S/Res/688 (1993).

181. *See* Security Council Resolution 853 of July 29, 1993, UN Doc. S/Res/853 (1993) concerning Azerbaijan, where the Security Council "calls once again for unimpeded access for international humanitarian relief efforts in the region, in particular in all areas affected by the conflict, in order to alleviate the increased suffering of the civilian population and reaffirms that all parties are bound to comply with the principles and rules of international humanitarian law." In Resolution 859 of Aug. 24, 1993 (S/Res/859 [1993]), the Security Council demanded in operative paragraph 3 "that all concerned facilitate the unhindered flow of humanitarian assistance, including the provision of food, water, electricity, fuel and communications, in particular to the 'safe areas' in Bosnia and Herzegovina."

Resolution 876 (1993) of Oct. 19, 1993, UN Doc. S/Res/876 (1993) concerning the situation in Abkhazia affirming "the right of refugees and displaced persons to return to their homes" (para. 5) and calling for "unimpeded access for international humanitarian relief assistance in the region." Security Council Resolution 898 (1994) of Feb. 23, 1994, UN Doc. S/Res/898 (1994), para. 18, "urges all parties to continue to facilitate unimpeded access to humanitarian assistance for the civilian population in need, and also to cooperate with the United Nations High Commissioner for Refugees and other humanitarian agencies operating in Mozambique to facilitate the speedy repatriation and resettlement of refugees and displaced persons."

182. Security Council Resolution 794 of Dec. 3, 1992, UN Doc. S/Res/794 (1992), preambular para. 7.

183. *Id.* at preambular para. 3.

184. *Id.* at para. 10.

185. Security Council Resolution 929 (1994) of July 22, 1994, UN Doc. S/Res/929 (1994).

186. Security Council Resolution 925 (1994) of June 8, 1994, UN Doc. S/Res/925 (1994), para. 4(a). The same goals were already set forth in Security Council Resolution 918 (1994) of Apr. 21, 1994, UN Doc. S/Res/918 (1994), para. 3; in its preambular paragraphs, the resolution referred, inter alia, to "the internal displacement of a significant percentage of the Rwandan population."

187. UNISOM II (Somalia): Security Council Resolution 814 (1993) of Aug. 26, 1993, UN Doc. S/Res/814 (1993), para. 12; Security Council Resolution 897 (1994) of Feb. 4, 1994, UN Doc. S/Res/897 (1994), para. 2(e). UNAMIR (Rwanda): Security Council Resolution 872 (1993) of Oct. 5, 1993, para. 3(f), UN Doc. S/Res/872 (1993); Security Council Resolution 925 (1994) of June 8, 1994, para. 4(a) UN Doc. S/Res/925 (1994); Security Council Resolution 965 (1994) of Nov. 30, para. 2(a), UN Doc. S/Res/965 (1994).

188. For a case of a non-international armed conflict, *see* Security Council Resolution 876 (1993) of Oct. 19, 1993, UN Doc. S/Res/876 (1993), para. 7, concerning the situation in Abkhazia (calling on all parties "for unimpeded access for international humanitarian assistance in the region").

189. *See* the second preambular paragraph in the quotation from Security Council Resolution 929 (1994) July 22, 1994, UN Doc. S/Res/929 (1994), and the preambular paragraph from Resolution 794 (1992) of Dec. 3 1992, UN Doc. S/Res/794 (1992).

190. The relationship between the obligation of states to respect a resolution of the Security Council calling for immediate or unimpeded access of humanitarian relief on the one hand and the principle (discussed in the previous section of this chapter) that humanitarian relief cannot be delivered without consent of the state concerned, on the other hand, remains unclear for the time being.

191. Convention on the Safety of United Nations and Associated Personnel, annexed to GA Res. 49/59, *adopted without a vote*, Dec. 9, 1994, not yet in force.

192. In order to enjoy the protections, privileges, and immunities extended

to these persons under that treaty, relief workers must qualify as "United Nations personnel" or "Associated personnel" as defined in the convention. It should be noted that ICRC personnel are not covered by this convention.

193. *See*, inter alia, Fourth Geneva Convention, Arts. 18–22; and Protocol I, Arts. 15, 16, 18 and 21–31.

194. *See* Compilation and Analysis.

195. *See* Compilation and Analysis, paras. 415–416.

196. *See* Compilation and Analysis, paras. 250–252.

197. For a full list of gaps and areas of normative weaknesses, *see id.* at paras. 415–16.

198. *See id.* at para. 109 (explaining how land mines pose significant dangers to civilians, especially internally displaced persons, both during and after the conclusion of hostilities).

Chapter Four

1. For a fuller discussion of the characteristics of complex emergencies, see Inter-Agency Standing Committee Working Group, "Report of Sixteenth Meeting," Geneva, November 30, 1994, pp. 28–32. A recent report of the UN secretary-general describes a complex emergency as "large-scale humanitarian crises in complicated political and military environments, often in the context of internal conflicts." See General Assembly, *Renewing the United Nations: A Programme for Reform,* Report of the Secretary-General, A/51/950 (United Nations, July 14, 1997), para. 180.

2. Other UN organizations play more marginal roles. The Food and Agriculture Organization, through its global information and early warning system, provides information to the United Nations on sudden population displacements as a result of drought and famine. It also participates in needs assessments missions in emergency situations. It is involved with the internally displaced mainly in the areas of resettlement and rehabilitation. The FAO, for example, has assisted returning internally displaced persons and refugees to adapt to new farming systems and agricultural environments. The International Labor Organization supports community-based income-generating and employment projects that benefit internally displaced persons.

3. In such cases, UNHCR must act within the limits of its resources, since activities for the internally displaced are not financed by UNHCR's general program but from special trust funds.

4. See General Assembly, "Office of the United Nations High Commissioner for Refugees," Resolution 48/116 (United Nations, December 20, 1993).

5. UNHCR, "Refugees and Others of Concern to UNHCR: 1996 Statistical Overview," Geneva, 1997.

6. In a 1994 note to its Executive Committee, UNHCR described the many new tasks its staff had been called upon to perform in defense of the internally displaced, in particular assisting the safe passage of civilians through front lines, relocating and evacuating civilians from conflict areas, assisting besieged popu-

lations who are unable or unwilling to move from their homes, and alerting governments and the public to human rights abuses. See Executive Committee of the High Commissioner's Programme, Sub-Committee of the Whole on International Protection, *Protection Aspects of UNHCR Activities on Behalf of Internally Displaced Persons*, EC/SCP/87 (UNHCR, August 17, 1994), pp. 11–12.

7. A UNHCR discussion paper found that "most" UNHCR staff "have a limited understanding of the meaning of protection in a country of origin, and are generally unfamiliar with the legal instruments which can be used for that purpose." See UNHCR, *UNHCR's Role in Protecting and Assisting Internally Displaced People*, Central Evaluation Section Discussion Paper EVAL/IDP/13/2 (Geneva, November 1993). Moreover, a UNHCR report on its operational experience with internally displaced persons emphasizes the difficulties faced by the organization in trying to extend protection to persons displaced in situations of internal conflict and points out that protection in such circumstances is often closer to ICRC's expertise than to its own. See Division of International Protection, UNHCR, *UNHCR's Operational Experience with Internally Displaced Persons* (Geneva, September 1994), pp. 78–82.

8. UNHCR, for example, has helped returning refugees and internally displaced persons to reintegrate in countries such as Nicaragua, Somalia, Tajikistan, and Afghanistan. In Rwanda, it has registered internally displaced persons for return, provided transport and relief, and drawn up draft principles to promote safe and secure returns in accordance with UNHCR principles for refugees. Further examples of UNHCR activities in support of reintegration of the internally displaced can be found in Executive Committee of the UN High Commissioner for Refugees, *Financial and Programmatic Implications of UNHCR Activities on Behalf of the Internally Displaced*, EC/1994/SC.2/CRP.13 (UNHCR, May 6, 1994). On the whole, when UNHCR assumes responsibility for the internally displaced, it considers that its activities must be consistent with its basic mandate "for protection and solutions." See IOM-FOM 33/93 in UNHCR, "UNHCR's Role with Internally Displaced Persons" Geneva, April 28, 1993.

9. Thomas G. Weiss and Amir Pasic, "Case Study on the Former Yugoslavia," in Roberta Cohen and Francis M. Deng, eds., *The Forsaken People: Case Studies of the Internally Displaced* (Brookings, 1998).

10. See Larry Minear and others, "Humanitarian Action in the Former Yugoslavia: The UN's Role 1991–1993," Thomas J. Watson Jr. Institute for International Studies and Refugee Policy Group, Occasional Paper 18 (Brown University, 1994), pp. 63–70; and Bill Frelick, "'Preventive Protection'" and the Right to Seek Asylum: A Preliminary Look at Bosnia and Croatia," *International Journal of Refugee Law*, vol. 4, no. 4 (1992), pp. 439–53.

11. Jacques de Milliano, Chairman, International Council of Médecins Sans Frontières, address to Parinac Oslo Global Conference, Oslo, June 9, 1994. See also the International Committee of the Red Cross, statement before UNHCR Sub-Committee of the Whole on International Protection, Executive Committee of the High Commissioner's Programme, Geneva, May 18, 1994. ICRC's statement challenged the view that priority should be given to in-country protection

to enable people to remain within their countries of origin: "To make this an a priori criterion would inevitably convey the impression that the interests of third countries [that is, countries reluctant to receive refugees] were being placed before those of the victims themselves."

12. Karin Landgren, "Danger-Safe Areas," *Refugees*, vol. 1 (UNHCR, 1996), pp. 16–19.

13. *UNHCR's Operational Experience*, p. 52.

14. Under these statutes, ICRC may offer its services to governments to protect and assist the civilian victims of internal strife. Recent resolutions of the International Red Cross and Red Crescent Movement have endorsed ICRC's involvement in these situations. See Jean-Philippe Lavoyer, "Refugees and Internally Displaced Persons: International Humanitarian Law and the Role of the ICRC," *International Review of the Red Cross*, no. 305 (March–April 1995); and Denise Plattner, "The Protection of Displaced Persons in Non-International Armed Conflicts," *International Review of the Red Cross*, no. 291 (November–December 1992).

15. In Rwanda, ICRC has cared for more than one million civilians, most of them displaced persons. This constitutes ICRC's largest relief operation to date. In Chechnya, ICRC has protected and assisted hundreds of thousands of people, many of them internally displaced.

16. This is particularly the case for prison visits. An agreement reached between ICRC and the UN Human Rights Field Operation in Rwanda in 1996 ("Guidelines for Coordination in the Field with Regard to Visits to Persons Deprived of their Freedom in Rwanda") provides for a division of labor in which ICRC standards are upheld with regard to prison visits.

17. In its reports, ICRC acknowledges the "irritation" expressed by UN bodies at its insistence upon its neutrality and independence. However, it demonstrates the "value" of this role by pointing out that it was ICRC that was needed in 1992 to visit UN military personnel detained by Somali factions, and Somalis held by UN forces. See International Committee of the Red Cross, "ICRC Special Report on Activities 1990–1995" (Geneva, November 1995), p. 10.

18. One hundred thirty-eight states have ratified Additional Protocol II relevant to noninternational armed conflict, whereas 188 states have ratified the Geneva Conventions.

19. General Assembly, "International Conference on the Plight of Refugees, Returnees and Displaced Persons in Southern Africa," Resolution 44/136 (United Nations, February 27, 1990). See also General Assembly, "International Conference on the Plight of Refugees, Returnees and Displaced Persons in Southern Africa," Resolution 43/116 (United Nations, December 8, 1988); and General Assembly, *Report of the Secretary-General*, A/44/520 (United Nations, September 28, 1989), p. 19. This decision developed by and large out of emergencies in Ethiopia and the Sudan in the mid-1980s when UNDP resident representatives were called upon to assume key roles in coordinating emergency response.

20. See United Nations Development Programme, "Manual for the Programming of UNDP Resources," (United Nations, April 1996), pt. III, p. 3.

21. Resident representatives/coordinators, for example, when providing information to the representative of the secretary-general on internally displaced persons, have sometimes failed to acknowledge problems of internal displacement that might require international attention. In one country where internally displaced persons faced serious protection problems, the resident representative/coordinator declined to provide information on the internally displaced to the task force on internally displaced persons. With regard to the Sudan, Médecins Sans Frontières, in a statement before the UN Commission on Human Rights, claimed that "the NGOs working with the internally displaced around Khartoum have repeatedly brought the plight of the displaced to the attention of the UNDP resident representative. However, no effective action appears to have been taken to improve their situation" (Geneva, April 11, 1996).

22. The Inter-Agency Standing Committee in 1997 recommended that resident coordinators report regularly on situations of internal displacement to the ERC and the representative of the secretary-general on internally displaced persons. As of this writing, however, the recommendation has not been implemented. The extent to which resident coordinators will be asked to report on protection and human rights issues also remains unclear.

23. In Kenya, for example, UNDP introduced a program intended to meet both the emergency and development needs of an estimated 300,000 internally displaced persons, although it was obstructed by the government. See Human Rights Watch/Africa, "Kenya: Old Habits Die Hard," New York, July 1995.

24. UNDP, "UNDP and Internally Displaced Persons in 1997," draft memorandum, November 18, 1996. See also Executive Board of the United Nations Development Programme and of the United Nations Population Fund, "Report of the Administrator," DP/1996/18/Add.2 (United Nations, March 15, 1996), p. 17; and UNDP, Emergency Response Division, "Building Bridges between Relief and Development," United Nations, 1996, pp. 12–14.

25. UNDP, "Manual for the Programming of UNDP Resources," pt. II.

26. In Burma, for example, UNDP development projects have been criticized for lending support to SLORC. See Aung San Suu Kyi, General Secretary of the National League for Democracy, letter to Gustave Speth, Administrator, UNDP, January 14, 1996. Human Rights Watch/Africa has criticized UNDP for failing to protest the Kenyan government's manipulation and obstruction of a project to facilitate the return of internally displaced persons to their homes in the Rift Valley. UNDP, the report said, "is damaging its credibility by being an implementing partner in a program in which blatant human rights violations are taking place, such as brutality against displaced persons, forced relocations and dispersal of camps." See Human Rights Watch/Africa, "Kenya: Old Habits Die Hard," pp. 7–10.

27. See World Food Programme, *Annual Report of the Executive Director 1994: Linking Relief to Development* (United Nations, April 26, 1995); and WFP, *Report to the Economic and Social Council*, WFP/EB.3/96/3 (United Nations, September 23, 1996).

28. Médecins Sans Frontières found acute malnutrition in camps of internally displaced persons when WFP assistance programs became development oriented

and were in the process of being terminated. See Curtis W. Lambrecht, "NGO Response Patterns to the Assistance, Protection and Development Needs of the Internally Displaced," Norwegian Refugee Council, July 1996. In the Sudan, an external evaluation prepared for DHA found "an implicit but steady withdrawal from, and down-grading of, the issue of war-displaced in Khartoum" by WFP and other UN agencies, despite "the persistence of some of the highest malnutrition rates among the Khartoum war-displaced." See Ataul Karim, Mark Duffield, and others, *OLS: A Review* (July 1996), p. 196.

29. It concluded that the "provision of assistance to the internally displaced remains inadequately addressed." See Inter-Agency Standing Committee Working Group, "Report of Eighteenth Meeting," Section on Burundi, Geneva, May 8, 1995.

30. UN Commission on Human Rights, *Report of the UN Special Rapporteur on Violence against Women*, E/CN.4/1995/42 (United Nations, November 22, 1994), para. 301.

31. See UN Expert Group, "Meeting on Refugee and Displaced Women and Children," EGM/RDWC/1990/WP.1 (United Nations, June 25, 1990).

32. See World Food Programme, Emergency Operations, *Protracted Refugee and Displaced Person Projects,* Report by the Executive Director, CFA:38/SCP:13 (United Nations, November 2, 1994).

33. WFP Executive Director, Letter on Internally Displaced Persons to all WFP Country Staff, Rome, August 18, 1995.

34. World Food Programme, *WFP Response to ECOSOC Resolution 1995/56,* Reports to the Economic and Social Council, WFP/EB.A/96/7 (United Nations, April 9, 1996), pt. 4, p. 5.

35. In a statement before UNHCR's Executive Committee in 1994, WFP's executive director observed, in the case of refugees: "Often food is distributed to camp elders who distribute down the hierarchy of their village as they see fit," even though distribution "family by family" would prove more effective. She emphasized that refugee women and their children are the primary victims of internal conflicts and should be given priority in efforts to ensure that entire families are fed. She also drew attention to the need to address the issue of food being diverted to the military, noting that despite a policy prohibiting this, in the camps in Goma for Rwandan refugees, "there is no delineation between feeding soldiers and non-soldiers and no opportunity to do so under the current circumstances." See Catherine Bertini, Executive Director, World Food Programme, statement to the Forty-Fifth Session of the Executive Committee of the High Commissioner's Programme, Geneva, October 3, 1994.

36. *WFP Response to ECOSOC Resolution 1995/56*, p. 5.

37. Negotiations with the government of Ethiopia and the Eritrean People's Liberation Front in the 1980s, for example, resulted in access to five million internally displaced persons in Eritrea and Tigray. More recently, negotiations with the government of Rwanda and the Rwandan Patriotic Front enabled WFP to mount cross-border operations into both northern and southern Rwanda. See World Food Programme, "Internally Displaced Persons," WFP Position Paper, Rome, June 1994.

38. In the Sudan, for example, WFP has been charged with allowing the government to exercise "a veto" over food distribution on political or ethnic grounds. See African Rights, "Humanitarianism Unbound?" London, November 1994, p. 14.

39. Two out of three tons of food aid provided in 1994 were distributed as relief assistance, and only one ton was used in support of development projects. See WFP, *Annual Report of the Executive Director* (United Nations, 1994).

40. Initially, UNICEF's main emphasis was on meeting emergency needs in Europe, but in 1950 this shifted to programs of long-range benefit to children in developing countries. See UNICEF, *Children in Situations of Armed Conflict*, E/ICEF/1986/CRP.2 (United Nations, March 10, 1986), p. 19.

41. Interviews with UNICEF staff, 1995 and 1996; and M. Rajan, "UNICEF Statement," Norwegian Government Round Table Discussion on Internally Displaced Persons, Geneva, February 15, 1995.

42. See UNICEF, "UNICEF Position on Internally Displaced Persons (IDPs)," February 15, 1996, p. 2; and Inter-Agency Task Force on Internally Displaced Persons, "UNICEF's Capacity to Provide Support to Internally Displaced Persons," Geneva, November 26, 1996.

43. See James P. Grant, "Refugees, Internally Displaced and the Poor: An Evolving Ethos of Responsibility," address at the Round Table on the Papal Document, UNICEF, March 9, 1993; and Iain Guest, "UNICEF's Cruel Choices," *Washington Post*, January 11, 1996, p. A23.

44. See UNICEF, *UNICEF Emergency Services: Mission and Strategies*, E/ICEF/1996/4 (United Nations, November 24, 1995); and *UNICEF Emergency Operations*, E/ICEF/1996/7 (United Nations, December 1, 1995).

45. See, for example, African Rights, "Humanitarianism Unbound?" pp. 14–15, 17, which criticizes UNICEF for insufficient attention to protection in the Sudan and Angola. A 1991 multidonor evaluation of UNICEF's role in emergencies also concluded that UNICEF should be more "critical" in its dealings with governments. Interview with UNICEF staff, April 1996.

46. It has also organized a center for traumatized children and has placed more than 10,000 uprooted children with foster families.

47. UNICEF, *State of the World's Children 1996* (United Nations, 1995). UNICEF has also drafted principles to guide agencies in assisting internally displaced persons that include the "protection of IDPs from human rights violations and unwarranted perpetration of atrocities." See Rajan, "UNICEF Statement."

48. Interviews with UNICEF staff, 1995 and 1996. See also UNICEF, "UNICEF Position on Internally Displaced Persons."

49. Economic and Social Council, *Children and Women in Emergencies: Strategic Priorities and Operational Concerns for UNICEF*, Executive Board, E/ICEF/1997/7 (United Nations, November 11, 1996), para. 35.

50. In the WHO Constitution, the words "special groups" are followed by "such as peoples of trust territories." In recent years, however, the term "special groups" has come to mean refugees, returning refugees, and internally displaced persons. See World Health Organization, Executive Board, *Emergency and Hu-*

manitarian Action, Report by the Director-General, EB95/23 (United Nations, November 14, 1994).

51. See World Health Organization, "Emergency and Humanitarian Action," Resolution of the Executive Board, EB95.R17 (United Nations, January 27, 1995); and WHO, Executive Board, *Emergency and Humanitarian Action.* In the Sudan, WHO requested funding to strengthen its presence in the field so that emergency health measures could be effectively carried out in displaced persons' camps and other areas. See Department of Humanitarian Affairs, United Nations Consolidated Inter-Agency Appeal for Sudan, January–December 1996, February 1996, p. 52.

52. Most emergency programs are in fact funded through extrabudgetary contributions; in 1995 WHO raised $40 million in extrabudgetary funds for emergency programs. See World Health Organization, *Collaboration within the United Nations System and with other Intergovernmental Organizations: Strengthening of the Coordination of Emergency Humanitarian Assistance,* Report by the Director-General, A49/27 (United Nations, March 25, 1996).

53. WHO, *Collaboration within the United Nations System and with other Intergovernmental Organizations.*

54. A research program it undertook in 1991, Health and Development for Displaced Populations (HEDIP), designed health care strategies along these lines. It organized pilot projects in Sri Lanka, Mozambique, and Croatia that sought to promote long-term development, foster reconciliation, and benefit entire communities, including the displaced. See World Health Organization, "The PHC [Primary Health Care] Philosophy and the Hedip Approach," PHCHED.Doc (Draft) (United Nations, October 25, 1993); Hedip Forum, "Newsletter of the WHO Programme Health and Development for Displaced Populations," 1993 and 1994; and Patricia Weiss Fagen and Birgitte Refslund Sorensen, "Evaluation of HEDIP," War-Torn Societies Project, UNRISD, Geneva, April 1995.

55. See Michael Toole, Centers for Disease Control, Department of Health and Human Services, Testimony before the U.S. Senate Subcommittee on Children, Family, Drugs, and Alcoholism, April 3, 1990, cited in Refugee Policy Group, "Internally Displaced Women and Children," Washington, D.C., February 1992. See also "Letter from Baidoa: The Need for Adult Therapeutic Care in Emergency Feeding Programs," *Journal of the American Medical Association,* vol. 270 (August 4, 1993); and Refugee Policy Group, "Humanitarian Assistance in Somalia 1990–1994," Washington, D.C., August 1994, pp. 89, 116, 120.

56. See WHO, "Emergency and Humanitarian Action," Resolution of the Executive Board, EB95.R17 (United Nations, January 27, 1995); and WHO, Executive Board, *Health and Medical Services in Times of Armed Conflict,* Report by the Director-General, EB95/24 (United Nations, November 7, 1994).

57. WHO, Executive Board, *Emergency and Humanitarian Action.*

58. IOM has fifty-five member states and forty-one observer states. It has a staff of more than one thousand persons and some seventy field offices. Its 1996 budget totaled $267 million. For a summary of its activities with the internally

displaced, see International Organization for Migration, "Internally Displaced Persons: IOM Policy and Programmes," April 1997.

59. International Organization for Migration, *IOM Strategic Planning: Toward the Twenty-First Century*," MC/1842 (May 9, 1995), pp. 6, 10.

60. IOM, "Internally Displaced Persons," pp. 7–8.

61. Richard Perruchoud, "Return Migration: Observations on the Mandate and Activities of IOM," International Organization for Migration, June 1994.

62. General Assembly, "Strengthening the Coordination of Humanitarian Emergency Assistance of the United Nations," A/Res/46/182 (United Nations, December 19, 1991).

63. Jacques Cuenod, *Report on Refugees, Displaced Persons and Returnees*, Report to Economic and Social Council, E/1991/109/Add.2 (United Nations, June 27, 1991), pp. 5 and 35.

64. OCHA, unlike DHA, will have no operational responsibilities, and de-mining, disaster mitigation, and its program on Iraq will be transferred to other agencies.

65. The heads of UNICEF, UNHCR, WFP, UNDP, FAO, and WHO are the full members of the IASC. Standing invitees are IOM, the Red Cross Movement (ICRC and the International Federation of the Red Cross and Red Crescent Societies), the high commissioner for human rights, and the representative of the secretary-general on internally displaced persons. The NGO consortia, International Council of Voluntary Agencies (ICVA), Interaction and the Steering Committee for Humanitarian Response, are invited to attend on a permanent basis. To assist it in its work, the IASC has established a working group and a number of task forces that deal with specific countries and thematic issues.

66. ECHA is composed of the heads of UNDP, UNHCR, UNICEF, WFP, the high commissioner for human rights, the under-secretaries general of peace-keeping and political affairs, and the head of the UN Relief and Works Administration for Palestine Refugees (UNRWA). Four executive committees were established under the secretary-general's 1997 reform program (peace and security, economic and social affairs, development operations, and humanitarian affairs) to assist with policy development and management. The chairs of the committees are part of a Senior Management Group that advises the secretary-general and oversees implementation of the reform program. See General Assembly, *Renewing the United Nations*.

67. Inter-Agency Task Force on Internally Displaced Persons, "Internally Displaced Persons," Report to the Inter-Agency Standing Committee, United Nations, November 1994, p. 2.

68. General Assembly, *Renewing the United Nations*, para. 186.

69. See, for example, Department of Humanitarian Affairs, Complex Emergency Division, "Field Coordination Units," United Nations, January 1996. Most of the resident and humanitarian coordinators in the fourteen countries listed are responsible for coordinating assistance to internally displaced persons.

70. Inter-Agency Task Force, "Internally Displaced Persons," p. 2.

71. The secretary-general's 1997 reform program does say that "funding re-

quirements for human rights field operations will be included in the CAP, where appropriate." See General Assembly, *Renewing the United Nations,* para. 191.

72. Inter-Agency Standing Committee, "Internally Displaced Persons," ECOSOC Review of the Capacity of the UN System in Humanitarian Assistance, March 17, 1997, p. 12.

73. See Inter-Agency Task Force on Internally Displaced Persons, "Draft Report to the Inter-Agency Standing Committee," October 1994; and Roberta Cohen and Jacques Cuenod, *Improving Institutional Arrangements for the Internally Displaced* (Brookings Institution–Refugee Policy Group Project on Internal Displacement, October 1995), pp. 48–50.

74. See Inter-Agency Task Force on Internally Displaced Persons, "Terms of Reference," Department of Humanitarian Affairs, May 1995.

75. Department of Humanitarian Affairs, "Minutes of Inter-Agency Meeting," October 25, 1995. An interagency mission sent to Sierra Leone and the subregion in 1995 commented that it was "struck by the low visibility and seeming lack of interest the situation attracts" and reported that "for the most part, the Sierra Leonean population is using its own coping mechanisms to meet the needs of the displaced." DHA Report on Inter-Agency Mission, July/August 1995, pp. 1, 4.

76. Task force members, for example, suggested that the situation in Lebanon should be addressed; others called attention to the situation in Turkey. In the case of Myanmar (Burma), the task force actually agreed that a special meeting on the country would be held, but it never took place. The representative of the secretary-general on internally displaced persons recommended that the task force undertake global monitoring of displacement and help ensure that his recommendations in different countries were carried out.

77. The task force had agreed on a mission after the NRC pointed out that protection problems of internally displaced persons were not being adequately addressed in Angola. However, IOM, UNICEF, and UNHCR subsequently opposed a mission, and it was decided instead that a local assessment mission would be undertaken with NRC participation.

78. Department of Humanitarian Affairs, "Report of the Inter-Agency Task Force on IDPs to the Inter-Agency Standing Committee," May 1, 1995–April 30, 1996.

79. The representative of the secretary-general on internally displaced persons, for example, found insufficient coordination in Tajikistan and Peru. In both cases, government officials began to question the presence of some of the agencies because they did not understand what their functions or activities were; there did not appear to be any unity.

80. Inter-Agency Task Force, "Internally Displaced Persons," p. 2.

81. Resident Coordinator for the Sudan, "1995 Annual Report," Office of the Resident Coordinator of the United Nations System's Operational Activities for Development in the Sudan, Khartoum, the Sudan, 1996.

82. United Nations Development Programme, "Change and Reform in UNDP: Highlights," *The Administrator,* October 1995. Rosters from which to

choose resident or humanitarian coordinators now include experienced staff from other UN agencies and NGOs.

83. The resident coordinator also appointed a special officer for internally displaced persons to lend support to the task force.

84. For example, in the cases of Myanmar (Burma), India, and Turkey.

85. Problems occurred in Afghanistan, Liberia, and Rwanda. See Resident Coordinator, "Annual Report on Operational Activities for Development of the United Nations System in Afghanistan in 1995," United Nations, April 1996, p. 10. In the case of Liberia, it was reported at interagency meetings in 1996 that coordination did not work well because of too many actors, namely, a resident coordinator, a humanitarian coordinator, and a special representative of the secretary-general.

86. The report also recommended that an official from each operational agency be seconded to the humanitarian coordinator's office to facilitate decisionmaking and to underscore that the humanitarian coordinator represents the system as a whole. See Randolph C. Kent, "Humanitarian Coordinator's End of Mission Report for Rwanda, 1 November 1994 to 1 November 1995," United Nations, New York, 1996.

87. Larry Minear and Randolph Kent, in "Case Study on Rwanda," in *The Forsaken People,* make recommendations to minimize overlap and duplication between resident or humanitarian coordinators and special representatives of the secretary-general. For example, they recommend that the resident or humanitarian coordinator act as deputy to the special representative for humanitarian and development activities and that all UN humanitarian and development organizations report to his or her office; also that the special representative have a second deputy, drawn from the UN's peacekeeping structure. This would bring together under one umbrella all the different components of the emergency situation.

88. Colin Scott, "Case Study on Liberia," in *The Forsaken People.*

89. For additional discussion of the tensions between UN political objectives and humanitarian principles, see Antonio Donini, "The Policies of Mercy: UN Coordination in Afghanistan, Mozambique, and Rwanda," Thomas J. Watson Jr. Institute for International Studies Occasional Paper 22 (Brown University, 1996), pp. 117–18.

90. The director general of WHO, Hiroshi Nakajima, in particular has called for a "common approach." He has warned that "disparities in approach" by UN agencies to violations of humanitarian law should be "a subject of concern" to all those involved in the provision of humanitarian aid. WHO, Executive Board, *Emergency and Humanitarian Action,* p. 4.

91. Lance Clark, "Comments and Suggestions on Annotated Agenda for Rwanda: Lessons Learned," Department of Humanitarian Affairs, New York, November 29, 1995.

92. The humanitarian coordinator in Rwanda has recommended that peacekeeping mandates coordinate their support of humanitarian activities specifically through the resident or humanitarian coordinator and that "relevant assets of the

military" be placed in "a more formal and predictable way at the disposal of the humanitarian community." See Kent, "Humanitarian Coordinator's End of Mission Report."

93. General Assembly Resolution 46/182, "Strengthening the Coordination of Humanitarian Emergency Assistance of the United Nations" (December 19, 1991), which sets out the policy framework for the Emergency Relief Coordinator, affirms that "emergency assistance should be provided in ways that will be supportive of recovery and long-term development. Thus, emergency measures should be seen as a step toward long-term development."

94. See, for example, UNHCR statement cited in Francis M. Deng, *Comprehensive Study to the Commission on Human Rights,* Commission on Human Rights, E/CN.4/1993/25 (United Nations, January 21, 1993), p. 26. See also UN High Commissioner for Refugees, statement to the World Conference on Human Rights, Vienna, June 15, 1993.

95. ECOSOC, "Enlargement of the Commission on Human Rights and the Further Promotion of Human Rights and Fundamental Freedoms," Resolution 1990/48 (United Nations, May 25, 1990).

96. Commission on Human Rights, "Internally Displaced Persons," Resolution 1996/52 (United Nations, April 19, 1996).

97. Commission on Human Rights, "Internally Displaced Persons," resolution contained in E/CN.4/1997/L.66 (United Nations, April 9, 1997).

98. See, for example, Commission on Human Rights, "The Situation of Human Rights in the Sudan," Resolution 1996/73 (United Nations, April 23, 1996); and "The Situation of Human Rights in Burundi," Resolution 1996/1 (United Nations, March 27, 1996).

99. Commission on Human Rights, "Internally Displaced Persons," Resolution 1994/68 (United Nations, March 9, 1994).

100. The field staff were asked to help create conditions of safety in areas of return and to "help redress existing problems and prevent possible human rights violations from occurring," in addition to other functions. For objectives of the UN Human Rights Field Operation in Rwanda, as set forth in "An Agreement between the United Nations and the Government of Rwanda on the Status of the Human Rights Mission in Rwanda," see African Rights, *Rwanda: "A Waste of Hope," The United Nations Human Rights Field Operation* (London: March 1995), p. 3.

101. It has dispatched small numbers of human rights field staff to the former Yugoslavia to monitor and report on human rights conditions. It has also called for the dispatch of field staff to Iraq and the Sudan, but political constraints have prevented deployment.

102. See General Assembly, "High Commissioner for the Promotion and Protection of All Human Rights," Resolution 48/141 (United Nations, 20 December 1993).

103. Ayala Lasso left his post and returned to Ecuador in early 1997 to become foreign minister; Mary Robinson, president of Ireland, succeeded him in the fall of 1997.

104. See Rene Degni-Segui, Special Rapporteur, *Report on Rwanda to the*

Commission on Human Rights, Commission on Human Rights Report, E/CN.4/ 1995/70 (United Nations, November 11, 1994). See also African Rights, *Rwanda: "A Waste of Hope"*; "Amateurs Posing as Professionals: The United Nations Human Rights Field Operation in Rwanda," *Human Rights Tribune,* Ottawa, Canada, June/July 1995; and Human Rights Watch/Africa and Federation Internationale des Droits de l'Homme, "Rwanda: The Crisis Continues," New York/ Paris, April 1995.

105. Philip Alston, "The United Nations High Commissioner for Human Rights," *ASIL Insight,* no. 8 (1995), p. 3.

106. See note 104.

107. An agreement signed in 1995 between the high commissioner and the United Nations Volunteers (UNV), for example, provides for UNV assistance in identifying qualified and experienced professionals for recruitment in field programs. In addition, the high commissioner has cooperated with the Commission of the European Communities (European Union), which has provided qualified and equipped personnel for the UN field operation in Rwanda. Cooperation has also been developed with the Organization for Security and Cooperation in Europe in the former Yugoslavia and in Abkhazia, Georgia. Agreements have also been signed with NGOs. General Assembly, *Report of the UN High Commissioner for Human Rights,* A/51/36 (United Nations, October 18, 1996), pp. 9– 11.

108. General Assembly, "Report on the Programme and Administrative Practices of the Centre for Human Rights," in *Review of the Efficiency of the Administrative and Financial Functioning of the United Nations,* A/49/892 (United Nations, April 26, 1995), annex, p. 4.

109. General Assembly, *Report of the UN High Commissioner for Human Rights,* A/50/36 (United Nations, November 2, 1995).

110. The office was opened in December 1996 as a joint undertaking with OSCE and the Georgian government. See UN High Commissioner for Human Rights, "HCHR News," December 1996–January 1997.

111. This accorded with a commission request to pay special attention to "situations which cause or threaten to cause mass exoduses." See Commission on Human Rights, "Human Rights and Mass Exoduses," Resolution 1995/88 (United Nations, March 8, 1995).

112. The high commissioner announced plans to send up to thirty-five observers to Burundi. See Commission on Human Rights, *Making Human Rights a Reality,* Report of the UN High Commissioner for Human Rights, E/CN.4/ 1996/103 (United Nations, March 18, 1996), pp. 24–26.

113. Human rights field presence is being planned in other countries with a view toward prevention. See Commission on Human Rights, "Situation of Human Rights in Haiti," Resolution 1996/58 (United Nations, April 19, 1996); and General Assembly, *Report of the UN High Commissioner for Human Rights,* A/ 51/36, para. 66.

114. Commission on Human Rights, "Internally Displaced Persons."

115. A UN report on Guatemala specifically calls for technical assistance programs for the internally displaced with regard to land, housing, official papers,

employment, and protection from harassment. See Commission on Human Rights, *Report on Assistance to Guatemala in the Field of Human Rights,* E/CN.4/1994/CRP.1 (United Nations, February 24, 1994). In Tajikistan, projects are needed to help strengthen the judicial system as it relates to land disputes and property law. See Francis M. Deng, *Report of the Representative of the Secretary-General on Internally Displaced Persons,* Commission on Human Rights, E/CN.4/1997/43 (United Nations, February 4, 1997), para. 18. In Colombia, where a human rights office was established in March 1997, a technical assistance program could be introduced that is directed at the prevention of violence and the protection of internally displaced persons.

116. Mary Robinson, statement to the Executive Committee of UNHCR, Geneva, October 14, 1997.

117. See *Human Rights Watch World Report 1996* (New York, 1996), pp. xviii–xix. See also Reed Brody, "Give the World a Clear Voice for Human Rights," *International Herald Tribune,* March 6, 1997.

118. Tadeusz Mazowiecki in fact resigned over this. See Letter dated July 27, 1995, E/CN.4/1996/9 (United Nations, August 22, 1995), annex 1; and "UN Envoy in Bosnia Quits at 'Hypocrisy,'" *International Herald Tribune,* July 28, 1995. For the high commissioner's statement on Rwanda, see United Nations Press Release HR/95/16, April 25, 1995.

119. Commission on Human Rights, "Internally Displaced Persons," Resolution 1993/95 (United Nations, March 11, 1993), and Resolution 1995/57 (United Nations, March 3, 1995).

120. The representative has visited the former Yugoslavia, the Russian Federation, Somalia, the Sudan, El Salvador, Sri Lanka, Colombia, Burundi, Rwanda, Peru, Tajikistan, and Mozambique. See General Assembly, *Note by the Secretary-General, Internally Displaced Persons,* A/51/483/Add.1 (United Nations, October 24, 1996), app., "Profiles in Displacement: Tajikistan." Also, the following reports of the Representative of the Secretary-General on Internally Displaced Persons: Commission on Human Rights, *Profiles in Displacement: Mozambique,* E/CN.4/1997/43/Add.1 (United Nations, February 24, 1997); *Profiles in Displacement: Peru,* E/CN.4/1996/52/Add.1 (January 4, 1996); *Note on the Mission to Rwanda,* E/CN.4/1995/50/Add.4 (February 16, 1995); *Profiles in Displacement: Burundi,* E/CN.4/1995/50/Add.2 (November 28, 1994); *Profiles in Displacement: Colombia,* E/CN.4/1995/50/Add.1 (October 3, 1994); *Profiles in Displacement: Sri Lanka,* E/CN.4/1994/44/Add.1 (January 25, 1994).

121. For compilation, see Commission on Human Rights, *Compilation and Analysis of Legal Norms,* Report of the Representative of the Secretary-General on Internally Displaced Persons, E/CN.4/1996/52/Add.2 (United Nations, December 5, 1995).

122. See Francis M. Deng, *Report of the Representative of the Secretary-General on Internally Displaced Persons,* Commission on Human Rights, E/CN.4/1995/50 (United Nations, February 2, 1995); Commission on Human Rights, *Report of the Representative of the Secretary-General on Internally Displaced Persons,* E/CN.4/1996/52 (United Nations, February 22, 1996); and Com-

mission on Human Rights, *Report of the Representative of the Secretary-General on Internally Displaced Persons*, E/CN.4/1997/43 (United Nations, February 4, 1997).

123. Francis M. Deng, "Internally Displaced Persons: An Interim Report to the United Nations Secretary-General on Protection and Assistance," UN Department of Humanitarian Affairs and Refugee Policy Group, December 1994, p. 16.

124. Deng, "Internally Displaced Persons: An Interim Report," p. 19.

125. The letter of understanding is dated July 31, 1996. In addition, UNDP's administrator sent out a notice to resident representatives/coordinators in 1994 suggesting steps they could take to assist the representative; and the executive director of WFP also called on relevant field staff to assist the representative with his missions and to provide him with information.

126. The government of Turkey, for example, has not yet agreed to receive a mission of the representative.

127. Deng, "Internally Displaced Persons: An Interim Report," p. 20.

128. Grant, "Refugees, Internally Displaced and the Poor."

129. The decision raises questions since UNHCR's refugee caseload in the Sudan has been gradually diminishing.

130. The camps, guarded by the Tutsi military, were regarded by many Hutus as "bases for Tutsi civilian militia." See U.S. Committee for Refugees, "Case Study on Burundi," in *The Forsaken People*, pp. 18, 20–21, 24.

131. UNHCR decided at the end of 1997 to undertake programs for the internally displaced. That same year, the Office of the High Commissioner for Human Rights set up a field office in Colombia and also began to consider undertaking programs for internally displaced persons.

132. Michael J. Toole, "Health Coordination in Emergencies: Options for The Role of WHO," Concept Paper, World Health Organization, 1996.

133. Human Rights Watch, *World Report 1996*, p. 79.

134. In Turkey, despite reports documenting the failure of the government to provide assistance to its internally displaced populations, UN agencies have not sought to monitor or in any way focus on the needs of up to two million Kurds reported to be internally displaced. See Human Rights Watch/Helsinki, "Turkey: Turkey's Failed Policy to Aid the Forcibly Displaced in the Southeast," New York, June 1996. To its credit, UNDP at the end of 1995 did manage to extend its development programs to Kurdish areas in the southeast and to include other UN agencies in development projects in the area.

135. The average response to the 1996 UN appeals for all countries was 65 percent, with donors providing about $1.7 billion of the $2.6 billion requested. UN appeal data constitute about half of overall funding for humanitarian emergencies. See United States Mission to the United Nations, "Humanitarian Emergencies 1997," New York, April 1997, pp. 15–21.

136. Steven Holtzman, "Post-Conflict Reconstruction," Environment Department Papers, World Bank, Washington, D.C., 1995. These figures do not include resources required for reconstruction.

137. The UN issued an appeal for $124 million, but only $56 million was forthcoming. See Bill Frelick, "Assistance without Protection," in *World Refugee Survey 1997* (Washington, D.C.: U.S. Committee for Refugees), pp. 31–32.

138. Minear and Kent, "Case Study on Rwanda."

139. WFP finds that assistance agencies have not done a good job of sending nonfood items to internally displaced persons, particularly fuel, fuel-efficient stoves, cooking pots, utensils, mills, and jerrycans (to haul water for cooking). It points out that when these items are delayed or unavailable, the cost-efficiency of food aid operations is compromised, and a greater labor burden is placed on women. See World Food Programme, *Report to the Economic and Social Council*, WFP/EB.3/96/3 (United Nations, September 23, 1996), paras. 77–78.

140. For the problems arising from an absence of coordination, see Donini, "The Policies of Mercy." Duplication among agencies is well known, with too many agencies providing the same service. In Rwanda, for example, more than 10,000 unaccompanied children were registered more than once because of a lack of coordination among the organizations involved. See International Committee of the Red Cross, "Challenges of the Nineties," November 1995, p. 14.

141. See Steven Holtzman, "Conflict-Induced Displacement through a Development Lens," paper prepared for Brookings, May 1997.

142. See Inspection and Evaluation Service, *Lessons Learned from the Burundi and Rwanda Emergencies"* (UNHCR, October 1996).

143. Minear and Kent, "Case Study on Rwanda."

144. See Donini, "The Policies of Mercy," pp. 123–24.

145. It described the organizational center as "weak, poorly resourced and lacking in organizational clarity." See *Humanitarian Aid and Effects,* vol. 3 of *The International Response to Conflict and Genocide: Lessons from the Rwanda Experience,* Joint Evaluation of Emergency Assistance to Rwanda (Copenhagen, March 1996), pp. 132–33.

146. Weiss and Pasic, "Case Study on the Former Yugoslavia."

147. The Norwegian Refugee Council brought this problem to the attention of the Inter-Agency Task Force on Internally Displaced Persons.

148. Inter-Agency Standing Committee, "Internally Displaced Persons: The Next Stage," Geneva, July 5, 1993.

149. In written communications to the Inter-Agency Task Force on Internally Displaced Persons in 1994, member agencies emphasized the importance of an integrated approach. WHO, for example, underscored the necessity of addressing not only the material needs of internally displaced persons but "access to information, freedom of movement and of association, the right to personal documents . . . and in general the right to full participation in the democratic process." UNDP endorsed "a comprehensive approach" in which "the human rights aspect intersects with the humanitarian, the political and the economic dimensions." FAO recommended that the "UN human rights system should operate within the existing UN operational mechanism for emergencies" so that "the welfare of the beneficiaries, including human rights, would be achieved." See responses of the World Health Organization, UN Development Programme, and the Food and Agriculture Organization to the Inter-Agency Task Force on Internally Displaced

Persons, Geneva, 1994. In a statement before UNHCR, the director of DHA's Geneva office pointed out that although DHA will keep its focus on the delivery of humanitarian assistance to internally displaced persons, "the human rights of internally displaced persons are of particular concern to us all and the balance between the provision of humanitarian assistance to them and the upholding of their human rights is crucial." See Charles LaMunière, statement before UNHCR Subcommittee of the Whole on International Protection, Executive Committee of the High Commissioner's Programme, Geneva, May 18, 1994.

150. Gradually, this has begun to change. A memorandum on a needs assessment mission to Tajikistan in 1996 included "protection" as one of the sectors that could be examined. although it was not listed as one of the mission's objectives. See Department of Humanitarian Affairs, "Tajikistan: Dates and Logistics of UN Needs Assessment Mission," September 24, 1996.

151. Sadako Ogata, opening statement of the High Commissioner for Refugees, at the Forty-Fifth Session of the Executive Committee of the High Commissioner's Programme, October 4, 1993, p. 3.

152. WFP, "Internally Displaced Persons."

153. Frederic Maurice and Jean de Courten, "ICRC Activities for Refugees and Displaced Civilians," *International Review of the Red Cross,* January–February 1991.

154. See, for example, Sadako Ogata, "Humanitarianism in the Midst of Armed Conflict," Statement to Brookings, Washington D.C., May 12, 1994.

155. Jennifer McLean, "The Provision of Humanitarian Assistance to the Internally Displaced in Chechnya," April 27, 1995 (unpublished paper).

156. See Weiss and Pasic, "Case Study on the Former Yugoslavia." See also Human Rights Watch, *World Report 1995* (New York, 1995), pp. xvii–xviii.

157. UNDP, Gender in Development Programme, "Support for Women in Internally Displaced Situations: Report of A Joint Mission of UNDP/UNICEF/UNIFEM/WHO/DHA," United Nations, October 18–November 5, 1993.

158. UNIFEM and UNICEF subsequently published the proceedings of a meeting on reproductive and mental health issues, which did draw attention to the problems faced by internally displaced women in select African countries. See UNIFEM/UNICEF, "Reproductive and Mental Health Issues of Women and Girls under Situations of War and Conflict in Africa," *Proceedings of an Experts Group Consultation* (Nairobi, 1994).

159. *Rebuilding Post-War Rwanda,* vol. 4 of *The International Response to Conflict and Genocide: Lessons from the Rwanda Experience,* Joint Evaluation of Emergency Assistance to Rwanda (Copenhagen, March 1886), p. 105.

160. In 1996, for the first time, UNICEF Khartoum conducted a gender evaluation of its emergency program activities, which, it said, should act as a benchmark for the further integration of gender perspectives into emergency programmes. See Department of Humanitarian Affairs, United Nations Consolidated Inter-Agency Appeal for the Sudan, January–December 1996, February 1996, p. 25.

161. UNIFEM/UNICEF, "Reproductive and Mental Health Issues," p. 14.

162. See Graça Machel, *Impact of Armed Conflict on Children,* Report of

the Expert of the Secretary-General to the UN General Assembly, A/51/306 (United Nations, August 26, 1996), paras. 81, 239.

163. Frederick C. Cuny, "Background Paper: Observations From Other Countries About Assistance for Displaced Persons," Intertect, 1988.

164. Report of the IOM and UN Unit for Humanitarian Assistance, Luanda, 1995.

165. In some cases they have not proved flexible enough to take on projects that do not fit strict development criteria; in other cases, their response has been slow because of bureaucratic procedures geared more to development than to emergencies; in still other instances, they have been short of the necessary resources.

166. Cuenod, *Report on Refugees, Displaced Persons and Returnees.*

167. *Rebuilding Post-War Rwanda,* p. 104.

168. More than 40 percent of official development assistance managed by the United Nations is dedicated to emergency relief operations. See UNDP, "Change and Reform in UNDP." In Rwanda, for example, only about 11 percent of donor grants during the period April 1994 to March 1995 was provided for rehabilitation and reconstruction. See *Rebuilding Post-War Rwanda,* p. 32. See also Peter D. Bell, "Rwanda Aid Doesn't Add Up," *Christian Science Monitor,* February 2, 1996, p. 18. Mozambique, however, is an exception to this rule.

169. See Frederick C. Cuny, "Humanitarian Assistance in the Post-Cold War Era," Working Paper, 1993; and Weiss and Pasic, "Case Study on the Former Yugoslavia."

170. In 1995 the United States proposed the consolidation of the emergency functions of UNHCR, WFP, UNICEF, and DHA into a new entity in order to avoid overlap. The suggestion met with considerable resistance from the agencies concerned as well as governments and was withdrawn. U.S. officials themselves acknowledged in interviews that the proposal was not "thought through." For its details, see Department of State, "Readying the United Nations for the Twenty-First Century: Some 'UN-21' Proposals for Consideration," Washington D.C., September 1995.

171. The case study on Rwanda, for example, calls attention to the need for greater coordination of policies inside Rwanda pertaining to the internally displaced with those relating to refugees in neighboring countries. See Minear and Kent, "Case Study on Rwanda."

172. Representative of the Kingdom of the Netherlands, statement to the Forty-Fourth Session of the UNHCR Executive Committee, Geneva, 1993.

173. See Sadako Ogata, statement of the High Commissioner for Refugees to the World Conference on Human Rights, Vienna, June 15, 1993.

174. The Executive Committee endorsed these limits. See General Assembly, *Conclusion of the Executive Committee of the High Commissioner's Programme,* A/AC.96/XLV/CRP.3 (United Nations, October 7, 1994).

175. UNHCR memoranda and interviews with senior UN staff.

176. Sadako Ogata, opening statement of the High Commissioner for Refugees, at the Forty-Sixth Session of the Executive Committee of the High Commissioner's Programme, UNHCR, Geneva, October 16, 1995. The high commis-

sioner noted that of the 27.4 million persons of concern to UNHCR, only about 14.5 million were refugees.

177. Weiss and Pasic, "Case Study on the Former Yugoslavia."

178. Andrew Natsios, President of World Vision, made this suggestion, in his personal capacity, at a UNICEF meeting on internally displaced persons in New York, May 31, 1996.

179. One instance of forceful coordination was found in the Sudan. See Francis M. Deng and Larry Minear, *The Challenges of Famine Relief: Emergency Operations in the Sudan* (Brookings, 1992), pp. xvii, 58–65.

180. Minear and Kent, "Case Study on Rwanda."

181. The report's specific recommendation was that "in major refugee emergencies, UNHCR in cooperation with DHA should seek to assume lead agency status with respect to both external and internal population displacements resulting from the same sets of causes so as to be in a position to develop and implement a comprehensive strategy." See UNHCR, "Lessons Learned from the Burundi and Rwanda Emergencies," p. 23.

182. World Food Programme, *Follow-up to Economic and Social Council Resolution 1995/56: Strengthening of the Coordination of Emergency Humanitarian Assistance of the United Nations,* WFP/EB.A/96/7 (United Nations, April 9 1996), pt. 4, p. 17. Graça Machel's report to the UN General Assembly also recommended that a "lead agency should be assigned overall responsibility for the protection and assistance of internally displaced persons." See Machel, *Impact of Armed Conflict on Children,* para. 90(d).

183. See General Assembly, *Profiles in Displacement: Tajikistan,* Note by the Secretary-General, A/51/483/Add.1, 24 (United Nations, October 1996), para. 95.

184. The United States has proposed that UNHCR and UNICEF sign an agreement on primary health care for internally displaced persons and refugees, and that UNHCR, UNICEF, and WFP reach agreements on relief supply operations. See Department of State, "Readying the United Nations." In the case of refugees, a memorandum of understanding between UNHCR and WFP provides that UNHCR will be responsible for food supplies if there are 5,000 or less refugees, but that WFP will assume responsibility if there are more than 5,000. A similar agreement might be considered in the case of the internally displaced, including when internally displaced persons are dispersed in urban areas. In such cases, UNICEF and UNDP, because of their development orientation, might do well to carve out specific responsibilities. In 1997 a memorandum of understanding was signed between UNHCR and IOM covering internally displaced persons, refugees, returnees, and other affected populations. See IOM, News Release, May 15, 1997.

185. See Salim Ahmed Salim, address before the Forty-Sixth Session of the Executive Committee of the High Commissioner's Programme, Geneva, October 16, 1995, p. 7.

186. See Minear and Kent, "Case Study on Rwanda."

187. For discussion of the use of humanitarian organizations as substitutes for political action, see José Maria Mendiluce, "War and Disaster in the Former

Yugoslavia: The Limits of Humanitarian Action," in *World Refugee Survey 1994* (Washington: U.S. Committee for Refugees, 1994); Eric E. Morris, "The Limits of Mercy: Ethnopolitical Conflict and Humanitarian Action," Massachusetts Institute of Technology, 1995, pp. 92–93; and African Rights, "Humanitarianism Unbound?"

188. Hiram A. Ruiz, "Case Study on the Sudan," in *The Forsaken People.*

189. Minear and Kent, "Case Study on Rwanda."

190. At the March 20, 1996, meeting of the Inter-Agency Task Force on Internally Displaced Persons, WHO reported that it did not have the funds to assist the government of Myanmar (Burma), but the task force did not go into the issue in depth.

191. Kofi A. Annan, "The Peacekeeping Prescription," in Kevin M. Cahill, ed., *Preventive Diplomacy* (Basic Books, 1996), pp. 178–79.

192. See Inter-Agency Task Force on Internally Displaced Persons, "Internally Displaced Persons: Preliminary Findings," Geneva, 1993.

193. Dennis McNamara, "Internally Displaced Persons: UNHCR's Perspective," paper presented at the symposium Internally Displaced Persons, International Committee of the Red Cross, Geneva, October 23–25, 1995, p. 64.

194. UNHCR's role, according to a letter from the secretary-general, authorized it only to provide "assistance," and the Human Rights Field Operation was not tasked with providing protection to internally displaced persons in camps.

195. Inter-Agency Task Force on Internally Displaced Persons, "Internal Review of the Case of the Kibeho Incident: Lessons for the Future," Geneva, November 1995.

196. The high commissioner for human rights estimated that $25 million would be needed by the Centre for Human Rights each year to adequately carry out field operations. See Commission on Human Rights, *Making Human Rights a Reality,* p. 33.

197. Human Rights Watch/Africa, *Africa, Failing the Internally Displaced: UNDP Displaced Persons Program in Kenya* (New York, June 1997).

198. In Tajikistan, for example, the government readily accepted UNHCR's human rights and protection activities because UNHCR was also providing humanitarian assistance. See Jennifer McLean and Thomas Greene, "Case Study on Tajikistan," in *The Forsaken People.*

199. "Note on Cooperation between United Nations High Commissioner for Refugees (UNHCR) and the United Nations Human Rights Field Operation in Rwanda (HRFOR)," Kigali, September 29, 1995.

200. The UN Assistance Mission in Rwanda (UNAMIR) was authorized to "contribute to the security and protection of displaced persons, refugees and civilians at risk." See Security Council, "The Extension of the Mandate and Deployment of the Two Additional Battalions of the UN Assistance Mission for Rwanda and Settlement of the Conflict in Rwanda," Resolution 925 (United Nations, June 8, 1994). The UN Protection Force in the former Yugoslavia was authorized to defend "safe areas" in Bosnia populated by displaced persons; it also was given human rights responsibilities in the "UN protected areas" of Croatia. See, for example, Security Council, Resolution 824 (United Nations,

May 6, 1993) Resolution 836 (United Nations, June 4, 1993) on Bosnia and Herzegovina, which declared that Sarajevo, Tuzla, Zepa, Gorazde, Bihac, and Srebrenica should be treated as "safe areas" and authorized UNPROFOR to "deter attacks against the safe areas."

201. See Annan, "The Peacekeeping Prescription," p. 177.

202. The High Commissioner for Human Rights' technical cooperation program in 1995 and 1996 began to provide some human rights training to civilian police officers and peacekeepers in the former Yugoslavia. See Commission on Human Rights, *Advisory Services in the Field of Human Rights,* Report of the Secretary-General to the Commission on Human Rights, E/CN.4/1996/90 (United Nations, March 20, 1996), pp. 1, 26.

203. A number of Western governments have introduced courses for the military in humanitarian and human rights issues. The government of Canada has instituted training for Canadian and international peacekeepers inclusive of a course on refugees and internally displaced persons and on human rights in modern peacekeeping, which provides skills in monitoring and protecting the human rights of civilians. See training programs of The Lester B. Pearson Canadian International Peacekeeping Training Centre, Nova Scotia. The Swedish Armed Forces International Centre has also developed a training program for peacekeeping forces that includes international humanitarian and human rights law.

204. A Human Rights Watch report examined five of the largest UN field operations in recent years—in Cambodia, El Salvador, Iraq, Somalia, and the former Yugoslavia—and found that with the exception of El Salvador, human rights concerns were given a low priority. See Human Rights Watch, *The Lost Agenda: Human Rights and UN Field Operations* (New York, June 1993).

205. See Cohen and Cuenod, *Improving Institutional Arrangements for the Internally Displaced,* pp. 82–86.

206. McLean and Greene, "Case Study on Tajikistan." In the Sudan, too, a "troubling lack of attention has been reported to involving the people and their local institutions" in self-sustaining occupations. See Deng and Minear, *The Challenges of Famine Relief,* p. 123.

207. UNHCR draft paper, Geneva, 1996.

208. Michael Priestly, Report to the Under-Secretary-General, Department of Humanitarian Affairs, September 21, 1994 (unpublished draft), p. 5.

209. See Cuenod, *Report on Refugees, Displaced Persons and Returnees.*

210. Minear and Kent, "Case Study on Rwanda." See also Bell, "Rwanda Aid Doesn't Add Up."

211. Minear and Kent, "Case Study on Rwanda."

212. For efforts to improve their operational relationship, see, for example, UNHCR, "Mozambique: An Account from a Lessons Learned Seminar on Reintegration," Geneva, June 24–25, 1996, pp. 11–12.

213. See Everett M. Ressler, "A Review of the Cross-Mandate Approach," Central Evaluation Section, UNHCR, January 1995. See also Dennis Gallagher and Susan Forbes Martin, "The Many Faces of the Somali Crisis: Humanitarian Issues in Somalia, Kenya and Ethiopia," Refugee Policy Group, December 1992.

214. See Peter Sollis and Christina M. Schultz, "Lessons of the PRODERE Experience in Central America," *RPG Focus,* October 1995. Carried out between 1989 and 1995, PRODERE supported the restoration of infrastructure as well as community-based income generating and development projects. In addition, it helped strengthen national human rights institutions and assisted displaced persons in securing legal documents and legal aid.

Chapter Five

1. See Thomas G. Weiss, "Nongovernmental Organizations and Internal Conflict," in Michael E. Brown, ed., *The International Implications of Internal Conflicts* (Cambridge, Mass.: MIT Press, 1996).

2. Statement of April 10, 1993, in Bangkok, quoted in H. L. Hernandez and S. Kuyuma, *Strengthening of the United Nations System Capacity for Conflict Prevention,* Joint Inspection Unit (United Nations, 1995), p. 53.

3. UNDP's five-year budget for Mozambique, for example, totals abut $60 million, whereas World Vision International spent more than $90 million in Mozambique in 1993 and again in 1994. See Weiss, "Nongovernmental Organizations and Internal Conflict," pp. 441, 446.

4. More than $8 billion of financial transfers from the industrialized to the developing world goes through NGOs (more than the amount being transferred through UN agencies). See Antonio Donini, "The Bureaucracy and the Free Spirits: Stagnation and Innovation in the Relationship Between the UN and NGOs," in Thomas G. Weiss and Leon Gordenker, eds., *NGOs, the UN, and Global Governance* (Boulder, Colo.: Lynne Rienner, 1996), p. 88.

5. Weiss, "Nongovernmental Organizations and Internal Conflict."

6. Andrew Natsios, "NGOs and the UN in Complex Emergencies: Conflict or Co-operation," *Third World Quarterly,* vol. 16 (September 1995), pp. 406–07. It is estimated that eight major families or federations of international NGOs have come to control almost half of an $8 billion market: CARE, World Vision, Oxfam, MSF, and Save the Children, and several coalitions of operational NGOs. See Donini, "The Bureaucracy and the Free Spirits," p. 91.

7. Care USA's annual budget, for example, is $456 million, and MSF's is $274 million. The International Federation of Red Cross and Red Crescent Societies, if one counts all its national member societies in 169 countries, has a staff of 263,000 and a $26 billion budget.

8. See, for example, Cyrus Vance and Herbert Okun, "Creating Healthy Alliances: Leadership and Coordination among NGOs, Governments and the United Nations in Times of Emergency and Conflict," in Kevin M. Cahill, ed., *Preventive Diplomacy* (New York: Basic Books, 1996), pp. 191–201.

9. Curtis W. Lambrecht, "NGO Response Patterns to the Assistance, Protection and Development Needs of the Internally Displaced," Norwegian Refugee Council, Geneva, July 1996 (hereafter Lambrecht report). As this chapter is drawn largely from this report, it is not continuously cited. The Lambrecht report drew on the surveys and other materials compiled for an earlier report, Ulrike

von Buchwald, "Response Systems of Non-Governmental Organisations to Assistance and Protection Needs of the Internally Displaced Persons," Norwegian Refugee Council, Geneva, March 31, 1996 (hereafter von Buchwald report).

10. Each was asked to designate a focal point on internally displaced persons within his or her organization, who was invited to participate in a debate about NGO activities on behalf of the internally displaced. In particular, the focal point was expected to complete a lengthy questionnaire about NGO policy and activities with regard to internally displaced persons and to provide suggestions on how responses to crises of internal displacement could be improved. The focal point was also invited to hold a round table discussion, based on the questionnaire, within his or her organization to stimulate dialogue. Four NGOs organized round tables, and the NRC guided and participated in the discussion. Other NGOs held informal discussions. Some engaged member organizations in the field in the discussions. A joint meeting of NGOs and UN agencies was then held to review the findings up to that point. See Lambrecht report.

11. Human Rights Watch, International Alert, International Islamic Relief Organization.

12. Caritas Internationalis, the International Federation of Red Cross and Red Crescent Societies, Jesuit Refugee Service, Lutheran World Federation, World Vision International, the Worldwide Fund for Nature International, and the World Council of Churches.

13. Care USA, Médecins Sans Frontières/Holland, and Oxfam/UK.

14. Von Buchwald report, table 1.

15. Lambrecht report.

16. World Council of Churches, "Statement on Uprooted People," Geneva, September 1995.

17. World Council of Churches, "A Call to Action: Accompanying Forcibly Displaced People and Denouncing the Violence Which Uproots Them," Addis Ababa, November 6–11, 1995.

18. Lambrecht report.

19. Lambrecht report.

20. Lambrecht report.

21. Lambrecht report.

22. See Lambrecht report.

23. The *Oslo Declaration and Plan of Action* (UNHCR, June 1994) was the result of six regional conferences organized by UNHCR and NGOs as a part of the partnership in action process. Recommendation 40 noted that some NGOs felt that a definition that limited itself to persons in refugee-like situations "may be too restrictive."

24. Von Buchwald report, p. 21.

25. Lambrecht report.

26. Hernandez and Kuyuma, *Strengthening of the United Nations System,* p. 56.

27. See Randolph C. Kent, "WorldAid '96," *Crosslines,* January 1997, p. 16.

28. Although ICVA ceased functioning in 1997, it may be reconstituted.

29. See Jan Borgen, "Internally Displaced Persons: An NGO Perspective on

Protection," Norwegian Refugee Council, April 1994, p. 23; Antonio Donini, "The Policies of Mercy: UN Coordination in Afghanistan, Mozambique, and Rwanda," Thomas J. Watson Jr. Institute for International Studies Occasional Paper 22 (Brown University, 1996), p. 49; and Jon Bennett, "Coordination, Competition and Control: NGOs on the Front Line," in Jim Whitman and David Pocock, eds., *After Rwanda* (New York: Macmillan, 1996), pp. 143–44.

30. Randolph C. Kent, "UN Humanitarian Coordinator's End of Mission Report for Rwanda, 1 November 1994 to 1 November 1995," New York, 1996, pp. 9–10.

31. See, for example, John Prendergast, *Crisis Response: Humanitarian Band-Aids in Sudan and Somalia* (London: Pluto Press, 1997); Alex de Waal, *Evil Days: Thirty Years of War and Famine in Ethiopia* (New York: Human Rights Watch, 1991); Michael Maren, *The Road to Hell* (New York: Free Press, 1997); Peter Shiras, "Humanitarian Emergencies and the Role of NGOs," in *After Rwanda* (London: Macmillan, 1996), pp. 106–17; Vance and Okun, "Creating Healthy Alliances"; and Donini, "The Policies of Mercy," pp. 45–52.

32. The code was sponsored by Caritas Internationalis, Catholic Relief Services, IFRC, the International Save the Children Alliance, LWF, OXFAM, and WCC, together with ICRC.

33. Humanitarian Community in Liberia, Mission Statement, June 1995. The NGOs who signed included Catholic Relief Services, LWF, MSF, OXFAM, and Save the Children Fund.

34. See Larry Minear, "New Opportunities and Dilemmas for Independent Agencies," *The Conrad Grebel Review*, vol. 13 (Fall 1995), pp. 339–41.

35. Lambrecht report.

36. See Larry Minear and Randolph Kent, "Case Study on Rwanda," in Roberta Cohen and Francis M. Deng, eds., *The Forsaken People: Case Studies of the Internally Displaced* (Brookings, 1998).

37. See De Waal, *Evil Days*, pp. 8–9; Prendergast, *Crisis Response*, pp. 139–41; Shiras, "Humanitarian Emergencies and the Roles of NGOs," pp. 114–15; and Maren, *The Road to Hell*, pp. 119–20.

38. Prendergast, *Crisis Response*, p. 149.

39. See, for example, Shiras, "Humanitarian Emergencies and the Roles of NGOs," p. 114.

40. Refugee Policy Group, "Internally Displaced Persons in Africa: Assistance Challenges and Opportunities," Washington, D.C., October 1992, p. 45.

41. Shiras, "Humanitarian Emergencies and the Role of NGOs."

42. International Federation of the Red Cross and Red Crescent Societies, "World Disasters Report: Under the Volcanoes (Special Focus on the Rwandan Refugee Crises)," 1994, p. 3.

43. See Statutes of the International Committee of the Red Cross and Red Crescent Movement.

44. See "MSF says Rwanda Expelled It for Atrocity Reports," *Reuters*, January 3, 1996.

45. African Rights, "Humanitarianism Unbound?," London, November 1994, p. 26.

46. Lambrecht report.

47. Rudy von Bernuth, statement at UNHCR meeting with NGOs, October 12 1995, *ICVA Forum*, vol. 1 (October 1995).

48. African Rights, "Humanitarianism Unbound?" p. 25.

49. See *Inter-Action*, October/November 1995, Médecins Sans Frontières, International Office (Brussels).

50. See, for example, Statement by Médecins Sans Frontières/Holland to the UN Commission on Human Rights (United Nations, April 11, 1996); and Joint Statement by Caritas Internationalis, Friends World Committee for Consultation, and World Council of Churches to the UN Commission on Human Rights, E/CN.4/1996/NGO/20 (United Nations, April 1996).

51. UNHCR, *Guidelines on the Protection of Refugee Women* (Geneva, July 1991). See also UNHCR, *Sexual Violence against Refugees: Guidelines on Prevention and Responses* (Geneva, March 1995); UNHCR, *Working with Refugee Women: A Practical Guide* (Geneva, September 1989); and UNHCR, *Refugee Children: Guidelines on Protection and Care* (Geneva, 1994).

52. See International Federation of the Red Cross and Red Crescent Societies, "Addressing Humanitarian Needs around Conflicts," *World Disasters Report 1995*, pp. 8–17.

53. See World Council of Churches, "Statement on Uprooted People," p. 7.

54. See for example, The Centre for Conflict Analysis and International Alert, "Conflict Resolution in the Former Soviet Union: Report of the Seminar Held at London School of Economics," March 27–28, 1995.

55. World Vision International, "Understanding Who We Are," p. 7; see also, Alan Whaites and David Westwood, "Displacement and Civil Society in Peru," *World Vision International* (Winter 1996).

56. Whaites and Westwood, "Displacement and Civil Society in Peru," pp. 10–11.

57. Human Rights Watch reports have increasingly focused on conditions of internally displaced populations. See, for example, its recent reports on the Sudan, Rwanda, Tajikistan, and Kenya. The U.S. Committee for Refugees also publishes reports on internally displaced populations. The Women's Commission for Refugee Women and Children has been devoting greater attention to internal displacement in its reports as well.

58. NGOs such as the Friends World Committee for Consultation, the Refugee Policy Group, and the World Council of Churches were the first to mobilize opinion at the commission, and their efforts led to the appointment of a representative on internally displaced persons. NGOs also have played an instrumental role in encouraging the commission to develop legal principles for the internally displaced. See statements in note 50 and Statement by Human Rights Watch to the Commission on Human Rights, E/CN.4/1996/NGO/41 (United Nations, 1996).

59. The International Council of Voluntary Agencies for example, has called upon UNHCR "to support ongoing NGO programmes of protection and assistance to the internally displaced, and the monitoring of their situation." See

ICVA, "The Human Rights of Refugees and Internally Displaced Persons," *Humanitarian Affairs Series,* no. 6, 1996, p. 7.

60. The program was eventually ended. See Human Rights Watch/Africa, "Kenya: Old Habits Die Hard," New York, July 1995.

61. See Hiram A. Ruiz, "Case Study on the Sudan," in *The Forsaken People*; and African Rights, *Food and Power in Sudan: A Critique of Humanitarianism* (London: 1997).

62. See Erin Mooney, "Presence, Ergo Protection? UNPROFOR, UNHCR and the ICRC in Croatia and Bosnia and Herzegovina," *International Journal of Refugee Law,* vol. 7, no. 3 (1995). See also Larry Minear and others, "Humanitarian Action in the Former Yugoslavia: The UN's Role 1991–1993," Thomas J. Watson Jr. Institute for International Studies and Refugee Policy Group, Occasional Paper 18 (Brown University, 1994).

63. Médecins Sans Frontières/Switzerland, Preface by Doris Schopper, President, *World in Crisis* (1997).

64. The term "humanitarian organization" or "humanitarian NGO" is used here to connote the operational organizations that address material humanitarian needs.

65. MSF/Belgium, for example, prepared a paper outlining atrocities committed by Russian forces in Chechnya, which it circulated to all Group of 7 embassies in Moscow before their April 1996 meeting in Moscow. See Thomas Greene, "Case Study on the Caucasus," in *The Forsaken People*.

66. Iain Guest and Francoise Bouchee-Saulnier, "International Law and Reality: The Protection Gap," in Médecins Sans Frontières, *World In Crisis* (1997), p. 83.

67. Médecins Sans Frontières, Conference on the Cooperation between Humanitarian Organisations and Human Rights Organisations, Amsterdam, February 9, 1996.

68. See Diane Paul, "The Role of Non-Governmental Organizations in the Protection of Civilians under Threat: Practical Considerations," Center for the Study of Societies in Crisis and the Jacob Blaustein Institute for the Advancement of Human Rights, 1996. This paper was discussed at the Conference on New Directions for the Protection of Civilians under Threat: Developing Field-Based Strategies, Jacob Blaustein Institute for the Advancement of Human Rights and the Center for the Study of Societies in Crisis, Washington, D.C., November 7, 1996. One of the proposals at the conference was that a handbook be developed on NGO protection of civilians under threat based on the paper.

69. There are, of course, risks. Humanitarian NGOs point out that human rights field staff could easily become targets and that humanitarian NGOs might jeopardize their presence through too close or visible an association with human rights staff. See Paul, "The Role of Non-Governmental Organizations."

70. Borgen, "Internally Displaced Persons," p. 3.

71. Borgen, "Internally Displaced Persons," p. 3.

72. Dennis Gallagher, remarks to conference, New Directions for the Protection of Civilians under Threat.

73. Lambrecht report.

74. UNHCR, *Oslo Declaration and Plan of Action*, Recommendation 1.

75. Humanitarian Assistance in Liberia: Principles and Protocols for Action.

76. See, for example, Roberta Cohen, "Strengthening Protection for Internally Displaced Persons," Refugee Policy Group, Washington, D.C., 1994; "Rwanda: Dilemmas of a Total Disaster," *World Disasters Report 1995*, p. 66; and African Rights, "Humanitarianism Unbound?" p. 10.

77. See Médecins sans Frontières, Conference on the Cooperation between Humanitarian Organisations and Human Rights Organisations, Amsterdam, February 9, 1996.

78. MSF, Conference on the Cooperation between Humanitarian Organisations and Human Rights Organisations, p. 69.

79. See, for example, the country reports contained in *Refugee Survey Quarterly*, vol. 14 (Spring/Summer 1995).

80. UNHCR, "Protection Aspects of UNHCR Activities on Behalf of Internally Displaced Persons," EC/SCP/87 (Geneva, August 17, 1994), p. 26.

81. See for example, "Towards a Common Agenda for Conflict Prevention," Norwegian Peoples' Aid and International Alert, May 15–16, 1995.

82. Cohen, "Strengthening Protection for Internally Displaced Persons," p. 6.

83. Steven Holtzman, "Conflict-Induced Displacement through A Development Lens," paper prepared for Brookings, May 1997, p. 23.

84. "Rwanda: Dilemmas of a Total Disaster," p. 67.

85. See for example, UNHCR, "Mozambique: An Account from a Lessons Learned Seminar on Reintegration," Geneva, 24–25 June 1996. See also Open Society Institute, *Protecting Eurasia's Dispossessed: A Guide for NGOs* (New York, 1996), pp. 18, 63; and Liliana Obregón and Maria Stavropoulou, "Case Study on Colombia," in *The Forsaken People*.

86. Open Society Institute, *Protecting Eurasia's Dispossessed*, pp. 18, 63.

87. "Programme of Action," Regional Conference to Address the Problems of Refugees, Displaced Persons, Other Forms of Involuntary Displacement and Returnees in the Commonwealth of Independent States and Relevant Neighboring States, Geneva, CISCONF/1996/5, 11 June 1996.

88. Lambrecht report.

89. Von Buchwald report, pp. 26, 32.

90. See Donini, "The Policies of Mercy," p. 51.

91. Greene, "Case Study on the Caucasus."

92. Boutros Boutros-Ghali, Foreword, in Weiss and Gordenker, eds., *NGOs, the UN, and Global Governance*, p. 11.

93. See von Buchwald report, table 9.

94. Adopted by the United Nations on December 9, 1994, the convention has not yet entered into force. See UN Document A/49/742, December 2, 1994. See also Open Society Institute, "Protecting Aid Workers: Prospects and Challenges," New York, September 1997.

95. UNHCR, *Oslo Declaration and Plan of Action*, Recommendation 54.

96. "The Role of NGOs in Complex Emergencies," *DHA News*, spec. ed. 93 (January–February 1994), p. 62.

Chapter Six

1. The OAU estimated that Africa had 10 million to 20 million internally displaced persons at the end of 1994. See the Addis Ababa Document on Refugees and Forced Population Displacement in Africa, adopted by the OAU/UNHCR Symposium, September 8–10, 1994.

2. The Addis Ababa Document, para. 18.

3. "Sudan, 'Potentially Explosive,'" *Reuters,* March 4, 1996.

4. See Salim A. Salim, Address of the OAU Secretary-General before the Forty-Sixth Session of the Executive Committee of the High Commissioner for Refugees Programme, October 1, 1995.

5. The mechanism is comprised of member states in the OAU executive and the secretary-general and his staff. See Chris J. Bakwesegha, "The Role of the Organization of African Unity in Conflict Prevention, Management and Resolution," OAU/UNHCR, September 1994.

6. Interview with Chris J. Bakwesegha, Head of the Conflict Management Division, OAU, December 1, 1994. The Arusha Accords between the Rwandan government and the Rwandan Patriotic Front provided for a broadly based transitional government, an electoral process, and refugee repatriation. These plans, however, were aborted when the plane carrying the president crashed, and conflict erupted, followed by genocide. For OAU initiatives in Burundi and other countries, see Bakwesegha, "Role of the Organization of African Unity," pp. 10–13; Ibrahima Sy, Observer of OAU to UN, statement before the Third Committee of the UN General Assembly, GA/SHC/3318, United Nations, November 10, 1995; Joint OAU/UNHCR Progress Report on the Implementation of the Plan of Action adopted by the Regional Conference, May 18, 1995; and Burgess Carr, "OAU and Burundi," ICVA Forum, Geneva, July 1996.

7. Council of Ministers, *Proposals for an OAU Mechanism for Conflict Prevention and Resolution,* Report of Secretary-General, CM/1710 (L.VI) (Organization of African Unity, Addis Ababa, 1992).

8. See William Drozdiak, "France Urges Africa to Form Peacekeeping Force," *Washington Post,* November 10, 1994, p. A54; and "War and Peacekeeping in Africa," editorial, *Washington Post,* November 14, 1994, p. A20.

9. In 1996, the United States proposed the creation of an African Crisis Response Force to be sent to countries where insurrection, civil war, or campaigns of genocide threaten mass civilian casualties. The force would not intervene in the fighting but would establish and protect safe areas where civilians could gather and receive humanitarian assistance. The United States, with the help of its European allies and possibly others, would train, equip, and deploy the force, which would be composed of troops from African countries but be under the overall control of the United Nations. See Thomas W. Lippman, "U.S. Presses for All-Africa Crisis Force," *Washington Post,* September 28, 1996, p. A1; and Michael O'Hanlon and Adekeye Adebajo, "Rapid-Reaction Force Could Help Alleviate African Misery," *Defense News,* January 13–19, 1997. U.S. training of African troops began in mid-1997, although the proposal has been substantially pared back and renamed the African Crisis Response Initiative. See James Ru-

pert, "U.S. Troops Teach Peacekeeping to Africans," *Washington Post,* September 16, 1997, p. A16.

10. Among the objections raised are the fact that many African countries do not have well-trained and reliable military forces. Political disputes between countries may also complicate agreement as to whom to assign to which conflicts, and some OAU member states oppose a step so clearly interventionist. It has also been argued that a neutral, international force, organized by the United Nations, would be more effective than a regional one.

11. It should nonetheless be noted that in 1996 the OAU endorsed the dispatch of an African force to defuse tensions and prevent genocide in Burundi, although none was actually formed. The OAU took the position that "if a military regime overthrows a government elected freely and fairly by the people, the OAU will act firmly." See statement of the OAU Secretary-General in Carr, "OAU and Burundi." The authors also met with Salim A. Salim, January 15, 1997.

12. Out of some eighty countries asked by the United Nations to lend support for a possible military force, no states outside Africa offered to send troops. See Salih Booker, "Burundi: Do the Right Thing," Council on Foreign Relations, New York, August 28, 1996. Nor was the United Nations able to act in a timely way to authorize an international force when hundreds of thousands of refugees were in danger of starvation in what was eastern Zaire in 1996, and African leaders urged the creation of a force. See Steven Lee Myers, "UN Fails to Authorize Peace Force for Zaire," *New York Times,* November 10, 1996, sec. 1, p. 18; and "African Leaders Urge UN to Deploy Force in Zaire," *Washington Post,* November 6, 1996, p. A14. On November 9, 1996, the Security Council did call on UN members to lay the groundwork for a force but did not authorize its deployment. Canada subsequently announced that it would establish an international force, but this turned out to be unnecessary when Rwandan refugees returned home en masse.

13. Council of Ministers, *Proposals for an OAU Mechanism,* pp. 12–13.

14. See African-American Institute, "Africa: Conflict Prevention and New Regional Initiatives," New York, May 24, 1994.

15. See Conclusions of the Seminar on Protection of African Refugees and Internally Displaced Persons, held in Harare, February 16–18, 1994, African Commission on Human & Peoples' Rights, Banjul, 1994. See also the Addis Ababa Document, 1994. Earlier in 1988 the OAU lent support to the International Conference on the Plight of Refugees, Returnees and Displaced Persons in Southern Africa, the first international conference in which displaced persons were a featured part.

16. The conference was held under the sponsorship of the OAU, UNHCR, UNIFEM, and the UN Economic Commission for Africa, and held in Addis Ababa. See Francis M. Deng, *Report of the Representative of the UN Secretary-General on Internally Displaced Persons,* General Assembly, A/50/558 (United Nations, October 20, 1995), p. 25.

17. The Commission of Twenty monitors the refugee situation in Africa and reports to the OAU Council of Ministers. An OAU Coordinating Committee on Assistance to Refugees in Africa, chaired by UNHCR, provides institutional

linkages between the commission and the wider international community, particularly international and nongovernmental organizations that provide support and assistance for refugees in Africa. See OAU/UNHCR, "Africa's Refugees."

18. See, for example, OAU Commission of Twenty, "Report on the Situation of Refugees, Returnees and Displaced Persons in Africa," to the Council of Ministers Sixty-First Ordinary Session, January 23–27, 1995, Addis Ababa; and OAU Commission of Twenty, "Report on Refugees," to the Council of Ministers Sixty-Second Ordinary Session, June 21–23, 1995, Addis Ababa.

19. The commission met with displaced populations, held discussions with the authorities, and gave a public interview. Interview with Mpotsch Ngung, Director of the OAU Bureau of Refugees, Displaced Persons, and Humanitarian Affairs, May 16, 1996. See also Mission of the OAU Commission of Twenty on Refugees to Guinea, Sierra Leone, Liberia, Côte d'Ivoire, and Nigeria, February 26–March 23, 1994, BR/5/MIS/94, Addis Ababa.

20. The *Plan of Action* of the Regional Conference on Assistance to Refugees, Returnees and Displaced Persons in the Great Lakes Region sought to promote the voluntary return of refugees and internally displaced persons combined with steps at rehabilitation and reconstruction.

21. In a 1995 overview of Africa, for example, the commission reported, with regard to the internally displaced, that the Sudan is "providing shelter, services and other facilities to its own displaced persons who opted to go to the Northern part of the country." See OAU Commission of Twenty, "Report on Refugees," p. 9. This hardly reflected the desperate conditions of hundreds of thousands of internally displaced Sudanese around Khartoum or other parts of the north, documented at length in UN and NGO reports and Hiram A. Ruiz, "Case Study on the Sudan," in Roberta Cohen and Francis M. Deng, eds., *The Forsaken People: Case Studies of the Internally Displaced* (Brookings, 1998).

22. The bureau, which is part of the OAU Secretariat, was established in 1968 to inform member states about refugee movements in Africa, to contribute to the needs of refugees, especially in the area of education, and to assist with the resettlement of individual refugees who have appropriate skills and qualifications. See OAU/UNHCR, "Africa's Refugees: Tackling the Crisis," Addis Ababa, October 1995.

23. See Lawyers Committee for Human Rights, *African Exodus: Refugee Crisis, Human Rights and the 1969 OAU Convention* (New York, July 1995), pp. 139–40, 143, 152–53, 164–65.

24. This unit was established in 1992 and has begun to include refugee and displaced women in its programs. See Lawyers Committee for Human Rights, *African Exodus*, p. 166.

25. See Lawyers Committee for Human Rights, *African Exodus*, pp. 153, 162.

26. Interview with Mpotsch Ngung, Director of the Bureau of Refugees, Displaced Persons and Humanitarian Affairs, May 16, 1996.

27. At its Eighteenth Ordinary Session in October 1995, the commission decided to organize a second seminar on the subject of refugees and internally

displaced persons in Africa. See International Commission of Jurists, "ICJ Newsletter," Geneva, October 1995. For resolution, see International Commission of Jurists, "ICJ Newsletter," January 1995, p. 2.

28. The commission for the first time in December 1995 held an extraordinary session on the situation in Nigeria and sent a mission to the country.

29. See Report of the Conference on the African Commission on Human and Peoples' Rights, The Fund for Peace, New York, June 24–26, 1991, pp. 34, 44–48. Human Rights Watch has urged the commission to publicize its reports and findings and take other steps as well to increase its impact, such as monitoring international humanitarian law so that it could address the behavior of insurgent movements in internal armed conflicts. See Human Rights Watch/Africa, Submission to the Twentieth Ordinary Session of the African Commission on Human and Peoples' Rights, Grand Bay, Mauritius, October 1996.

30. L. Muthoni Wanyeki, "Africa-Human Rights: Sharpening the Teeth of Continental Watchdog," *InterPress Service,* August 1, 1996.

31. Interview with Chris J. Bakwesegha, December 1, 1994.

32. Lawyers Committee, *African Exodus,* p. 162.

33. Francis M. Deng and others, *Sovereignty as Responsibility: Conflict Management in Africa* (Brookings, 1996), p. 142.

34. ECOWAS's authority to intervene is conditioned on the conflict having been engineered and supported actively from outside and being likely to endanger the security and peace of the entire community. See, for example, W. Ofuatey-Kodjoe, "The ECOWAS Intervention in Liberia: Regional Organization and the Resolution of Internal Conflicts," Ralph Bunche Institute on the United Nations, Occasional Papers Series 17, April 1994.

35. Nigeria, for example, led other African states in May 1990 to block the initiative by UN Secretary-General Perez de Cuellar to bring the Liberian situation before the UN Security Council. Instead, Nigeria presented an ECOWAS "Peace Plan" for Liberia to the Security Council; and when the council declined to endorse it, ECOWAS dispatched ECOMOG to Liberia. The ECOMOG intervention, initially composed of troops from Nigeria and Ghana, later broadened, however, to include troops from other countries, and the members of ECOWAS joined in a common effort to achieve a settlement in Liberia. See Colin Scott, "Case Study on Liberia," in *The Forsaken People.*

36. See Timothy Weaver, "Liberia: Deadly Dreams of Power," *Crosslines Global Report* (September 1993), pp. 7–8; and Africa Watch, "Waging the War to Keep the Peace: The ECOMOG Intervention and Human Rights," New York, June 1993, p. 8.

37. Colin Scott, "Humanitarian Action and Security in Liberia, 1989–1994," Thomas J. Watson, Jr. Institute for International Studies Occasional Paper 20 (Brown University, 1995), p. 10.

38. Scott, "Humanitarian Action and Security in Liberia," p. 10. See also Scott, "Case Study on Liberia."

39. Africa Watch, "Waging the War," p. 8.

40. Report of the Inter-Agency Mission to Sierra Leone and the Sub-Region,

September 5, 1995, p. 18, contained in Inter-Agency Standing Committee Working Group Meeting, Geneva, 27 September 1995. See also Médecins Sans Frontières, *World in Crisis* (London, 1997), pp. 116–17.

41. ECOMOG's failure to contain the fighting in April 1996 has been attributed to the shrinking size of the force (reduced to 6,000 by 1995), lagging pay, and a sharp falling off of logistical support for it. According to one UN official, the forces were "not motivated, not rotated and not paid often enough." See Jonathan C. Randal, "Liberian Fighting Raises Doubts on Peace Force," *Washington Post*, April 23, 1996, p. A12.

42. The OAU designated a special envoy to participate in the major talks in Geneva and Cotonou, but did not monitor ECOMOG's role in respect of the civilian population.

43. UNOMIL, a 303-person UN observer force, was dispatched to Liberia in 1993 to monitor the cease-fire organized by the joint UN-OAU-ECOWAS effort; to implement the Cotonou agreement for the formation of a transitional government and elections; and to monitor violations of humanitarian law. Africa Watch repeatedly urged UNOMIL to make public its reports on violations of humanitarian and human rights law by the warring factions and by ECOMOG troops. UNOMIL, however, considered its reports to be intended for UN headquarters only. See Africa Watch, "Waging the War."

44. See Scott, "Case Study on Liberia," which describes how UN humanitarian operations extended only to helping civilians on one side of the conflict, in line with ECOMOG's political/military objectives.

45. SADC, created by treaty in 1992 to promote common economic, political, and social values and systems in southern Africa, replaced the Southern African Development Coordination Conference (SADCC), which had been founded in 1979 to reduce the region's economic dependence on South Africa. See Europa Publications, *Africa South of the Sahara 1995* (London, 1994).

46. See Terrence Lyons, memorandum for this study, Brookings Institution, March 2, 1996.

47. Lyons, memorandum, March 2, 1996. See also Thomas Ohlson and Stephen John Stedman with Robert Davies, *The New Is Not Yet Born: Conflict Resolution in Southern Africa* (Brookings, 1994), pp. 212–13.

48. See, for example, OAU/UNHCR, "Africa's Refugees," p. 6.

49. *Africa Research Bulletin*, Blackwell Publishers Ltd., July 1–31, 1996, p. 12329.

50. Interview with K. Mbuende, Executive Director, SADC, March 20, 1996.

51. IGAD was established in 1986 to deal with desertification and food security issues, but its meetings of heads of state have proved useful for discussions of conflict resolution initiatives. See Deng and others, *Sovereignty as Responsibility*, p. 137; and Deng, "Mediating the Sudanese Conflict: A Challenge for the IGADD," *CSIS Africa Notes*, no. 169, February 1995.

52. UNDP, "Area-Based Development-Oriented Programme for the Reintegration of Uprooted Populations and Rehabilitation in the Horn of Africa," Working Paper, 1994.

53. CSCE began in 1972 as an intergovernmental process to promote East-

West cooperation which was formalized with the signing of the Helsinki Final Act on August 1, 1975. Under the Final Act and subsequent documents, participating states pledged to implement commitments in the areas of military security, economic and environmental cooperation, and human rights and humanitarian questions. Compliance was monitored by follow-up meetings or review conferences. CSCE had a particularly strong influence in the area of human rights.

54. Representatives from OSCE countries facilitated the mediation of the Nagorno-Karabakh dispute between Armenia and Azerbaijan leading to a ceasefire. The OSCE also played a critical role in Chechnya in 1995, negotiating an armistice between Russian troops and Chechen rebels. And its actions helped secure the withdrawal of Russian troops from Estonia in 1995. For a critical evaluation of its missions, see Commission on Security and Cooperation in Europe, "CSCE Missions," Washington D.C., September 1, 1992; and David Shorr, "From Treaties to Crises," *Foreign Service Journal*, vol. 70 (December 1993).

55. Long-term missions have been stationed in Macedonia, Moldova, Estonia, Latvia, Georgia, and other areas. A mission in Kosovo, however, which sought to ease tensions between the Albanian and Serb populations, was expelled by the Federal Republic of Yugoslavia. For a discussion of long-term missions, see John J. Maresca, "An Important Role for an Evolving CSCE: Preventive Diplomacy," *International Herald Tribune*, August 23, 1994; Shorr, "From Treaties to Crises;" "CSCE Works to Develop Its Conflict Prevention Potential," *NATO Review*, April 1994, p. 18; and OSCE, Decisions by the Rome Council Meeting, December 1, 1993.

56. The high commissioner is reported to have been effective in the Baltic States and Macedonia and has also been active in the case of the Hungarian minority in Slovakia, the Tatars in Ukraine, and others. See Konrad J. Huber, "The CSCE and Ethnic Conflict in the East," *RFE/RL Research Report*, vol. 2 (July 1993); Shorr, "From Treaties to Crises;" CSCE, "High Commissioner on National Minorities of the Conference on Security and Cooperation in Europe," 1994; Helsinki Commission, *CSCE Digest*, vol. 18, Washington (March 1995), p. 5; and Rachel Brett, "Human Rights and the OSCE," *Human Rights Quarterly*, vol. 18 (August 1996), p. 692.

57. The Lisbon Summit Declaration of 1996 in fact lists "involuntary migration" as an acute problem "within the human dimension." See OSCE, Lisbon Document 1996, Ref. 5/174/96 (3 December 1996). For a critical evaluation of ODIHR's work, see "The 1995 OSCE Meeting on Human Dimension Issues," A Report Prepared by the Staff of the Commission on Security and Cooperation in Europe, Washington, D.C., January 1996, pp. 4–6, 57–59.

58. When the declaration referred to displaced persons, it meant those externally displaced. See "Helsinki Summit Declaration," in *CSCE Helsinki Document 1992: The Challenges of Change* (Helsinki, July 10, 1992). When CSCE's Council of Ministers requested the organization's main decisionmaking bodies to address the subject of mass migration, its focus was also on refugees and those displaced externally. See Jacques Eric Roussellier, letter, CSCE Office for Democratic Institutions and Human Rights, Warsaw, September 27, 1994.

59. This was true for the Human Dimension Seminar on migration held in

1993. See Rachel Brett and Elaine Eddison, "Migration, Refugees and Displaced Persons: Report on the CSCE Human Dimension Seminar," Papers in the Theory and Practice of Human Rights no. 4, Human Rights Centre, University of Essex, 1993. Similarly, a 1994 Parliamentary Assembly Declaration recommended that the organization "prevent involuntary movements" of refugees. See Vienna Declaration of the CSCE Parliamentary Assembly, Vienna, July 4–8, 1994. The 1995 OSCE Meeting on Human Dimension Issues held in Warsaw likewise paid no attention to the issue of internal displacement. See Rapporteurs' reports, in "The 1995 OSCE Meeting on Human Dimension Issues," pp. 63–71.

60. The Regional Conference to Address the Problems of Refugees, Displaced Persons and Other Forms of Involuntary Displacement and Returnees in the Commonwealth of Independent States (CIS) and Relevant Neighboring States was convened in Geneva on May 30–31, 1996 by UNHCR, IOM, and OSCE at the request of the UN General Assembly to provide a forum for the discussion of population displacement and elaborate a nonbinding program of action for the CIS countries. See Report of the Conference, CISCONF/1996/6, July 4, 1996; and Programme of Action, CISCONF/1996/5, June 11, 1996.

61. Commission on Security and Cooperation in Europe, CSCE Digest, vol. 18 (March 1995), p. 5.

62. See Jennifer McLean and Thomas Greene, "Case Study on Tajikistan," in The Forsaken People; and Commission on Security and Cooperation in Europe, CSCE Digest, vol. 17 (January 1994), p. 2.

63. See Commission on Security and Cooperation in Europe, "The OSCE in Post-Dayton Bosnia," CSCE Digest, vol. 19 (January 1996).

64. See, for example, Netherlands Kurdistan Society, "Forced Evictions and Destruction of Villages in Dersim (Tunceli) and the Western Part of Bingol, Turkish Kurdistan, September–November 1994," Amsterdam, 1995.

65. The mandate of the high commissioner precludes him from dealing with "situations involving organized acts of terrorism." Terrorism, however, is a highly political and emotive term; it is up to the high commissioner to decide whether it applies to a given situation and whether it is organized. The high commissioner also has to decide at what point a situation is a conflict precluding his involvement since his mandate confines his role to addressing situations prior to their development into conflicts. See Brett, "Human Rights and the OSCE," pp. 690–92.

66. The Federal Republic of Yugoslavia (Serbia and Montenegro) was suspended from membership.

67. Another nonconsensual instrument is the Mechanism for Discussion and Clarification of Unusual Military Activities, adopted in 1990. Under this mechanism, a state with a "security concern" about another state's activities may request clarification, which must be provided within forty-eight hours. If there is no satisfaction, the requesting state may call a meeting of participating states at the Conflict Prevention Centre. This mechanism has been invoked by Hungary and by Austria with regard to airspace incursions by the Federal Republic of Yugoslavia. The Emergency Meeting Mechanism, adopted in 1991, is also nonconsensual. Under this mechanism, a state may request clarification regarding a developing emergency and the state in question is obligated to respond. If the

situation remains unresolved, a request may be made to the Committee of Senior Officials to hold a two-day emergency session. If twelve or more states second the request, a meeting will be held no later than three days from that time. This mechanism was invoked in 1991 and 1992 in connection with the Yugoslav crisis. Since the Permanent Council began holding regular weekly meetings, however, this mechanism has not been used.

68. A state can be forced to receive a fact-finding mission if six participating states agree, and immediately, if ten participating states agree. The provision was adopted in 1991 and has been invoked in very few cases. No enforcement machinery exists to compel acceptance if a state refuses to receive a mission, but states have themselves invited missions or given their consent rather than undergo the political pressure of a mandatory process. This has been the case for Croatia, Estonia, and Moldova.

69. Report of OSCE's Parliamentary Assembly's Delegation to Turkey, May 1–6, 1995, p. 18.

70. See Human Rights Watch/Helsinki, "Tajikistan," New York, May 1996, pp. 4, 26–27. In Bosnia, OSCE staff have been found to be inexperienced in human rights monitoring; moreover, the six-month field contracts given to staff do not assure the continuity of presence needed for successful monitoring. Interview with NGO representative stationed on the ground in Sarajevo, June 1996.

71. See Chris Hedges, "U.S. Envoy Told Staff to Be Optimistic on Bosnia Vote," New York Times, June 5, 1996, p. A3; "Commission Questions Bosnia's Readiness for Free and Fair Elections in Letter to Christopher," CSCE News Release, Washington, D.C., June 11, 1996; and Mike O'Connor, "An Intimidation Persists, Doubts Grow on Bosnia Vote," New York Times, September 4, 1996, p. A14.

72. Commission on Security and Cooperation in Europe, CSCE News Release, Washington D.C., March 23, 1995. The OSCE Assistance Group has been engaged in political mediation; its efforts are intended to support the return of displaced persons and foster the observance of human rights. See Tim Guldimann, "The OSCE Assistance Group to Chechnya—Experience Report," Washington, D.C., March 11, 1997.

73. See, for example, Human Rights Watch/Helsinki, "Russia: Caught in the Crossfire," New York, March 1996, pp. 5–6.

74. "CSCE Works to Develop Its Conflict Prevention Potential," NATO Review, April 1994, p. 21.

75. A NATO declaration in 1994, for example, affirmed that NATO countries "remain deeply committed to further strengthening the CSCE" as an instrument of preventive diplomacy and conflict prevention. "CSCE Works to Develop Its Conflict Prevention Potential," NATO Review, p. 22.

76. The WEU, founded in 1948, was intended to become the European Community's defense component; since its inception, however, it has been overshadowed by NATO. Composed of nine West European states, it can draw upon the forces of its member nations for peacekeeping and peace enforcement operations. Although it has thus far not developed a serious independent capability for such actions, on June 19, 1992, it decided to create a standing military force. See

"West European Force to Be Formed," *Washington Post,* June 20, 1992, p. A18. See also David S. Huntington, "A Peacekeeping Role for the Western European Union," in Abram Chayes and Antonia Handler Chayes, eds., *Preventing Conflict in the Post-Communist World* (Brookings, 1996).

77. The tenuous nature of the cease-fire has been largely responsible, but problems have also arisen over the size of the force, the countries from which it should come, and the resources. In particular, the United States and Russia could not reach agreement over the extent to which WEU or CIS troops should be deployed. Nonetheless, in Bosnia, for the first time, NATO forces and Russian troops have been deployed together and this could become a precedent for greater cooperation in support of OSCE activities.

78. See John M. Goshko, "UN Approves Italy-Led Force for Albania," *Washington Post,* March 29, 1997, p. A14.

79. The Commission of the European Communities has provided fifty or more personnel to the UN field operation in Rwanda, and has agreed to fund the deployment of a team of UN human rights observers in Burundi.

80. The European Union, for example, has not yet accepted Turkey as a member, primarily because of its human rights record. See "Europeans Shut the Door on Turkey's Membership in Union," *New York Times,* March 27, 1997, p. A13.

81. The Council of Europe, created in 1949 and headquartered in Strasbourg, has thirty-nine members, including East European states and Russia. Its three organs are said to correspond to executive, legislative and judicial functions: the Committee of Ministers, composed of foreign ministers, which is the major decisionmaking body; the Parliamentary Assembly, selected by the parliaments of member countries, which passes recommendations for action by the ministers; and the European Commission and Court of Human Rights, which seek compliance with the provisions of the European Convention for the Protection of Human Rights and Fundamental Freedoms. The council seeks to harmonize human rights and economic and social standards among its members and has prepared more than two hundred intergovernmental agreements to this end.

82. See Human Rights Watch/Helsinki, "Turkey: Violations of the Right of Petition to the European Commission of Human Rights," New York, April 1996. The 800 number may even be higher: the *Turkish Daily News,* Ankara, December 6, 1996 reported that the state minister and deputy government spokesman, Gurcan Dagdas, asserted that of 6,000 cases brought to the European Commission, 1,500 have been against Turkey.

83. See Jean E. Manas, "The Council of Europe's Democracy Ideal and the Challenge of Ethno-National Strife," in Chayes and Chayes, eds., *Preventing Conflict,* pp. 110–12. See also Human Rights Watch/Helsinki, "HRW Calls on Council of Europe to Suspend Consideration of Russian Membership," Human Rights Watch Update, New York, March 1995.

84. See Human Rights Watch/Helsinki, "Turkey"; and Stephen Kinzer, "Europe Slaps Turkey," *New York Times,* September 25, 1996, p. A5. See also Human Rights Watch/Helsinki, "Russian Federation: A Review of the Compliance of the Russian Federation with Council of Europe Commitments and Other Human

Rights Obligations on the First Anniversary of its Accession to the Council of Europe," New York, February 1997.

85. When there is an interruption of the democratic process in a member state, the OAS Permanent Council has been authorized, since 1991, to meet immediately and decide upon a course of action; and in 1997, the OAS's 1948 Charter was amended to permit suspension of an illegitimate government. Although the charter prohibits intervention in internal affairs, the overwhelmingly democratic nature of the region now makes it easier to override lingering inhibitions about interference. See Tom Farer, "Collectively Defending Democracy in a World of Sovereign States: The Western Hemisphere's Prospect," International Centre for Human Rights and Democratic Development, Canada, 1993, pp. 18–20; and Christina Cerna, "Universal Democracy: An International Legal Right or the Pipe Dream of the West?" *New York University Journal of International Law and Politics,* vol. 27 (Winter 1995).

86. Cerna, "Universal Democracy?" See also Thomas W. Lippman, "Joint Effort Helps Head Off Coup Threat in Paraguay," *Washington Post,* April 26, 1996, p. A30.

87. Organization of American States, "Legal Situation of Refugees, Returnees, and Displaced Persons in the American Hemisphere," General Assembly Resolution, AG/Res.1214 (XXIII-O/93) (Washington, D.C., June 11, 1993).

88. Organization of American States, "Situation of Refugees, Returnees, and Displaced Persons in the American Hemisphere," General Assembly Resolution, AG/Res. 1336 (XXV-O/95) (Washington, D.C., June 9, 1995).

89. Organization of American States, "Situation of Refugees, Returnees, and Displaced Persons in the Hemisphere," General Assembly Resolution, AG/Res. 1416 (XXVI-0/96) (Washington, D.C., June 3, 1996).

90. Organization of American States, *Annual Report of the Inter-American Commission on Human Rights 1993* (Washington D.C., 1994), p. 559.

91. Among the conflicts identified are those between displaced persons and those who have occupied their property during their absence. Interview with Senior Political Officer at the U.S. Mission to the OAS, Washington D.C., April 19, 1996.

92. Robert Goldman, "Internally Displaced Persons: Global and Regional Initiatives, Specific Protection Needs and the Importance of an Inter-Agency Framework," *Memoria del Coloquio Internacional: 10 Años de la Declaración de Cartagena sobre Refugiados,* Inter-American Institute of Human Rights–UNHCR, San José, Costa Rica, December 1994.

93. A 1994 report on Guatemala, for example, called on the government to cease military harassment of the displaced and to extend them legal recognition. See Inter-American Commission on Human Rights, *Special Report on the Human Rights Situation in the So-Called "Communities of Peoples in Resistance in Guatemala"* (Washington, D.C., 1994). A report on the forcible displacement of the Miskito Indians in Nicaragua made the far-reaching recommendation that compensation be awarded to the Miskitos for the damage done to their property. See Inter-American Commission on Human Rights, *Report on the Situation of Human Rights of a Segment of the Nicaraguan Population of Miskito Origin and Resolu-*

tion on the Friendly Settlement Procedure Regarding the Human Rights Situation of a Segment of the Nicaraguan Population of Miskito Origin (Washington, D.C., 1984). See also the commission's *Fourth Report on the Situation of Human Rights in Guatemala* (Washington, D.C., June 1, 1993); *Report on the Situation of Human Rights in Peru* (Washington, D.C., March 12, 1993); and *Reports on the Situation of Human Rights in Haiti* (Washington, D.C., March 9, 1993, and February 9, 1995).

94. Organization of American States, *Annual Report of the Inter-American Commission on Human Rights,* p. 559.

95. The rapporteur selected was commission member Robert K. Goldman, Professor of Law at the Washington College of Law of American University. See Inter-American Commission on Human Rights, Press Release 3/96, March 8, 1996.

96. Organization of American States, *Annual Report of the Inter-American Commission on Human Rights,* p. 539.

97. IIHR was created in 1980 as an autonomous international body by agreement between the Inter-American Court of Human Rights and the Costa Rican government. Through its research and studies it seeks to promote the human rights objectives of the inter-American system.

98. Inter-American Institute of Human Rights, Program of Refugees, Repatriated and Displaced Persons and Human Rights, Aide Memoire on Technical Meeting of the Permanent Consultation on Internal Displacement in the Americas, San José, Costa Rica, April 15, 1993. See also Memoria Coloquio Internacional, Inter-American Institute of Human Rights–UNHCR.

99. The Guatemala report, "Informe Final Misión In Situ A Guatemala," CPDIA, Costa Rica, 1996, contains twenty-two recommendations to the government for improving the conditions of the internally displaced.

100. For example, CPDIA and IIDH have given technical support to church organizations in Colombia which provide legal aid, develop statistics on the internally displaced and organize campaigns to prevent violence against displaced populations. They also have developed human rights training programs for displaced indigenous women in Guatemala in collaboration with local women's organizations. Interview with Cristina Zeledon, Director of CPDIA, May 23, 1996.

101. See Carlos Alberto Sarti Castaneda, "In Search of Human Security in Central America," in *Regional Responsibilities and the United Nations System,* ACUNS Reports and Papers 1994, no. 2, p. 72.

102. In 1994 the representative of the UN secretary-general and CPDIA undertook missions to Colombia within six months of one another without planning or coordination. Although they did in the end supplement each other's work, a regular institutional link would avoid duplication and strengthen collaborative efforts.

103. The LAS's main purpose is to coordinate political, economic and social policy among Arab states, especially in regard to matters touching on the Arab-Israeli conflict.

104. The declaration was the result of a series of seminars on asylum and

refugee law in the Arab world, organized by the International Institute of Humanitarian Law together with the Faculty of Law of Cairo University, under the sponsorship of UNHCR. See International Institute of Humanitarian Law, *Cairo Declaration on the Protection of Refugees and Displaced Persons in the Arab World*, November 19, 1992.

105. See Seminaire Regional sur Les Deplacements Internes de Populations dans les Pays Arabes, Droits de l'Homme et Droit International Humanitaire, Tripoli, Lebanon, June 10–12, 1995. The conference was organized by the Centre for Human Rights of Jinane University in Tripoli, Lebanon, with the support of IOM, UNHCR, UNFPA, and ICRC. It should be noted that in 1997, in Jordan, UNHCR organized a regional consultation on population displacements in central, southwest Asia and the Middle East as a result of wars and civil conflicts. While its main focus was refugees, it also referenced the problem of internal displacement, which could stimulate some attention to this issue in the region. See UNHCR, press release, "UNHCR Holds Regional Meeting on Population Displacement," Washington, D.C., March 10, 1997.

106. Interview with Khalid M. Khalid Abdalla, Chief Representative, Washington, D.C., Office, League of Arab States, January 25, 1996.

107. Interview with Khalid M. Khalid Abdalla. The LAS did take political initiatives with respect to Somalia. For example, in August 1996 it called on the Somali factions to work out a peaceful settlement and offered to sponsor negotiations to end the fighting. The LAS, together with the OAU and the Organization of the Islamic Conference, also cooperated directly with the United Nations in negotiations with the Somali parties and in establishing the UN Operation in Somalia.

108. In 1982, for example, the United Nations held a seminar in Sri Lanka to promote regional arrangements for the promotion and protection of human rights in Asia. See United Nations Report, A/37/422, annex. Similar workshops were held in subsequent years. See Commission on Human Rights, *Report of the Secretary-General on Regional Arrangements for the Promotion and Protection of Human Rights in the Asian and Pacific Region*, E/CN.4/1995/44 (United Nations, November 28, 1994), and Centre for Human Rights, Fourth Workshop on Regional Human Rights Arrangements in the Asian and Pacific Region, United Nations, 1996.

109. In 1994, for example, the Friedrich Naumann Foundation organized a conference on regional systems for the protection of human rights that focused largely on the establishment of a regional human rights system for the Asian and Pacific region. See *Report of the Secretary-General on Regional Arrangements*.

110. *Report of the Secretary-General on Regional Arrangements*.

111. Sidney Jones, "Regional Institutions for Protecting Human Rights in Asia," in American Society of International Law, *Proceedings of the 89th Annual Meeting: Structures of World Order*, April 5–8, 1995, p. 480.

112. Founded in 1967 as a quasi-defense arrangement against communism, ASEAN today includes Brunei, Indonesia, Laos, Malaysia, Myanmar (Burma), the Philippines, Singapore, Thailand, and Vietnam, with Cambodia in observer status.

113. Jones, "Regional Institutions for Protecting Human Rights in Asia," pp. 476–77; and Sarasin Viraphol, "Human Rights: An Asian Perspective," in Don M. Snider and Stuart J. D. Schwartzstein, eds., *The United Nations at Fifty: Sovereignty, Peacekeeping, and Human Rights* (Washington: Center for Strategic and International Studies, 1995), p. 62.

114. ASEAN nations and neighboring states contributed most of the troops and civilian police for the United Nations Transitional Authority in Cambodia (UNTAC). See H. L. Hernandez and S. Kuyama, *Strengthening of the United Nations System Capacity for Conflict Prevention*, Joint Inspection Unit (United Nations, 1995), para. 230.

115. ASEAN in fact claims that it has been working "quietly" behind the scenes to achieve a peaceful reconciliation in Myanmar (Burma). See Michael Richardson, "ASEAN Ignores West on Burma," *International Herald Tribune*, July 20–21, 1996; and Seth Mydans, "Southeast Asia Bloc Admits Burmese and Two Others," *New York Times*, June 1, 1997, sec. 1, p. 10.

116. Dialogue partners include Japan, India, China, Australia, New Zealand, and the Republic of Korea, as well as Russia, the United States, Canada and the European Union.

117. SAARC is composed of India, Pakistan, Bangladesh, Nepal, Sri Lanka, Bhutan, and the Maldives. See Union of International Associations, *Yearbook of International Organizations 1994/1995*, vol. 1 (Munich: K. G. Saur, 1994), pp. 1377–78; and Madhavi Basnet, "South Asia's Regional Initiative on Human Rights," *Human Rights Brief*, Center for Human Rights and Humanitarian Law, Washington College of Law, American University (Winter 1997), pp. 10–11.

118. General Assembly, *Report of the Secretary-General: International Decade for Natural Disaster Reduction*, A/50/201; E/1995/74 (United Nations, June 20, 1995), pp. 6–7.

119. For example, Forum Asia (based in New Delhi and Bangkok) and the Asian Cultural Forum on Development have coordinated large numbers of local NGOs throughout Asia for lobbying work at UN human rights and other conferences and have increased outreach to the media. See Jones, "Regional Institutions for Protecting Human Rights in Asia," pp. 479–80. Other groupings include the Regional Council on Human Rights in Asia founded in 1982 in Manila, the Asian Legal Resource Centre founded in 1984 in Hong Kong, and the Asian Human Rights Commission founded in 1984 in Hong Kong. The latter two have drafted a "Charter of Asian Human Rights." See Jones, "Regional Institutions for Protecting Human Rights in Asia," and *Human Rights Tribune*, Ottawa, February–March, 1995. In addition, there is a South Asia Forum for Human Rights founded in 1993 in Kathmandu comprising NGOs from Bangladesh, Bhutan, India, Maldives, Nepal, Pakistan, and Sri Lanka; an All-Asia Bar Association, founded in 1981 in Japan; and an Asian Coalition of Human Rights Organizations established in Australia in 1982. See Human Rights Internet Reporter 10, Washington, September–December 1984, cover page and pp. 203–05; and Basnet, "South Asia's Regional Initiative on Human Rights."

120. Chapter 8 of the UN Charter provides that regional agencies or arrange-

ments may deal with matters relating to peace and security, provided they are consistent with the UN Charter.

121. Francis Deng, "Curative Prevention: Breaking the Cycle of Displacement," in Kevin M. Cahill, ed., *Preventive Diplomacy: Stopping Wars before They Start* (New York: Basic Books, 1996), p. 230.

122. The General Assembly adopted a declaration in December 1994 on the enhancement of cooperation between the United Nations and regional arrangements or agencies in the maintenance of international peace and security. The Security Council welcomed the offer made by the UN secretary-general to help regional organizations develop a capacity for preventive action, peacemaking and where appropriate, peacekeeping, especially in the case of Africa. See Hernandez and Kuyama, *Strengthening of the United Nations System*, para. 216; and General Assembly, Boutros Boutros-Ghali, *An Agenda for Peace,* Report of the Secretary-General on the Work of the Organization, A/47/277, S/24111 (United Nations, June 17, 1992); and *Supplement to an Agenda for Peace,* January 3, 1995. See also General Assembly, *Renewing the United Nations: A Programme for Reform,* Report of the Secretary-General, A/51/950 (United Nations, July 14, 1997), para. 116.

123. In Rwanda, the OAU was found not to have been given needed resources or UN cooperation at critical stages in the emergency to enable it to play a more significant role. See *Synthesis Report,* vol. 5 of *The International Response to Conflict and Genocide: Lessons from the Rwanda Experience,* Joint Evaluation of Emergency Assistance to Rwanda (Copenhagen, March 1996), pp. 23, 49. In Liberia, abuses by ECOMOG against internally displaced persons and others in the civilian population were not effectively curbed by UNOMIL.

124. In the UN secretary-general's 1997 reform program, the "codeployment of field operations" is identified as an example of a complementary effort as well as the designation of a joint UN-OAU Special Representative for the Great Lakes Region of Africa. See General Assembly, *Renewing the United Nations,* para. 116. A series of institutional steps to strengthen cooperation is further suggested in Hernandez and Kuyama, *Strengthening of the United Nations System,* paras. 235–42. In addition, a reinterpretation of chapter 8 of the UN Charter has been proposed so that the UN's relationship with regional bodies becomes more cooperative than hierarchical. See S. Neil MacFarlane and Thomas G. Weiss, "The United Nations, Regional Organizations, and Human Security: Building Theory in Central America," in *Regional Responsibilities and the United Nations System,* ACUNS, no. 2 (1994), p. 8.

Chapter Seven

1. Randolph C. Kent, "World Aid and Global Visions," *Crosslines,* vol. 5, WorldAid'96 Special Supplement (January 1997), p. 8.

2. General Assembly, "Strengthening the Coordination of Humanitarian

Emergency Assistance of the United Nations," A/Res/46/182 (United Nations, December 19, 1991). For earlier efforts at early warning, see Roberta Cohen, "Introducing Refugee Issues into the United Nations Human Rights Agenda," Refugee Policy Group, Washington, D.C., January 1990, pp. 8–10; and Roberta Cohen, "Human Rights and Humanitarian Emergencies," Refugee Policy Group, Washington, D.C., September 1992.

3. See Department of Humanitarian Affairs (DHA), *Consultations on Early Warning of New Flows of Refugees and Displaced Persons: A Report to the Administrative Committee on Coordination* (United Nations, 1995). Participating in the Consultation were UNHCR, UNICEF, UNDP, UNIFEM, UNEP, FAO, UNESCO, WHO, WFP, the Centre for Human Rights, the Department of Political Affairs, and in an observer capacity, IOM and ICRC.

4. See, in particular, Maria Stavropoulou, "Human Rights and 'Early Warning' in the United Nations," *Netherlands Quarterly of Human Rights*, vol. 14 (1996).

5. Commission on Human Rights, *Report of the Special Rapporteur on Extra Judicial, Summary, or Arbitrary Executions*, E/CN.4/1994/7/Add.1 (United Nations, August 11 1993), paras. 20–22, 70–86.

6. Commission on Human Rights, *Internally Displaced Persons*, Resolution 1995/57 (United Nations, 3 March 1995).

7. Diane Paul, "Beyond Monitoring and Reporting, Strategies for Field-Level Protection of Civilians Under Threat," Background Paper for Conference on New Directions for the Protection of Civilians Under Threat, Jacob Blaustein Institute for the Advancement of Human Rights and Center for the Study of Societies in Crisis, Washington D.C., November 7, 1996, p. 26.

8. Paul, "Beyond Monitoring and Reporting," p. 26.

9. For discussion of the potential role of business in humanitarian emergencies, see "Another View of Relief Inc.," *Crosslines*, vol.5, WorldAid'96 Special Supplement (January 1997), pp.23–24.

10. *Synthesis Report*, vol. 5 of *The International Response to Conflict and Genocide: Lessons from the Rwanda Experience*, Joint Evaluation of Emergency Assistance to Rwanda (Copenhagen, March 1996). See chapter 5, "Overall Findings and Recommendations."

11. Regional Conference to Address the Problems of Refugees, Displaced Persons, Other Forms of Involuntary Displacement and Returnees in the Countries of the Commonwealth of Independent States and Relevant Neighboring States, *Programme of Action*, CISCONF/1996/5 (United Nations, June 11, 1996), para. 98.

12. *Synthesis Report*, p. 21.

13. In southern Africa in 1992, for example, early warning was combined with a coordinated international response to prevent a major famine due to drought. See Jan Eliasson, "Humanitarian Challenges for the UN: Ethical Standards as Reality Rather than Pious Hope," *DHA News, 1993 in Review* (January–February 1994).

14. Early warning of the possible spread of the Yugoslav conflict to Macedonia resulted in the deployment of the UN preventive force and OSCE observer mis-

sion with the aim of reducing ethnic tensions and preventing the outbreak of violence.

15. Economic and Social Council, *Review of the Capacity of the United Nations System for Humanitarian Assistance,* Report of the Secretary-General, E/1997/98 (United Nations, July 10, 1997), para. 37.

16. Letter of Understanding between the Representative of the Secretary-General on Internally Displaced Persons and the Under-Secretary-General for Humanitarian Affairs, July 31, 1996.

17. Inter-Agency Standing Committee Working Group, New York, September 9, 1997.

18. See Francis M. Deng, and others, *Sovereignty as Responsibility: Conflict Management in Africa* (Brookings, 1996), p. 34.

19. Terrence Lyons, "Thoughts on Multilateral Intervention to Reconstruct Collapsed States," research note (Brookings, 1997), p. 1. See also Preliminary report of the Arusha Consultation, cited in Francis M. Deng, "Reconciling Sovereignty with Responsibility: A Basis for International Humanitarian Action," in John W. Harbeson and Donald Rothchild, *Africa in World Politics: Post-Cold War Challenges,* 2d. ed. (Boulder, Colo.: Westview Press, 1995), p. 303.

20. Its antecedents include Article 27 of the International Covenant on Civil and Political Rights, which addresses minority rights. The Committee on Human Rights, which monitors implementation of the Covenant, issued a General Comment on this article in 1994. The International Convention on the Elimination of All Forms of Racial Discrimination also includes ethnic groups within its purview.

21. The 1995 Framework Convention for the Protection of National Minorities, adopted in the context of the Council of Europe, is the first multilateral treaty pertaining exclusively to the protection of national minorities. A 1992 European Charter for Regional or Minority Languages, also adopted in the context of the Council of Europe, contains measures of affirmative state action for promoting the use of regional or minority languages in the fields of education and culture. The 1975 Helsinki Act and subsequent documents adopted by the OSCE, in particular the 1990 Copenhagen Document, also pertain to minority rights. For an analysis of the weaknesses and strengths of the Framework agreement, see Geoff Gilbert, "The Council of Europe and Minority Rights," *Human Rights Quarterly,* vol. 18 (February 1996), pp. 160–89. For discussion of the OSCE process, see Jane Wright, "The OSCE and the Protection of Minority Rights," *Human Rights Quarterly,* vol. 18 (February 1996), pp. 190–205.

22. See Hurst Hannum, "Minorities, Indigenous Peoples, and Self-Determination," Louis Henkin and John Lawrence Hargrove, eds., *Human Rights: An Agenda for the Next Century* (Washington, D.C.: American Society of International Law, 1994), pp. 1–16; Roberta Cohen, "UN Human Rights Bodies: An Agenda for Humanitarian Action," in Life and Peace Institute, *The Challenge to Intervene: A New Role for the United Nations?* (Uppsala, 1992), pp. 79–81; and The Atlantic Council of the United States, "Ethnic Conflicts: Old Challenges, New Dimensions," July 1995.

23. See, for example, The Kampala Document: Towards a Conference on Security, Stability, Development and Cooperation in Africa (CSSDCA), Kam-

pala, Uganda, May 19–22, 1991, which says that Africa is on the way toward achieving its own Helsinki process. The document was adopted at a meeting organized by the Africa Leadership Forum jointly with the OAU and the UN Economic Commission for Africa. The Brookings Institution Africa Project is currently undertaking a research program to promote the principles in The Kampala Document.

24. Deng and others, *Sovereignty as Responsibility*, p. 214.

25. UNA–USA, "Inalienable Rights, Fundamental Freedoms: A UN Agenda for Advancing Human Rights in the World Community," New York, 1996, p. 57.

26. See Articles I and VIII, Convention on the Prevention and Punishment of the Crime of Genocide, UN General Assembly Resolution 260 A (III), December 9, 1948.

27. Deng and others, *Sovereignty as Responsibility*, p. 215.

28. ODIHR, for example, held a roundtable on "The Role of Ombudsmen in Conflict Prevention, Conflict Resolution and Confidence Building" in June 1996 in Budapest. In addition, ODIHR holds roundtables and seminars to foster the sharing of national experiences among new human rights institutions in Eastern Europe and Central Asia and their more established counterparts in western democracies. See Erin Mooney, "Strategies for Prevention and Protection," paper prepared for this study, May 1997.

29. See Erin Mooney, "CIS Conference on Refugees and Forced Migrants," *International Journal of Group and Minority Rights*, vol. 4 (1996/97), pp. 79–85.

30. See Arthur C. Helton, "The CIS Migration Conference: A Chance to Prevent and Ameliorate Forced Movements of People in the Former Soviet Union," *International Journal of Refugee Law*, vol. 8 (1996), pp. 167–79.

31. See Statement of the UN High Commissioner on Human Rights to the 50th Session of the General Assembly (United Nations, November 21, 1995).

32. Jan Borgen, "Internally Displaced Persons: An NGO Perspective on Protection. Check-list of Activities," paper presented on behalf of Norwegian Refugee Council to the Parinac Conference, Budapest, Hungary, April 25–27, 1994, p. 9.

33. Jan Borgen, "Institutional Arrangements for Internally Displaced Persons: The Ground-Level Experience, Norwegian Refugee Council, 1995, p. 17.

34. Paul, "Beyond Monitoring and Reporting," p. 24. For workshops in Peru and Colombia, see UN Commission on Human Rights, Francis M. Deng, *Profiles in Displacement: Peru and Profiles in Displacement: Colombia*, E/CN.4/1996/52/Add.1 (United Nations, January 4, 1996), p. 28, and E/CN.4/1995/50/Add.1 (United Nations, October 3, 1994), p. 26.

35. See, for example, *Oslo Declaration and Plan of Action* (1994); and CIS Conference, *Programme of Action*, CISCONF/1996/5. See also Borgen, "Internally Displaced Persons: An NGO Perspective on Protection"; and, with respect to strengthening human rights protection more generally, Claude E. Welch Jr., *Protecting Human Rights in Africa: Roles and Strategies of Non–Governmental Organizations* (University of Pennsylvania Press, 1995).

36. The Open Society Institute, for example, has opened a legal aid office in Tajikistan to clarify the status of displaced persons as either refugees or internally

displaced persons and to resolve issues concerning the protection of their human rights. See Open Society Institute, "Legal Aid Office Encounters Initial Success in Tajikistan," *Forced Migration Alert,* no. 16 (February 19, 1997).

37. For a list of the training programs recently conducted by ODIHR for enhancing the role of NGOs in building civil society, see *From Budapest to Lisbon: Review Activities of the ODIHR, November 1994–November 1996* (Warsaw: OSCE-ODIHR, October 1996), pp. 25–26. See also Mooney, "Strategies."

38. Statement of the UN High Commissioner for Human Rights to the Fifty-First General Assembly, November 14, 1996. See also General Assembly, *Report of the UN High Commissioner for Human Rights,* A/51/36 (United Nations, October 18, 1996), para. 49; and *Preliminary Report of the UN High Commissioner for Human Rights on the Implementation of the Plan of Action for the UN Decade for Human Rights Education,* A/51/506, October 16, 1996.

39. See also *Compilation and Analysis of Legal Norms, Part II: Legal Aspects Relating to the Human Right to Be Protected against Arbitrary Displacement,* Report of the Representative of the Secretary-General on Internally Displaced Persons to the UN Commission on Human Rights, to be presented in 1998. See also Maria Stavropoulou, "The Right Not to be Arbitrarily Displaced," *American University Journal of International Law and Policy,* vol. 9 (1994), pp. 689–749.

40. World Bank Operational Directive 4.30 8, para. 8, Washington, D.C., June 29, 1990; OECD, Guidelines for Aid Agencies on Involuntary Displacement and Resettlement, OECD/GD (91), Washington, D.C., 1991, p. 201. These are consistent with the principles developed by the reprsentative of the secretary-general.

41. Boutros Boutros-Ghali, *An Agenda for Peace: Preventive Diplomacy, Peacemaking and Peacekeeping,* Report of the Secretary-General (United Nations, 1992), p. 9.

42. *Plan of Action,* Regional Conference on Assistance to Refugees, Returnees and Displaced Persons in the Great Lakes Region, Bujumbura, February 12–17, 1995.

43. Specifically, the UN Security Council and secretary-general reportedly discouraged the OAU from playing a significant role in the monitoring and implementation of the Arusha accords. See *Synthesis Report,* "Overall Findings and Recommendations."

44. General Assembly, *Report of the UN High Commissioner for Human Rights,* A/51/36, para. 40.

45. See, for example, *Synthesis Report;* Roberta Cohen, "Who Will Respond to Burundi?" *Christian Science Monitor,* February 14, 1996, p. 20; and Lionel A. Rosenblatt, "It's Not So Simple to Make Rules about Humanitarian Aid," *International Herald Tribune,* April 5–6, 1997.

46. Sadako Ogata, "A Haven for Refugees," *Washington Post,* May 4, 1997, p. C7.

47. Mohamed Sahnoun, *Somalia: The Missed Opportunities* (Washington: U.S. Institute of Peace Press, September 1994).

48. InterAction, Letter to U.S. General Brent Scowcroft, November 19, 1992, p. 1, in Larry Minear and Thomas G. Weiss, *eds., Mercy under Fire: War and*

the Global Humanitarian Community (Boulder, Colo.: Westview Press, 1995), p. 123.

49. See Mooney, "Strategies," citing Romeo A. Dallaire, "Rwanda: From Peace Agreement to Genocide in Less than Twelve Months," paper presented to the Singapore Conference on Humanitarian Action and Peace-keeping Operations: Debriefing and Lessons, February 24–26, 1997, p. 16.

50. Romeo A. Dallaire, "The Changing Role of UN Peacekeeping Forces: The Relationship between UN Peacekeepers and NGOs in Rwanda," in Jim Whitman and David Pocock eds., *After Rwanda: The Coordination of United Nations Humanitarian Assistance* (Basingstoke: Macmillan, 1996), p. 209.

51. Bill Frelick, " 'Preventive Protection' and the Right to Seek Asylum: A Preliminary Look at Bosnia and Croatia," *International Journal of Refugee Law,* vol. 4 (1992), pp. 439–54; Andrew Shacknove, "From Asylum to Containment," *International Journal of Refugee Law,* vol. 5 (1993), pp. 516–33; and Mikhael Baruteiski, "The Reinforcement of Non-Admission Policies and the Subversion of UNHCR: Displacement and Internal Assistance in Bosnia-Herzegovina (1992–1994)," *International Journal of Refugee Law,* vol. 8 (1996), pp. 49–110.

52. UNHCR, *The State of the World's Refugees: In Search of Solutions* (Oxford University Press, 1996), p. 53.

53. Erin Mooney, "In-Country Protection: Out of Bounds for UNHCR?" in Frances Nicholson and Patrick Twomey, eds., *Refugee Rights and Realities: Evolving International Concepts and Regimes* (Cambridge University Press, forthcoming).

54. General Assembly, *Renewing the United Nations: A Programme for Reform,* Report of the Secretary-General, A/51/950 (United Nations, July 14, 1997), para. 180. See also Bill Frelick, "Assistance without Protection: Feed the Hungry, Clothe the Naked, and Watch Them Die," in *World Refugee Survey 1997* (Washington, D.C.: U.S. Committee for Refugees, 1997), pp. 24–33.

55. Jean-Luc Blondel, "Assistance to Protected Persons," *International Review of the Red Cross* (September–October, 1987), p. 453.

56. UNHCR, Central Evaluation Section Discussion Paper, *UNHCR's Role in Protecting and Assisting Internally Displaced People,* EVAL/IDP/13/2 (Geneva, November 1993), para. 77.

57. UNHCR, Information Notes on former Yugoslavia, 1/94 (January 1994), p. ii.

58. Mooney, "Strategies," citing Nicole Gnesotto, "Lessons of Yugoslavia," Chaillot Paper 14 (Paris: Western European Union Institute for Security Studies, 1994), p. 48.

59. Interview with Jacques Cuenod, Refugee Policy Group, Geneva, 1996.

60. See Convention and Protocol Relating to the Status of Refugees and the Statute of the Office of the United Nations High Commissioner for Refugees.

61. See UNHCR, Executive Committee of the High Commissioner's Program, Conclusion 72 on Personal Security of Refugees (Geneva, 1993); and UNHCR, Executive Committee of the High Commissioner's Programme, Sub-Committee of the Whole on International Protection, *The Personal Security of Refugees,* EC/1993/SCP/CRP.3 (Geneva, May 5, 1993). In this document, the

term "personal security" or "safety" is used rather than "physical protection" because "the effects of insecurity," it is said, "affect the whole person and the entire community of which he or she is a member" (para. 5). Violations of personal security include "killing, military and armed attacks, rape and other forms of sexual abuse, beatings, intimidation, abduction, involuntary servitude, robbery, forced recruitment, and arbitrary or inhumane detention."

62. See Guy S. Goodwin-Gill, "The Language of Protection," *International Journal of Refugee Law,* vol. 1 (1989), pp. 15–17.

63. Guy S. Goodwin-Gill, *The Refugee in International Law,* 2d ed. (Oxford: Clarendon Press, 1996), p. 207.

64. UNHCR, Executive Committee of the High Commissioner's Programme, Sub-Committee of the Whole on International Protection, *Protection Aspects of UNHCR Activities on Behalf of Internally Displaced Persons,* EC/SCP/87 (Geneva, August 17, 1994), pp. 11–12.

65. See "The ICRC, the League and the Report on the Re-appraisal of the Role of the Red Cross," *International Review of the Red Cross* (January–February 1979), p. 19. See also Vitit Muntarbhorn, "Protection and Assistance for Refugees in Armed Conflicts and Internal Disturbances: Reflections on the Mandates of the International Red Cross and Red Crescent Movement and the Office of the United Nations High Commissioner for Refugees," *International Review of the Red Cross,* no. 265 (July–August 1988), p. 352.

66. Goodwin-Gill, "The Language of Protection," pp. 16–17. See also Arthur C. Helton, "UNHCR and Protection in the 90s," *International Journal of Refugee Law,* vol. 6 (1994), pp. 1–5.

67. Frederick C. Cuny, "Refugees, Displaced Persons, and the United Nations System," in Charles William Maynes and Richard S. Williamson, eds., *U.S. Foreign Policy and the United Nations System* (New York: Norton, 1996), p. 202; and Diane Paul, "The Role of Non-Governmental Organizations in the Protection of Civilians Under Threat: Practical Considerations," Background Paper for Conference on New Directions for the Protection of Civilians under Threat, the Jacob Blaustein Institute for the Advancement of Human Rights and the Center for the Study of Societies in Crisis (Washington, D.C.: November 7, 1996), p. 16.

68. Statement of Caritas Internationalis, Commission of the Churches on International Affairs of the World Council of Churches and the Friends World Committee for Consultation to the UN Commission on Human Rights, Geneva, March 7, 1997.

69. UNHCR, *International Legal Standards Applicable to the Protection of Internally Displaced Persons: A Reference Manual for UNHCR Staff* (Geneva, 1996).

70. Africa Watch, "Somalia, Beyond the Warlords: The Need for a Verdict on Human Rights Abuses," New York, March 7, 1993, pp. 20–22.

71. Mary Anderson, "Development and the Prevention of Humanitarian Emergencies," in Thomas G. Weiss and Larry Minear, eds., *Humanitarianism Across Borders: Sustaining Civilians in Times of War* (Boulder, Colo.: Lynne Rienner, 1993), p. 30.

72. Curtis Lambrecht, "Protection," paper prepared for this study, 1996, p. 8.

73. Lambrecht, "Protection," citing "Addressing Humanitarian Needs around Conflicts," *World Disasters Report 1996* (Geneva: International Federation of the Red Cross and Red Crescent Societies, 1995), p. 15.

74. Mooney, "Strategies," citing Open Society Institute, *Forced Migration: Repatriation in Georgia*, Special Report (New York, June 1995), p. 23.

75. Peace Brigades International, an international NGO, regularly employs this tactic by attending mass demonstrations as well as smaller gatherings of political activists and labor organizations. See Paul, "Beyond Monitoring and Reporting," p. 26.

76. Lambrecht, "Protection," citing UNHCR, "Social Services in Refugee Emergencies" (UNHCR, 1991), p. 8.

77. Lambrecht, "Protection," citing Ulla Blomqvist, "Community Participation in a Refugee Emergency—Focusing on Community Mobilisation, Women and Youth: A Report from the Rwandan Camps in the Kagera Region of Tanzania," Radda Barnen (Swedish Save the Children), 1995.

78. Jan Borgen, "Institutional Arrangements for Internally Displaced Persons," p. 15.

79. Francis M. Deng, *Report of the Representative of the Secretary-General on Internally Displaced Persons*, Commission on Human Rights, E/CN.4/1995/50 (United Nations, February 2, 1995).

80. United Nations Development Programme, Gender in Development Programme, "Support for Women in Internally Displaced Situations, Report of a Joint Mission of UNDP/UNICEF/UNIFEM/WHO/DHA" (United Nations, October 18–November 5, 1993), p. 13.

81. Lambrecht, "Protection," p. 11.

82. Jennifer McLean, "Government Focal Points for Displacement Issues," memorandum prepared for this study, March 19, 1997.

83. In Guatemala, the UNHCR-funded National Commission to Aid Repatriates, Refugees, and Displaced Persons (CEAR) has been concentrating mainly on refugees while the national land agency, INTA, is reported not to be supportive of internally displaced persons' claims or credit applications. The Accord for the Resettlement of Persons Uprooted by the Armed Conflict, formulated in June 1994, was intended to assist internally displaced persons after the signing of a peace agreement which was completed in December 1996. It remains to be seen whether the accord's provisions will be effectively implemented with regard to the internally displaced. See U.S. Committee for Refugees, "State of the World's IDPs," paper prepared for Brookings, 1996. Similarly, despite the existence in Kenya of a National Committee for Displaced Persons that brings together representatives from the government, donors, UNDP and NGOs, the government has continued to commit abuses against internally displaced persons. See Human Rights Watch/Africa, *Failing the Internally Displaced: The UNDP Displaced Persons Program in Kenya* (New York, June 1997).

84. Francis M. Deng, *Profiles in Displacement: Peru, Report of the Representative of the Secretary-General on Internally Displaced Persons*, E/CN.4/1996/52/

Add.1 (United Nations, January 4, 1996), p. 32; and Maria Stavropoulou, "Case Study on Peru," in Roberta Cohen and Francis H. Deng, eds., *The Forsaken People: Case Studies of the Internally Displaced* (Brookings, 1998).

85. See Liliana Obregón and Maria Stavropoulou, "Case Study on Colombia," in *The Forsaken People*.

86. Francis M. Deng, *Profiles in Displacement: Sri Lanka, Report of the Representative of the Secretary-General on Internally Displaced Persons*, E/CN.4/1994/44/Add.1 (United Nations, January 25, 1994), para. 67. See also Court Robinson, "Sri Lanka: Island of Refugees," U.S. Committee for Refugees, Washington, D.C., 1991, p. 19.

87. Francis M. Deng, *Profiles in Displacement: Sri Lanka*, para. 68.

88. In some cases, many basic needs except for food have not been adequately met and in some areas even food assistance has not reached those in need. See H. L. Seneviratne and Maria Stavropoulou, "Case Study on Sri Lanka," in *The Forsaken People*.

89. Seneviratne and Stavropoulou, "Case Study on Sri Lanka."

90. U.S. Committee for Refugees, "State of the World's IDPs."

91. CIS Conference, *Programme of Action*, CISCONF/1996/5, paras. 50, 52.

92. CIS Conference, *Programme of Action*, CISCONF/1996/5, para. 126.

93. Thomas Greene, "Case Study on the Caucasus," in *The Forsaken People*.

94. José Maria Mendiluce, "War and Disaster in the Former Yugoslavia: The Limits of Humanitarian Action," in *World Refugee Survey 1994* (Washington: U.S. Committee for Refugees, 1994), p. 14.

95. Opening Statement of the United Nations High Commissioner for Refugees at the Forty-Fourth session of the Executive Committee of the High Commissioner's Programme, 4 October 1993, p. 3.

96. Umesh Palwankar, ed., *Report on the Symposium on Humanitarian Action and Peace-keeping Operations, 22–24 June 1994* (Geneva: ICRC, 1994), p. 104.

97. Seneviratne and Stavropoulou, "Case Study on Sri Lanka."

98. See, for example, Erin Mooney, "Presence, *ergo* Protection?" *International Journal of Refugee Law*, vol. 7, no. 3 (pp. 413–19; and Erin Mooney, "Internal Displacement and the Conflict in Abkhazia: International Responses and their Protective Effect," *International Journal of Group Rights*, vol. 3, no. 3 (1995/96), pp. 197–226. See also Frelick, "Assistance Without Protection."

99. See Mooney, "Presence, *ergo* Protection?"

100. Tadeusz Mazowiecki, *Situation of Human Rights in the Territory of the Former Yugoslavia*, Report of the Special Rapporteur, E/CN.4/1995/57 (United Nations, January 9, 1995), para. 122.

101. "Memorandum Concerning the Implementation of the Mandate of the Special Rapporteur on the Situation of Human Rights in the Territory of the Former Yugoslavia," to the Secretary-General, September 4, 1992, cited in Roman Wieruszewski, "Case Study on the Former Yugoslavia: The International Mechanisms, Their Efficiency and Failures," in Arie Bloed, Liselotte Leicht, Manfred Nowak, and Allan Rosas, eds., *International Studies in Human Rights*, vol. 30: *Monitoring Human Rights in Europe: Comparing International Procedures and Mechanisms* (Dordrecht: Martinus Nijhoff, 1993), p. 294.

102. Manfred Nowak, "Beyond Bookkeeping, Bringing Human Rights to Bosnia," *World Today,* vol. 52 (April 1996), p. 102. Nowak resigned as UN Expert on Missing Persons on July 27, 1995.

103. General Assembly, *Report of the High Commissioner for Human Rights on the Human Rights Field Operation for Rwanda,* Note by the Secretary-General, A/50/743 (United Nations, November 13, 1995), annex.

104. Human Rights Watch, *The Lost Agenda: Human Rights and the UN Field Operations* (New York, 1993), pp. 2, 22.

105. Wilbert van Hovell, UNHCR Senior Protection Officer for the former Yugoslavia, cited in Roberta Cohen, "International Protection for Internally Displaced Persons," in Louis Henkin and John Lawrence Hargrove, eds., *Human Rights: An Agenda for the Next Century* (Washington, D.C.: American Society of International Law, 1994), p. 25.

106. Paul, "Beyond Monitoring and Reporting," p. 45.

107. Mooney, "Strategies," citing Humanitarian Law Centre, "Kosovo Albanians I: Repression and Discrimination," Spotlight Report 6, August 1993, in *Spotlight On: Human Rights Violations in Times of Armed Conflicts* (Belgrade, 1995), p. 54.

108. The FRY expelled the OSCE mission in retaliation for the suspension of its membership in the organization and similarly restricted access by the UN human rights special rapporteur and field staff in the belief that after the Security Council's imposition of the embargo and the adoption of various condemnatory resolutions, the United Nations as a whole was biased against the Serbs.

109. Paul, "The Role of Non-Governmental Organizations in the Protection of Civilians Under Threat," p. 21.

110. Larry Minear and Thomas G. Weiss, *Humanitarian Action in Times of War: A Handbook for Practitioners* (Boulder, Colo.: Lynne Rienner, 1993), p. 9.

111. Julia Taft, President, InterAction, cited in *Crosslines,* vol. 5, World-Aid'96 Supplement (January 1997), p. 14.

112. Cuny, "Refugees, Internally Displaced Persons and the United Nations System," p. 208.

113. Human Rights Watch/Africa, *Failing the Internally Displaced.*

114. United Nations, Inter-Agency Standing Committee, Recommendations, May 1997.

115. Lambrecht, "Protection" (the paper provides a detailed typology of advocacy efforts), pp. 12–14.

116. Cuny, "Refugees, Displaced Persons and the United Nations System," p. 188.

117. Mendiluce, "War and Disaster in the Former Yugoslavia," p. 14.

118. Marion Harrof-Tavel, "Neutrality and Impartiality: The Importance of These Principles for the Red Cross and Red Crescent Movement and the Difficulties Involved in Applying Them," *International Review of the Red Cross* (November–December, 1989), pp. 541–42.

119. Lambrecht, "Protection," p. 13.

120. Human Rights Watch/Africa, *Failing the Internally Displaced,* pp. 113–15.

121. Médecins sans Frontières, *Deadlock in the Rwandan Refugees Crisis: Virtual Standstill on Repatriation* (Amsterdam, July 1995), pp. 7, 9.

122. Lucas van den Broeck, "The Bankruptcy of 'Humanitarian' Policy," *Crosslines,* vol. 5 (January 1997), p. 10.

123. Kofi Annan, "UN Reform: The First Six Weeks," Statement by the UN Secretary-General, New York, February 13, 1997.

124. Letter of Understanding, July 31, 1997.

125. Larry Minear, and others, "Humanitarian Action in the Former Yugoslavia: The UN's Role, 1991–1993," Thomas J. Watson Jr. Institute for International Studies and Refugee Policy Group, Occasional Paper 18 (Brown University, 1994), p. 114.

126. In Somalia, Cambodia and the former Yugoslavia, there have been reports of peacekeepers engaged in disreputable practices, ranging from black marketeering to actual torture. See, for example, John Tagliabue, "Photos of Troops Abusing Somalis in '93 Shock Italians," *New York Times,* June 14, 1997, sec. 1, p. 4; African Rights, *Somalia: Human Rights Abuses by the United Nations Forces* (London, July 1993); and Roy Gutman, "UN Forces Accused of Using Serb-Run Brothel," *Washington Post,* November 2, 1993, p. A12.

127. See Roberta Cohen, "Refugee and Internally Displaced Women: A Development Perspective," Brookings Institution–Refugee Policy Group Project on Internal Displacement, November 1995. See also *Rebuilding Post-War Rwanda,* vol. 4 of *The International Response to Conflict and Genocide: Lessons from the Rwanda Experience,* Joint Evaluation of Emergency Assistance to Rwanda (Copenhagen, March 1996), p. 105.

128. Among the conferences drawing attention to the plight of displaced women were the Regional Conference on the Legal Status of Refugee and Internally Displaced Women in Africa, sponsored by the OAU, UNHCR, UNICEF and the Economic Commission for Africa, Addis Ababa, 1995; the World Summit For Social Development, Copenhagen, 1995; and the Fourth World Conference on Women, Beijing, 1995. The Addis Ababa conference focused on the legal problems facing displaced women, in particular with regard to land ownership and inheritance, and called for the strengthening of legal protections through the enunciation of standards and through institutional arrangements. See Francis M. Deng, *Report of the Representative of the Secretary-General on Internally Displaced Persons,* General Assembly, A/50/558 (United Nations, October 20, 1995), paras. 84 and 102.

129. UNDP, "Support for Women in Internally Displaced Situations."

130. See UNHCR, *Sexual Violence against Refugees: Guidelines on Prevention and Response* (Geneva, 1995); and UNHCR, *Guidelines on the Protection of Refugee Women* (Geneva, 1991).

131. Francis M. Deng, *Report of the Representative of the Secretary-General on Internally Displaced Persons,* Commission on Human Rights, E/CN.4/1996/52 (United Nations, February 22, 1996), para. 46.

132. Human Rights Watch/Africa Watch/Women's Rights Project, "Seeking Refuge, Finding Terror: The Widespread Rape of Somali Women Refugees in North Eastern Kenya," New York, 1993, pp. 4, 12.

133. Paul, "Beyond Monitoring and Reporting," pp. 33–34.

134. Human Rights Watch reports that there may have been at least 250,000 rapes in Rwanda. See Human Rights Watch/Africa, "Shattered Lives: Sexual Violence during the Rwandan Genocide," New York, 1996; and "Rape as a Weapon of War," *Peacework* (March 1997). In the case of Liberia, see UNDP, "Support for Women in Internally Displaced Situations."

135. See, for example, UNHCR, *Review of the Implementation and Impact of UNHCR's Policy on Refugee Women*, EVAL/FEM/13, December 1993, paras. 80–82.

136. Graça Machel, *Impact of Armed Conflict on Children*, Report of the Expert of the Secretary-General to the UN General Assembly, A/51/306 (United Nations, August 26, 1996); and A/51/306/Add. 1 (United Nations, September 9, 1996).

137. General Assembly Resolution, "The Rights of the Child," A/Res/51/77 (United Nations, February 20, 1997).

138. UNICEF Executive Board, *Children and Women in Emergencies: Strategic Priorities and Operational Concerns for UNICEF*, E/ICEF/1997/7 (United Nations, November 11, 1996, para. 35).

139. Machel, *Impact of Armed Conflict on Children*, para. 289.

140. UNHCR, internal paper, 1996, pp. 8–9, 14.

141. World Food Programme, *WFP Response to ECOSOC Resolution 1995/56*, Reports to the Economic and Social Council, WFP/EB.A/96/7 (Part IV) (United Nations, April 9, 1996), pp. 5, 17.

142. See, for example, Cynthia Weber, *Simulating Sovereignty: Intervention, the State and Symbolic Exchange* (Cambridge University Press, 1995), p. 8.

143. See Francis M. Deng, "Frontiers of Sovereignty in Africa," in Francis M. Deng and Terrence Lyons, eds., *African Reckoning: A Quest for Good Governance* (Brookings, forthcoming).

144. See Deng, "Frontiers of Sovereignty in Africa."

145. See Security Council Resolutions 706 (1991) and 688 (1991) on Iraq. See also Security Council Resolution 834 (1993) on Angola; Resolution 822 (1993) on the Nagorno-Karabakh conflict in Azerbaijan; Resolution 820 (1993) on Bosnia-Herzegovina; Resolution 916 (1994) on Mozambique; and Resolution 931 (1994) on Somalia. For a detailed survey of the relevant General Assembly and Security Council resolutions, including overviews of four major cases (Liberia, Iraq, former Yugoslavia, Somalia) of humanitarian action in the absence of governmental consent, see Martin Griffiths, Iain Levine, and Mark Weller, "Sovereignty and Suffering," in John Harriss, ed. *The Politics of Humanitarian Intervention* (London: Pinter, 1995), pp. 35–60.

146. Commission on Human Rights, *Compilation and Analysis of Legal Norms*, Report of the Representative of the Secretary-General on Internally Displaced Persons, E/CN.4/1996/52/Add.2 (United Nations, December 5, 1995), paras. 359–81. On the applicability of this right to NGOs, the European Parliament refers to a "right of non-governmental organizations to intervene even without the agreement of the authorities in the territory of a country" in order

to assist victims of war or natural disasters, as a corollary of the right of individuals to receive humanitarian assistance. See European Parliament (Rapporteur J. W. Bertens), *Report on the Right of Humanitarian Intervention*, A3-02227/94 (April 8, 1994), p. 14, in Reinhard Marx, "A Non-Governmental Human Rights Strategy for Peacekeeping?" *Netherlands Quarterly of Human Rights*, vol. 14, no.2 (1996), p. 126.

147. Ogata, "A Haven for Refugees."

148. Interviews with UN Secretariat officials, 1996.

149. Hiram A. Ruiz, "Case Study on the Sudan," in *The Forsaken People.*

150. Operation Lifeline Sudan is exemplary of the contact needed with insurgent forces to reach displaced populations, see Ruiz, "Case Study on the Sudan." In Sri Lanka, the operation of UNHCR's open relief centers in the north has been reportedly undermined by its not having obtained formal consent from the LTTE. See Seneviratne and Stavropoulou, "Case Study on Sri Lanka." In Liberia, the limiting of the UN assistance operation to the "Greater Monrovia" area failed to reach many internally displaced persons in rebel territory. See Colin Scott, "Case Study on Liberia," in *The Forsaken People.*

151. Cornelio Sommaruga, President of the International Committee of the Red Cross, Lecture, Oslo, January 31, 1997.

152. See African Rights, *Somalia, Operation Restore Hope: A Preliminary Assessment* (London: May 1993), pp. 20–24. See also Security Council Resolution 794 on Somalia, December 3, 1992.

153. Yasushi Akashi, "The Use of Force in a United Nations Peace-keeping Operation: Lessons Learnt from the Safe Areas Mandate," *Fordham International Law Journal*, vol. 19 (1995), p. 320.

154. Mooney, "Presence, *ergo* Protection?" p. 433, citing "UN Bosnia Commander Wants More Troops, Fewer Resolutions," *New York Times*, December 31, 1993, p. A3.

155. Security Council, S/1994/1389 (United Nations, 1 Dec 1994), para. 41.

156. Security Council Resolutions 819 (16 April 1993) and 824 (6 May 1993), respectively, on the former Yugoslavia "demands" and "declares," under Chapter VII of the Charter, that all parties treat Srebrenica, Sarajevo, Tuzla, Zepa, Gorazde, and Bihac and their surrounding areas as "safe areas."

157. Security Council Resolution 836 (June 4, 1993) only required the "withdrawal of military or paramilitary units other than those of the Government of Bosnia and Herzegovina" (para. 5). Bosnian Serbs thus used this as an excuse for their attacks. In the case of Srebrenica, UNPROFOR did pressure government forces to demilitarize, but the Bosnian Serbs nonetheless overran the area. At the same time, Bosnian government forces engaged in forcible conscription of Muslim males and also tolerated the eviction of non-Muslims from their homes. See UN Commission on Human Rights, *Reports of the Special Rapporteur on the Situation of Human Rights in the Former Yugoslavia*, E/CN.4/1994/3 (United Nations, May 5, 1993), paras. 66, 70-1; E/CN.4/1994/47 (United Nations, November 17, 1993), paras. 144–46; and E/CN.4/1995/57 (United Nations, January 9, 1995), para. 23.

158. Security Council, *Report of the Secretary-General on Bosnia and Herzegovina,* S/1995/444 (May 30, 1995), para. 36; see also S/1994/1389 (December 1, 1994), para. 34.

159. For efforts made by UNAMIR, in cooperation with the government, to disarm the camps, see UN Commission on Human Rights, Report of the Representative of the Secretary-General on Internally Displaced Persons, *Note on the Mission to Rwanda,* E/CN.4/1995/50/Add.4, February 16, 1995, para. 11. Basically, however, the acts and omissions both of French forces in Operation Turquoise and UNAMIR troops enabled Hutu militants responsible for the genocide to regroup and rearm within the displaced persons camps and thereby create security problems within them, including extortion of food deliveries. See African Rights, *Rwanda: "A Waste of Hope":The United Nations Field Operation* (London: March 21, 1995), p. 7; *Early Warning and Conflict Management,* vol. 2 of *The International Response to Conflict and Genocide: Lessons from the Rwanda Experience,* Joint Evaluation of Emerging Assistance to Rwanda (Copenhagen: March 1996), p. 55. See also Larry Minear and Randolph C. Kent, "Case Study on Rwanda," in *The Forsaken People.*

160. See, for example, Security Council Resolution 836 (June 4, 1993), para. 5.

161. See Security Council, *Report of the Secretary-General on Bosnia and Herzegovina,* S/1994/555 (United Nations, May 9, 1994), para. 13. It should be noted that following the designation of the safe areas, the Secretary-General called for 34,000 troops, see UN document A/225939 (March 18, 1993). The Security Council, however, instead chose the "light option" of 7,600 reinforcements and even this limited number of forces took over a year to deploy and suffered from acute shortages of essential equipment, see *Report of the Secretary-General on Bosnia and Herzegovina,* S/1994/1389 (United Nations, December 1, 1994), para. 54. Although UNPROFOR was authorized to call upon NATO air power, NATO air power was used sparingly, limited at the direction of the Secretary-General to pinprick attacks "against artillery, mortar positions, or tanks . . . determined by UNPROFOR to be responsible for attacks against civilian targets within those [safe] areas." See Letter of the Secretary-General to NATO, April 18, 1994, cited in Mooney, "Presence, *ergo* Protection?" p. 417.

162. See Security Council Resolution 836 (June 4, 1993), para. 9. See also Mooney, "Presence, *ergo* Protection?" pp. 413–19.

163. Security Council Resolution 929 (June 22, 1994), para. 3 referring to Resolution 925 (8 June 1994), para. 4 (a).

164. Security Council Resolution 925, para. 5.

165. A UN internal evaluation found that UNAMIR did not interpret its mandate to mean protecting internally displaced persons against attacks by government forces, see Report of the Inter-Agency Task Force on Internally Displaced Persons, November 1995. According to "200 Rwandans, Army in Standoff," *Washington Post,* April 26, 1995, p. A25, the UN Special Representative in Rwanda considered UNAMIR to be restricted by its mandate to using its weapons only in self-defense. The case study on Rwanda also emphasizes that UNAMIR could act only in self-defense and in the protection of UN installations, see Minear and Kent, "Case Study on Rwanda," n. 20.

166. See Republic of Slovenia, Ministry of Foreign Affairs, "Proposals Concerning the Measures for Voluntary Return Home of the Displaced Persons and Refugees from Bosnia and Hercegovina," Statement to the International Conference on the Former Yugoslavia, Geneva, July 29, 1992, cited in Tom Argent, "Croatia's Crucible: Providing Asylum for Refugees from Bosnia and Hercegovina," U.S. Committee for Refugees, Washington, D.C., October 1992, p. 18. Supporting this proposal, a spokesperson from the French Foreign Ministry reportedly expressed the view of the majority of the countries participating in the conference in arguing, "We have to try to keep them in Yugoslavia." See "France Says On-the-Spot Safe Havens Best Refugee Policy," *Reuters,* July 30, 1992, cited in Bill Frelick, "Preventive Protection and the Right to Seek Asylum: A Preliminary Look at Bosnia and Croatia," *International Journal of Refugee Law,* vol. 4, no. 4 (1992), p. 443.

167. See, for example, Bill Frelick, "Preventing Refugee Flows: Protection or Peril?" *World Refugee Survey 1993* (Washington, D.C.: U.S. Committee for Refugees), p. 9. He notes that "while the rhetoric of 'Operation Provide Comfort' was humanitarian, and the military was, in fact, mobilized for purposes that were, in part, humanitarian, something else was going on: the prevention of a refugee flow."

168. Karin Landgren, "Safety Zones and International Protection: A Dark Grey Area," *International Journal of Refugee Law,* vol. 7, no. 3 (1995), pp. 436–58.

169. UNHCR, *Note on International Protection,* A/AC.96/815 (United Nations, 1993), para. 20.

170. Rosalyn Higgins, "The New United Nations and Former Yugoslavia," *International Affairs,* vol. 69, no. 3 (1993), p. 469.

171. Minear and Kent, "Case Study on Rwanda."

172. See, for example, Greene, "Case Study on the Caucasus"; see also a recent report on internal displacement in the Philippines which recommends that donors "link relief, rehabilitation, and development assistance to recipients' commitment to working towards a just and lasting peace." See Hiram A. Ruiz, "Internal Displacement in the Philippines," U.S. Committee for Refugees, Washington, D.C., 1997.

173. The government of Sri Lanka, for example, reacted strongly when the representative of the secretary-general on internally displaced persons made this observation, on the grounds that his mandate did not include conflict resolution. See Commission on Human Rights, *Profiles in Displacement: Sri Lanka,* Report of the Representative of the Secretary-General on Internally Displaced Persons, E/CN.4/1994/44/Add.1 (United Nations, January 25, 1994), para. 146; and Statement by the Delegation of Sri Lanka to the Fifty-First session of the Commission on Human Rights (United Nations, February 24, 1995).

174. See Francis M. Deng, "Internal Displacement in Context: Themes from Country Missions," Refugee Policy Group, Washington, D.C., Summer 1995; and Hiram A. Ruiz, "Case Study on the Sudan," in *The Forsaken People.*

175. Some internally displaced persons have also been reported to be directly

pressured to return for political reasons, see Stavropoulou, "Case Study on Peru."

176. Deng, "Internal Displacement in Context," p. 8. See also Seneviratne and Stavropoulou, "Case Study on Sri Lanka."

177. UN humanitarian and development agencies in Rwanda set up Operation Retour in an effort to control the return process and mitigate government actions, but this failed. See Minear and Kent, "Case Study on Rwanda"; Deng, "Displacement in Context;" and Commission on Human Rights, Report of the Representative of the Secretary-General on Internally Displaced Persons, *Note on the Mission to Rwanda*.

178. By legal safety is meant amnesties or public assurances of personal safety, integrity, non-discrimination and freedom from fear of persecution or punishment upon return; physical security includes protection from armed attacks, and mine-free routes and if not mine-free than at least demarcated settlement sites. By material security is meant access to land or means of livelihood. See UNHCR, *Handbook on Voluntary Repatriation: International Protection* (Geneva, 1996), p. 12.

179. Human Rights Watch/Africa, *Failing the Internally Displaced*.

180. Human Rights Watch/Africa, *Failing the Internally Displaced*, p. 12.

181. Borgen, "Institutional Arrangements for Internally Displaced Persons," p. 18.

182. The Convention on the Prohibition of the Use, Production, Transfer and Stockpiling of Anti-Personnel Landmines and on Their Destruction was adopted in Oslo on 18 September 1997; it will enter into force six months after forty governments accede to its provisions.

183. See David P. Forsythe, "The United Nations, Human Rights, and Development," *Human Rights Quarterly*, vol. 19 (May 1997), pp. 334–49; World Bank, "A Framework for World Bank Involvement in Post-conflict Reconstruction," April 25, 1997, p. iii; and Human Rights Watch/Africa, *Failing the Internally Displaced*, p. 3.

184. Statement by UN Secretary-General Kofi Annan, "UN Reform: The First Six Weeks," United Nations, New York, February 13, 1997. For discussion of the neglect of human rights in reconstruction programs, see Human Rights Watch, *The Lost Agenda: Human Rights and UN Field Operations* (New York, June 1993).

185. Ambassador Walter Gyger, Head of Switzerland's UN Mission, cited in Randolph C. Kent, "Building Bridges," *Crosslines*, WorldAid'96 Supplement, vol. 5 (January 1997), p. 14.

186. Steven Holtzman, "Conflict-Induced Displacement through a Development Lens," paper prepared for Brookings, May 1997, p. 1.

187. Holtzman, "Conflict-Induced Displacement," p. 3.

188. Randolph C. Kent, "Building Bridges," p. 14.

189. The expansion in 1997 of the UN Consolidated Appeals Process (CAP) to include initial rehabilitation and recovery needs reflects the intent to integrate relief and development planning more effectively. See chapter 4.

190. Jennifer McLean and Thomas Greene, "Case Study on Tajikistan," in *The Forsaken People.*

191. See World Bank, "A Framework for World Bank Involvement in Post Conflict Reconstruction," p. 15.

192. Holtzman, "Conflict-Induced Displacement," pp. 3–4.

193. Holtzman, "Conflict-Induced Displacement," pp. 4–5.

194. Holtzman, "Conflict-Induced Displacement," pp. 5–6, 27.

195. Holtzman, "Conflict-Induced Displacement," p. 9.

196. Holtzman, "Conflict-Induced Displacement," pp. 16–17.

197. Holtzman, "Conflict-Induced Displacement," pp. 11–12.

198. Holtzman, "Conflict-Induced Displacement," pp. 12–13.

199. Holtzman, "Conflict-Induced Displacement," p. 16.

200. Holtzman, "Conflict-Induced Displacement," pp. 20–21.

201. Holtzman, "Conflict-Induced Displacement," p. 21.

202. Holtzman, "Conflict-Induced Displacement," pp. 22–23.

203. Holtzman, "Conflict-Induced Displacement," p. 26.

204. Cohen, "Refugee and Internally Displaced Women," p. 5.

205. Holtzman, "Conflict-Induced Displacement," p. 24.

206. Holtzman, "Conflict-Induced Displacement," p. 24.

207. Holtzman, "Conflict-Induced Displacement," p. 24–25.

208. Holtzman, "Conflict-Induced Displacement," p. 25.

209. Holtzman, "Conflict-Induced Displacement," p. 25.

210. Holtzman, "Conflict-Induced Displacement," pp. 25–26.

211. Holtzman, "Conflict-Induced Displacement," p. 27.

212. Holtzman, "Conflict-Induced Displacement," pp. 7, 26.

213. Holtzman, "Conflict-Induced Displacement," p. 37.

214. International aid to Mozambique, for example, represented at least 75 percent of its GNP. See Holtzman, "Conflict-Induced Displacement," pp. 28–29.

215. Holtzman, "Conflict-Induced Displacement," pp. 28–29.

216. Holtzman, "Conflict-Induced Displacement," p. 30.

217. Holtzman, "Conflict-Induced Displacement," p. 33.

218. Holtzman, "Conflict-Induced Displacement," p. 33.

219. Holtzman, "Conflict-Induced Displacement," p. 36.

220. Holtzman, "Conflict-Induced Displacement," p. 38.

221. Cohen, "Refugee and Internally Displaced Women," p. 22.

222. Cohen, "Refugee and Internally Displaced Women," p. 26.

223. Cohen, "Refugee and Internally Displaced Women," p. 28.

224. Cohen, "Refugee and Internally Displaced Women," p. 28.

225. UNHCR reports such programs in Sri Lanka, Afghanistan and Tajikistan. See UNHCR, *Financial and Programmatic Implications of UNHCR Activities on Behalf of the Internally Displaced,* EC/1994/SC.2/CRP.13 (Geneva, May 6, 1994). See also UNHCR, "UNHCR and Refugee Women," 1995, pp. 19–20.

226. Cohen, "Refugee and Internally Displaced Women," p. 24.

227. Cohen, "Refugee and Internally Displaced Women"; and Commission on Human Rights, *Report of the Representative of the Secretary-General on Inter-*

nally Displaced Persons, E/CN.4/1997/43 (United Nations, February 4, 1997), para. 33.

228. Barbara Crossette, "The Second Sex in the Third World," *New York Times,* September 10, 1995, sec. 4, p. 1; and Cohen, "Refugee and Internally Displaced Women," pp. 34–35.

229. See for example, UNDP, "Support for Women in Internally Displaced Situations," p. 13.

230. Commission on Human Rights, *Report of the Representative of the Secretary-General on Internally Displaced Persons,* E/CN.4/1996/52 (United Nations, February 22, 1996), para. 50.

231. Francis M. Deng, *Profiles in Displacement: Burundi,* Report of the Representative of the Secretary-General on Internally Displaced Persons, Commission on Human Rights, E/CN.4/1995/50/Add.2 (United Nations, November 28, 1994), p. 21.

232. General Assembly, Platform for Action, Fourth World Conference on Women, A/CONF.177/L.5/Add.9 (United Nations, September 13, 1995); Regional Conference on the Legal Status of Refugee and Internally Displaced Women in Africa, Addis Ababa, August 1–4, 1995.

233. Forsythe, "United Nations, Human Rights, and Development," pp. 346–47.

234. Holtzman, "Conflict-Induced Displacement," p. 6.

Index

Abkhazia, 262
Addis Ababa Regional Conference on the Legal Status of Refugee and Internally Displaced Women in Africa, 302
Advocacy, 268–69
Afghanistan: assistance to, 63–64, 137, 140, 161; during the cold war, 5, 63; conflict in, 292; effects of conflict, 34; ethnic factors, 22; as a "forgotten emergency," 147; internal displacement, 4, 19, 24, 29, 56, 57, 59; nongovernmental organizations, 63, 64, 193, 210–11; refugees in, 57, 63–64; women, 60, 64
Africa: assistance to, 45, 135, 160, 167; children, 44; ethnic groups, 21; Great Lakes region, 136, 162, 175, 184, 252, 288; internal displacement, 20, 40–47, 160, 214, 218–19; military and enforcement capacity, 215–16, 220–22, 252; refugee population, 214; women, 42. See also individual countries
African Centre for Democracy and Human Rights Studies, 219
African Charter, 219
African Commission on Human and Peoples' Rights, 218
Africa, South. See South Africa
Agenda for Peace (1992), 251, 252, 254
Agriculture, 295–96
Aid. See Internal displacement; Organizations; United Nations; individual countries
Akagera National Park, 25
Akashi, Yasushi, 144
Albania, 227, 237
Algeria, 40, 295

American Convention, 96, 104
American Convention on Human Rights, 230
American Council for Voluntary International Action (InterAction), 193
Angola: assistance to, 45, 129, 136, 142, 147–48, 161, 166; during the cold war, 5, 19; conflict in, 292; effects of conflict, 34; human rights monitoring, 146, 178; internal displacement, 4, 19, 24, 37, 40, 41, 297; nongovernmental organizations, 192; protection, 163; Southern African Development Community, 222
Annan, Kofi, 176–77, 180, 254–55, 270
Apartheid. See South Africa
Armenia, 27, 49–50, 211
Article 19, 147
Arusha Accords (1993, Rwanda), 215
ASEAN. See Association of Southeast Asian Nations
Asia: government response to internal displacement, 61; internal displacement, 56, 59, 60, 64; nongovernmental organizations, 235–36; protection, 62; refugees, 64; regional organizations, 234–36. See also individual countries
Assistance. See Internal displacement; Organizations; United Nations; individual countries
Association of Southeast Asian Nations (ASEAN), 214, 234–35
Ayala Lasso, José, 153, 154, 155–56
Azerbaijan: Armenians in, 49–50; ethnic issues, 54, 261, 286; internal displacement, 48, 51–52, 285, 297; nongovernmental organizations, 211;

401

regional depopulation, 24. *See also* Nagorno-Karabakh

Barre, Siad, 20
Barzani, Masoud, 63
Bellamy, Carol, 139
Bertini, Catherine, 136
Bosnia and Herzegovina: assistance to, 5, 54, 55, 135, 171, 264; elections, 226; "ethnic cleansing," 24, 49; human rights monitoring, 267; internal displacement, 17, 29, 30, 48, 50; military intervention, 281; Organization for Security and Cooperation in Europe, 225, 226, 237; protection in, 162, 165, 255; safe areas, 54, 175, 268, 281, 282, 283; Sarajevo, 28, 49; women and children, 51, 165, 274. *See also* Muslims
Boutros-Ghali, Boutros, 187, 211, 251
Burma. *See* Myanmar
Burundi: assistance to, 27, 136, 152, 160, 172, 216, 253; children, 139; ethnic issues, 41, 42; human rights monitoring, 155, 163; internal displacement, 28, 34, 40; massacres, 278; Organization of African Unity mission, 215; resettlement, 288; women, 42, 260

"Cairo Declaration on the Protection of Refugees and Displaced Persons in the Arab World," 233
Cambodia: assistance to, 27, 129, 135, 136, 137, 167; civil war, 235; during the cold war, 5, 19, 20; government role, 61; internal displacement, 56, 58, 60, 260
CARE USA, 189
Caritas Internationalis, 189, 190
Cartagena Declaration, 16
Catholic Church, 69, 70, 160
Caucasus, 47–48
CCPR. *See* Covenant on Civil and Political Rights
CDR (Centre for Documentation on Refugees). *See* United Nations High Commissioner for Refugees
Centers for Disease Control, 2
Central America. *See* Latin American
CEDAW. *See* Convention on the Elimination of Discrimination against Women
Centre for Documentation on Refugees (CDR). *See* United Nations High Commissioner for Refugees
CESCR. *See* Covenants on Economic, Social and Cultural Rights

Chechnya: assistance to, 54–55, 132, 165, 173; effects of conflict, 34; internal displacement, 48, 50–51, 52, 53; as an "internal matter," 278; Organization for Security and Cooperation in Europe, 224, 226–27; Russian Federation in, 226–27. *See also* Russian Federation
Children: discrimination against, 136; education, 111–13, 297; effects of displacement, 25–26, 42, 43; internally displaced, 51, 65, 91, 165–66; prohibitions of the Geneva Conventions, 83; protection, 44, 109–10, 138–39, 274–75; registration of, 104; standard of living, 100; as victims, 292. *See also* Convention on the Rights of the Child; United Nations Children's Fund; Women and girls
China, 234
CIS. *See* Commonwealth of Independent States
Civilians: in Africa, 215; assistance to, 115, 116–17; internally displaced, 84, 90–91, 105, 197; International Committee of the Red Cross, 131; land mines and, 97, 289; protection, 256; protections of Geneva Conventions, 82, 83, 90, 102–03; rape of, 96; relief workers, 121; subsistence and survival needs, 100–103, 108; United Nations operations, 200; witnessing, 197
Civil wars, 5–6; access to populations in need, 277; Africa, 40; Angola, 292; Asia, 58; Central America, 70; effects of, 292–93; Geneva Conventions, 82–83; Lebanon, 57, 58–59; Liberia, 220, 292; Tajikistan, 57
Code of Crimes against the Peace and Security of Mankind, 88
Cold war, 4, 5, 19, 20, 63, 71
Colombia: assistance to, 68, 69, 160; civil war, 65; drug cartels, 65; government role, 67; internal displacement, 17, 28, 29, 34, 65, 261; legal rights, 68; nongovernmental organizations, 160; Permanent Consultation on Internal Displacement in the Americas, 231; rehabilitation, 295; self-help, 70, 259; standard of living, 66
Commission of Twenty on Refugees, 218
Committee on Economic, Social and Cultural Rights, 100, 102
Committee on the Elimination of Racial Discrimination, 86
Commonwealth of Independent States (CIS), 72, 136, 209, 242, 247, 262
Communism, 56

Compilation and Analysis of Legal Norms, 122, 123, 125, 152, 206
Conference on the Plight of Refugees, Returnees, and Displaced Persons in Southern Africa (SARRED, *1988*), 5
CONDEG. *See* National Council of the Displaced in Guatemala
Conference on Security and Cooperation in Europe (CSCE). *See* Organization for Security and Cooperation in Europe
Conflict: African, 215–16; causes of, 21; cost-effectiveness, 253; development during and following, 295–303; displacement and, 22, 23, 213, 291–304; good governance and, 244; Inter-Governmental Authority on Development, 222–23; national security, 87; Organization for Security and Cooperation in Europe, 223; prevention, 237, 251–54, 294–95; prohibition of forced movement, 89–90; public order, 87; state of emergency, 90; tensions, disturbances, and disasters, 77–80, 105, 114–15, 127. *See also* Legal issues
Conflict, armed: legal framework, 80–85, 96–97, 99, 102–03, 104, 111; occupations, 117–18; relief for civilian populations, 116–18; role of the United Nations, 120; role of the World Health Organization, 141; safety of relief personnel, 121. *See also* Geneva Conventions
Conflict resolution and management: effective national institutions, 246–48; internal displacement and, 293, 300; nongovernmental organizations, 248–49, 300; postconflict reconstruction, 12; role of local community, 259; strategies for international response, 284–85; strategies for protecting minorities, 245–46; World Bank and, 291
Congo. *See* Democratic Republic of the Congo
Convention against Torture, 106
Convention on the Elimination of All Forms of Radical Discrimination, 86
Convention on the Elimination of Discrimination against Women, 93–94, 95, 96, 104
Convention on the Non-Applicability of Statutory Limitations to War Crimes and Crimes against Humanity, 89
Convention on the Prevention and Punishment of the Crime of Genocide, 246

Convention on the Rights of the Child (CRC; United Nations), 79, 100, 109, 112, 138–39, 275
Convention on the Safety of United Nations and Associated Personnel, 120–21
Coordination Bureau for International Humanitarian Aid, 262
Coordinators and coordination: development and relief agencies, 295; emergency coordination, 172–74; in-field coordination, 149–51, 162; nongovernmental organizations, 192–93, 204–05, 212, 271; regional organizations, 222, 227–28; strengthening of, 174–75; United Nations, 222, 271. *See also* United Nations Emergency Relief Coordinator
Council of Churches, 46
Council of Europe, 228, 237, 245
Covenant on Civil and Political Rights (CCPR): Article *4*, 79–80, 104; Article *7*, 95, 106–07; Article *9*, 98; Article *11*, 100; Article *12*, 78, 87, 104; Article *17*, 88; Article *23*, 109; Article *26*, 86; interpretation of, 95, 98–99. *See also* Laws; Legal issues
Covenants on Economic, Social and Cultural Rights (CESCR): Article *2*, 114; Article *6*, 93; Article *7*, 93; Article *11*, 89, 100, 114; Article *12*, 95, 102; Article *13*, 109; responsibilities of, 79, 100. *See also* Law; Legal issues
CPDIA. *See* Permanent Consultation on Internal Displacement in the Americas
CRC. *See* Convention on Rights of the Child
Crimes: detention for, 99–100; displacement, 92, 250; homicide, 82; against humanity, 89; international criminal tribunals, 108–09; internationally recognized, 81; rape, 96, 274; unlawful transfer or confinement, 91
Croatia, 48, 49, 50, 51, 54, 261
Croat-Muslim Federation, 49
CSCE (Conference on Security and Cooperation in Europe). *See* Organization for Security and Cooperation in Europe
Cuba, 29
Cyprus: ethnic issues, 50, 261; internal displacement, 37, 38, 47, 50, 286; Pan-Cyprien Refugee Committee, 56; urban-rural tensions, 51

Dayton Peace Accord, 106, 109, 225, 285, 299
Declaration on the Rights of Persons Belonging to National or Ethnic, Religious, or Linguistic Minorities, 245
Democratic Republic of the Congo (Zaire): assistance to, 27, 129, 160; ethnic issues, 40–41; internal displacement, 40, 42, 152; Organization of African Union conflict resolution, 215
Deng, Francis M., 156
Dependency, 10, 25, 207–08, 259, 295
Detention, 97–100
Development: financial institutions and, 250, 303; funding, 183; human rights and protection needs, 177, 268; integration with relief, 182–84, 289–91; investments, 296; postconflict reconstruction, 298–303; relief in the context of, 10, 12, 16–17; resettlement and rehabilitation, 291, 294–303; strategies in conflict-induced displacement, 291–304; transition from relief to rehabilitation, 151, 167; women in, 300–301. See also Financial institutions
DHA. See United Nations Department of Humanitarian Affairs
Disasters: assistance following, 6, 16; disaster management teams (DMTs), 148–51, 172; displacement following, 16, 17–18, 127; early warning systems, 242; man-made, 16–17; Southern African Development Community, 222
Discrimination, 86, 93–94, 95–96, 136. See also Ethnic issues
Displacement. See Internal displacement
Documentation, 103–04
Doe, Samuel, 20

Early warning system, 240–42, 258
ECHA. See Executive Committee on Humanitarian Affairs
ECMM. See European Community Monitoring Mission
ECOMOG. See Economic Community of West Africa Monitoring Group
Economic and Social Council (ECOSOC). See United Nations Economic and Social Council
Economic Community of West Africa Monitoring Group (ECOMOG), 220–22, 283
Economic Community of West African States (ECOWAS), 47, 220–22, 252

Economic issues: civil wars, 293; "criminalization," 297; displaced populations, 25–26, 60–61, 66, 295; employment opportunity, 93–94, 295; ethnic factors, 22; inequalities, 303; migration due to poverty, 17; postconflict development, 298–99; sanctions, 277; standard of living, 60–61, 66, 67, 100, 114
ECOSOC. See United Nations Economic and Social Council
ECOWAS. See Economic Community of West African States
Education, 111–13. See also Training and education
EEC (European Economic Community). See European Union
Eliasson, Jan, 144
El Salvador: assistance to, 69; civil war, 64; ethnic factors, 22; human rights monitoring, 266; internal displacement, 4, 19–20, 28, 37–38; self-help, 266
Emergency relief coordinator (ERC). See United Nations emergency relief coordinator
Employment. See Economic issues
Environmental issues, 25, 296
ERC (emergency relief coordinator). See United Nations emergency relief coordinator
Eritrea, 19, 20, 37–38
Ethiopia: assistance to, 184, 195, 201; during the cold war, 19; displacement and relocation, 16, 19, 20, 37–38, 40, 41; ethnic issues, 40–41; media coverage, 3. See also Muslims
Ethnic issues: assistance, 261; "ethnic cleansing," 24, 41, 71, 86, 89, 274, 281; increase in conflict, 21–22; indigenous peoples, 91–92, 249–50; internal displacement, 5, 47–56, 58–59, 71, 245, 250; multiethnic programs, 199, 249; numbers of ethnic groups, 21; prevention and protection, 274; reconciliation, 300. See also Discrimination; Kurds; Muslims; individual countries
EU. See European Union
Europe: assistance to internally dislocated, 53–56; denial of asylum to Tamils, 30; ethnic dislocation, 47–56; living conditions, 51–53; minority protection, 245. See also Organization for Security and Cooperation in Europe
European Commission Monitoring Mission, 237

European Community Monitoring Mission (ECMM), 266–67
European Convention, 96, 99
European Council on Refugees and Exiles, 56
European Court on Human Rights, 107, 228
European Economic Community (EEC). *See* European Union
European Human Rights Convention, 107
European Union (EU), 222, 228, 266
Europe, Eastern, 20, 47–48
Europe, Western, 12
Eviction, 89
Executive Committee on Humanitarian Affairs (ECHA), 143

Families, 109–11. *See also* Children; Women and girls
Females. *See* Women and girls
Financial institutions, 250, 299, 302. *See also* individual institutions
Food, 100–03, 108, 136, 137. *See also* World Food Programme
Fourth World Conference on Women, 302
Freedom House, 247
Funding: crises, 175; development, 298; government response to donations, 179; Inter-American Commission on Human Rights, 231; internally displaced, 161; nongovernmental organizations, 188, 208; Organization for Security and Cooperation in Europe, 227; Organization of African Unity, 216, 218, 219–20; for rehabilitation, 167, 183; reintegration programs, 208, 303; United Nations programs, 155, 291, 301

Geneva Conventions (*1949*): application to internal displacement, 84–85; Article *3* (Common), 81–82, 99, 101, 102, 103, 112, 115, 116, 121, 256; Article *4*, 84, 111, 112; Article *7*, 103; Article *14*, 101; Article *16*, 94, 103; Article *18*, 103, 115; Article *19*, 103; Article *23*, 116; Article *24*, 111, 112; Article *26*, 111; Article *54*, 101; Article *55*, 101, 103, 117; Article *56*, 103; Article *59*, 117; Article *61*, 118; Article *69*, 118; Article *70*, 116–17; Article *71*, 121; Article *74*, 111; Article *78*, 91; Article *81*, 118; Article *85*, 121; Article *147*, 91; Fourth Convention, 99, 101, 103, 111, 112, 116, 117, 118; International Committee of the Red Cross, 131, 132; Part II, 84, 111; protection in, 256; Protocol I, 84–85, 91,
94, 99, 101–02, 103, 111, 116, 117, 118, 121; Protocol II, 82–83, 90, 99, 101, 102–03, 105, 108, 111, 112, 115, 121, 256; ratification of, 132–33; status as international law, 91. *See also* Conflict, armed; Laws; Legal issues
Genocide, 89, 277–78. *See also* Rwanda
Georgia: ethnic issues, 261; government assistance plan, 52–53; internal displacement, 48, 50, 51, 55; nongovernmental organizations, 262; resettlement, 55, 154; sense of community, 259; UN mission, 55
Ghana, 29, 40–41, 44
Girls. *See* Women and girls
Governments: community building, 199; deportation and extradition, 107; documentation and registration, 103–04; duties of protection and subsistence needs, 96, 100–01, 207; effects of coordination, 204–05; emergency response capacity, 261; governance, 244–46, 248, 294; humanitarian and development agencies, 179; human rights monitoring, 178, 198; internal displacement, 250, 285; occupations, 117–18; Organization for Security and Cooperation in Europe, 225–26; provision of assistance, 113, 114–15, 167, 195; refusal of access and assistance, 190, 225, 263, 267, 269, 276, 278; refusal to grant asylum, 130; response to advocacy, 270; restrictions of residence and movement, 105; right to accept or refuse assistance, 115–20, 127–28, 133, 277; sovereignty, 7, 233, 235, 251, 275–80; weak, 279–80. *See also* Laws; Legal issues; Recommendations and solutions; individual countries
Grant, James, 159–60
Great Lakes region. *See* Africa
Guatemala: assistance to, 129, 299; civil war, 65; elections, 260; ethnic factors, 22; government role, 67–68, 70; internal displacement, 19–20, 28, 36–37, 65, 105, 261; International Committee of the Red Cross and, 133; legal rights, 68; legal system, 247; nongovernmental organizations, 70, 199; Organization of American States, 228, 229, 251; Permanent Consultation on Internal Displacement in the Americas, 231; self-help, 70, 259; standard of living, 66; training in, 249
Guiding principles. *See* Recommendations and solutions

Haiti, 34, 64, 228, 236–37, 251
Hansen, Peter, 144
Health issues. *See* Public health
Herzegovina. *See* Bosnia and Herzegovina
Holtzman, Steven, 292
Humanitarian assistance: effectiveness, 9–11, 259, 290; funding for, 183; human rights issues, 201, 204; political consequences, 268; protection, 178–79
Humanitarian emergencies, 8, 10
Humanitarian law. *See* Geneva Conventions; Laws; Legal issues
Human rights: abuse as a cause of displacement, 22; advocacy, 196; application of international human rights law, 78–84; armed conflict situations, 80–85; cruel and inhuman treatment, 95, 106–07, 123; derogable, 79–80, 96, 98, 99, 104, 105, 250; enforcement measures, 280–84; guiding principles, 305–16; humanitarian protection, 278; international, 93; liberty and security of person, 98; life, 114; limitations and restrictions, 79–80; movement and residence, 78, 86–90, 92, 104–07, 123, 249–51, 286–87; Organization for Security and Cooperation in Europe, 224; peacekeeping units and, 180; privacy, 89; property and restitution, 108; in protection programs, 206, 265–67; religion, 86; resettlement programs, 289; responsibility for violations, 81; role in conflict, 244–45; subsistence needs, 100–03; training for, 206–07; United Nations human rights system, 151–59, 163–66, 185–86. *See also* Geneva Conventions; Laws; Legal issues; Universal Declaration of Human Rights
Human rights movement, 4
Human Rights Watch: focus of, 189, 190; monitoring by, 262–63, 267; policy on forced relocation, 197; reliance on humanitarian organizations, 204; United Nations and, 200
Hussein, Saddam. *See* Iraq

IASC. *See* United Nations Inter-Agency Standing Committee
ICRC. *See* International Committee of the Red Cross
ICVA. *See* International Council of Voluntary Agencies
IFRC. *See* International Federation of Red Cross and Red Crescent Societies

IGAD. *See* Inter-Governmental Authority on Development
IIDH. *See* Inter-American Institute of Human Rights
ILO. *See* International Labor Organization
IMF. *See* International Monetary Fund
India: assistance to, 62–63, 161; government role, 61; internal displacement, 56, 57, 58, 59; Kashmir dispute, 59, 235
Indigenous peoples, 91–92, 249–50
Indochina, 234–35
Information: early warning system, 240–41; human rights violations, 203–04; internal displacement, 209, 226, 232, 233, 242–44; nongovernmental organization networks, 249; protection concerns, 269; statistics, 31–35, 243–44
Institutional arrangements. *See* Organizations, operational; United Nations; individual organizations
InterAction. *See* American Council for Voluntary International Action
Inter-Agency Standing Committee (IASC). *See* United Nations Inter-Agency Standing Committee
Inter-agency task force on internally displaced persons. *See* United Nations inter-agency task force on internally displaced persons
Inter-American Commission on Human Rights, 69, 90, 108, 229–32, 242. *See also* Organization of American States
Inter-American Convention on Violence against Women, 95
Inter-American Institute of Human Rights (IIDH), 231, 232
Inter-American Human Rights Court, 230
Inter-Governmental Authority on Development (IGAD), 222–23, 279
Internal displacement: access to those displaced, 6, 58, 127–28, 152, 176, 277, assistance, 2–3, 6–7, 45, 72, 113–22, 184–86, 224; causes, 3, 11–12, 18, 19–23, 78, 80, 127–28; cold war and, 19; community issues, 258–60; comparison with refugees, 1, 2, 27, 29–30, 129–30; definitions, 16–19, 31; detention, 97–100; effects, 1–2, 5–6, 23–26, 41–43, 71, 78, 93, 195, 293; forced, 85–92; government role, 71–72, 74; guiding principles, 305–16; identification of, 33–35; international concern, 2–5, 6–7; military interventions, 10–11; needs resulting from, 77, 92–113, 203; numbers of

displaced, 1, 3, 15, 29, 31, 33, 129, 214; resettlement and reintegration, 35–39, 128, 166–68; self-help, 64, 259; statistics, 31–35; as a special category, 26–29; violence toward, 94–97; women, 301. *See also* Civilians; Ethnic issues; Legal issues; Protection; Recommendations and solutions

International Alert, 189, 197, 199

International Committee of the Red Cross (ICRC): assistance to internally displaced, 3, 8, 27, 45–46, 72, 115, 118, 131, 159; Chechnya, 54–55; development of principles for the internally displaced, 75; Lebanon, 63; mandates and capacities, 131–33, 197; neutrality, 269; Permanent Consultation on Internal Displacement in the Americas, 231; protection activities, 10, 164–65, 202, 256–57; responsibilities, 131; training and education, 249; work with the United Nations, 173. *See also* Organizations, operational

International community: assistance to internally displaced, 8–13, 27, 113–22; concerns and aid, 4; conflict management, 246; early warning system, 241; humanitarian relief, 276–77; India, 62–63; internal displacement and, 250; Iraq, 63; Myanmar, 62; protection needs, 110, 200; rights of internally displaced, 109

International Conference on Central American Refugees (CIREFCA, *1989*), 5, 28, 69

International Convention on the Elimination of All Forms of Racial Discrimination, 86

International Convention on the Suppression and Punishment of the Crime of Apartheid, 86

International Council of Voluntary Agencies (ICVA), 193

International Criminal Tribunal (Yugoslavia), 108–09

International Federation of Red Cross and Red Crescent Societies (IFRC), 189, 190, 196, 201

International Human Rights Law Group, 267

International human rights movement. *See* Human rights movement, international

International Islamic Relief Organization, 189

International Labor Organization (ILO) Convention No. *169* concerning

Indigenous and Tribal Peoples in Independent Countries, 91, 106

International Monetary Fund (IMF), 299

International Organization for Migration (IOM): in Angola, 166; assistance to internally displaced, 8, 45, 68, 159; mandate and capabilities, 141–42, 173, 262; mobility of internally displaced, 35; Permanent Consultation on Internal Displacement in the Americas, 231. *See also* Organizations, operational

International Red Cross and Red Crescent Movement, 115, 131, 194, 198

IOM. *See* International Organization for Migration

Iraq: assistance to, 63, 118–19, 140; ethnic issues, 60; government role, 61; internally displaced and refugees, 4–5, 17, 56, 57; lack of access, 34; nongovernmental organizations, 63; safe area for Kurds, 30, 59, 62, 63, 281, 283; Security Council Resolution *688*, 63; standard of living, 61; women, 60. *See also* Kurds; Muslims

Israel, 57, 58–59

Jesuit Refugee Service (JRS), 189, 197

Judiciary, 246, 247

Kashmir, 29, 235

Kenya: ethnic issues, 40–41, 42; human rights monitoring, 178; internal displacement, 40, 178, 261, 268; nongovernmental organizations, 46–47, 200, 209; protection concerns, 269

Kibeho massacre. *See* Rwanda

Kurdistan, 63

Kurds: in Azerbaijan, 297; in Iraq, 17, 20, 30, 57, 59, 60, 278, 281; media coverage, 3–4; in Turkey, 5–6, 20, 48, 51, 225–26, 228

Kuwait, 108

Land mines, 37, 41, 97, 141, 289, 297

LAS. *See* League of Arab States

Latin America: assistance to, 70–71, 135, 167, 184; civil wars during the cold war, 19–20, 65; conflicts in, 20; ethnic issues, 70; government role, 67; internal displacement, 31, 64–66, 70; legal rights, 68; protection, 68, 202; self-help, 69–71, 72. *See also* individual countries

Laws: armed conflict, 80–85; against forced displacement, 85–92; gaps in, 122–25; genocide in, 277–78; refugee law, 85, 257; right to provide assistance,

115; sovereignty, 276; tensions, disturbances, and disasters, 77–80, 105, 114–15; against violence, 96; of war, 84. *See also* Legal issues; individual documents

Laws, humanitarian: arbitrary displacement, 249–50; in armed conflict, 74, 80–81, 84, 90, 96, 99, 104; children's issues, 112; destruction of property and pillage, 108; International Committee of the Red Cross, 256–57; obligation to accept assistance, 277; protection of internally displaced, 93, 96, 104, 105, 129, 256; protection of relief workers, 121–22. *See also* Geneva Conventions

Laws, human rights: applicability of, 74–75, 77–84; arbitrary displacement, 92, 250; in armed conflict, 74–75; children's issues, 112; documentation and registration, 104; movement and residence, 105; obligation to accept assistance, 277; protection of internally displaced, 129; protection of relief workers, 120–21; provision of assistance, 114; restrictions and derogations, 80; right to employment, 93

Lawyers Committee for Human Rights, 218

League of Arab States (LAS), 214, 232–34

Lebanon: assistance to, 63; civil war, 57, 58–59, 63, 292; ethnic issues, 58–59; government role, 61, 262; internal displacement, 29, 56, 57, 59, 60; nongovernmental organizations, 63; standard of living, 60–61

Legal issues: armed conflict, 80–85, 96–97, 99, 101, 102–03, 104, 111, 115; children, 275; documentation, 103–04; insufficient or inadequate legal protection, 122–25; internally displaced, 7–8, 73–74, 75–76; judiciary, 246, 247, 251; limitations and derogations, 79–80; Permanent Consultation on Internal Displacement in the Americas, 231; principles on internally displaced persons, 76, 157; property and housing rights, 24–25, 87–89, 107–09; protection, 255, 257; recommendations, 122–25; refugees, 2; sovereignty, 7, 233, 235, 251, 275–80; state responsibilities, 7; women's rights, 302. *See also* Laws; individual documents

Liberia: assistance to, 45, 136, 144, 172, 283; conflict in, 34, 220–22, 292; coordinators, 150; economy, 297; elections, 260; human rights monitoring,

146; internal displacement, 20, 28, 40, 41–42, 43; lack of access, 137; nongovernmental organizations, 46, 47, 194, 204; protection, 43, 44, 163, 165, 204, 252; rape, 274; United Nations response, 213; women, 165, 272

Lutheran World Federation (LWF), 189, 190, 191

Macedonia, 242, 253, 295

Machel, Graça, 139, 166

Mauritania, 190

Médecins sans Frontières (MSF): *1996* conference for human rights organizations, 205; assistance for internally displaced, 202; human rights considerations, 196; mission areas, 190; MSF/Netherlands, 267; policy of witnessing or "temoignange," 197; watchdog role, 200, 201

Media, 3–4, 242, 247, 270

Mengistu, Haile Mariam, 19. *See also* Ethiopia

Methodist Church, 46

Middle East, 21. *See also* individual countries

Military interventions: in cases of internal displacement, 10–11; effectiveness, 280; peacekeeping units, 45, 119–20, 180, 183–84, 242, 272, 278, 280; safe areas, 282

Monrovia, 220–22, 283

Mozambique: assistance to, 27, 45, 135, 136, 137, 141–42, 166, 167; during the cold war, 5, 19; health issues, 43; internal displacement, 19, 20, 24, 31, 37, 40, 41; land mines, 289; nongovernmental organizations, 193; protection, 44; South African Development Community, 222

MSF. *See* Médècins sans Frontières

Mujahedin, 57–58. *See also* Afghanistan

Muslims: Bosnia, 17, 49, 282; Ethiopia, 17; India, 58, 59; Iraq, 17, 59, 60; Lebanon, 58–59; the Philippines, 58

Myanmar (Burma): assistance to, 62, 147; ethnic issues, 60; government role, 61; internal displacement, 17, 22, 34, 56, 58, 59–60, 152, 161; lack of access, 34. *See also* Muslims

Nagorno-Karabakh: Armenia and, 261; displaced in Azerbaijan, 51–52, 261, 285, 286; fact-finding mission, 224; government assistance, 54; peacekeeping force, 252

National Council of the Displaced in Guatemala (CONDEG), 65
National security, 87
NATO. *See* North Atlantic Treaty Organization
Natural disasters. *See* Disasters
Neutrality. *See* Political issues
NGOs. *See* Nongovernmental organizations
NGOs in Disaster Relief, 194
Nicaragua, 19–20, 37–38, 69
Nigeria, 40, 220
Nongovernmental organizations (NGOs): assistance to internally displaced, 8, 45, 46, 55–56, 69, 72, 189–90, 268; codes of conduct, 194–95, 198, 211; coordination, 192–93, 212; definition of internal displacement, 18, 191; disaster management teams, 148; early warning system, 241–42; funding, 188; human rights issues, 196, 200–01, 203–04, 235–36; information systems, 243, 248, 271; interaction with the United Nations, 47, 187–88, 193, 210; international and local, 208–09, 212; monitoring of, 262–63; neutrality, 269; protection by, 195–207, 210, 271; protection for, 11–12, 211; role and mandates, 187–90, 191–93, 196–97, 202, 207–08, 210–11, 247–48; United Nations and, 200, 211, 212; weaknesses, 188, 191–95; women's issues, 301. *See also* individual countries; individual organizations
North Atlantic Treaty Organization (NATO), 227, 237, 252, 282, 285
Norwegian Refugee Council, 188–89, 243, 248

OAS. *See* Organization of American States
OAU. *See* Organization of African Unity
OCHA. *See* United Nations Office for the Coordination of Humanitarian Affairs
OECD. *See* Organization for Economic Cooperation and Development
Ogata, Sadako, 254
OLS (Operation Lifeline Sudan). *See* Sudan
Open Society Institute, 56, 248, 262–63
Operation Lifeline Sudan (OLS). *See* Sudan
Operation Provide Comfort, 62. *See also* Iraq
Operation Turquoise, 282–83
Organizational arrangements. *See* Organizations, operational

Organization for Economic Cooperation and Development (OECD), 250–51
Organization for Security and Cooperation in Europe (OSCE), 11: Commonwealth of Independent States conference, 242; formation of networks, 249; international intervention, 251; monitoring role, 262, 266–67; peacekeeping capability, 237, 252; protection for minorities, 245; role and mandate, 56, 214, 223–26; strengthening its capacity, 226–27; training programs, 246–47
Organization of African Unity (OAU), 11, 214: awareness meetings and commissions, 216–17; conflict prevention, 215, 251; definition of refugees, 15; early warning system, 242; funding, 216, 218, 219–20; internal displacement policies, 217, 218; noninterference in internal affairs, 214–15; Peace Fund, 216; protection activities, 217
Organization of American States (OAS), 11, 214, 228–29, 236–37, 249, 251. *See also* Inter-American Commission on Human Rights
Organizations, operational: coordination and the emergency relief coordinator, 143–51; principal organizations, 128–42; recommendations for improvement of the international system, 168–86; representative of the secretary-general on internally displaced persons, 156–59; United Nations human rights system, 151–56; weaknesses of the international system, 159–68. *See also* Recommendations and solutions; United Nations; individual organizations
Organizations, regional: in Africa, 214–23; enforcement capabilities, 252; role in conflict prevention, 251; role in conflict resolution, 11, 213–14; role in internal displacement, 236–38; United Nations and, 252. *See also* Recommendations and solutions; individual organizations
OSCE. *See* Organization for Security and Cooperation in Europe
Oslo Declaration and Plan of Action, 29, 191, 204, 207
OXFAM, 189, 190, 207

Pakistan, 30, 301
Palestinians, 57, 233

PAR. *See* Proyecto de Apoyo a la Repoblación (Peru)

Paraguay, 228, 356–37, 251

PARINAC (partnership in action process). *See* United Nations High Commissioner for Refugees

Peace and reconstruction, 5

Peacekeeping, 215. *See also* United Nations

Permanent Consultation on Internal Displacement in the Americas (CPDIA), 18, 69, 191, 231–32, 244

Persian Gulf War. *See* Iraq

Peru: assistance to, 68, 129, 147; civil war, 65; government role, 67; internal displacement, 29, 34, 36, 65, 66–67, 261; legal rights, 68; nongovernmental organizations, 67, 69–70, 191, 199; resettlement, 286; self-help, 69–70, 259; Shining Path, 36, 65, 66–67; standard of living, 67

Philippines, 56, 58, 62

Political issues: assistance, 194–95; combating violence, 280–81; conflict resolution, 284; depoliticizing aid, 195; ethnic and minority issues, 246; humanitarian aid, 268; human rights advocacy, 196; internal displacement, 263, 285; neutrality, 196–97, 269; postconflict development, 298–99; role of nongovernmental organizations, 188, 193–95; role of the United Nations, 278–79

Prevention, 30, 215, 237, 240–54

PRODERE. *See* United Nations Development Program for Displaced Persons, Refugees, and Returnees in Central America

Property rights. *See* Legal issues

Protection: children, 44, 109–10, 138–39, 272–75; community-based, 205–06, 258–60; concepts and forms of, 10, 142, 198–202, 254–58; development of legal and organizational framework, 75–76, 145–46, 176–77; following disasters, 16–17; against forced displacement, 85–92; guiding principles, 307–15; human rights and, 206; integrated with assistance, 254–72; internally displaced, 28, 92–113, 155, 162–66, 178–80, 257, 263, 280; international mechanisms, 263–64; national mechanisms, 260–63; nongovernmental organizations, 195–207; through presence, 264–65; property, 107–09; relief workers and organizations, 120–22, 137, 267, 271; in

the return process, 287–89; right to, 278; against violence, 94; women, 44, 139, 165, 198, 202, 203, 260; United Nations role, 162–66. *See also* Security

Proyecto de Apoyo a la Repoblación (PAR, Peru), 67

Psychosocial issues, 202

Public health, 43, 87, 102–03, 105, 140

Public order, 87, 105

Quadripartite Agreement on Voluntary Return of Refugees and Displaced Persons to Abkhazia, 55

Quick-impact projects (QIPs), 167, 291, 295, 301

Rape. *See* Crimes

Recommendations and solutions: assistance to internally displaced, 9, 11, 12–13, 72, 127, 236–38; Association of Southeast Asian Nations, 235; children, 274–75; conflict resolution, 284–85; enforcement measures, 280–84; guiding principles, 197, 257–58, 280, 286–87, 305–16; financial institutions, 302–03; funding, 303; governments, 244–46; in-country coordination, 148–49, 150–51, 174–81; internal displacement, 239–40; international development efforts, 12; League of Arab States, 233, 234; legal framework, 85, 122–25; monitoring and oversight, 221; nongovernmental organizations, 192, 195, 202–07, 208–12, 271; Organization for Security and Cooperation in Europe, 226–27; Organization of African Unity, 218–19; Organization of American States, 229, 230; Permanent Consultation on Internal Displacement in the Americas, 232; preventive strategies, 240–54; protection, 202–07, 255, 257–58, 259–75, 287–89; regional organizations, 236–38; resettlement and rehabilitation, 293–304; safe areas, 124, 281–84; sovereignty as responsibility, 275–80; United Nations, 139, 154–56, 157–59, 181–82, 270–72, 274–75, 278–80, 283, 285, 287, 288; weaknesses in the international relief system, 159–86; women, 124, 203, 272–75. *See also* Training

Refugee Convention (*1951*): Article *33*, 107; application to internally displaced, 75; "cessation clause," 36, 37–38; definition of refugees, 16; principle of *non-refoulement*, 106

Refugee Policy Group, 195, 231

Refugees: Afghans, 57; assistance for, 159–60; children's issues, 110, 112; comparison with internally displaced, 1, 2, 27, 29–30, 129–30; definition of, 2, 16, 85; detention, 99; in Latin America, 69; numbers of, 3, 214; Palestinian, 57; protection, 129, 255; restriction and prevention, 30; repatriation, 35–36, 41, 106; safe areas and, 283. *See also* Laws; United Nations High Commissioner for Refugees

Regional Seminar on Internal Displacement of Populations in Arab States, Human Rights and Humanitarian Law, 233

Resettlement and reintegration, 285–87, 296–97, 315–16. *See also* Development

Restitution of Land Rights Act of *1994* (South Africa), 38–39

Robinson, Mary, 155

Rural areas: effects of displacement, 24–25, 41, 51–52; internal displacement into, 59; reintegration to, 300; rural-to-urban migration, 35

Russian Federation, 34, 48, 50, 54. *See also* Chechnya

Rwanda: Arusha Accords (*1993*), 215; assistance to, 5, 119–20, 132, 140, 161, 168, 172, 253, 254; coordination in, 150, 162; early warning, 241, 242; economy, 297; genocide, 278; human rights monitoring, 146, 152, 153–54, 163, 266; internal displacement in, 22, 25, 27, 29, 40, 152–53; International Committee of the Red Cross and, 132; Kibeho massacre, 44, 163, 177–78, 180, 266; nongovernmental organizations, 192, 193; political issues, 175, 285; property disputes, 155; protection, 44, 162–63, 165, 179; quick-action trust funds, 183; rape, 274; resettlement, 41, 287, 288; safe areas, 281, 282–83; United Nations response, 213, 252, 270, 282, 288; use of aid, 195

SAARC. *See* South Asian Association for Regional Cooperation

SADC. *See* Southern African Development Community

Safe areas: Bosnia, 54, 175, 268, 281, 282, 283; demilitarization, 281, 283; human rights staff, 266; Iraq, 30, 59, 62, 63, 281, 283; right to refuge in, 105; Yugoslavia, 156, 200, 259

Safety. *See* Protection; Security

Salim, Salim Ahmed, 214–15, 236

Samper, Ernesto, 67

Sanctions, 277, 279

SARRED. *See* Conference on the Plight of Refugees, Returnees, and Displaced Persons in Southern Africa

Save the Children Fund-US, 193

Security, 10, 90–91, 104–05. *See also* Protection

Security Council. *See* United Nations

Security Council Resolution *688* (*1991*), 63

Separatism, 23

Serbs. *See* Bosnia-Herzegovina

Shining Path. *See* Peru

Sierra Leone: assistance to, 45, 46, 129, 136, 144; child malnutrition, 43; internal displacement, 34, 35, 40, 162; as a "neglected" emergency, 147; nongovernmental organizations, 46, 200

Slavonia, 49

SLORC. *See* State Law and Order Restoration Council (Burma)

Slovenia, 49

Solutions. *See* Recommendations and solutions

Somalia: assistance to, 45–46, 119–20, 136, 137, 173, 195, 268; community-based strategies, 258–59; coordinators, 149; delivery of relief, 5; ethnic factors, 22; internal displacement, 19, 20; International Committee of the Red Cross, 131; League of Arab States, 233; military intervention, 281; nongovernmental organizations, 187; public health, 140; United Nations response, 213, 254

Sommaruga, Cornelio, 280

South Africa: apartheid, 22, 37–39, 86; economic issues, 42–43; ethnic issues, 40–41; internal displacement, 31, 37–38, 40–47; living conditions, 43; property claims, 38–39; protection problems, 43–44; refugee repatriation, 41

South African Land Act of *1913*, 38

South Asian Association for Regional Cooperation (SAARC), 235

Southern African Development Community (SADC), 222

Soviet Union, 47–48, 57, 59, 209, 248

Sri Lanka: assistance to, 64; conflict in, 20, 59, 292; coordinators, 149; ethnic issues, 60; government role, 61–62, 261–62; internal displacement, 28, 30, 56, 57, 58, 59; lack of access, 34; nongovernmental organizations, 64; protection, 265; resettlement, 286; women, 60

Speth, James Gustave, 216
Standard of living. *See* Economic issues
Starvation. *See* Civilians
State Law and Order Restoration Council
    (SLORC, Burma), 22
States. *See* Governments
Statistics. *See* Information
Subsistence. *See* Human rights
Sudan: assistance to, 46, 129, 130–31, 136,
    147, 152, 160, 195, 284; children, 139;
    conflict in, 20, 292; ethnic issues, 42;
    famine in *1980*s, 16; Inter-Governmental
    Authority on Development, 223;
    internal displacement, 5, 28, 29, 40, 41,
    43, 152, 160; lack of access, 34, 137, 152;
    media coverage, 3; Operation Lifeline
    Sudan, 4, 46, 138, 200, 279; political
    issues, 175; protection, 44; refugees,
    160; resettlement, 286; United Nations
    in, 4, 147, 160–61, 279
Superpowers. *See* Cold war; individual
    countries
Syria, 58

Tajikistan: assistance to, 129, 140, 166,
    172–73, 182; civil war, 59; ethnic factors,
    22; government role, 61; human rights
    monitoring, 153, 163, 178; internal
    displacement, 28, 56, 57, 61; judicial
    system, 247; Organization for Security
    and Cooperation in Europe, 225, 226,
    237; protection for returnees, 288;
    rehabilitation and development, 290;
    United Nations in, 172–73
Taylor, Charles, 220–21
Telecommunications. *See* Media
Television. *See* Media
Tibet, 29
Training and education: children, 111–13,
    297; conflict resolution, 249; internal
    displacement, 226, 249, 271–72, 290,
    295; military intervention units, 283;
    national institutions, 246; protection,
    201, 206–07, 271–72; rights of children,
    275; United Nations peacekeeping units,
    280; women, 300. *See also* Education;
    Recommendations and solutions
Tribunals, war crime, 108–09, 132, 274
Turkey: assistance to, 53, 55, 161, 225;
    internal displacement, 5–6, 29, 48, 51,
    225; International Committee of the
    Red Cross and, 133; Iraqi Kurds, 30,
    62, 283; lack of access, 34; Organization
    for Security and Cooperation in Europe,
    225–26; rural-to-urban migration, 35;
    United Nations in, 147, 161

Uganda, 40, 160, 292
UNAMIR. *See* United Nations Assistance
    Mission for Rwanda
UNDP. *See* United Nations Development
    Programme
UNEP. *See* United Nations Environmental
    Programme
UNHCR. *See* United Nations High
    Commissioner for Refugees
UNICEF. *See* United Nations Children's
    Fund
UNIFEM. *See* United Nations
    Development Fund for Women
United Nations: assistance for internally
    displaced, 47, 68, 69, 114–15, 126–27,
    171–72, 277; definition of internal
    displacement, 17–18; development of
    framework for protection of displaced,
    76; estimates of internal displacement,
    34; ethnic and minority issues, 245–46;
    freedom of movement, 88; funding, 155,
    161; human rights system, 151–56;
    International Committee of the Red
    Cross and, 132; lack of response, 213;
    observer mission, 221; peacekeeping
    units, 45, 119–20, 180, 183–84, 242, 272,
    278, 280; rapid deployment force, 253–
    54; regional organizations and, 237–38;
    responsibilities and role, 131, 253; right
    of repatriation, 106; Security Council
    actions, 118–20; Special Rapporteur on
    Torture, 95; Special Rapporteur on
    Violence against Women, 136. *See also*
    Recommendations and solutions;
    individual agencies; individual countries
United Nations Assistance Mission for
    Rwanda, 282, 288
United Nations Centre for Human Rights,
    153, 178, 181, 266
United Nations Charter: Articles 55 and
    56, 78–79, 114; enforcement actions,
    121; human rights in, 93; international
    provision of assistance, 113, 118–20, 236
United Nations Children's Fund
    (UNICEF): assistance for internally
    displaced, 8, 45, 46, 159, 160, 171, 173,
    274; gender perspectives, 165–66;
    Permanent Consultation on Internal
    Displacement in the Americas, 231;
    mandate and capacities, 137–39, 171,
    174; women, 301. *See also*
    Organizations, operational
United Nations Commission on Human
    Rights, 151–56, 200
United Nations Declaration on the Rights
    of Indigenous Peoples, 92

United Nations Department of Humanitarian Affairs (DHA), 143, 144–45, 146–48, 240, 242

United Nations Development Fund for Women (UNIFEM), 165–66, 296, 301

United Nations Development Program for Displaced Persons, Refugees, and Returnees in Central America (PRODERE), 28, 184, 269–70, 291

United Nations Development Programme (UNDP): assistance for internally displaced, 8, 28, 47, 167; emergency fund, 168; Kenya, 200, 288; mandate and capacities, 133–35; neutrality, 269; nongovernmental organizations and, 208; Permanent Consultation on Internal Displacement in the Americas, 231; Peru, 68; rehabilitation fund, 291. *See also* Organizations, operational

United Nations Economic and Social Commission for Asia and the Pacific, 238

United Nations Economic and Social Council (ECOSOC), 152

United Nations emergency relief coordinator (ERC): assistance for internally displaced, 8, 127; development of early warning system, 240–41; information system, 242–43; role of, 127, 133–34, 137, 143–51, 158, 173

United Nations Environmental Programme (UNEP), 296

United Nations High Commissioner for Human Rights, 153–56, 207, 243

United Nations High Commissioner for Refugees (UNHCR): assistance for internally displaced, 2, 8, 46, 55, 129, 130, 159, 160, 170–71, 173, 256; assistance for refugees, 2, 129–30, 159–60, 255; Central America, 69; Centre for Documentation on Refugees, 243; children's issues, 110, 112–13; Declaration on Violence against Women, 95–96; definition of internal displacement, 18; establishment and development, 2, 45; guidelines, 35–36, 85, 198; human rights, 151; information system, 243; mandates and capacities, 128–31, 165, 165, 174, 208, 262; manual on internally displaced persons, 75; neutrality, 269; partnership in action process (PARINAC), 205, 211; protection activities, 10, 29–30, 200, 202, 211, 256, 260, 264, 288; quick-impact projects, 167, 291, 295, 301; training and education, 207, 249; United

Nations Children's Fund and, 138, 139; women's issues, 94, 301. *See also* Organizations, operational

United Nations Inter-Agency Standing Committee (IASC): humanitarian coordinator, 149–50; internally displaced persons, 144, 146, 148, 157, 163, 174; nongovernmental organizations, 211; protection activities, 145, 163, 268; responsibilities and role, 127, 174, 175–76, 177

United Nations inter-agency task force on internally displaced persons, 146–48, 161–62

United Nations Observer Mission in Georgia (UNOMIG), 55

United Nations Office for the Coordination of Humanitarian Affairs (OCHA), 143

United Nations Protection Force (UNPROFOR, former Yugoslavia), 282

United Nations Relief and Works Agency for Palestine Refugees in the Near East (UNRWA), 57

United Nations secretary-general, 9, 16, 156–59, 181–82

United Nations Sub-Commission on Prevention of Discrimination and Protection of Minorities, 88

United States, 62, 215

United States Agency for International Development (USAID), 68

United States Committee for Refugees (USCR): causes of internal displacement, 20–21; end of internal displacement, 37–38; monitoring by, 262–63; overview of regional displacement, 15; statistics on internally displaced, 31, 37, 39, 58; Turkey, 48

Universal Declaration of Human Rights: Article *9*, 98; Article *13*, 78, 87, 104; Article *16*, 109; Article *17*, 108; Article *25*, 95, 102; interpretation of state obligations, 79. *See also* Human rights; Laws; Legal issues

UNOMIG. *See* United Nations Observer Mission

UNPROFOR. *See* United Nations Protection Force

UNRWA. *See* United Nations Relief and Works Agency for Palestine Refugees in the Near East

Urban areas: effects of displacement, 25, 28, 41–42, 43, 51–52; internal displacement into, 59, 66, 71; reconstruction, 300; rural-to-urban migration, 35, 268, 293

USAID. *See* United States Agency for
International Development
USCR. *See* United States Committee for
Refugees

Vietnam, 29, 235
Violence, 94–97, 259, 274, 294–95. *See
also* Crime; Land mines; Protection

War. *See* Conflict; Laws
Warlordism, 6, 58, 268
WCC. *See* World Council of Churches
Weapons Convention, 97
West European Union (WEU), 227, 237,
252
WFP. *See* World Food Programme
WHO. *See* World Health Organization
Women and girls: in Africa, 216–17;
"Cairo Declaration on the Protection of
Refugees and Displaced Persons in the
Arab World," 233; discrimination
against, 136; education opportunities,
112–13; effects of displacement, 26, 42;
employment opportunities, 93–94;
gender-specific violence, 95–96;
internally displaced, 51, 60, 65–66, 165–
66; protection, 44, 139, 165, 198, 202,
203, 260, 272–75; return and
reintegration, 300–303
Women's Commission on Refugee Women
and Children, 273
Women's Convention, 96
World Bank: Dayton Accords, 299;
displacement, 250–51; mine clearance
programs, 289; in Pakistan, 301;
postconflict reconstruction, 168, 291,
292–93, 294, 302–03
World Conference on Human Rights, 109
World Council of Churches (WCC), 189,
190, 197, 199, 231

World Court, 79
World Food Programme (WFP): assistance
for internally displaced, 8, 46, 161, 163,
173, 200; mandate and capacities, 135–
37, 164, 174; Permanent Consultation on
Internal Displacement in the Americas,
23; United Nations and, 136. *See also*
Organizations, operational
World Health Organization (WHO):
assistance for internally displaced, 8,
159; mandate and capacities, 139–41;
Myanmar, 176; Sudan, 160. *See also*
Organizations, operational
World Summit on Children, 110
World Vision, 189, 199
World Wide Fund for Nature
International, 189

YMCA. *See* Young Men's Christian
Association
Young Men's Christian Association
(YMCA), 46
Yugoslavia: assistance to, 129, 130, 136,
140, 165, 171, 172; conflicts in, 20;
elections, 260; human rights monitoring,
146, 152, 178, 265, 266–67; internal
displacement in, 47–49, 254, 285;
International Committee of the Red
Cross and, 132; Organization for
Security and Cooperation in Europe,
225, 237; political issues, 175; protection
in, 162, 202; resettlement, 106, 286; safe
areas, 156, 200, 259; United Nations
response, 266; UNPROFOR, 282

Zaire. *See* Democratic Republic of the
Congo
Zimbabwe, 222

ALSO AVAILABLE IN LAUREL-LEAF BOOKS:

CANYONS, *Gary Paulsen*
THE CROSSING, *Gary Paulsen*
THE ISLAND, *Gary Paulsen*
NIGHTJOHN, *Gary Paulsen*
THE CAR, *Gary Paulsen*
THE NIGHT THE WHITE DEER DIED, *Gary Paulsen*
SNOWBOUND, *Harry Mazer*
SOMEONE'S MOTHER IS MISSING, *Harry Mazer*
WHO IS EDDIE LEONARD?, *Harry Mazer*
SHADOW OF A HERO, *Peter Dickinson*

Gary Paulsen

with illustrations by
Ruth Wright Paulsen

LAUREL-LEAF BOOKS

FATHER WATER, MOTHER WOODS

Essays on
Fishing and Hunting
in the North Woods

Published by
Bantam Doubleday Dell Books for Young Readers
a division of
Bantam Doubleday Dell Publishing Group, Inc.
1540 Broadway
New York, New York 10036

ISBN: 0-440-21984-1

RL: 7.4

Reprinted by arrangement with Delacorte Press

Printed in the United States of America

April 1996

10 9 8 7 6 5 4 3 2 1

OPM

This book is dedicated to the memory of Nick Allemenos,
a casualty of our times.

Contents

Foreword   xi

Fishing

Down by the Power Dam   3

Working the Ditches   20

First Strike   28

Fishing for Bulls   37

Sucker Hunting   42

The Ninth Street Bridge   46

Lazy Fishing   53

Walleye Fishing   61

Northerns in the Lily Pads   75

Bobber Fishing   80

Fishing Madness   84

Fishhouse Dreams   90

Camping

Running the River   97

Hunting

Fool Hens   117
First Shot   135
Bow Hunting   145
Duck Hunting   168

In the thirty to forty thousand letters a year that come asking about *Hatchet* there are many diversities—questions about Brian, how his life is getting on, how he likes high school, is he old enough now to get married, have children; some readers have even done videos depicting different aspects of Brian's life, and more than once media has asked where he lives so he could be interviewed for magazines or papers.

But there is one thread that permeates nearly all the letters.

Almost without exception there is an overwhelming desire to know how it all started, where *Hatchet* began.

It is a simple question, but like so many simple questions it has a complex answer. The knowledge that went into writing *Hatchet* came from my life, and the forces that shaped and guided that life started not in the woods but in the throes of alcoholism.

I was one of the wasted ones.

The ones who turned away.

It was before foster homes or attempts to understand and help children from "problem" families; before machinery existed to catch young people who fell through the cracks, dropped by the wayside, were lost in the mist, and all those other cliches that are applied to familial casualties—the young walking wounded of the society. I was one of them, one of the emotionally injured, who awakened crying in the night, the boys who saw with wide eyes and could say nothing.

In those days, there were no programs to help, no government agencies, but the problems were still there; the abuse and alcohol and emotional strain and pain—all existed then and before then, except that when a young person had trouble, there wasn't any way to fix it. The young would either have to stand and take it, which many did, to great and lasting harm, or they could cut and run.

I ran to the woods and rivers of northern Minnesota.

It was, I suppose, a kind of self-fostering—perhaps a subconscious seeking of help from nature—although we did not think of it in those terms. It was simpler. In the normal run of things our lives hurt. When we were in the woods or fishing on the rivers and lakes our lives didn't hurt. We did what didn't hurt, and as it didn't hurt more and more, we spent more and more time in the woods and on the rivers—a natural flow of survival.

It also, in a very direct way, led to the novel *Hatchet* for it was there, on the soft winding rivers and quiet blue lakes, in the quick splash of fall color, the hiss of line going off a reel, the soft crack of an old .22 rifle sighted on grouse (fool hen), the shaking hands that aimed at first deer with a straight bow and homemade arrows—it was there that *Hatchet* was born.

Fishing

Down by the
Power Dam

Every year it is necessary for fishing to start. Even though it has gone on year-round it must have a beginning each year, and fishing always started in the spring.

In the small northern town in Minnesota where we were raised it is possible that everything started in the spring, but fishing was the most important thing, and it became vital to watch for the signs that it would begin.

There were two primary indications.

One was the car on the ice.

Pollution was not then considered nor discussed, and each year the town would put an old car on the frozen ice of the river and tie wires from the car to a clock on a tree on the bank. The idea was that when the ice started to go out the car would fall through the ice, trip the clock, and there would be an exact record of when this event occurred.

Much was made of this whole business. It was not just a way to dispose of old cars—although over the years the bottom of the river became littered with them, and God only knows how many fishing lures were lost by people trying to fish around the cars and catching their hooks on door handles or bumpers. More importantly, the old car on the ice became a contest that occupied the whole town.

Everybody guessed at the exact moment when the ice would progress enough into the "rotten" stage (also known as "honeycomb ice," which I would come to know intimately and with horror later, running dog teams on small lakes and the Bering Sea) and allow the car to drop to the bottom.

It started that simply. At the courthouse or the library there was a large bulletin board, and for a dollar you could sign the board and write down your guess to win the car-through-the-ice raffle. Of course, you never met anyone who had won, but only those who knew somebody who had won, and therein, in the winning, the simplicity was lost.

The raffle dominated the town. Merchants competed with each other to put up prizes for the winner so that along with a sizable cash award there were dozens, hundreds of other prizes, and all of them had to do with summer and most of them had to do with fishing.

Rods, reels, life jackets, lures, anchors, boats, picnic baskets, motors—it was said that a person could win the raffle and be set for life as far as fishing or summer was concerned, and as the time approached people would find reasons to walk or drive along the river to see the old car.

"Oh, I had to run down to the elevator and check on grain prices," they would say. "The car has one wheel through but she's still hanging there."

"My aunt's been feeling poor," they would say, about an aunt they hadn't spoken to in twelve years, "and I thought I should stop by and check on her. The car has both rear wheels down now. She's just hanging there, teetering . . ."

"Your aunt?"

"No, the car, you ninny—the car on the ice."

And as the time grew still closer there were those who would come and sit with bottles in paper sacks and fur caps and boogers hanging out their noses and drink and spit and scratch and wait and sometimes pray; just sit there and wait for the car to fall and make their fortunes.

Naturally it never happened when anybody thought it would happen, but it always signaled the end, the final end of winter.

And the beginning of spring. Also, when the ice became that rotten it began the signal to the fish that spawning was close.

The second indication was the light.

All winter the light had been low, flat, cold. In midwinter it became light in the morning at nine or so and began to get dark at three-thirty or four in the afternoon on a cloudy day, and most of the time it seemed to be dark and cold.

But as spring came and the ice became rotten on the river the light moved, was a thing alive. The sun came back north, like an old friend that seemed to have been gone forever, and it changed everything, changed the way things looked. There was still snow, still cold at night, but during the day it was brighter, clearer; everything seemed bathed in soft gold.

People changed as well. During the winter, talk —what talk there was—was always short and to the point and almost always seemed to be on weather-related problems: how difficult it was to start a car in the cold, who was sick with a cold, who was getting sick, who had been sick and was getting well only to get sick again, how it was necessary to drain the car radiators at night (this was before antifreeze) and refill them with warm water when it was time to start them the next day and how they almost never started and wasn't it a shame that the car companies, the Car Companies with all their money, couldn't design a car to start in the winter?

The light changed all that, made the winter end, though there was still more cold weather, still more mornings when nostril hairs stuck to the insides of your nose and the combed ducktails froze on the way to school, more days when it was possible to play the joke where somebody talks somebody else—and where do they keep coming from, the ones who can be talked into these things?—into pushing their tongue out on a frozen propane tank where it would stick and leave a piece of tongue-skin.

The light changed all things.

It was the same sun, and it seemed to come up at the same time, but it rose higher and made gold, new gold that altered everything. Jacobsen's Bakery, where we would get free fresh hot rolls sometimes in the morning to carry when we delivered papers—two rolls each, one in the mouth and one still hot in the pocket of the jacket for later—the bakery was transformed. It had been an old brick building with a loading ramp on the back for the truck to get the fresh bread, and now, in the new gold light it became a bright castle of fresh-bread smells and beauty rising out of the alley next to the Montgomery Ward (always, always called the Monkey Wards) store.

The trees near the library, still without leaves, still with scrabbly arms that reached into the sky, did not seem ominous now but reaching. And the library seemed to shine with warmth and beckoned in the new light, and it became impossible to believe in winter any longer, only in the newness of spring.

And fishing.

For a moment, a day, a week—for a time that felt forever, everything hung, balanced on the edge.

The car . . . didn't . . . *quite* . . . fall through the ice, the light promised but spring did not seem to come, the trees tried but didn't quite bud.

Just for a moment in the year. Just for a flick of time, everything hung and we would daily go to where the first signals would be, the first true movement of spring.

Down to the dam.

The river wound through town without any purpose, a lazy snake. It seemed to barely move as it crawled beneath the Ninth Street bridge, an eighth of a mile wide, past the swimming beach, and under the First Street bridge approaching the dam.

Here it changed. At the south end of town, years before, they had put a dam straight across the whole river. It was made with two floodgates that could be lowered or raised with large screw-wheels, and at the side, over a wide spillway, they had erected a power plant.

The backed-up river fought to get through the spillway and in so doing turned two large, whining turbines that furnished electricity to the town, and none of this mattered to us when the light changed and the car came near to falling through the ice.

At the lower end of the building housing the turbines the water came out in a spillway. With the whine of the turbines mixing into the thundering roar of the water pounding out of the spillway it was difficult to hear anything but the dam, the power of it.

But when the sun rose high enough to bring the soft light into the recesses of the spillway, or perhaps it was because there was a smell to the rotting of the ice on the river or the way the sun hit the ice—for whatever reason, the fish began to dance.

Old rhythms, old, very old music drove them. For all the time there is, the fish have run in the spring, and they have memory built into their genes, of being born upstream, always upstream, and their parents and their grandparents and their great-grandparents—all have the same memory coded into them.

When the light was just so and the smell was just so, they must run, they must dance, they must get back upstream to lay eggs and fertilize them, and it does not matter that man has put the dam there to stop them, does not matter that there is the whirling death of the turbine there to shred and destroy them.

It was a thing to see, this dance, this run—a thing almost not to be believed. Carp, sheepshead, suckers, walleyes, and northern pike—all made the run, or tried to. Not at once. There is timing that has been worked out over the ages so that first the walleyes and northerns, then the carp and suckers, each in its turn tried, separated only by days, but separate.

And they could not make it.

None of them could get through the turbines. Even if they could in some way swim against the horrendous speed of the water being driven out of the spillway, the blades of the turbine would destroy them, and above that there was a mesh screen that would stop them.

They were completely doomed to failure, and yet each spring they tried to make the run and the dance and the water became alive with them. The spillway was perhaps thirty feet across and six or seven feet deep and when the run was on, the water was filled with fish rolling over one another, seething and fighting to get up to the turbines; but even that was difficult. Not just because of the speed of the water or the power of the force kicked out by the turbines, but because of the boys who had come to fish the run.

It was the first open-water fishing of the year and it was very important—as perhaps all fishing is very important.

There was great skill involved. Just getting to the water was a problem. Now and then a child fell into the spillway and was sucked downstream to drown, and be fished out miles later, and to keep that from happening, the town had put fencing around the dam and spillway. The fencing was elaborate. Chain link and steel pipes ten feet tall and angling out at the top to keep anyone from getting over, with barbwire at the very top to further discourage the boys, and none of it worked. It is possible that it slowed us, but only momentarily, and then we were over to hang on the outside of the fence, much more exposed to danger now than before because it was necessary to balance on a narrow ledge of concrete while clutching the fence with one hand and fishing with the other.

So many of us did this, climbed the fence and hung on the wires to fish, that sometimes it seemed a virtual net of lines went down into the water and it was a wonder any of the fish could get through.

It was not fishing in the pure sense of the word so much as snagging. While running, the fish don't eat—or nearly don't. Northerns will hit a lure now and then, but the others ignore bait and so it was necessary to snag them, which might seem crude, but there was an art to it.

Everything was done by feel, the feel of the line, the feel of the hook. The snag was a large triple-hook with a heavy sinker wired to the bottom of it with stovepipe wire, hung on the end of a steel leader and thirty-pound test line. All of this had to be done by hand because only one hand was available and it was impossible to use a rod and reel with one hand.

The hook had to be swung in a large arc upstream to where the water pounded out of the spillway, a looping arc just above the water, back and forth and back and forth, all with the movement of the arm and body while hanging onto the chain-link fence, out over the roaring water with the fingers clawed into the wire of the fence, always further and further until the hook and sinker drop just exactly, almost delicately, at the precise point the water exits the turbine.

It was here, fighting to get into the shredding turbines, that the mass of fish congregated, pushing and driving, rolling belly-over-back so thick there seemed to be no water between them.

Here the hook drops.

Just perfectly *here*.

Too deep and it falls below the seething fish into the rocky bottom of the spillway and is swept back beneath them; too shallow and it slides over their backs.

Perfect.

Once in ten, once in twenty tries it can be done right. Lean out, and out, so far as to nearly fall, then swing, again, again, and then finally, at last, the perfect toss.

The hook drops into the roiling mass of fish and water and begins moving back through them.

And it is here that practice, wisdom, patience, knowledge pay off. If the hook is jerked too soon, it won't be in the right place, will skid off the side or back of a fish and come up with nothing but silver scales stuck to it.

All by feel. The hook moves back through the fish and where it is, what the hook is doing, must be felt.

The line is wrapped around the hand, sometimes with a cheap cloth glove to keep it from cutting and the fingers cut off the glove so the line can be felt. The line leaves the hand out over the back of the index finger, lies across the finger so the movement of the hook can be sensed.

There are differences so subtle they cannot be told, cannot be taught—tiny bits of knowledge, of feeling, as fine and pure as those of any neurosurgeon.

The hook moves, bumping off fish, rolling down their sides, scraping; and all of it comes up through the line across the finger.

Until the hook nudges, ever so gently, into the nose of a fish, directly into the center of the nose. It hesitates slightly, seems to bounce, sends a live signal up through the line across the finger, and exactly then the hook must be jerked upward, with a sharp short motion, to set the hook into the lower jaw of the fish.

If one in twenty tries brings the hook into the right place, it is another one in twenty that the hook hits the nose right, lines up correctly, and angles the right way to allow the hook to set in the bony plate of the lower jaw.

The effect is electric.

The fish runs, cuts across the current so the power of the spillway is added to the power of the fish. If it is a large sheepshead or walleye, it is bad enough—the sudden lunge all comes into the hand wrapped in line. But if a northern pike is snagged, and set—twenty or more pounds—it can be nearly fatal. Not only is the line around the hand the only connection, the other hand is the only bond with the fence, and if the fish cuts out across the current, catches it right, swings back downstream, it pulls sideways at the hand so hard it is almost impossible to hang on and boys caught by surprise have been snatched from the wire and into the spillway to drown. But if it all works right, if all is perfect, there is the fish. Eight, ten, twenty pounds of northern or walleye or sheepshead or carp on the bank, swung out and wide with the free hand to land on the bank to be unhooked. And then the line is thrown back out, swinging, further and further.

Every bit of it completely illegal. It is the worst time to take fish, when they spawn, and once and sometimes twice a day the game warden comes by with a knife and cuts the lines and lets the hooks fall into the water and tells us if he catches us there again he will arrest us, but we know he is only saying that to scare us and when he is gone second hooks come out, or third or fifth—however many it takes.

There are too many things against the fish for them to win.

If they were just to eat, the fish, if they were just for food for the table for the boys, it might be all right to take them with snag hooks when they run, but it is not.

There is the whole winter against them, a whole winter of cold and dark, and so the fish, the running of them into the power plant, comes to mean more than just food.

It means the end of winter, the beginning of spring. The whole town talks of it.

"Are the fish running yet?" they ask. "Are they moving at the dam?"

And everybody wants to taste it, taste the spring with fresh fried fish dipped in batter and eaten with the last of the potatoes from the year before, taken up from the basement where they've been stored, and fried all crisp in butter with salt and pepper; or to strip the eggs from the fish into a frying pan with butter and fry them until they look like scrambled eggs.

The town lusts for the fish, and the boys who work the snag hooks are from poor families. There is no extra money, often no money at all, and so the fish became a part of how the boys live.

As soon as a fish was landed, a large one, the boy would run the two blocks from the dam to the center of uptown and hit the bars.

The Joliette Lounge, the Lumberjack Corner, the Woodsman Cafe and Beer Hall. Carp and suckers were not worth as much as the other fish and could be used only for smoking, which was good enough, if not the full freshness of spring, but northern pike and walleyes, if they were large enough, brought top money.

A nickel a pound.

Work the bars. The fish hanging on a piece of wire or twine; hit the front end of the bar, dark, smelling of stale beer and sweeping compound on the floor to soak up the spit and spill and puke, bars with grimy mirrors and no stools, only places to stand, with men leaning on their elbows, drinking from the tall brown-wet bottles—hit the front end and hold the fish out like a prize, a contest won.

"How much?" Beery breath, weaving men unshaven, hard to see in the dark of the bar.

"A dime."

"For the whole fish?"

How drunk *is* the son of a bitch? "No—a pound. He's a good one, go twelve, fifteen pounds. . . ."

"Hell, kid, he ain't ten."

"Come on—he's an easy twelve. . . ."

"Ten."

"Eleven."

Laughter, other men cutting in. "Hell, Swen, buy the damn fish. . . ."

And he bends. "All right, eleven pounds, a nickel a pound."

"A dime."

"That's it, kid—take a nickel or nothing. Feed it to your cat."

"I don't have a cat—seven cents."

"Damn, kid—all right. Six and that's it."

"Six. Times eleven pounds. That's sixty-six cents. . . ."

And at last the money, the pay, and then back to the dam at a run to find a place on the wire and unroll the line and start swinging the hook out and out to feel it come back, while another boy takes another fish to the bars to make money.

Sometimes riches—more money than can be imagined. Sometimes a huge fish—twenty pounds —and a drunk that forgets all the rules and pays the full dime a pound.

Two dollars.

Sometimes more—five, six fish in a day taken on the snag hooks at the dam, and a good day, the best day of all, the best day ever, earning nine dollars—a full day's pay for a grown man working for a dollar and a nickle an hour, which was the wage then, when boys made only two dollars and fifty cents and sometimes only a dollar a day doing mean-grunt work from sunup to sundown on the farms.

Nine dollars. Nine incredible dollars in one day to be jammed tightly into the pocket and hoarded and hidden from the larger boys and spent slowly on secret pleasures.

Candy, malts for a quarter and hamburgers, more candy until the belly bulges and then the next day back once more to the dam and the swinging hooks and the roaring water.

Spring and first fishing.

Working the
Ditches

Snagging fish below the dam was the start of spring, but there were other, different beginnings as well.

The country around the town was flat farmland, the richest in the world, it was said, soil so black you could see into it the way you see into a black marble, but flat, absolutely flat with no hills.

And no natural drainage.

The snow melts and the fields stand in water and mud and would stand that way into summer because there is a clay base down a couple of feet that won't allow the water to sink except for the ditches.

Somewhere in the past, in times before we were born, great projects dug ditches for miles and miles to drain the farms—some ditches thirty miles long, straight through the farmlands, with side ditches heading into networks of fields, so that on an aerial photo hanging in the feed store, flyblown and greasy, the ditches look exactly like the canals of Mars.

The fish do not know these are drainage ditches; they think they are creeks. After a time, some of them would nose up the ditches, in the spring when the runoff water was pouring out, push further and further up and lay eggs, and the spawning ground was imprinted on the new fish and then still more new fish until the ditches became an accepted spawning area for thousands and thousands of them.

Walleyes and northern pike run first, and because the snagging at the dam is going on at the same time, they are not bothered.

But after the walleyes and northerns come the suckers, and by that time the snagging at the dam is over. Then we would take spears or bows and work the ditches for suckers.

It was not easy. Using a spear with eight or ten tines it seemed impossible to miss, but the fish could move sideways, or appear to, and many times they were not where they seemed to be when the spear was jabbed. After a bit, a technique evolved— and for some reason it had to be relearned each year. The spear had to be held with the point in the water just over their backs and pushed forward and down almost delicately—too far and the spear would hit the rocks lining the bottom of the ditch and bend or break; too little and the spear would not penetrate far enough for the barbs to take hold.

Shooting them with a bow was also tricky at first. There were no fish arrows then to buy in the stores, and no money to buy them if they had been available. Bows were of lemonwood with fiber backing and arrows were homemade from cedar shafts that cost a nickel each and turkey feathers. A small hole could be drilled through the front of a field point and a tiny nail put through the hole and bent back to make a barb, then a forty-pound test fishing line was tied from another hole in the point back to the reel on the bow. The "reel" was a plastic water glass taped to the bow so that it tapered down to the front. The line had to be carefully wound on the glass each time, one wrap laid precisely next to the last so it would spin off (this was before spinning reels as well, which can be used now) without making the arrow fly off sideways.

It was all very involved, and if a shot was missed it might take five minutes to get ready for another one. For that reason we liked to get very close before shooting, and finally one boy found that you didn't need the reel or line at all. The ditch was shallow, and if you shot down, the arrow would go through the fish and pin them to the bottom.

There was no limit on suckers.

Gunnysacks were carried on a cord around the neck to drop the fish in when they were speared or shot, working up the ditch in the spring sunshine, walking in the icy water until our legs were blue—nobody could afford hip boots or waders—when we would stop and build a fire and warm feet and legs, working the ditches that way until the sacks weighed sixty or seventy pounds.

When the sack became too heavy to carry we would stop and use a pocketknife to gut all the fish, then continue on until even with gutted fish the weight was too much and the fish would be loaded on bicycles as a burro would be loaded, huge bags on the sides and top to push the miles home.

The suckers were not only for direct cooking and eating.

An old man—forty at least—had a smoke-shed set up on the edge of town. If you helped him, he would smoke your fish for half of them.

The suckers had to be split the long way down the back with a sharp knife and coarse salt hand-rubbed into the inside meat. Then they were hung over poles in the smoke-shed and a round-the-clock fire had to be made outside in the firepit. A buried stovepipe carried the smoke into the smoke-shed from the hardwood branches that were burned.

Hours turned to days turned to weeks—or so it seemed. The sucker run in the ditches lasted at most two weeks but it seemed much longer.

A constant procession of boys and bicycles moved from the ditches back into the old man's smoke-shed, and it did not matter that he was using the boys' work to get free fish, did not matter that we spent days with eyes burning from the smoke, spent days sitting in clouds of smoke, days and nights stoking and damping the fire to keep the smoke moving evenly through the racks of fish, did not matter that he kept half and maybe more than half to sell in the stores and at church suppers and to an endless line of cars that came to buy from him.

None of it mattered except the fish.

When they were done, when they were all shot with arrows and speared and gutted and carried and salted and smoked and at last were done, it was worth it.

First tastes were compared, measured against each other the way wine is compared.

The meat is soft-hard, gentle-leathery golden-brown, the color of caramel and deep honey mixed, and simply has to be eaten.

It comes off in strips, tastes delicately of salt and smoke—not of wood, but the taste of the smoke so that it seems that the forest itself is in the meat of the fish; a bite is like being there in the woods, a bite is part of a memory.

Except that the meat, the work in the meat, is too expensive to eat—the way farm workers cannot afford to eat the meat they grow and must instead eat venison and sell the beef and pork for money.

The fish must be sold, the work in the cold ditches must be sold.

If the taste of fresh cooked fish means spring to the town, the taste of fresh smoked fish means luxury.

Everybody wants it. There is no problem selling —we could sell ten times as much as we get. When we start down the street with the gunnysack the people find us, hunt us.

"How much?" they ask and it is not like in the bar with the snagged fish. No dickering.

"Fifty cents a side," we say. "Flat."

A nod and money. Half a fish, half a dollar—a dollar a fish, which sounds good, but to get a fish, one fish in the sack to sell, is a day at the ditch, another fish for the old man, nights working at the smoke-shed for the old man, and then . . . then to not eat the fish.

To *not* eat the fish.

To take a taste of the smoky-salt-golden-meat and then not eat the fish. . . .

Impossible.

It takes four, five fish to get just one to sell. Dreams of money, of wealth, die with a taste, one taste.

Pepsi for a nickel a bottle, two Pepsis and sit on the back porch of the apartment building while they drink and fight inside, two Pepsis and sit there and eat strips of smoked fish cut and washed down with cold Pepsi, eat until even the hair is greasy with it and every cat in the neighborhood is there with you, sitting there eating the fish in the spring sunshine and reading a Zane Grey western or an Edgar Rice Burroughs science fiction novel. . . .

No, not riches from selling the fish. Other riches, but not money from selling. Only fish to eat, to sit and read and eat.

Sometimes a dogfish is snagged or speared or shot. They are like an eel, long and wriggly with a fin that starts halfway down the back to wrap around the tail and up the belly. Most throw them away, consider them rough fish, but the old man at the smoke-shed knows a recipe, has secret salts and seasoning and smokes them. It is oily, almost greasy, and hard to eat at first—the first bite. But after that there is something there, some new edge of taste and we sit with the old man outside the smoke-shed and eat the dogfish—peeling long strips to lay on coarse bread and eat with strong hot tea sticky with sugar while the old man tells, weaves stories about fishing, smuggling booze across the Canadian border during Prohibition, stories of wild runs at night while federal agents shoot at the night-boats, glamorous stories of ugly things.

Spring ends there. . . .

Not in the ditches with cold blue legs, not at the power dam swinging the snag hook to bump the noses of the rolling fish nor in the bars hustling the drunks nor selling the smoked suckers on the street nor hiding on the back porch of the apartment to drink Pepsi and read and eat but there. . . .

At night by the smoke-shed eating the eellike dogfish and coarse bread and drinking hot tea, listening to old stories from the old man and petting the dog that eats all the bones and skin and heads from the smoked fish and is so fat his legs cannot hold him up for more than a few minutes at a time.

There.

Spring and first fishing end sitting by the smoke-shed on the soft nights as the buds turn to leaves even on the hardwoods and the stars lose their brittle winter look and take on the soft shape of summer, and the dog lays his head in a lap to beg and to be petted.

There it ends.

And summer begins.

First Strike

In reality it is not possible to draw an exact line and say here one kind of fishing becomes another, just as it is not possible to draw an exact line in any part of life to separate it from another.

Summer fishing came in so many different forms, became so many different arts, that there must be a start to it, a beginning and a middle and an end just to be able to see it.

The start was where the river passed a smaller stream that entered the river by the Ninth Street bridge.

Though summer had come, always lying back hiding was the cold snap—a late killing frost that caught everybody off guard so often that it seemed people would come to expect it and not set their garden vegetables out. But they are always surprised by the frost, and have to wrap paper around the plants in small cones until the backyards of everybody in town seem to be full of buried elves with only their hats showing.

But the frost does more than kill plants. Something about it affects the fish, and where the stream comes into the river just after the frost and even during the frost the northern pike come to feed. It is perhaps that they think it is fall, or perhaps the cold makes small fish come there and the big ones follow.

And they are truly big—some of them like twenty-pound green sharks, filled with teeth and savagery.

Fishing for them was done one way and one way only—casting lures. Two lures worked the best, and everybody who came to work where the stream flows into the river used one or sometimes both of them. The best was a red-and-white daredevil—a spoon that is silver on one side with red and white stripes on the other and a single triple-hook at the bottom, or business end. The new ones didn't seem to work very well until they were scuffed and scratched by teeth tearing at the paint on them. Most of us tried rubbing them on rocks or concrete to scuff them up a bit, but it didn't work as well as having it done by teeth. The other lure was called a plug—a simple cylindrical piece of wood painted red in the front and white in the back with two small silver eyes and a "lip" made of stamped metal to pull the plug under when it was reeled in.

The rigs used then would not be considered usable by modern fishermen. This was all before glass or carbon rods and spinning reels or free-wheeling casting reels, and casting with them was a true art, a balance of coordination and luck. The line used was of a heavy braid—there were no monofilaments then either—rolled on a drum reel with thumb-busting side drive handles that had to spin with the drum when a cast was made.

Everything was in the thumb. The right thumb rested on the line drum, and the rod—a clunker made of spring steel and by modern standards about as flexible as casting with a tire iron—had to be whipped overhead and forward with great force at the same instant the thumb had to be lifted from the drum to allow the lure to pull the line out. But not all the way. If the thumb came up too much, the line would go too fast and cause a backlash—a tangle on the reel sometimes so hideous the line had to be cut from the drum with a pocketknife, hacked off, and replaced completely. But the thumb couldn't be pressed too hard either, or the lure wouldn't go anywhere.

And then, just as the lure entered the water the thumb had to act as a gentle brake and stop the line drum.

All to start just one cast.

And almost no casts produced a fish. It might take sixty or seventy casts to entice a northern to strike, and then it didn't always pay off.

If the daredevil was used it had to be allowed to wobble down into the water no more than a foot, and then the rod had to be put in the left hand and the right hand had to grip the handles, and the line had to be reeled in as fast as the hand could move to make the spoon roll and flip and flash silver and red. Then, just before shore the daredevil had to be stopped, cold, for half a second in case there was what was called a "follow-up" to give a fish time to hit it just then.

The plug was slightly different. Because it was of wood it floated and so the cast had time to be developed correctly. The cast could be placed with more time, the plug allowed to drift into position, and then the reeling started at one's leisure.

The lip on the front of the plug worked as a water scoop so that the faster the plug was reeled in the deeper it would dive, and the depth could be controlled that way. Some worked the tip back and forth to the right and left while reeling, but it didn't seem to help, just as spitting or peeing on the lure— another trick used by some—also didn't seem to help. Once somebody scrounged some blood from a butcher in a small bucket and dipped the lures in the blood, and that had some effect but made us stink for days of rotten blood and fish slime. It didn't bother us, but in school there was a noticeable reaction.

Again, as with the daredevil, when the plug was

close to shore it was stopped for half a moment to allow a possible follow-up strike, but really the cast was always everything. And though many—most—casts did not catch fish, each and every cast had to be made with art and skill and the hope, the prayer was always there that it would work; that *this* cast would work *this* time.

The problem was the cold. It was necessary to work the line in just the right place, reeling the braided line through the fingers to be able to "feel" when the first hit came, if it came. Braided line soaked up water, and this squeezed out on the finger, ran down the wrist, and dripped on the waist or legs—depending on where the reel was held.

Wet, cold hour after hour, each perfect cast followed by each perfect cast waiting for that moment, that split part of a moment when it comes.

The strike.

They are never the same. Daredevil strikes are different from plug strikes as cold-weather strikes are different from summer strikes, and every fish seemed to strike differently.

Northern pike are the barracuda of fresh water and when the mood is on them they will hit, tear at anything that moves. Mother loons keep their babies on their backs so the northerns won't get them, and baby ducks get nailed constantly. Northerns eat anything and everything. In their guts we found bottlecaps, can openers, cigarette lighters, bits of metal, nails, wire, pieces of glass and once, complete, a pair of sunglasses that fit one of the boys perfectly.

But they're picky. Not always, but sometimes. And they must be coerced, persuaded, into biting—begged, enticed.

A cast can be "dropped," the lure allowed to settle, then reeled in fast, then allowed to settle again and once more reeled fast—to make it seem sick or wounded. It can be skittered across the surface, then suddenly stopped, skittered and stopped, teased and teased, looking, waiting for *the* moment:

The strike.

It always comes like lightning. Sometimes there is just the tiniest hint, a small grating of their teeth on the lure as they come in for the hit, but usually there is no warning. One second the reel is turning and the lure is coming in, and the next there is a slashing blow and the line stops, begins to sizzle out, cuts the finger, and the rod bends, snaps down, and in some cases, if it is a large fish and a steel rod, it stays bent in a curve.

It is impossible to judge size. Three pounds seems like six, six like twelve and over. One cold, clear morning a miracle came. A cast, one clean cast with a daredevil that slipped into the water like a knife, clean and in and halfway back, the reel spinning as fast as it would go; there was a small grating on the lure and then a tremendous slashing strike, a

blow that nearly tore the rod away, and the line cut the water, sizzled off to the right so fast it left a wake.

Seventeen pounds.

A great green torpedo of a fish that tore the water into a froth, a fight that slashed back and forth until at last the fish was tired, until it nosed finally into the bank, where it could be dragged up onto the grass to lie, green and shining, the tail flapping, and a voice, a small voice notes the sadness of the fish and whispers in the mind and the words come out:

"Let it go."

"Are you crazy?"

"Let it go—it's too, too much fish to keep like this. Let it go. . . ."

"Nobody will believe it."

"We saw it. That's enough. Let him go."

And so it is.

Somebody has a scale, a spring with a needle that slides, and the fish is weighed, and the lure is removed, and it is laid in the shallows. It wiggles twice, a left and right squirm, and it's gone.

"It will learn," somebody says. "It will never strike again."

But he is wrong.

Four of us that day catch the same fish and release him, and each time he fights and each time he slides back into the river and disappears like a green ghost, and there are many other springs and thousands of other casts and hundreds of fish caught and eaten when it snaps cold where the stream comes into the river, but never the same again.

Never that same slamming surge of the first large strike.

Seventeen pounds.

Fishing for Bulls

F ishing during the cold snap where the stream comes into the river is not always sure and is over in a short time, often only a day, two days, never more than a week, and is considered a small treat, a bonus for the boys who are purists.

There were other kinds of temporary fishing as well.

Just as the time for fishing starts, the panfish come into the shallows to spawn. These are not the later types of panfish to be caught in droves and bucketsful, but the first, the big ones that cannot be caught later because they stay deep, where it is impossible to get a lure or bait down to them through the clouds of small ones.

"Bulls," we call them. Not minnows or six-inch-long worm-eaters but truly large sunfish with flashing yellow bellies, bluegills over a pound, over two pounds, panfish to fight like northerns when they take the worm, and still, even with bait, even with a worm, there is art.

Nothing is left to chance, no part of the ritual is omitted. This was before anybody thought of fly-fishing for panfish, and the boys were too poor for the split-bamboo rods of that time anyway—and lures specifically for panfish (wigglers, small bugs, etc.) were far in the future. All to be had were the spring-steel casting rods and the thumb-busting early Shakespeare reels used for all fishing.

But there were ways to make the heavy gear act like lighter equipment.

A tiny hook was used and a small sinker set well above—two feet at least—a gut leader, a twist knot with the end fed through to tie the hook to the leader, many with different knots, so that there were always arguments about who had the better knot, who could hold the largest "bull" sunfish (actually females) with his knot; gear arguments that would go on all summer, go on all year, go on all of lives, though we could not see that then while we worked the shallows when the big sunfish and bluegills came in to spawn.

It is possible that the lure, the bait, the place-ment of it made no difference, but nobody believed that, nobody could believe it. We would put the worm on the long shank hook a certain way, thread the head and part of the body full on the hook to keep it from pulling off if nibbled, but the tease loop was more important, most important. Down the hook, where it bent around the bottom, a loop of worm would be left loose to wiggle.

The tease loop.

And then the rest of the worm on the remainder of the hook except for a half inch of tail to complement the tease loop.

The delivery was perhaps not important, as the lure or bait was perhaps not important, but we believed it to be and so worked the steel rods with our wrists, whipped them back and forth with six or eight feet of line, slammed them to get some action out of them, flipped the line forward and back and forward again to get it to land perfectly on the edge of the old weeds where the fish came to spawn.

But not like casting for northerns, this—not anything like it. When they are hitting—though the boys did not believe it—probably a bare hook would do as well as a baited one.

Sometimes they could be seen lying there and when the hook hit the water they would cut sideways, hit the hook so fast they would move the line to the side with a small hissing noise.

And fight. A two-pound sunfish, splashing gold up through the water, seemed to fight more than a five-pound northern or walleye. They would get the flat side toward the rod and run, planing off the flatness of their body, using it like a lever to fight the pull of the line, and it was never sure that they would be landed.

And one in three, perhaps only one in four, would wind up on the piece of wire used for a stringer to be brought to the pan.

Now fishermen fillet all fish as often as they can, cut the steaks off the side even when they are small, and fry them in deep fat with factory-prepared batter and factory-prepared grease and factory-prepared seasoning so that the fish all seem to be factory-processed. Like fish sticks.

But with the bulls, the water could be tasted in them, how they lived could be tasted, what they were. The fish were gutted and the egg sack saved. They were not filleted but scaled and the head cut off just in front of the hump of meat that came down to the fish's forehead.

This hump was the "sweet meat," along with northern tails, walleye cheeks, bullhead backs, and crawfish tails—all were special parts for the one who caught the fish to either eat as earned privilege or give away as a way to show respect, the way Inuit give away the best whale blubber.

The cooking varied, but always around a set method—frying.

The best was with bear grease. No grease, no lard nor shortening will ever equal strained bear grease for frying fish, pancakes, potatoes, or doughnuts. It is clear and stays liquid at room temperature and tastes of leaves and woods, and mixes with the taste of the fish, the water, the soft summer air.

The sunfish are fried whole in a large pan in a base of bear grease. Next to the fish the egg sack is cut open and the eggs are fried, and on the other side a pile of thinly sliced—thin as paper—raw potatoes are fried and the whole pan covered with a metal pie pan that is used as a plate so that while the food is cooking the steam carries heat and taste into the metal.

The cooking is finished when the skin lifts easily off the fish and is crunchy or when the smell has driven past where it can be tolerated or when hunger takes over.

Salt and pepper are sprinkled generously over the top, and it is eaten with the same knife used to clean the fish.

And all of this is better if done on a small fire made of dry poplar or hardwood on the shore near where the fish is caught along the edge, after snagging at the dam and spearing and casting for the big northerns, but still well before true summer fishing begins.

Sucker Hunting

When it was still cool at night but warming to hot in the days, when a jacket was too much during the day but not quite enough at night, there was a time for shooting suckers in the shallow lagoons.

Spawning was over for the suckers, the bottom feeders. They had run the ditches and streams that came in to the river and laid their eggs and in clouds of numbers they had been speared and shot and smoked and sold and eaten.

But they grew still in numbers, each female laying thousands and thousands of eggs until even the predators, the slashing northerns and schools of walleyes, couldn't keep them down, and the rivers and lakes teemed with them, huge blankets of them, gray backs touching gray backs so that when seen in the shallows it seemed they could be walked upon.

When the nights were cold and the days were

warm, sometimes, not always but sometimes, some of the suckers would come out of the rivers and lakes to lie in the shallow lagoons along the edge or in the backwater swamps where the water is rarely over one or two feet deep. Later in the summer the weeds and water lilies would grow to clog the lagoons, but early in the season the weeds weren't there and the suckers could be seen, would show like small dark logs just beneath the surface.

They were too fast to be speared and wouldn't take bait—and were not good to hook anyway as their mouths are too soft—but they were perfect to hunt with bows.

An old boat was used. None of us could afford a new one nor indeed afford anything but a free one so we would scrounge and dig and come up with an old bait boat made with cross-boards for a floor. Caution had to be used as the boards were simply nailed up from the bottom with common box nails, and if stood on directly their nails wouldn't hold and we would plummet straight through the bottom. By sitting on the seats and spreading our weight, we managed to make it all hold together, and paddles were fashioned out of old boards, carved and hacked with saws and hatchets.

Turns were taken. One person sat straddling the front of the boat, the bow with the arrow and fishing line ready, while the other sat in the stern paddling. The lagoons were entered slowly, carefully, and it was not a patched-up old bait boat with hacked paddles any longer but a slim canoe, a birchbark canoe gliding silently over the water from a time before, a time from books read and movies seen, a time before white men.

The fish seemed to think the boat was a log and moved slowly away as it approached, but even so, from a sitting position it was hard to hit them. The arrow almost invariably went high, and then came the laborious job of rewinding the line on the plastic water glass fastened to the bow, carefully laying it in rows so it would furl off evenly when the next shot was taken. If this were not done correctly sometimes the arrow would go out about twenty feet, the line would snarl and stop, and the arrow would snap back at the face of the shooter, point first; this could make for a lot of sudden activity in a boat that was about ready to fall apart, and almost all of the boys had a scar somewhere on their face from arrows hitting them.

Finally a position was found where the shooter kneels but raises up, and by shooting beneath the fish, almost as if there were another fish below the fish to aim at, it was possible to start making hits.

All of it was much slower than spearing or shooting them in a stream. If they were hit solidly near the back it was easy to boat them, but if the arrow passed through the main body, or worse, back by the tail, the fish ran and often cut back under the boat. Then it was necessary to manage the bow, the line—not stepping on the floorboards of the boat—a quiver full of homemade arrows, and the front paddle all at the same time.

It was, of course, impossible, and usually if the fish cut and ran under the boat, in the excitement somebody would step through the bottom of the boat and in moments it was full of water, floating just beneath the surface while the fight with the fish went on.

It is perhaps just as well that this type of fishing did not last long as most of the time seems to have been spent on the shore trying to get a fire going with wet matches to dry out clothes or feathers on arrows or hammering the boards back onto the bottom of the boat with a rock while the shoals and schools of suckers moved mockingly back and forth slowly across the lagoon just beneath the surface in the late spring sun.

The Ninth
Street Bridge

Real summer comes first when the lily pads and weeds along the edge of the river began to grow. It does not happen slowly, does not seem to occur gradually. One day the pads are not there and the weeds are all dry and brittle from winter and the next day the pads appear and the weeds are green and the summer water has life it did not have before.

The second sign of true summer is when the rock bass start biting down by the Ninth Street bridge.

It is thought that they start biting simply because the water temperature reaches a certain point—that would probably be the scientific answer. Or the weeds get a certain height, or the moon moves into a quadrant of the sky it must be in to make them hungry.

Whatever the reason, when they "come to start

biting," as the old people say, it marks the start of true summer fishing, and in this business of the Ninth Street bridge there are the first seeds of the real art.

It is not enough then nor now to simply bait a hook and lower it into the water and catch a fish and eat a fish. It has perhaps never been enough.

There are a hundred ways to do everything, but this principle seems truer of fishing by the Ninth Street bridge than of other things. Nothing is ignored in the search for perfection.

The rod, the kind of line, the hook—all are argued over, discussed to death.

"If the line is heavy you won't feel their mouth on the hook. . . ."

"Too much weight and they'll spit the bait. . . ."

"Wash your hands before you bait up or the stink will drive them back—nothing's as bad as man-stink. . . ."

It is likely that if a bent pin were hooked to a piece of baler twine and some bait wiped on the pin, the rock bass would bite, but nobody believes it, nobody wants to believe it.

It must take more.

And so the ritual begins. Any worm would work, but the worms from Halverson's backyard over near the corner of his clothesline back by his mother's favorite flower bed in that crumbly dirt that smells of sheep manure just after it has rained . . .

Those worms, those worms are the best.

They must then be carried right. Best is an old lard bucket with some of the dirt from where the worms were dug and a little water to keep the dirt moist plus just a dab of Steve's father's stale beer to "feed" the worms and kill the man-stink. (The beer is open for much argument—as to whether it works or not, what kind of beer is best, how stale it must be, and the best way to make it stale. Steve contends two days open is enough, but Wayne Kline swears that it takes longer, and Harvey Overton says none of it works unless you pee in the dirt on top of the beer, except that nobody likes to reach into the can for a worm if Harvey pees in it.)

Types of worms—large, fat, short, thin—also make for discussion and for a long time it was thought the sex of the worms mattered. This until it was found that worms are dual sexed; but none of it, none of the talk of baits or rigs or time of day or temperature or peeing or not peeing . . .

None of it compares to the complication of the actual fishing for the rock bass.

All fishing is complex, but this first true summer fishing seems the most important. Later in the summer mistakes can and will be made but this first time things must be perfect, and even the arrival at the bridge must be accomplished carefully.

Rods are carried across the handlebars, hooked in thumbs, and the bikes are old, fat-tired, hard to pedal, but are ridden carefully across the bridge and allowed to coast to a stop lest there be any undue noise. This in spite of the fact that trucks cross the bridge regularly and rattle the old timbers until dirt falls in.

Bikes are hidden. Chrome reflects light into the water so they are pulled well back and laid carefully, quietly on their sides and the edge of the bridge abutment approached.

The water moves past the rocks and concrete sidewall dark and murky, still looking muddy from the spring ditch runoff, coiling in tight eddies and swirls, making black holes where the year before or the year before that Roger Vetrum who was just fourteen and a doctor's only son and the papers said had everything to live for fell in and went under not three times but just the once. Just the one time and he didn't come up and never came up until they found him two days later a quarter of a mile downstream with mud in his eyes and his mouth, packed and dark and thick and bite marks where the turtles had been at him.

Along the abutment wall is where the rock bass are, nose up into the current, smelling for food.

The worm goes on the hook one of two ways. A small hook. Either the worm is threaded full on the hook, the metal shank and curve going through the body so it is hard to pull loose, or it is threaded on in loops with a tail left on to wiggle and tease in case the fish are not biting well.

A heavy sinker is used to fight the current, or a light one is used and the bait swung forward and dropped to drift back.

Willy read an article in *Field and Stream* about fishing. In the article the writer talked about "presenting the bait" to the fish, and only Willy read it, so for summer after summer in conversations about fishing he was an expert:

"Yes," he would say. "But that all depends on how you present the bait."

"No," he would say. "That depends on how you present the bait."

And while we laughed at him and made fun of him, we all secretly, in our hearts, thought he was right.

We all thought it mattered, and we thought of it that way—not as throwing the hook in the water or lowering it but as "presenting the bait."

It had to be "felt" into the fish's mouth, lowered along the wall high to let the current float it back, slowly lowering the line and the bait until it comes to a rock bass.

They don't bite hard, don't seem to bite at all. They come to the worm and in some way make a grating feeling on the bait, a rubbing feel/sound that somehow comes up the line and can be felt with a wet—not dry, but wet—finger and thumb just where the line goes into the reel.

Still it is not time to set the hook. Many times fish are lost because the hook is set too soon. Waiting is everything. The grating starts and then the fish will move away, come back, must be coaxed to bite. The bait must be raised, lowered, teased until the grating comes again and maybe even a third time, and then, when the bait is well in the fish's mouth, the hook can be set with an almost gentle but sudden raise of the rod tip.

The rock bass are seldom very large. A pound is rare. But they are very active and fight hard and often get loose from the hook, and, it was thought, learned from the experience to not bite again. At least we thought that until Duane Severson caught the same one twice, having dropped it by mistake the first time after landing it and recognizing a scar on its back from where a northern pike raked it.

The first one seems to take the longest, and some days they never bite and stringers go home empty. But when they start it can be hot and heavy for a time and usually enough are caught for a large meal for a family, and there is something special about the rock bass from the bridge. They are scaled but the heads left on for flavor and fried in clean fat, the fish rolled in a crushed-cracker batter, cooked until the skin just comes away from the meat and eaten the same day as they are caught, while everybody talks about catching them, bragging on this or laughing about something or another while chins get greasy and there is the knowledge that a whole summer is waiting to happen.

Lazy Fishing

After the rock-bass fishing down by the Ninth Street bridge there came the first "lazy fishing." There were times all summer when fishing would get lazy, but the first lazy fishing was a reaction to winter, to the length, the coldness, the depth of it.

When the first warm night came, a good solid warm day, perhaps even hot, followed by an early evening when the dog would barely raise his head when somebody walked by the hardware store— when it became that warm and soft something would pass between everybody and without really talking about things, without knowing how it happened, it was time for bullhead fishing.

Bullheads are northern catfish. Always fairly small—a pound and a half would be large—they were considered by the unintelligent to be rough fish, not worth eating. In fact in some small lakes and swamps they were poisoned out so "good" fish —walleyes—could be planted.

The poor knew better. The boys knew then why they would later come to be called such things as "fresh water lobster" and "fish filet mignon."

Because the state considered them to be rough fish—as they did perch and dogfish—there was virtually no limit and almost no control on the way they were fished.

The idea was to spend a whole night on a riverbank catching bullheads and dozing and then eat them with watermelon for dessert, but here too there was a form. A way that things must be done.

The place to fish was important, and many things entered into picking the right location. Since it was in the north there would be mosquitoes after dark—hordes of them—and so a small fire would have to be maintained with poplar leaves or grass thrown on the coals now and then to make smoke to drive them away. A place with dry firewood had to be found on the bank of the river where it left town and it had to be next to an eddy in the current so there would be a hole.

The bullheads like holes. Deep, dark, still holes.

They never bit during the day and only started about ten-thirty on a warm summer evening and after they started the biting was steady most of the night.

We did set lines and fished with rods as well. The

set lines we made by putting a hook and leader every four or five feet. Each hook was baited with worms or cut-up pieces of dead rotten chicks from the hatchery in town and the line thrown out with a rock to weight the end for distance. The set line would be left on the bottom where it fell for most of the night until most or all of the hooks were filled. (It is perhaps important to note that almost all of these methods are illegal in the north now.)

Along with the set we would work with rods with just one hook on the end. The advantage of a rod and reel was that we could cast past holes where there were only small bullheads and perhaps get larger ones, or a walleye—although walleyes were rare then in that river.

The bullheads bit like Huns. They would come in and swallow everything whole, taking the bait and hook and line well down their throats. They were very hard to get off the hook, requiring pliers, and were dangerous to work with because they had a spine in the top of their back and one on either side that had a mild poison on them and would hurt and swell when they got you. We quickly discovered a way to hold them, from the belly, with the palm against the belly and the thumb up in back of one spine and two fingers up alongside the other-side fin, and they could be worked off the hook and put on the cord stringer.

Biting ran in fits and starts. When they bit, they

bit hard and came fast, but when they stopped—sometimes for half an hour or more—it was time to nap or put a little wood on the fire and talk.

Talk. On our backs with the stars up above us, showing through wisps of smoke, the fire warming one side then another when we turned, talked and talked through the dark night.

Talked of girls.

Geraldine this and Sharon that, Shirley and Linda and Dianne—girls and more girls to talk about, dream about, sing about. This one to take to a movie, a scary movie, so scary that in the bad parts of the movie maybe she would throw her arms around . . . dreams and wishes, stories hoped to come true. We'd be walking along the sidewalk and she would be there and she would smile and her bicycle would be broken or her cat up a tree or, or, or . . . and she would be helped, saved, and she would be so grateful. . . . All night stories, dreams, prayers. When I get older and the pimples are gone and I have some money and my hair goes into a perfect flattop and I have the right clothes and I have a car, oh yes, a car like Harlan's '34 Dodge with the windshield that cranks up and I am popular, *then* she'll wish she'd gone out with me, been nicer to me, seen me.

In the middle of the night, finally, sleep comes and the fire dies and there is nothing until the first gray line comes up across on the east side of the river and the morning birds sing.

The set lines are pulled in and almost always there is a fish on each hook. They are added to the stringer, and if somebody thought ahead they remembered to bring the washtub and a wagon for hauling it. River water is put in the tub and all the bullheads are dumped in—upwards of a hundred of them—and taken home to clean. Depending on where they are to be cooked sometimes the fish are cleaned at the river, the guts let to slide with the current and feed other bullheads and snapping turtles that come up from the muddy bottom to strike at and grab the fish heads like something from a monster movie. That's if the cooking is at Wayne's house because his mother doesn't understand about things and doesn't want fish guts around even though we promised to turn them into the garden, which makes for good potatoes. But at other places there are cats and dogs to eat the guts and heads and the fish are taken home because some swear that the longer the heads are left on the better bullheads taste, although it is hard to see how they could taste better.

Hard to see how anything could taste better.

The fish are cleaned, the heads cut off and the meat washed in cool water and wiped with a towel to get the slime off the skin—they have no scales. The meat is a rich reddish color and when they are clean and wiped they are dipped in batter made from eggs and stale beer and then rolled in cracker crumbs mixed with pepper and fried in butter. They are done when the skin separates from the meat and the flakes of meat open like a book when they are pulled with a fork. There are some who fillet the bullheads but they are generally considered foolish because that takes away the skin, and the skin—crackling and tasting of butter—lends flavor to the meat and is itself good to eat.

You cannot catch enough of them. Maybe there aren't enough of them in the whole world. Jimmy Breshkov said once that it's impossible to keep up; that you could fish and catch bullheads and clean bullheads and fry bullheads and eat bullheads and by the time you buried the bones in the garden and went back to the river you would be hungry again and you could just keep going that way forever, catching and cleaning and eating them, but Jimmy is the same one who says ants never die because it's never been proven. He says nobody has ever seen an ant die of old age and Jimmy says that they're like the weeds in the Sargasso Sea that never die—one end shrivels off while the other end grows and they live forever, and he says there are plants that were alive when Columbus came through and so it must be true of ants as well.

But the bullheads *do* taste good, even if Jimmy is

wrong, and it is tempting always in the summer to try his theory and see if it works; see if it's possible to eat your way through a summer on bullheads and raw-fried potatoes and watermelon for dessert.

Walleye Fishing

These summers were long ago, so long ago that cigarettes were given to high school students by cigarette companies as a way to get them started and hooked; so long ago nobody had television and there were shows on the radio to listen to in the nights, back when portable radios cost an arm and a leg and took close to four pounds of batteries just to keep the tubes going for an hour and a half; and African-American people were kept from voting in the South and other places and did not have schools they could attend except for shacks. So very long ago that a teacher could—and often did—take a hardwood cane to a wiseass student (it made welts that lasted a week), and there were dress codes and curfews and tent revival meetings in the middle of town, and almost no drugs except what doctors prescribed and not a glimmer of the horror of AIDS, and all the streams and lakes in the north had not been fished out by greedy people.

There were truly large fish, many of them. Northern pike were considered not very good to eat because of the Y-bones down the side. They were eaten when caught but not favored and sometimes released. Once Duane Severson's father won a fishing trip up into Canada by bush-plane at a saloon raffle, and when Duane came back he told stories of not keeping any northern pike under twenty pounds and had the pictures to prove it. After that only really large northerns were kept and eaten, and even when Bill Wenstrom found a French recipe for baking northerns with the slime still on and they turned blue, people didn't eat them much if there were other fish available.

Walleyes were the cream of fish and while nobody yet called the big ones "lunkers," they were thought of that way.

The problem was that in the town the river had been pretty much fished out as far as big fish were concerned. So many people came down to the banks in the summer and worked there with rods and reels and set lines that respectable fish were virtually wiped out.

To catch big walleyes it was necessary to go out of town.

People who had money—we thought of them as rich people though they were probably only lower-middle class—had sleek wooden boats and trailers and would head out to the many lakes that surrounded the area, but we could never afford such luxury. Other people had canoes and would work the rivers and streams with them, but we could not afford even that until later.

There was the river.

It moved through town like a muddy huge worm, headed south below the power plant and dam and came from the north. South it went shallow, and so much farmland drained into it that the chemicals used by farmers for fertilizer and herbicide leached from the fields to the river and killed everything.

But north it came from the woods, was fed by a thousand small streams and swamps where fish could hatch and grow large and not be poisoned. North of town even a mile it was a different river, covered over with large trees that were so full of leaves they almost met overhead, making it a green tunnel filled with birdsongs and rustling brush so that it became impossible not to think of every Johnny Weissmuller Tarzan movie ever seen at Saturday matinees.

More than a mile north, two, four, six miles up the river, it was almost literally a wilderness that seemed untouched by humans. There were wolves there, big slab-sided gray wolves that sometimes showed in the brush on the banks, and bear that

worked the muddy sides of the river for clams, trying to stay ahead of the raccoons who hit the clams
and crayfish like Genghis Khan hit Asia.

And fish.

Here in the north part of the river, well north of
town, there were fish that had never seen a lure or a
line.

Really big fish.

There were holes along the banks, muddy swirls
that were ten, twelve feet deep, and down there in
the dark water, just above the muddy bottom waiting for food were walleyes, their yellow eyes glowing
in the murk.

Ten-, eleven-, twelve-pound walleyes.

The Cadillac of fish, according to an article
Wayne had read in *Sports Afield*.

The difficulty was getting to them.

A walleye-fishing expedition started with finding
a boat, and it was always difficult and sometimes
seemed impossible and always made the trip seem
more important than a fishing trip could ever be.

Willy's uncle had a sister-in-law who owned an
old beat-up cedar rowboat except that she didn't
have any oars, but Harlan's father worked with a
man who had a set of oars in his garage that he
never used, but Willy's uncle's sister-in-law needed
the boat that weekend because her nephew was
coming to visit so maybe we should ask the nephew
to come, except that he was a total jerkoff who had

never been fishing and was from the city and thought he was something else (cool) only he wasn't, but it didn't matter because Steve found an old wooden bait boat that only leaked a little and we could carve paddles out of two boards. . . .

And finding the boat was only the beginning. The initial walleye expedition also started so many side endeavors that it was difficult to remember the true reason for it all.

When a boat was located, and oars either carved or found, there was still the gear. What rods to take, the kinds of hooks, the line, the bait . . .

The bait.

Walleyes almost never rose to a lure—this was before the realistic minnow lures used now. They ate food, real food, and the two kinds of bait that worked the best were night crawlers (not just plain worms) and frogs.

Both difficult to get.

Night crawlers couldn't be dug because they were thought to be too deep. (Duane Severson used an extension cord plugged into a garage outlet and jammed two wires into the ground, trying to "shock" the night crawlers up; it might have worked, but Duane grabbed hold of the two wires just as his brother plugged the cord in and the experiment was called off rather suddenly.) But across the Ninth Street bridge in the woods near town there were old rotten logs, and during or just after a

rain, if the logs were tipped quickly, the night crawlers were there and could be taken and stored in fresh
dirt in a coffee can in the icebox—in those homes
where this had not been tried before and the worms
forgotten until a mother found them when they
rotted. The smell of rotten worms in an icebox had
a very dampening effect on family help for walleye
expeditions.

Frogs were harder still.

There were almost no frogs in town. They had to
be found in the river outside the city limits and
stored to take in buckets on the trip. The difficulty
lay in storing frogs. They couldn't be kept in the
icebox—at least not since Wayne had tried it and
his mother opened the icebox to have about thirty
of them jump out at her.

Much research had been done on storing frogs. It
took a week and more to gather them, and they had
to be saved in a cool, damp place, and they could
get out of almost any container.

Nobody was sure but it was thought that
Wayne's dad or grandfather came up with the idea
of the frog pit.

Whoever thought of it, frog pits sprang up all
over the neighborhood. In back of every garage, the
edges of gardens—anywhere and everywhere.

Two feet wide, three feet long, and at least three
feet deep so the frogs couldn't jump out, the pits
would be covered with a piece of tin and some loose

grass or straw, and the earth would keep it cool and damp. They were perfect, and in the week before a walleye expedition everybody involved in the trip would be working along the river in both directions from town gathering frogs to put in the pit.

This was very important. Walleyes hit only fresh frogs and it might take four or five frogs to get a single fish. Fishing all night could take a person dozens of frogs and a three-day trip with three or four boys. . . .

It took a lot of frogs.

This meant that after the week of gathering there might be four, five hundred frogs in a pit. Sometimes more than one pit was used, but frequently mothers and fathers objected and had the pits filled in and so often all the frogs would be in one pit—a deep, squirming, slimy mass of frogs crawling over each other about a foot deep.

For those of us who liked frogs and used them for bait it was a lovely sight. For others it was not always so lovely and there is probably still talk of the time Dennis Hansen's mother was hanging clothes and stepped back from her clothesline directly into a pit full of frogs. This was long before women wore jeans or slacks very much and she had a dress on and sank with bare legs into a foot and a half of fresh frogs. The frogs immediately tried to use her legs to climb out and legend has it the sound she made—not a scream so much as a banshee wail—

cracked the leaded glass windows on St. Mary's Church nearly a block away.

Once the frogs and night crawlers were gathered, along with a can or two of regular worms in case no walleyes were found and it was necessary to fish for bullheads or panfish, it was time to turn to equipment.

It is probable that nothing is so important as equipment. Ever. Without equipment it is impossible to catch fish—the whole reason for the expedition would be lost without equipment.

Tackle boxes were not then the expensive and detailed, complete items they are now. None of us had anything new. Old rusty tackle boxes were found in the town dump with hinges gone and were fixed and sanded and painted carefully with names on them written with airplane model paint called dope for reasons that have never become clear. The tackle inside was usually limited to an extra roll of braided line, eight or nine snelled gut leaders (so called because they were then made with cat's guts, as were tennis rackets and violin and guitar strings), and a small metal container with a rotating window for hooks in case the snelled hooks broke or were lost. There was also a scaler made by screwing three bottle caps to a wooden handle and an old pair of needle-nose pliers for getting hooks out when they went too deep. A knife might also be included except that it was usually not in the tackle box but carried in a pocket or on a belt.

There was also "secret" equipment. No matter how close the boys were, everybody had at least one secret kind of lure or bait or idea to try for the really big one.

The lunker.

These secrets often cost money, and by selling papers in bars at night, waiting for the drunks to get juiced enough to hustle them for an extra quarter, or setting pins at the bowling alley or mowing yards or even caddying at the country club for the rich fat ones, it was possible to get enough money for special lures or a scent to squirt on bait or even a new reel to be hidden until just the right moment. Maybe to drop it in a conversation.

"Yeah, I was going to try working that deep place over by the bank with some of this new stuff on the bait. I sent for it through *Field and Stream. . . .*"

And a boy would pull out a small glass bottle of scent or maybe a new lure he'd been hiding, and even if it didn't work very well—and it seemed none of them did—it was still worth it just for the effect.

Finally it was all there.

Gear, more gear, equipment that had been cleaned and reels oiled with fine oil and knives sharpened and frogs and night crawlers put in buckets or cans, and everything had been checked and rechecked and rechecked again until it seemed things would be worn out from handling, and the boat was loaded, repacked, and reloaded, and on an early morning the expedition would at last be started.

Of course, it never worked like the plan.

Plans were always definite. Nights were spent sleeping over and making plans; talking until dawn about where it would be, how it would be, why it would be. Willy would actually draw pencil maps showing the whole river from where we started with detailed docks and houses along the way, every bend lined in accurately with possible holes where walleyes might be. There were drawings of these walleyes and other sketches of bullheads and northerns that looked like monsters, and the maps lost nothing because Willy had never been up the river on such an expedition before or maybe both eyes on a walleye seemed to be on the same side of the head. It was the effort that counted, and when a bend appeared on the real river that wasn't on the map or when the map showed a dock or house that wasn't really on the river nobody made fun of Willy. He kept a notebook and made corrections carefully, measuring distances with his eye and plotting possible good fishing locations as the boys rowed up the river.

Somehow all the boats we ever had were impossible to row easily, probably because they were old and heavy and always loaded way past good sense so there were only two or three inches of freeboard between the edge of the boat and the water. Three or four boys, what seemed tons of gear, a boat that was at best simply heavy, at worst waterlogged and just looking for an excuse to sink or capsize—all being powered by homemade paddles or old oars.

The trip was the hardest part.

Always when it started there was talk of getting far north.

"We've got to get up to the wild part," someone would say. "Where there aren't any people."

But miles take on new meaning when you are bucking the current; and there were some bends in the river where the current gained speed on the outside edge and it was quite possible to paddle or row as hard as we could and still the boat would sit in the same place, endlessly nosing into the current.

A trip that started by measuring miles on Willy's map ended with blisters and aching muscles not in miles but in effort, not in reaching wilderness but in reaching as far as one could reach before collapsing on the oars or paddles.

It was wild enough. Farms disappeared soon heading north, and within two miles the river closed in with thick brush and snarled wild grapevines that produced grapes so sour even Willy, who read a lot and called the grapes "Indian candy" and said Indians loved them, couldn't eat more than one or two without puckering and throwing up.

A place to stop was found, was fallen into, was delivered by God, at the end of the day just when dusk was coming, bringing the inevitable clouds of mosquitoes. It is important to note that this was not "camping." Camping was an art form in and of itself and had almost nothing to do with fishing.

Walleye expeditions were different from northern pike expeditions because walleyes always bit best in the night and northerns in the day and walleyes were for food more than sport, although there were those who said walleye meat wasn't all that good, was kind of flat, not as good as bullheads.

When a place was selected, a lean-to was erected and a fire made—the lean-to not to sleep in but for shelter in case it rained, and the fire not for cooking but to make smoke to keep mosquitoes away while the work at hand was performed, the hard work of fishing.

Frogs were hooked through the lower lip and left alive and moving, except by Willy, who stunned them by hitting them against a log before hooking them through the brain, which of course killed them. His argument was that they died anyway, drowned, but others pointed out that they moved for a while and during that time the big walleyes would go for them, and like many differences it was never resolved.

The frogs were hooked on a snelled leader, then a fairly heavy sinker was crimped on the line—this was prior to the rubber-twister sinkers and all that existed were the straight lead sinkers with fold-over tabs—about four feet above the hook, and the whole business was cast out into the middle of a hole or eddy or deep spot and left to sink on the bottom.

Walleyes were notoriously slow-mouthed and would come in the night, nose the frog, and work their mouth around it, and all of this must be felt with two fingers on the line; the different stages must be felt in the darkness with a low fire to make smoke and talking in whispers when talking at all. When the walleye first approached, when he opened his mouth and moved it over the frog, when he closed his mouth and his teeth grated gently on the line—everything about them had to be sensed through forty feet of braided nylon line and a gut leader. And when it was time, when the fish's mouth was over the frog, when all of that was *felt* to be correct, the hook could be set.

The hands lowered gently from the line to the cork handle of the rod, the handle was grasped slowly, carefully, and in a sudden swooping motion the rod raised up and back to drive the hook sticking through the frog's lip up and into the roof of the walleye's mouth, slamming past the barbs to hook him.

Many small ones are caught. The night is long, and though they stop biting well before dawn and many small ones are caught, nobody stops fishing until there is light and it is necessary to sleep, because there is always hope; there is always the soft prayer that in the bottom of the river, in the murk, there is a fish so large, a lunker of all lunkers waiting there, waiting to take your frog and your rod and whip them, twist them, and make you fight for your very place on shore.

That it never comes, that four-, five-pounders are there but the great gray-green monsters never come through the long night, or another long night, does not matter.

It is the trying that counts.

Northerns in
the Lily Pads

Day expeditions, when not working for walleyes but for northern
pike, were similar to night-fish-
ing trips except that more art was involved.

Fishing for walleyes took skill, but it was largely
static, slow—sitting for hours in the smoke from the
campfire, touching the line with the fingers, waiting
for the grating of their teeth.

Northern pike were an entirely different matter.

There were three times to fish for northerns. The
first was in the spring, right after the suckers ran,
when the northerns took lures readily. The second
time was in the middle of summer, and the last time
was in the fall.

Fishing for northerns in the summer was like
mounting a big-game hunt in Africa. It was very
serious and focused on one thing and one thing
only: using artificial lures to catch northern pike,
preferably lures made by hand.

Nobody seemed to know when self-made lures started but everybody knew why—none of the boys could afford factory-made except for the red-and-white or black-and-white spoons known as daredevils. The daredevils worked well enough in the spring, and even through the summer, but usually worked only on smaller fish and were very hard to use in thick weeds or snags because they sank so quickly and the hooks were exposed so openly. Wooden plugs, made in the shape of a large minnow and painted to look like a fish or a red-and-white spark plug would float until the reeling-in phase of the cast started—when a lip would pull them under and set up the action. This meant the plug could be cast into a bad place next to a dead tree or snag—where large northerns liked to hunt for smaller fish—then pulled gently and slowly along the surface until it was clear and the fast-reeling retrieve could be started.

Plug-making went on all winter, a way to remember summer fishing when the snow was deep. Treble hooks and lip-spoons and eyelets could be ordered from sporting goods mail-order houses, and good plugs could be made for fifteen or twenty cents. They were carved of soft pine and sanded in the streamlined shape of a minnow or small fish and painted with airplane model dope, either with rib bones down the side and a dark back and green sides and bottom, or simply red and white—the front, or head, bright red and the rest of the body white.

Offbeat plugs first appeared one winter when a new boy moved in and had never fished for northerns. He painted realistic plugs like minnows, showing not just ribs but eyes and gill slits and mouths, like Flying Tiger aircraft. He also started the thought that the bigger the plug the bigger the fish, which culminated in Gene Tray making a plug nearly a foot long with five sets of treble hooks down the bottom and the end of a kitchen spoon for a diving lip under the chin. It looked good and everybody was anxious to try it, but it proved a disaster because his reel wasn't strong enough to take the weight of the plug during a cast. The first time he tried it the line fed out about ten feet and snarled in a horrendous backlash. It hung, the plug moving close to a hundred and fifty miles an hour, and hit the end of the line, bent the rod out and down and whipped up, around and back and buried three sets of hooks in the back of Gene's head. Four of the hooks went in well past the barb, driven in with tremendous force, some of them stuck deep in the skull itself, and the boys couldn't get them out even with fishing pliers. It was four miles back to town on bicycles, and Gene had to pedal all the way in with that wooden fish hanging out of the back of his head and that pretty much marked the end of trying with big plugs.

Moving out for northerns usually meant something of a military operation. In the summer the big northerns seemed to hole up where it was almost impossible to get to them. There were small lakes out around town where a boat wouldn't fit, but we could work to the shore through thick brush and we would bicycle out to them. Some lakes were ten miles away, and this was before thin-tired—what were called "English"—bicycles. We had huge steel beasts with fat balloon tires and shock-absorber front forks that weighed sixty or seventy pounds, and pedaling them ten miles on a gravel road, especially if the wind was wrong, could be a nightmare.

Northerns struck best early in the morning and in the evening, so we would leave when it was still dark, three-thirty or four in the morning, rods across the handlebars, hoping to reach the lake when it was still good for fishing.

They were very wary, so when we arrived at the lake each person would take a sector and work down to the shore through the brush carefully, quietly.

All these lakes were thick with lily pads. It was difficult to fish by casting over the pads because they would snag the plug and ruin the return. We would wade in, moving slowly, until the water was waist deep and we were at the edge of the pads, and then cast up and down the side of the pad bed, working the plug along the sides in smooth runs. The plugs would go deeper the harder they were reeled, and that gave some control of depth so the speed could be held to keep the plug two or three feet down, scooting and wobbling like an injured fish.

The northerns hid back in the pads, cruising there while they hunted panfish and minnows, and when the sun hit the lure they would come out like tanks, slashing and hitting so hard that if a boy wasn't ready they'd take the rod out of his hands.

Not huge—up to four, five pounds—these fish. But they fought like tigers and the plugs never hooked them that securely and often they would get off. And it seemed *always* the big ones would get away; always it was the one to tell about, the one to hold up hands about, the one to lie about that raised its ugly green head and slashed this way and that in the sunlight and the plug was gone, shaken loose to cartwheel away while the picture, the same picture as on the cover of every *Field and Stream* and *Outdoor Life, the* picture, burned itself into the eyes and mind forever.

Bobber Fishing

When a thing is done in the summer it is really never done; the fishing cycles, feeds back on itself and returns, so that the summer roars by and seems endless at the same time. When walleyes have been fished for it is time to do northerns, and then bullheads and northerns again and walleyes once more, around and around until it is not possible to say it is summer or just time to fish—until summer *is* fishing.

There is one other kind of fishing to make the summer—that is when we fished not to fish at all, but to be resting. It is perhaps not art then, but there is a kind of great joy in it.

Hole fishing.

Some of the boys sneered at it but there came a day each summer when somebody mentioned "bobber" fishing. It took courage to say it—we had become purists by then and some of us even filed the

barbs off the hook to make the fish harder to catch
—and the idea of throwing a line out with a red-
and-white wooden bobber seemed to lack purpose.

But the truth was that fishing that way was too
alluring not to do, and so we snorted and made fun
and joked and teased but still went to fetch our cane
poles and lines and bobbers and bicycled out of
town to the best panfish hole.

A small hook set three feet below the bobber
with a light sinker and a gob of worms brought up
sunfish and bluegills by the hundreds, and it was
mesmerizing watching the bobber as it hung there
on the glass of the afternoon water. Then a nudge,
another nudge, and suddenly it would go under as
the fish ran, and a boy would pull up another sunfish flashing gold in the light—a calendar picture—
swing the pole back and around and put the fish in
a bucket of water to fry later.

Mostly to lie back, bobber fishing; mostly to
soak up the sun and daydream. The fish are a minor
part of it, a thing to justify lying back on a summer
bank in deep grass, watching clouds make summer
pictures in the sky and talking of what will come
with life, with age, with time, and now and then to
see the bobber sink and to pull in another fish.

"You know," Willy said one time when we were
lying there. "All the thinking parts of living must be
like bobber fishing. You lean back and your mind
gets all flat and bam, you discover electricity. . . ."

Willy was the one who later found out about fly-fishing and started a craze that went for nearly half a summer. He read in an article in *Outdoor Life* about fly-fishing for trout on rivers in the Rocky Mountains and thought the boys should try it. The problem was there were no mountains and no streams and no trout. But Willy wasn't one to see the problems, only the solutions, and he rigged up a kind of fly rod with a cane pole.

Nobody had flies so he made some with hair cut from his mother's poodle. She found out about it even though he took it from underneath where it didn't really show and that was nearly the end of fly-fishing, and in a way it was just as well. Once all the boys got into it the poodle wouldn't have had enough hair anyway. But about then Jimmy found an old stuffed deer head in the attic of his garage and that gave everybody enough hair.

The hair was crudely tied to small hooks with wrapped, braided fishing line, painted with airplane model dope, and then we had to find some fish.

Of course not all fish will rise to a fly and it would be many years before trout were stocked, but Willy tried along the lily pads one day when we were bobber fishing, and the sunfish and bluegills rose.

That's all it took, and for the rest of that summer fly-fishing was all the rage. None of us had fly rods or the right kinds of line or reels but that didn't stop anybody. We made flies with anything we could get —the deer hair, tinfoil, bits of old diapers, string, even bare hooks painted gold with dope.

The fish rose to them all. They would hide back under the lily pads from the northerns who cruised the outside edges looking for food, and when the fly plunked down between two pads they couldn't resist and came barreling out to hit it.

That was the same summer that Wayne found an old pair of rubber swim goggles and we took turns swimming around the lily pads watching the sunfish and northerns until Wayne saw a musky that ran maybe twenty or twenty-five pounds but looked like it weighed a hundred. He wouldn't go in again. Said it looked too mean, like it could take something right off you, and his fear was infectious enough that it scared all the boys and that stopped the diving.

Fishing Madness

Some fished for fun and some for something else and a few were driven crazy by it, so that they became complete purists. As summer ended the true addicts, the ones who even when young knew they would be fishing for the rest of their lives, restlessly moving along a bank or working out of a boat—as the last weeks in summer came, those who thought of only fishing prepared for the kind that almost always ended in failure.

Musky fishing.

Muskies are a cousin to northern pike only usually much larger. Thirty- and forty-pounders were not uncommon then (although they are rare now) and they fought hard enough that they sometimes tired the fisherman before they could be brought to shore or alongside the boat.

Everything about them was myth. Size, the way they fought, what kind of lure they struck—all rumors, sayings, dreams. It was said that it took a thousand casts to get a strike, ten strikes to get a fish, and a hundred strikes to get a big one. Many (this author included) have fished for muskies with lures for years, all their lives, and never landed one, and so everything known about them comes from somebody else. Somebody's cousin who knew a friend who met somebody who was using a large silver spoon for a lure and had a thirty-, forty-, fifty-pound musky take his rod completely away, over the side and gone and done, though he was strong and held hard.

The method was simple. A good reel, stout line (thirty- to forty-pound test), a steel leader (muskies' teeth cut through line like butter) and a good lure. The lures were very expensive and we could not afford more than one, so care had to be taken to get the right one. Many said the best lure was a large silver or golden spoon with red-jewel bug-eyes and everybody knew somebody who knew somebody who had had a strike on this bug-eye. The problem was that they were steel and weighed close to a quarter pound, and when they hit the water you had to start reeling as fast as you could because they sank like a stone and would catch every snag there was on the bottom. Another lure that worked well, or that was said to work well, looked like a baby duck with big treble hooks hanging out its bottom (muskies loved to eat baby ducks and loons) and little orange legs that rotated when the lure was pulled across the water. The advantage here was that the lure floated and was controllable and wasn't so easily lost, but it cost so much that many either went with the bug-eye or tried making their own baby ducks. The procedure was the same in any event. Cast out as far as possible and reel in as fast as the crank will turn.

Then do it again.

And again.

And again.

Alone in the hot sun on the bank, over and over until your arm seems about to come off, until it is agony to cast even one more time.

Then again.

And again.

Musky fishing, along with fall fishing, is the purest form—not just of fishing but of torture. To stand for hours, days, casting and recasting and never a hit, never a strike, never a follow-up.

It's madness.

And everyone who tries it must go back; though they live forever, they always must go back and try it one more time. There's always the chance that on the next cast, the very next cast, a green-backed submarine will come up from the dark weeds and the line will hiss out so fast it burns your thumb and it's—all—right—there, on the next cast.

Madness.

•   •   •

Finally summer is done, not suddenly, but with a last flurry of fishing, a last time at the hole with cane poles, a last night of bullheads, a last try at the walleyes or working the rock bass down by the Ninth Street bridge. A day comes when leaves start to dry and curl up and there is a coolness in the air. Fishing begins to end.

Except for some.

With the first frost, and first ice on the edge of the river, the sane ones quit. The ones with lives, with families, oil their reels and wrap them in soft rags for the next year; prepare themselves for winter fishing.

But there are a few diehards who know the secret that the old-timers talked about sometimes sitting around the smokehouses eating salty smoked fish and drinking beer cooled in a tub of water.

Just as the ice comes, just with the first hard freeze and when the wind starts bringing storms down from Canada and there is new snow starting to show and stay—just then, when all the boats are put away and motors drained of oil and people are settling in for winter . . .

Just then the big northerns come out to play.

It is a hard time to fish. Nothing goes right. It is best to use lures and work where a river runs into a lake or where a stream runs into a river, working the lure across the opening. The lure must move across the current at an angle and seem to be sliding sideways while it moves, slipping along with a jerk and wobble. Again, a bug-eyed spoon seemed to work best, but most couldn't afford them and so used homemade plugs. Brightness seemed to be most effective and a flash-white plug with a red head, reeled in as fast as a hand could turn a reel handle to make it run deep and keep it wobbling and jerking as rapidly as possible, could be made almost irresistible.

Each cast was torture. The weather had to be cold for the big ones to come and that made it almost impossible to fish. Bundled in coats, we would stand in ice mixed with water in old five-buckle overshoes, and every time the line came in it had to be squeezed between thumb and forefinger to compress the water out of it or it would freeze on the reel in a solid lump. This meant that water was constantly dripping down the hand and freezing on the fingers and in the cuff along the wrist. Feet wet, frozen, water freezing all down the front, snow falling and winter coming, and one more cast.

When they hit, and they hit often, it was with the complete savagery of desperation. Either from instinct or knowledge, the fish knew winter was coming, and knew that they had to eat and build up fat for the lean times; and the old ones, the big ones, knew it better than the small young ones. So almost every cast brought a strike from a large fish, and the strikes came from the side or bottom—it was hard to tell—and seemed to drive the lure sideways or up as if it were getting hit by a train.

Soon the fingers were numb, and the hands, and feet, and the pain came, and everything inside said quit now, quit, the year is done, summer fishing is done.

But something held, something pulled, and it seemed always there was one more cast, and one more strike and one more big northern until it was the last day, dark on the last day, snow falling heavily and people getting ready for Thanksgiving and still a part says it isn't over, summer can't be over, and still one more cast. . . .

Fishhouse
Dreams

Sometimes cold weather came long before snow and there was enough time for the rivers and lakes to freeze without snow accumulating on the ice. This period would not last long but when it came, as soon as the ice was thick enough to hold weight, we would skate on it.

Not to just skate or play hockey but to go and see country. The rivers became ice highways that led to lakes, small frozen streams, openings into the wilderness that usually lasted only a week or so and demanded exploration. Skates allowed speed and we flew through the early winter, and while most of these explorations were for hunting, now and then they led to fishing.

Light brought the fish to the surface, or as close to the surface as they could get, rubbing their backs along the ice, and skating above them we could see them. Somebody thought of chopping a hole through the ice—usually only a couple of inches deep—and trying to "herd" the fish into the opening where they could be netted, and after trying for hours we finally caught a northern in a dip net, and after that we always tried to do this when the ice froze before the snow came.

When the ice finally became thick enough to hold serious weight—usually by early December—the ice fishing season would start. There were two methods. Nobody could afford fancy augers so usually an old axe was used to cut a hole in the ice and we fashioned homemade tip-ups to use for rigs. A tip-up was just a stick across the hole and another across that, the two bolted or tied in the middle to make a cross. From the end of one, a line was tied with a sinker and hook, and it hung about six or eight feet below the ice with a piece of raw chicken or a silver pickled minnow (if they could be afforded) bought from the bait shop.

Then everybody went to shore and gathered firewood enough for a bonfire, which was made on the ice not too far from the hole. The boys would stand by the fire watching the tip-ups and waiting for a fish to come along.

When a fish took the bait—usually a panfish, crappie or bluegill—the one stick would flip up in the air and the fish could be jerked up. It was simple and not really fishing so much as just taking fish.

The other method involved using a fishhouse. In the winter people would put small houses on all the

lakes and rivers, huts really. In the floor of each house a hole was cut and a similar hole cut in the ice beneath the fishhouse. Inside the fishhouse it was kept dark, and hours could be spent watching down in the green hole, jigging a lure up and down to draw northerns in where they could be speared with a ten-tined, foot-wide spear.

There were many dreams in fishhouses. Dreams of summer, dreams of ends and beginnings and of how it all started when the car fell through the ice and would all start again next spring. A little stove burned sticks and shavings and kept the fishhouse toasty and comfortable, and all that had to be done was to sit and stare down in the emerald-green hole, watching the lure and waiting for the northerns. When they came it was suddenly, impossibly quick. One second there was the lure, the next a huge fish either nosing it or taking it—slash, and it was there —and then the lunge with the spear, trying to put the tines across his back and missing often. So fast, so lightning-fast that they could move away while the spear was on the way down.

And then the green again; the deep green from the water coming up through the hole while we waited, waited for another fish, waited for deep winter, waited for the end of the white blanket that covered all things, waited for the end of cold, blue cold.

Waited for summer and fishing to start again.

Camping

Running the
River

There came a time in the almost exact center of the summer when, as impossible as it was to believe, fishing paled. Not permanently. Not even for long enough to measure.

"Let's go down to the Ninth Street bridge and catch some rock bass," somebody suggests, and everybody shakes his head.

"We did that yesterday."

"We could go out for frogs. There are bullfrogs just thick out by Peterson's slough. . . ."

"We've got all the frogs we need."

"Well then, what?"

A pause, a breath, because this cannot be wasted —this time, this only time when the sun is still there and the sky is still there and the soft days and softer nights are still there, and if there is no fishing and it is still too fine and wonderful to stay inside, to stay in town, well then, what?

"Let's go camping."

And there it is. How could nobody think of it each summer until this moment, when it is so logical, so right? And suddenly there is nothing else, no other thing in the whole world than to go camping.

But first, as with hunting and fishing, first there is the planning.

Where to go?

Hours, days, spent on just where to go when always, never changing, there is the river. It is the highway to all things, the river, winding muddy and slow and inviting, a road to all the adventure in all the books. Books by Twain and London and Burroughs, books about rivers and of rivers and in rivers, read and reread, dreamed and redreamed, and so there is never really any choice, and talk goes on until somebody at last says it:

"Let's run up the river."

And then more planning. How to get a boat when there is no boat, this time not even one to borrow from Wayne's aunt, nothing but the old bait boat with the boards nailed across which never works but is all there is, and it is dragged up on the shore at the edge of the swamp and all the boards renailed and bits of rag tucked in the cracks with a screwdriver.

"Don't worry," somebody says. "It'll leak at first until the wood swells and then she'll tighten right up."

"Hell," another one says. "Columbus crossed in a boat worse than this. We're just running the river for a couple of days. It'll work fine."

And everybody nods and nobody asks how four boys and gear are going to fit into the old flat-bottom bait boat.

We just know; all will fit in and the wood will swell and the leaks will stop and there is that . . . that thing, that smell, that fresh adventure calling from up the river so it will all work out.

Gear is selected. No fishing this time, no hunting, only to go and lie by the river with a fire at night and look up at the stars and talk about what will be, could be, should be.

Gear for comfort.

An old army surplus pup tent and a piece of canvas for a tarp because it always rains. The tent for two men will sleep three boys easily, four if the tarp is used.

Blankets. This was before sleeping bags. Blankets and an old quilt are wrapped and rolled in the tents but they will not be needed because even in rain, even in clouds and wind and rain, it is still summer and the nights are hot and damp, and a single blanket works to help keep the mosquitoes off when the fire dies down and the smoke is gone.

But still blankets, two, three for each boy, more blankets than can fit in the boat, and the largest part of planning hasn't yet begun.

Food is next. Hunting and fishing take "fixin's," flour to cook fish or a pan to cook meat, but all food is carried on camping. Enough food for thirty days is carried. Everything that has ever been wanted and can be afforded is taken except by Bill, whose father is a grocer. He has to bring all past-dated fruit and vegetables because his father will not give him things that can be sold.

Wayne brings all the cans of Spam he can find because he loves Spam, cooked, raw, sliced, in chunks, Spam, and Kool-Aid made from spring water and cupfuls, not spoonfuls, but cups of sugar.

Marshmallows and hot dogs and a stream of cans of pork-and-beans and soft tasteless white bread and jars of peanut butter that doesn't stick to the roof of your mouth and some that does and grape jelly in small jars with cartoons on the sides and more marshmallows and more beans and cans of corned beef hash and large potatoes and tinfoil to bake them in the fire until they are burned black and taste like charcoal and bags of cookies, Oreos and the kind that are filled with marshmallow, and there are never enough in the box, and still more hot dogs and one, one jar of pickles and two more loaves of bread and one last bag of marshmallows and two pounds of raw hamburger to fry in an old pan, all in a pile on the bank next to the boat.

And that was just for one boy.

Food for the masses, food for towns, was stacked

on the bank next to the bait boat. Food until it couldn't possibly all fit in the boat, stacked and waiting and still one boy not there, still to come one more pile and at the last, disaster.

Every last thing is thought of and no matter how many times the camping is done there is always some last-minute disaster that seems to come to ruin everything.

When Bruce comes to the boat, all his food in sacks on his bicycle, there is another boy with him helping to push the bicycle, a last-minute boy.

"This is Gilson," Bruce says. "He's an exchange student from South America. They sent him up early so he could work on his English." And then the curse, the words that nobody wants to hear, the doom words. "Pa says we've got to take him with us."

Five boys then. Gilson, it turns out, cannot speak more than forty or so words in English, many of them almost wonderfully foul and almost all of them used completely in the wrong context.

"I am damn," he says, smiling at us. "Is the boat screw?"

Nobody wants to take him.

"He'll be fine," Bruce says, trying to put the best light on it. "All he does is smile and give everybody the finger. . . ."

And since Bruce is one of the all-for-one and one-for-all summer gang that camps and fishes, since that is the way it is, we must take Gilson or leave Bruce, and it is unthinkable to leave Bruce.

With gear and paddles and five boys, when the boat is pushed away from shore and an attempt is made to paddle it upstream, it is impossible, and only two inches of freeboard exist between floating and sinking and the wood hasn't swelled yet so it leaks.

"Son of a bitch," Gilson says. "Water more boat. . . ."

Command decisions are made, all mistakes. As heavy as the boat rides it will not paddle upstream, hangs like a half-sunken log in the current, and Wayne says what everybody is thinking.

"We'll float downstream—it'll be easier to paddle her back light."

It makes no logical sense. Except for some of the food being gone (eaten), all the other gear and all the boys would still be with the boat, and it wouldn't be any lighter. But it somehow sounds sensible and the boat is moved into middle current and catches the river and slides off out of town.

Hot morning sun beating down. Steering the boat now and then with an idle push of the homemade paddles. Drifting on through town, the boat really just on the verge of sinking, portaging the short walk around the dam and reloading and finding the current again.

The boat moves deceptively fast. The current

seems sluggish, more so as the morning turns to noon and the day-heat comes, but as slow as it seems, the river is moving fast, faster than a quick walk, carrying boys and food away from town.

Some notice. Wayne has science knowledge and uses his fingers as a gauge to measure progress against dead trees on the bank and says, "You know, we're moving right along" and "I think we're hitting at least four point six miles an hour" and "I've been calculating, and if we're moving at four point six miles an hour and we've been drifting for four hours, we've come roughly eighteen point four miles. . . ."

But nobody listens.

The day is warm, the sky is completely open and blue; and in broken English, almost crippled English, and awe-inspiring gestures Gilson has revealed that he is almost a year older than anybody in the boat, lives in Rio de Janeiro, that there are prostitutes there and that he has availed himself of them not once but—holding up his fingers—four times.

Telling all this, using the limited language and his hands, takes considerable time, and the audience —at an age when hormones run wild—is raptly attentive and does not notice the current or the distance traveled. There are many questions of a technical nature and each answer takes Gilson considerable time.

Mile floats past aimless mile while Gilson struggles to describe how it was to Know Things, and when disaster comes it happens so fast and with such finality that it almost isn't accepted.

Gilson's hand is in the air—something to do with female anatomy—he is struggling for a word, the perfect word, when there is a slight bumping sound beneath the hull and without further warning a short limb from a sunken snag jams through the boards and rips the entire bottom out of the boat.

A half-second hangs, Gilson's hand in the air, all eyes on the hand, the boat bottom gone; half a second, and then everything, everything goes under.

The boat, already waterlogged, sinks like a stone and all the gear with it. There is time for nothing but survival. It has happened so fast Gilson's hand is still in the air when he goes under, his eyes wide. Somebody has time for half of a foul word and then five boys are in and under the muddy water.

Three heads come up sputtering, then four, and finally Gilson, who—it turns out—cannot, could not swim but has learned quickly how to do a cross between a paddlewheel riverboat and a thrashing dog and comes up in a spray of muddy water and eloquent Latin-based curses.

"All right," Wayne starts, treading water, "whose job was it to check the bottom boards?"

But again, nobody listens, and Gilson—having had his fill of river water—wheels and aims for shore, leaving a rooster tail like a speedboat.

The problem is that there isn't a shore. The river has been winding deeper and deeper into thick forest, really northern jungle, and the undergrowth grows to the edge of the river and out, so thick it is hard to push an arm through it, let alone a body, so thick it prevents Gilson from leaving the river, from doing anything but hang on a limb staring at the muddy water around him whispering softly: "Snakes? Is snakes here?"

Wayne finds a hole away from the bank, two feet across, high enough to crawl where a beaver has dragged a log down the bank, and he pulls himself up out of the water and disappears into the green wall as if he's been swallowed.

"Come on." His voice is muffled, within a few feet, and it's almost impossible to hear him. "It's nice in here. . . ."

He has lied. We all follow him, slipping up from the water in the mud of the river's side and into the greenness, the thick green of the forest, but he has lied to us.

It is not "nice."

As soon as we are out of the sun and into green —so thick it wraps us, so close and cloying that Bruce hisses, "It's like being in a jar of lime Kool-Aid"—as soon as we clear the direct light of the sun, the mosquitoes find us.

Hordes, clouds, a mass so thick they cover all skin, sting the eyes, every inch they can reach, millions of them come at us so terribly that Gilson—who is almost totally urban and knows nothing of forests except for stories of the Brazilian rain forests and headhunters and snakes—Gilson goes mad with the mosquitoes, screaming and trying to run away from them. He is quickly tangled in hazel brush and wild grapevines, fights free and scrambles back down the tunnel to the river, where he sits submerged up to his neck refusing to come back out.

"We need a fire," Wayne says. "To make some smoke to drive them away."

"All the matches were in the boat. . . ."

"Not all. I have some in my waterproof pocket container, along with salt and pepper."

"You would. . . ."

But nobody complains when he scrapes some kindling together and uses one of the matches to start a small smudge fire that, miraculously, does work; the whiffs of smoke drive the mosquitoes away, and after convincing Gilson to leave the river and come under the protection of the smoke, there is time to consider the predicament.

"How far," somebody asks, "do you think we came down the river?"

"Twenty-four point seven miles." Wayne coughs.

Everybody stares at Wayne.

"How do you know that?"

"Well if we were doing four point six miles an hour and we traveled . . ."

"All right, all right."

"Of course the river winds a lot. In a straight shot we're probably fourteen or fifteen miles from town. If we walk at an average of three miles an hour it's going to be five, six hours. But the woods are so thick I don't think we'll make two, maybe a mile and a half an hour. Say twelve, sixteen hours of walking."

Everybody has been silent except Gilson, who is looking for snakes again and does not seem to understand that there are no poisonous snakes in the north woods.

"What if we cut straight out?" Bruce points away from the river. "What's out there?"

"Ten, twelve miles of woods and then the highway. God knows how many swamps. We're better off walking straight back to town. . . ."

"I'm hungry." Lloyd has been silent all this time. Like Gilson he did not know how to swim and learned on the way down with the boat and has been quiet since he came to shore. Until now. "I could eat rotten fish. . . ."

"All the food went down with the boat."

"I know. I'm still hungry."

"Keep it to yourself."

"I'm *still* hungry." As if he thought it would go away by talking about it.

Argument followed discussion followed argument, standing in the smoke from leaves thrown on the fire, and nothing is agreed on by all people. Two think it would be wise to strike for the highway and two think it would be smartest to follow the river, with Gilson dissenting in ignorance. It is decided to vote and to give Gilson a chance to vote as well, though he has almost no idea of what is happening, and explaining it to him—as explaining that there are no poisonous snakes or jaguars in northern Minnesota—borders on the absurd. Any sound, the crack of a twig on the fire, Lloyd farting—any little sound and Gilson jumps a foot in the air and heads back for the river.

Finally a vote is cast, and with much yelling and gesticulating Gilson casts his vote for following the river.

"Hell," Lloyd says, "he thinks he's voting for a ride to town."

"It don't matter." Wayne shakes his head. "Elections are elections. The vote is done. We follow the river."

It was much easier to say than to do. There are game trails, but they wind like snakes and go in no consistent direction for more than ten or fifteen yards, and trying to move off the trails is like hitting a wall. Vines and thorns catch at clothing and skin, hold, impale, and soon everybody is cut and bleeding.

"How far do you think we've come?" Lloyd asks after half an hour.

"Maybe fifty yards. I can still see the smoke from our smudge hanging in the trees back there."

"How fast does that make us?"

"We'll get home," Wayne says, looking up at the sky—for what reason nobody can define except that it gives him an air of knowledge—and calculating, "day after tomorrow, late in the day. If we keep moving at this speed and don't stop to rest, or sleep or eat."

"Eat, hell. There ain't nothing to eat."

"Snakes?"

"No, Gilson. No snakes. None. Not any snakes."

It is at this precise instant Gilson steps on a snake. It is a garter snake, completely harmless except to frogs, about two feet long and just trying to cross the trail. Gilson steps on the tail and the snake responds by biting at his ankle. Garter snakes have no teeth and the response is purely automatic and cannot hurt, but Gilson looks down just as the snake is striking and there is nothing in the world that can stop him.

He makes a sound like a muffled steam whistle and leaves. Simply leaves. One instant Gilson is there, in the middle of the group, and the next he is gone, vanished, having gone straight ahead in a shower of falling brush and ripping vines.

"Well," Wayne says, watching him go, "he's heading in the right direction and leaving a good trail. Let's follow him."

Gilson makes almost a hundred and fifty yards before wearing down, and his trail makes for easy walking until we come up on where he has stopped.

"Morte," he says, and we would not know what he means except that Wayne had seen the word in a comic book about Cisco Kid.

"It's death," he says. "He thinks he's dying."

"He sure made it easy getting here, breaking trail for us." Lloyd looks back at the distance covered. "Did anybody think to pick up the snake? We could use it again. Kind of keep him going with it."

But nobody has thought of the snake, and after a moment Gilson is dragged to his feet—Wayne says he is confessing his sins by this time and wants to listen in case there's anything good about the prostitutes—and we start again, weaving through the brush.

It is nightmarish going. Slow enough so the mosquitoes can follow easily, and the undergrowth and trees keep away any chance of breeze to force them down.

We are savaged by them. At first it helps to brush them away, but there are too many and at last we can only slog along, swollen with bites, thirsty and hungry, until near dark.

"Now," Lloyd says, "I'm *really* hungry."

"We can't travel in the dark," Wayne says. "Not without seeing the stars."

Everybody gathers wood for a fire. Everybody

except Gilson, who has cleared a spot with his foot and is standing in the middle looking for snakes, and soon a fire is going and the mosquitoes are once again at bay. Working through the day has dried our clothing, and the fire raises spirits and Lloyd has amassed enough wood to burn for several nights, let alone one, and talk starts up about Gilson and the prostitutes and it is some time before anybody notices that Wayne is gone.

"Where did he go?" Lloyd asks.

"Did anybody hear a scream or anything?"

"Snakes?"

"Wayne!"

There is nothing, no sound. Somebody throws more wood on the fire, heaps it until the flames go up fifteen feet, and we search in the light from the fire but there is no sign.

"What could have happened?" Lloyd moves closer to the fire. "He was right here and then he just disappeared. . . . God, you don't suppose a bear took him, do you?"

"I don't think a bear would *want* him."

"We'd have heard something. A yell, something. . . ."

"We should look for him."

"In the dark?"

Wayne was gone. More yelling was done, even Gilson forgetting the "jungle" long enough to add his voice but there was no answer and it was decided

—after much argument—to wait until daylight to look for him.

"Maybe he went back to the river, fell in and drowned . . ."

All knew stories of boys who drowned in the river. Never girls, always boys going down in the murky water and not coming up because the temperature was so low it kept the bodies from generating gas to make them float. Put just that way. "The bodies don't generate gas to make them float. . . ."

But looking in the dark at the river would aid nothing, and others might drop in and drown and so, finally, more wood and still more wood is put on the fire and everybody lies strangely quiet, looking at the flames, until Lloyd starts:

"You know, I liked Wayne. Always have. . . ."

"Yeah, he's all right. A little too full of numbers and stuff but not bad. . . ."

And more until an hour has passed, everybody thinking Wayne has dropped in the river and getting sadder and sadder until there is a sound, a crackling in the brush, and Wayne comes into the firelight.

Everybody is startled and jumps, including Gilson, who heads for the river again in the dark and has to be tackled and dragged back.

"What are you carrying?"

Wayne is holding a large object in his hands and when he gets into the light Lloyd identifies it.

"A shovel?"

He has an old scoop shovel, the handle long rotted away, and it is filled with eggs.

"Eggs?" Lloyd says. "Where'd you get eggs?"

"There's a farm. Not half a mile away." He is still breathing hard from trotting. "I heard a chicken squawk earlier and thought I should go investigate it. The people were gone but I found the chicken coop and the eggs and this old shovel to cook in. Oh, there's a driveway. We can walk out tomorrow, get to the highway and hitch home. . . ."

Three dozen eggs, mixed brown and white, and eager hands cracked them in the shovel until they were a large puddle. Then onto the fire, the shovel full of eggs, stirred with a stick as they fry, burn, smoke, smell, bits of rust and dirt and God knows what else from the shovel until the eggs are done and then—with great flair—Wayne produces his waterproof salt and pepper shakers to season the eggs.

Then to eat them. A full day without food and the eggs with salt and pepper and hot, eaten with fingers, a fair share each. Not enough to fill, and dry without grease, but, God, so delicious and wonderful that once Lloyd—who likes food more than anything—turns so his face catches the light and it can be seen he is crying, chewing eggs and crying softly.

Then around the fire, lying down, the smoke and heat keeping the insects away, the forest a black wall to the edge of the light, we lie, dozing in and out, while Gilson—content, safe by the flames—picks up the story of the prostitutes exactly where he left off when the boat sank beneath him. And just before sleep, just before the last moment of the day goes under, Bill says:

"Hell, this is fun. Where we going to sink next year?"

And everybody nods, agrees, and tries to remember if last year's camping was as good as this year's. . . .

Hunting

Hunting

Fool Hens

Hunting always began with excitement. Not ordinary breath-catching, first-girl, first-love, first-success, first-child, first-time excitement.

Nothing that superficial.

The kind of hunting almost didn't matter—just the act. To hunt.

It always started in the fall.

Summer was fishing, and then school—God, school, the great bother of it all—trying, trying to fit in, trying to be part of, trying to understand, trying to learn, trying to be accepted, trying to look right, trying to act right, feel right, say right, do right, be right.

And failing at all, most, all. Grades bad, clothes wrong, never any money, hair that never worked into a flattop or a ducktail—just impossible. To wear wrong clothes and be from the wrong place in town and have the wrong parents and think the wrong thoughts and to feel, to suspect, to know that everyone is looking, pointing, laughing. School.

All summer, fishing, camping, looking for the best places and largest fish. Talking of dreams and some hopes and large brags, and when school started the same boys came with the same problems. School became not a place to learn so much as a way to meet, to talk. In the halls between classes, some-times in class with notes passed back and forth, drawings, maps, all aimed at one point—hunting. To plan hunting. Study hall was perfect. Whole notebooks could be moved back and forth while the football coach who monitored study hall stared out the window or at the ceiling or dozed. Physical education was the same. Everybody had to run but it was easy to hide in back of the bleachers outside or in the gym and talk, sometimes sneaking drags on forbidden cigarettes while plans were made.

Planning was perhaps the most important thing, a constant. During school but also afterwards on the walk home or at night while setting pins in the bowling alley or selling newspapers or hiding from parents—always there was planning.

The plans varied with the kind of hunting con-templated but were still everything; where to go, what kind of equipment, expected game, how to find the game, how to bring the game home, how to prepare the game; and it was always "the game," ever since one boy read the phrase in *Sports Afield*.

Plans allowed the excitement to live, to continue, even when it wasn't possible to hunt, but even planning didn't change one other constant.

In the fall, toward the end of September, the first hunt was always grouse.

Ruffed grouse, sometimes erroneously called partridge, also fool hens, spruce hens—it didn't matter.

They were the first.

The state picked a day when grouse season opened, a day late in September when it was legal to go into the woods after them, but it didn't ever mean anything.

There was another day that counted more.

Summer died hard, hanging on with hot muggy days that never seemed to end, hung on well into September. Gardens came into full ripening, and the boys would "go gardening"—work around town in late August nights from one backyard garden to the next with a salt shaker to use on vine-ripened tomatoes eaten fresh from the plants, tomatoes that tasted of summer and earth and dust and night all at once, tomatoes to bite hard and make the juice run down the chin, to eat until it was hard to walk.

Summer died hard, with high-moon nights in the playgrounds, swinging and teasing Sharon or Darlene or Mary, pushing them higher and higher on the swings until they shone in the moon all pigtails and legs and teeth and laughter.

Summer died hard, going to the fair to play the draglines and pitch nickels onto saucers to get the big stuffed toys that never came, never came, or to pay the small start money at the hootchy-kootchy tent where the woman danced for half a dollar on a wooden platform outside and a dollar inside, except that the boys were said to be too young to be inside, the boys who would hunt. Luckily there were holes in the canvas that could be enlarged only a little with a pocketknife, and the inside was lighted with a large bulb hanging in the middle that made it easy to see all the parts of the dance until Sonny Burton pushed too hard and the bouncer inside saw the canvas bulge and came out to chase us away.

Summer died hard, setting pins at the bowling alley where the pits were so hot Kyle Nova passed out, and a man who had too much beer threw the ball anyway and the boys thought it killed Kyle. The man had to leave when all the pinsetters came out of the pits and started throwing pins at him even though Kyle wasn't killed but only had a broken finger. The boys set his alley for him for three weeks until he could work again while he sat up in the open back window above the pits and talked about going all the way with Clair Severson who had big ones, which the boys found later was a lie but it didn't matter because it was a good story anyway

and got better when Clair found out about it and hit Kyle with a bicycle, a whole bicycle, and like to killed him.

Summer died hard when people sat on their porches of an evening under yellow light and listened to the moths hitting the bulb and drank basement beer out of quart jars and talked of working at the grain elevator or hatchery until the young ones were asleep in the porch swing and had to be carried in and put to bed without awakening.

Summer died hard.

But it happened in one night. Somebody would reach for a tomato or flip a cigarette out the back window of the bowling alley between balls and it would be there.

The cool. The fall cool. A corner of a touch of cool air, a chill on the back of the hand, a puff of breath that showed, a kiss on the temple from the north, from all the way north where it is always cool.

Fall had come.

And there is nothing else then—nothing else but hunting grouse.

But first the excitement, and the excitement begins with equipment.

The boys who hunted, the orphans of the woods, did not have money, and so many of the ways to hunt now were not available to them. Auto-loading shotguns, super-trained dogs, cars, special coats, vests to hold shells or birds, boots—all of that was not available then.

Choices had to be made. A new pair of boots cost close to six dollars, half a week's wages setting pins and selling papers to the drunks in the bars along the river. A box of .22 long-rifle cartridges was thirty cents. A pair of boots was the same as twenty boxes of long rifles. Twenty boxes at fifty shells a box was a thousand rounds, and a boy without money could hunt an entire fall and winter on a thousand rounds; shoot cans and grouse and rabbits and hunt until spring and use any other money for school clothes or food or a book, sometimes a book. On hunting or fishing or the woods.

We had to use what equipment we could get. Most had a cheap single-shot .22 rifle. New they could be bought for eleven dollars and ninety-five cents, but it was always possible to find a used one in somebody's garage or hanging on a nail on a back porch for two or three dollars. Work guns. Kill-the-steer-for-slaughter guns. Guns for shooting the skunk in the henhouse, the weasel in the coop, the stray cat with the duckling, the rats killing baby rabbits—utility guns for everything from rabid dogs to a needed deer. They were not necessarily good rifles. A rough maple or even pine stock and a stamped metal trigger; hard to load, with a knob that had to be pulled back to cock the rifle when it was time to fire, and a safety so crude that it practically ensured accidental discharge. First gun—no, second gun. First was a Daisy Red Ryder lever-action BB gun with the leather thong on the side, but the first real gun, the first rifle, was the .22 single-shot. And the feeling that came with the rifle; the knowing that came with it, the way of it to go back and forward in time. To go back until it was the same rifle as the Minutemen held at Concord, the same as the flintlocks used to hunt when hunting was all, and to go forward from the .22 and the boy until he was a man standing in a rank in the hot Colorado sun with other men who were once boys while a sergeant slammed an M1 .30 caliber air-cooled semiautomatic shoulder weapon into his hands and told him how it would be to kill another man with such a weapon—the same rifle. The same boy. The same man.

For the boys it was also usually the only gun. Everything else was too expensive. Some boys had even older rifles, antique rolling-block Stevens .22 rifles with an external hammer. They were loaded by dropping a small block and (usually) picking the fired cartridge case out the rear with a pocketknife; rifles that spit back every time they were fired, and left pits of powder in the eye that lasted until the boys were men, and then old men, who would be bankers or write books.

One boy had a J. C. Higgins model .410 single-shot break-open shotgun that his father had won in a raffle. He was the envy of all with the new gun but the shells were fantastically expensive—a dollar eighty a box for only twenty-five shells—and when he shot something it was full of BB shot that had to be spit out when you ate the meat. Still, the gun was a thing of beauty and easy to load and shoot, and even the boys who sneered at it and talked of spitting BBs and how it didn't take skill to shoot things with it, even those who knew it all and could speak with the corner of the mouth lifted, secretly wanted such a gun, such a new gun to hunt with.

One boy had a Mossberg .22 semiautomatic rifle that would take sixteen rounds in a tube in the stock and had a covered front sight and a molded strip in the handgrip with places for the fingers. It was an elegant rifle—everybody agreed—and had been designed during the Second World War to teach shooting to soldiers, which gave it extra mystique. But it weighed a great deal and everybody thought it made the owner a bad shot because if he missed with the first there was the second and if he missed with the second there was the third and on and on until he had spit out sixteen shells and missed with them all. With the single-shot there was a tendency to wait just that half a second to ensure a clear hit, and generally the waiting made the owner a better shot. That was, at least, the expressed feeling among the boys who could not own the better rifle and had to stick with the single-shots because of bad luck or lack of money.

Whatever the gun, the first cool night in September, when there would be frost on the edges of leaves in the morning, the night before the first hunting morning, the world changed.

It was not slow, this change—and in some ways it was inside the boys. Summer died that night and the knowledge that there would be grouse hunting the next morning changed everything, changed the whole world.

Suddenly everything that had lain dormant all summer, every little thing about fall and hunting, became important.

During the day in school fall stories from the year before are taken up where they were left off the previous autumn. This grouse that was taken, that grouse that got away, six, eight shots and all misses, one impossible shot and the grouse fell. Notes are passed talking about the forty-acre stand of poplar and pine four miles south of town and how it must be full of grouse because it has been left alone all summer, how there must be fifteen, twenty, fifty, a hundred grouse in there, hiding in there, just waiting to be taken. Notes passed and taken on the state of equipment. This rifle is that good, this sight is knocked loose and needs to be checked—endless talks, notes about shells, triggers, guns, bullets.

And the day crawls, doesn't crawl, stops right in

the middle of study hall. The large white clock on the wall with the big numbers and the second hand that normally moves—slowly, but moves—stops dead.

Somebody has to drop a notebook on the floor or cough or fart to relieve the tension and get the clock moving again. The clock drags itself around, staggering toward the end of the day and still it isn't over, still it doesn't hurry.

At home, hidden from prying eyes, is the equipment for hunting. It is there, waiting, but there is another variable to handle first—parents. Parents who may have other plans for the next day like school or chores; or worse, parents who drink and say no to all things, no matter what is asked.

It is better to hide from them and wait while the day grinds along until they are so drunk it is safe to go home, to go inside and prepare for the next day.

Sleep is impossible.

The gun is checked, rechecked, the boots oiled with Crisco, bullets wiped and tied into the sock that holds them, then it is untied and they are rechecked again, three, four more times, and the clock next to the bunk, the old brass clock with the hammer that gongs back and forth between two bells, is still sitting on nine o'clock. Like the school clock it doesn't move. The alarm is muted with bits of cloth so it won't awaken the parents and no sooner are the eyes closed than they open in worry:

Will the alarm be heard when it goes off? *If* it goes off? What if it goes off at the wrong time and it is too late to meet the boys down by the hatchery and they go alone and the first day of hunting is ruined because it will be necessary to hunt alone and it is hard to hunt alone?

What if that?

What if?

Sleep comes. At last it comes, but it is not deep, and it is not dreamless sleep. The mind works all the time sleep is tried, and it keeps waiting for the bell on the alarm. Waiting so hard that in ten minutes it awakens, forces eyes to open, forces muscles to contract, forces the body to sit up, look at the alarm.

Ten minutes have passed. That's all.

Sleep comes again.

Ten more minutes.

And so the night goes—bouncing from ten-minute sleep to ten-minute sleep until at last deep sleep comes, deep drooling-out-the-corner-of-the-mouth sleep; so deep that it is not possible to hear the alarm when it goes off and were it not for one of the boys stopping by and tapping on the window, opening day would be lost. But Jimmy comes by on his way and throws small rocks at the window and wakens the sleeper, ends the deep sleep.

Then up.

Pitch dark. Black. So dark and black that it seems incredible that day could ever come. Quietly down the hallway past the parents' door lest they awaken, to open the back door and let Jimmy in. Quieter still, a frying pan on the stove, not scraping or clanging because, God, if they awaken they'll ruin it all, ruin everything for the rest of life if they come out because of kitchen noise. Jimmy sitting in the corner, leaning his head against the wall with an impatient look on his face because *he* was on time, *he* was able to get up early, *he* had his gear and food all ready, and it was important, it was everything, to get out of town and into the woods while it was still dark, to not waste a moment of daylight non-hunting. A little lard in the pan and four eggs from the icebox, no, five eggs to fry until they are burned on the outside edges, burned and crisp and crackling with the yolks and parts of the whites still runny. Pepper dusted over them, and salt, three eggs eaten out of the pan with pieces of bread to soak up the grease and yolk while Jimmy sits in the corner glaring, angry; no talk, not even whispers, just sitting there, fuming. Two more eggs folded into bread and wrapped in wax paper and tucked into a paper sack and rolled into a jacket pocket for later.

Then gear, boots on, jacket, hat, shells—make certain of shells, check the shells twice, three times —rifle, gloves.

And out.

It is still dark, almost pitch—Jimmy needn't have brewed up—and there is new frost, first frost lining the edges of trees and grass, the tops of propane tanks.

Air catches on the sides of the nostrils, cold, crisp, no smells—clean air—and for a moment the boys stop and listen to the town, pull the air in and listen, looking at the dark sky and the glow from the town lights.

Then away.

Down Fifth Street four blocks to the railroad, walking easily, rifles over shoulders not loaded, not loaded until the woods.

Across the tracks, then turn and move with them, talking in low sounds, breath "whuffing" out in front of faces, sting of cold on cheeks, the sandwiches still warm in the jacket pocket, warm against the side, and Jimmy speaking of a hunt before, last year, year before, talking about working along the river and catching mallards, something about ducks but not all clear . . . fuzzy words in the dark morning.

Past the coal tower where they used to store coal to fill the steam-fired locomotives, looming up like a monster in the dark, a roosting place for pigeons to be hunted later, not with guns but with slingshots using marbles, hunted in the dark and coal dust, to come home flat black except for eyes and loaded with pigeons for pies and roasting.

Then to the hatchery, where three other boys are waiting, Harvey's face glowing as he smokes an Old

Gold corktip—he is the only one to smoke steady yet, though all will try it because all agree it makes Harvey look older—and the boys set off walking in single file.

Off the tracks, walking faster now because there is grayness in the east—not light yet, just not as dark, but dawn will come fast when it comes, and light in town is wasted; light anywhere but in the woods is wasted.

Three blocks to the Fourth Street bridge, over the river with ice along the edges where the water is still. A muskrat slides off a log into the water with a soft splash. Across and then left, past a cornfield, another, then along half a mile of dirt road. Well out of town now, but still another half a mile to the woods. The first stand of woods. Walking silently now. To talk is to scare the game. One foot flat in front of the other, just walking, moving through the early morning.

Still not light but definitely gray now and the edges of things starting to show; bushes, trees, the side of the road. Frost-rimmed and colder now, just before dawn, the coldest time of the day; breath comes in spurts, and Jimmy whispers there is a hunting moon, which seems dumb because there is no moon at all but maybe that's what he means.

Finally to the woods, the first hunting woods.

It is a stand of hazel brush and poplar, fifth, sixth growth—maybe tenth. Nobody knows. It has been logged for paper and trash wood so many times it is little more than a thick bramble covering forty or so acres. There are swamps and some balsam here and there and deer and rabbits and, of course, grouse.

The boys stop there, wait for a moment: Wayne, who is often quiet and shoots well but doesn't brag; Sonny, who shoots well but does brag and lies, so nobody listens to him; and Harvey, who as far as anybody can remember has never hit a single animal that he has aimed at in his entire life though he has a good semiautomatic rifle and seems to spray bullets every time he sees a grouse or rabbit; and Bennie and Sam. We wear hand-me-downs. Old coats, old boots—none can afford good, new equipment—shells carried in pockets, army surplus ammo belts. Two boys wear sheepskin flight helmets though the day will probably be warm and they will swelter in them. Runny noses, half of us sniffling, hawking, spitting. Nods, greetings, hushed teases: ". . . I see Jimmy got your ass up" and ". . . spend all night pulling your pud?"

More plans are made. Plans *must* be made. Not original hunting plans. They were done in school, at the bowling alley in the pits, walking home from school, hiding from drunken parents in basements.

But immediate plans. Field plans.

How to hunt the woods.

It is always the same. Every year. Two boys with good weapons on either end to catch the animals that try to go around the sweep-through. The same two boys. Harvey with the semiautomatic who has never hit anything on one end, and Bennie with the single-shot four-ten on the other end because he dreams of getting a good wing shot on a flying grouse, and everybody has at least once had to duck because Bennie tracked on a grouse and let go without thinking where he was aiming. Two boys have pits from the shot that went through coats and sweaters and made it into skin. With him working the right end of the sweep, only those on his left will have to worry when a bird gets up. Sam claims to hold the record at dropping—hitting the ground flat in the split second between the time Bennie cocks the four-ten and actually pulls the trigger— but others swear to have actually ducked the shot, dropped between the moment when he fires and the one when the shot arrives. It doesn't matter who is on the end really, because no animals ever try to get around them. It is a myth, but still it is part of the hunting plan in the early morning just before the hunt starts and must every year be discussed.

This boy on the left, this one next, this one next, everybody moving as quietly as possible, no yelling or other loud noises, lined up on the dirt road along the edge of the woods, bolts pulled back, .22 long rifle loaded, bolts in, safety on, barrel up, ready.

And it is still too dark to hunt.

So it is, standing, waiting to move, too far from

the next boy to talk, watching the sun slide with agonizing slowness up over the woods to show first individual trees, then limbs, and, finally, leaves and small branches; to stand and wait, half asleep, numb with sleep, waiting for the light. To wait, to stand and wait, and try to make things happen, and they will not happen.

To hunt grouse.

First Shot

There are worlds to live in, all different, all important, all complete. At night there is the world at the bowling alley, back in the dark pits soaked in sweat, deafened by the crashing of balls slamming into hardwood pins, a cigarette hanging always out the side of the mouth, naked from the waist up, working two alleys screaming joyful curses at the other pinsetters while earning the unheard-of wealth of seven cents a line, eleven cents if it's league night; setting two alleys each night without a break until eleven-thirty, every weeknight, earning twelve dollars a week. With tips that they throw down the gutters if they get a good game, sometimes a dollar in the fingerhole of the ball if they are trying to impress a girl wearing tight slacks—and inspiring almost terminal lust in the pinsetters when she throws her ball, leaning over without thinking of the view she is presenting the four pairs of testosterone-driven eyes in the dark of the pits. Or perhaps she knows, like Willy said, knows and really wants the boys in the pit to see while they slam back and forth from alley to alley, scooping up the ball to flip it carelessly into the ball-return chute and bending to grab two and sometimes three pins in each hand to slide them easily into the pin racks before jerking them down in one motion, all in one motion.

There is the world of the bars. Before setting pins and sometimes on the weekends later at night, working through the bars to sell newspapers; waiting until the men in the bar get juiced to sell more papers, to hustle more money; the bars where the men drink beer out of the bottles with water running down the side in droplets, standing at the bar with no stools while they talk of work and women and woods and fishing and women and cars and trucks and women in raw terms, naked words.

There is the world of home. Where they fight and drink and scream and make up and fight and drink and scream; the world where it is necessary to hide in the basement of the tenement building in back of the furnace, around in back on the old easy chair with the springs sticking through the stuffing and a single light hanging with the filaments showing and read, read books to take away thoughts; fly them away to other worlds, other times, other lives that are better than the life in the basement.

There is the world of the back alleys. Where in

some mysterious way it is always dark, and pennies are pitched and sometimes on dares or challenges more than pennies—nickels, a dime, but never larger because a quarter or half dollar is simply too much money to waste, to gamble; to work all night setting pins for seven cents a line and then bet the farm, shoot the wad, dump the load all on a pitched coin in an alley is too much. Alleys where much is decided by scuffling, called fighting then but always ending before anybody had more than a blackened eye or bloody nose; before weapons, except for Tip, who had a switchblade his father brought back from Germany where it was said he took it off a dead German during the War except that on the blade it said MADE IN U.S.A., which everybody ignored because we wanted to believe it came off a dead German killed by Tip's father, who was a for-real war hero. It made a better story. Tip never used the switchblade except to show off because he pulled it on Wayne Hallock once and Wayne hit him so hard with a garbage-can lid that Tip swore he saw God in the stars—that's how he put it, "I saw God-in-the-stars." The alley world where it was always dark and dreams were always low and pride always high.

But the world of the woods, the world when the road is left, stepped from softly, the world in the trees in the early morning with low fog hanging and ice crystals glimmering on tree limbs—the world of the first morning of the first day of the first hunt is a world so old, so wonderfully ancient that it is always completely new.

Everything changes.

The light is not the same light that comes from the sun. It starts in fusion, is born in cosmic explosions and heat, but when it at last reaches the woods it is altered, shaped, bent and warped and molded into something close to sculpture. The morning light wraps a tree, catches the ice, becomes a dance, almost light-music. Things seen every day—a limb, a leaf, stones, swamp grass—all take on a change with the morning light and it stops not just one boy but all the boys; stops all of us just inside the woods.

Stops us to change.

No longer the town boys, no longer the drunk-parent boys or the alley boys or the bar boys or the bowling alley boys—not any of those now, not even boys now. Oh no.

Deerslayer.

Last of the Mohicans.

Buffalo Bill.

The light changes the woods and the woods change us. We aren't wearing hand-me-downs or army surplus ammo belts, not carrying two-dollar worn-out .22 single-shots with cracked stocks, not standing in worn boots with too-large canvas hunting caps stuffed with newspaper to keep them above the ears.

We are *hunters*.

Buckskin-clad, eyes alert, rifle (it could easily be a Kentucky, a flintlock with curly maple stock and silver dressing) poised, balanced gracefully up and out to the left, the oiled barrel catching the same morning light while we crouch/step/flow into the woods; part of it, part of the light, the cold, the leaves on the ground, the air, part of it all.

Hunters.

And there are things to hunt.

There are the grouse.

Some say grouse are little more than a really dumb wild chicken, but they are wrong. Grouse live in the woods alone, without clothes, without fire, with nothing to help them but themselves, and they have not only survived, they have thrived, grown.

Everything that eats meat hunts them. Fox, wolf, lynx, bobcat, raccoon (sometimes), wild house cats, neighborhood dogs, snakes (when they are chicks), skunks, weasels, owls, hawks, and boys with .22 rifles on the first morning of hunting.

They are at the same time easy to hunt and almost impossible to hunt. Later there are rules, later in life there are ethics to this business, and no hunter worth his salt would ever shoot one sitting, would always try for a wing shot and very often miss, if he hunted them at all.

But not the boys.

With a .22 rifle it is impossible to shoot them

flying, and so they must be hunted sitting, and over the eons, over the hundreds of thousands of years they have existed, grouse have learned one thing to absolute perfection.

They have learned to sit.

It is an art, the way they sit. With their coloration—speckled gray to brown, bars and stripes mixed with spots—they blend perfectly with where they choose to hide: in brush, at the base of clumps of willows amidst fallen leaves and grass. They sit still—no, more than still. They become what they are in; become a part of the earth, cease to exist as a bird, as something alive.

It is entirely possible to look right at a grouse, know that it is there, have it pointed out and still not see it—and continue to not see it until it explodes into flight beneath your feet in the thunder that comes from air compressing between their wings and bodies when they fly.

Tip says often, every fall he says it, says it again and again until everybody is sick of it but it is still true; he says that hunting grouse—except he calls them partridge, which they're not, because articles in *Field and Stream* said they're not—is like hunting morel mushrooms in the spring. For morels everything must be perfect; a wet spring followed by soft, warm weather, all well before the grass comes green or any plants have yet recovered from winter enough so they can grow and hide the mushrooms, and then on one night, a soft spring warm night, they come.

Except it is hard to see them. Overnight they come, little Christmas-tree-shaped, spear-point, gnome-hat mushrooms pop up on the north sides of shallow slopes and along the south banks of lakes and rivers in the brush and willows, but for some reason they are almost invisible. They can be thick all around and not show themselves until something happens, some mysterious magical thing triggers, and the shape enters the brain, the little triangle shape, and then it is impossible to *not* see them and morels are everywhere, bags of them, to fry in fresh butter and eat with fresh bread.

Just so with grouse.

It isn't that the grouse are seen, are hunted, are known, as much as the place where the grouse *sits* is seen, known. Less a shape than a bend in the light, a corner, a shadow that makes the brain think of grouse.

And it is there.

Right *there.*

Sitting still, they freeze and don't move, don't breathe, don't blink, and the old-timers are full of stories of how they don't move. Sit on a limb until you reach up and grab them, fool birds, sit on a nest while you reach under and take eggs, sit on a branch while the branch is sawed off and taken out of the woods and home and nailed to a barn wall and the neighbors are called to come and see the stupid bird sitting on the limb on the barn wall.

They have lived by sitting, and it is what allows boys with old single-shot .22s to hunt them, take them, eat them.

But not always.

There is something about their stillness, their solidness that causes a frantic feeling, a need to hurry, to make the shot before they can fly and so the rifle is raised and the barrel aimed in the general direction of the grouse and the trigger jerked.

To miss.

"What's that?" Somebody yells from down the line. "What the hell are you shooting at?"

"Grouse."

"Did you get him?"

A cry that, a tease, a curse.

"Did you get him?"

"Did you get him?"

A vicious question, a question of worth, a challenge question.

"Did you get him?"

"No."

"What the hell. . . ."

And the grouse holds while fumbling fingers jerk the bolt of the rifle open. The empty shell does not extract. Close the bolt and jerk it open again and the shell still does not come out.

And the grouse holds. There, ten, eight, four feet

away at the base of a willow standing perfectly solid the grouse still holds.

Out with the pocketknife. Swearing under the breath. Damn gun never works. The same swear as all hunters when they miss. It is the gun, the bow, the spear, the club that is deficient.

Pick at the jammed empty shell casing with the pocketknife. Pick. Pick.

The grouse holds.

Finally the empty case slides out. Drop the knife. It can be found later. A new shell from a jacket pocket. Jammed in. No, wrong end. Backwards. There, lead in the bore, pushed in with a thumb.

Still the grouse holds.

Raise the rifle, aim quickly, pull the trigger.

Nothing. Forgot to pull back the cocking spring. Reach up, jerk it back and let go before the trigger engages.

The rifle fires.

Well away from the grouse, a foot above, two feet above.

"Did you get him?"

"Did you *get* him?"

Damn—a hiss under the breath, a curse at the soul of the rifle, the man who invented the rifle, the men who invent all rifles, the souls of all grouse.

Still the grouse holds.

Another jam. Kneel slowly to pick up the pocketknife where it was dropped, and now at last it is too much.

While kneeling, one hand groping for the knife, off-balance, the eyes are dropped for one second, less, a part of a second, and that is when it happens.

The grouse detonates, blows from the ground in the sound of thunder, and it startles so completely that it is hard not to pee, not to scream and pee and run, and then it is done.

"Did you *get* him?"

A hesitation, a breath, a lifetime excuse.

"No. I missed him. He flew."

Many grouse will come and many will be missed and some will be taken. They will be eaten stuffed with dandelion greens and baked with new red potatoes fresh from the garden garnished with fresh goat butter and salt. They will be eaten cold from a plate with fingers while winter comes and eaten baked with strips of bacon over them to keep the meat moist and eaten stuffed with wild rice taken over the side of a canoe in the late summer and eaten with corn on the cob dripping with butter and salt. They will be eaten for almost all the falls that come, and each and every time a bite is taken, each time the taste comes from the rich breast meat, the memory will be there.

"Did you *get* him?"

"No. I missed him. He flew."

Bow Hunting

All of hunting was everything when fall came; there didn't seem to be anything else. School, setting pins, even girls—all of it faded compared to hunting.

But bow hunting was more demanding than other forms, took more effort, more art, and so became perhaps more important.

This was in the time before compound bows or aluminum or fiberglass arrows or even full recurve bows. Laminated glass bows were just coming into use and so were very expensive for the boys— twenty-nine ninety-five for a semi-recurve Bear Cub (the cheapest Bear bow available), which amounted to three weeks setting pins and not spending anything on candy, food, clothes, or movies at the Carousel Theater where movie and a popcorn and candy bar could go close to fifty cents.

In other words, buying a bow was an impossibility.

For that reason most of the boys did not have modern equipment. Straight wooden bows were carried by most and could be purchased through catalogs for seven or eight dollars. They usually seemed to come at about thirty-five-pounds' pull but lost it fast, because once they were strung and carried strung for a day of hunting the wood would take a "set" and lose some of its spring tension. A more accurate pound weight would probably be in the neighborhood of twenty-eight pounds unless one of the slightly more expensive fiber-backed bows could be found. These were a stage before laminate fiberglass bows and, while not as good as equipment now, were some better than plain wood.

Most boys couldn't afford to buy any bow and made their own for shop projects where the best wood—lemonwood—could be bought for as little as a dollar through the school. Mr. Halverson, who taught shop, also hunted with a bow and would help shave and balance the limbs to get proper pull and true flight, and it is hard to think of bows without seeing Mr. Halverson's hand pulling the small shaving plane along a bow-limb and the curls of wood coming up over his scarred thumb while he smiled and sucked on an unlit pipe and talked of moose hunting in Canada or trying to wing-shoot pheasants with arrows in South Dakota.

Arrows were a problem as well. They cost so much to buy "factory-made"—twenty-eight cents apiece—that buying was simply out of the question. Six, seven, even ten arrows could be lost in a day while hunting, and to lose that much wealth in one day was inconceivable.

A hundred cedar shafts could be purchased mail-order for two dollars and fourteen cents. Nocks to take the string were half a cent each, and for points it was found that empty .38 special-cartridge cases slid perfectly and glued on the wooden shafts and made as good a blunt—the best point for hunting small game—as could be purchased from archery suppliers. The police department had boxes of empty .38 special cases from target firing and would always part with twenty or so when asked.

Mail-order feathers were expensive, but they were always slaughtering turkeys down at the hatchery by the railroad tracks, and they would let boys stand as the turkeys were hooked up to the overhead track and pull wing feathers off as the turkeys were sent into the killing room. One afternoon would give enough feathers for a whole year.

The feathers could be held between two thin boards and the spine sanded off to make a base to glue to the arrow in just a few moments. Ben Pearson Archery sold a clamp-jig to put feathers on three at a time for two dollars, and it was guaranteed to last a lifetime no matter how many arrows were made. Duco cement was used to glue the feathers on, and they could be cut into a streamlined shape with sewing scissors as long as a mother didn't know it.

The arrows wobbled a bit and sometimes broke easily, and often—almost always—missed, but they only cost four cents each, and if by a miracle they were brought onto the target right they got the job done.

The sleeve out of an old leather flight jacket left over from the war made a good quiver, held on with an old belt over the shoulder, and as many as twenty arrows could be carried into the woods for hunting.

Hunting was different with a bow.

With a gun anything was possible, ranges could vary, targets as well. Once the initial excitement was over and aiming could be accomplished, the little .22 single-shot became deadly anywhere from point blank to pushing fifty yards—using long-rifle cartridges—and it would take anything from grouse and rabbits to a deer or bear (those larger animals cannot be legally taken with a .22, but have been killed that way, as well as moose and elk). For many years the .22 was known as a camp gun or work gun and was all many woods-runners—trappers, guides, lumber-scalers—would carry, using it to get camp meat as well as for protection. But the gun removes the animal from consideration in a way, makes the activity less hunting and more killing, and makes it possible to hunt an animal without knowing as much about it as bow hunting requires.

Hunting with a bow changes all things, even the way to move. With the bows then used, and the crude arrows, twenty yards was a long shot, an almost unheard-of shot on grouse or rabbits. Fifteen, twenty *feet* was more realistic—and closer was better.

To get that close to game it is mandatory to know the game, to study it, to know that rabbits come to the edges of clearings in the early morning or late afternoon or that grouse will move toward gravel (for their gizzards) in the evenings before they roost so they can digest their food while they sleep. Hunting with a bow it must be known that having a dog will make grouse jump up sooner but they will land in trees to avoid the dog and might give a good tree-shot; or that a dog will run a rabbit but rabbits are territorial and hate to leave their usual area so will run in a circle, and if you stand and wait they sometimes will come back around and might give you a chance for a running shot—difficult to hit but challenging to try. . . .

The real beauty of hunting with a bow is that there is no noise. A shot doesn't scare all the game in the area, and even the animal being shot at often isn't startled. Because it is so hard to hit anything, especially something as small as a grouse—smaller yet when it is remembered that it must be hit in the

middle of the middle or the arrow will brush through the feathers without hitting the body of the grouse—it is easy to shoot all the arrows carried without hitting the bird. Failure is much more common than success. The area that must be caught by the arrow is only as big as a fist, and if the bird is twenty feet away, sitting in willows or brush, hitting something that small with a wooden bow and wooden homemade arrows, driving the back end of a .38 special blunt into a target that small is close to impossible. Once I shot fourteen arrows at a grouse sitting at the base of a clump of willows not ten feet away, every arrow I had with me, and the grouse was still there, and stayed there while I carefully reached forward, pulled one of the arrows out of the ground, knocked it on the string and shot one more time—this time brushing the grouse enough to startle it and make it fly away.

But when it is learned, when the bow is understood and used as it was meant to be used, used as an extension of the mind and within its limits, the bow can be deadly. When shooting a true bow—not a sight-mounted compound with aluminum arrows (really almost a different kind of gun)—a true bow with no sight, it takes more practice, practice, until the fingers are calloused from the string and the shoulders are corded with the effort, driving the shafts into hay bales again and again. When it is done enough, when the practice has gone on so long that everything is automatic, a strange thing happens.

The arrow becomes alive. Without a sight, when it is at full draw and tucked back under the chin, the wood of the arrow sings and it is alive and the flight can be "felt." Looking down the shaft the center of the center, *inside* the core of the center of the middle of the target can be seen. When that feeling is right, when the arrow is part of the mind and the mind is part of the arrow and the release comes smoothly and the string takes the arrow correctly, the arrow has no choice but to go to that place, the center of the aimed place.

Some hunts with bows were disasters. No rabbits or grouse, all the arrows either lost because they snaked beneath the grass and couldn't be found or broke when they hit stumps, to leave the boys walking home with empty quivers and no meat. Sometimes all the boys would hunt for all the day, and there would be one rabbit, one grouse.

But not always. There was a time when all the wolves and coyotes and fox had been trapped out by the state—trying to control without knowing how to control. Since the wolves, coyotes, and fox were the only thing really holding the rabbits down, and since rabbits reproduce like, well, rabbits, the numbers became staggering. It was common to walk down a mile of dirt country road in the fall and count fifty, a hundred rabbits just sitting in the ditch or jumping back into the woods. They began to get tularemia—a disease transmittable to humans —and the state decided it was necessary to hunt the rabbits out, or at least take them down to a manageable number. Since almost no adults hunted them, the job fell on the boys, and it came at about the time bow hunting was at its peak. The rabbits were not wasted; after being checked for the disease and found clear, the carcasses were used for orphanages and poor farms. This was long before welfare or food stamps, and all extra or confiscated game was used for orphans and the poor.

Nobody counted all the rabbits taken, but limits were not checked, nor encouraged, and many, many thousands of them were killed.

On a day the boys were using wood bows and homemade arrows, in the high time of that hunt with empty .38 special-cartridge cases for blunts— on one single day the boys worked an eighty-acre stand of brush and poplar and took over a hundred rabbits. A hundred rabbits to get and tie the back legs to each other to drape across bicycles and cart back to Eckert Feed and Fur Supply, where old man Eckert paid a dime a rabbit.

Later there were larger hunts. Later there were days using .22 rifles when three and four hundred rabbits were taken—all carried into town draped over hand-pushed bicycles to be sold for a dime each. The state paid the money through old man

Eckert and then gave the meat to the poor and orphans, and it was not until years later that the boys found out Eckert was getting a quarter a rabbit and pocketing fifteen cents a rabbit for himself. And it was not for many years that the boys found out Eckert was rich and owned vast holdings of land west of town, many hundreds of acres, the same acres the boys hunted; not for many years that the boys found out that old man Eckert had lived through the death camps in Europe and now spent almost all of the money he made giving the boys a dime a rabbit and keeping fifteen cents a rabbit— spent all of the money he made helping other survivors of the camps find a life.

But none of the later hunts with the rifle or even still later hunts for love or hunts for life or hunts in the army or hunts in art equaled the hunt with bows when the rabbits were so many that they filled the woods and ditches and roads.

The first deer hunt with a bow started almost a year before the actual hunt took place.

A deer is so big a thing to kill with an arrow, so big and beautiful a thing, that the preparation becomes perhaps more important than the hunt itself, a kind of prayer.

Sometimes the rabbits died fast when the blunt took them, and always the grouse died fast, but there were times when the rabbits were hit wrong and then the death came not so fast, not so clean, more like a natural death than a hunting death, more like a wolf death or coyote death or fox death or weasel death or owl death for the rabbit—a death to make the hunter think of the animal. And when that happened, when the arrow hitting the rabbit did not end him fast but let him scream in the high-pitched death scream that rabbits have, it made deer hunting seem impossible.

There was too much animal for an arrow. It was forgotten then that almost all animals had given lives to arrows; that men in armor, men in blue cavalry, men in leather leggings had all died from arrows, died in hundreds, died in thousands, fell in rows to wooden shafts and steel or stone points.

A deer seemed so big. But then the excitement set in, a boy told another boy that somebody last year had taken an enormous buck—a six-, eight-, ten-pointer that dressed out at a hundred eighty, hundred ninety, two twenty-five pounds; that the buck had been taken with one arrow shot at forty, fifty, eighty yards and the deer just dropped.

Just dropped.

Clean.

That's how the boy said it—like some are dirtier than others; like there is a clean way to kill, to die. As if such a thing could be.

Soon it is too much, the excitement, and there comes a decision to hunt deer with a bow.

Preparation takes time—a year—and money. Practice is vital. The only way to bring a deer down is to get a good shot, a proper shot, a correct shot.

There are many bad shots. An arrow through the stomach, an arrow through a leg, an arrow through a rump, an arrow across the front of the chest, an arrow across the edge of the neck—all of these could kill the deer, let the deer bleed to death, but not kill it right away. A gut shot will kill but it might take hours, days, and if there is no blood trail to follow, the deer will wander off and die where it cannot be found. It will not be a clean kill.

There are many more bad places to hit a deer than there are proper places and so, practice. Cardboard cutouts of deer life-size are made and pinned to hay bales and shot at until they hang in tatters. Again and again at ten, twenty, even thirty yards the cardboard is hit, hit properly in its cardboard heart, hit correctly in its cardboard lungs—hit again and again until the cardboard deer dies a clean cardboard death.

But it is not the same when life is real—not ever the same.

First there is the matter of the arrow.

A deer cannot be killed with a blunt that works on a rabbit or a grouse. It takes a special point—a broadhead.

But broadheads are expensive—a quarter each just for the points—and they bend and get their edges ruined easily, so it is not feasible to practice with them. On top of that, the broadheads used then were just simple, flat two-bladed points that were difficult to mount on the shaft straight. Because they were flat-sided and quite large they tended to "fight the feathers," and cause the arrow to plane off in strange directions. Tip swore he shot one once that went all the way around in a circle and almost killed him but nobody saw it and almost nobody believed him.

Because the broadheads cost so much and break so easily and are seldom shot at targets, there are terrible problems with accuracy that make it extremely difficult to get a deer, but still the attempt continues.

Still the preparation goes on.

Each broadhead is mounted as straight as possible, glued with melted ferrule cement that dries hard as iron, and is then sharpened, and sharpened, and sharpened. . . .

For a broadhead to work it must cut effortlessly.

Even primitive man knew this. The boys once found a stone arrowhead in a block of dried and cracked clay near the edge of a river. The head was of black flint and shined like new when wet. Wayne held it up to the light and said, "Look, the light comes through," and as he twisted it to see the sun better, the old edges, buried in clay for hundreds, maybe thousands of years, the scalloped and shaped edges, slid in his grasp and nearly took a finger off with one small slicing action.

There were none of the razor-blade inserts when we hunted that make the modern heads so deadly, and the flatheads used then had to be hand-sharpened.

First a small file was used to shape a shallow, gradual edge on each side of the point. Considering that there may be twelve points—if such extravagance can be afforded—and each point has four edge-sides to file, the initial honing down can take considerable time. A week, two weeks can be spent, every spare moment used to file the heads. After the filing there is the actual sharpening, using an oilstone, and since no head is good unless it is as sharp as a razor and can literally shave the hair off an arm, this process may take longer than the filing. (It is, really, never done; Tip and Wayne argue that the points will get dull—lose their fine edge—just being exposed to air and they carry small stones while they're hunting and resharpen the heads during breaks or sometimes while walking down a road or —once with Wayne—while sitting in church, much to the distress of Wayne's mother, who hit him so hard with a hymnal he thought she'd dropped a pew on him.)

Much was not understood then about hunting deer with a bow. It is known now about camouflage, about hiding and hunting from stands. But then most people just walked quietly through the woods until a shot presented itself. Those who could afford them bought soft leather moccasins to make the walking silent—or as silent as it could be on dry leaves and grass—but most made their own moccasins from patterns found in magazines and books.

But even then the need for silence was understood, and the boys practiced walking constantly, feet straight ahead, weight down on the ball of the foot to step slowly, carefully, silently ahead, stopping every three or four steps to look into, into the *inside* of the woods, to look for a line, a curve, or a slight motion that could mean a deer.

It often never comes.

Days can be spent walking through woods, the bow held in the left hand with a broadhead nocked to the string, one finger holding the arrow against the bow, walking and looking and smelling and listening—waiting.

Waiting.

And sometimes if movement is not right or the boys aren't lucky—sometimes a whole season can be spent looking, waiting, hunting for nothing; nothing except walking through the beauty of autumn days in the thick forest, moving through color and clean air and the soft light of a million dappled leaves while the act of hunting forces all the things seen, all the beauty into the mind, but it is not until later, until years and a life later, that it is understood. When it becomes known that the reason for hunting is not the deer, never has been the deer, never would be the deer; the reason for hunting is just that: to hunt.

To hunt the sun, the wind, the trees—to hunt the beauty. In time, in memory, it all becomes more important than the deer, than the quarry.

Than the kill.

When it comes, it is not so much, and still it is more than anything before it and makes a sadness that will not go away even with life, even with all of life.

Everything, every aspect of it is remembered for all the rest of the time there is; everything.

It is early morning.

It is early morning and there are no clouds so the sun comes cleanly up in the east and filters new light through the chill air to make everything seem overly defined, almost to having cutting edges. Leaves are not just part of trees, part of the forest, but jump out in the morning air like small paintings, each a work of art alone. A rock catches light and becomes alive, seems to move; a tree limb stands out against the sky like an etching, caught and held in the new sun.

It is early morning and cold enough so the air sticks in the nose and sounds seem more clear, sharper than they do at other times; a grouse moves, leaves rustle, and it could be anything—a moose, a bear, a deer.

There is a deer, but not yet.

First there is the woods.

It is an eighty-acre patch of poplar. At one time it had been cleared land, a part of a small hundred-and-sixty-acre homestead, but the farmer who cleared the land had been driven out by the Depression of the 1930s. He had built a log house with two rooms and a loft and had tried to keep a family alive and happy on a hundred and sixty acres with eighty acres clear and eighty in brush and woods. But there was no market for anything the farmer grew, and he could not make enough for taxes, and so it went back to the state. And then back to nature. The poplars grew fast, and by the time of the hunt the trees were thirty feet high and the ground covered in hazel brush about waist high. The eighty acres can't be walked through in a straight line. The hunter must weave around the clumps of hazel, and it is hard because the ends of the bow snag and catch and the arrow shaft keeps banging against poplar trees, rattling and making enough noise to scare away any game within miles.

Any game but a deer—this deer, this special deer. But not yet.

There is the boy.

He hunts alone this time. Many times he has hunted this stand of woods with the other boys and taken grouse and rabbits with the blunts, walked through the woods in a line abreast. But this time Tip is sick and Wayne is on a trip and this has happened and that has happened, and he decided to come alone. He sometimes liked to hunt alone because he was alone so much of the time when he was in town because of his parents. He tries to have the right clothes, the right equipment, but there is no money, has never been any money, and so he must make do. He wears an old field jacket, so ragged it hangs almost in rags, but it is military green and seems to blend in and he thinks it is his lucky jacket because he was wearing it the day he got a shot at a twelve-point buck. He missed, but still he saw the buck, and though the shot went wide and missed he was of the thought that when hunting with a bow a miss was almost as important as hitting because actually hitting a deer seemed impossible—something in *Sports Afield* articles that always happened to somebody else.

He had many great misses. There was the twelve-pointer, and a spike buck that ran past him ten feet away, and a four-pointer he nearly stepped on and a six-pointer that stood perfectly still while he released a perfect, aimed shot that was heading exactly at the buck's heart but stuck in a two-inch sapling that stood in front of the deer. Misses all, arrows gone, skipping off tree limbs or rocks, flying away in small zips of light. So many misses that bow hunting for deer seemed not real to him—something done for fun alone; a kind of dance.

Until this day, this morning.

When it came, when it happened, it did not work the way it did in his dreams. There was a small clearing where the homestead cabin once stood. It had fallen in on itself and for the most part was a rotting mass of old logs and boards. But one wall still stood about four feet high, and as he approached the wall he caught a slight movement along the top of the wall out of the corner of his eye.

He froze, watching. Once he had seen a wolf hunting in a field. The wolf moved slowly, listening and watching, stopping absolutely still when there was any movement—a bird flying overhead, a mouse rustling in the grass, a bug—anything. The boy did the same when he hunted.

For a moment, for three breaths, he saw nothing and had nearly decided it must have been a small bird flitting by when it came again.

Along the top of the wall a line of fuzz seemed to move sideways. At first he couldn't make it work in his mind—a moving, horizontal fuzzy line. Then it moved again and he understood.

It was the back of a deer moving along the other side of the wall with its head down out of sight.

He held his breath, waiting, leaning forward as if his body were being pulled.

How far? he thought. Not fifteen, not even ten

yards. Feet. Twenty feet. The deer was moving along the wall not twenty feet from him, and with that thought, in that same instant, the deer appeared from in back of the logs.

It was a doe.

The light caught her as she came into view. She was losing the red summer color and had a brown coat, full and bushy so she looked almost unnaturally fat. The morning was cool and there were small jets of steam from her nostrils, little spurts that caught the morning sun and looked golden, almost like fire.

She had her head turned slightly away and had no knowledge, no idea the boy was there.

I'm so close, he thought—so close I could spit to her. He had never been this close to a live deer.

The bow.

He had completely forgotten the bow.

He let his eyes move down and saw that the arrow was still nocked to the string. Nothing in his thinking seemed to work right. I must do something, he thought—what? Oh yes, shoot. I must shoot. Still his arms did not move, seemed frozen.

But now things happened to take the decision away from the boy.

The doe had kept her head away from the boy but now she began to turn, the graceful neck arched, began to come around.

She would see him in a second, less, half a second. Less. No time.

Without thinking, without aiming or hesitating he raised the bow, drew the arrow to his chin and released—all in one motion.

There was a soft "thrummm" from the bowstring and the arrow left, flew from the bow, spiraling once and the boy saw the feathers seem to disappear against the side of the doe.

It didn't look like she'd been hit—the feathers just seemed to vanish.

She twitched slightly.

Not a jump. A small twitch, no more, and she turned to look at him, saw the boy standing, looked not just at him but up, into his eyes.

Then she turned away, walked slowly to the edge of the clearing and lay down in some tall grass there.

I missed her, he thought. Clean. For the moment he could not see her and he stepped forward to get a better view.

Then he saw the arrow.

It was lying on the ground six feet past where the doe was standing, just lying there, not buried in the grass or dirt.

From the point to the feathers it was completely red, totally covered with blood.

Oh, he thought. I hit her.

The red numbed him. He wasn't sure what he expected if he actually hit a deer. He always knew what to do when he missed a deer because he missed them all the time. When he missed he swore and made up an excuse—there was a crosswind, he shot too fast, the arrow planed on the point. A million excuses.

But he had no excuse for hitting a deer.

And he wanted one now badly.

He looked over in the grass, holding the bloody arrow, and saw the doe, watched the doe, and she looked at him once more, looked directly at him, into him, and he very much wanted an excuse for hitting the doe.

Then she turned away, turned her head away and stared into the clearing, ignoring him, stared through the clearing and through the woods and maybe through the sky, through everything, and she laid her head down—almost in sleep, the movement, though he knew better, knew that he had in less than a second ended something beautiful, something that could never be again, ended this doe— and she died. She laid her head down and took a last breath, in and out, pulled her back legs closer to her front and died.

Was no more.

Her world, the boy thought, *I have ended her world,* and the boy would live, would have a life and take a million breaths and eat and sleep and love and dance and have first things, first times, but not the doe.

She would have nothing. No world.

And he would never forget it; would remember everything, every aspect of it; would remember her color and the grass and the blood on the arrow and her last breath going out in steam, going out of her with her life—would remember the last of her for the rest of his life.

Duck Hunting

After grouse, after rabbits, after bow hunting for deer, but before the long winter hunts, there was duck hunting.

Sometimes it was walking along the river out of town, starting in the cold mornings, the rainy cold mornings of late October when nobody sane went outside.

Teal flew along the river, their wings whistling, and were difficult to hit because they flew so fast and never seemed to reveal themselves until it was too late to raise the old single-barrel sixteen-gauge and shoot.

Jump-shooting mallards was better. Wayne had a smokey-black Lab named Ike after the president, and he would retrieve with a lily-soft mouth no matter who shot the duck. North of town there were chains of swamps with open, small potholes of dark water where the mallards would sit. It was hard to walk because the peat under the swamp-grass was unfrozen and springy and frequently allowed a foot to go through down into the mud, where it tried to suck a boot off. But a rhythm could be felt after a time, and it was possible to move forward. Because the grass was so deep the mallards would be surprised, and it was while they were rising, their wings pounding to give them altitude—it was then that sometimes a shot could be taken, and Ike would watch with even brown eyes for the mallard to fall. At the moment it was hit, when it went from the beauty of a flying duck to the broken form of death —at that moment Ike would leap forward into the pothole and sometimes be waiting when the duck hit the water.

But there was an uncle . . .

Walk-hunting was fine except that it was limited and so clumsy that some of the art was lost.

But there was an uncle who had a duck-boat and an old truck and a rusty brown Chesapeake retriever named Robby, and the uncle and Robby took the boy out one morning to hunt ducks, and though the boy never hunted that way again it was in him and his mind from then on.

The uncle had just come back from fighting in Korea and would be in the boy's life for only one year before the uncle would move on to Montana, where he would hole up and think on what he had done and seen in Korea.

He loved the dog and took it with him everywhere, talked to it as if it were a person, and sometimes would even read to the dog out of books he carried that had strange-sounding names the boy could not understand, though there were several of them on the dashboard of the truck and the boy could read the titles on the spine. Titles like *The Collected Writings of Plato* and *Aristotelian Thinking*.

The boy did not sleep the whole night before and was up waiting when the uncle arrived at four o'clock.

It was pitch-dark and cold—so cold there was ice on the puddles left by rain during the night. The truck was a 1940 Ford with a cranky heater, but Robby was in the front seat with the uncle and climbed on the boy as soon as he got in the truck. The dog was warm and smelled of dog food and outside, and the boy cuddled with him while they drove north out of town to the flat swampy lakes that sat squat in the middle of the main migratory flight path.

At some point on the drive in the old truck through the dark morning the boy fell asleep with his face buried in the dog's neck-fur. He was awakened by the sound of the uncle talking.

"We'll work that stand of rice on the south end of the lake."

The voice was soft, even.

"Come in there quiet, before first light, and try

to catch the early-dawn movers like we did last time. . . ."

The boy nodded, but he felt the dog move and cock his ears and lean away and realized the uncle was talking to the dog and not him.

"May be some geese moving, too," the uncle said. "Most of them are already gone south but there might be a few." The uncle poured hot coffee from a thermos expertly, while driving, popped the cork back in the mouth of the thermos and then produced a half pint of Calvert Reserve from his duck-coat pocket and dropped a generous amount in the hot coffee. The smell of the whiskey on top of the hot coffee immediately filled the cab of the truck, but the boy pretended not to notice because he did not like drinking. To hide the smell of the whiskey he buried his nose in the dog's fur again.

The uncle spoke no more but sipped the coffee in silence while they drove for another half hour. Then he turned off the main road and killed the headlights and drove for ten or fifteen minutes in darkness so black the boy could see only a dim bulk of trees to the side of the track.

The dog knew where they were and became excited when the uncle stopped the truck.

Without speaking he climbed out of the truck and moved around to the rear. He pulled rubber boots out of the back end and jerked them on over his regular boots, then waited while the boy—who was already wearing rubber boots because that's all he had—came around the truck to help with the duck-boat.

The boat was twelve feet long, flat on the bottom and pointed at both ends so it would slide through the swamp-grass more easily. In the center was a seven-foot-long cockpit where two men and a dog could sit if they remained still and patient.

They put the boat in the water—or rather the uncle guided the boy, because it was still so dark he could see nothing—and the dog jumped in without having to be told.

The uncle brought two guns and handed the boy one—a sixteen-gauge Ithaca pump as old or older than he was—and put boxes of shells in the boat.

"Get in."

The boy was so excited that he tripped and stumbled and would have fallen had the uncle not caught him and helped him.

The boy moved to the front of the boat, and the uncle climbed in the back and laid his shotgun down and a large gunnysack down, stood and worked the pole with the steel expanding feet against the grass to propel the boat through the weeds and stands of rice.

It was still dark, but now the boy could see outlines, edges, and he watched ahead of the boat and made out the shape of a blind just before the boat bumped into it. The uncle poled back, moved the nose over, and worked slowly to the front of the blind. When the boat was in a small patch of clear water, he opened the sack and pulled out decoys, arranged them in a kind of fan, each held down with a lead sinker and a cord. Then he turned the boat and slid it back inside the blind, where he squatted down and laid the pole to the side on the grass.

"We'd better load—the light will come fast now when it comes."

He flipped his shotgun over, and the boy did the same with the Ithaca pump, loaded it with three high-base shells from the box on the floor of the boat and studied the weapon in the new morning light.

The boy had never seen such a gun. All the bluing was worn, but it had been kept in perfect shape and coated with a light film of fine oil that jumped to his fingers and somehow to his mouth and he could taste the steel, taste the bluing, taste all the hunts the gun had been on, taste the years of the gun.

He loaded it, and when he worked the pump to chamber a shell the action was so worn it almost worked itself, closed with a soft "snicking" sound that made him shiver and expect something he did not understand—some great adventure.

When the ducks came, the first ducks, they were high, just spots in the barely lighted sky, and the

uncle used a call to make the mallard feeding chuckle, and for a moment nothing happened. Then a small flock of eight or ten ducks set their wings and broke off in a long glide down toward the blind.

The boy could not stand it and when the ducks were still well out range he rose and fired, wobbling the boat and startling both the uncle and the dog.

The ducks veered away and the sudden explosion brought up hundreds of them that had been in the weeds around the boat. The boy stared, open-mouthed, while the uncle fired from a sitting position; once, twice, and two of the jumpers fell.

Before they hit the weeds Robby was over the side and heading for them. He brought one back within a minute—while the boy still stared—and went back for the other without being told. This one he found after working the weeds with his head down, belly-deep in swampwater, and carried it back with a wing flapping because the duck was still alive. The uncle quickly killed it and then turned to the boy and said, simply, "Maybe next time will be better."

And the next time was better.

A flock came in again high, specks in the gray-dawn sky, and the uncle called again, used the soft low chuckling sound from the call, and once more a group broke from the flock and started the glide down.

"I'll shoot left," the uncle whispered. "You right."

It was almost impossible to wait. The ducks seemed to hang in the air, caught on currents of wind that wouldn't let them down.

But they came, floating in a curve well out to the side to give them approach and landing room, and it seemed they would hit the water any second.

But this time the boy waited, watching the uncle out of the corner of his eye, waited until he couldn't stand it, and then waited even more until it seemed the ducks were going to land, were on their final approach, barely skimming the water near the decoys, and at last the uncle raised his shotgun and the boy did too and aimed at the duck on the right, aimed just in front of him and pulled the trigger.

Two ducks fell. The uncle had fired at exactly the same moment. The boy heard the pump work on the uncle's gun, did the same with his, and aimed at a mallard working to get high, flying straight up away from the water, and the boy fired and saw the duck break.

That's how it looked. How he thought of it. The duck broke. Its wings etched against the sky, broken and falling, the neck curved over backwards and he thought then, could not help but think then of the doe, the way the doe looked when she lay down in the grass and put her head over and down, and he had the first moment of true doubt; doubt that

THE OXFORD

Essential Dictionary
of New Words

THE OXFORD

Essential Dictionary
of New Words

EDITED BY
Erin McKean

BERKLEY BOOKS, NEW YORK

THE OXFORD ESSENTIAL DICTIONARY OF NEW WORDS

A Berkley Book / published by arrangement with
Oxford University Press, Inc.

PRINTING HISTORY
Berkley edition / July 2003

For information address: Oxford University Press, Inc.,
198 Madison Avenue, New York, New York 10016.

ISBN: 0-425-19097-8

BERKLEY®
Berkley Books are published by
The Berkley Publishing Group, a division of Penguin Group (USA) Inc.,
375 Hudson Street, New York, New York 10014.
BERKLEY and the "B" design are trademarks
belonging to Penguin Group (USA) Inc.

PRINTED IN THE UNITED STATES OF AMERICA

10 9 8 7 6 5 4 3 2 1

Contents

Staff	vi
Preface	vii
Introduction: What is a New Word?	viii
How to Use This Dictionary	xii
Using the Pronunciation Key	xv
Oxford Dictionary of New Words	1
New Words by Subject Area	301
Quick Syllabification Guide	324
Oxford Dictionaries	328
Finding New Words	330

Staff

Senior Editor:	Erin McKean
Managing Editor:	Constance Baboukis
Editors:	Christine Lindberg
	Carol Braham
	Orin Hargraves
	Enid Pearsons
Editorial Assistant:	Ryan Sullivan

Preface

The *Oxford Essential Dictionary of New Words* is a helpful, up-to-the-minute guide to the constantly changing vocabulary of American and World English. Whether it is used as a companion to a larger dictionary or as a book to browse through, this collection of new words will help you understand the latest developments in technology, law, medicine, politics, and popular culture.

The *Oxford Essential Dictionary of New Words* presents both the flashy and obvious new words (*flexecutive, IM, kidult*) as well as 'stealth' new words, such as *camper* (in the sense 'happy camper,') *must-have*, and *roaming*. This allows for a fuller picture of how our language is changing and growing, and for a more complete understanding of the creativity and inventiveness of speakers of English.

This *Dictionary* is intended to showcase new words and new senses that are not represented or are underrepresented in current dictionaries of contemporary English. Example sentences and etymologies are included wherever possibly to put words in both current and historical context, and essential grammatical information and full pronunciations are given to ensure confident, correct use of tricky words. The *Oxford Essential Dictionary of New Words* is a handy reference to be carried with you to enhance your reading and comprehension wherever you go.

Introduction:
What is a New Word?

New words are the tip of the iceberg of lexicography. They stick up and attract all the attention, yet at least eighty percent of the work done on any dictionary isn't about new words at all. It lies below the surface, invisible. Because of the showy, flaunting, extroverted visibility of certain new words, lexicographers can get tired of the assumption that tracking and defining these words is the be-all and end-all of their job. The tracking of new words, although exciting, rewarding, and occasionally glamorous, is usually complicated and headache-inducing. This cephalalgic quality is due to the fuzzy nature of the words "new" and "word."

The general idea of what constitutes a new word is simple. A new word is a novel arrangement of letters with a meaning not quite duplicated by any other arrangement of letters. This is the ideal form of a new word. Like most ideals, this is rarer than we'd like. Real-world new words are messier. For one thing, new "words" are often made up of more than one word—they're *multiword lexical units*, to be technical. These are words like *call center, cancer cluster,* and *carbon sink,* just to flip through the C's. Often, "new" words are merely new senses of an existing word—stilll exciting for the lexicographer, but often just a source of irritation and "what's the language coming to?" for the layperson. It's also quite common for journalists and pundits to be all agog over a 'new' word (especially a slangy one) only to find, upon consulting the *Oxford English Dictionary,* that it was first used hundreds of years ago.

For the lexicographer, choosing new words to include in a conventional dictionary can be frustrating and tantalizing. A new word must earn its place in the dictionary by showing that people are using it—lots of people, in lots of different places. A new word, no matter how apt or shiny or endearing, won't justify its place in any one-volume dictionary unless the lexicographers are convinced that it's not just a flashy fashionable mirage, there for a season and then gone. Of course, by the time lexicographers amass this kind of evidence, the obvious newness of the word has usually rubbed off, and it's been assimilated into the general vocabulary. This is great for proving that the new word is a stolid citizen of the English language, but not so great for creating excitement and feeling like a linguistic explorer. Every lexicographer has a few favorite new-word candidates for which the evidence of widespread use is not quite up to standard, and like a perennial runner-up in a beauty contest, each revision sees these candidates less and less likely to be included. This doesn't mean that they're not 'real' words, but just that they're not used by enough people to be elected to that most democratic of reference works, the general-purpose dictionary. Like those beauty contest runners-up, they're still beautiful, but not appealing enough to mass taste.

Thus this collection of new words. Some of these words just barely missed their chance in the last round of dictionary revision, and are included here, making slightly delayed debuts. Some are poised on the brink of inclusion in the next round of dictionary revision, and are trying their wings here. Some of these words, especially new variant forms, are understudies, only a few citations of use away from getting that starring role. And some of these words are merely embryonic, used once or twice (these are often called *nonce words*) and still gestating. They may emerge to a full and satisfying life in a general dictionary, or they may be stillborn and wither away. Some of the words in the book are old words that have acquired a new figurative meaning so slowly and stealthily that the general reader should not have even noticed the change (*expenditure*, for example, has come to be used in nonmonetary contexts, and the entry for it in this book is a reflection of that change.) We have included these "new" words in this book to highlight this type of language change. Some of these words have already been included in the very latest editions of contemporary American English dictionaries, and are included here to direct more attention to their existence. Other new words that we've included here are words that may have appeared in other dictionaries as undefined forms at the end of a entry or as undefined words in a list, but that we have decided deserve full definitions and entries (*fallacious* and *outdrink* are examples of this kind of entry.) Many other new words in this book are the result of functional shifts, whereby an existing word comes to be used with another grammatical function—most often another part of speech. This last category is very interesting to the lexicographer and the student of language, and we have included many of this kind of new word in this book.

In this book the goal is to showcase these nascent words for education and entertainment. Some of these words are useful, some are edifying, and some are merely amusing. Many of these words are like concept cars at an auto show—they're just to show what could be done, not what people will be driving next year or even next decade. Many of the definitions given are sketches because the words themselves are even more mutable than the general run of English vocabulary, and because finding one or two more examples of use could recast what the lexicographer believes the word to mean.

Included in this book are words, phrases, and senses that have come into being or prominence since 1990, and which, at the time of writing, still seemed to have the gloss of newness about them. The idea is to cover as wide a variety of new words as possible in a book that is not bound as tightly by the expectations of authority that coil around the general dictionary. This book is intended to be more of a showcase and a display of new words rather than a chance to give them a firm lexicographical imprimatur.

In order to make this book more useful, we have also included a series of indexes to the words by subject matter, including Abbreviations, Arts and Music, Business, Computing, Encyclopedic Terms, Food and Clothing, Language, Law, Politics, and Government, Lifestyle, Medicine and Health, People and Society, Popular Culture, Religion, Science and Technology, Sports, and World English. These indexes put words in context and let you use the dictionary outside of the normal constraints of alphabetical order.

In addition, we have included a long list of possible derivatives, with their syllabification and parts of speech. These derivatives are words formed by adding prefixes and suffixes to existing words, and their definitions are readily understood from the meanings of the root word and the prefix or suffix. They are included here as aids to syllabification and spelling.

Some of the words in this book also appear in three recent Oxford dictionaries, *The New Oxford Dictionary of English, The New Oxford American Dictionary,* and the *Oxford American College Dictionary.* These words have been included where their omission would seem to be an oversight or if they are necessary to understand the definition of a newer word.

In compiling this book I and the rest of the US Dictionaries staff have relied heavily on the collegial and cheerful help of the lexicographers of the Oxford University Press UK, especially Sara Hawker, James McCracken, Judy Pearsall, Catherine Soanes, Angus Stevenson, and the extremely goodhearted and generous Elizabeth Knowles. In addition, the help of Jesse Sheidlower, Suzanne Pinnington, Stuart Jenkins, and Michael Profitt of the *Oxford English Dictionary* was invaluable. Of course, any infelicities, clunkers, or outright errors are mine.

—Erin McKean
Senior Editor, US Dictionaries
Oxford University Press

How to Use the
Oxford Essential Dictionary of New Words

The "entry map" below explains the different parts of an
entry.

Syllabification

Pronunciation set off
with slashes / /

in•vac•u•ate /in'vækyōō‚āt/
  ▸ **verb** [trans.] confine (people) to a space
in an emergency.
  ■ use a defined space in this way: *these designs permit us
to invacuate tenants to a safe haven within the building.*
-DERIVATIVES **in•vac•u•a•tion** noun
-ORIGIN on the pattern of *evacuate.*

Subsenses
signalled by ■

Etymology section

Examples in *italic*

Derivative section,
derivatives in **bold face**

land /lænd/
Grammar information in square brackets [ ]
  ▸ **noun** [in combination] figurative a particular sphere of activity or group of people: *the blunt, charmless climate of
techno–land.*
-PHRASES **the land of the free** the United States of
America.

Phrases in **bold face**

min•i•stroke /'minē‚strōk/
  ▸ **noun** a temporary blockage of the blood supply to the
brain, lasting only a few minutes and leaving no noticeable symptoms or deficits. Also called TRANSIENT ISCHEMIC
ATTACK.

Cross references in BOLD SMALL CAPITALS

Main entries and other boldface forms

Main entries appear in boldface type, as do inflected forms, idioms and phrases, and derivatives. The words PHRASES and DERIVATIVES introduce those elements. Main entries and derivatives of two or more syllables show syllabification with centered dots.

Parts of speech

Each new part of speech is introduced by a small right-facing arrow.

Senses and subsenses

The main sense of each word follows the part of speech and any grammatical information (e.g., [trans.] before a verb definition). If there are two or more main senses for a word, these are numbered in boldface. Closely related subsenses of each main sense are introduced by a solid black box. In the entry for **invacuate** above, the main sense of "confine (people) to a space in an emergency" is followed by a related sense, "use a defined space in this way."

Example sentences

Example sentences are shown in italic typeface; certain common expressions appear in bold italic typeface within examples.

Cross references

Cross references to main entries appear in small capitals. For example, in the entry **ministroke** seen previously, a cross reference is given in bold small capitals to the entry for TRANSIENT ISCHEMIC ATTACK.

Usage notes

Usage notes appear in boxes after the entry to which they refer:

par•tial-birth a•bor•tion /ˈpärsHəl ˌbərTH əˈbôrsHən/
  ▸ **noun** a late-term abortion of a fetus that has already died, or that is killed before being completely removed from the mother.
  USAGE: The term **partial-birth abortion** is used primarily in legislation and pro-life writing about this procedure. Pro-choice, scientific, and medical writing uses the term *D&X*, for *dilation and extraction*.

Appendix

A handy appendix at the back of the book features a list of further derivatives with syllabification and parts of speech.

Key to the Pronunciations

This dictionary uses a simple respelling system to show how entries are pronounced, using the following symbols:

æ	*as in*	**hat** /hæt/, **fashion** /ˈfæsHən/, **carry** /ˈkærē/
ā	*as in*	**day** /dā/, **rate** /rāt/, **maid** /mād/, **prey** /prā/
ä	*as in*	**lot** /lät/, **father** /ˈfäTHər/, **barnyard** /ˈbärn‚yärd/
b	*as in*	**big** /big/
CH	*as in*	**church** /CHərCH/, **picture** /ˈpikCHər/
d	*as in*	**dog** /dôg/, **bed** /bed/
e	*as in*	**men** /men/, **bet** /bet/, **ferry** /ˈferē/
ē	*as in*	**feet** /fēt/, **receive** /riˈsēv/
er	*as in*	**air** /er/, **care** /ker/
ə	*as in*	**about** /əˈbowt/, **soda** /ˈsōdə/, **mother** /ˈməTHər/, person /ˈpərsən/
f	*as in*	**free** /frē/, **graph** /græf/, **tough** /təf/
g	*as in*	**get** /get/, **exist** /igˈzist/, **egg** /eg/
h	*as in*	**her** /hər/, **behave** /biˈhāv/
i	*as in*	**guild** /gild/, **women** /ˈwimin/
ī	*as in*	**time** /tīm/, **fight** /fīt/, **guide** /gīd/, **hire** /hīr/
ir	*as in*	**ear** /ir/, **beer** /bir/, **pierce** /pirs/
j	*as in*	**judge** /jəj/, **carriage** /ˈkærij/
k	*as in*	**kettle** /ˈketl/, **cut** /kət/
l	*as in*	**lap** /læp/, **cellar** /ˈselər/, **cradle** /ˈkrādl/
m	*as in*	**main** /mān/, **dam** /dæm/
n	*as in*	**honor** /ˈänər/, **maiden** /ˈmādn/
NG	*as in*	**sing** /siNG/, **anger** /ˈæNGgər/
ō	*as in*	**go** /gō/, **promote** /prəˈmōt/
ô	*as in*	**law** /lô/, **thought** /THôt/, **lore** / lôr/
oi	*as in*	**boy** /boi/, **noisy** /ˈnoizē/
o͝o	*as in*	**wood** /wo͝od/, **football** /ˈfo͝ot‚bôl/, **sure** /sHo͝or/

o͞o	*as in*	food /fo͞od/, **music** /ˈmyo͞ozik/
ow	*as in*	mouse /mows/, **coward** /ˈkowərd/
p	*as in*	put /po͝ot/, **cap** /kæp/
r	*as in*	run /rən/, **fur** /fər/, **spirit** /ˈspirit/
s	*as in*	sit /sit/, **lesson** /ˈlesən/
SH	*as in*	shut /SHət/, **social** /ˈsōSHəl/, **action** /ˈækSHən/
t	*as in*	top /täp/, **seat** /sēt/
ṭ	*as in*	butter /ˈbəṭər/, **forty** /ˈfôrṭē/, **bottle** /ˈbäṭl/
TH	*as in*	thin /THin/, **truth** /tro͞oTH/
TH	*as in*	then /THen/, **father** /ˈfäTHər/
v	*as in*	never /ˈnevər/, **very** /ˈverē/
w	*as in*	wait /wāt/, **quick** /kwik/
(h)w	*as in*	when /(h)wen/, **which** /(h)wiCH/
y	*as in*	yet /yet/, **accuse** /əˈkyo͞oz/
z	*as in*	zipper /ˈzipər/, **musician** /myo͞oˈzisHən/
ZH	*as in*	measure /ˈmeZHər/, **vision** /ˈviZHən/

Foreign Sounds

KH	*as in*	Bach /bäKH/
N	*as in*	en route /äN ˈro͞ot/, **Rodin** /rōˈdæN/
œ	*as in*	hors d'oeuvre /ôr ˈdœvrə/, **Goethe** /ˈgœtə/
Y	*as in*	Lully /lYˈlē/, **Utrecht** /ˈY,treKHt/

Cutbacks

A hyphen will replace a section of a pronunciation when that section would be repeated redundantly. Cutbacks will occur primarily in three areas:

a) where the headword has a variant pronunciation:

quasiparticle /ˌkwäzīˈpärṭəkəl, ˌkwäzē-/

b) in derivative blocks:

dangle /ˈdæNGgəl/
dangler /-glər/
dangly /-glē/

Note: Cutbacks always refer back to the headword pronunciation, not the preceding derivative.

c) at irregular plurals:

> **parenthesis** /pə'renTHəsis/
> **parentheses** /-ˌsēz/

Stress marks

Stress marks are placed before the affected syllable. The primary stress mark is a short vertical line above the letters ['] and signifies greater pronunciation emphasis should be placed on that syllable. The secondary stress mark is a short vertical line below the letters [ˌ] and signifies a weaker pronunciation emphasis.

Additional information

- Some pronunciations show a letter within parenthesis to indicate this as a variant pronunciation. For example, some people say the d in sandwich, others do not.

- Variant pronunciations, separated by semicolons, are generally listed with the more common pronunciation first.

- A hyphen sometimes serves to separate syllables where the pronunciation would otherwise be confusing.

- Generally, only the first of two identical headwords will have a pronunciation given.

- Where a derivative adds a common suffix to the headword, the derivative may not have a pronunciation. A pronunciation will not be shown for suffixes such as "-less," "-ness," "-ly," each time they appear in derivatives.

A

AAVE
▶ **abbreviation** Linguistics African-American Vernacular English.

abs /æbz/ informal
▶ **plural noun** the abdominal muscles.

ac•cess charge /'ækses ˌCHärj/ (also **ac•cess fee** /'ækses ˌfē/)
▶ **noun** a charge made for the use of computer or local telephone-network facilities.

ac•cor•di•on sched•ul•ing /ə'kôrdēən ˌskejo͞oliNG/
▶ **noun** the practice of continually adjusting the work schedule of part-time or temporary workers to accommodate a company's changing labor requirements.

a•cha•ry•a /ə'CHärēə/
▶ **noun** (in India) a Hindu or Buddhist spiritual teacher or leader.
■ an influential mentor.
-ORIGIN early 19th cent.: from Sanskrit *ācārya* 'master, teacher.'

ac•id re•flux /'æsid 'rēfləks/
▶ **noun** the flow of stomach contents back into the esophagus, usually after a meal.

ack•ers /'ækərz/
▶ **plural noun** Brit. informal money.
-ORIGIN 1930s (originally used by British troops in Egypt as a name for the piaster, an Egyptian monetary unit): probably an alteration of Arabic *fakka* 'small change, coins.'

ACMOS
> ▸ a system of alternative medicine that combines princi-
ples of acupuncture with modern technology and bio-
physics.
 –ORIGIN acronym from *Analysis of the Compatibility of
Matter on the Organism and its Synergy.*

a•cous•tic shock /ə'ko͞ostik 'sHäk/
> ▸ **noun** damaged hearing suffered by the user of an ear-
phone as a result of sudden excessive noise in the device.

ac•tion•a•ble /'æksHənəbəl/
> ▸ **adjective** Law giving sufficient reason to take legal action:
an actionable assertion. ■ able to be done or acted on;
having practical value: *insightful and actionable information on the effect advertising is having on your brand.*

ac•tive bar•ri•er /'æktiv 'bærēər/
> ▸ **noun** a barrier that allows passage of defined agents
while preventing or impeding others, in particular:
■ a security barrier that responds to attempted entries
with sensors or personnel. ■ a physical or chemical barrier that intercepts contaminants, debris, or the like.

ac•tive•wear /'æktiv,wer/
> ▸ **noun** clothing designed to be worn for sports, exercise,
and outdoor activities.

act the mag•got /'ækt тнə 'mægət/
> ▸ **phrase** Irish informal behave in a foolishly playful way.

ac•u•point /'ækyo͞o,point/
> ▸ **noun** any of the supposed energy points on the body
where needles are inserted during acupuncture or
where manual pressure is applied during acupressure.

ad•min•is•tra•tive law /əd'mini,strātiv 'lô; -strətiv/
  ▸ **noun** legislative requirements, typically for businesses, issued by government agencies in published regulations.

a•do•bo /ə'dōbō/
  ▸ **noun** (pl. **a•do•bos**) a spicy dish or sauce, in particular: ■ a Filipino dish of chicken or pork stewed in vinegar, garlic, soy sauce, bay leaves, and peppercorns. ■ a paste or marinade made from chili peppers, vinegar, herbs, and spices, used in Mexican cooking to flavor meat or fish.
  –ORIGIN Spanish, literally 'marinade.'

a•dre•nal•ized /ə'drēnl,īzd/
  ▸ **adjective** affected with adrenalin.
  ■ informal excited, charged, or tense: *they possess an adrenalized vigor that distinguishes them from other bands.*

ADSL
  ▸ **abbreviation** asymmetric digital subscriber line, a technology for transmitting digital information over standard telephone lines that allows high-speed transmission of signals from the telephone network to an individual subscriber, but a slower rate of transmission from the subscriber to the network.

ad•ult•es•cent /,ædl'tesənt; ə,dəl-/
  ▸ **noun** informal a middle-aged person whose clothes, interests, and activities are typically associated with youth culture.
  –ORIGIN 1990s: blend of *adult* and *adolescent.*

ad•vanced place•ment /əd'vænst 'plāsmənt/ (abbreviation: **AP**)
  ▸ **noun** the placement of a student in a high school course that offers college credit if successfully com-

pleted: [as adj.] *advanced placement English and chemistry courses.*

ad•ven•ture /æd'venCHər/
▸ **adjective** (of an activity) daring and exciting: *adventure sports.*

ad•ver•game /'ædvər,gām/
▸ **noun** a downloadable or Internet-based computer game that advertises a brand-name product by featuring it as part of the game.
–DERIVATIVES **ad•ver•gam•ing** noun
–ORIGIN blend of *advertisement* and *game.*

aer•i•al lad•der /'erēəl 'lædər/
▸ **noun** a long extension ladder, especially on a fire engine, used to reach high places.

aer•o•dyne /'erə,dīn/
▸ **noun** any heavier-than-air aircraft that derives its lift principally from aerodynamic forces.

aer•o•med•i•cal /,erō'medikəl/
▸ **adjective** relating to medical issues associated with air travel.

aer•o•med•i•cine /,erō'medisən/
▸ **noun** a branch of medicine relating to conditions specific to flight.

af•fect•ed class /ə'fektid ,klæs/
▸ **noun** a defined group affected by legislation or prevailing practice, especially one adversely affected by discrimination.

af•flu•en•tial /,æflōō'enCHəl/ informal
▸ **adjective** rich and socially influential: *the daughter of an affluential businessman.*

▸**noun** a rich and socially influential person: *the local afflu-entials have driven up property values.*
–ORIGIN 1970s: blend of *affluent* and *influential.*

af•flu•en•za /ˌæflo͞o'enzə/
▸ **noun** a psychological malaise supposedly affecting young wealthy people, symptoms of which include a lack of motivation, feelings of guilt, and a sense of isola-tion.
–ORIGIN 1970s: blend of *affluent* and *influenza.*

Af•fri•la•chian /ˌæfri'lāCHən/
▸**noun** an African American who is native to or resides in Appalachia: [as adj.] *Affrilachian poets.*

a•flut•ter /ə'flət̬ər/
▸ **adjective** [predic.] in a state of tremulous excitement: *he has the physique that could send a thousand female hearts aflutter.*

Af•ri•can Eve hy•poth•e•sis /'æfrikən 'ēv hī,päTHəsis/
▸**noun** another term for EVE HYPOTHESIS.

af•ter•care /'æftər,ker/
▸ **noun** childcare for the period between the end of the school day and the end of the parent's work day: *an af-tercare facility at the local YMCA.*

age-mate /'āj ,māt/
▸ **noun** a person or animal that is the same age as an-other.

gent /'ājənt/
▸**noun** Computing an independently operating Internet pro-gram, typically one set up to locate information on a specified subject and deliver it on a regular basis.

age of rea•son /ˈāj əv ˈrēzən/
▸ noun 1 (**Age of Reason**) the Enlightenment.
2 (especially in the Roman Catholic Church) the age at which a child is held capable of discerning right from wrong.

ag•glu•tin•o•gen /əˈglo͞otnəjən/
▸ noun Biology an antigen that stimulates the production of an agglutinin (a substance that causes the clumping together of bacteria or red blood cells).

ag•gre•ga•tor /ˈægrəˌgātər/
▸ noun Computing an Internet company that collects information about other companies' products and services and distributes it through a single Web site.

a•hi /ˈähē/
▸ noun the Japanese name for yellowfin tuna.

❡ **ai•lur•o•phile** /īˈlo͞orəˌfīl; āˈlo͞or-/
▸ noun a cat lover.

air ball /ˈer ˌbôl/
▸ noun Basketball a shot that misses the backboard, rime, and net entirely.

air•date /ˈerˌdāt/
▸ noun the date on which a particular television or radio program is scheduled to be broadcast.

air•pot /ˈerˌpät/
▸ noun a container for storing and dispensing coffee or other beverages that maintains a constant temperature by use of thermal glass insulation.

aj•o•wan /ˈæjəˌwän/
▸ noun an annual plant (*Trachyspermum ammi*) of the

parsley family, with feathery leaves and white flowers, native to India.
■ the aromatic seeds of the ajowan plant, used as a culinary spice. ■ the essential oil of the ajowan plant.
-ORIGIN from Hindi *ajvāyn*.

a•lert /ə'lərt/
▸ **noun** a signal on an electronic device that prompts the user to do something or attracts their attention: *a vibrating alert is a discreet alternative to a ringing phone.*

a•li•as•ing /'ālēəsiNG/
▸ **noun** Computing the distortion of a reproduced image so that curved or inclined lines appear inappropriately jagged, caused by the mapping of a number of points to the same pixel.

a-life /'ā ˌlīf/
▸ **noun** short for artificial life (the production or action of computer programs or computerized systems that stimulate the characteristics of living organisms).

A-list /'ā ˌlist/ (or **B-list** /'bē ˌlist/)
▸ **noun** a real or imaginary list of the most (or, for B-list, second-most) celebrated or sought-after individuals, especially in show business: [as modifier] *an A-list celebrity.*

Al•len wrench /'ælən ˌrenCH/ (Brit. **Allen key** /-ˌkē/)
▸ **noun** trademark an L-shaped metal bar with a hexagonal head at each end, used to turn bolts and screws bearing recessed sockets.
-ORIGIN 1960s: from the name of the manufacturer, the *Allen* Manufacturing Company, of Hartford, Connecticut.

all-night•er /ˌôl 'nītər/
▸ **noun** informal an event or activity that continues throughout the night, especially a study session before

an examination: *he would do an all-nighter, the way he used to in school.*

al-Nak•ba /æl 'nækbä/
▸ **noun** Palestinian term for the events of 1948, when many Palestinians were displaced from their homeland by the creation of the new state of Israel.
–ORIGIN from Arabic, literally 'the disaster.'

al Qae•da /æl 'kīdə; 'kādə/, (also **al-Qa'i•dah, al-Qae•da**) a militant Islamic fundamentalist group. Founded in the late 1980s to combat the Soviets in Afghanistan, its goal is to establish a pan-Islamic caliphate by collaborating with Islamic extremists to overthrow non-Islamic regimes and to expel Westerners and non-Muslims from Muslim countries.
–ORIGIN Arabic, literally 'the base.'

alt. (also **alt-**)
▸ **combining form** denoting a version of something that is intended as a challenge to the traditional version: *an alt.classical quartet.*
–ORIGIN 1990s: abbreviation of *alternative*, influenced by the *alt.* prefix of some Internet newsgroups.

al•tar girl /'ôltər ‚gərl/
▸ **noun** a girl who acts as a priest's assistant during a service, especially in the Roman Catholic Church.

alt.coun•try /'ôlt 'kəntrē/ (also **alt-coun•try**)
▸ **noun** a style of country music that is influenced by alternative rock.

am•a•kho•si /‚æmə'kōsē/
▸ **plural noun** S. African tribal leaders regarded collectively.
–ORIGIN Zulu and Xhosa, plural of *inkosi* 'ruler, chief.'

AMBER A•lert /'æmbər ə,lərt/ (also **Am•ber A•lert**)
‣ **noun** an emergency response system that disseminates information about a missing person, usually by means of radio or television broadcasts: *our state's AMBER Alert became operational last September.*
■ a public announcement or alert that uses this system: *the AMBER alert gave a description of the suspected abductor.*
–ORIGIN acronym from America's Missing: Broadcast Emergency Response, named after Amber Hagerman, a child kidnapped in Texas in 1996.

am•bu•lo•ce•tus /,æmbyələ'sētəs/
‣ **noun** a large carnivorous amphibian (*Ambulocetus natans*, order Cetacea) of the Eocene epoch, an early ancestor of today's whales.
–ORIGIN modern Latin, from Latin *ambulare* 'to walk' + *cetus* 'whale.'

am-dram /'æm ,dræm/
‣ **noun** [treated as sing. or pl.] informal amateur dramatics.

a•men cor•ner /'āmen ,kôrnər/
‣ **noun** (in some Protestant churches) seats, usually near the preacher, occupied by those who lead responses from the congregation.

amp /æmp/ informal
‣ **verb** (often **amp something up**) **1** play (music) through electric amplification: *their willingness to amp up traditional songs virtually began the folk-rock genre.*
2 [as adj.] (**amped** or **amped up**) informal full of nervous energy, especially through taking amphetamines or similar drugs.

Am•pa•kine /'æmpə,kīn/
‣ **noun** (trademark) any of a class of synthetic compounds that facilitate transmission of nerve impulses in the

brain and appear to improve memory and learning capacity.
-ORIGIN 1990s: from *AMPA* (an acronym denoting certain receptors in the brain) + Greek *kinein* 'to move.'

am•scray /ˈæmˌskrā/
▸ verb leave quickly; scram.
-ORIGIN Pig Latin for *scram*.

an•ac•ro•nym /əˈnækrənim/
▸ noun an acronym of which the constituent letters are taken from words that are unfamiliar to most people (e.g. *Nicam, scuba*).
-ORIGIN 1980s: from Greek *an-* 'without' + *acronym*.

an•a•tom•i•cal•ly cor•rect /ˌænəˈtämik(ə)lē kəˈrekt/
▸ adjective (of a doll) having the sexual organs plainly represented.

An•drew•sar•chus /ˌændrooˈsärkəs/
▸ noun a very large carnivorous mammal (*Andrewsarchus mongoliensis*, order Creodonta) of the Eocene epoch.
-ORIGIN modern Latin: from the name of the US paleontologist Roy Chapman *Andrews* (1884-1960), who led the expedition on which the animal's fossils were found, + Greek *arkhos* 'ruler.'

andro-
▸ combining form of men; male: *androcentric*.
-ORIGIN from Greek *anēr, andr-* 'man.'

an•dro•pause /ˈændrəˌpôz/
▸ noun a collection of symptoms, including fatigue and a decrease in libido, experienced by some older men and attributed to a gradual decline in testosterone levels.
-DERIVATIVES **an•dro•pau•sal** /ˈændrəˌpôzəl/ **adjective**

-ORIGIN 1960s: from **andro-**, on the pattern of *meno-pause*.

an•dro•stene•di•one /ˌændrōstēn'dīōn/
▸ **noun** an androgenic steroid from which testosterone and certain estrogens are derived in humans.

an•eu•ploid /'ænyo͞oˌploid/
▸ **adjective** Genetics not euploid.
-DERIVATIVES **an•eu•ploi•dy** noun

an•gel•ol•o•gy /ˌānjə'läləjē/
▸ noun theological dogma or speculation concerning angels: *Gnostic angelology influenced Pseudo-Dionysius.*
-DERIVATIVES **an•gel•ol•o•gist** /ˌānjə'läləjist/ noun
-ORIGIN mid 19th cent.

an•gi•o•sta•tin /ˌænjēō'stætn/
▸ noun Medicine a drug used to inhibit the growth of new blood vessels in malignant tumors.

an•gry white male /'æNGgrē ˌ(h)wīt 'māl/
▸ noun derogatory a politically conservative or anti-liberal white man.

an•guish /'æNGgwisH/
▸ **verb** [intrans.] be extremely distressed about something: *I spent the next two weeks anguishing about whether I'd made the right decision.*

an•i•mal
▸ **adjective** /'ænəməl/ [attrib.] Biology relating to or denoting the pole or extremity of an embryo that contains the more active cytoplasm in the early stages of development. The opposite of VEGETAL.

an•ti•a•li•as•ing /ˌæntēˈālēəsiNG; ˌæntī-/
▸ noun the reduction of jagged edges on diagonal lines in digital images: *is there a way to turn off antialiasing for NSPDFImageRep classes?*
–DERIVATIVES **an•ti•a•li•as** verb

an•ti•ma•lar•i•al /ˌæntēməˈlerēəl; ˌæntī-/
▸ adjective (of a drug) used to prevent malaria.
▸ noun an antimalarial drug.

an•ti•roll /ˌæntēˈrōl; ˌæntī-/
▸ adjective designed to prevent vehicles from rolling over when turning: *if the track is very bumpy, then antiroll bars are not your best bet.*

An•tis•the•nes /ænˈtisTHəˌnēz/ (*c.*445–*c.*360 BC), Greek philosopher and teacher, regarded as the founder of the school of Cynics. A pupil and friend of Socrates, he believed that happiness is based on virtuous action rather than ease and pleasure, and that virtue, once acquired, cannot be lost.

an•ti•ter•ror•ism /ˌæntēˈterəˌrizəm; ˌæntī-/
▸ noun the prevention or abatement of terrorism: *a meeting of experts on antiterrorism* | [as adj.] *antiterrorism measures.*

An•y•town /ˈenēˌtown/
▸ noun (also **Anytown USA**) any real or fictional place regarded as being typical of American small-town appearance or values: *the party was looking for that elusive candidate from Anytown.*

Ao•ra•ki-Mount Cook /owˈrækē ˌmownt ˈko͝ok/
official name for Mount Cook, the highest peak in New Zealand: 12,349 feet (3,764 m).

ap•pre•cia•tive /ə'prēsH(ē)ətiv/
▸ **adjective** feeling or showing gratitude or pleasure: *an appreciative audience* | *the team is very **appreciative** of your support.*
–DERIVATIVES **ap•pre•cia•tive•ly** adverb; **ap•pre•cia•tive•ness** noun

aq•ua /'äkwə; 'æk-/
▸ **noun** (especially in pharmaceutical and commercial use) water.
–ORIGIN Latin.

ar•a•mid /'ærəmid; 'er-/
▸ **noun** any of a class of synthetic polymers, related to nylon, that yield fibers of exceptional strength and thermal stability.
–ORIGIN 1970s: from *ar(omatic)* + *(poly)amid(e)*.

-arch
▸ **combining form** (forming nouns) denoting a ruler or leader: *monarch.*
–ORIGIN Greek *arkhos* 'ruling,' from *arkhein* 'to rule.'

ar•chive /'ärkīv/
▸ **noun** a complete record of the data in part or all of a computer system, stored on an infrequently used medium.
▸ **verb** create an archive of (computer data): [intrans.] *we began archiving in June* | [trans.] *neglecting to archive our files was a costly oversight.*

arc•to•phile /'ärktə,fīl/
▸ **noun** a person who collects or is very fond of teddy bears.
–DERIVATIVES **arc•to•phil•i•a** /,ärktə'filēə/ noun; **arc•toph•il•ist** /ärk'täfilist/ noun; **arc•toph•il•y** /-filē/ noun
–ORIGIN 1970s: from Greek *arctos* 'bear' + *philos* 'loving.'

a•re•li•gious /ˌāriˈlijəs/
▸ **adjective** not influenced by or practicing religion: *areligious rationalism was the prevalent trend.*

ar•e•ol•o•gy /ˌerēˈäləjē/
▸ **noun** the study of the planet Mars.
‑DERIVATIVES **ar•e•o•log•i•cal** adjective; **ar•e•ol•o•gist** noun & adjective
‑ORIGIN late 19th cent.: from *Ares* (Greek equivalent of the Roman war god Mars) + *-ology* (denoting a subject of study or interest).

ar•gan /ˈärgən/
▸ **noun** an evergreen Morocccan tree or shrub (*Argania spinosa*, family Sapotaceae) that has hard, heavy wood and yields seeds whose oil is used in cosmetics and cooking.
‑ORIGIN Moroccan Arabic, from Berber *argān*.

arm can•dy /ˈärm ˌkændē/
▸ **noun** informal a sexually attractive companion accompanying a person, especially a celebrity, at social events: *the athletes and their arm candy clustered around the bar.*

ar•my brat /ˈärmē ˌbræt/
▸ **noun** informal a child of a career soldier, especially one who has lived in various places as a result of military transfers.

ar•ri•vi•der•ci /əˌrēvəˈderCHē/
▸ **exclamation** goodbye until we meet again.
‑ORIGIN late 19th cent.: from Italian, literally 'to the seeing again.'

arse /ärs/ Brit. vulgar slang
▸ **verb** [trans.] make a botched attempt at something: *we'll make sure we haven't completely arsed up your system.*

ar•ti•fi•cial climb•ing /ˌärtə'fiSHəl 'klīmiNG/
▸ **noun** the sport of climbing on an indoor or outdoor wall whose surface simulates a mountain: *artificial climbing can be done regardless of the weather.*

ar•ti•fi•cial life /ˌärtə'fiSHəl 'līf /
▸ **noun** see **a-life.**

art•sy-craft•sy /'ärtsē 'kræftsē/ (chiefly Brit. also **art•y-craft•y** /'ärtē 'kræftē/)
▸ **adjective** informal interested or involved in making decorative artistic objects, especially ones perceived as quaint or homespun: *she had a lot of artsy-craftsy friends.*

ash•tang•a /æsH'täNGə/ (also **as•tang•a** /æs-/)
▸ **noun** a type of yoga based on eight principles and consisting of a series of poses executed in swift succession, combined with deep, controlled breathing.
-ORIGIN from Hindi *aṣṭaṇ* or its source, Sanskrit *ashṭaṇga* 'having eight parts,' from *ashtán* 'eight.'

as•i•a•go /ˌäsē'ägō/
▸ **noun** a strong-flavored cow's milk cheese made in northern Italy.
-ORIGIN named after *Asiago,* the plateau and town in northern Italy where the cheese was first made.

ASP
▸ **abbreviation** application service provider, a company providing Internet access to software applications that would otherwise have to be installed on individual computers.

ass-back•ward /'æs'bækwərd/ (also **ass-back•wards**) informal
▸ **adverb** in a manner contrary to what is usual, expected,

or logical: *I never did like to do anything simple when I could do it ass-backwards.*

▸**adjective** contrary to what is usual, expected, or logical: *they are taking an ass-backward approach to crime.*

as•sist•ed liv•ing /əˈsistid ˈlivɪNG/
▸ **noun** housing for the elderly or disabled that provides nursing care, housekeeping, and prepared meals as needed.

A•sta•na /əˈstänə/
a city in Kazakhstan, the capital since 1997; pop. (1990) 281,400. Former name **Akmola.**

as•tang•a /æsˈtäNGə/
▸ **noun** variant spelling of ASHTANGA.

as•tro•bi•o•lo•gy /ˌæstrōbīˈäləjē/
▸ **noun** the science concerned with life in space.

a•sym•met•ri•cal war•fare /āsəˈmetrikəl ˈwôrfer/
▸ **noun** warfare involving surprise attacks by small, simply armed groups on a nation armed with modern high-tech weaponry.

@
▸ **symbol for** 'at', used:
■ to indicate cost or rate per unit: *30 dictionaries @ $29.99 each.* ■ in Internet addresses between the user's name and the domain name: *murrayj@oup-usa.org.*

-athon
▸ **suffix** forming nouns denoting an action or activity which is carried on for a very long time or on a very large scale, typically to raise funds for charity: *talkathon | walkathon.*
-ORIGIN on the pattern of *(mar)athon.*

at sign /'æt ˌsīn/
▸ **noun** the symbol @.

at•tach•ment /ə'tæcHmənt/
▸ **noun** a computer file appended to an e-mail.

au na•tu•rel /ˌō næcHə'rel/
▸ **adjective & adverb** humorous naked: [as adv.] *the remote beach where we'd been camping au naturel.*

au•ric•u•lo•ther•apy /ôˌrikyəlō'THerəpē/
▸ **noun** a form of acupuncture applied to points on the ear in order to treat other parts of the body.
–ORIGIN 1970s: from Latin *auricula* 'external part of the ear' + *therapy*.

Ausch•witz Lie /'owsHvits 'lī/ (also **Ausch•witz lie**)
▸ **noun** the assertion that the Holocaust did not take place or that the number of deaths is exaggerated: *he was accused of using the Internet to spread the Auschwitz Lie.*
–ORIGIN from *Auschwitz,* a concentration camp in Poland.

auto-
▸ **combining form** relating to cars: *autocross.*
–ORIGIN abbreviation of *automobile.*

au•to•dial /'ôtōˌdīl/
▸ **verb** (**au•to•dialed, au•to•dial•ing**; Brit. **au•to•dialled, au•to•dial•ling**) [intrans.] Computing (of a modem) automatically dial a telephone number or establish a connection with a computer.

au•to•e•rot•ic as•phyx•i•a /'ôtō-i'rätik æs'fiksēə/
▸ **noun** asphyxia (suffocation) that results from intentionally strangling oneself while masturbating, in an

attempt to heighten sexual pleasure by limiting the oxygen supply to the brain.

au•tog•ra•phy /ôˈtägrəfē/
▸ noun an autobiography.

au•to•mat•ed clear•ing•house /ˈôtə‚mātid ˈkliriNG‚hows/
▸ noun the clearing and settlement system used by US commercial banks and other institutions.

au•to•pa•thog•ra•phy /‚ôtōpəˈTHägrəfē/
▸ noun an autobiography dealing primarily with the influence of a disease, disability, or psychological disorder on the author's life.
–ORIGIN blend of *autobiography* and *pathography*.

AYT
▸ abbreviation Computing informal (in e-mail) are you there?

B

ba•by•moth•er /'bābē͵məTHər/ (or **ba•by•fa•ther** /'bābē ͵fäTHər/)
▸ **noun** black English the mother (or father) of one or more of one's children.

bach /bæCH/ informal
▸ **verb** [intrans.] N. Amer. & Austral./NZ (especially of a man) live alone and do one's own cooking and housekeeping: *Baldy bached in a hut down the road a bit.*
▸ **noun** NZ a small vacation house.
 –ORIGIN late 19th cent. (as a verb): abbreviation of *bachelor.*

ba•cha•ta /bä'CHätä/
▸ **noun** a style of romantic music originating in the Dominican Republic.
 ■ a bachata song.
 –ORIGIN Caribbean Spanish, literally 'a party, good time.'

back cat•a•log /'bæk ͵kætl͵ôg; -͵äg/ (also Brit. **back catalogue**)
▸ **noun** all the works previously produced by a recording artist or record company: *the owner of the Elvis Presley back catalog.*

back•door sell•ing /bæk'dôr 'seliNG/
▸ **noun** the selling by wholesalers directly to the public, seen as detrimental to retailers.

back•drop /'bæk͵dräp/
▸ **verb** (**back•dropped, back•drop•ping**) give a background of: *the picture of a single tree backdropped by mountains was stunning.*

back•stab•bing /'bæk,stæbiNG/

▸ noun the action or practice of criticizing someone in a treacherous manner while feigning friendship: *we were due for another round of Aaron's backstabbing.*

▸ **adjective** (of a person) behaving in such a way: *the backstabbing little weasel.*

–DERIVATIVES **back•stab** verb; **back•stab•ber** noun

back•sto•ry /'bæk,stôrē/

▸ noun (pl. **back•sto•ries**) a history or background created for a fictional character in a film or television program: *a brief prologue detailing our hero's backstory.*

bac•te•rize /'bæktə,rīz/

▸ verb [trans.] (**be bacterized**) treat with bacteria: *the bacterized seedlings were more resistant than the nonbacterized ones.*

–DERIVATIVES **bac•te•ri•za•tion** /,bæktərə'zāsHən/ noun

bag /bæg/

▸ verb (**bagged, bag•ging**) [trans.] informal fit (a patient) with an oxygen mask or other respiratory aid.

–DERIVATIVES **bag•ger** noun

ba•guette /bæ'get/

▸ noun a slim, rectangular handbag with a short strap.

bail /bāl/

▸ verb [intrans.] informal abandon a commitment, obligation, or responsibility: *just two days before the conference, the keynote speaker bailed.*

■ (**bail on**) let (someone) down by failing to fulfill a commitment, obligation, or responsibility: *he looks a little like the guy who bailed on me.*

Baka /'bäkə/

▸ noun (pl. same) **1** a member of a nomadic Pygmy

people inhabiting the rain forests of southeastern Cameroon and northern Gabon.
2 the Bantu language of the Baka.
–ORIGIN the name in Baka.

bald•head /'bôld,hed/
▸ **noun** (among Rastafarians) a person who is not a Rastafarian.

bal•lo•tin /'bælətin/
▸ **noun** a deep decorative cardboard box, slightly larger at the top and with broad flaps, in which chocolates are sold.
–ORIGIN French, from *ballot* 'a small package of goods.'

bal•lo•tine /'bælətēn/
▸ **noun** a piece of roasted meat that has first been boned, stuffed, and folded or rolled into an egglike shape.
–ORIGIN mid 19th cent.: French, ultimately from *balle* 'a package of goods.'

bam•boo cur•tain /bæm'bōō 'kərtn/
▸ **noun** (often **the Bamboo Curtain**) a political, economic, and ideological barrier between China and noncommunist countries.
–ORIGIN 1950s: blend of *bamboo* (alluding to China) and *iron curtain* (a notional political barrier).

bam•my /'bæmē/ (also **bam•mie**)
▸ **noun** (**bam•mies**) (in the West Indies) a flat roll or pancake made from cassava flour.
–ORIGIN probably from a West African language.

ban•deau /bæn'dō/
▸ **noun** (pl. **ban•deaux** /bæn'dō/) [modifier] a woman's strapless top formed from a band of fabric fitting around the bust: *a bandeau bikini top.*

ban•do•bast /'bændə,bæst/
▸ **noun** variant spelling of BUNDOBUST.

Ban•ja Lu•ka /'bænjə 'lo͞okə/
a town in northern Bosnia–Herzegovina; pop. 195,000 (1991).

Bar•ca•loung•er /'bärkə,lownjər/
▸ **noun** trademark a type of deeply padded reclining chair.
-ORIGIN 1970s: from the name of Edward J. *Barcolo*, who acquired the original license to manufacture the chairs, and *lounger*.

Bar•ce•lo•na chair /,bärsə'lōnə ,CHer/
▸ **noun** trademark an armless chair with a curved stainless steel frame and padded leather cushions.

bar•do /'bärdō/
▸ **noun** (in Tibetan Buddhism) a state of existence between death and rebirth, varying in length according to a person's conduct in life and manner of, or age at, death.
-ORIGIN Tibetan *bár-do*, from *bar* 'interval' + *do* 'two.'

bare•back•ing /'ber,bækiNG/
▸ **noun** vulgar slang the practice of having anal intercourse without a condom.

barf bag /'bärf ,bæg/
▸ **noun** a bag provided for airplane passengers for use in case of vomiting associated with motion sickness.

bar•hop /'bär ,häp/ (also **bar hop**)
▸ **verb** (**bar•hopped, bar•hop•ping**) [intrans.] [noun] (**barhopping**) visit several bars in succession, having a drink in each.
-DERIVATIVES **bar•hop•per** noun

bar·i·a·trics /ˌberēˈætriks/
▸ **noun** the branch of medicine that deals with the study and treatment of obesity.
–DERIVATIVES **bar·i·a·tric** adjective

bar·i·at·ric sur·ger·y /ˌberēˈætrik ˈsərjərē/
▸ **noun** surgical removal of parts of the stomach and small intestines to induce weight loss.

ba·ri·sta /bəˈrēstə/
▸ **noun** a person who serves in a coffee bar.
–ORIGIN 1980s: Italian, 'barman.'

bark·i·tec·ture /ˈbäriˌtekCHər/
▸ **noun** humorous the art or practice of designing and constructing doghouses. ■ the style in which a doghouse is designed or constructed: *the property also included an elaborate doghouse that was a stunning example of pampered pooch barkitecture.*

Bar·num ef·fect /ˈbärnəm iˌfekt/
▸ **noun** Psychology the tendency to accept certain information as true, such as character assessments or horoscopes, even when the information is so vague as to be worthless.
–ORIGIN named after P. T. Barnum (1810–91), US showman renowned for his promotion of sideshow oddities; the word *Barnum* was in use from the mid 19th cent. as a noun in the sense 'nonsense, humbug.'

bar·rique /bəˈrēk/, French
▸ **noun** a wine barrel, especially a small one made of new oak in which Bordeaux and other wines are aged.
–ORIGIN late 18th cent.: French.

bashert /bæˈSHert/
▸ **noun** (in Jewish use) a person's soulmate, especially

when considered as an ideal or predestined marriage partner.
-ORIGIN Yiddish, 'fate, destiny.'

bas•i•lo•sau•rus /ˌbæsələ'sôrəs/
▸ **noun** a large marine cetacean (*Basilosaurus isis*) of the Eocene epoch, having a long, slender body and vestigial fore and hind limbs.
-ORIGIN modern Latin, from Greek *basileus* 'King' + *sauros* 'lizard.'

bas•ket-weav•ing /'bæskit,wēviNG/
▸ **noun** humorous a college course that is thought to be very easy.

bass-ack•ward /'bæs'ækwərd/ (also **bass-back•wards** /'bæs 'bækwərdz/)
▸ **adverb & adjective** jocular variant of ASS-BACKWARD.

bat•tered child syn•drome /'bætərd 'CHīld ,sindrōm/
▸ **noun** the set of symptoms, injuries, and signs of mistreatment seen on a severely or repeatedly abused child.

bat•tered wom•an syn•drome /'bætərd 'wŏŏmən ,sindrōm/
▸ **noun** the set of symptoms, injuries, and signs of mistreatment seen in a woman who has been repeatedly abused by a husband or other male figure.

bat•ter•ing par•ent syn•drome /'bæt̯əriNG 'perənt ,sindrōm/
▸ **noun** the set of symptoms and signs indicating a psychological disorder in a parent or child-care provider resulting in a tendency toward repeated abuse of a child.

bat•tler /'bætlər/
▸ **noun** chiefly Austral./NZ a person who refuses to admit defeat in the face of difficulty.

ba•zil•lion /bə'zilyən/
▸ **cardinal number** informal a very large exaggerated number: *you were going a bazillion miles per hour!*
-ORIGIN 1980s: probably a blend of *billion* and *gazillion* (also a large exaggerated number).

b-ball /'bē ,bôl/
▸ **noun** informal basketball.
-ORIGIN 1980s: contraction.

beard /bird/
▸ **noun** informal a person who carries out a transaction, typically a bet, for someone else in order to conceal the other's identity.
■ a person who pretends to have a romantic or sexual relationship with someone else in order to conceal the other's true sexual orientation.

Bea•tle /'bētl/ **adjective** characteristic of the Beatles: *a Beatle jacket.*

bed-block•ing /'bed ,bläkiNG/
▸ **noun** Brit. the long-term occupation of hospital beds, chiefly by the elderly, due to a shortage of suitable care elsewhere.

beef /bēf/
▸ **noun** informal a criminal charge: *getting caught with pot in the sixties was a narco beef.*

Bee•mer /'bēmər/ (also **Bea•mer**)
▸ **noun** informal a car or motorcycle manufactured by the company BMW.

-ORIGIN 1980s (originally US): representing a pronunciation of the first two letters of *BMW* (Bayerische Motoren Werke AG) + *-er*.

Beige Book /'bāzн ‚bŏŏk/
▸ **noun** a summary and analysis of economic activity and conditions, prepared with the aid of reports from the district Federal Reserve Banks and issued by the central bank of the Federal Reserve for its policy makers before a Federal Open Market Committee meeting.

Bel•fast sink /'belfæst 'siNGk/
▸ **noun** Brit. a type of deep rectangular kitchen sink, traditionally made of glazed white porcelain.

Bel•li•ni /bə'lēnē/
▸ **noun** (pl. **Bel•li•nis**) a cocktail consisting of peach juice mixed with champagne.
-ORIGIN from the name of Venetian painter Giovanni *Bellini* (c. 1430–1516): the cocktail is said to have been invented in Venice during a major exhibition of the artist's work in 1948.

Belt•way ban•dit /'beltwā ‚bændit/
▸ **noun** informal a company that does a large percentage of its business as a federal government contractor.
-ORIGIN from the use of *Beltway* as a nickname for Washington, DC.

beng•a /'beNGgə/
▸ **noun** a style of African popular music originating in Kenya, characterized by a fusion of traditional Kenyan music and a lively arrangement of guitars, bass, and vocals.
-ORIGIN 1980s: from Luo (a Kenyan language).

ben•to /ˈbentō/
▸ **noun** (pl. **ben•tos**) a lacquered or decorated wooden Japanese lunchbox.
■ a Japanese-style packed lunch, consisting of such items as rice, vegetables, and sashimi (raw fish with condiments).
-ORIGIN Japanese.

be•suit•ed /biˈso͞otid/
▸ **adjective** (of a person, especially a man) wearing a suit: *a quiet, besuited bank manager.*

be•ta-ad•ren•er•gic /ˈbātə ˌædrəˈnərjik/
▸ **adjective** of, relating to, or being a beta receptor (stimulation of which results in increased cardiac activity): *observing the effects of beta-adrenergic stimulation in aging rats.*

BEV
▸ **abbreviation** Linguistics black English vernacular, any of various nonstandard forms of English spoken by black people.

BGH
▸ **abbreviation** bovine growth hormone.

bhu•na /ˈbo͞onə/ (also **bhoo•na**)
▸ **noun** a medium-hot dry curry originating in Bengal, prepared typically by frying meat with spices at a high temperature: *lamb bhuna.*
-ORIGIN 1950s: from Bengali, Urdu *bhunnā* 'to be fried,' ultimately from Sanskrit *bhrajj* 'to fry, parch, roast.'

bi•bi /ˈbēbē/
▸ **noun** (pl. **bi•bis**) Indian a wife.

bib•li•cist /'biblisist/
▸ **noun** a person who interprets the Bible literally.
–ORIGIN mid 19th cent.: from *biblic(al)* + *-ist*.

bi•coast•al /bī'kōst̲l/
▸ **adjective** living on, taking place in, or involving both the Atlantic and Pacific coasts of the US: *a bicoastal businessman.*
–DERIVATIVES **bi•coast•a•lite** /bī'kōst̲l,īt/ noun

big air /'big 'er/
▸ **noun** a high jump in sports such as skateboarding, snowboarding, and BMX.

big crunch /'big 'krənCH/
▸ **noun** Astronomy a contraction of the universe to a state of extremely high density and temperature (a hypothetical opposite of the big bang).

big hit•ter /'big 'hitər/
▸ **noun** another term for HEAVY HITTER.

big•o•rex•i•a /,bigə'reksēə/
▸ **noun** informal another term for MUSCLE DYSMORPHIA.
–DERIVATIVES **big•o•rex•ic** adjective & noun
–ORIGIN *big* + Greek *orexis* 'appetite,' on the pattern of *anorexia.*

big tent /'big 'tent/
▸ **noun** used in reference to a political party's policy of permitting or encouraging a broad spectrum of views among its members: [as modifier] *we're running a big-tent campaign.*

bike /bīk/ informal
▸ **verb** chiefly Brit. cause (a letter or package) to be delivered by bicycle or motorcycle: *I'll get them to bike the scripts over.*

bio- /'bīō/
▶ **combining form** relating to or involving the use of toxic biological or biochemical substances as weapons of war: *bioterrorism.*

bi•o•a•cou•stics /ˌbīōəˈko͞ostiks/
▶ **plural noun** [treated as sing.] the branch of acoustics concerned with sounds produced by or affecting living organisms, especially as relating to communication.

bi•o•as•tro•naut•ics /ˌbīōˌæstrəˈnôṭiks/
▶ **noun** the study of the effects of space flight on living organisms.

bi•o•chem•i•cal /ˌbīōˈkemikəl/
▶ **adjective** relating to the chemical processes and substances that occur within living organisms.
▶ **noun** a biochemical substance.
–DERIVATIVES **biochemically** adverb

bi•o•cli•ma•tol•o•gy /ˌbīōˌklīməˈtäləjē/
▶ **noun** the study of climate in relation to living organisms and especially to human health.
–DERIVATIVES **bi•o•cli•mat•o•log•i•cal** /-ˌklīməṯlˈäjikəl/ adjective

bi•o•com•put•ing /ˌbīōkəmˈpyo͞oṭiNG/
▶ **noun** the design and construction of computers using biochemical components.
■ an approach to programming that seeks to emulate or model biological processes. ■ computing in a biological context or environment.

bi•o•con•ver•sion /ˌbīōkənˈvərzHən/
▶ **noun** the conversion of organic matter, such as animal or plant waste, into a source of energy through the action of microorganisms.

bi•o•e•lec•tron•ics /ˌbīōilek'träniks; -ˌēlek-/
▸ **noun** the study and application of electronics in medicine and biological processes.
-DERIVATIVES **bi•o•e•lec•tron•ic** adjective; **bi•o•e•lec•tron•i•cal•ly** /-ik(ə)lē/ adverb

bi•o•film /'bīōˌfilm/
▸ **noun** a thin but robust layer of mucilage adhering to a solid surface and containing a community of bacteria and other microorganisms.

bi•o•in•for•mat•ics /ˌbīōˌinfər'mætiks/
▸ **plural noun** [treated as sing.] the science of collecting and analyzing complex biological data such as genetic codes.
-DERIVATIVES **bi•o•in•for•mat•ic** adjective

bi•o•log•ic /ˌbīə'läjik/
▸ **adjective** of or relating to biology or living organisms: *biologic therapy involves treatment with substances that can stimulate the immune system.*

bi•o•ma•ter•i•al /ˌbīōmə'tirēəl/
▸ **noun** synthetic or natural material suitable for use in constructing artificial organs and prostheses or to replace bone or tissue.

bi•o•me•te•o•rol•o•gy /ˌbīōˌmētēə'räləjē/
▸ **noun** the study of the relationship between living organisms and weather.

bi•o•met•ric read•er /'bīəˌmetrik 'rēdər/
▸ **noun** an electronic device that determines identity by detecting and matching physical characteristics.

bi•o•met•rics /ˌbīə'metriks/
▸ **noun** [treated as sing.] the science and methodology of identifying people by means of unique biological char-

acteristics. Such biological markers include facial features, fingerprints, and voice.

-DERIVATIVES **bi•o•met•ric** adjective

bi•o•met•ric sig•na•ture /'bīə,metrik 'signəCHər/
▸ **noun** the unique pattern of a bodily feature such as the retina, iris, or voice, encoded on an identity card and used for recognition and identification purposes.

bi•o•pi•ra•cy /,bīō'pīrəsē/
▸ **noun** the practice of commercially exploiting naturally occurring biochemical or genetic material, especially by obtaining patents that restrict its future use, while failing to pay fair compensation to the community from which it originates.

bi•op•sy /'bīäpsē/
▸ **verb** (**bi•op•sies, bi•op•sied, bi•op•sy•ing**) [trans.] conduct a biopsy on (tissue removed from a living body): *the lesions may be malignant melanomas and should be biopsied.*

bi•o•sat•el•lite /,bīō'sæṭl,īt/
▸ **noun** an artificial satellite that serves as an automated laboratory, conducting biological experiments on living organisms.

bi•o•sur•ge•ry /,bīō'sərjərē/
▸ **noun** the medical use of maggots to clean infected wounds, especially in cases where a patient is resistant to conventional antibiotic treatment.

bi•o•tech /'bīō,tek/
▸ **noun** of, related to, or created by biotechnology.
▸ **adjective** genetically modified: *biotech corn.*
-ORIGIN shortened form of *biotechnological.*

bi•o•te•lem•e•try /ˌbīōtəˈlemitrē/
▸ **noun** the detection or measurement of human or animal physiological functions from a distance using a telemeter: *a review of underwater biotelemetry, with emphasis on ultrasonic techniques.*
–DERIVATIVES **bi•o•tel•e•me•tric** /ˌbīōˌteləˈmetrik/ adjective

bi•o•ter•ror•ism /ˌbīōˈterəˌrizəm/
▸ **noun** the use of infectious agents or other harmful biological or biochemical substances as weapons of terrorism.
–DERIVATIVES **bi•o•ter•ror•ist** noun

bi•o•ther•a•py /ˌbīōˈTHerəpē/
▸ **noun** (pl. **bi•o•ther•a•pies**) the treatment of disease using substances obtained or derived from living organisms.

bi•o•trans•for•ma•tion /ˌbīōˌtrænsfərˈmāSHən/
▸ **noun** the alteration of a substance, typically a drug, within the body.

bi•o•war•fare /ˌbīōˈwôrfer/
▸ **noun** biological warfare, the use of toxins of biological origin or microorganisms as weapons of war.

Bir•ken•stock /ˈbərkənˌstäk/
▸ **noun** trademark a type of shoe or sandal with a contoured cork-filled sole and a thick leather upper.
■ [as modifier] denoting people concerned with political correctness or conservationist issues: *home builders are no longer content to leave environmentalism to the Birkenstock crowd.*
–ORIGIN 1970s: from the name of the manufacturer.

birth•ing cen•ter /ˈbərTHiNG ˌsentər/
▸ **noun** a medical facility, specializing in childbirth, that is less restrictive and more homelike than a hospital.

birth•ing room /ˈbərTHiNG ˌro͞om; ˌro͝om/
▸ **noun** a room in a hospital or other medical facility that is equipped for labor and childbirth and is designed to be comfortable and homelike.

bitch-slap /ˈbiCH ˌslæp/
▸ **verb** (**bitch-slapped**, **bitch-slap•ping**) informal deliver a stinging blow to (someone), typically in order to humiliate them: *I would have bitch-slapped him for talking that way.*
–ORIGIN 1990s: originally black English, referring to a woman hitting or haranguing her male partner.

bi•zar•ro /biˈzärō/
▸ **adjective** informal bizarre: *another one of Frenchie's bizarro parties.*

black bot•tom pie /ˈblæk ˌbätəm ˈpī/
▸ **noun** pie with a bottom layer of chocolate cream or custard and a contrasting top layer, usually of whipped cream.

blad•dered /ˈblædərd/
▸ **adjective** Brit. informal extremely drunk.

blade /blād/
▸ **verb** informal skate using in-line skates.
–DERIVATIVES **blad•er** noun
–ORIGIN shortened form of the verb *rollerblade*, from the generic use of the trademark *Rollerblades.*

blame•storm•ing /ˈblām,stôrmiNG/
▸ **noun** group discussion regarding the assigning of responsibility for a failure or mistake.
–ORIGIN 1990s: on the pattern of *brainstorming.*

bleed•ing edge /ˈblēdiNG ˈej/
▸ **noun** the very forefront of technological development.
–ORIGIN 1980s: on the pattern of *leading edge, cutting edge.*

bling-bling /ˈbliNG ˌbliNG/
> ▸ **noun** informal expensive, ostentatious clothing and jewelry, or the wearing of them: *behind the bling-bling: are diamonds worth it?*
-ORIGIN 1990s: perhaps imitative of light reflecting off jewelry, or of jewelry clashing together.

blip•vert /ˈblipvərt/
> ▸ **noun** a television commercial of a few seconds' duration.
-ORIGIN from *blip* + *(ad)vert(isement)*.

B-list /ˈbē ˌlist/
> ▸ noun see **A-list.**

bloat•ware /ˈblōtˌwer/
> ▸ **noun** software that requires an amount of disk storage space that is grossly incommensurate with its utility: *none of the programs on this page is bloatware, so they can be downloaded fairly quickly.*

BLOB
> ▸ **noun** Computing binary large objects.
-ORIGIN acronym.

blog /bläg/
> ▸ **noun** a weblog.
> ▸ **verb** [noun] (**blogged, blog•ging**) add new material to or regularly update a weblog.
-DERIVATIVES **blog•ger noun**

blonde mo•ment /ˈbländ ˈmōmənt/
> ▸ **noun** humorous an instance of being silly or scatter-brained: *sorry, guys, I was just having another blonde moment.*
-ORIGIN late 20th cent.: from the stereotypical perception of blonde-haired women as unintelligent.

bloot•er /ˈbloȯtər/
▸ **verb** [trans.] Scottish hit or kick (something) hard and wildly: *he blootered the ball over the bar.*
–ORIGIN 1980s: earlier senses include 'blunder' and 'talk foolishly,' but ultimately of unknown origin.

blue dog Dem•o•crat /ˈbloȯ ˌdôg ˈdeməˌkræt/ (also **Blue Dog Dem•o•crat**)
▸ **noun** a Democrat from a Southern state who has a conservative voting record.

Blue•tooth /ˈbloȯˌtoȯTH/
▸ **noun** trademark a standard for the short-range wireless interconnection of cell phones, computers, and other electronic devices.
–ORIGIN 1990s: said to be named after King Harald *Bluetooth* (910–985), credited with uniting Denmark and Norway, as Bluetooth technology unifies the telecommunications and computing industries.

blunt /blənt/
▸ **noun** slang a hollowed-out cigar filled with marijuana.

BMI
▸ **abbreviation** body mass index.

boat neck /ˈbōt ˌnek/
▸ **noun** a type of wide neckline on a garment that passes just below the collarbone.

bo•ba tea /ˈbōbə ˌtē/
▸ **noun** another term for BUBBLE TEA.

Bo•bo /ˈbōbō/
▸ **noun** (pl. **Bo•bos**) informal a person having both the values of the counterculture of the 1960s and the materialism of the 1980s; a bourgeois Bohemian.
–ORIGIN 1990s: abbreviation.

bod•gie /'bäjē/
▸ **adjective** Austral./NZ informal worthless or inferior; false: *a bodgie secondhand car with bodgie number plates.*

bod•i•ly /'bädl-ē/
▸ **adverb** in one mass; as a whole: *the committee arrived, bodily, and demanded access to the transcripts.*

bod•y dys•mor•phic dis•or•der /'bädē dis'môrfik dis,ôr-dər/ (abbreviation: **BDD**)
▸ **noun** a psychological disorder in which a person becomes obsessed with imaginary defects in their appearance.

bod•y im•age /'bädē ,imij/
▸ **noun** the subjective picture or mental image of one's own body.

bod•y mass in•dex /'bädē ,mæs ,indeks/ (abbrev.: **BMI**)
▸ **noun** (pl. **bod•y mass in•di•ces** or **in•dex•es**) a weight-to-height ratio, calculated by dividing one's weight in kilograms by the square of one's height in meters and used as an indicator of obesity and underweight.

bod•y me•chan•ics /'bädē mə,kæniks/
▸ **plural noun** [treated as sing. or pl.] exercises designed to improve posture, coordination, and stamina.

boer•bull /'bôrbŏŏl; 'bŏŏr-/ (also **boer•bul**)
▸ **noun** S. African a large dog crossbred from the mastiff and indigenous African dogs.
-ORIGIN 1960s: from Afrikaans *boerboel,* from *boer* (commonly applied to indigenous plants and animals) + *boel,* from Dutch *bul* (as in *bulhond* 'mastiff').

bo•gart /'bōgärt/
▸ **verb** [trans.] informal selfishly appropriate or keep (some-

thing, especially a marijuana cigarette): *don't bogart that joint, my friend.*
-ORIGIN 1960s: from US actor Humphrey *Bogart* (1899–1957), who often smoked in films.

BOGOF /'bägôf/
▸ **abbreviation** buy one, get one free.

bo•keh /bō'kā/
▸ **noun** Photography the visual quality of the out-of-focus areas of a photographic image, especially as rendered by a particular lens.
-ORIGIN from Japanese.

bok•ken /'bäkən/
▸ **noun** a wooden sword used as a practice weapon in kendo, the Japanese martial art of fencing.

bol•li•to mi•sto /bô'lētō 'mēstō/
▸ **noun** (pl. **bol•li•ti mi•sti** /bô'lētē 'mēstē/) an Italian dish of mixed meats, such as chicken, veal, and sausage, boiled with vegetables in broth.
-ORIGIN Italian, literally 'boiled mixed (meat).'

bol•ter /'bōltər/
▸ **noun** Austral./NZ informal an outsider in a sporting event or other competition.

bomb /bäm/
▸ **noun** informal **1** (**da** (or **the**) **bomb**) an outstandingly good person or thing: *the site would really be da bomb if its content were updated more frequently.*
2 a marijuana cigarette; a joint.

bom•bo•ra /bäm'bôrə/
▸ **noun** chiefly Australia **1** a submerged offshore reef or rock.

2 a potentially dangerous wave that breaks over a submerged offshore reef or rock.

book•mark /'boŏk,märk/
▸ **verb** [trans.] Computing make a record of (the address of a file, Internet page, etc.) to enable quick access by a user.

boo•mer•ang kid /'boōmə,ræNG ,kid/ (also **boo•mer•ang•er** /'boōmə,ræNGər/)
▸ **noun** informal a young adult who goes back to live with a parent after a period of independence: *I have a boomerang kid at home just when I'm ready to retire!*
-ORIGIN allusion to a *boomerang,* which is thrown so as to return to the thrower.

boot-cut /'boōt ,kət/
▸ **adjective** (of jeans or other trousers) flared very slightly below the knee, so as to be worn comfortably over boots.

boot•strap /'boōt,stræp/
▸ **verb** [trans.] start up an enterprise, especially one based on the Internet, with minimal resources: *they are bootstrapping their stations themselves, not with lots of dot-com venture capital.*

boo•ty call /'boōtē ,kôl/
▸ **noun** informal a sexual invitation or rendezvous.
-ORIGIN 1990s: from *booty* (slang for 'buttocks') and *call.*

boo•ty•li•cious /,boōtl'isHəs/
▸ **adjective** informal sexually attractive.
-ORIGIN early 21st cent.: from *booty* (slang for 'buttocks'), on the pattern of *delicious.*

bor•ga•ta /bôr'gätə/
‣ **noun** (pl. **bor•ga•tas** or **bor•ga•te** /bôr'gätē/) an organized branch of the Mafia.
–ORIGIN 1960s: from Italian *borgatà* 'district, village.'

bo•ride /'bôrīd/
‣ **noun** a binary compound of boron with a metallic element.

Bos•man rul•ing /'bäzmən 'rōōliNG/
‣ **noun** a European Court ruling that obliges professional soccer or other sports clubs to allow players over the age of 25 to move freely between clubs once their contracts have expired.
–ORIGIN 1990s: named after Jean-Marc *Bosman* (1964–), a Belgian soccer player who brought a legal case that resulted in the ruling.

bot /bät/
‣ **noun** informal Austral./NZ a person who persistently begs or borrows from others.

Bo•tox /'bō,täks/
‣ **noun** trademark a drug prepared from the bacterial toxin botulin, used medically to treat certain muscular conditions and cosmetically to remove wrinkles by temporarily paralyzing facial muscles.
–DERIVATIVES **Bo•toxed** adjective
–ORIGIN 1990s: from *bo(tulinum) tox(in)*.

Bo•tox par•ty /'bōtäks ,pärtē/
‣ **noun** a social event at which guests receive Botox injections from a doctor and mingle with each other for mutual support.
–ORIGIN on the pattern of *Tupperware party*.

bot•tle bill /'bätl ˌbil/
‣ **noun** any of several state laws that require refundable deposits on beverages sold in recyclable bottles and cans.

bot•tle jack /'bätl ˌjæk/
‣ **noun** a large bottle-shaped jack used for lifting heavy objects.

bot•tom feed•er /'bätəm ˌfēdər/
‣ **noun** informal, derogatory a member of a group of very low social status who survives by any means possible.

bou•tique ho•tel /boo'tēk hō,tel/
‣ **noun** a small stylish hotel, typically one situated in a fashionable urban location.

bo•vine growth hor•mone /'bōvīn 'grōTH ˌhôrmōn/ (abbreviation: **BGH**)
‣ **noun** a natural hormone in cattle that helps regulate growth and milk production and that may be produced artificially and given to dairy cattle to increase the yield of milk. Also called **bo•vine so•ma•tro•pin** /'bōvīn ˌsōmə'trōpin/.

boy band /'boi ˌbænd/ (or **girl band** /'gərl ˌbænd/)
‣ **noun** a pop group composed of attractive young men (or young women) whose music and image are designed to appeal primarily to a young teenage audience.

bra•ce•ro /brä'serō/
‣ **noun** (pl. **bra•ce•ros**) a Mexican laborer allowed into the United States for a limited time as a seasonal agricultural worker.
-ORIGIN 1970s: Spanish, literally 'laborer,' from *brazo* 'arm.'

brach•y•ther•a•py /ˌbrækē'THerəpē/
▸ noun the treatment of cancer, especially prostate cancer, by the insertion of radioactive implants directly into the tissue.

Bra•dy Bill /'brādē ˌbil/ (also **Bra•dy Law**)
▸ noun common name for the Brady Handgun Violence Protection Act, a law enacted by Congress in 1993 that requires a waiting period for handgun purchases and background checks on those who wish to purchase them.
–ORIGIN named for former White House press secretary James S. Brady (1940–), who campaigned for the bill after being shot and seriously wounded in the 1981 assassination attempt on President Ronald Reagan.

brain fin•ger•print•ing /'brān ˌfiNGgərprintiNG/
▸ noun the recording and analysis of an individual's neurological responses to images and words flashed on a screen, especially to determine if the person is telling the truth.

brand ex•ten•sion /'brænd ik,stensHən/
▸ noun an instance of using an established brand name or trademark on new products, so as to increase sales.

brand train /'brænd ˌtrān/ (or **brand sta•tion**)
▸ noun a subway train or station in which most or all advertisements are sponsored by a single company or organization: *brand trains are an expensive but effective way to advertise your product.*

brane /brān/
▸ noun Physics an extended object with any given number of dimensions, of which strings in string theory are examples with one dimension. Our universe is a 3-brane.
–ORIGIN abbreviation of *membrane*.

brane world /ˈbrān ˌwərld/ (also **brane-world**)

▸ **noun** Physics a world model in which our space-time is the result of a 3-brane moving through a space-time of higher dimension, with all interactions except gravity being confined to the 3-brane.

Bra•zil•ian /brəˈzilyən/ (also **Bra•zil•ian wax•ing** /brəˈzil-yən ˈwæksiNG/)

▸ **noun** a style of waxing a woman's pubic hair in which almost all the hair is removed, with only a very small central strip remaining.

break•beat /ˈbrākˌbēt/

▸ **noun** a repeated sample of a drumbeat, usually forming a fast syncopated rhythm, used a basis for dance music.
■ dance music featuring breakbeats.

breath•ar•i•an /breTHˈerēən/

▸ **noun** a person who believes that it is possible, through meditation, to reach a level of consciousness where one can obtain all the nutrients one needs from the air or sunlight.

bre•sao•la /breˈsowlə/

▸ **noun** an Italian dish of raw beef cured by salting and air-drying, served typically in slices with a dressing of olive oil, lemon juice, and black pepper.
-ORIGIN Italian, from *bresada*, past participle of *brasare* 'braise.'

brew•ski /ˈbrооskē/

▸ **noun** (pl. **brew•skis** or **brew•skies**) informal a beer.
-ORIGIN 1980s: from *brew* + a fanciful ending, perhaps after the common Slavonic surname suffix *-ski*.

bricks and mor•tar /ˈbriks ən ˈmôrtər/

▸ **noun** used to denote a business that operates in the

physical world rather than (or as well as) over the Internet: [as modifier] *the bricks-and-mortar banks.*

bride•zil•la /brīd'zilə/
▸ **noun** an overzealous bride-to-be who acts irrationally or causes offense: *I like to think I wasn't a bridezilla in the months, days, and hours leading up to our wedding.*

bridge mix /'brij ‚miks/
▸ **noun** a mixture of various bite-size candies, especially nuts, raisins, and chocolates.

Bril•lo pad /'brilō ‚pæd/
▸ **noun** trademark a pad made of steel wool impregnated with soap, used for scouring pans.
■ [as modifier] denoting wiry or tightly curled hair: *she had a foot-high Brillo-pad hairdo.*

broast /brōst/
▸ **verb** [trans.] cook (food) by a combination of broiling and roasting: [as adjective] (**broasted**) *broasted chicken.*
-ORIGIN 1980s: blend of *broil* and *roast.*

broc•ci•flow•er /'bräkə‚flowər/ (also **broc•co•flow•er**)
▸ **noun** a light green vegetable that is a cross between broccoli and cauliflower: *this recipe calls for brocciflower but I can't find it here.*
-ORIGIN blend of *broccoli* and *cauliflower.*

broc•co•li rabe /'bräkəlē ‚räb/ (also **broc•co•li raab**)
▸ **noun** a leafy green vegetable with broccolilike buds and bitter-flavored greens.

bro•chure•ware /brō'sнōōr‚wer/
▸ **noun** Web sites or Web pages produced by converting a company's printed marketing or advertising material into an Internet format, typically providing little or no

opportunity for interactive contact with prospective customers.

bron•to•there /'bräntəTHir/
▸ **noun** a large ungulate mammal (*Embolotherium andrewsi*) of the Eocene epoch with a hornlike bony growth on the nose.
–ORIGIN modern Latin, from Greek *brontē* 'thunder' + *thērion* 'wild beast.'

bronz•er /'bränzər/
▸ **noun** a cosmetic liquid or powder applied to the skin to give it color or shine, typically to give the appearance of a suntan.

broom•ball /'broo͞om,bôl; 'broo͞om/
▸ **noun** a game similar to ice hockey in which players run rather than skate and use rubber brooms or broom handles to push a ball into the goal.

brown goods /'brown ,goo͞odz/
▸ **plural noun** television sets, audio equipment, and similar household appliances.

B2B
▸ **abbreviation** business-to-business, denoting trade conducted via the Internet between businesses.

B2C
▸ **abbreviation** business-to-consumer, denoting trade conducted via the Internet between businesses and consumers.

bub•bie /'boo͞obē; 'bəbē/
▸ **noun** informal (in Jewish use) one's grandmother.
–ORIGIN from Yiddish *bubeleh* 'grandmother.'

bub•ble tea /'bəbəl ˌtē/
▸ noun a cold, frothy drink made with iced tea, sweetened milk or other flavorings, and usually with sweet black balls or "pearls" made from tapioca. Also called **BOBA TEA, PEARL TEA.**

buck•et hat /'bəkit ˌhæt/
▸ noun a simple soft cloth hat with a brim.

buck•le bun•ny /'bəkəl ˌbənē/
▸ noun a woman who is a follower or devotee of rodeos and cowboys.

build•out /'bild,owt/
▸ noun the growth, development, or expansion of something: *the rapid buildout of digital technology.*

bull•dust /'bool,dəst/
▸ noun Austral./NZ **1** coarse dust.
2 vulgar slang nonsense; rubbish.

bul•let point /'boolit ˌpoint/
▸ noun each of several items in a list, typically the ideas or arguments in an article or presentation and typically printed with a bullet before each for emphasis.

bull-necked /'bool,nekt/
▸ adjective (of a man) having a thick, strong neck: *a beefy, bull-necked cop.*
–DERIVATIVES **bull neck** noun

bum /bəm/ informal
▸ verb (**bummed, bum•ming**) [trans.] (**be bummed out**) make (someone) feel upset or disappointed: *I was really bummed out when he forgot my birthday.*

bunce /bəns/
▸ **noun** Brit. informal money or profit gained by someone: *they can turn their hand to many jobs as long as there's a bit of bunce in it.*
–ORIGIN early 18th cent.: origin unknown.

bun·do·bust /'bəndə,bəst/ (also **ban·do·bast** /'bændə ,bæst/,)
▸ **noun** Indian arrangements or organization: *why all these big crowds and strict police bundobust, he wondered.*
–ORIGIN Urdu, from Persian *band-o-bast* 'tying and binding.'

bun·ker bust·er /'bəŋkər ,bəstər/ (also **bun·ker-bust·er**)
▸ **noun** a bomb designed to penetrate deep into the ground or rock before exploding or detonating.

bun·ny-boil·er /'bənē ,boilər/
▸ **noun** informal a woman who acts vengefully after having been spurned by her lover.
–ORIGIN with reference to the movie *Fatal Attraction* (1987), in which a rejected woman boils her lover's pet rabbit.

bun·ny hug·ger /'bənē ,həgər/ (also **bun·ny-hug·ger**)
▸ **noun** informal, chiefly derogatory **1** an animal lover or supporter of animal rights.
2 an environmentalist or conservationist.

bunt·ing /'bəntiNG/ (also **bunt·ing bag**)
▸ **noun** a hooded sleeping bag for babies.
–ORIGIN 1920s: origin uncertain.

bup·kis /'boŏpkis/
▸ **noun** informal nothing at all: *you know bupkis about fundraising.*
–ORIGIN from Yiddish.

bu•pro•pi•on /byōō'prōpēən/
> ▸ noun an antidepressant drug ($C_{13}H_{18}ClNO$) that is also given to relieve the symptoms of nicotine withdrawal. Also called ZYBAN (trademark).
> –ORIGIN 1970s: from *butane* + *propionic*.

bur•ka /'bŏŏrkə/
> ▸ noun a long, loose garment covering the whole body, worn in public by many Muslim women.
> –ORIGIN from Urdu and Persian *burka'*, from Arabic *burk̲u'*.

burn /bərn/
> ▸ verb (past and past participle **burned** or chiefly Brit. **burnt**) [trans.] produce (a compact disc) by copying from an original or master copy.
> ▸ noun a hot, painful sensation in the muscles experienced as a result of sustained vigorous exercise: *feel the burn.*

burn•er /'bərnər/
> ▸ noun a device for producing a compact disc by copying from an original or master copy.

burn rate /'bərn ˌrāt/
> ▸ noun the rate at which an enterprise spends money, especially venture capital, in excess of income: *the corporation lays off workers to cut burn rate.*

bur•qa /'bŏŏrkə/
> ▸ noun variant spelling of BURKA.

bush•meat /'bŏŏSH,mēt/
> ▸ noun the meat of African wild animals.

butch•er's block /'bŏŏCHərz ˌbläk/
> ▸ noun a sturdy wooden kitchen table with a square top on which food may be chopped.

Bu•tey•ko method /boōˈtākō ˈmeтнəu̇/
▸ **noun** a technique of controlled breathing claimed to alleviate asthma.
-ORIGIN 1990s: named after Ukrainian physiologist Konstantin *Buteyko* (1923–), who devised the technique.

butt heads /ˈbət ˈhedz/
▸ **verb phrase** informal engage in conflict or be in strong disagreement: *the residents continue to butt heads with the mall developers.*

butt•in•sky /bəˈtinskē/
▸ **noun** informal an interfering person.
-ORIGIN early 20th cent.: from *butt in* and *-ski*, formed in humorous imitation of the final element in many Russian names.

but•ton man /ˈbətn ˌmæn/
▸ **noun** informal a hired killer.

buzz•y /ˈbəzē/
▸ **adjective** (**buzz•i•er, buzz•i•est**) informal (especially of a place or atmosphere) lively and exciting: *a buzzy bar with live music.*

BYOG Austral./NZ
▸ **abbreviation** bring your own grog.

C

ca•cha•ca /kə'sHäsə/
▸ **noun** a Brazilian white rum made from sugar cane.
-ORIGIN mid 19th cent.: Brazilian Portuguese, from Portuguese *cacaça* '(white) rum.'

CAFE
▸ **abbreviation** Corporate Average Fuel Economy.

cai•pi•ri•nha /,kīpē'rēnyä; ,kīpə'rinyə/
▸ **noun** a Brazilian cocktail made with cachaca, lime or lemon juice, sugar, and crushed ice.
-ORIGIN Brazilian Portuguese, from *caipira* 'yokel.'

call cen•ter /'kôl ,sentər/
▸ **noun** an office set up to handle a large volume of telephone calls, especially for taking orders and providing customer service.

cam•girl /'kæm,gərl/
▸ **noun** a girl or woman who poses for a webcam.

camp•er /'kæmpər/
▸ **noun** informal a person in a specified mood: *I understand that this is necessary, but I am not a happy camper.*

can•cer clus•ter /'kænsər ,kləstər/
▸ **noun** a statistically higher than average occurrence of cancer among the residents of a particular geographic area.

cane /kān/
▸ **verb** [trans.] Brit. informal take (drink or drugs) in large quantities: *the others were probably out **caning it** in some bar.*

caned /kānd/
▸ **adjective** Brit. informal intoxicated with drink or drugs.

can•no•li /kə'nōlē/
▸ **plural noun** a dessert consisting of small deep-fried pastry tubes with a creamy filling, typically of sweetened ricotta cheese.
-ORIGIN Italian, from *canna* 'reed.'

can•yon•ing /'kænyəniNG/ (also **can•yon•eer•ing** /ˌkænyə'niriNG/)
▸ **noun** the sport of exploring a canyon by rappelling, rafting, jumping into a waterfall, etc.: *an exciting weekend of bungee-jumping and canyoning.*

cap /kæp/
▸ **noun** Finance short for capitalization: [as modifier] *mid-cap companies* | *small-cap stocks.*

ca•peesh /kə'pēsh/
▸ **exclamation** informal do you understand?: *Upstairs is off limits. Capeesh?*
-ORIGIN 1940s: from Italian *capisce* third person singular present tense of *capire* 'understand.'

cap•el•li•ni /ˌkæpə'lēnē/
▸ **plural noun** pasta in the form of very thin strands.
-ORIGIN 1950s: Italian, diminutive of *capello* 'hair.'

cap•sule en•do•scope /'kæpsəl ˌendəskōp/
▸ **noun** another term for VIDEO PILL.
-DERIVATIVES **cap•sule en•dos•co•py** /'kæpsəl en'däskəpē/ **noun**

car•bon sink /'kärbən ˌsiNGk/
▸ **noun** Ecology a forest, ocean, or other natural environment viewed in terms of its ability to absorb carbon dioxide from the atmosphere.

car•ci•no•ma•to•sis /ˌkärsəˌnōməˈtōsis/
▸ **noun** the widespread dissemination of carcinoma in the body.

car•di•nal sin /ˈkärdnəl ˈsin; ˈkärdn-əl/
▸ **noun** chiefly humorous a serious error of judgment: *he committed the cardinal sin of criticizing his teammates.*

care work•er /ˈker ˌwərkər/
▸ **noun** Brit. a person employed to support and supervise vulnerable, infirm, or disadvantaged people, or those under the care of the state.

car•go pants /ˈkärgō ˌpænts/
▸ **plural noun** loose-fitting casual cotton pants with large patch pockets halfway down each leg.

cark /kärk/
▸ **verb** Australian (often **cark it**) die: *he'll own the whole company when his dad carks it.*

car•nap•per /ˈkärˌnæpər/ (also **car•nap•er**)
▸ **noun** a person who steals cars: *that shopping mall is attractive to pickpockets and carnappers.*
-ORIGIN on the pattern of *kidnapper.*

Car•o•lin•i•an /ˌkærəˈlinēən/
▸ **noun** a native or inhabitant of South or North Carolina.
▸**adjective 1** of or relating to South or North Carolina.
2 denoting a forest region extending from South Ontario to South Carolina.

car•pen•ter pants /ˈkärpəntər ˌpænts/
▸ **plural noun** loose-fitting pants with many pockets of various sizes and loops for tools at the tops or sides of the legs.

car•riage house /ˈkærij ˌhows/
▸ **noun** a building for housing a horse-drawn carriage, typically such a building that has been converted into a dwelling.

carve•out /ˈkärvˌowt/
▸ **noun 1** an entity separated from a larger one and given separate treatment, in particular:
■ a dot-com spinoff. ■ a class of employees treated separately with regard to benefits. ■ a class of medical treatments treated separately with regard to insurance coverage: *the carveout and the basic plan sometimes toss the bill back and forth and the patient gets left in the lurch.*
2 the activity of effecting such a separation.

cash ma•chine /ˈkæsн məˌsнēn/
▸ **noun** another term for ATM.

ca•si•ta /kəˈsētə/
▸ **noun** a small house or other building, especially a wooden cabin.
-ORIGIN early 19th cent.: from Spanish, diminutive of *casa* 'house.'

ca•su•al Fri•day /ˈkæzнōōəl ˈfrīdā/
▸ **noun** Friday as a designated day of the week when organizations allow employees to dress more casually than on other workdays.

cat•e•go•ry kill•er /ˈkætəgôrē ˌkilər/
▸ **noun** a large store, typically one of a chain, that specializes in a particular type of discounted merchandise and becomes the dominant retailer in that category.

ca•te•nac•cio /ˌkätəˈnäcн(ē)ō; ˌkætnˈæcнēō/
▸ **noun** Soccer a very defensive system of play, especially one employing a sweeper.

-ORIGIN 1970s: Italian, literally 'bolt', from *catena* 'chain' + the pejorative suffix *-accio*.

ca•the•dral ceil•ing /kə'THēdrəl 'sēliNG/
▸ **noun** a pointed or slanting ceiling of a room that rises through more than one floor.

ca•va•quin•ho /ˌkävə'kēnyō/
▸ **noun** (pl. **ca•va•quin•hos**) a type of small, four-stringed guitar resembling a ukulele, popular in Brazil and Portugal.
-ORIGIN Portuguese.

CCU
▸ **abbreviation** ■ cardiac care unit. ■ coronary care unit. ■ critical care unit.

CDM
▸ **abbreviation** cold dark matter.

CDMA
▸ **abbreviation** Electronics Code Division Multiple Access, a generic term denoting a wireless interface based on code division multiple access technology.

Ce•leb•ra /sə'lebrə/
▸ **noun** trademark a synthetic drug used in the management of arthritic pain.
-ORIGIN 1990s: an invented word.

ce•leb•re•al•i•ty /sə,lebrē'ælitē/ (often as **ce•leb•re•al•i•ty TV**)
▸ **noun** television shows that feature well-known people or celebrities interacting in real situations contrived for purposes of entertainment: *many former stars welcome celebreality as a way of getting themselves back in the public eye.*
-ORIGIN blend of *celebrity* and *reality*.

cell•y /'selē/ (also **cell•ie**)

▸ **noun** (pl. **cell•ies**) informal a cell phone: *I'll try her on her celly.*

■ a person who uses a cell phone: *my friends are all cellies and addicted to text messaging.*

cell yell /'sel ,yel/

▸ **noun** informal loud talking on a cell phone: *I was annoyed by cell yell in the doctor's waiting room.*

ce•roc /sə'räk/

▸ **noun** a type of modern social dance having elements of rock and roll, jive, and salsa.

-ORIGIN 1990s: invented word, apparently coined in English from French *ce* 'this' + *roc* 'rock.'

CFO

▸ **abbreviation** chief financial officer.

cgi

▸ **abbreviation** common gateway interface (a script standard for writing interactive programs generated by visitors to web pages, such as forms and searches).

cgi-bin /'sējē'ī ,bin/

▸ **noun** a server directory where cgi programs are stored: [as adj.] *cgi-bin files.*

cha•lu•pa /chə'lōōpə/

▸ **noun** (in Spain and Latin America) a small light boat or canoe.

■ a fried tortilla in the shape of a boat, with a spicy filling.

-ORIGIN late 19th cent.: Spanish, ultimately related to Dutch *sloep* 'sloop.'

cha•mise /CHə'mēz; SHə-/ (also **cha•mi•so** /CHə'mēsō/)
▸ noun (pl. **cha•mis•es** or **cha•mi•sos**) an evergreen shrub (*Adenostoma fasciculatum*) of the rose family, with small narrow leaves, common in the chaparral of California.
-ORIGIN mid 19th cent.: from Mexican Spanish *chamiso*.

chan•nel-hop /'CHænl ,häp/
▸ verb [intrans.] (**chan•nel•hopped, chan•nel•hop•ping**) informal **1** another term for channel-surf (as with a television's remote control).
2 travel across the English Channel and back frequently or for only a brief trip.
-DERIVATIVES **chan•nel-hop•per noun**

Chap•ter 7 /'CHæptər 'sevən/
▸ noun protection from creditors granted to individuals or companies who legally file for bankruptcy, providing for liquidation of certain assets to pay debts.

Chap•ter 13 /'CHæptər THər'tēn/
▸ noun protection from creditors granted to individuals who legally file for bankruptcy, providing for repayment of debts by a court-approved plan.

char•ac•ter code /'kæriktər ,kōd/
▸ noun Computing the binary code used to represent a letter or number.

charge•back /'CHärj,bæk/
▸ noun a demand by a credit-card provider for a retailer to make good the loss on a fraudulent or disputed transaction.
■ (in business use) an act or policy of allocating the cost of an organization's centrally located resources to the individuals or departments that use them.

chase the drag•on /'chās ᴛʜə 'drægən/
▸ **verb phrase** informal smoke heroin.

chat group /'chæt ˌgro͞op/
▸ **noun** a group of people who communicate regularly via the Internet, usually in real time but also by e-mail.

chat•ter•bot /'chætər,bät/
▸ **noun** a computer program designed to interact with people by simulating human conversation.
–ORIGIN 1990s: blend of *chatter* and *(ro)bot*.

Chat•tis•garh /'chətēs,gär/
a state in central India, formed in 2000 from the southeastern part of Madhya Pradesh; capital, Raipur.

chees•y /'chēzē/
▸ **adjective** (**chees•i•er, chees•i•est**) hackneyed and obviously sentimental: *an album of cheesy pop hits.*

chef /shef/
▸ **verb** (**cheffed, chef•fing**) [intrans.] (**cheffing**) informal work as a chef: *I cheffed for wealthy tourists on chartered yachts* | [as noun] *cheffing is hard work.*
–ORIGIN early 19th cent.: French, literally 'head.'

chem•i•cal /'kemikəl/
▸ **noun** an addictive drug.

chib /chib/ Scottish
▸ **noun** a knife used as a weapon.
▸ **verb** (**chibbed, chib•bing**) [trans.] stab (someone): *you can be chibbed easily by one of the knife-wielding maniacs roaming the streets.*

Chick•en Lit•tle /'chikən 'litl/
▸ **noun** an alarmist or pessimist; a person who panics easily.

-ORIGIN 1990s: from the name of a character in a children's story who repeatedly warns that the sky is falling.

chick flick /'CHik ˌflik/
▸ **noun** informal, chiefly derogatory a movie that appeals to young women.

chick lit /'CHik ˌlit/
▸ **noun** informal, chiefly derogatory literature that appeals to young women.

child•mind•er /'CHīldˌmīndər/
▸ **noun** Brit. a person who looks after other people's children in his or her own house for payment.
-DERIVATIVES **child-mind•ing noun**

child sup•port /'CHīld səˌpôrt/
▸ **noun** court-ordered payments, typically made by a noncustodial divorced parent, to support that parent's minor child or children.

chi•me•ne•a /ˌCHiməˈnāə; -ˈnēə/
▸ **noun** a free-standing clay fireplace or oven that consists of a hollow bulbous body, open at the front, in which a fire may be lit, tapering to a short chimneylike smoke vent.
-ORIGIN 1990s: Spanish, 'chimney.'

chi•nois /sHinˈwä/
▸ **noun** a cone-shaped sieve with a closely woven mesh for straining sauces.

choc•cy /'CHäkē; 'CHô-/
▸ **noun** (pl. **choc•cies**) Brit. informal chocolate.
◼ a chocolate candy.

cho•ki•dar /'CHôkiˌdär/
▸ **noun** variant spelling of CHOWKIDAR.

chow•hound /ˈCHowˌhownd/
▸ **noun** informal a very enthusiastic eater.
–ORIGIN early 20th cent.: (originally US military slang) from *chow* + *hound*.

chow•ki•dar /ˈCHôkiˌdär/ (also **cho•ki•dar** /ˈCHôkiˌdär/)
▸ **noun** (in India) a watchman or gatekeeper.
–ORIGIN from Urdu *caukīdār*, from *caukī* 'toll house' + *-dār* 'keeper.'

chro•ma•key /ˈkrōməˌkē/
▸ **noun** a technique by which a block of a particular color in a video image can be replaced either by another color or by a separate image, enabling, for example, a weather forecaster to appear against a background of a computer-generated weather map.
▸ **verb** (**chro•ma•keys, chro•ma•keyed, chro•ma•key•ing**) [trans.] manipulate (an image) using this technique.

chron•o•ther•a•py /ˌkränəˈTHerəpē/
▸ **noun** the treatment of an illness or disorder by administering a drug at a time of day believed to be in harmony with the body's natural rhythms.

chud•dies /ˈCHədēz/
▸ **plural noun** Brit. informal (chiefly among British Asians) underpants.
–ORIGIN 1990s: Anglo-Indian, perhaps an alteration of *churidars* (long, fitted pants worn in India).

chud•dy /ˈCHədē/ (also **chut•ty** /ˈCHət̲ē/)
▸ **noun** Austral./NZ informal or dialect chewing gum.
–ORIGIN 1940s: origin uncertain; probably an alteration of *chewed*.

chuff /CHəf/
▸ **noun** chiefly Brit. informal a person's buttocks or anus.
–ORIGIN 1940s: origin uncertain.

chuff•ing /'CHəfiNG/
▸ **adjective** N. English used for emphasis or as a mild expletive: *the whole chuffing world's gone mad.*
-ORIGIN 1980s: origin uncertain; perhaps related to CHUFF.

church•key /'CHərCH,kē/
▸ **noun** a metal device with a bottle opener at one end and a triangular head at the other for punching a hole in cans.
-ORIGIN origin unknown.

chy•ron /'kīrän/
▸ **noun** trademark an electronically generated caption superimposed on a television or movie screen.
-ORIGIN 1970s: origin uncertain.

cig•a•rette pants /,sigə'ret ,pænts/
▸ **plural noun** women's pants with straight, very narrow legs.

cir•cu•lar po•lar•i•za•tion /'sərkyələr ,pōləri'zāSHən/
▸ **noun** Physics polarization of an electromagnetic wave in which either the electric or the magnetic vector executes a circle perpendicular to the path of propagation with a frequency equal to that of the wave. It is frequently used in satellite communications.

cit•y /'sitē/
▸ **noun** (pl. **cit•ies**) [with modifier] informal a place or situation characterized by a specified attribute: *the staff was in turmoil—it was panic city.*

civ•ic cen•ter /'sivik 'sentər/
▸ **noun** a municipal building or building complex, often publicly financed, with space for conventions, sports events, and theatrical entertainment.

civ•il un•ion /'sivəl 'yo͞onyən/
▸ **noun** a legally recognized union of a same-sex couple, with rights similar to those of marriage.

cla•fou•tis /klæ'fo͞otē/
▸ **noun** (pl. same) a type of flan made of fruit, typically cherries, baked in a sweet batter.
–ORIGIN French, from dialect *clafir* 'to stuff.'

clam•dig•gers /'klæm,digərz/
▸ **plural noun** close-fitting calf-length pants for women.

clean room /'klēn ,ro͞om; ,ro͝om/
▸ **noun** an environment free from dust and other contaminants, used chiefly for the manufacture of electronic components.

clear•skin /'klir,skin/ (also **clean•skin** /'klēn,skin/)
▸ **noun** Austral./NZ **1** an unbranded animal.
2 informal a person without a police record.

click rate /'klik ,rāt/ (also **click-through rate** /'klik 'THro͞o ,rāt/)
▸ **noun** Computing the percentage of people downloading a Web page who access a hypertext link to a particular advertisement.

clicks and mor•tar /'kliks ən 'môrtər/
▸ **noun** used to refer to a traditional business that has expanded its activities to operate also on the Internet.

click•stream /'klik,strēm/
▸ **noun** Computing a series of mouse clicks made by a user while accessing the Internet, especially as monitored to assess a person's interests for marketing purposes.

click-through /'klik ,THro͞o/
▸ **noun** Computing the ratio of clicks that an Internet ad receives to page views of the ad.

cli•mate change /'klīmət ˌCHānj/
▸ **noun** long-term, significant change in the climate of an area or of the earth, usually seen as resulting from human activity.

cli•mate jump /'klīmət ˌjəmp/
▸ **noun** a sudden and drastic change in climate: *scientists fear that a climate jump would be more harmful than gradual global warming.*

clip•per /'klipər/ (also **clip•per chip** /'klipər CHip/)
▸ **noun** a microchip that inserts an identifying code into encrypted transmissions, allowing them to be deciphered by a third party having access to a government-held key.

closed cap•tion /'klōzd 'kæpsHən/
▸ **noun** one of a series of subtitles to a television program, accessible through a decoder.
▸ **verb** (**closed-caption**) [trans.] [usually as noun **closed-captioning**] provide (a program) with closed captions.

close en•coun•ter /'klōs en'kowntər/
▸ **noun** a supposed encounter with a UFO or with aliens.
-PHRASES **close encounter of the first** (or **second**, etc.) **kind** used to describe encounters involving increasing degrees of complexity and apparent exposure of the witness to aliens.

clo•sure /'klōzHər/
▸ **noun** a feeling that an emotional or traumatic experience has been resolved.

club-sand•wich gen•er•a•tion /'kləb 'sæn(d)wiCH jenə ˌrāsHən/
▸ **noun** a generation of people responsible for the care of their children, grandchildren, and parents or other

aging relatives: *typically members of the club-sandwich generation also have busy careers.*
-ORIGIN from *club sandwich,* a sandwich using three slices of bread, on the pattern of *sandwich generation,* a generation responsible for the care of their children and parents.

coach•er /'kōCHər/
▸ noun Austral. a docile cow or steer used as a decoy to attract wild cattle.

coast•eer•ing /'kōstiriNG/
▸ noun the sport of jumping off a cliff into the ocean and swimming or exploring caves along the coast: *you need to wear a helmet and wetsuit if you want to go coasteering.*

co•bot /'kōbät/
▸ noun a computer-controlled robotic device designed to assist a person in a task that requires maneuvering in a tight space: *on automobile assembly lines, cobots guide workers in moving heavy or bulky parts.*
-ORIGIN blend of *collaborative* and *robot.*

cod /käd/ Irish informal
▸ noun a foolish person: *he's making a cod of himself.*

code•share /'kōd,SHer/
▸ noun a marketing arrangement in which two airlines sell seats on a flight that one of them operates: [as adj.] *Qantas is a codeshare partner with both American Airlines and Alaska Airlines in North America.*
■ a flight or aircraft in which such an arrangement is in effect.

cod•ol•o•gy /kä'däləjē/
▸ noun Irish informal foolish or untrue talk or writing; nonsense.

coked /kōkt/
▸ **adjective** informal having taken a large amount of cocaine:
*he was obviously drunk or **coked up***.

cold war•rior /'kōld 'wôrēər/
▸ **noun** a person who promotes a cold war.

col•lat•er•al dam•age /kə'læt̬ərəl 'dæmij/
▸ **noun** unintended damage to property or persons who
are in the vicinity of a military target.

col•or ther•a•py /'kələr ˌTHerəpē/
▸ **noun** a system of alternative medicine based on the use
of color, especially projected colored light.

col•tan /'kältæn/
▸ **noun** a dull metallic mineral composed of columbite
and tantalite, and refined to produce tantalum.
–ORIGIN early 21st cent.: from *col(umbite)* + *tan(talite)*.

com•bi•na•tion ther•a•py /ˌkämbə'nāSHən ˌTHerəpē/
▸ **noun** treatment in which a patient is given two or more
drugs (or other therapeutic agents) for a single disease.

com•bin•er /kəm'bīnər/
▸ **noun** any of various electronic devices that combine
signals, in particular:
■ a device that couples different frequencies to a single
antenna. ■ a component of a cipher that combines two
data sources to encrypt text. ■ an electrical transformer
comprising several smaller ones.

comb•o•ver /'kōm ˌōvər/ (also **comb-o•ver**)
▸ **noun** hair that is combed over a bald spot in an attempt
to cover it.

com•men•tar•i•at /ˌkämən'terēət/
▸ **noun** members of the news media considered as a class.

-ORIGIN late 20th cent.: blend of *commentary* and *proletariat*.

com•mu•ni•ty bank /kə'myo͞onitē ˌbæNGk/
▸ **noun** a commercial bank that derives funds from and lends money to the community where it operates, and is not affiliated with a multibank holding company.

co•mor•bid•i•ty /ˌkōmôr'biditē/
▸ **noun** the simultaneous presence of two chronic diseases or conditions in a patient: *the comorbidty of anxiety and depressive disorders is not uncommon.*

com•plete game /kəm'plēt 'gām/
▸ **noun** Baseball a statistic credited to a pitcher who pitches from start to finish in a regulation game.

com•pli•ance /kəm'plīəns/
▸ **adjective** undertaken or existing mainly in order to comply with an earlier treaty, order, or law: *Canada's WTO compliance legislation ignores skyrocketing drug costs.*

com•press /kəm'pres/
▸ **verb** [trans.] reduce the dynamic range of (a sound signal).

com•put•er•ese /kəmˌpyo͞otə'rēz; -'rēs/
▸ **noun** the jargon associated with computers.
■ the symbols and rules of a computer programming language.

con•cur•rent /kən'kərənt/
▸ **adjective** agreeing or consistent.

con•densed tan•nin /kən'denst 'tænin/
▸ **noun** any of various tannins occuring naturally in plants with antioxidant properties, comprising polymers of flavonoids linked by a carbon-to-carbon bond.

con•joined twins /kən'joind 'twinz/
‣ **plural noun** technical term for Siamese twins.

con•jun•to /kän'ho͝ontō; -'həntō/
‣ **noun** (pl. **con•jun•tos**) (in Latin America or Hispanic communities) a small musical group or band.
-ORIGIN Spanish, literally 'an ensemble, group.'

con•si•glie•re /ˌkänsil'yerē/
‣ **noun** (pl. **con•si•glie•ri** pronunc. same) a member of a Mafia family who serves as an adviser to the leader and resolves disputes within the family.
-ORIGIN Italian, literally 'a member of a council.'

con•sign•ment shop /kən'sīnmənt ˌSHäp/ (or **con•sign•ment store**)
‣ **noun** a store that sells secondhand items (typically clothing and accessories) on behalf of the original owner, who receives a percentage of the selling price.

con•sil•i•ence /kən'silēəns/
‣ **noun** agreement between the approaches to a topic of different academic subjects, especially science and the humanities.
-DERIVATIVES **con•sil•i•ent** adjective
-ORIGIN mid 19th cent.: from *con(current)* + Latin *-silient-*, *-siliens* 'jumping' (as in *resilience*).

con•struc•tion pa•per /kən'strəkSHən ˌpāpər/
‣ **noun** a type of thick colored paper used for making models, designs, and other craftwork.

con•tact /'käntækt/
‣ **verb** [trans.] touch: *I winced as my blister contacted the floor.*

con•tent /'käntent/
‣ **noun** information made available by a Web site or other electronic medium: [as modifier] *online content providers.*

-DERIVATIVES **con•tent•less** adjective
-ORIGIN late Middle English: from medieval Latin *contentum* (plural *contenta* 'things contained').

con•tin•gen•cy fee /kən'tinjənsē ˌfē/
▸ noun a sum of money that is paid to a lawyer by a client only in the eventuality of a case being brought to a successful conclusion.

con•trol freak /kən'trōl ˌfrēk/
▸ noun informal a person who feels an obsessive need to exercise control over themselves and others and to take command of any situation.
-DERIVATIVES **con•trol freak•er•y** noun

con•ver•sion van /kən'vərzHən ˌvæn/
▸ noun a motor vehicle in which the area behind the driver has been converted into a living space.

Cool•Max /'kōōlˌmæks/
▸ noun trademark a polyester fabric that draws perspiration along its fibers away from the skin, used chiefly in sportswear.
-ORIGIN 1980s: an invented name, probably from *cool* + *max(imum)*.

co•op•e•ti•tion /kōˌäpə'tisHən/
▸ noun collaboration between business competitors, in the hope of mutually beneficial results.
-ORIGIN 1980s: blend of *cooperative* and *competition*.

co•or•di•na•tion com•pound /kōˌôrdn'āsHən ˌkämpownd/
▸ noun Chemistry a compound containing coordinate bonds, typically between a central metal atom and a number of other atoms or groups.

cop•y•left /'käpē,left/
▸ **noun** an arrangement whereby software or artistic work may be used, modified, and distributed freely on condition that anything derived from it is bound by the same conditions.
–DERIVATIVES **cop•y•left•ed adjective**
–ORIGIN 1980s: on the pattern of *copyright*.

co•qui /'kōkē/ noun
▸ a singing tree frog (*Eleutherodactylus coqui*), native to Puerto Rico, that has become an invasive pest in Hawaii.

cord blood /'kôrd ,bləd/
▸ **noun** blood from the human umbilical cord, a source of stem cells.

core asset /'kôr 'æset/
▸ **noun** an asset of an entereprise considered to be essential to its success: *we are attracted to their core assets and strong management team.*

core com•pe•ten•cy /'kôr 'kämpətənsē/
▸ **noun** a defining capability or advantage that distinguishes an enterprise from its competitors.
■ a defined level of competence in a particular job or academic program.

cork•er /'kôrkər/ informal
▸ **adjective** NZ informal very good; excellent: *there's nothing quite like corker rock n' roll shows.*

co•ro•ni•al /kə'rōnēəl/
▸ **adjective** relating to a coroner.

cor•po•rat•ize /'kôrp(ə)rə,tīz/
▸ **verb** [trans.] convert (a government organization) into an independent commercial company.
–DERIVATIVES **cor•por•a•ti•za•tion noun**

cor·po·ra·tor /ˈkôrpəˌrātər/
▸ **noun** Indian an elected member of a municipal corporation.

co-sleep·ing /ˈkō ˈslēpiNG/
▸ **noun** the practice of sleeping in the same bed with one's infant or young child: *co-sleeping often facilitates a good breastfeeding relationship.*

cos·me·ceu·ti·cal /ˌkäzməˈso͞otikəl/
▸ **noun** a cosmetic that has or is claimed to have medicinal properties.
–ORIGIN 1980s: blend of *cosmetic* and *pharmaceutical.*

cos·mo·pol·i·tan /ˌkäzməˈpälitn̩/
▸ **noun** a citrusy vodka cocktail, commonly made with Cointreau, cranberry juice, and lime juice.

cost cen·ter /ˈkôst ˌsentər/
▸ **noun** a department or other unit within an organization to which costs may be charged for accounting purposes.

cot-case /ˈkät ˌkās/
▸ **noun** Brit. informal an eccentric or mad person.

cough·er /ˈkôfər/
▸ **noun** a person with a chronic cough.

coulrophobia /ˌkōlrəˈfōbēə/
▸ **noun** extreme or irrational fear of clowns.
–ORIGIN from Greek.

coun·ter·ter·ror·ism /ˌkowntərˈterəˌrizəm/
▸ **noun** political or military activities designed to prevent or thwart terrorism.

-DERIVATIVES **coun•ter•ter•ror•ist** /ˌkowntər'terərist/ noun

coun•try•pol•i•tan /ˌkəntri'pälitn/ (also **Coun•try•pol•i•tan**)
▸ **noun** a type of country music that resembles pop music, usually characterized by orchestrated arrangements: *he prefers traditional country music but likes the sound of the string section in countrypolitan.*
▸ **adjective** relating to or denoting an architectural style that combines country charm with sophistication: *this magazine features moderately priced countrypolitan homes.*
-ORIGIN on the pattern of *cosmopolitan.*

coun•ty clerk /'kowntē 'klərk/
▸ **noun** an elected county official who is responsible for local elections and maintaining property ownership records.

cov•er sheet /'kəvər ˌSHēt/
▸ **noun** a page placed before a manuscript or report, typically with the name of the author, title of the book or report, and date.
■ a page sent as the first page of a fax transmission, identifying the sender, number of pages, etc.

co•vert cou•ture /'kōvərt kōo'tōor/
▸ **noun** the design and manufacture of subtly customized versions of fashionable clothing and accessories: *models and young starlets are the best customers for covert couture, and carry the handbags to prove it.*

cram•ming /'kræmiNG/
▸ **noun** the practice of charging a customer for telephone services that were not requested, authorized, or used: *cramming often shows up as unexplained 900-number charges.*
-DERIVATIVES **cram•mer noun**

cre•den•tial /krə'denCHəl/

▶ **verb** [trans.] [usually as adjective] (**credentialed**) provide with credentials.

-ORIGIN late Middle English: from medieval Latin *credentialis*, from *credentia* 'believing, believability.' The original use was as an adjective in the sense 'giving credence to, recommending,' frequently in *credential letters* or *credential papers*, hence the noun *credentials* (mid 17th cent.).

cre•vette /krə'vet/

▶ **noun** Brit. a shrimp or prawn, especially as an item on a menu.

-ORIGIN French.

cringe•wor•thy /'krinj,wərTHē/

▶ **adjective** informal causing feelings of embarrassment or awkwardness: *the play's cast was excellent, but the dialogue was unforgivably cringeworthy.*

CRM

▶ **abbreviation** customer relationship management, denoting strategies and software that enable a company to organize and optimize its customer relations.

cron•ing /'krōniNG/

▶ **noun** (especially among feminists in the US and Australasia) a celebration or ceremony to honor older women.

-ORIGIN 1990s: blend of *crone* + *crowning*.

cross-con•tam•i•na•tion /'krôs kə,tæmə'nāSHən/

▶ **noun** the process by which bacteria or other microorganisms are unintentionally transferred from one substance or object to another, with harmful effect.

cross-par•ty /'krôs 'pärtē/
> ▶ **adjective** involving or relating to two or more political parties: *a cross-party committee of senators.*

crowd-pleas•er /'krowd ˌplēzər/
> ▶ **noun** a person or thing with great popular appeal: *once again, the group has produced an album which is bound to be a crowd-pleaser.*
> –DERIVATIVES **crowd-pleas•ing** adjective

crowd-surf /'krowd ˌsərf/
> ▶ **verb** [intrans.] be passed in a prone position over the heads of the audience at a rock concert, typically after having jumped from the stage.

crow•eat•er /'krō͵ēt̬ər/
> ▶ **noun** Austral. informal a South Australian.

crown mold•ing /'krown 'mōldiNG/
> ▶ **noun** an ornamental molding around the wall of a room just below the ceiling. Also called **cornice**.

cru•been /'krōōbēn/
> ▶ **noun** Irish a boiled pig's foot as food.
> –ORIGIN mid 19th cent.: from Irish *crúibín*, diminutive of *crúb* 'claw, hoof.'

cru•ci•ver•bal•ist /krōōsi'vərbəlist/
> ▶ **noun** a person who enjoys or is skilled at solving cross-word puzzles.
> –ORIGIN 1970s: from Latin *crux*, *cruci-* 'cross' and *verbalist*.

crush space /'krəSH ˌspās/
> ▶ **noun** space in the common area of a performance venue that can accommodate the largest crowd expected.

cryp•to•spo•ri•di•o•sis /ˌkriptōspəˌrīdēˈōsis/
▸ **noun** an intestinal disease caused by infection with cryptosporidium, causing diarrhea and vomiting.

crys•tal heal•ing /ˈkristl ˈhēliNG/ (also **crys•tal ther•a•py**)
▸ **noun** in alternative medicine, the use of crystals for their professed healing properties.

C2C
▸ **abbreviation** consumer-to-consumer, denoting transactions conducted via the Internet between consumers.

cube farm /ˈkyo͞ob ˌfärm/
▸ **noun** a large open-plan office divided into cubicles for individual workers.

cud•dle pud•dle /ˈkədl ˌpədl/
▸ **noun** informal **1** a whirlpool or hot tub: *all the new, overpriced houses in this area come with eurokitchens and cuddle puddles.*
2 a group of people lying on the floor with their bodies intertwined: *the ravers had collapsed in a cuddle puddle by six a.m.*

cued speech /ˈkyo͞od ˈspēCH/
▸ **noun** a type of sign language that uses hand movements combined with mouth shapes to communicate to the hearing impaired.

Cul•len skink /ˈkələn ˈskiNGk/
▸ **noun** a Scottish soup made from smoked haddock, potatoes, onions, and milk.
-ORIGIN 1980s: from the name of *Cullen*, a village on the Moray Firth in NE Scotland, + Scots *skink* 'soup made from shin of beef,' probably from Middle Low German *Schinke* 'ham.'

cul•tu•ra•ti /ˌkəlCHə'rätē/
▸ **plural noun** well-educated people who appreciate the arts.
–ORIGIN 1980s: blend of *culture* and *literati*.

cul•ture war /'kəlCHər ˌwôr/
▸ **noun** a conflict between groups with different ideals, beliefs, philosophies, etc.

cup-holder cui•sine /'kəp ˌhōldər kwiˌzēn/
▸ **noun** food that is packaged to fit in a car or other vehicle's cup holder: *I like to eat on the go, so I buy soups and other cup–holder cuisine.*

cup•ping /'kəpiNG/
▸ **noun** (in Chinese medicine) a therapy in which heated glass cups are applied to the skin along the meridians of the body, creating suction and believed to stimulate the flow of energy.

cup•ro /'k(y)o͞oprō/
▸ **noun** a type of rayon made by dissolving cotton cellulose with cuprammonium salts and spinning the resulting solution into filaments.
–ORIGIN 1980s: an invented word, probably from *cuprammonium* (an ion formed from coppers salts and ammonia).

cush•ty /'ko͞oSHtē/
▸ **adjective** Brit. informal very good or pleasing: *he's got a cushty setup.*
–ORIGIN 1920s: from Romany *kushto*, *kushti* 'good,' perhaps influenced by *cushy*.

cusp•ing /'kəspiNG/
▸ **noun** Architecture a formation consisting of cusps.

cus•tom•ize /'kəstə,mīz/
▸ verb [trans.] modify (something) to suit a particular individual or task: *the software can be customized to the developing needs of your students.*
–DERIVATIVES **cus•tom•i•z•able** adjective; **cus•tom•i•za•tion** noun

cut lunch /'kət 'lənCH/
▸ noun Austral./NZ a packed lunch.

cy•ber•at•tack /'sībərə,tæk/
▸ noun Computing an effort by hackers to damage or destroy a computer network or system: *the conference addressed the possibility of a cyberattack on our communications infrastructure.*
–DERIVATIVES **cy•ber•at•tack•er** noun

cy•ber•cash /'sībər,kæsH/
▸ noun 1 funds used in electronic financial transactions, especially over the Internet.
2 money stored on an electronic smart card.

cy•ber•chon•dri•ac /,sībər'kändrē,æk/
▸ noun a person who reads health or medical information on the Internet and develops imaginary physical symptoms and ailments: *in Internet chat rooms I can meet other cyberchondriacs who sympathize with me.*
–DERIVATIVES **cy•ber•chon•dri•a** /,sībər'kändrēə/ noun

cy•ber•crime /'sībər,krīm/
▸ noun crime conducted via the Internet or some other computer network: *as international tensions increase, cybercrime often escalates.*

cy•ber•law /'sībər,lô/
▸ noun laws, or a specific law, relating to Internet and computer offenses, especially fraud, copyright infringement, etc.

cy•ber•mall /'sībər,môl/
> ▸ **noun** a commercial Web site through which a range of goods may be purchased; a virtual shopping mall on the Internet.

cy•ber•naut /'sībər,nôt; -,nät/
> ▸ **noun** Computing a person who wears sensory devices in order to experience virtual reality.
> ■ a person who uses the Internet.
> –ORIGIN 1990s: from *cyber-*, on the pattern of *astronaut* and *aeronaut*.

cy•ber•pet /'sībər,pet/
> ▸ **noun** an electronic toy that simulates a real pet and with which human interaction is possible: *you'll have to feed your cyberpet when it gets hungry.* (Also called **dig•i•pet** or **vir•tu•al pet**.)

cy•ber•pho•bi•a /,sībər'fōbēə/
> ▸ **noun** fear of or anxiety about computing or information technology; reluctance to use computers, especially the Internet: *a few bad online experiences shouldn't lead to cyberphobia.*
> –DERIVATIVES **cy•ber•phobe** noun;; **cy•ber•pho•bic** adjective

cy•ber•porn /'sībər,pôrn/
> ▸ **noun** pornography viewable on a computer screen, especially accessed on the Internet: *the anti-spam filter is set to block cyberporn, but some gets through anyway.*

cy•ber•shop /'sībər,sнäp/
> ▸ **verb** [intrans.] (**cy•ber•shopped, cy•ber•shop•ping**) [often as noun] (**cybershopping**) purchase or shop for goods and services on a Web site: *people who cybershop often end up buying the item at a shopping mall.*
> ▸**noun** (also **cy•ber•store** /'sībər,stôr/) a Web site that sells

or provides information about retail goods or services: *the retailer's cybershop sometimes has different prices than in its mail-order catalog.*
-DERIVATIVES **cy•ber•shop•per** noun

cy•ber•slack•er /'sībər,slækər/
▸ **noun** informal a person who uses their employer's Internet and e-mail facilities for personal activities during working hours.
-DERIVATIVES **cy•ber•slack•ing** noun

cy•ber•squat•ting /'sībər,skwätiNG/
▸ **noun** the practice of registering names, especially well-known company or brand names, as Internet domains, in the hope of reselling them at a profit.
-DERIVATIVES **cy•ber•squat•ter** noun

cy•ber•stalk•ing /'sībər,stôkiNG/
▸ **noun** the repeated use of electronic communications to harass or frighten someone, for example by sending threatening e-mails.
-DERIVATIVES **cy•ber•stalk•er** noun

cy•ber•surf•er /'sībər,sərfər/
▸ **noun** a person who habitually uses or browses the Internet.
-DERIVATIVES **cy•ber•surf•ing** noun

cy•ber•ter•ror•ism /,sībər'terə,rizəm/
▸ **noun** the politically motivated use of computers and information technology to cause severe disruption or widespread fear in society.
-DERIVATIVES **cy•ber•ter•ror•ist** noun

cy•brar•i•an /sī'brerēən/
▸ **noun** a librarian or researcher who uses the Internet as

an information resource: *my company employs cybrarians to keep track of competing Web sites.*
-ORIGIN blend of *cyber-* and *librarian.*

cy•clic re•dun•dan•cy check /'sīklik ri'dəndənsē ˌCHek; 'siklik-/ (also **cy•clic re•dun•dan•cy code**) (abbreviation: **CRC**)

▸ **noun** Computing a data code that detects errors during transmission, storage, or retrieval.

D

da /də/
▸ **adjective** nonstandard spelling of *the*, used in representing informal speech.

DAB
▸ **abbreviation** digital audio broadcasting.

dag /dæg/
▸ **noun** Austral./NZ, informal an awkward adolescent.
■ an unfashionable or socially conservative person.

dag•ga /ˈdægə/
▸ **noun** chiefly S. African marijuana.
–ORIGIN late 17th cent.: from Afrikaans, from Khoikhoi *dachab* .

dag•ger•board /ˈdægər,bôrd/
▸ **noun** a board that slides vertically through the keel of a sailboat to reduce sideways movement.

dai•sy-cut•ter /ˈdāzē ,kətər/
▸ **noun** informal an immensely powerful aerial bomb that derives its destructive power from the mixture of ammonium nitrate and aluminum powder with air.
–ORIGIN early 20th cent.: so named because the bomb explodes just above ground level.

dam•i•an•a /,dæmē'ænə/
▸ **noun** a small shrub native to Mexico, whose leaves are used in herbal medicine and in the production of a liqueur, and also reputedly possess aphrodisiac qualities.
• *Turnera diffusa*, family Turneraceae.

dark bi•ol•o•gy /'därk bī'äləjē/
▸ **noun** scientific research related to biological weapons.

dark en•er•gy /'därk 'enərjē/
▸ **noun** Physics a theoretical repulsive force that counter-
acts gravity and causes the universe to expand at an accelerating rate: *Einstein's theories allow for the possible existence of dark energy.*

DARPA /'därpə/
▸ **abbreviation** Defense Advanced Research Projects
Agency.

da•shi /'däsʜē/
▸ **noun** stock made from fish and kelp, used in Japanese
cooking.

da•ta•point /'dætə,point; 'dātə-/
▸ **noun** an identifiable element in a data set: *software that
can quickly process tens of thousands of datapoints.*

da•ta set /'dætə ,set; 'dātə/
▸ **noun** a collection of related sets of information that is
composed of separate elements but can be manipulated
as a unit by a computer.

da•ta smog /'dætə ,smäg; 'dātə/
▸ **noun** informal an overwhelming excess of information, especially from the Internet.

date rape /'dāt ,rāp/
▸ **verb** [trans.] (of a man) rape (a woman) he is dating or
with whom he is on a date.

date-rape drug /'dāt ,rāp ,drəg/
▸ **noun** a drug that causes temporary loss of memory or
inhibition, surreptitiously given to a girl or a woman so
that her date may sexually abuse or rape her.

day trad•ing /ˈdā ˌtrādiNG/

▸ **noun** Stock Exchange a form of securities trading in which individuals buy and sell shares (usually over the Internet) over a period of a single day's trading, with the intention of profiting from small price fluctuations.

-DERIVATIVES **day trad•er** noun

DDoS

▸ **abbreviation** distributed denial of service, the intentional paralyzing of a computer network by flooding it with data sent simultaneously from many individual computers.

dead-ball line /ˈded ˈbôl ˌlīn/

▸ **noun** Soccer the part of the goal line to either side of the goal.

dead white Eu•ro•pe•an male /ˈded ˈ(h)wīt ˌyərəˈpēən ˈmāl; ˌyo͝orə-/ (also **dead white male**)

▸ **noun** informal a writer, philosopher, or other significant figure whose importance and talents may have been exaggerated by virtue of his belonging to a historically dominant gender and ethnic group.

death met•al /ˈdeTH ˌmetl/

▸ **noun** a form of heavy metal music using lyrics preoccupied with death, suffering, and destruction.

de Cle•ram•bault's syn•drome /də ˌklerəmˈbōz ˌsindrōm/

▸ **noun** Psychiatry another term for EROTOMANIA.

-ORIGIN from the name of Gatin *de Clérambault* (1872–1934), French psychiatrist, who first described it.

de•com•pile /ˌdēkəmˈpīl/

▸ **verb** [trans.] Computing produce source code from (compiled code).

-DERIVATIVES **de•com•pi•la•tion** /dē,kämpəˈlāsHən noun; **de•com•pil•er** noun

de•con•di•tion•ing /ˌdēkən'dɪsHəniNG/
▸ **noun** Psychiatry the reform or reversal of previously conditioned behavior, especially in the treatment of phobia
and other anxiety disorders in which the fear response
to certain stimuli is brought under control.

deep brain stim•u•la•tion /'dēp 'brān ˌstimyə,lāsHən/
▸ **noun** a nonsurgical treatment to reduce tremor and to
block involuntary movements in patients with motion
disorders. Small electric shocks are delivered to the
thalamus (especially in the treatment of multiple scle-
rosis) or the globus pallidus (especially in the treatment
of Parkinson's disease), rendering these parts of the
brain inactive without surgically destroying them.

deep e•col•o•gy /'dēp i'kälərjē/
▸ **noun** an environmental movement and philosophy that
regards human life as just one of many equal components of a global ecosystem.

deep mag•ic /'dēp 'mæjik/
▸ **noun** any of the techniques used in the development of
software or computer systems that require the pro-
grammer to have esoteric theoretical knowledge: *some
hackers use deep magic to tweak existing software.*
-ORIGIN probably from C.S. Lewis's *Narnia* books.

deep-pan /'dēp ˌpæn/
▸ **adjective** Brit. (of a pizza) baked in a deep dish and having a thick dough base.

deep throat /'dēp 'THrōt/
▸ **noun** a person who anonymously supplies information
about covert or illegal action in the organization where
they work.
-ORIGIN 1970s: the title of a pornographic film of 1972,
first applied in this sense as the name ('Deep Throat')
of an informant in the Watergate scandal.

deep-vein throm•bo•sis /'dēp ˌvān THräm'bōsis/
▸ **noun** thrombosis in a vein lying deep below the skin, especially in the legs.

de•flesh /dē'flesH/
▸ **verb** [trans.] remove the flesh from.

de•frag /dē'fræg/
▸ **verb** [trans.] (**de•fragged, de•frag•ging**) Computing (of software) reduce the fragmentation of (a file) by concatenating parts stored in separate locations on a disk: *the safe way to defrag your files.*

de•fund /dē'fənd/
▸ **verb** [trans.] prevent from continuing to receive funds: *the California legislature has defunded the Industrial Welfare Commission.*

de•hull /dē'həl/
▸ **verb** [trans.] remove the hulls from (fruit, seeds, or grain).

de•husk /dē'həsk/
▸ **verb** [trans.] remove the husk or husks from (grain).

de•ink /dē'iNGk/
▸ **verb** [trans.] remove ink from (paper being recycled).

de•in•stall /ˌdē-in'stôl/ (*Brit.* also **de•in•stal**)
▸ **verb** (**de•in•stalls** also **de•in•stals, de•in•stalled, de•in•stal•ling**) [trans.] remove (an application or file) from a computer. ■ humorous to fire someone: *I worked there for three months but then the company lost funding and I was deinstalled.*
-DERIVATIVES **de•in•stal•la•tion** /ˌdē-instə'lāsHən/ noun; **de•in•stall•er** noun

de•junk /dē'jəNGk/
‣ **verb** [trans.] informal clear (a room or other space) by disposing of clutter and unwanted possessions: *dejunk the house before you move.* | figurative *how to dejunk your life.*

de•li•cense /dē'līsəns/ (*Brit.* **de•li•cence**)
‣ **verb** [trans.] deprive of a license.

de•link /dē'liNGk/
‣ **verb** [often as noun] (**delinking**) break the connection between (something) and something else: *the possibility of delinking from the international economic system.*

Del•phi tech•nique /'delfī tek,nēk/
‣ **noun** a method of group decision-making and forecasting that involves successively collating the judgments of experts.
–ORIGIN in allusion to the ancient Greek oracle at *Delphi.*

de•mine /dē'mīn/
‣ **verb** [trans.] remove explosive mines from: *the money will be used to demine a field in Afghanistan.*
–DERIVATIVES **de•min•er** noun

de•mu•tu•al•ize /dē'myōōCHŌōə,līz/
‣ **verb** [intrans.] (of a mutual insurance company) convert to a publicly held corporation: *the measure will be especially helpful to smaller insurers that want to demutualize.*
–DERIVATIVES **de•mu•tu•al•i•za•tion** noun

de•na•zi•fy /dē'nätsə,fī/
‣ **verb** (**de•na•zi•fies, de•na•zi•fied, de•na•zi•fy•ing**) [trans.] remove Nazi influence from.
–DERIVATIVES **de•na•zi•fi•ca•tion** noun

den•dri•mer /'dendrəmər/
> ▸ **noun** a synthetic polymer with a branching, treelike structure.
-ORIGIN 1990s: from Greek *dendron* 'tree' + *-i-* + *-mer*.

den•tex /'den,teks/
> ▸ **noun** (pl. same or **den•tex•es**) a sea bream of the genus *Dentex*, especially *D. dentex* of the Mediterranean and the North African Atlantic coast.
-ORIGIN modern Latin (genus name), from Latin.

de•part /di'pärt/
> ▸ **verb** [trans.] leave (one's job).

De•pres•sion glass /də'presHən ,glæs/
> ▸ **noun** machine-pressed, tinted glassware that was mass-produced in the US from the late 1920s to the 1940s and often used as giveaways to persuade customers to purchase goods.

de•queue /dē'kyo͞o/
> ▸ **verb** [trans.] (**de•queued, de•queu•ing** or **de•queue•ing**) Computing remove (an item of data) from a queue.

de•re•cho /də'rāCHō/
> ▸ **noun** (pl. **de•re•chos**) a storm system that moves a long distance rapidly and brings winds that can devastate an area several miles wide.
-ORIGIN late 19th cent.: Spanish, literally 'direct, straight.'

DES
> ▸ **abbreviation** Computing data encryption standard.

des•ig•nat•ed driv•er /'dezig,nātid 'drīvər/
> ▸ **noun** a person who abstains from alcohol at a social gathering so as to be fit to drive others home.

de•sign•er stub•ble /dɪˈzīnər ˌstəbəl/
▸ **noun** beard stubble that is deliberately groomed to look fashionable or trendy: *is that designer stubble or did you forget to shave this morning?*

desk din•ing /ˈdesk ˌdīnɪNG/ (also **desk-din•ing**)
▸ **noun** the eating of a meal at one's desk in an office: *desk dining is antisocial but it saves time and money.*
‑DERIVATIVES **desk din•er noun**

de•sol•der /dēˈsädər/
▸ **verb** [trans.] remove solder from.

des•per•ate /ˈdespərit/
▸ **adjective** Irish informal very bad: *that beer's desperate—it's a wonder you've the nerve to offer it for sale.*

des•ti•na•tion /ˌdestəˈnāsHən/
▸ **noun** [as modifier] denoting a place that people will make a special trip to visit: *a destination restaurant.*

des•ti•na•tion charge /ˌdestəˈnāsHən ˌCHärj/
▸ **noun** a fee added to the price of a new car to cover the cost of shipping the vehicle from the manufacturer to the dealer.

de•vel•op•men•tal de•lay /diˌveləpˈmentl diˈlā/
▸ **noun** the condition of a child being less developed mentally or physically than is normal for its age.

de•vo•ré /dəˈvôrā/ (also **de•vo•re**)
▸ **noun** [usu. as modifier] a velvet fabric with a pattern formed by burning the pile away with acid: *a devoré top.*
‑ORIGIN 1990s: from French *dévoré*, lit. 'devoured,' past participle of *dévorer.*

de•wax /dēˈwæks/
▸ **verb** [trans.] remove wax from: *linoleum needs to be de-waxed using a strong solvent.*

dhikr /'dikər/ (also **zikr** /'zikər/)

▸ **noun** Islam a form of devotion, associated chiefly with Sufism, in which the worshipper is absorbed in the rhythmic repetition of the name of God or his attributes.

■ a Sufi ceremony in which this is practiced.

–ORIGIN from Arabic *d̲ikr* 'remembrance.'

DHTML

▸ **abbreviation** Computing dynamic HTML.

DI

▸ **abbreviation** direct injection.

di•al-a•round /'dīl ə,rownd/

▸ **adjective** used to describe a telephone service that requires callers to dial a special access code that enables them to bypass (or 'dial around') their chosen long-distance carrier in order to obtain a better rate.

dick•wad /'dik,wäd/

▸ **noun** vulgar slang a contemptible person.

–ORIGIN 1980s: from *dick* in the sense 'penis' + *wad*.

dic•tion•ar•y at•tack /'dikSHə,nerē ə,tæk/

▸ **noun** an attempted illegal entry to a computer system that uses a dictionary headword list to generate possible passwords.

dig•i•cam /'diji,kæm/

▸ **noun** a digital camera.

dig•i•pet /,diji'pet/

▸ **noun** see CYBERPET.

dig•it•al cam•er•a /'dijitl 'kæm(ə)rə/

▸ **noun** a camera which produces digital images that can

be stored in a computer, displayed on a screen, and printed.

dig•it•al com•pact cas•sette /'dijiṯl 'kämpækt kə'set/ (abbreviation: **DCC**)
▸ **noun** a format for tape cassettes similar to ordinary audiocassettes but with digital rather than analog recording.

dig•it•al com•pres•sion /'dijiṯl kəm'presHən/
▸ **noun** a method of reducing the number of bits (zeros and ones) in a digital signal by using mathematical algorithms to eliminate redundant information.

dig•it•al di•vide /'dijiṯl di'vīd/
▸ **noun** the gulf between those who have ready access to computers and the Internet, and those who do not.

dig•it•al lock•er /'dijiṯl 'läkər/
▸ **noun** Computing an Internet service that allows registered users to access music, movies, videos, photographs, video games, and other multimedia files.

dig•it•al sig•na•ture /'dijiṯl 'signəCHər/
▸ **noun** Computing a digital code (generated and authenticated by public key encryption) that is attached to an electronically transmitted document to verify its contents and the sender's identity.

dig•it•al tel•e•vi•sion /'dijiṯl 'telə,vizHən/
▸ **noun** television broadcasting in which the pictures are transmitted as digital signals that are decoded by a device in or attached to the receiving television set.

di•hy•dro•ep•i•an•dro•ste•rone /dī'hīdrō,epēæn'drästə,rōn/ (abbreviation: **DHEA**)
▸ **noun** a naturally occurring weak androgenic steroid

hormone produced by the adrenal glands with benefits such as the prevention of aging, the improvement of sexual function, the enhancement of athletic performance, and the treatment of osteoporosis.

din•kum /ˈdiNGkəm/
▸ **adverb** Austral./NZ, informal really, truly, honestly.

di•rect deb•it /diˈrekt ˈdebit; dīˈrekt/
▸ **noun** a payment system whereby creditors are authorized to debit a customer's bank account directly at regular intervals.

dirt•bag /ˈdərtˌbæg/
▸ **noun** informal a very unkempt or unpleasant person.

dirt•y /ˈdərtē/
▸ **adjective** (**dirt•i•er, dirt•i•est**) informal using illegal drugs.

dirt•y rice /ˈdərtē ˈrīs/
▸ **noun** a Cajun dish consisting of white rice cooked with onions, peppers, chicken livers, and herbs.

dis•cern•ment /diˈsərnmənt/
▸ **noun** (in Christian contexts) perception in the absence of judgment with a view to providing spiritual guidance.

dis•con•nect /ˌdiskəˈnekt/
▸ **noun** a discrepancy or lack of connection: *there can be a disconnect between boardrooms and IT departments when it comes to technology.*

di•sease man•age•ment /diˈzēz ˌmænijmənt/
▸ **noun** a system that seeks to manage the chronic conditions of high-risk, high-cost patients as a group.

dish•pan hands /'dɪsʜ,pæn ,hændz/
> ▸ **plural noun** red, rough, or chapped hands caused by sensitivity to or excessive use of household detergents or other cleaning agents.

Dis•ney•land /'dɪznē,lænd/
> ▸ **noun** a theme park in Anaheim, California, that opened in 1955. [ORIGIN: from Walt *Disney*]
> ■ a large, bustling place filled with colorful attractions.
> ■ a place of fantasy or make-believe: *their own think tank, their own Disneyland of future ideas* | [as adj.] *Disneyland conceptions of defense which have no genuine relevance.*

dis•play ad /dis'plā ,æd/
> ▸ **noun** a large advertisement, especially in a newspaper or magazine, that features eye-catching type or illustrations.

dis•sent /di'sent/
> ▸ **noun** a statement by a judge giving reasons as to why he or she disagrees with a decision made by the other judges in a court case.

dis•tant ear•ly warn•ing /'distənt 'ərlē 'wôrnɪnɢ/ (abbreviation: **DEW**)
> ▸ **noun** a radar system in North America for the early detection of a missile attack.

dis•trib•ute /di'stribyōōt/
> ▸ **verb** [trans.] [as adj.] (**distributed**) Computing (of a computer system) spread over several machines, especially over a network.
> –DERIVATIVES **dis•trib•ut•a•ble** adjective

Dix•ie Cup /'diksē ,kəp/
> ▸ **noun** trademark a brand of disposable paper cup.

djem•be /'jembə; -bā/
▸ **noun** a kind of goblet-shaped hand drum originating in West Africa.
–ORIGIN French *djembé*, from Mande *jembe*.

DLL
▸ **abbreviation** dynamic link library.

DNR
▸ **abbreviation 1** Department of Natural Resources.
2 do not resuscitate, an instruction not to attempt the resuscitation of a terminally ill patient after cardiac arrest in the hospital.

DNS
▸ **abbreviation** Computing domain name system.

Dob•son u•nit /'däbsən ˌyo͞onit/ (abbreviation: **DU**)
▸ **noun** a unit of measurement for the total amount of ozone in the atmosphere above a point on the earth's surface, one Dobson unit being equivalent to a layer of pure ozone 0.01 mm thick at standard temperature and pressure.
–ORIGIN 1980s: from the name of G. M. B. *Dobson* (1889–1976), British meteorologist.

doc•u•soap /'däkyəˌsōp/
▸ **noun** a documentary, usually produced for television and having elements of soap opera, following people in a particular occupation or location over a period of time.
–ORIGIN 1990s: blend of *documentary* and *soap (opera)*.

dog•gy style /'dôgē ˌstīl/ (also **dog•gy fash•ion** /'dôgē ˌfæsHən/)
▸ **noun** a sexual position in which the woman, usually supporting herself on her hands and knees, is penetrated from behind by the man.

DOHC
> ▸ **abbreviation** dual overhead cam (engine).

DOI
> ▸ **abbreviation** Computing digital object identifier, a unique identifying number allocated to a Web site.

dol•phin-safe /'dälfin ,sāf; 'dôl-/
> ▸ **adjective** (on canned tuna labels) indicating that the tuna has been harvested using fishing methods that are not harmful to dolphins.

do•main name /dō'mān ,nām/
> ▸ **noun** Computing a series of alphanumeric strings separated by periods, such as *www. oup-usa. org*, serving as an address for a computer network connection and identifying the owner of the address. The last three letters in a domain name indicate what type of organization owns the address: for instance, .com stands for commercial, .edu for educational, and .org for nonprofit.

do•nate /'dō,nāt; dō'nāt/
> ▸ **verb** [trans.] Chemistry & Physics provide or contribute (electrons or protons).

dong quai /'dôNG 'kwā; 'kwī/,
> ▸ **noun** an aromatic herb native to China and Japan, the root of which is used by herbalists to treat premenstrual syndrome and menopausal symptoms.
> •*Angelica sinensis*, family Umbelliferae.
> –ORIGIN from Chinese *dāngguī*.

do-noth•ing /'dōō,nəTHiNG/ informal
> ▸ **adjective** taking no action; doing nothing: *a weak, divided, do-nothing government.*
▸**noun** an idle or irresponsible person: *a shiftless lot of do-nothings.*

doo•bry /ˈdo͞obrē/ (also **doo•brey** or **doo•brie**)
▸ **noun** (pl. **doo•bries** also **doo•breys**) Brit. informal used to refer to a person or thing whose name one cannot recall, does not know, or does not wish to specify: *you know, the little plastic doobry that covers the connector.*
-ORIGIN 1950s: of unknown origin.

door•knock /ˈdôr,näk/
▸ **verb** [intrans.] Austral./NZ campaign by making door-to-door house visits.

do•pa•min•er•gic /,dōpəmiˈnərjik/
▸ **adjective** Biochemistry releasing or involving dopamine as a neurotransmitter.
-ORIGIN 1960s: from *dopamine* + Greek *ergon* 'work' + *-ic.*

do-rag /ˈdo͞o ,ræg/
▸ **noun** black slang a scarf or cloth worn to protect one's hairstyle.
-ORIGIN 1990s: from *hairdo.*

DoS
▸ **abbreviation** denial of service, an interruption in an authorized user's access to a computer network, typically one caused with malicious intent.

dos•ser /ˈdäsər/
▸ **noun** Brit. informal, derogatory an idle person.

DOT
▸ **abbreviation** directly observed therapy, a method of supervising patients to ensure that they take medication as directed.

dot-bomb /ˈdät 'bäm/ (also **dot bomb** or **dot.bomb**)
▸ **noun** informal an unsuccessful dot-com: *many promising Internet start-ups ended up as dot-bombs.*
-DERIVATIVES **dot-bomb verb** [intrans.]

dot-com /'dät 'käm/ (also **dot.com**)
- ▸ **noun** a company that conducts its business on the Internet.
- ▸**adjective** of or relating to business conducted on the Internet.
- -DERIVATIVES **dot-com•er noun**
- -ORIGIN 1990s: from '.com' in an Internet address, indicating a commercial site.

dou•la /'dōōlə/
- ▸ **noun** a woman giving support, help, and advice to another woman during pregnancy and during and after the birth.
- -ORIGIN 1960s: modern Greek, from Greek *doulē* 'female slave.'

down•burst /'down,bərst/
- ▸ **noun** a strong downward current of air from a cumulonimbus cloud, which is usually accompanied by intense rain or a thunderstorm.

down•wind•er /'down'windər/
- ▸ **noun** a person living downwind of a nuclear test site or reactor, where the risk from fallout or radiation leaks is greatest.

drag-and-drop /'dræg ən 'dräp/ Computing
- ▸ **verb** [trans.] move (an icon or other image) to another part of the screen using a mouse or similar device, typically in order to perform some operation on a file or document.
- ▸**adjective** of, relating to, or permitting the movement of images in this way.

dress-down Fri•day /'dres,down 'frīdā/
- ▸ **noun** another term for CASUAL FRIDAY.

drill /dril/
▸ verb [intrans.] (**drill down**) Computing access data that is in a lower level of a hierarchically structured database.
-DERIVATIVES **drill•er** noun

drink /driNGk/
▸ noun (**drinks**) a social gathering at which alcoholic drinks are served: *would you like to come for drinks on Sunday?*

drop /dräp/
▸ verb (**dropped, drop•ping**) [trans.] Brit. informal (of a DJ) select and play (a record): *various guest DJs drop quality tunes both old and new.*
-DERIVATIVES **drop•pa•ble** adjective

drop box /'dräp ˌbäks/
▸ noun a secured receptacle into which items such as returned books or videotapes, payments, keys, or donated clothing can be deposited.

drop-ship /'dräp ˌSHip/
▸ verb (**drop-shipped, drop-ship•ping**) [trans.] move (goods) from the manufacturer directly to the retailer without going through the usual distribution channels.
-DERIVATIVES **drop ship•ment** noun

drug mule /'drəg ˌmyo͞ol/
▸ noun a person who transports illegal drugs by swallowing them or concealing them in a body cavity.

drum /drəm/
▸ verb (**drummed, drum•ming**) [trans.] Austral./NZ informal, dated give (someone) reliable information or a warning: *I'm drumming you, if they come I'm going.*

dry•er sheet /'drīər ˌSHēt/
▸ noun a fabric softener sheet.

dry mount•ing /'drī ˌmowntiNG/
> **noun** Photography a process in which a print is bonded to a mount using a layer of adhesive in a hot press.
-DERIVATIVES **dry-mount** /'drī ˌmownt/ **verb**; **dry-mount•ed** adjective

DSL
> **abbreviation** digital subscriber line, a technology for the high-speed transmission of digital information over standard telephone lines.

DTV
> **abbreviation** digital television.

DU
> **abbreviation** ■ depleted uranium. ■ Dobson unit(s).

dub-dub-dub /'dəb 'dəb 'dəb/
> **noun** Computing, informal short form used instead of pronouncing the three letters in the abbreviation WWW (World Wide Web).

dul•ce de le•che /'dōōlsā də 'lācHā/
> **noun** a traditional Argentinian dessert made by caramelizing sugar in milk.

dumb•size /'dəm,sīz/
> **verb** [intrans.] (of a company) reduce staff numbers to levels so low that work can no longer be carried out effectively.
-ORIGIN 1990s: humorously, on the pattern of *downsize*.

dump•er /'dəmpər/
> **noun** a large metal container for trash.

dump•ster div•ing /'dəmpstər ˌdīviNG/
> **noun** the practice of raiding dumpsters to find discarded

items that are still useful, can be recycled, and have value.

Dun•geons and Drag•ons /'dənjənz ən 'drægənz/
▸ noun trademark a fantasy role-playing game set in an imaginary world based loosely on medieval myth.

dur•wan /dər'wän/
▸ noun Indian a porter or doorkeeper.
–ORIGIN late 18th cent.: Urdu *darwān*, from Persian.

Dust•bust•er /'dəst,bəstər/
▸ noun trademark a hand-held vacuum cleaner.

dutch•ie /'dəCHē/
▸ noun W. Indian a large, heavy cooking pot.
–ORIGIN from *Dutch oven*.

Dutch•man /'dəCHmən/ (or **Dutch•wom•an** /'dəCH,wŏŏmən/)
▸ noun (pl. **Dutch•men** /'dəCH,men/ or **Dutch•wom•en** /'dəCH,wimin/) S. African derogatory an Afrikaner.

du•vet day /d(y)ŏŏ'vā ,dā/
▸ noun Brit., informal an unscheduled extra day's leave from work, taken to alleviate stress or pressure and sanctioned by one's employer.

dwell time /'dwel ,tīm/
▸ noun technical time spent in the same position, area, stage of a process, etc.

DWEM
▸ abbreviation DEAD WHITE EUROPEAN MALE.

DWM
▸ **abbreviation** dead white male, used to describe a writer, philosopher, or other significant figure whose importance and talents may have been exaggerated by virtue of his belonging to a historically dominant gender.

dy•nam•ic link li•brar•y /dī'næmik 'liNGk ˌlībrerē; -brəry/ (abbreviation: **DLL**)
▸ **noun** a collection of subroutines stored on disk, which can be loaded into memory and executed when accessed by a running program.

dy•nam•ic pric•ing /dī'næmik 'prīsiNG/
▸ **noun** the practice of pricing items at a level determined by a particular customer's perceived ability to pay.

dys•mor•phi•a /dis'môrfēə/
▸ **noun** Medicine deformity or abnormality in the shape or size of a specified part of the body: *muscle dysmorphia*.
-DERIVATIVES **dys•mor•phic adjective**
-ORIGIN late 19th cent.: from Greek *dusmorphia* 'misshapenness, ugliness,' from *dus- dis-* + *morphē* 'form.'

E

e¹
▸ **symbol for** (€) euro(s).

e² /ē/
▸ **noun** (plural **e's**) an e-mail system, message, or messages: *there are fifty e's in my inbox just waiting for me.*
▸**verb** (**e'd, e'•ing**) [trans.] **1** send an e-mail to (someone): *how many times did you e him today?*
2 send (a message) by e-mail: *can you e that to me?*

ear can•dy /'ir ˌkændē/
▸ **noun** informal light popular music that is pleasant and entertaining but intellectually undemanding.

ear•ly doors /'ərlē dôrz/
▸ **adverbial phrase** Brit. informal early on, especially in a game or contest: *you should try to wind up their star player early doors.*
-ORIGIN apparently originally with reference to admission to a music hall some time before the start of the performance.

ear•ly a•dopt•er /'ərlē ə'däptər/
▸ **noun** a person who starts using a product or technology as soon as it becomes available.

ear•ly warn•ing sys•tem /'ərlē 'wôrnıNG ˌsistəm/
▸ **noun** a network of radar stations established at the boundary of a defended region to provide advanced warning of an aircraft or missile attack.
■ a condition, system, or series of procedures indicating a potential development or impending problem.

e-book /'ē ˌbo͝ok/
▸ **noun** an electronic version of a printed book that can be read on a personal computer or hand-held device designed specifically for this purpose. ▪ a dedicated device for reading electronic versions of printed books.

e-busi•ness /'ē ˌbiznis/
▸ **noun** another term for E-COMMERCE.

ec•o•con•sum•er /'ekōkən,so͞omər; 'ēkō-/
▸ **noun** a consumer who makes purchasing decisions partly or largely on the basis of ecological issues: *a large number of sophisticated ecoconsumers are descending upon some destinations that are not capable of delivering the expected services.*

ec•o•lodge /'ekō,läj; 'ēkō-/
▸ **noun** a type of tourist accommodation designed to have the minimum possible impact on the natural environment in which it is situated.

e-com•merce /'ē ˌkämərs/
▸ **noun** commercial transactions conducted electronically on the Internet.

e•con•o•box /i'känə,bäks/
▸ **noun** informal a car that is small and economical rather than luxurious or stylish.

ec•o•nom•ic mi•grant /'ekə,nämik 'mīgrənt; 'ēkə-/
▸ **noun** a person who travels from one country or area to another in order to improve their standard of living.

e•con•o•my-class syn•drome /i'känəmē ˌklæs ˌsindrōm/
▸ **noun** deep-vein thrombosis said to be caused by periods of prolonged immobility on long-haul flights.

ec•o•phys•i•ol•o•gy /ˌekōˌfizēˈäləjē; ˌēkō-/
▸ **noun** Biology the study of the interrelationship between the normal physical function of an organism and its environment.

ec•o-war•ri•or /ˈekō ˌwôrēər; ˈēkō-/
▸ **noun** a person actively involved in preventing damage to the environment.

ed•a•ma•me /ˌedəˈmämā/
▸ **noun** a Japanese dish of salted green soybeans boiled in their pods, typically served as a snack or appetizer.
-ORIGIN Japanese, literally 'beans on a branch.'

EEA
▸ **abbreviation** European Economic Area, a free-trade zone created in 1994, composed of the states of the European Union together with Iceland, Norway, and Liechtenstein.

EEO
▸ **abbreviation** equal employment opportunity.

Ee•yor•ish /ˈēyôrisн/ (also **Ee•yore•ish**)
▸ **adjective** pessimistic or gloomy: *they were an Eeyorish bunch, always looking on the dark side of life.*
-ORIGIN 1990s: from *Eeyore,* the name of a donkey in A. A. Milne's *Winnie-the-Pooh* (1926), characterized by his gloomy outlook on life.

ef•face /iˈfās/
▸ **verb** [trans.] cause (a memory or emotion) to disappear completely: *whole sections of the memory of the world have been effaced.*

ef•fer•ent /ˈefərənt/ Physiology
▸ **adjective** conducted or conducting outward or away from something.
▸ **noun** an efferent nerve fiber or vessel.

ef•fing /ˈefiNG/
> ▸ **adjective** informal a euphemistic substitute for the word *fucking*.

E-fit /ˈē ˌfit/
> ▸ **noun** an electronic picture of a person's face made from composite photographs of facial features, created by a computer program.
-ORIGIN 1980s: from *e-* 'electronic' and *fit*, on the pattern of *Photofit* (trademark method of creating a composite picture of a crime suspect's face).

EFM
> ▸ **abbreviation** electronic fetal monitor.

EGD
> ▸ **noun** a technology or system that integrates a computer display with a pair of eyeglasses, using a lens or mirror to reflect images into the eyes: *some EGDs are designed to clip right on to your eyeglasses.*
-ORIGIN abbreviation of 'eyeglass display.'

e•gest /ēˈjest/
> ▸ **verb** [trans.] formal (of a cell or organism) excrete (waste matter): *the bacteria were egested by toads into the reservoir.*
-DERIVATIVES **e•ges•tion** noun
-ORIGIN late Middle English (as *egestion*): from Latin *egest-*, from the verb *egerere* 'expel,' from *e-* (variant of *ex-*) 'out' + *gerere* 'bear, carry.'

e•go•surf /ˈēgō,sərf/
> ▸ **verb** [intrans.] informal search the Internet for instances of one's own name or links to one's own Web site.
-DERIVATIVES **e•go•surf•ing** noun

e•gres•sion /ēˈgreSHən/
> ▸ **noun** the action of going out or leaving a place: *the*

egression of root segments was most noticeable in the group of peat pots.

-ORIGIN from the verb *egress* 'go out of' + *-sion* (on the pattern of *regression*), resulting in another form of the noun *egress*.

el•der•care /'eldər₁ker/
▸ **noun** care of the elderly or infirm, provided by residential institutions, by paid daily help in the home, or by family members.

e•lec•tron•i•ca /ilek'tronikə; ēlek-/
▸ **noun 1** a popular style of music deriving from techno and rave and having a more ambient, esoteric, or cerebral quality.
2 electronic devices or technology considered collectively.
-ORIGIN 1990s: from *electronic* + *-a* Greek and Latin plural ending of neuter nouns.

e•lec•tron•ic mu•sic /ilek₁tränik 'myōōzik; ₁ēlek-/
▸ **noun** music created using synthesizers and other electronic instruments.

e•lec•tron•ic or•gan•iz•er /ilek₁tränik 'ôrgə₁nīzər; ēlek-/
▸ **noun** a pocket-sized computer used for storing and retrieving information such as addresses and appointments.

el•e•va•tor talk /'eləvātər ₁tôk/
▸ **noun** brief and superficial talk that is suitable for an elevator ride.
■ an example of this that summarizes an idea: *an elevator talk about the purpose of the conference.*

ELSS
▸ **abbreviation** Aerospace extravehicular life support system.

ELT
▸ abbreviation English language teaching.

em•bry•ec•to•my /ˌembrē'ektəmē/
▸ noun (pl. **em•bry•ec•to•mies**) the surgical removal of an embryo, especially one implanted outside the uterus in an ectopic pregnancy.

em•bry•op•a•thy /ˌembrē'äpəTHē/
▸ noun (pl. **em•bry•op•a•thies**) a developmental defect in an embryo or fetus.

e•merg•ing mar•ket /i'mərjiNG 'märkit/
▸ noun a market, typically in a developing economy, that is expected to become profitable soon: *the portfolio excludes emerging market securities because they tend to be highly volatile.*

e•mo /'ēmō/ (also **e•mo•core** /'ēmō,kôr/)
▸ noun a style of rock music resembling punk but having lyrics that deal with more emotional subjects.
–ORIGIN 1990s: short for *emotional hardcore.*

em•ploy•ment /em'ploimənt/
▸ noun the utilization of something: *economies can be achieved by the full employment of existing facilities.*

en•a•bled /en'ābəld/
▸ adjective [in combination] adapted for use with the specified application or system: *WAP-enabled cell phones | Java-enabled browsers.*

en•act /en'ækt/
▸ verb [trans.] (**be enacted**) take place: *walkers stopped to watch, aware that some tragedy was being enacted.*

en•clave /'enklāv; 'äNGklāv/
▸ noun a secured area within another secured area: *the*

cost of a security service is going to be proportional to the size of the enclave that you must secure.

end•i•an /'endēən/
▸ **adjective** Computing denoting or relating to a system of ordering data in a computer's memory whereby the most significant (**big endian**) or least significant (**little endian**) byte is put first.
-ORIGIN 1980s: a reference to Swift's *Gulliver's Travels*, in which the Lilliputians were divided into two camps, those who ate their eggs by opening the 'big' end and those who ate them by opening the 'little' end.

en•dow /en'dow/
▸ **verb** [trans.] informal (**be endowed**) have breasts or a penis of specified size: *the girl on page three is well endowed.*

end use /'end ˌyo͞os/
▸ **noun** the application or function for which something is designed or for which it is ultimately used.

en•gulf /en'gəlf/
▸ **verb** [trans.] powerfully affect (someone); overwhelm: *it was a feeling of anguish so great that it threatened to engulf him.*

en•ne•a•gram /'enēəˌgræm/
▸ **noun** a nine-sided figure used in a particular system of analysis to represent the spectrum of possible personality types.
-ORIGIN from Greek *ennea* 'nine' + *-gram* 'something written or recorded.'

e•no•ki /i'nōkē/ (also **e•no•ki mush•room** /i'nōkē 'məsH ˌro͞om; -ˌro͞om/)
▸ **noun** an edible Japanese mushroom (*Flammulina velutipes*, family Agaricaceae), growing in clusters, with slender stems and small caps.

-ORIGIN 1980s: from Japanese *enoki-take*, from *enoki* 'nettle-tree' + *take* 'mushroom.'

en•queue /en'kyú/
▸ verb [trans.] (**en•queued, en•queuing** or **en•queue•ing**) Computing add (an item of data) to a queue.

en•ti•tle•ment pro•gram /en'tītlmənt ˌprōgræm; prōgrəm/
▸ noun a government program that guarantees certain benefits to a particular group or segment of the population. *at risk are Social Security and other entitlement programs.*

en•vi•ro /en'vīrō/
▸ noun (pl. **en•vi•ros**) informal an environmentalist.
▸ adjective environmental.

en•vi•ron•men•tal au•dit /en'vīr(ə)n'mentl 'ôdit/
▸ noun an assessment of the extent to which an organization is observing practices that seek to minimize harm to the environment.

EQ
▸ abbreviation equalizer, specifically a graphic equalizer (often as **graphic EQ**).

e•qual time /'ēkwəl 'tīm/
▸ noun (in broadcasting) a principle of allowing equal air time to opposing points of view, especially to political candidates for two or more parties.

e•ro•to•ma•nia /iˌrätə'mānēə; iˌrō-/
▸ noun excessive sexual desire.
■ Psychiatry a delusion in which a person (typically a woman) believes that another person (typically of higher social status) is in love with them.

ESV
> ▸ **abbreviation** earth satellite vehicle.

e-tail•er /'ē ˌtālər/
> ▸ **noun** a retailer selling goods via electronic transactions on the Internet.
> –ORIGIN 1990s: blend of *e-* 'electronic' and *retailer*.

ETV
> ▸ **abbreviation** educational television.

eup•loid /'yo͞oploid/
> ▸ **adjective** Genetics having an equal number of all the chromosomes of the haploid set.
> –DERIVATIVES **eup•loid•y** /'yo͞oploidē/ **noun**
> –ORIGIN early 20th cent.: from *eu-* 'good, normal' + *-oid*, as in *diploid, haploid*.

eu•ro•creep (also **Eu•ro•creep**) /'yo͞orō,krēp/
> ▸ **noun** informal the gradual acceptance of the euro in European Union countries that have not yet officially adopted it as their national currency.

Eu•ro•land /'yo͞orō,lænd/ (also **eu•ro•land**)
> ▸ **noun** the economic region formed by those member countries of the European Union that have adopted the euro.

Eur•o•zone /'yo͞orə,zōn/ (also **eur•o•zone**)
> ▸ **noun** another term for EUROLAND.

Eve hy•poth•e•sis /'ēv hī,päTHəsis/ (also **Af•ri•can Eve hy•poth•e•sis**)
> ▸ **noun** the hypothesis (based on study of mitochondrial DNA) that modern humans have a common female ancestor who lived in Africa around 200,000 years ago.

e•vent cre•a•tion /i'vent krē,āsHən/
‣ **noun** the activity of planning, organizing, and staging public events: *select "Forms" if you want the ability to notify certain users at the time of event creation.*

ev•i•dence-based /'evədəns ,bāst/
‣ **adjective** Medicine denoting disciplines of health care that proceed empirically with regard to the patient and reject more traditional protocols: *evidence-based nursing.*

ev•o•lute /'evə,lo͞ot/
‣ **adjective** Zoology & Botany rolled outward at the edges: *an evolute shell.*

ex•clude /ik'sklo͞od/
‣ **verb** [trans.] Brit. expel (a student) from school.

ex•cus•al /ik'skyo͞ozəl/
‣ **noun** the action or fact of excusing or being excused, typically from an official duty or requirement: *if any members of the jury felt unable to serve that long, they would be considered for excusal.*

ex•cuse /ik'skyo͞os/
‣ **noun** a note written by a doctor or parent excusing a student from school or from a school activity.

ex•o•plan•et /'eksō,plænit/
‣ **noun** a planet that orbits a star outside the solar system.

ex•pan•sion team /ik'spænsHən ,tēm/
‣ **noun** a new team added to an established professional league.

ex•pen•di•ture /ik'spendiCHər/
‣ **noun** the use of energy, time, or other resources: *work is the expenditure of energy.*

ex•pense /ik'spens/
▸ **verb** [trans.] informal charge (something) to an expense account: *I can expense the refreshments.*

ex•press lane /ik'spres ˌlān/
▸ **noun** (on a highway) a lane for through traffic, having fewer exits than the other lanes.
■ (in a grocery store) a checkout aisle for shoppers buying only a few items.

ex•ten•sion /ik'stensʜən/
▸ **noun** 1 (**extensions**) lengths of artificial hair woven into a person's own hair to create a long hairstyle.
2 Computing an optional suffix to a file name, typically consisting of a period followed by several characters, indicating the file's content or function.
–DERIVATIVES **ex•ten•sion•al adjective**
–ORIGIN late Middle English: from late Latin *extensio(n-)*, from *extendere* 'stretch out.'

ex•te•ri•o•rize /ik'stirēəˌrīz/
▸ **verb** [trans.] make exterior; give exterior form to.
–DERIVATIVES **ex•te•ri•o•ri•za•tion noun**

ex•tern /'eksˌtərn/,
▸ **noun** 1 a nonresident doctor or other worker in a hospital.
2 (in a strictly enclosed order of nuns) a sister who does not live exclusively within the enclosure and goes on outside errands.
▸ **verb** [trans.] SE Asian banish (someone considered politically undesirable) from a region or district: *he was externed for inciting communal tension in Mumbai.*
–DERIVATIVES **ex•tern•ment noun**
–ORIGIN mid 16th cent. (as an adjective in the sense 'external'): from French *externe* or Latin *externus*, from *exter* 'outer.' The word was used by Shakespeare to

mean 'outward appearance'; current noun senses date from the early 17th cent.

ex•tra•net /'ekstrə,net/
▸ **noun** an intranet that can be partially accessed by authorized outside users, enabling businesses to exchange information over the Internet in a secure way.
-ORIGIN 1990s: from *extra-* 'outside' + *net*, by analogy with *intranet*.

ex•tra•so•lar /,ekstrə'sōlər/
▸ **adjective** outside the solar system: *extrasolar planets*.

ex•treme /ik'strēm/
▸ **adjective** designating a sport or variety of sport requiring unusual stamina, daring, or strength: *extreme skiing*.

Ex•tro•py /'ekstrəpē/ (also **ex•tro•py**)
▸ **noun** the pseudoscientific principle that life will expand indefinitely and in an orderly, progressive way throughout the entire universe by the means of human intelligence and technology.
-DERIVATIVES **Ex•tro•pi•an** /ek'strōpēən/ **adjective & noun**
-ORIGIN 1980s: from *ex-* 'out' + a shortened form of *entropy*.

eye•ball /'ī,bôl/ informal
▸ **verb** [trans.] look or stare at closely: *we eyeballed one another*.
▸ **plural noun** (**eyeballs**) readers or consumers, especially of online content: *the big portal sites are fighting for eyeballs*.
-PHRASES **give someone the hairy eyeball** informal stare at someone in a disapproving or angry way, especially with partially lowered eyelids. **up to the** (or **one's**) **eyeballs** informal used to emphasize the extreme degree of an undesirable situation: *he's up to his eyeballs in debt*.

F

fab
   ▸ **noun** Electronics a microchip fabrication plant.
   ■ a particular fabrication process in such a plant.
   -ORIGIN late 20th cent.: abbreviation of *fabrication*.

fab•less /ˈfæblis/
   ▸ **adjective** denoting or relating to a company that designs microchips but contracts out their production rather than owning its own factory.
   -ORIGIN 1980s: from *fab* 'a microchip fabrication plant' + *-less*.

face•print /ˈfās,print/
   ▸ **noun** a digital scan or photograph of a human face, used for identifying individuals from the unique characteristics of facial structure: *hidden cameras and faceprints are used to single out individuals in a crowd.*
   -ORIGIN on the pattern of *fingerprint*.

face•print•ing /ˈfās,printiNG/
   ▸ **noun** the process of creating a digital faceprint and using software to compare it with a database of photographs, especially to identify known criminals: *the suspect's faceprint was matched up with a photo on file at the police precinct.*
   -ORIGIN on the pattern of *fingerprinting*.

fa•cial pro•fil•ing /ˈfāsHəl ˈprōfiliNG/
   ▸ **noun** the recording and analysis of a person's facial characteristics, especially to assist in identifying an individual: *the police have set up a system of facial profiling at major sporting events.*

fa•ience /fī'äns; fā-/
▸ **noun** Architecture molded glazed or unglazed terracotta blocks used structurally or as cladding.
-ORIGIN late 17th cent. (originally denoting pottery made at Faenza, Italy): from French *faïence*, from *Faïence*, the French name for *Faenza*.

fail•o•ver /'fāl,ōvər/
▸ **noun** Computing a method of protecting computer systems from failure, in which standby equipment automatically takes over when the main system fails.

fail•te /'foiltə/ Scottish & Irish
▸ **exclamation** welcome.
▸**noun** an act or instance of welcoming someone.
-ORIGIN Gaelic.

fair•ness doc•trine /'fernis ,däktrin/
▸ **noun** a former federal policy requiring television and radio broadcasters that presented one side of a controversy to provide the opportunity for opposing points of view to be expressed at no charge.

fair-trade a•gree•ment /'fer 'trād ə,grēmənt/
▸ **noun** an agreement, typically illegal, between a manufacturer of a trademarked item in the US and its retail distributors to sell the item at a price at or above that designated by the manufacturer.

fair use /'fer 'yōōs/
▸ **noun** (in US copyright law) the doctrine that copyright material may be quoted verbatim without need for permission from or payment to the copyright holder, provided that attribution is clearly given and that the material quoted is reasonably brief in extent.

faith-based /'fāTH,bāst/
▸ **adjective** affiliated with, connected with, or based on religion or a religious group: *should faith-based charities get government funding?*

fake bake /'fāk 'bāk/ (also **fake-bake**) informal
▸ **noun** the process of getting a sunless tan, as under sunlamps or by applying a sunless-tanning lotion: *a salon in my neighborhood is advertising reasonable prices for fake bakes.*
▸ **verb** [intrans.] to get a sunless tan: *in the winter months, she likes to fake-bake about once a week.*

fal•la•cious /fə'lāSHəs/
▸ **adjective** based on a mistaken belief: *fallacious arguments.*
-DERIVATIVES **fal•la•cious•ly** adverb; **fal•la•cious•ness** noun
-ORIGIN early 16th cent.: from Old French *fallacieux*, from Latin *fallaciosus*, from *fallacia* 'deception,' from *fallac-*, *fallax* 'deceiving.'

Fa•lun Gong /'fälo͞on 'go͞oNG; 'gäNG/ (also **Fa•lun Da•fa** /'fälo͞on 'däfä/)
▸ **noun** a spiritual exercise and meditation regime with similarities to t'ai chi ch'uan, practiced predominantly in China.
▪ a Taoist-Buddhist sect practicing Falun Gong.
-ORIGIN 1990s: Chinese, literally 'wheel of law.'

fam•i•ly hour /'fæm(ə)lē ,ow(ə)r/
▸ **noun** a period in the evening during which many children and their families watch television, especially 8 to 9 p.m.: *they protested against the increase in sexual content in shows aired in the family hour.*

far gone /'fär 'gôn/
▸ **adjective** informal very intoxicated or ill.

far•i•na•ceous /ˌfærə'nāSHəs/
▸ **adjective** consisting of or containing starch.
-ORIGIN mid 17th cent.: from late Latin *farinaceus*, from Latin *far* 'grain.'

farm•ers' mar•ket /'färmərz 'märkit/
▸ **noun** a market where local farmers and growers sell their produce directly to the public.

fas•ci•a /'fæsH(ē)ə; 'fā-/ (also **fa•ci•a**)
▸ **noun** a covering, typically a detachable one, for the front part of a cellular phone.

fash•ion•is•ta /ˌfæsHə'nēstə/
▸ **noun** informal **1** a designer of haute couture.
2 a devoted follower of fashion.
-ORIGIN 1990s: from *fashion* + Spanish suffix *-ista*, as in *Sandinista, turista.*

fa•toush /fæ'tōōsH/
▸ **noun** a Middle Eastern salad consisting of tomatoes, cucumber, and other vegetables together with croutons made from toasted pita bread.
-ORIGIN Arabic.

fauj•dar /'fôjdär/ (also **fau•ji•dar** /'fôji,där/)
▸ **noun** Indian a police officer.
-ORIGIN late 17th cent. (in the sense 'Mogul state official in charge of the police'): from Persian *fawjdār* 'military commander,' from Arabic *fawj* 'troop' + Persian -*dār* 'holding, holder.'

par•ty fa•vor /'pärtē ˌfāvər/
▸ **noun** a small inexpensive gift given to guests at a party.

feath•er /'feᴛʜər/
 ▸ **verb** [trans.] blend or smooth delicately: *feather the paint in, in a series of light strokes.*

feck /fek/
 ▸ **verb** Irish vulgar slang used as a euphemism for 'fuck.'
 –ᴅᴇʀɪᴠᴀᴛɪᴠᴇꜱ **feck•ing adjective & adverb**

fe•da•yeen /ˌfedä'yēn/ (also **fi•da•yeen** /ˌfidä'yēn/)
 ▸ **plural noun** Arab guerrillas operating especially against Israel.
 –ᴏʀɪɢɪɴ 1950s: from colloquial Arabic *fidā'iyīn*, plural of classical Arabic *fidā'ī* 'one who gives his life for another or for a cause,' from *fadā* 'to ransom someone.' The singular *fedai* (from Arabic and Persian *fidā'ī*) had previously been used (late 19th cent.) to denote an Ismaili Muslim assassin.

Fed•er•al O•pen Mar•ket Com•mit•tee /'fed(ə)rəl 'ōpən 'märkịt kə,mitē/
 ▸ **noun** a committee of the Federal Reserve Board that meets regularly to set monetary policy, including the interest rates that are charged to banks.

Fed•er•al Reg•is•ter /'fed(ə)rəl 'rejəstər/
 ▸ **noun** a daily publication of the US government that issues proposed and final administrative regulations of federal agencies.

fee•bate /'fē,bāt/
 ▸ **noun** a system of charges and rebates whereby energy-efficient or environmentally friendly practices are rewarded while failure to adhere to such practices is penalized.
 –ᴏʀɪɢɪɴ 1990s: blend of *fee* and *rebate.*

feed /fēd/
> ▸ **verb** (past and past participle **fed**) [trans.] informal satisfy (a drug habit): *users who commit crime to feed their habit.*
▸**noun** a broadcast distributed by a satellite or network from a central source to a large number of radio or television stations: *a satellite feed from Washington.*

feel-good fac•tor /ˈfēlˌgo͝od ˌfæktər/
> ▸ **noun** Brit. a widespread feeling of well-being and financial security, viewed as a factor in increased consumer spending.

feet first /ˈfēt ˈfərst/
> ▸ **adverb phrase** in a dead condition, as in a coffin: *they hoped to be carried feet first out of the house they lived in for twenty-five years.*

feh /fe/
> ▸ **exclamation** conveying disapproval, displeasure, or disgust: *The greatest writer in the English language? Feh!*
–ORIGIN Yiddish.

feis /fesH/
> ▸**noun** (pl. **feis•ean•na** /ˈfesHənə/) an Irish or Scottish festival of music and dancing.
–ORIGIN Irish *feis, fess* 'meeting, assembly.'

fen•flu•ra•mine /fenˈflo͝orəˌmēn/
> ▸ **noun** Medicine a prescription drug once prescribed for obesity, withdrawn from the US market in 1997 because of safety concerns. Also called FEN-PHEN.

fen-phen /ˈfen ˌfen/
> ▸ **noun** a shortened form of FENFLURAMINE.

Fer•mi-Di•rac sta•tis•tics /ˈfərmē dəˈræk stəˌtistiks/ **plural noun** [treated as sing.] Physics a type of quantum statistics used to describe systems of fermions.

-ORIGIN 1920s: named after Italian-born US atomic physicist Enrico *Fermi* (1901–54) and English theoretical physicist Paul A. M. *Dirac* (1902–84).

fi•bro•my•al•gia /ˌfībrōmīˈaljə/
▸ **noun** a chronic disorder characterized by widespread musculoskeletal pain, fatigue, and tenderness in localized areas.

fi•da•yeen /ˌfidäˈyēn/
▸ **plural noun** variant of FEDAYEEN.

fig•ure-hug•ging /ˈfigyər ˌhəgiNG/
▸ **adjective** (of a garment) fitting closely to the contours of a woman's body: *a low-cut, figure-hugging dress.*

fil•ter /ˈfiltər/
▸ **noun** Computing a piece of software that processes text, for example to remove unwanted spaces or to format it for use in another application.
▸ **verb** [trans.] Computing process or treat with a filter.
2 (of light or sound) enter a place slowly or in small quantities: *sunlight filtered in through the thin curtains.*

fi•nan•cial /fəˈnænCHəl/
▸ **adjective** W. Indian & Austral./NZ (of a member of a club or society) paid-up.
▸ **plural noun** (**financials**) shares in financial companies.
■ financial data about a company: *take a look at their financials.*

fin•ger•pick /ˈfiNGgər,pik/
▸ **verb** play (a tune) on a guitar or banjo by using the fingernails or small plectrums on the fingertips to pluck the strings.

fin•ish /ˈfiniSH/
▸ **verb** [trans.] reduce to utter exhaustion or helplessness.

fin•ish•er /ˈfinisHər/
> ▸ noun Brit. (in soccer) a player who scores a goal: *he is one of the best finishers at the club.*

first-line /ˈfərst ˌlīn/
> ▸ adjective of first resort: *first-line drugs for HIV exposure.*

First Na•tion /ˈfərst ˈnāsHən/
> ▸ noun (in Canada) an indigenous American Indian community officially recognized as an administrative unit by the federal government or functioning as such without official status.

fist /fist/
> ▸ verb [trans.] clench (the hand or fingers) into a fist: *she fisted her hands on her hips.*

fit /fit/
> ▸ verb (**fit•ted** or **fit, fit•ting**) [intrans.] have an epileptic fit: *he started fitting uncontrollably.*

Fitz•roy /ˈfitsˌroi/ a shipping forecast area covering part of the Atlantic off of northwestern Spain, west of the Bay of Biscay. Formerly (until 2002) called *Finisterre.*

flang•er /ˈflænjər/
> ▸ noun an electronic device that alters a sound signal, used especially in popular music.

flan•nel pan•el /ˈflænl ˌpænl/
> ▸ noun informal a section in a magazine, newspaper, or other publication that lists the contributors or advertises the contents.

fla•vi•vi•rus /ˈflāvəˌvīrəs/
> ▸ noun a virus whose genome consists of positive RNA, that is capable of reproducing in its arthropod vector, and that causes a number of serious human diseases in-

cluding yellow fever, dengue, Japanese encephalitis, and West Nile encephalitis.
• family *Flaviviridae,* three genera.

fla•vor en•hanc•er /ˈflāvər enˌhænsər/
▸ noun a chemical additive, e.g., monosodium glutamate, used to intensify the flavor of food.

flex•ec•u•tive /flekˈsekyətiv/
▸ noun an executive or high-level employee who has flexible hours and can choose to work in any location: *flexecutives often work at home and come into the office only for important meetings.*
–ORIGIN blend of *flexible* and *executive.*

flex•wing /ˈfleksˌwiNG/
▸ noun a collapsible fabric delta wing, as used in hang gliders.

flight sim•u•la•tor /ˈflīt ˌsimyəlātər/
▸ noun a machine designed to resemble the cockpit of an aircraft, with computer-generated images that mimic the pilot's view and mechanisms that move the entire structure in imitation of an aircraft's motion, used for training pilots.

flip /flip/
▸ verb (flipped, flip•ping) [trans.] 1 buy and sell (a property) quickly and profitably using fraudulent evaluation of its worth: *within one week of starting I flipped a property for a quick $3,000 profit.*
2 access the nonpublic parts of (a Web site): *if you want to learn who the main IT contact at a company is, just flip their Web site.*

float /flōt/
▸ noun a light object held for support by a person learning to swim.

flood•wa•ter /ˈfləd͵wôt̬ər, -͵wä-/ (also **flood•wa•ters**)
  ▸ **noun** water left by flooding.

floor /flôr/
  ▸ **noun** the bottom surface of a vehicle: *she retrieved the groceries from the floor of the car.*

FOAF
  ▸ **abbreviation** friend of a friend, a story or rumor that has no definite source and cannot be authenticated: *investigations never do succeed in finding the FOAF who started any of these yarns.*

foam par•ty /ˈfōm ͵pärtē/
  ▸ **noun** a party, especially in a nightclub, at which guests dance and play in foam or soap suds: *she ruined her new shoes at a foam party.*

food bank /ˈfo͞od ͵bæNGk/
  ▸ **noun** a place supplying food to poor or destitute people.

foo fight•er /ˈfo͞o ͵fītər/
  ▸ **noun** an unidentified flying object of a kind reported by US pilots during World War II, usually described as a bright light or ball of fire.
  -ORIGIN 1940s: from 'Where there's foo there's fire,' a nonsense catchphrase from the US *Smoky Stover* cartoon strip.

foost•er /ˈfo͞ostər/
  ▸ **verb** [intrans.] Irish busy oneself in a restless or agitated way: *he was foostering around in his room.*
  -ORIGIN late 19th cent.: from Irish *fústar* 'bustle, fussy behavior.'

foot•ed /ˈfo͞otid/
  ▸ **adjective 1** having a foot or feet: *a footed bowl.*
  2 [in combination] having a foot or feet of a specified type or number: *a quick-footed running back.*

foot•fall /ˈfo͝otˌfôl/
▸ **noun** the number of people entering a store or shopping area in a given time.

foot-tap•ping /ˈfo͝ot ˌtæpiNG/
▸ **adjective** having or creating a strong rhythmical musical beat: *foot-tapping gospel hymns.*

foot•y /ˈfo͝otē/ (also **foot•ie** or **foot•er**)
▸ **noun** Austral./NZ informal term for *rugby.*

fore•part /ˈfôrˌpärt/
▸ **noun** the part situated at the front of something; the foremost part: *the forepart of the brain.*

for•ma•tion /fôrˈmāsHən/
▸ **noun** a thing that has been formed: *strange black rock formations.*

for•ward con•tract /ˈfôrwərd ˌkäntrækt/
▸ **noun** Finance an informal agreement traded through a broker-dealer network to buy and sell specified assets, typically currency, at a specified price at a certain future date. Compare with FUTURES CONTRACT.

foun•da•tion gar•ment /fownˈdāsHən ˌgärmənt/
▸ **noun** a woman's supportive undergarment, such as a girdle or corset.

four-by-four /ˈfôr bī ˌfôr; -bə-/ (also **4X4**)
▸ **noun** a vehicle with four-wheel drive.

frag•ile X syn•drome /ˈfrajəl ˈeks ˌsinˌdrōm, ˈfrajīl/
▸ **noun** a genetic condition mainly affecting males in which a mutation of a gene on the X chromosome typically causes learning disabilities, decreased attention span, and hyperactivity.

frag•ment re•ten•tion film /ˈfrægmənt riˌtenCHən ˌfilm/
‣ **noun** a polymer-based transparent film on a pane of glass that prevents fragments scattering in the event of breakage.

frame /frām/
‣ **noun** Computing a graphic panel in a display window, especially in an Internet browser, that encloses a self-contained section of data and permits multiple independent document viewing.

Frank•en•food /ˈfræNGkənˌfo͞od/
‣ **noun** informal, derogatory genetically modified food.
-ORIGIN 1990s: from *Franken(stein)* + *food*.

free fall /ˈfrē ˌfôl/
‣ **noun** a rapid decline that cannot be stopped: *her career seemed about to go into free fall*.

free-to-air /ˈfrē to͞o ˈer/
‣ **adjective** denoting or relating to television programs broadcast on standard public or commercial networks, as opposed to satellite, cable, or digital programs available only to fee-paying viewers.

French-cut /ˈfrenCH ˈkət/
‣ **adjective 1** Cooking sliced obliquely: *French-cut green beans.*
2 (of women's panties) cut so as to reveal much of the upper thigh.

friend of Dorothy /ˈfrend əv ˈdôrəˌTHē/
‣ **noun** informal a homosexual man.
-ORIGIN from the name of *Dorothy*, a character played by the actress Judy Garland (a gay icon) in the movie *The Wizard of Oz* (1939).

front bot•tom /'frənt 'bätəm/
▸ **noun** Brit. informal used euphemistically to refer to the female genitals, especially in contexts involving children.

fro-yo /'frō ˌyō/
▸ **noun** informal frozen yogurt.

fro•zen smoke /'frōzən 'smōk/
▸ **noun** another term for aerogel (a very low-density substance resulting when moisture is removed from a gel).

fruit ac•id /'frōōt ˌæsid/
▸ **noun** another term for alpha-hydroxy acid (an organic acid derived from fruit and milk sugars).

FTA
▸ **abbreviation** Free Trade Agreement, used to refer to that signed in 1988 between the US and Canada.

Fu•ji•ta scale /fōō'jētə ˌskāl, 'fōōjētä/ (also **F-scale**)
▸ **noun** a standard scale that rates the intensity of a tornado based on the amount and type of damage it causes: *the Fujita scale rating depends on a somewhat subjective assessment of property damage.*
-ORIGIN named for Japanese-born US meteorologist Tetsuya (Ted) *Fujita* (1920–98).

full-fig•ured /'fŏŏl 'figyərd/
▸ **adjective** (of women's clothing) designed for larger women.

func•tion•al med•i•cine /'fəNGkSHənl 'medisən/
▸ **noun** medical practice or treatments that focus on optimal functioning of the body and its organs, usually involving systems of holistic or alternative medicine: *you don't have to have a disease to benefit from functional medicine.*

fun•nel cake /ˈfənl ˌkāk/
▸ **noun** a cake made of batter that is poured through a funnel into hot fat or oil, deep-fried until crisp, and served sprinkled with powdered sugar.

fur•nish•ing /ˈfərniSHiNG/
▸ **adjective** denoting fabrics used for curtains, upholstery, or floor coverings: *they create historic furnishing textiles for the finest museums.*

fu•sion /ˈfyo͞ozHən/
▸ **adjective** referring to food or cooking that incorporates elements of both Eastern and Western cuisine: *their fusion fare includes a sushi-like roll of gingery rice and eel wrapped in marinated Greek grape leaves.*

fu•tures con•tract /ˈfyo͞ocHərz ˌkänträkt/
▸ **noun** Finance an agreement traded on an organized exchange to buy or sell assets, especially commodities or shares, at a fixed price but to be delivered and paid for later. Compare with FORWARD CONTRACT.

G

ga•blet /ˈgāblit/
▸ **noun** Architecture a small ornamental gable over a buttress or similar feature.
-ORIGIN late Middle English: from *gable* 'the part of a wall that encloses the end of a pitched roof' + *-et*, diminutive suffix.

gain•shar•ing /ˈgān‚SHeriNG/
▸ **noun** an incentive plan in which employees or customers receive benefits directly as a result of cost-saving measures that they initiate or participate in.

ga•lac•tos•a•mine /gəlakˈtäsə‚mēn; -min; -ˈtōsə-/
▸ **noun** Biochemistry an amino acid, $C_6H_{13}NO_5$, derived from the sugar galactose.
-ORIGIN early 20th cent.: from *galactose* + *amine*.

game face /ˈgām ‚fās/
▸ **noun** a sports player's neutral or serious facial expression, displaying determination and concentration.

gang-bang /ˈgæNG ‚bæNG/
▸ **verb** [trans.] informal **1** (of a group of people) rape (someone).
2 [as noun] (**gang-banging**) the violent activities of a criminal gang.

gang•sta rap /ˈgæNGstə ‚ræp/
▸ **noun** rap music with lyrics about gangs, crime, and violence.
-ORIGIN 1980s: alteration of *gangster*.

gan•sey /ˈgänzē/
▸ **noun** Brit. & W. Indian a sweater or T-shirt.
–ORIGIN late 19th cent.: representing a pronunciation of *Guernsey*.

ganz•feld /ˈgänz‚feld; ˈgæns-/ (also **Ganz•feld**)
▸ **noun** a technique of controlled sensory input used in parapsychology with the aim of improving results in tests of telepathy and other paranormal phenomena.
–ORIGIN late 20th cent.: from German, literally 'whole field.'

GAPA
▸ **abbreviation** ground-to-air pilotless aircraft.

gap year /ˈgæp ‚yir/
▸ **noun** chiefly Brit. a period, typically an academic year, taken by a student as a break between high school and college.

gas•sy /ˈgæsē/
▸ **adjective** (**gas•si•er, gas•si•est**) (of a person) flatulent.

gas•tor•nis /gæˈstôrnis/
▸ **noun** a huge flightless bird (*Gastornis geiselensis*) of the Eocene epoch.
–ORIGIN modern Latin, from the name of the French scientist Gaston *Planté* (1834–89), who found the first specimen, + Greek *ornis* 'bird.'

gas•tro•porn /ˈgæstrə‚pôrn/ (also **gas•tro•por•nog•ra•phy** /‚gæstrōpôrˈnägrəfē/)
▸ **noun** videos, photographs, or descriptions of food that are intended to be sexually suggestive: *the menu was full of the flowery adjectives that characterize gastroporn.*
–ORIGIN blend of *gastronomy* and *pornography*.

gas•tro•pub /ˈɡæstrəˌpəb/
▸ **noun** Brit. a pub that specializes in serving high-quality food.
–ORIGIN 1990s: blend of *gastronomy* and *pub*.

gate•way drug /ˈɡātwā ˌdrəɡ/
▸ **noun** a drug that supposedly leads the user on to more addictive or dangerous drugs.

ga•tor /ˈɡātər/
▸ **verb** [usually **be gatored**] Computing cause a competitor's advertisement to appear on (a commercial Web site).
■ cause (a Web-site visitor) to view a competitor's advertisement: *he was gatored with an ad for a competitor while visiting his own company's site.*
–ORIGIN from *Gator,* the name of the software that creates this effect.

gay•dar /ˈɡāˌdär/
▸ **noun** informal the supposed ability of homosexuals to recognize one another by means of very slight indications.
–ORIGIN 1990s: blend of *gay* and *radar.*

geas /ɡesʜ/
▸ **noun** (pl. **geas•a** /ˈɡesʜə/) (in Irish folklore) an obligation or prohibition magically imposed on a person.
–ORIGIN Irish.

gel•cap /ˈjelˌkæp/
▸ **noun** a gelatin capsule containing liquid medication or other substance to be taken orally.

gel pen /ˈjel ˌpen/ (also **gel•ly pen** /ˈjelē ˌpen/ or **gel•ly** (pl. **gel•lies**))
▸ **noun** a type of pen that uses a gel-based ink, combining the permanence of oil-based ballpoint ink and the

smooth glide of water-based ink: *she especially likes scented gel pens in metallic colors.*

gen•der bend•er /'jendər ˌbendər/
▸ **noun** a device for changing an electrical or electronic connector from male to female, or from female to male.

Gen•er•a•tion D /'jenərāsʜən 'dē/
▸ **noun** the generation of people with great interest or expertise in computers and other digital devices: *technology marketers focus on Generation D.*
-ORIGIN from an abbreviation of *digital generation.*

ge•net•i•cal•ly mod•i•fied /jə'netik(ə)lē 'mädə,fīd/
▸ **adjective** (of an organism) containing genetic material that has been artificially altered so as to produce a desired characteristic: *consumers are entitled to know if they're eating genetically modified food.*

ge•net•ic blue•print /jə'netik 'bloo̅,print/
▸ **noun** [not in technical use] a gene or genome map: *a global consortium of scientists plan to sequence the genetic blueprint of the banana within five years.*

ge•net•ic pol•lu•tion /jə'netik pə'loo̅sʜən/
▸ **noun** the spread of altered genes from genetically engineered organisms to other, nonengineered organisms, especially by cross-pollination.

gen•lock /'jen,läk/
▸ **noun** a device for maintaining synchronization between two different video signals, or between a video signal and a computer or·audio signal, enabling video images and computer graphics to be mixed.
▸ **verb** [intrans.] maintain synchronization between two signals using the genlock technique.
-ORIGIN 1960s: from *generator* + the verb *lock.*

ge•no•mics /jē'nōmiks; -'näm-/
▸ **plural noun** [treated as sing.] the branch of molecular biology concerned with the structure, function, evolution, and mapping of genomes.
-ORIGIN 1980s: from *genome* 'the complete set of genes present in an organism' + *-ics*.

gen•o•type /'jenə,tīp; 'jē-/
▸ **verb** [trans.] Biology investigate the genetic constitution of (an individual organism).
-ORIGIN verbal usage of the noun *genotype*.

ge•o•cach•ing /'jēō,kæsHiNG/
▸ **noun** the recreational activity of hunting for and finding a hidden box of objects by means of Global Positioning System (GPS) coordinates posted on a Web site: *hardcore geocaching sometimes involves mountain climbing.*
-ORIGIN blend of *geographical* and *cache* 'hide something in a safe place.'

ge•o•code /'jēə,kōd/
▸ **noun** the characterization of a region or neighborhood based on population statistics such as the average age or income of its inhabitants, used especially for marketing purposes.

ge•o•mat•ics /,jēə'mætiks/
▸ **plural noun** [treated as sing.] the application of computerization to information in geography and related fields.
-DERIVATIVES **ge•o•mat•ic** adjective
-ORIGIN 1980s: blend of *geography* and *informatics* 'the science of processing data for storage and retrieval.'

ge•o•met•ric /,jēə'metrik/
▸ **noun** a geometric pattern: *I don't want a floral for the couch; how about a nice geometric?*

ge•o•spa•tial /ˌjēōˈspāsHəl/
  ▸ adjective Geography relating to or denoting data that is associated with a particular location.

ge•o•ther•mal /ˌjēōˈTHərməl/
  ▸ adjective of, relating to, or produced by the internal heat of the earth: *some 70% of Iceland's energy needs are met from geothermal sources.*
  –DERIVATIVES **ge•o•ther•mal•ly** adverb

get-go /ˈget ˌgō/
  ▸ noun [in sing.] informal the very beginning: *the quintet experienced difficulties **from the get-go**.*

gey /gī/
  ▸ adverb Scottish very; considerably: *he was gey fond of you.*
  –ORIGIN early 18th cent.: variant of *gay.*

GHz
  ▸ abbreviation gigahertz.

gi•nor•mous /jiˈnôrməs; jī-/
  ▸ adjective informal, humorous extremely large; enormous: *ginormous spiders made of balloons that hung from the ceiling.*
  –ORIGIN blend of *gigantic* and *enormous.*

GLA
  ▸ abbreviation gamma linolenic acid.

glam•a•zon /ˈglæməˌzän; -zən/
  ▸ noun informal a glamorous, powerfully assertive woman.
  –ORIGIN 1990s: from *glam* + *Amazon.*

glögg /gləg/ (also **glugg**)
  ▸ noun a type of Scandinavian mulled wine made with brandy, almonds, raisins, and spices.
  –ORIGIN Swedish.

glurge /glərj/
▸ **noun** informal inspirational but overly sentimental stories, poems, etc., that are circulated on the Internet: *I'm usually annoyed by glurge because most of it is so hard to believe.*
▸ **verb** [trans.] [usually **be glurged**] send glurge to (someone): *when I've been glurged I sometimes forward the e-mail to friends.*
-ORIGIN origin uncertain.

glu•te•al /'glo͞ote͞el/
▸ **noun** (usually **gluteals**) a gluteus muscle in the buttocks.

GM
▸ **abbreviation** genetically modified.

goal•hang•er /'gōl,hæNGər/
▸ **noun** Soccer derogatory a player who spends much of the game near the opposing team's goal in the hope of scoring easy goals.

go com•man•do /gō kə'mændō/
▸ **verb phrase** informal wear no underpants.

God•zil•la /gäd'zilə/
▸ **noun** informal a particularly enormous example (of something): *a Godzilla of a condominium tower.*
-ORIGIN from the name of a huge prehistoric monster featured in a series of Japanese films from 1955.

gold•en hour /'gōldən ,ow(ə)r/
▸ **noun** [in sing.] Medicine the first hour after a traumatic injury, when emergency treatment is most likely to be successful.

gold•en rai•sin /'gōldən 'rāzən/
▸ **noun** a small, light brown, seedless raisin used in foods such as cookies and cakes, or eaten as a snack.

gold•en rice /ˈgōldən ˈrīs/
  ▸ **noun** a genetically modified variety of rice containing large amounts of the orange or red plant pigment beta-carotene, a substance important in the human diet as a precursor of vitamin A.

Go•li•ath /gəˈlīəTH/ (also **go•li•ath**) **noun** a person or thing of enormous size or strength: *the two unassuming hippies took on a corporate Goliath.*
  -ORIGIN in allusion to the biblical *Goliath*, a Philistine giant slain by David.

go•mer /ˈgōmər/
  ▸ **noun 1** military slang an inept or stupid colleague, especially a trainee.
  2 informal (used by doctors) a troublesome patient, especially an elderly one.
  -ORIGIN 1960s: origin uncertain; sense 1 perhaps from the television character *Gomer* Pyle, a bungling Marine Corps enlistee; sense 2 perhaps an acronym from *get out of my emergency room.*

goo•ber /ˈgo͞obər/
  ▸ **noun** informal often offensive a person from the southeastern US, especially Georgia or Arkansas.
  ■ derogatory an unsophisticated person.
  -ORIGIN late 19th cent.: from an earlier sense 'peanut,' from Kikongo *nguba.*

good oil /ˈgo͝od ˈoil/
  ▸ Austral./NZ informal reliable information.
  -ORIGIN figurative use referring to lubricating oil and the successful running of a machine.

goof•us /ˈgo͞ofəs/
  ▸ **noun** informal a foolish or stupid person (often used as a term of abuse).
  -ORIGIN 1920s: based on *goof.*

goo•gle /'go͞ogəl/
‣ **verb** [intrans.] informal use an Internet search engine, particularly google.com: *she spent the afternoon googling aimlessly.* ■ [trans.] search for the name of (someone) on the Internet to find out information about them.
–ORIGIN from *Google*, the proprietary name of a popular Internet search engine.

go•pu•ra /'gōpərə/ (also **go•pu•ram** /'gōpərəm/)
‣ **noun** (in southern India) a large pyramidal tower over the entrance gate to a temple precinct.
–ORIGIN mid 19th cent.: Sanskrit *gōpura* 'city gate,' from *gō* 'eye' and *pura* 'city.'

go•ra /'gôrə/
‣ **noun** (pl. **go•ras** or **go•ray** /'gôrā/) (fem. **go•ri** /'gôrē/) (in India, and among British Asians) a white person.
–ORIGIN originally a term in the Jewish community in India for people who refrained from marrying Indians.

gosht /gōsʜt/
‣ **noun** Indian red meat (beef, lamb, or mutton): [as adj.] *gosht biryani.*
–ORIGIN from Hindi *gośt.*

go south /'gō 'sowʜ/
‣ **verb phrase** (**goes south, go•ing south;** past **went south** /'went 'sowʜ/ past part **gone south** /'gôn 'sowʜ/) informal fall in value, deteriorate, or fail: *my stock portfolio hasn't exactly gone south, but it's seen better days* | *don't drink that milk—it went south a few days ago.*

go-team /'gō ˌtēm/
‣ **noun** a group of investigators who can be dispatched immediately to investigate accidents, attacks, and the like: *a go-team from the National Transportation Safety Board is en route to the scene.*

go-to guy /ˈgō ˈtoͦ ˌgī/
▸ **noun** informal a person who can be relied upon for help or support.
■ Sports a member of a sports team who can be relied on to score points if given the opportunity.

gov•ern•ess•y /ˈgəvərnisē/
▸ **adjective** having or showing characteristics considered to be characteristic of a governess, especially primness or strictness: *her governessy tone.*

GPRS
▸ **abbreviation** general packet radio services, a technology for radio transmission of small packets of data, especially between cellular phones and the Internet.

grab /græb/
▸ **noun 1** [usually with modifier] Computing a frame of video or television footage, digitized and stored as a still image in a computer memory for subsequent display, printing, or editing: *a screen grab from Wednesday's program.*
2 a mechanical device for clutching, lifting, and moving things, especially materials in bulk.
■ [as adj.] denoting a bar or strap for people to hold on to for support or in a moving vehicle: *a grab rail.*
–DERIVATIVES **grab•ber noun**

grand•kid /ˈgrænd,kid/
▸ **noun** informal a grandchild.

gran•u•lar /ˈgrænyələr/
▸ **adjective** technical characterized by a high level of granularity: *a granular database.*

gran•u•lar•i•ty /ˌgrænyəˈleritē/
▸ **noun** the quality or condition of being granular. ■ technical the scale or level of detail present in a set of data.

grat•i•fi•ca•tion /ˌgrætəfiˈkāSHən/
▸ **noun** pleasure, especially when gained from the satisfaction of a desire: *a thirst for sexual gratification.*
■ a source of pleasure.

graunch /grônCH/
▸ **verb** [trans.] informal, chiefly Brit. & NZ damage (something): *she sat massaging a shoulder she'd graunched last week.*

gray /grā/ (Brit **grey**)
▸ **adjective** S. African relating to an ethnically mixed residential area.
▸ **verb** [trans.] (**gray something out**) Computing display a menu option in a light font to indicate that it is not available.

gray goods /ˈgrā ˌgo͞odz/
▸ **plural noun** computing equipment.

great /grāt/
▸ **adjective** [predic.] Irish (of two people) on very close or intimate terms: *one of the boys was very **great with** her.*

green jer•sey /ˈgrēn ˈjərzē/
▸ **noun** (in a cycling race involving stages) a green knit shirt worn each day by the rider accumulating the highest number of points, and presented at the end of the race to the rider with the highest overall points total.

green•tail•ing /ˈgrēnˌtāliNG/
▸ **noun** the sale of goods that are not harmful to the environment or were produced in conformity with environmental standards: *organic gardening is part of our commitment to greentailing.*
-ORIGIN blend of *green* 'not ecologically harmful' and *retailing.*

green•wash /'grēn,wäSH; -,wôSH/
▸ **noun** disinformation disseminated by an organization so as to present an environmentally responsible public image: *the recycling bins in the cafeteria are just feeble examples of their corporate greenwash.*
-DERIVATIVES **green•wash•ing noun**
-ORIGIN 1980s: from *green* 'not ecologically harmful,' on the pattern of *whitewash.*

grid /grid/
▸ **noun** Computing a number of computers linked together via the Internet so that their combined power may be harnessed to work on difficult problems.

G-ride /'jē ,rīd/
▸ **noun** informal a stolen car.
-ORIGIN perhaps from the name *Grand Theft Auto,* a video game.

grinds /grīndz/
▸ **plural noun** Irish private tutoring: *experienced teacher offers grinds in Physics and Irish, to all levels.*

grom•met /'grämit/
▸ **noun** informal, chiefly Austral. a young or inexperienced surfer or skateboarder.
-ORIGIN of uncertain origin.

ground•ed /'growndid/
▸ **adjective** well balanced and sensible: *for someone so young, Chris is extremely grounded.*

Ground Ze•ro /'grownd 'zirō/
▸ **noun** [in sing.] the site of the World Trade Center in New York, destroyed by terrorists on September 11, 2001.

Group of Eight /ˈgro͞op əv ˈāt/ (abbreviation: **G8**) the eight leading industrial nations (US, Japan, Germany, France, UK, Italy, Canada, and Russia), whose heads of government meet regularly.

grrrl /grrl/ (also **grrl**)
▸ **noun** a young woman perceived as independent and strong or aggressive, especially in her attitude to men or in her sexuality.
–ORIGIN 1990s: a variant of *girl*, as in *riot grrrl*, with the *grrr* representing the sound of an animal growling.

grudge match /ˈgrəj ˌmæCH/
▸ **noun** a contest or other competitive situation involving personal antipathy between the participants.

guai•fen•e sin /gwīˈfenəsin/
▸ **noun** an expectorant used in cough syrups and sometimes for pain relief from fibromyalgia.

gua•ra•na /gwəˈränə/
▸ **noun 1** a substance prepared from the seeds of a Brazilian shrub, used as a tonic or stimulant.
2 the shrub (*Paullinia cupana*) of the soapberry family that yields guarana.
–ORIGIN mid 19th cent.: from Tupi.

guay•a•ber•a /ˌgīəˈberə/
▸ **noun** a lightweight open-necked Cuban or Mexican shirt with two breast pockets and two pockets over the hips, typically having short sleeves and worn untucked.
–ORIGIN 1970s: Cuban Spanish, apparently originally from the name of the *Yayabo* river, influenced by Spanish *guayaba* 'guava.'

gub /gəb/ (also **gub•ba** /ˈgəbə/ or **gub•ber** /ˈgəbər/)
▸ **noun** chiefly derogatory (among Australian aboriginals) a white person.

-ORIGIN 1940s: of uncertain origin: perhaps an alteration of *government* or *garbage*.

guil•lo•tine /ˈgiləˌtēn; ˈgēə-/
▸ noun a device for cutting that incorporates a descending or sliding blade, used typically for cutting paper, card, or sheet metal.
▸ verb [trans.] cut (paper, card, etc.) with a guillotine.

guilt /gilt/
▸ verb [trans.] informal make (someone) feel guilty, especially in order to induce them to do something: *Celeste had been guilted into going by her parents.*

gut•kha /ˈgo͞otkə/
▸ noun a sweetened mixture of chewing tobacco, betel nut, and palm nut, originating in India as a breath freshener.
-ORIGIN 1990s: from Hindi 'a shred; small piece.'

gut-wrench•ing /ˈgətˌrenCHiNG/
▸ adjective informal extremely unpleasant or upsetting: *the film is a gut-wrenching portrait of domestic violence.*

gym /jim/
▸ noun informal a place, typically a private club, providing a range of facilities designed to improve and maintain physical fitness and health.

gyo•za /ˈgyōzə/
▸ noun a Japanese dish consisting of wonton wrappers stuffed with pork and cabbage.

H

Ha•des /ˈhādēz/ informal hell.

hair•weav•ing /ˈherˌwēviNG/
▸ **noun** the process of interweaving a hairpiece with one's own hair.

hal•lou•mi /häˈloomē/
▸ **noun** a mild, firm, white Cypriot cheese made from goats' or ewes' milk, used especially in cooked dishes.
-ORIGIN 1990s: from Egyptian Arabic *ḥalūm*, probably from Arabic *ḥaluma* 'to be mild.'

ham-and-egg•er /ˌhæm ən ˈegər; ənd/
▸ **noun** informal an ordinary, average person.

hand•ed•ness /ˈhændidnis/
▸ **noun** the tendency to use either the right or the left hand more naturally than the other: *our research on human handedness is ongoing.*

hand•phone /ˈhændˌfōn/
▸ **noun** SE Asia a cordless or cellular phone.

hands-free /ˈhændz ˈfrē/
▸ **adjective** (especially of a telephone) designed to be operated without using the hands.

hand•span /ˈhændˌspæn/
▸ **noun** the width of a person's hand, as measured when the fingers and thumb are spread out: *the boat was hardly more than a handspan above the waterline.*

hand-wav•ing /ˈhænd ˌwāviNG/
▸ **noun** the use of gestures and insubstantial language

meant to impress or convince: *their patriotic hand-waving lacked sincerity* | [as adj.] *her path of logic and hand-waving explanations.*

hand•wring•ing /ˈhændˌriNGiNG/
‣ **noun** the clasping together and squeezing of one's hands, especially when distressed or worried.
■ an excessive display of concern or distress: *his customary handwringing about the need for more local aid.*

hard•bod•y /ˈhärdˌbädē/
‣ **noun** (pl. **hard•bod•ies**) informal a person with very toned or well-developed muscles: *he felt intimidated by all the hardbodies on the beach.*
-DERIVATIVES **hard•bod•ied** adjective

hard core /ˈhärd ˈkôr/
‣ **noun** the most active, committed, or doctrinaire members of a group or movement.
■ popular music that is experimental in nature and typically characterized by high volume and aggressive presentation. ■ pornography of an explicit kind.

hard•gain•er /ˈhärdˈgānər/
‣ **noun** (in bodybuilding) a person who does not find it easy to gain muscle through exercise.

Har•ring•ton /ˈhæriNGtən/
‣ **noun** a man's short lightweight jacket with a collar and a zipped front.
-ORIGIN from the name of Rodney *Harrington*, a character in the 1960s television series *Peyton Place*, who was associated with the garment.

hat /hæt/
‣ **noun** a symbolic hat, used in metaphoric phrases that refer to one's character, including:

•

■ **be all hat and no cattle** tend to talk boastfully without acting on one's words. ■ **black hat** (or **white hat**) used in reference to the bad (or good) party in a situation: *we are the good guys—the black hats lost.* [ORIGIN: from the color of hat traditionally worn by the bad (or good) character in movie Westerns.]

hate crime /ˈhāt ˌkrīm/
‣ **noun** a crime motivated by racial, sexual, or other prejudice, typically one involving violence.

ha•wa•la /həˈwälə; -ˈvälə/
‣ **noun** a system of transferring money traditionally used in Arabia and India, whereby the money is paid to an agent who then instructs an associate to pay the final recipient.
–ORIGIN from Arabic, literally 'change, transform.'

haze /hāz/
‣ **verb** [trans.] obscure with a haze: *a clump of islands, very green, but hazed in cloud and mist.*

head shop /ˈhed ˌSHäp/
‣ **noun** a store that sells drug-related paraphernalia.

head•shot /ˈhed,SHät/
‣ **noun 1** a photograph of a person's head.
■ a frame, or a sequence of frames, of videotape or motion-picture film that captures a close-up of a person's head.
2 a bullet or gunshot aimed at the head.

head•space /ˈhed,spās/
‣ **noun** informal the notional space occupied by a person's mind: *to play, you enter the headspace of a female bounty hunter.*

head-trip /'hed ˌtrip/
▸ noun **1** an intellectually stimulating experience.
2 an act performed primarily for self-gratification.

health care /'helTH ˌker/
▸ noun [often as adjective] the organized provision of medical care to individuals or a community: *health-care professionals.*

heart•sink pa•tient /'härtˌsiNGk ˌpāsHənt/
▸ noun Brit. informal (among doctors) a patient who makes frequent visits to a doctor's office, complaining of persistent but unidentifiable ailments.

heart•worm /'härtˌwərm/
▸ noun a parasitic nematode worm (*Dirofilaria immitis*, class Phasmida) that infests the hearts of dogs and other animals.

heav•y hit•ter /'hevē 'hiṯər/ (also **big hit•ter**)
▸ noun informal an important or powerful person.

heav•y mob /'hevē 'mäb/
▸ phrase Brit. informal a group of strong or violent criminals or bodyguards.

heft•y /'heftē/
▸ adjective (**heft•i•er, heft•i•est**) done with vigor or force: *with one hefty swing of the bat, Cuddyer has tied the game.*

height•ism /'hīṯizəm/
▸ noun prejudice or discrimination against someone on the basis of their height.
–DERIVATIVES **height•ist** adjective & noun

help desk /'help ˌdesk/
▸ noun a service providing information and support to the users of a computer network.

high-band /'hī 'bænd/
▸ **adjective** relating to or denoting a video system using a relatively high carrier frequency, which allows more bandwidth for the signal.

high-con•cept /'hī 'känsept/
▸**adjective** (especially of a movie or television plot) having a striking and easily communicable idea.

high-main•te•nance /'hī 'māntənəns/
▸**adjective** needing a lot of work to keep in good condition.
■ informal (of a person) demanding a lot of attention: *if Martin could keep a high-maintenance girl like Tania happy, he must be doing something right.*

high•veld /'hī,velt/
▸**noun** a region of veld situated at a high altitude, especially the region in Transvaal, South Africa, between 4,000 and 6,000 feet (1,200 and 1,800 m) above sea level.
–ORIGIN late 19th cent.: partial translation of Afrikaans *hoëveld.*

hi•jab /hi'jäb/
▸**noun** a head covering worn in public by some Muslim women.
■ the religious code that governs the wearing of such clothing.
–ORIGIN from Persian, from Arabic *ḥajaba* 'to veil.'

hink•y /'hiNGkē/
▸ **adjective** (**hink•i•er, hink•i•est**) informal (of a person) dishonest or suspect: *he knew the guy was hinky.*
■ (of an object) unreliable: *my brakes are a little hinky.*
–ORIGIN 1950s: of obscure origin.

hired gun /'hīrd 'gən/
▸ **noun** informal **1** a hired bodyguard, mercenary, or assassin.
2 an expert brought in to resolve complex legal or financial problems or to lobby for a cause.

his•to•ry-sheet•er /'hist(ə)rē ,SHēt̬ər/
▸ **noun** Indian a person with a criminal record.

hit /hit/
▸ **noun** Computing an instance of a particular Web site's being accessed by a user: *the site gets an average 350,000 hits a day.*

ho•key-po•key /'hōkē 'pōkē/
▸ **noun** NZ informal a kind of brittle toffee or a type of toffee-flavored ice cream.

hole /hōl/
▸ **noun** a shortcoming, weakness, or flaw in a plan or argument: *intriguing as it sounds, the theory is full of holes.*

hol•i•day /'häli,dā/
▸ **noun** chiefly Brit. [with modifier] a short period during which the payment of installments, tax, etc., may be suspended: *a pension holiday.*

hol•i•day sea•son /'hälidā ,sēzən/
▸ **noun** the period of time from Thanksgiving until New Year, including such festivals as Christmas, Hanukkah, and Kwanzaa.

Hol•o•caust de•ni•al /'hälə,kôst di,nīəl; 'hōlə-/
▸ **noun** the belief or assertion that the Holocaust did not happen or was greatly exaggerated.

home•room /ˈhōmˌro͞om; -ˌro͝om/
> ▸ **noun** a classroom in which a group of students assembles daily with the same teacher before dispersing to other classes.

home stud•y /ˈhōm ˌstədē/
> ▸ **noun** an assessment of prospective adoptive parents to see if they are suitable for adopting a child.

ho•mo•ge•ne•ous /ˌhōməˈjēnēəs/
> ▸ **adjective** Chemistry denoting a process involving substances in the same phase (solid, liquid, or gaseous): *homogeneous catalysis.*

ho•mog•e•ny /həˈmäjənē/
> ▸ **noun** Biology correspondence of structure or organs due to common descent.

hon•ey•trap /ˈhənēˌtræp/
> ▸ **noun** a stratagem in which an attractive person entices another person into revealing information.

hooch /ho͞oCH/
> ▸ **noun** informal a shelter or improvised dwelling.
> -ORIGIN 1950s (originally military slang): perhaps from Japanese *uchi* 'dwelling.'

hood•ie /ˈho͝odē/ (also **hood•y**)
> ▸ **noun** [pl. **hoodies**] informal a hooded sweatshirt or jacket: *they were casually dressed in hoodies and jeans.*

ho•tel•ing /hōˈteliNG/
> ▸ **noun** the short-term provision of office space to a temporary worker.
> ■ the short-term letting of surplus office space to employees from other companies.

hot press /'hät ˌpres/
> ▸ **noun** Irish a cupboard that houses or is adjacent to a water heater, and in which clothes and linens are placed in order to extract their dampness.
> -ORIGIN from the *hot* temperature inside the *press* (Irish for 'cupboard').

hot•tie /'hät̲ē/ (also **hot•ty**)
> ▸ **noun** (pl. **hot•ties**) informal a sexually attractive person, especially a young woman: *he got mad when I said his sister was a hottie.*

HR
> ▸ **abbreviation** human resources (the personnel department of an organization).

hryv•na /'(h)rivnyə; -nēə; hə'riv-/ (also **hryv•nia**)
> ▸ **noun** the basic monetary unit of Ukraine, equal to 100 kopiykas.
> -ORIGIN from Ukrainian *gryvnya* '3-kopek coin of pre-independent Ukraine,' from Old Russian *grivina* 'necklace, ring, coin.'

HSGT
> ▸ **abbreviation** high speed ground transit.

hue•vos ran•che•ros /ˌ(h)wevōs rän'CHerōs/
> ▸ **plural noun** a dish of fried or poached eggs served on a tortilla with a spicy tomato sauce, originating in Mexico.
> -ORIGIN 1980s: Spanish *huevos* 'eggs' + *rancheros* 'ranch-style.'

huff /həf/
> ▸ **verb** [trans.] informal sniff fumes from (gasoline or solvents) for a euphoric effect, the consequences of which may be lethal.
> -DERIVATIVES **huff•er** noun; **huff•ish** adjective

hunt•ing /ˈhəntiNG/
▸ **noun** [in combination] the activity of searching for something: *house-hunting*.

hy•brid car /ˈhībrid ˈkär/
▸ **noun** a car with a gasoline engine and an electric motor, each of which can propel it.

hy•dro•fluoro•car•bon /ˌhīdrōˈfloŏrə,kärbən; -ˈflôr-/ (abbreviation: **HFC**)
▸ **noun** Chemistry any of a class of partly chlorinated and fluorinated hydrocarbons, used as an alternative to chlorofluorocarbons.

hy•per•fli•er /ˈhīpər,flīər/
▸ **noun** a person who travels a great deal, especially for business: *surrounded by laptop-toting hyperfliers in the airline club.*
 –ORIGIN 1990s: from *hyper-* 'excessively, above normal' + *flier* 'a person or thing that flies, especially in a particular way.'

hy•per•i•cin /hīˈperəsin/
▸ **noun** a substance found in St John's wort, credited with chemical and pharmacological properties similar to those of antidepressants.
 •A polycyclic quinone; chem. formula: $C_{30}H_{14}O_8$.
 –ORIGIN early 20th cent.: from *hypericum* 'a yellow-flowered plant' + *-in*, chemical suffix.

hy•po•cen•ter /ˈhīpə,sentər/
▸ **noun** the point on the earth's surface directly above or below an exploding nuclear bomb.

hy•po•spray /ˈhīpō,sprā/
▸ **noun** (chiefly in science fiction) a device used to introduce a drug or other substance into the body through the skin without puncturing it.

hys•ter•i•cal re•al•ism /hi'sterikəl 'rēə,lizəm/
  ▸ **noun** realistic fiction that is characterized by overblown prose and intellectual digressions: *that new novel is an 800-page example of hysterical realism.*

I

ICANN
> ▸ **abbreviation** Internet Committee for Assigned Names and Numbers, the nonprofit organization that oversees the use of Internet domains.

ICC
> ▸ **abbreviation** International Criminal Court.

ich•thus /'ikᴛʜəs/
> ▸ **noun** an image of a fish used as a symbol of Christianity.
> -ORIGIN from Greek *ikhthus* 'fish,' an early symbol of Christianity: the initial letters of the word are sometimes taken as short for I*esous* C*hristos*, T*heou* U*ios*, S*oter* (Jesus Christ, Son of God, Savior).

i•con•ize /'īkə,nīz/
> ▸ **verb** [trans.] **1** Computing reduce (a window on a video display terminal) to a small symbol or graphic.
> **2** treat as an icon: *in the land of his birth, Lenin has been iconized.*

ICT
> ▸ **abbreviation** information and computing technology.

i•den•ti•ty pol•i•tics /ī'dentiṯē ,pälətiks/
> ▸ **plural noun** [treated as sing.] a tendency for people of a particular religion, race, social background, etc., to form exclusive political alliances, moving away from traditional broad-based party politics.

ill-tem•pered /'il 'tempərd/
> ▸ **adjective** irritable or morose.
> -DERIVATIVES **ill-tem•pered•ly adverb**

il·lus·tra·tive /i'ləstrətiv; 'ilə,strātiv/
▸ **adjective** relating to pictorial illustration: *the illustrative arts.*

IM
▸ **abbreviation** Computing ■ instant message. ■ instant messaging.
▸**verb** [trans.] (**IM's, IM'd, IM'ing**) send an online message to (someone) by using an instant messaging system: *when I am online I like to IM my friends because it's faster than e-mail* | [intrans.] *parents were surprised to learn how much time their kids spend IM'ing.*

IMAP /'ī,mæp/
▸ **abbreviation** Computing Internet Mail Access Protocol.

im·mu·no·blot·ting /,imyənō'blätiNG; i,myōō-/
▸ **noun** a technique for analyzing or identifying proteins in a mixture, involving separation by electrophoresis followed by staining with antibodies.

i-Mode /'ī ,mōd/
▸ **noun** a technology that allows data to be transferred to and from Internet sites via cell phones.
-ORIGIN early 21st cent.: from *I* (referring to the user's ability to interact directly with the Internet) + *mode.*

im·pres·sion /im'presHən/
▸ **noun** an instance of a pop-up or other Web advertisement being seen on computer users' monitors: *we can guarantee 10,000 unique impressions weekly.*

in-box /'in, bäks/
▸ **noun** Computing the window in which an individual user's received e-mail messages and similar electronic communications are displayed.

in•cur•a•ble /inˈkyo͞orəbəl/
> **adjective** figurative (of a person or behavior) unable to be changed: *an incurable optimist.*
-DERIVATIVES **in•cur•a•bly adverb**

in•fo•me•di•ar•y /ˌinfōˈmēdē͏ˌerē/
> **noun** an Internet company that gathers and links information on particular subjects on behalf of commercial organizations and their potential customers.
-ORIGIN 1980s: from *info(rmation)* + *-mediary*, on the pattern of *intermediary*.

in•for•ma•tion scent /ˌinfərˈmāsHən ˌsent/
> **noun** visual or textual cues provided on a Web site to suggest what information it or its links may contain.
■ the perceived usefulness of a page based on such information: *the scientists determined the strength of the information scent by analyzing users' actions, the links, and other data.*

in•for•ma•vore /inˈfôrməˌvôr/
> **noun** a consumer of information: *an informavore's behavior is guided by the adaptive tendency to jointly minimize acquisition costs and maximize information gain.*
-ORIGIN from *informa(tion)* + *-vore* 'one who consumes or devours,' on the pattern of *carnivore, herbivore.*

in•nit /ˈinit/ Brit. informal
> **contraction** isn't it (often used in conversation when seeking confirmation or as a general filler): *it's the easiest way, innit?* | *we all want to get highly paid jobs, innit?*
USAGE: The word **innit** arose as an informal way of saying "isn't it," especially in questions in spoken English where the speaker is seeking confirmation of a statement, as in *weird that, innit?* More recently, however, **innit** has developed into a general-purpose 'filler,' being used in questions in speech or very informal writ-

ing both to seek confirmation or merely for emphasis, as in the following examples: *I play it quite often, innit?* | *you'd better hurry on over, innit?* (meaning "hadn't you?"). This extended use is especially common among young people.

in one's pelt /'in ˌwənz 'pelt/
▸ **adjective phrase** Irish informal naked: *the attention of the crowd shifted to an odd little man, quite nearly in his pelt.*

in•side /'inˌsīd/
▸ **adjective** [attrib.] known or done by someone within a group or organization: *they were accused of selling shares while in possession of inside information.*

in•sight med•i•ta•tion /'insīt medəˌtāsHən/
▸ **noun** a form of Buddhist mediation practiced with the intention to gain insight into reality.

in•sourc•ing /'inˌsôrsiNG/
▸ **noun** the practice of using an organization's own personnel or other resources to accomplish a task.
■ the practice whereby an organization provides its own personnel to accomplish specialized tasks for a client, at the client's place of business.
–DERIVATIVES **in•source** verb

in•stant mes•sag•ing /'instənt 'mesijiNG/ (abbreviation: **IM**)
▸ **noun** Computing the exchange of typed messages between computer users in real time via the Internet: *instant messaging is fun, but it interrupts whatever else I'm doing.*
–DERIVATIVES **in•stant mes•sage** noun

in•tel /'intel/
▸ **noun** [often as modifier] informal military intelligence; information: *I need some intel, and I need it fast.*
–ORIGIN 1980s: abbreviation.

in•tel•li•gent de•sign /in'telijənt di'zīn/
▸ **noun** the theory that life, or the universe, cannot have arisen by chance and was designed and created by some intelligent entity.

in•ter•op•er•a•bil•i•ty /,intər,äp(ə)rə'bilitē/
▸ **noun** the ability of two or more systems with different architecture, platforms, or the like to share information: *in many buildings, interoperability means that the front-end controls for the various systems in the building all terminate in the same room.*

in•ter•pre•ta•tive /in'tərpri,tātiv/ (also **in•ter•pre•tive** /in 'tərpritiv/)
▸ **adjective** relating to or providing an interpretation: *activities are designed to reinforce students' interpretative skills.*
-DERIVATIVES **in•ter•pre•ta•tive•ly** (also **in•ter•pre•tive•ly**) adverb

in•tra•der•mal /,intrə'dərməl/
▸ **adjective** situated or applied within the layers of the skin: *they offer a facial procedure of intradermal pigmentation, similar to tattooing and known as "permanent cosmetics."*
-DERIVATIVES **in•tra•der•mal•ly** adverb

in•tra•net /'intrə,net/ (also **In•tra•net**)
▸ **noun** Computing a local or restricted communications network, especially a private network created using World Wide Web software.

in•tra•pre•neur /,intrəprə'noor; -'nər/
▸ **noun** an entrepreneur operating within an organization and developing its capabilities or resources.
-ORIGIN from *intra-* 'within' + *(entre)preneur.*

in•vac•u•ate /in'vækyoo,āt/
▸ **verb** [trans.] confine (people) to a space in an emergency.

■ use a defined space in this way: *these designs permit us to invacuate tenants to a safe haven within the building.*
–DERIVATIVES **in•vac•u•a•tion** noun
–ORIGIN on the pattern of *evacuate*.

IP ad•dress /ˈīˈpē ə,dres/
▸ **noun** Computing a unique string of numbers separated by periods that identifies each computer attached to the Internet. It also usually has a version containing words separated by periods.

ir•ri•tat•ing /ˈiri,tātiNG/
▸ **adjective** causing anger, annoyance, or impatience: *an irritating child.*
■ causing inflammation or other discomfort to a body part: *the substance may be irritating to eyes and skin.*
–DERIVATIVES **ir•ri•tat•ing•ly** adverb

Is•lam•o•pho•bi•a /is,lämə'fōbēə; iz-/
▸ **noun** a hatred or fear of Islam or Muslims, especially as a political force.

Is•mail Sa•ma•ni Peak /ˈismīl sə'mänē 'pēk/ one of the principal peaks in the Pamir Mountains of Tajikistan, rising to 24,590 feet (7,495 m). It was the highest mountain in the former Soviet Union. Former names: **Mount Garmo** (until 1933), **Stalin Peak** (1933–62), **Communism Peak** (1962–98).
–ORIGIN named after the 9th-century founder of the Tajik nation.

i•so•bu•tyl•ene /,īsə'byo͞otl,ēn/,
▸ **noun** Chemistry an easily liquefied hydrocarbon gas, $(CH_3)_2C=CH_2$, used in the making of butyl rubber.

ISP
▸ **abbreviation** Internet service provider.

is•sues /ˈisHo͞oz/
> ▸ **plural noun** informal personal problems or difficulties: *emotions and intimacy issues that were largely dealt with through alcohol* | *I never met anyone with so many issues.*
> –DERIVATIVES **is•sue•less** adjective

-ista
> ▸ **suffix** informal forming nouns denoting a person associated with a particular activity, often with a derogatory intent: *fashionista.*
> –ORIGIN from the Spanish suffix -*ista*, as in *Sandinista.*

ISV
> ▸ **abbreviation** independent software vendor.

it girl /ˈit ˌgərl/
> ▸ **noun** a young woman who has achieved celebrity because of her socialite lifestyle.
> –ORIGIN coined by American screenwriter Elinor Glyn (1864–1943) with reference to American actress and sex symbol Clara Bow (1905–65), who starred in Glyn's romantic comedy *It* (1927). The current usage dates from the 1960s.

ITV (also **iTV**)
> ▸ **abbreviation** interactive television.

I•vo•ri•an / īˈvôrēən/
> ▸ **adjective** relating to the Ivory Coast or its people.
> ▸ **noun** a native or inhabitant of the Ivory Coast.

ix•nay /ˈiksˌnā/ informal
> ▸ **exclamation** (**ixnay on/to**) used in rejecting something specified: *ixnay to corporate control!*
> ▸ **verb** [trans.] cancel or stop: *the group has ixnayed the rest of its North American tour.*
> –ORIGIN 1930s: pig Latin for *nix.*

J

jack /jæk/
▸ **verb** [trans.] informal take (something) illicitly; steal: *what's wrong is to jack somebody's lyrics and not acknowledge the fact.*
■ rob (someone): *I got jacked in broad daylight.*
–ORIGIN 1990s: from *hijack.*

jack up /'jæk 'up/
▸ **phrasal verb** NZ informal arrange or organize (something): *we'll jack up a revised proposal before the end of the week.*

Jac•o•be•an /ˌjækə'bēən/
▸ **adjective** denoting the architectural style prevalent during the reign of James I of England (1603–25), consisting of a blend of Gothic and classical features.

jal•fre•zi /jäl'frāzē/
▸ **noun** (pl. **jal•fre•zis**) a medium-hot Indian dish consisting of chicken or lamb with fresh chili peppers, tomatoes, and onions.
–ORIGIN 1980s: from Bengali *jalfrezi*, from *jal* 'hot.'

Jane Doe /'jān 'dō/
▸ **noun** Law an anonymous female party, typically the plaintiff, in a legal action.
■ informal a hypothetical average woman.
–ORIGIN mid 19th cent.: the female equivalent of *John Doe.*

jas•per /'jæspər/ (also **jas•per•ware** /'jæspərˌwer/)
▸ **noun** a kind of fine hard porcelain developed by English potter Josiah Wedgwood (1730–95) and used for Wedgwood cameos and other delicate work.

jazz funk /'jæz ˌfəNGk/
▸ noun a style of popular dance music incorporating elements of jazz and funk.

Jed•i /'jedī/ (also **Jed•i knight** /'jedī ˌnīt/)
▸ noun (pl. same or **Jed•is**) a member of the mystical knightly order in the *Star Wars* films, trained to guard peace and justice in the universe.

jeet kune do /'jēt ˌkōōn 'dō/
▸ noun a modern martial art incorporating elements of kung fu, fencing, and boxing, devised by the American actor Bruce Lee (1941–73).
-ORIGIN 1990s: from Cantonese, literally 'the way of the intercepting fist.'

je•fe /'hefā/
▸ noun informal a boss or leader; a person in charge of something.
-ORIGIN late 19th cent.: Spanish from French *chef* 'chief.'

jerk /jərk/
▸ verb [trans.] [usually as adj.] (**jerked**) prepare (pork or chicken) by marinating it in spices and barbecuing it over a wood fire.

Jhar•kand /'järkænd/ a state in northeastern India, formed in 2000 from the southern part of Bihar; capital, Ranchi.

jig•gy /'jigē/
▸ adjective (**jig•gi•er,jig•gi•est**) informal **1** uninhibited, especially in a sexual manner: *the script required her to get jiggy with Leonardo.*
2 trembling or nervous, especially as the result of drug withdrawal.
-ORIGIN 1930s: from *jig* + *-y.*

ji•had•i /ji'hädē/ (also **je•had•i**)
‣ **noun** (pl. **ji•had•is**) a person involved in a jihad (Islamic holy war); an Islamic militant.
–ORIGIN from Arabic *jihādi*, from *jihād*.

jis•som /'jizəm/
‣ **noun** vulgar slang variant of jism (semen).

job spill /'jäb ˌspil/
‣ **noun** a situation in which job-related work or anxiety encroaches on one's leisure time: *your headaches may be related to job spill, so try to reduce your workload.*
–ORIGIN on the pattern of *oil spill*.

jock•ey shorts /'jäkē ˌSHôrts/ (also **Jock•ey shorts** or **Jock•eys**)
‣ **plural noun** trademark men's close-fitting underpants with a short leg.

jocks /jäks/
‣ **plural noun** informal jockey shorts.

john•ny /'jänē/
‣ **noun** (pl. **john•nies**) informal (also **rub•ber john•ny** /'rəbər 'jänē/) a condom.

joined-up /'joind 'əp/
‣ **adjective** (of handwriting) written with the characters joined; cursive.
■ (especially of a policy) characterized by coordination and coherence of thought; integrated: *a joined-up approach to rural poverty, public services, and employment.*

join•er•y /'joinərē/
‣ **noun** the activity or skill of a joiner.

Jor•dan•esque /ˌjôrdn'esk/
‣ **adjective** resembling the basketball player Michael Jordan in skill or agility: *a brand of basketball that features no*

spectacular alley-oops, no Jordanesque jams, and no shot-swatting seven-footers.

joy•pad /'joi,pæd/
▸ **noun** an input device for a computer game that uses buttons to control the motion of an image on the screen.
–ORIGIN late 20th cent.: blend of *joystick* and *keypad*.

juice box /'jo͞os ,bäks/
▸ **noun** a small disposable carton containing a single serving of fruit juice: *only juice boxes (no cans, no bottles) are allowed in the cafeteria.*

juke /jo͞ok/ informal
▸ **noun** (also **juke joint** /'jo͞ok ,joint/) a roadhouse, nightclub, or bar, especially one providing food, drinks, and music for dancing.
▸ **verb** [intrans.] **1** dance, especially to the music of a jukebox: *a middle-aged couple juked to the music.*
2 (in sports) make a sham move to mislead an opponent.
■ move in a zigzag fashion: *I juked down an alley.*
–ORIGIN 1930s: from Gullah *juke* 'disorderly.'

jump the shark /'jəmp T͟Hə 'sHärk/
▸ **verb phrase** informal (of a television series or a movie) reach a point when far-fetched events are included merely for the sake of novelty, suggesting a decline in quality and creativity.
–ORIGIN with allusion to an episode in 1977 of the television series *Happy Days*, in which a central character (the Fonz) jumps over a shark on water skis.

jump•sta•tion /'jəmp ,stāsHən/
▸ **noun** Computing a site on the World Wide Web containing a collection of hypertext links, usually to pages on a particular topic.

june•teenth /ˌjōōn'tēnTH/
▸ **noun** a festival held annually on the nineteenth of June by African Americans (especially in the southern states), to commemorate emancipation from slavery in Texas on that day in 1865.
– ORIGIN 1930s: blend of *June* and *(nine)teenth*.

junk sci•ence /'jəNGk ˌsīəns/
▸ **noun** untested or unproven theories when presented as scientific fact (especially in a court of law).

just war /'jəst 'wôr/
▸ **noun** a war that is deemed to be morally or theologically justifiable.

K

ka-ching /kəˈCHiNG/ (also **ker-ching** /kərˈCHiNG/)
> ▸ **noun** used to represent the sound of a cash register, especially with reference to making money: *the highlight will be a month-long gig at a casino in the US Virgin Islands. Ka-ching!*
> –ORIGIN imitative.

kan•ga•roo care /ˌkæNGgəˈrōō ˌker/
> ▸ **noun** a method of caring for a premature baby in which the infant is held in skin-to-skin contact with a parent, typically the mother, for as long as possible each day.

ka•pai /ˈkəpī/
> ▸ **adjective** NZ very pleasant; good, fine.
> ▸ **adverb** in a pleasant way; very well.
> –ORIGIN mid 19th cent.: from Maori *ka pai*.

kark /kärk/
> ▸ **verb** variant form of CARK.

ka•ro•shi /kəˈrōSHē; ˈkär,ō-/
> ▸ **noun** death by overwork: *the government has acknowledged that too much time on the job can result in karoshi.*
> –ORIGIN Japanese.

keech /kēKH/
> ▸ **noun** Scottish informal excrement.
> ■ rubbish: *maybe this keech about "microclimate" was true.*
> –ORIGIN early 19th cent.: from *cach*, Scots variant of *cack*.

keen /kēn/
> ▸ **adjective** (of activity or feeling) intense: *there could be keen competition to provide this service.*

kei•ret•su /kā'retsōō/
▸ **noun** a form of conglomerate in Japan, formed by cross-holdings or close cooperation among different companies.

Ken•tuck•y colo•nel /ken'təkē 'kərnl/
▸ **noun** an honorary commission given by the state of Kentucky to individuals noted for their public service and their work for the advancement of Kentucky.

ker•a•to•mi•leu•sis /ˌkerətōmī'lōōsis/
▸ **noun** the surgical reshaping of the cornea, carried out in order to correct a refractive error.
–ORIGIN 1990s: from *kerato-* 'of the cornea' + Greek *smileusis* 'carving.'

key•pal /'kē,pæl/
▸ **noun** a person with whom one becomes friendly by exchanging e-mails; an e-mail pen pal.
–ORIGIN 1990s: from *key* + *pal*, by analogy with *pen pal*.

kha•bar /'kəbər/
▸ **noun** Indian the latest information; news.
–ORIGIN mid 19th cent.: from Urdu and Persian *k̲h̲abar*, from Arabic.

ki•a•su /'kēə,sōō/ SE Asian
▸ **noun** a grasping, selfish attitude.
▸ **adjective** (of a person) very anxious not to miss out on an opportunity; grasping.
–ORIGIN from Chinese, 'scared to lose.'

kick up /'kik 'əp/
▸ **phrasal verb** (of the wind) become stronger.

kid /kid/
▸ **verb** (**kid•ded, kid•ding**) [intrans.] behave in a silly way: *no more* **kidding around**, *it's time to get to work*.

kid•ult /ki'dəlt; 'kid,əlt/
▸ noun informal an adult with childish tastes.

kill•er app /'kilər 'æp/
▸ noun informal a feature, function, or application of a new technology or product that is presented as virtually indispensable or much superior to rival products.

kill•ing field /'kiliNG ,fēld/
▸ noun (usually **killing fields**) a place where a heavy loss of life has occurred, typically as the result of massacre or genocide during a time of warfare or violent civil unrest.

kink /kiNGk/
▸ noun an unusual sexual preference: *I didn't know that was his kink, but it's okay.*

ki•san /ki'sän/
▸ noun Indian an agricultural worker; a peasant.
–ORIGIN 1930s: Hindi *kisān*, from Sanskrit *kṛṣāṇa* 'person who plows.'

kite•surf•ing /'kīt,sərfiNG/ (also **kite•board•ing**) /'kīt ,bôrdiNG/
▸ noun the sport or pastime of riding on a modified surfboard while holding on to a specially designed kite, using the wind for propulsion.
–DERIVATIVES **kite•surf•er** noun

kit•ten heel /'kitn ,hēl/
▸ noun (on a shoe) a type of low curvy heel, typically between 1 and 2 inches in height.

klep•to•crat /'kleptə,kræt/
▸ noun a ruler who uses their power to steal their country's resources.

-DERIVATIVES **klep•toc•ra•cy** /klep'täkrəsē/ noun; **klep•to•crat•ic** adjective

-ORIGIN 1960s: from Greek *kleptēs* 'thief' + -crat.

Kling•on /'kliNGän/
▸ **noun 1** a member of a warlike humanoid alien species in the television series *Star Trek* and its derivatives and sequels.
2 the language of the Klingons.
-ORIGIN 1960s: invented name.

kloof /klōof/ S. African
▸ **noun** a steep-sided wooded ravine or valley.
▸ **verb** [intrans.] [usu. as noun] (**kloofing**) explore kloofs as a sport.
-ORIGIN Afrikaans, from Middle Dutch *clove* 'cleft.'

knock•out /'näk,owt/
▸ **adjective** designating a genetically modified organism in which a normally functioning gene has been deactivated or eliminated: *a series knockout chicken DT40 cell-lines.*

knowl•edge /'nälij/
▸ **noun** information held on a computer system.

knowl•edge base /'nälij ,bās/
▸ **noun 1** a store of information or data that is available to draw on.
2 the underlying set of facts, assumptions, and rules that a computer system has available to solve a problem.

knowl•edge man•age•ment /'nälij ,mænijmənt/
▸ **noun** efficient handling of information and resources within a commercial organization.

knowl•edge work•er /ˈnälij ˌwərkər/
▸ **noun** a person whose job involves handling or using information.

Kol•ka•ta /kälˈkätə; -ˈkətə/ official name (since 2000) for Calcutta, India.

kon•fyt /kônˈfāt/
▸ **noun** S. African a preserve containing whole fruit or pieces of fruit.
–ORIGIN mid 19th cent.: Afrikaans, from Dutch *konfijt*, probably from French *confiture*.

kop /kôp/
▸ **noun** S. African (especially in place names) a hill or peak.
–ORIGIN Afrikaans, from Dutch, literally 'head.'

ko•piy•ka /kôˈpēkə/
▸ **noun** a monetary unit of Ukraine, equal to one-hundredth of a hryvna.
–ORIGIN 1990s: Ukrainian from Russian *kopeĭka* 'kopek.'

Kraut•rock /ˈkrowtˌräk/
▸ **noun** an experimental style of rock music associated with German groups of the 1970s, characterized by improvisation and strong, hypnotic rhythms.
–DERIVATIVES **Kraut•rock•er** noun

Krav Ma•ga /ˈkräv məˈgä/
▸ **noun** a form of self-defense and physical training, first developed by the Israeli army in the 1940s, based on the use of reflexive responses to threatening situations.
–ORIGIN 1990s: from Hebrew, 'contact combat.'

K•u-band /ˈkāˈyo͞o ˌbænd/
▸ **noun** a microwave frequency band used for satellite

communication and broadcasting, using frequencies of about 12 gigahertz for terrestrial reception and 14 gigahertz for transmission.

-ORIGIN 1990s: from *Ku* (arbitrary serial designation) + *band*.

Kui•per belt /ˈkīpər ˌbelt/
▶ **noun** a region of the solar system beyond the orbit of Neptune, believed to contain many comets, asteroids, and other small bodies made largely of ice.

-ORIGIN 1990s: named after Gerard P. *Kuiper* (1905—73), Dutch-born US astronomer.

L

lac•tiv•ist /'læktəvist/
  ▸ **noun** informal humorous an advocate for breastfeeding, especially one who promotes the right to breastfeed a child in public places.
  –ORIGIN a blend of *lactation* and *activist*.

lad•ette /læ'det/
  ▸ **noun** Brit. informal a young woman who behaves in a boisterously assertive or crude manner and engages in heavy drinking sessions.
  –ORIGIN 1990s: from *lad* + *-ette*.

la•dy•boy /'lādē,boi/
  ▸ **noun** (in Thailand) a transvestite.

lair•y /'lerē/
  ▸ **adjective** (**lair•i•er, lair•i•est**) Brit. informal **1** cunning or conceited.
  2 ostentatiously attractive; flashy.
  3 aggressive or rowdy: *a couple of lairy people pushed me around.*
  –ORIGIN mid 19th cent. (originally Cockney slang): alteration of *leery*. Sense 2 was originally Australian slang and dates from the early 20th cent.

lamp /læmp/
  ▸ **verb** [trans.] Brit hit or beat (someone).
  –ORIGIN early 19th cent.: of uncertain origin; perhaps related to *lam*.

land /lænd/
  ▸ **noun** [in combination] figurative a particular sphere of activity or group of people: *the blunt, charmless climate of techno-land.*

-PHRASES **the land of the free** the United States of America.

land•mark /'lænd,märk/
▸ **noun** a building or monument of historical importance.

lane /lān/
▸ **noun** Astronomy a dark streak or band that shows up against a bright background, especially in a spiral galaxy.
-ORIGIN Old English, related to Dutch *laan*; of unknown ultimate origin.

lan•guage en•gi•neer•ing /'læŋgwij ,enjə,niriNG/
▸ **noun** any of a variety of computing procedures that use tools such as machine-readable dictionaries and sentence parsers in order to process natural languages for industrial applications such as speech recognition and speech synthesis.

La Ni•ña /lä 'nēnyə/
▸ **noun** a cooling of the water in the equatorial Pacific, which occurs at irregular intervals and is associated with widespread changes in weather patterns complementary to those of El Niño, but less extensive and damaging in their effects.
-ORIGIN Spanish, literally 'the girl child,' after *El Niño*.

lan•iard /'lænyərd/
▸ **noun** variant spelling of LANYARD.

lank /läNGk/
▸ **adjective** S. African informal **1** very numerous or plentiful: *come and share our braai—we've got lank meat.*
2 very good; fantastic: *dad's got a lank new car.*
-ORIGIN sense 1 is perhaps from Afrikaans *geld lank* 'money galore;' sense 2 may be related to Afrikaans *lank nie sleg nie* 'not at all bad.'

large /lärj/
▸ **verb** [intrans.] (**large it**) Brit. informal enjoy oneself in a lively way with drink or drugs and music: *I can't go, but large it for me, okay?*

la•ser gun /ˈlāzər ˌgən/
▸ **noun** a hand-held device with a laser beam.
■ (in science fiction) a weapon using a laser beam.

la•ser point•er /ˈlāzər ˌpointər/
▸ **noun** a pen-shaped pointing device that contains a small diode laser that emits an intense beam of light, used to direct attention during presentations.

la•ser tweez•ers /ˈlāzər ˈtwēzərz/ (also **op•ti•cal tweez•ers** /ˈäptikəl ˈtwēzərz/)
▸ **noun** Physics a device that uses light from a 10-watt laser to move individual molecules within cells.

lashed /læsʜt/
▸ **adjective** Brit. informal very drunk.

LASIK /ˈlāzik/
▸ **noun** corrective eye surgery in which a flap of the corneal surface is raised and a thin layer of underlying tissue is removed using a laser.
-ORIGIN 1990s: acronym from *laser-assisted in situ keratomileusis.*

late•ish /ˈlātisʜ/
▸ **adjective & adverb** variant spelling of LATISH.

lat•er•al /ˈlætərəl/
▸ **adjective** chiefly Brit. involving lateral thinking: *he's very creative in a lateral way.*

la•va tube /'lävə ˌt(y)o͞ob; 'lævə/ (also **la•va tun•nel** /'lävə ˌtənl; 'lævə/)
▸ noun a natural tunnel within a solidified lava flow, formerly occupied by flowing molten lava.

lead bal•loon /'led bə'lo͞on/
▸ noun (in phrase **go over like a lead balloon**) (of something said or written) be poorly received: *his suggestion of moving to a part-time schedule went over like a lead balloon.*

learn•fare /'lərnˌfer/
▸ noun a welfare system in which attendance at school, college, or a training program is necessary in order to receive benefits.
–ORIGIN 1990s: from *learn,* on the pattern of *workfare.*

left-brained /'left ˌbrānd/
▸ adjective having the left part of the brain as the dominant or more efficient part, often said to indicate abilities in language, mathematics, and logical reasoning.

left coast /'left 'kōst/
▸ noun the West Coast of the United States, especially California: *America's left coast should be on everyone's vacation list.*

leg-rope /'leg ˌrōp/
▸ noun Austral./NZ (in surfing) a rope attached to a surfboard and tied to the surfer's ankle to prevent the board being washed away by the surf.

lem•ma /'lemə/
▸ noun (pl. **lem•mas** or **lem•ma•ta** /'lemətə/) a word or phrase defined in a dictionary or entered in a word list.

leop•ard lil•y /ˈlepərd ˌlilē/
▸ **noun** a lily resembling a tiger lily, native to the southwestern US.
•*Lilium pardalinum*, family Liliaceae.

leu•cite /ˈloōˌsīt/
▸ **noun** a potassium aluminosilicate mineral, crystallizing in the tetrahedral system and typically found as grey or white glassy trapezohedra in volcanic rocks.
–ORIGIN late 18th cent.: from Greek *leukos* 'white' + *-ite*.

lev•el /ˈlevəl/
▸ **noun** a floor within a multistory building.
▸**verb** (**le•veled, lev•el•ing**; Brit. **lev•elled, lev•el•ling**) [trans.] make equal or similar: *Woods dunked to level the score.*

lev•el•er /ˈlevələr/ (Brit. **lev•el•ler**)
▸ **noun** a situation or activity in which distinctions of class, age, or ability are immaterial: *he valued the sport because it was a great leveler.*

life coach /ˈlīf ˌkōCH/
▸ **noun** a person who counsels and advises clients on matters having to do with careers or personal life: *she went to a life coach for a skills assessment.*

life•style drug /ˈlīfstīl ˌdrəg/
▸ **noun** a drug used to improve the quality of life rather than alleviating or curing disease: *Viagra is the ultimate lifestyle drug.*

life vest /ˈlīf ˌvest/
▸ **noun** a buoyant or inflatable vest for keeping a person afloat in water.

like /līk/
▸ **adverb** informal used to convey a person's reported attitude or feelings in the form of direct speech (whether or

not representing an actual quotation): *so she comes into the room and she's like "Where is everybody?"*

like a shag on a rock /ˌlīk ə ˈSHæg än ə ˈräk; ôn/
▸ **phrase** Austral. in an isolated or exposed position.

lime•scale /ˈlīmˌskāl/
▸ **noun** Brit. a hard white substance deposited by water on the inside of pipes, pots, etc.

line a•breast /ˈlīn əˈbrest/
▸ **phrase** Nautical a formation in which a number of ships travel side by side.

line a•head /ˈlīn əˈhed/
▸ **phrase** Nautical a formation in which a number of ships follow one another in a line.

line a•stern /ˈlīn əˈstərn/
▸ **phrase** a formation in which a number of aircraft follow one another in a line.

lin•guis•tic pro•fil•ing /liNGˈgwistik ˈprōfiliNG/
▸ **noun** the analysis of a person's speech or writing, especially to assist in identifying or characterizing an individual or particular subgroup: *linguistic profiling revealed that the bomber was probably an uneducated southerner.*

Lin•ux /ˈlinəks/
▸ **noun** Computing, trademark an operating system modeled on Unix, whose source code is publicly available at no charge.
-ORIGIN 1990s: from the name of *Linus* Benedict Torvalds (b. 1969), a Finnish software engineer who wrote the first version of the system, + *-x*, as in *Unix*.

li•on /ˈlīən/
▸ **noun** (usually **literary lion**) a notable or famous author.

li•pec•to•my /li'pektəmē; lī-/
▸ noun (pl. **li•pec•to•mies**) any surgical procedure carried out to remove unwanted body fat, usually by suction.
–ORIGIN 1990s: from *lip(o-)* + *-ectomy*.

li•po•dys•tro•phy syn•drome /ˌlīpə'distrəfē ˌsindrōm; ˌlipə-/
▸ noun a metabolic disease in which fat distribution in the body becomes abnormal, often as a result of taking protease inhibitor drugs. Fat is lost from the face, arms, and legs, and is built up in other places, especially the breasts, abdomen, and back of the neck.

-lish /lish/
▸ suffix forming nouns denoting a blend of a particular language with English, as used by native speakers of the first language: *Japlish*.

lit•er•a•cy hour /'litərəsē ˌow(ə)r/
▸ noun Brit. a period in school set aside for developing reading skills, introduced as a daily requirement in English primary schools in 1998.

loan word /'lōn ˌwərd/
▸ noun a word adopted or borrowed from another language.

lock•box /'läkˌbäks/
▸ noun a lockable container; a safe.
■ a delivery mailbox provided with a lock.

loft /lôft; läft/
▸ noun 1 part of a room on a higher level than the rest of the room.
2 a living space that may or may not have been converted from industrial or commercial space, characterized by an open floor plan with few interior walls.

lo•gis•tics /ləˈjistiks; lō-/
▸ **plural noun** the commercial activity of transporting goods to customers.

look•ism /ˈlo͝ok,izəm/
▸ **noun** prejudice or discrimination on the grounds of a person's appearance.
–DERIVATIVES **look•ist** noun & adjective

look•up /ˈlo͝ok,əp/
▸ **noun** [usually as modifier] the action of systematic electronic information retrieval.
■ a facility for lookup: *you need an online dictionary with fast phonetic lookup.*

loon•y tunes /ˈlo͞onē ˌt(y)o͞onz/ informal
▸ **adjective** crazy; deranged: *it sounds a little loony tunes.*
▸**plural noun** crazy or deranged people.
–ORIGIN 1980s: from *Looney Tunes* the name of an animated cartoon series that began in the 1930s, featuring Bugs Bunny and other characters.

loos•ey-goos•ey /ˈlo͞osē ˈgo͞osē/
▸ **adjective** informal relaxed and comfortable.
–ORIGIN 1980s: fanciful formation from *loose* + *goosey.*

los•ing•est /ˈlo͞oziNGist/
▸ **adjective** informal losing more often than others of its kind; least successful: *the losingest club in baseball history.*

lost prop•er•ty /ˈlôst ˈpräpərtē; ˈläst/
▸ **noun** the British term for LOST-AND-FOUND.

lounge•core /ˈlownj,kôr/
▸ **noun** songs from the 1960s and 1970s, including easy

listening music, orchestral verions of rock songs, and television or movie theme songs.
-ORIGIN 1990s: blend of *lounge* and (HARD) CORE.

love•ware /ˈləvˌwer/
▸ **noun** informal Computing computer software that is distributed freely, with the developer asking for the users to think kindly of the developer or of a dedicatee in lieu of payment.

low-main•te•nance /ˈlō ˈmāntənəns/
▸ **adjective** requiring little work to keep in good condition: *low-maintenance lawns.*
■ informal (of a person) independent and not demanding a lot of attention.

low post /ˈlō ˌpōst/
▸ **noun** Basketball an offensive position on the court close to the basket.

LRD
▸ **noun** (plural **LRDs** or **LRD's**) an organ donor who is genetically related to the recipient: *brothers and sisters commonly volunteer to be LRDs.*
-ORIGIN abbreviation of *living related donor.*

LSE
▸ **abbreviation** London Stock Exchange.

LTR
▸ **abbreviation** long-term relationship (used in personal advertisements).

lunch box /ˈlənCH ˌbäks/
▸ **noun** informal a fool; an inept person.

LURD /lərd/
▸ **noun** (plural **LURDs** or **LURD's**) an organ donor who is genetically unrelated to or has no prior relationship with the recipient: *they were the first hospital in the region to do transplants with LURDs.*
–ORIGIN abbreviation of *living unrelated donor.*

lurk•er /'lərkər/
▸ **noun** a user of Internet chat rooms or newsgroups who does not participate: *I read somewhere that most newsgroups have an average of a hundred lurkers for each active poster.*

lush /ləSH/
▸ **adjective** Brit. informal sexually attractive.

LW
▸ **abbreviation** long wave.

ly•o•cell /'līə,sel/
▸ **noun** a strong synthetic fiber made from reconstituted cellulose, used in carpets and in apparel when blended with other fibers.

ly•sim•e•ter /lī'simitər/
▸ **noun** a device for measuring mass changes due to leaching and evaporation, undergone by a body of soil.
–ORIGIN late 19th cent.: from Greek *lusis* 'loosening' + *-meter.*

M

M
▸ **abbreviation** money, when used with a following numeral in measures of money supply: *broad money, M3, grew by an annualized 9.7%.*

mac•chi•a•to /ˌmäkē'ätō/
▸ **noun** espresso coffee with a dash of frothy steamed milk.
–ORIGIN 1970s: from Italian, literally 'stained, marked.'

mag /mæg/ Australian/NZ informal
▸ **verb** (**magged, mag•ging**) [intrans.] chatter incessantly.
▸ **noun** a gossip or chat.
–ORIGIN early 19th cent.: originally English dialect; related to *magpie*.

mag•got /'mægət/
▸ see ACT THE MAGGOT.

mag•got•y /'mægətē/
▸ **adjective 1** full of maggots.
2 Australian/NZ informal angry or bad-tempered: *Scotty got a bit maggoty about all this.*

mag•ne•tar /'mægni,tär/
▸ **noun** Astronomy a neutron star with an extremely strong magnetic field.
–ORIGIN 1990s: from *magnetic* + *-ar* on the pattern of *pulsar* and *quasar*.

ma•hal /mə'häl/
▸ **noun** Indian **1** a mansion or palace: [in names] *the Taj Mahal.*

2 living quarters set aside for a particular group of people: *the whole servant mahal has been buzzing with the gossip.*
-ORIGIN early 17th cent.: from Urdu and Persian *mahal(l)*, from Arabic *mahall*, from *hall*, 'stopping-place, abode.'

main man /'mān 'mæn/
▸ **noun** informal **1** a close and trusted friend.
2 the most important person in a team, organization or situation: *now their main man can give his loving fans a big present by helping his team go all the way.*

ma•ki /'mäkē/ (also **ma•ki zu•shi** /'mäkē 'zo͞oshē/)
▸ **noun** a Japanese dish consisting of sushi and raw vegetables wrapped in seaweed.
-ORIGIN 1970s: Japanese, from *maki-* (combining form of *maku* 'roll up') + *-zushi*, sushi.

mal•fat•ti /mäl'fätē/
▸ **plural noun** dumplings or gnocchi made with spinach and ricotta.
-ORIGIN 1980s: Italian, from *malfatto*, 'badly made' (because they resemble ravioli without their pasta envelopes).

mal•ware /'mæl,wer/
▸ **noun** Computing software that is intended to damage or disable computers and computer systems: *protect your computer against viruses and other malware.*
-ORIGIN blend of *malicious* and *software.*

man•age•ment in•for•ma•tion sys•tem /'mænijmənt ,infər,māshən ,sistəm/
▸ **noun** (abbreviation **MIS**) a computerized information-processing system designed to support the activities of company or organizational management.

Man•ches•ter /'mæn,CHestər; 'mænCHi-/ (also **man•ches•ter**)
▸ **noun** S. African & Australian/NZ household linen.

man•ny /'mænē/
▸ **noun** (pl. **man•nies**) a male nanny: *My husband would like us to hire a manny for our two boys.*
–ORIGIN 1990s: blend of *man* and *nanny*.

MAOI
▸ **noun** Medicine monamine oxidase inhibitor, a type of antidepressant drug.

March Mad•ness /'märCH 'mædnis/
▸ **noun** informal the time of the annual NCAA college basketball tournament, generally coinciding with the month of March.

mar•go•sa /mär'gōsə/
▸ **noun** a tropical Old World tree that yields mahoganylike timber, oil, medicinal products, and insecticide. Also called *neem*.
•*Azadirachta indica*, family Meliaceae.
–ORIGIN Portuguese *amargosa*, feminine of *amargoso* 'bitter.'

mark•er /'märkər/
▸ **noun** a distinctive feature or characteristic indicative of a particular quality or condition: *identification with one's own language has always been a marker of nationalism* | *using gene expression, one can simultaneously track multiple markers associated with potency, specificity and toxicology.*

mar•ra /'mærə/
▸ **noun** variant spelling of MARRER.

mar•rer /'mærər/ (also **mar•ra** /'mærə/, **mar•row** /'mærō/)
▸ **noun** N. English & Scottish **1** a friend, companion, or work-

mate (often used as a form of address): *come here, mar-rer, we need to talk.*
2 something that forms a pair with something else; a counterpart or twin.
-ORIGIN late Middle English: probably from Old Norse *margr* 'many,' also 'friendly, communicative.'

mar•riage of con•ven•ience /ˈmærij əv kənˈvēnyəns/
▸ **noun** a marriage that is arranged for practical, financial, or political reasons.

mar•row /ˈmærō/
▸ **noun** variant spelling of MARRER.

Mar•sanne /märˈsän/
▸ **noun** a variety of white wine grape originating in the northern Rhône area of France.
-ORIGIN from *Marsanne,* the name of a town in southern France.

Mar•y Jane /ˈmerē ˈjān/
▸ **noun 1** a flat, round-toed shoe for women and girls, with a single strap across the top.
2 informal marijuana.
-ORIGIN 1920s: from the female given name *Mary Jane.*

mash /mæsн/
▸ **verb** [trans.] US & Caribbean informal attack or assault: *they both got **mashed up** pretty bad.*

mash-up /ˈmæsн ˌəp/
▸ **noun** informal a recording created by digitally combining and synchronizing instrumental tracks with vocal tracks from two or more different songs: *we all compete to make the craziest mash-ups.*

mas•sive•ly par•al•lel /ˈmæsivlē ˈpærəˌlel/
▸ **adjective** (of a computer) consisting of many individual processing units, and thus able to carry out simultane-

ous calculations on a substantial scale: *a massively parallel computer with 168 processors.*

MAT /mæt/
▸ **noun** a technology that uses chemicals, usually petrolatum, dimethicone, and polyquaternium, to reduce the ability of bacteria to adhere to the skin: *the company is developing MAT-containing soaps.*
–ORIGIN abbreviation of *Microbial Anti-attachment Technology.*

ma•tu•ri•ty /məˈCHŌŌrəṯē, -ˈt(y)ŌŌrə-/
▸ **noun** (pl. **ma•tu•ri•ties**) an insurance policy, security, etc. having a fixed maturity date.

Mc•Man•sion /məkˈmænsHən/
▸ **noun** a large modern house that is considered ostentatious and lacking in architectural integrity: *let's hope it happens before David Geffen erects cyclone fences on either side of his Malibu McMansion to keep away the riff-raff.*

m-com•merce /ˈem ˌkämərs/
▸ **noun** electronic commerce conducted on cellular phones.

Mc•Tim•o•ney /məkˈtimənē/
▸ **noun** [as modifier] denoting a gentle form of chiropractic treatment involving very light and swift movements of the practioner's hands.
–ORIGIN 1970s: named after John *McTimoney* (1914–80), its British inventor.

ME
▸ **abbreviation 1** Medical Examiner.
2 myalgic encephalitis, another name for chronic fatigue syndrome.

mean•while /'mēn'(h)wīl/
▶ **adverb** informal on the other hand: *he has said little, mean-while, about how he plans to live his life.*

meat•space /'mēt,spās/
▶ **noun** informal the physical world, as opposed to cyber-space or a virtual environment: *I'd like to know a little more before we talk about a get-together in meatspace.*

med•al /'medl/
▶ **verb** (**med•aled, med•al•ing**; British **medalled, med•al•ling**) [intrans.] win a medal in a sporting event: *Larsen medaled in 4th place in the 3,200 meter run.*

me•di•a•scape /'mēdēə,skāp/
▶ **noun 1** communications media as a whole: *the rapidly changing mediascape in Belgium.*
2 [in sing.] the world as presented through, or perceived by, the mass media: *the vast, ubiquitous mediascape we in-habit today.*

me•di•a stud•ies /'mēdēə ,stədēz/
▶ **plural noun** [usually treated as sing.] the study of the mass media, especially as an academic subject.

me•di•um /mēdēəm/
▶ **noun** (pl. **me•di•a** /'mēdēə/ or **me•di•ums**) a particular form of storage material for computer files, such as magnetic tape or discs.

Mé•doc /mā'dôk; -'däk/
▶ **noun** (pl. same or **Mé•docs**) a red Bordeaux wine pro-duced in Médoc, the area along the left bank of the Gironde estuary in SW France.

Meg•a•loc•er•os /,megə'läsərəs/
▶ **noun** a very large extinct deer of the Pleistocene epoch, of which the Irish elk was the main example.

-ORIGIN modern Latin, from Greek *megas*, *megalo-* 'great' + *keras* 'horn.'

meg•a•pix•el /'megə,piksəl/
▸ **noun** one million pixels; used as a measure of the resolution in digital cameras: [in comb.] *a 3.2-megapixel camera*

men in black /'men in 'blæk/
▸ **phrase** informal anonymous dark-clothed men who, to prevent publicity, supposedly visit people who have reported an encounter with a UFO or an alien.

men's move•ment /'menz ,mōōvmənt/
▸ **noun** a movement aimed at liberating men from their traditional roles in society.

mer•chant ac•count /'mərCHənt ə,kownt/
▸ **noun** a bank account that enables the holder to accept credit cards for payment: *it took several weeks to set up a merchant account for her Web site.*

mess /mes/
▸ **noun** [usually in sing.] (**a mess of**) informal a large amount or quantity of: *she made us a mess of collards and biscuits.*

met•a /'metə/
▸ **noun** short for META KEY.
▸ **adjective** (of a creative work) referring to itself or to the conventions of its genre; self-referential.
-ORIGIN 1980s: from *meta* in the sense 'beyond'.

met•a•da•ta /'metə,dætə; -,dātə/
▸ **noun** a set of data that describes and gives information about other data.

met•a key /ˈmetə ˌkē/
> ▸ **noun** Computing a function key on a keyboard that is activated by simultaneously holding down a control key.

me•thaq•ua•lone /məˈTHækwəˌlōn/
> ▸ **noun** trademark a sedative and sleep-inducing drug. Also called QUAALUDE (trademark).
> -ORIGIN 1960s: from elements of its chemical name *meth-* + *-a-* + *qu(inine* + *a(zo-* + *-o)l* + *-one.*

mez•za•lu•na /ˌmetsəˈlōōnə/
> ▸ **noun** a utensil for chopping herbs, vegetables, etc., with a semi-circular blade and a handle at each end.
> -ORIGIN 1950s: from Italian, literally 'half moon.'

mi•cro•ar•ray /ˈmīkrō-əˌrā/
> ▸ **noun** a grid of DNA segments of known sequence that is used to test and map DNA fragments, antibodies, or proteins.

mi•cro•brows•er /ˈmīkrōˌbrowzər/
> ▸ **noun** Computing a small Internet browser for use with cellular phones and other handheld devices.

mi•cro•chip /ˈmīkrōˌCHip/
> ▸ **verb** (**mi•cro•chipped, mi•cro•chip•ping**) [trans.] implant a microchip under the skin of (a domestic animal) as a means of identification.

mi•cro•cin•e•ma /ˈmīkrōˌsinəmə/
> ▸ **noun** a genre consisting of low-budget alternative or independent films and videos: *she took a course in microcinema at the state college.*
> ■ a small room or theater used to show such films and videos: *the campus has three microcinemas.*

mi•cro•cred•it /'mīkrō,kredit/
▶ noun the lending of small amounts of money at low interest to new businesses in the developing world. ■ such a loan considered individually: *microcredits should not be considered a substitute for long-term investment in infrastructure.*

mi•cro•e•lec•tro•me•chan•i•cal /,mīkrō-i,lektrōmə'kæni-kəl/
▶ adjective denoting systems or compenents relating to microscopic electronic machines that are typically built on computer chips: *optical true-time delay devices with microelectromechanical mirror arrays.*
-DERIVATIVES **mi•cro•e•lec•tro•me•chan•ics** noun

mi•cro•scoot•er /'mīkrō,skōōtˌər/
▶ noun a small two-wheeled foldable aluminium scooter, used by children and adults.

mi•cro•site /'mīkrə,sīt/
▶ noun 1 a auxiliary Web site with independent links and address that is accessed mainly from a larger site.
2 a small part of an ecosystem that differs markedly from its immediate surroundings.

mid•dl•es•cent /,midl'esənt/
▶ adjective 1 middle-aged, but typically still maintaining the interests and activities of younger people.
2 in technical use people forty to sixty years of age.
-DERIVATIVES **mid•dl•es•cence** /,midl'esəns/ noun
-ORIGIN 1960s: blend of *middle* + *adolescent*.

mid•dle•ware /'midl,wer/
▶ noun Computing software constituting the interface between a database and a client: *we can help your organization achieve business process integration through the use of customized middleware.*

mile-high club /'mīl 'hī ˌkləb/
▶ **phrase** humorous used in reference to having sex on an aircraft: *she joined the mile-high club by making love on a flight between New York and LA.*

mi•lieu ther•a•py /mil'yŏŏ ˌTHerəpē; mēl'yœ/
▶ **noun** psychotherapy in which the patient's social environment is controlled or manipulated with a view to preventing self-destructive behavior.

mind•share /'mīnd,sHer/
▶ **noun** consumer awareness of a product or brand, as contrasted with market share: *a light-hearted measurement of which famous artists have the greatest mindshare in our culture.*

ming•er /'miNGər/
▶ **noun** British informal, derogatory an unattractive or unpleasant person or thing. *Why can't anyone see that Spencer is a complete minger?*
–ORIGIN 1990s: from MINGING.

ming•ing /'miNGiNG/
▶ **adjective** British informal foul-smelling.
■ very bad or unpleasant: *what I'd really like to do is burn that minging beige jacket he has glued to him all the time.*
–ORIGIN 1970s: perhaps from Scots dialect *ming* 'excrement.'

min•i•camp /'minē,kæmp/
▶ **noun** a session run by a professional sports team to train particular players, or to test potential new players, before the main preseason training.

min•i•stroke /'minē,strōk/
▶ **noun** a temporary blockage of the blood supply to the brain, lasting only a few minutes and leaving no notice-

able symptoms or deficits. Also called TRANSIENT ISCHEMIC ATTACK.

mis•con•fig•ure /ˌmiskən'figyər/
> ▸ **verb** [trans.] [often as adj.] (**misconfigured**) Computing configure (a system or part of it) incorrectly: *misconfigured Windows systems.*
-DERIVATIVES **mis•con•fig•u•ra•tion** /ˌmiskən,figyə'rā-SHən/ **noun**

mis•er•a•bi•lism /'miz(ə)rəbə,lizəm/
> ▸ **noun** gloomy pessismism or negativity: *the duo spent much of the eighties exploring the lonely outer reaches of miserabilism.*
-DERIVATIVES **mis•er•a•bi•list** noun & adjective

mis•sion creep /'miSHən ,krēp/
> ▸ **noun** a gradual shift in objectives during the course of a military campaign, often resulting in an unplanned long-term commitment. ■ such a development in a nonmilitary context, resulting in undesirable policies or consequences: *the IMF's mission creep has been consistently endorsed by the Treasury Department as a way of furthering U.S. economic foreign policy.*

mitch /miCH/
> ▸ **verb** [intrans.] informal chiefly Irish play truant from school: *we're looking for three young fellows who've **mitched** from school* | [trans.] *he would mitch school and go down to the docks.*
-ORIGIN late Middle English (in the obsolete sense 'pilfer'): apparently from Old French *muchier* 'hide, lurk.'

mobe /mōb; 'mōbē/ (also **mo•bey** /'mōbē/)
> ▸ **noun** British informal a cellular phone.
-ORIGIN 1990s: shortening of *mobile.*

mo•chac•ci•no /ˌmōkə'cHēnō/
▸ noun (pl. **mo•chac•ci•nos**) a cappuccino containing chocolate syrup or chocolate flavoring.
–ORIGIN 1990s: blend of *mocha* and *cappucino*.

mock•u•men•ta•ry /ˌmäkyə'ment(ə)rē/
▸ noun a television program or film that takes the form of a serious documentary in order to satirize its subject.
–DERIVATIVES **mock•u•men•tar•i•an** noun
–ORIGIN 1960s: blend of *mock* and *(doc)umentary*.

moe•ri•the•ri•um /ˌmirə'THirēəm/
▸ noun a medium-sized mammal of the late Eocene and Oligocene epochs with a long snout and short legs, related to modern elephants.
•*Moeritherium trigodon.*
–ORIGIN modern Latin, from the name of Lake *Moeris* in Egypt, where the first fossils were found + Greek *thērion* 'wild beast.'

moi /mwä/
▸ exclamation (usually **moi?**) humorous me? (used especially when accused of something that one knows one is guilty of).
–ORIGIN French, 'me.'

mo•jo /'mōjō; -hō/
▸ noun a Cuban sauce or marinade containing garlic, olive oil, and sour oranges.
–ORIGIN probably from Spanish *mojo* 'wet' from *mojar* 'make wet.'

mo•lec•u•lar e•lec•tron•ics /mə'lekyələr ilek'träniks; ˌēlek-/
▸ plural noun [treated as sing.] a branch of electronics in which individual molecules perform the same function as microelectronic devices such as diodes.

–DERIVATIVES **mo•lec•u•lar e•lec•tron•ic** adjective *molecular electronic materials and inorganic particles*

mol•et•ron•ics /ˌmäliˈträniks/
▸ plural noun [treated as sing.] short for MOLECULAR ELECTRON-ICS.
–DERIVATIVES **mol•et•ron•ic** adjective

mom-and-pop /ˈmäm ən ˈpäp/
▸ adjective denoting a small store or business of a type often run by a married couple: *most of the town relies on a local mom-and-pop ISP for their email.*

mom•my track /ˈmämē ˌtræk/
▸ noun informal a career path for women who sacrifice some promotions and pay raises in order to devote more time to raising their children.
–DERIVATIVES **mom•my track•er** noun; **mom•my track•ing** noun

mom•pa•ra /mämˈpärə/ (also **mam•pa•ra**)
▸ noun S. African derogatory an unsophisticated country person.
–ORIGIN Fanakalo, literally 'a fool,' also 'waste material.'

mon•o•brow /ˈmänəˌbrow/
▸ noun informal a pair of eyebrows that meet above the nose, giving the appearance of a single eyebrow.
–DERIVATIVES **mon•o•browed** adjective

mon•ster truck /ˈmänstər ˌtrək/
▸ noun a pickup truck on an elevated chassis with oversized tires, especially one that competes in various motor sports.

mon•tu•no /mänˈto͞onō/
▸ noun (pl. **mon•tu•nos**) an improvised passage in a rumba.

mon•ty /'mäntē/
> ▸ noun (in phrase **the full monty**) British informal the full amount expected, desired, or possible: *they'll do the full monty for a few thousand each.*
-ORIGIN perhaps from *the full Montague Burton,* 'Sunday-best three-piece suit' (from the name of a tailor.)

mo•tor vo•ter law /'mōtər ˌvōtər ˌlô/
> ▸ noun another name for the National Voter Registration Act of 1993, designed to reverse declining voter registration by allowing voters to register at motor vehicle departments when they renew their driver's licenses.

moul•vi /'mo͞olvē/ (also **maul•vi, mol•vi**)
> ▸ noun (pl. **moul•vis**) (especially in India) a Muslim doctor of the law.
-ORIGIN from Urdu *maulvī,* from Arabic *mawlawī* 'judicial' (adjective used as a noun), from *mawlā* 'mullah.'

mouse /mows/
> ▸ noun (pl. **mice** /mīs/) a dull light brown color reminiscent of a mouse's fur: *her blonde hair dulled to mouse.*

mouse•trap /'mows,træp/
> ▸ verb [trans.] Computing (often as **mouse•trap•ping**) to block (a user's) efforts to exit from a Web site, usually one to which he or she has been redirected: *mousetrapping is a tactic commonly used by pornographic Web sites.*

mouth•feel /'mowTH,fēl/
> ▸ noun the physical sensations in the mouth produced by a particular food: *this Cabernet has a dense, tightly woven mouthfeel, with complex, chewy and velvety tannins.*

MPEG /'em,peg/
> ▸ noun an international standard for encoding and compressing video images.
-ORIGIN 1990s: from *Motion Pictures Experts Group.*

MP3
> **noun** a standard for compressing audio files, used especially as a way of downloading music from the Internet.
-ORIGIN 1990s: from **MPEG** + *Audio Layer-3*.

Mud•ville /ˈməd,vil/
> **noun** the world of baseball.
-ORIGIN from the fictional locality in the 1888 poem *Casey at the Bat.*

mug•gle /ˈməgəl/ (also **Mug•gle**)
> **noun** informal an unimaginative or boring person: *this video game won't appeal to muggles.*
-ORIGIN used in the sense 'nonwizard' in J.K. Rowling's *Harry Potter* books, but of uncertain origin.

mullet /ˈməlit/
> **noun** a man's hairstyle in which the hair is cut short at the front and sides and left long at the back.
-ORIGIN 1990s: of unknown origin.

mul•ti•cast /ˈməlti,kæst; ,məltiˈkæst/
> **verb** (past and past part. **mul•ti•cast**) [trans.] send (data) across a computer network to several users at the same time.
> **noun** a set of data sent across a computer network to many users at the same time.

mul•ti•cul•ti /,məltēˈkəltē; ,məltī-/ informal
> **adjective** multicultural.
> **noun 1** popular music incorporating ethnically disparate elements.
2 an advocate of cultural diversity.
-ORIGIN 1990s: rhyming alteration of *multicultural.*

mul•ti•pur•pose de•vice /,məltēˈpərpəs di,vīs; ,məltī-/ (abbreviation: **MPD**)

▸ **noun** a device, especially an electronic device, that combines two or more functions or whose functionality can be altered: *a good choice for small offices is a multipurpose device for printing, faxing, scanning, and copying.*

mul•ti•slack•ing /ˌməltēˈslækiNG; ˌməltī-/
▸ **noun** informal the practice of using a computer at work for tasks or activities that are not related to one's job: *most employers tolerate a certain amount of multislacking.* See also CYBERSLACKER.
–DERIVATIVES **mul•ti•slack•er noun**
–ORIGIN *multi-* + *slacking* 'working slowly or lazily,' on the pattern of *multitasking,* the simultaneous execution of multiple computer tasks by a single processor.

mul•ti-u•til•i•ty /ˌməltēyo͞oˈtilitē; ˌməltī-/
▸ **noun** a privatized utility that has extended or combined its business to offer its customers additional services (especially those of another privatized utility).

mul•ti•verse /ˈməlti͵vərs/
▸ **noun** the universe considered as lacking order or a single ruling and guiding power.

mup•pet /ˈməpit/
▸ **noun** British informal an incompetent or foolish person.
–ORIGIN 1990s: from *Muppet,* the generic name given to various puppets and marionettes created by Jim Henson (1936–90) for the children's television programs *Sesame Street* and *The Muppet Show.*

mur•ri /ˈmərē/
▸ **noun** (pl. same or **mur•ris**) Australian an Aboriginal (used by the Aboriginals to refer to themselves).
–ORIGIN from Kamilaroi (and other Aboriginal languages) *mari* 'the Aboriginal people,' 'people generally.'

mus•cle dys•mor•phi•a /ˈməsəl disˌmôrfēə/
▸ **noun** a psychological disorder marked by a negative body image and an obsessive desire to have a muscular physique: *a large proportion of people with muscle dysmorphia are weightlifters or bodybuilders.*
-ORIGIN *muscle* + *dysmorphia* 'abnormality in the shape or size of a body part.'

must-have /ˈməst ˈhæv/
▸ **adjective** essential or highly desirable: *the must-have blouse of the season.*
▸ **noun** an essential or highly desirable item: *this season's must-have is an ostrich bowling bag.*

must-read /ˈməst ˈrēd/
▸ **noun** informal a piece of writing that should or must be read: *it's a must-read for anyone interested in the geologic history recorded in the landscape.*

must-see /ˈməst ˈsē/
▸ **noun** informal something that should or must be seen, especially a remarkable sight or entertainment: *this sassy and superior suspense thriller is a must-see.*

mu•ti /ˈmo͞otē/
▸ **noun** South African informal medicine of any kind.

myth•i•fy /ˈmiTHəˌfī/
▸ **verb** mythicize: *as success mythified their reputation, the stormtroopers grew in distinctiveness.*
-DERIVATIVES **myth•i•fi•ca•tion** /ˌmiTHəfəˈkāSHən/ noun

N

nad
▶ **abbreviation 1** nothing abnormal detected.
2 no appreciable response.

nads /nædz/
▶ **plural noun** vulgar slang a man's testicles.
– ORIGIN 1960s: shortening of *gonads*.

nag•ware /'næg,wer/
▶ **noun** informal Computing computer software that is free for a trial period and thereafter frequently reminds the user to pay for it.

nail wrap /'nāl 'ræp/
▶ **noun** a type of beauty treatment, in which a nail strengthener, usually containing fibers, is either brushed on or applied with adhesive.

nak•fa /'näkfə/
▶ **noun** (pl. same or **nak•fas**) the basic monetary unit of Eritrea, equal to one hundred cents.
– ORIGIN 1990s: from *Nakfa*, the name of the town where the country's armed struggle against the Ethiopian regime was launched.

na•na /'nænə/
▶ **noun** British a child's word for a grandmother.

nan•dro•lone /'nændrə,lōn/
▶ **noun** an anabolic steroid with tissue-building properties, used unlawfully to enhance performance in sports.
– ORIGIN 1950s: shortened form of its chemical name *norandrostenolone*.

nan•ny cam /'nænē ˌkæm/
▸ **noun** a webcam or CCTV camera in a private home for parents to monitor their childcarer.

nan•o- /'nænō; 'nānō; 'nænə; 'nānə/
▸ **combining form** submicroscopic: *nanotube.*

nan•o•bac•te•ri•um /ˌnænōbæk'tirēəm; ˌnānō-/
▸ **noun** (pl. **nan•o•bac•te•ri•a**) a kind of microorganism about a tenth the size of the smallest normal bacteria, claimed to have been discovered in living tissue and in rock.

nan•obe /'nænōb; 'nā-/
▸ **noun** another term for NANOBACTERIUM.

nan•o•wire /'nænōˌwīr; 'nānō-/
▸ **noun** a nanometer-scale rod made of semiconducting material, used in miniature transistors and some laser applications.

Nas•sau /'næsô/
▸ **noun** Golf an eighteen-hole match in which the players bet on the first nine holes, the second nine holes, and the entire round.

nas•ty•gram /'næstēˌgræm/
▸ **noun** Computing a particularly offensive e-mail message.

nav•i•gate /'næviˌgāt/
▸ **verb** Computing move around a Web site, file, the Internet, etc.: *We've added features that make our site much easier to navigate.*

ned /ned/
▸ **noun** Scottish informal a hooligan or petty criminal.
■ a stupid or loutish boy or man.

-ORIGIN early 19th cent.: perhaps from *Ned* (shortening of *Neddy,* a child's word for a donkey).

Ned Kel•ly /'ned 'kelē/
▸ **phrase** (in the phrase **as game as Ned Kelly**) audaciously bold.

need-blind /'nēd ,blīnd/
▸ **adjective** of or denoting a university admissions policy in which applicants are judged solely on their merits, irrespective of their ability to pay for tuition.

need•y /'nēdē/
▸ **adjective** (**need•i•er, need•i•est**) (of a person) needing emotional support; insecure.

net me•ter•ing /'net ,mētəriNG/
▸ **noun** a system in which solar panels or other renewable energy generators are connected to a public-utility power grid and surplus power is transferred onto the grid, allowing customers to offset the cost of power drawn from the utility: *when the wind turbine generates more power than we need, the net metering program gives us kilowatt credits for future use.*
-ORIGIN surplus energy, measured by an electric meter, is netted from the amount passing from the utility to the customer.

net•work ap•pli•ance /'netwərk ə,plīəns/
▸ **noun** a relatively low-cost computer designed chiefly to provide Internet access and without the full capabilities of a standard personal computer.

neu•ral com•pu•ter /'n(y)o͝orəl kəm'pyo͞otər/
▸ **noun** a computer using neural networks.
-DERIVATIVES **neu•ral com•put•ing** noun

neu•ro•com•pu•ter /'n(y)o͞oro̅kəm,pyo͞otər/
▸ noun another term for NEURAL COMPUTER.

neu•tro•pe•ni•a /,n(y)o͞otrə'pēnēə/
▸ noun Medicine the presence of abnormally few neutrophils in the blood, leading to increased susceptibility to infection.
-DERIVATIVES **neu•tro•pe•nic** /,n(y)o͞otrə'pēnik; -'penik/ **adjective**
-ORIGIN 1930s: from *neutral* + Greek *penia* 'poverty, lack.'

new e•con•o•my /'n(y)o͞o i'känəmē/
▸ noun new industries, such as biotechnology or the Internet, that are characterized by cutting-edge technology and high growth.

news peg /'n(y)o͞oz ,peg/
▸ noun an aspect or angle of a story that makes it newsworthy: *Talese further expanded traditional journalistic practice by delaying a story's news peg until as late in a story as he could manage.*

New York min•ute /'n(y)o͞o ,yôrk 'minət/
▸ noun informal a very short time; a moment: *you mention that price and she'll be out of here in a New York minute.*

nib•ble /'nibəl/
▸ verb [intrans.] informal show cautious interest in a commercial opportunity: *there's a Hollywood agent nibbling.*
▸ noun [in sing.] informal a show of interest in a commercial opportunity: *so far we've got a few nibbles but nothing we can bank on.*

ni•gi•ri zu•shi /'nigərē 'zo͞oSHē/
▸ noun a type of sushi consisting of a small ball of rice,

smeared with wasabi sauce and topped with raw fish or
other seafood.
-ORIGIN 1990s: Japanese, from *nigiri-* (combining form
of *nigiru* 'clasp, clench, roll in the hands') + *-zushi sushi.*

Ni•hang /ni'häNG/
▸ **noun** (in India) a member of a militant fundamentalist
Sikh movement.
-ORIGIN late 19th cent.: Persian *nihang*, literally 'croco-
dile.'

9/11 /'nīn i'levən/ (also **Sep•tem•ber 11th** /sep'tembər
i'levənTH/) September 11, 2001. On this date two hi-
jacked commercial airliners were flown into the World
Trade Center in New York. Another airliner was crashed
into the Pentagon, and one went down in a field in
Pennsylvania.

nip•py /'nipē/
▸ **adjective** (**nip•pi•er, nip•pi•est**) informal Scottish & Canadian
(of food) sharp-tasting; tangy.

no•ce•bo /nə'sēbō/
▸ **noun** a negative belief concerning a medical treatment
or procedure that produces a detrimental effect on a
person's health for purely psychological or psychoso-
matic reasons.
-ORIGIN 1960s: from Latin, literally 'I shall cause
harm,' from *nocere* 'to harm,' on the pattern of *placebo*.

no-kill /'nō ˌkil/ (also **no kill**)
▸ **noun** a policy or an animal shelter in which abandoned,
neglected, or lost animals are not put to sleep even if no
home can be found for them: *there are thousands of no-
kills that rescue pets.*
▸ **adjective** opposed to or not killing animals that live in
shelters: *find out if the organization has a no-kill policy.*

no-mark /'nō ˌmärk/
▸ **noun** British informal an unimportant, unsuccessful, or worthless person.
-ORIGIN 1980s: perhaps from the idea of performing badly in school.

non•cus•to•di•al /ˌnänkəs'tōdēəl/
▸ **adjective** Law **1** not having custody of one's children after a divorce: *the relationship between the children and their noncustodial father was virtually destroyed.*
2 not involving incarceration: *all offenders in the sample received a noncustodial sentence, and most of them received fines or probation.*

non•dig•i•tal /nän'dijiṯl/
▸ **adjective 1** not represented by numbers, especially binary codes; not digitized: *nondigital items have only their location information (catalog records) in the digital library, as it happens in a traditional automated library situation.*
2 not using the Internet or computers: *nondigital submissions will be accepted only until February 1st.*

non-net /'nän 'net/
▸ **adjective** (of an amount) including tax and other sums in addition to the net amount.

noo•dle /'nōōdl/
▸ **verb** [intrans.] informal improvise or play casually on a musical instrument: *tapes of him noodling on his farfisa organ* | [as noun] (**noodling**) *ambient synthesizer noodling.*
-ORIGIN mid 19th cent.: of unknown origin.

No•ro•vi•rus /'nôrəˌvīrəs/
▸ **noun** a virus similar to the Norwalk virus that causes outbreaks of gastroenteritis in dense populations.

Nor•walk vi•rus /'nôrwôk ˌvīrəs/
▸ **noun** a virus that can cause epidemics of severe gastro-enteritis.
-ORIGIN 1970s: from *Norwalk*, a town in Ohio where an outbreak of gastroenteritis occurred from which the virus was isolated.

nos•tal•gic /nä'stæljik/
▸ **noun** a nostalgic person.

no-till•age /'nō 'tilij/
▸ **adjective** designating a method of planting in which soil is not tilled but instead is planted by insertion of seeds in small slits, weeds being controlled by other means: *a no-tillage tomato production system using hairy vetch and subterranean clover mulches.*

nought•ies /'nôtēz/
▸ **plural noun** the decade from 2000 to 2009.
-ORIGIN 1990s: from *nought*, on the pattern of *twenties*, *thirties*, etc.

no•vel•a /nō'velə/
▸ **noun** another term for TELENOVELA.

no•wheres•ville /'nō(h)werzˌvil/
▸ **noun** informal used to describe a place or situation of no significance, promise, or interest: *an unhappy girl stuck in rural Nowheresville, KS.*

no wor•ries /'nō 'wərēz/
▸ **phrase** informal, chiefly Australian all right; fine.

NSAID /'enˌsed/
▸ **abbreviation** non-steroidal anti-inflammatory drug.

NU
> ▸ **abbreviation** Nunavut (in official postal use).

nu- /ˈn(y)oo/
> ▸ **combining form** informal respelling of 'new,' used especially in names of new or revived genres of popular music: *nu-metal bands* | *nu-disco*.

nu•cle•ar thresh•old /ˈn(y)ooklēər ˈTHreSH(h)ōld/
> ▸ **noun** a point in a conflict at which nuclear weapons are or would be brought into use.

num•ber one /ˈnəmbər ˈwən/ informal
> ▸ **phrase** (**number one, number two, etc.**) the shortest, or next shortest, etc., men's haircut, produced with electric hair clippers.

nump•ty /ˈnəm(p)tē/
> ▸ **noun** (pl. **nump•ties**) Scottish informal a stupid or ineffectual person.
> –ORIGIN 1990s: from obsolete *numps* 'a stupid person,' of unknown origin.

nu•tri•ge•no•mics /ˌn(y)ootrijēˈnōmiks; -ˈnäm-/
> ▸ **plural noun** [treated as sing.] the scientific study of the interaction of nutrition and genes, especially the role of diet in causing disease: *nutrigenomics holds great promise in fighting obesity and cancer.*
> –ORIGIN blend of *nutrition* and *genomics* 'analysis of an organism's complete set of genes.'

nvCJD
> ▸ **abbreviation** new variant Creutzfeldt–Jakob disease.

O

ob•ten•tion /əbˈtenCHən; äb-/
‣ **noun** the action of obtaining something.
–ORIGIN early 17th cent.: French, or from late Latin *ob-tentio(n-)*, from *obtinere* 'obtain, gain.'

of•fice park /ˈôfis ˌpärk; ˈäfis/
‣ **noun** an area where a number of office buildings are built together on landscaped grounds.

of•fice-park dad /ˈôfis ˌpärk ˌdæd; ˈäf-/ (abbreviation: **OPD**)
‣ **noun** a white middle-class father, aged 25 to 50, employed in a suburban white-collar job: *pollsters noted that office-park dads tended to vote Republican in the last election.*

off-la•bel /ˈôf ˈlābəl; ˈäf-/
‣ **adjective** (of a drug) prescribed in a way or for a condition not covered by the original FDA approval: *off-label use of Botox to reduce wrinkles* | [as adverb] *this drug is used off-label to help with seizures.*

oh•no•sec•ond /ˈōˈnōˌsekənd/
‣ **noun** Computing, informal a moment in which one realizes that one has made an error, typically by pressing the wrong key.

oil /oil/
‣ **noun** Austral./NZ informal information or facts: *Young had some good oil on the Adelaide races.*

old-growth /ˈōld ˈgrōTH/
‣ **adjective** (of a tree, forest, etc.) never felled; mature: *upland mesic forest habitats were predominately old-growth.*

old-time /ˈōld ˌtīm/
> ▸ **adjective** denoting ballroom dances in which a sequence of dance steps is repeated throughout, as opposed to modern dancing in which steps may be varied.

o•le•o•chem•i•cal /ˌōlēōˈkemikəl/
> ▸ **noun** a chemical compound derived industrially from animal or vegetable oils or fats.

one-shot /ˈwən ˌSHät/
> ▸ **adjective** informal achieved with a single attempt or action: *there is no one-shot solution to the problem.*
> ■ done, produced, or occurring only once: *a one-shot deal.*

one-on-one /ˈwən än ˌwən; ôn/ (also chiefly British **one-to-one** /ˈwən tə ˈwən/)
> ▸ **noun** informal a face-to-face encounter.

one-trick po•ny /ˈwən ˌtrik ˈpōnē/
> ▸ **noun** a person or thing with only one special feature, talent, or area of expertise: *competitors rounded on the middleware firm for being a one-trick pony.*

OPD
> ▸ **abbreviation** office-park dad.

o•pen class•room /ˈōpən ˈklæsˌro͞om; -ˌro͝om/
> ▸ **noun** an approach to elementary education that emphasizes spacious classrooms where learning is informally structured, flexible, and individualized.
> ■ a spacious instructional area shared by several groups of elementary students that facilitates such an approach and the movement of students from one activity to another.

o•pen en•roll•ment /ˈōpən enˈrōlmənt/
> ▸ **noun** a period during which a health insurance com-

pany or HMO is statutorily required to accept applicants without regard to health history.
■ such a period when employees can change insurance plans offered by their employer, without proof of insurability.

o•pen mar•riage /'ōpən 'mærij/
▸ **noun** a marriage in which both partners agree that each may have sexual relations with others.

op•er•a win•dow /'äp(ə)rə ˌwindō/
▸ **noun** a small fixed window usually behind the rear side window of an automobile.

op•ti•cal turn•stile /'äptikəl 'tərnstīl/
▸ **noun** an access control system without barriers in which those attempting to enter are evaluated by CCTV or other visual means.

op•tion•aire /ˌäpSHə'ner; 'äpSHəˌner/
▸ **n.** a person whose great wealth is based on owning or exercising employee stock options: *aspiring optionaires need to be aware of tax consequences.*
-ORIGIN on the pattern of *millionaire*.

or•tho•ker•a•tol•o•gy /ˌôrTHōˌkerə'täləjē/
▸ **noun** the temporary reshaping of the cornea (usually overnight) with specially-made rigid contact lenses, in order to correct myopia.

or•tho•rex•i•a /ˌôrTHə'reksēə/
▸ **noun** an obsession with eating foods that one considers healthy.
■ (also **or•tho•rex•i•a ner•vo•sa** /ôrTHə'reksēä nər 'vōsə/) a medical condition in which the sufferer systematically avoids specific foods in the belief that they are harmful.

-DERIVATIVES **or•tho•rex•ic** adjective & noun
-ORIGIN 1990s: from *ortho-* + Greek *orexia* 'appetite,' after *anorexia*.

OST
▸ **abbreviation** original soundtrack.

os•te•o•sper•mum /ˌästēōˈspərməm/
▸ **noun** a plant or shrub of the daisy family, native to Africa and the Middle East, some varieties of which are cultivated for their yellow or violet flowers.
•Genus *Osteospermum*, family *Compositae*.
-ORIGIN mid 19th cent.: modern Latin, from Greek *osteo-* 'bone' + Greek *sperma* 'seed.'

out•draw /ˌowtˈdrô/
▸ **verb** (past **out•drew** /ˌowtˈdro͞o/; past participle **out•drawn** /ˌowtˈdrôn/) [trans.] (of a person or event) attract a larger crowd than (another person or event): *smaller theme parks seem to be outdrawing the big ones.*

out•drink /ˌowtˈdriNGk/
▸ **verb** (past **out•drank** /ˌowtˈdræNGk/; past participle **out•drunk** /ˌowtˈdrəNGk/) [trans.] drink more than (another person): *crazy Aunt Kathy outdrinks anyone!*

out•gross /ˌowtˈgrōs/
▸ **verb** [trans.] surpass in gross income or profit: *the film has outgrossed all other movie comedies.*

out•hit /ˌowtˈhit/
▸ **verb** (past and past participle **out•hit; out•hit•ting**) [trans.] surpass (someone) in hitting; hit a higher score than: *the Tigers outhit Boston for a 7-5 victory.*

out•punch /ˌowtˈpənCH/
▸ **verb** [trans.] surpass (an opponent) in punching ability:

Tunney opened fast, outpunching Jack in a heated first round.

out•sprint /ˌowt'sprint/
▸ **verb** [trans.] sprint faster than (someone): *JT just managed to outsprint the third girl by one second to win the class race.*

o•ver•breed /ˌōvər'brēd/
▸ **verb** (past and past participle **o•ver•bred** /ˌōvər'bred/) breed or cause to breed to excess: *the cats are overbred and their immune system is too weak to fight infections.*

o•ver•con•nect•ed•ness /ˌōvərkə'nektidnis/
▸ **noun** a social malaise characterized by an obsessive need to keep in constant touch with people or events by means of cell phones, the Internet, and other communications technology: *overconnectedness is the downside of living in a high-tech society.*

o•ver•dry /ˌōvər'drī/
▸ **verb** (**o•ver•dries, o•ver•dried, o•ver•dry•ing**) [trans.] cause to become too dry: *a gas dryer should dry laundry thoroughly, without overdrying the fabrics.*

o•ver•fund /ˌōvər'fənd/
▸ **verb** [trans.] provide more funding for (something) than is necessary or permitted: *at such time, the plan would probably become an overfunded defined benefit plan.*

o•ver•hit /ˌōvər'hit/
▸ **verb** [trans.] (in sporting contexts) hit (a ball) too strongly or too far: *Marat Safin was overhitting, mucking up volleys, but he won anyway.*

o•ver•hype
▸ **verb** /ˌōvər'hīp/ [trans.] make exaggerated claims about

(a product, idea, or event); publicize or promote excessively: *preschool is overhyped.*
▸**noun** /'ōvər,hīp/ excessive publicity or promotion: *how will Mike strategize the overhype of the new coach?*

o•ver•keen /,ōvər'kēn/
▸ **adjective** excessively keen or enthusiastic: *it seems that the police have been overkeen in interrogating Chileans and Peruvians about APEC protests.*

o•ver•lay•er /'ōvər,lāər/
▸ **noun** a top or covering layer: *the sulfided surface is then reacted with a metal salt to form an insoluble metal-S overlayer on the semiconductor.*

o•ver•loud /,ōvər'lowd/
▸ **adjective** excessively noisy or loud: *Orli deliberately chose jukebox tracks just to upset him: overloud songs with frenetic beats and impenetrable lyrics.*

o•ver•pack /,ōvər'pæk/
▸ **verb** [trans.] **1** pack too many items into (a container). **2** add a protective layer to items or material packed in a container: *could the liquids be shipped without overpacking?*

o•ver•shirt /'ōvər,SHərt/
▸ **noun** a loose shirt worn over other garments.

o•ver•spin /'ōvər,spin/
▸ **noun** a rotating motion given to a ball when throwing or hitting it, used to give it extra speed or distance or to make it bounce awkwardly: *overspin is used to place the ball out in front of a teammate so that it runs along the ground.*

o•ver•stored /,ōvər'stôrd/
▸ **adjective** **1** stored for too long a period: *superficial blotches on overstored fruit.*

2 supplied with more retail stores than the market demands: *general economic conditions have led to the area being overstored.*

o•ver•stud•y
▸ noun /'ōvər͵stədē/ excessive study.
▸ verb /͵ōvər'stədē/ study too long or too intensely: *if your child is a high achiever, but overstudies for fear of not receiving an A+, help her to gradually study a little less.*

o•ver•sweet /͵ōvər'swēt/
▸ adjective **1** excessively sweet in taste.
2 excessively sentimental or maudlin: *if oversweet metaphors like this are your bag, then you're really going to like BaggerVance.*

o•ver•tip /͵ōvər'tip/
▸ verb (**o•ver•tipped, o•ver•tip•ping**) [trans.] give (someone) an excessively generous tip: *the food was so cheap that I overtipped the waitress.*

o•ver•wear /'ōvər͵wer/
▸ noun outer clothing.

ox•a•zo•lid•i•none /͵äksəzō'lidn͵ōn/
▸ noun any of a class of synthetic antibiotics that inhibit protein synthesis, used against gram-positive bacteria.

Ox•y•Con•tin /͵äksē'käntin/
▸ noun trademark a synthetic analgesic drug that is similar to morphine in its effects.

ox•y•gen bar /'äksəjən ͵bär/
▸ noun an establishment where people pay to inhale pure oxygen for its reputedly therapeutic effects.

oys•ter bar /ˈoistər ˌbär/
▸ **noun 1** a hotel bar, small restaurant, or other place where oysters are served.
2 (especially in the southeastern US) an oyster bed.

oys•ter sauce /ˈoistər ˌsôs/
▸ **noun** a sweet and salty sauce made with oyster extracts, used especially in Asian cooking.

P

pad site /ˈpæd ˌsīt/
▸ **noun** a building lot adjacent to a shopping center or mall.

pain•ful /ˈpānfəl/
▸ **adjective** informal very bad: *their attempts at reggae are painful.*

Pakh•tun /pækˈto͞on/
▸ **noun** a variant form of *Pashtun.*

pal•am•pore /ˈpæləmˌpôr/
▸ **noun** Indian a type of chintz cloth, used especially for bedspreads.
■ a palampore bedspread.
-ORIGIN late 17th century.: origin uncertain; perhaps from Portuguese *palangapuz(es)* plural, from Urdu, Persian *palangpoš* 'bedcover,' or perhaps from *Pālanpur,* a town in Gujarat, India.

Palm Pi•lot /ˈpäm ˈpīlət/
▸ **noun** trademark a hand-held computer.

Pa•loo•ka•ville /pəˈlo͞okəˌvil/
▸ **noun** informal **1** a state of obscurity: *defeat would have meant a one-way trip to Palookaville.*
2 an economically depressed, working-class community: *he's the sort of kid who's making his first million when his classmates are still pumping gas in Palookaville.*

pan•cha•kar•ma /ˌpənCHəˈkärmə/
▸ **noun** (in Ayurvedic medicine) a fivefold detoxification treatment involving massage, herbal therapy, and other procedures.

–ORIGIN 1980s: from Sanskrit *panca* 'five' + *karman* 'action.'

pan•ic dis•or•der /'pænɪk dɪsˌôrdər/
▸ **noun** a psychiatric disorder characterized by recurrent or unexpected panic attacks with no rational origin.

pan•ic room /'pænɪk ˌro͞om; ˌro͞om/
▸ **noun** another name for a safe room.

pa•ni•no /pæ'nēnō/
▸ **noun** (plural **pa•ni•ni** /pə'nēnē/) a sandwich, usually toasted, made with a baguette or with Italian bread.
–ORIGIN 1950s: from Italian, literally 'bread roll.'

pants /pænts/
▸ **plural noun** Brit. informal rubbish; nonsense: *he thought we were going to be absolute pants.*

par•a•chute /'pærəˌsHo͞ot/
▸ **verb** appoint or be appointed in an emergency or from outside the existing hierarchy: *an old crony of the CEO was controversially **parachuted into** the job.*

par•al•lel port /'pærəlel ˌpôrt/
▸ **noun** Computing a connector for a device that sends or receives several bits of data simultaneously on multiple wires.

Par•a•mo•tor /'pærəˌmōtər/
▸ **noun** trademark a motorized steerable parachute, powered by a motor and propeller strapped to the pilot's back.
–DERIVATIVES **par•a•mo•tor•ing noun**

par•a•site store /'pærəˌsīt ˌstôr/
▸ **noun** a retail store that would not generate any traffic but for its location adjacent to a more successful store.

par•tial-birth a•bor•tion /ˈpärsHəl ˌbərTH əˈbôrsHən/
▸ **noun** a late-term abortion of a fetus that has already died, or that is killed before being completely removed from the mother.
USAGE: The term **partial-birth abortion** is used primarily in legislation and pro-life writing about this procedure. Pro-choice, scientific, and medical writing uses the term *D&X*, for *dilation and extraction*.

par•ti•cle beam /ˈpärtikəl ˌbēm/
▸ **noun** a concentrated stream of subatomic particles, generated to cause particle collisions that will shed new light on their nature and structure.
■ such a stream used in an antimissile defense weapon.

Pass•face /ˈpæsˌfās/
▸ **noun** trademark **1** a security system in which a user must recognize pictures of human faces in order to gain access to a computer or computer network: *their site uses Passface because it's less hackable than regular passwords.*
2 (**pass•face**) a digital photograph of a human face that is used for identification in a Passface system: *the company uses cameras and passfaces to make sure only authorized employees get through the door.*
–ORIGIN on the pattern of *password*.

pat•er•a /ˈpætərə/
▸ **noun** (pl. **pat•er•ae** /ˈpætərē/) a broad, shallow bowl-shaped feature on a planet's surface.

pat•ter of ti•ny feet /ˈpætər əv ˈtīnē ˈfēt/
▸ **phrase** humorous (in full **the patter of tiny feet**) used in reference to the presence or imminent birth of a child: *I had long ago given up hope of ever **hearing the patter of tiny feet**.*

pat•tress /ˈpætrɪs/
▸ **noun** a block fixed to a wall or ceiling to receive an electric light switch, ceiling rose, etc.
–ORIGIN late 19th cent.: alteration of *pateras*, plural of *patera*.

p-book /ˈpē ˌbo͝ok/ (**pbook**)
▸ **noun** a book printed on paper, as distinguished from one in electronic form: *I prefer reading p-books, but I sometimes use the search capabilities of digitized text.*
–ORIGIN abbreviation of *paper book.*

pearl tea /ˈpərl ˌtē/
▸ **noun** another term for BUBBLE TEA.

pech /peKH/
▸ **verb** [intrans.] Scottish, Irish, & N. English breathe hard or with difficulty; pant: *by the time he reached the second floor, he was peching.*
▸ **noun** a gasping or labored breath; pant: *a pech uphill takes us to the canal.*

pelt /pelt/
▸ SEE IN ONE'S PELT.

pep•per spray /ˈpepər ˌsprā/
▸ **noun** an aerosol spray containing oils derived from cayenne pepper, irritant to the eyes and respiratory passages and used as a disabling weapon.

per•ma•lanc•er /ˈpərməˌlænsər/ (also **per•ma•temp** /ˈpərmə,temp/)
▸ **noun** a long-term freelance, part-time, or temporary worker who does not have employee benefits: *the permalancers always have to park in the temporary spaces.*
–ORIGIN blend of *permanent* and *freelancer.*

per•ma•temp /ˈpərmə,temp/
▶ another term for PERMALANCER.
–ORIGIN a blend of *permanent* and *temporary.*

pes•ter pow•er /ˈpestər ,powər/
▶ noun the ability of children to nag adults, especially to influence their parents to make certain purchases: *advertisers encourage the use of pester power, especially at Christmas.*

PETA /pētə/
▶ abbreviation People for the Ethical Treatment of Animals.

phar•ma•co•ge•nom•ics /,färmə,kōjē'nämiks; -'nōmiks/
▶ plural noun [treated as sing.] the branch of genetics concerned with determining the likely response of an individual to therapeutic drugs.
–DERIVATIVES **phar•ma•co•ge•nom•i•cist** /,färmə,kōjē 'nämisist/ noun
–ORIGIN 1990s: from *pharmaco-* + *genomics.*

phar•ma•co•phore /ˈfärməkə,fôr/
▶ noun a part of a molecular structure that is responsible for a particular biological or pharmacological interaction that it undergoes.

phase•out /ˈfāz,owt/
▶ noun an act of discontinuing a process, project, or service in phases.

phi•los•o•pause /fə'läsə,pôz/
▶ noun a supposed period in a scientist's career during which they reflect on philosophical issues and explanations: *after winning a prestigious prize, the physicist took time off to indulge in a philosopause.*

-ORIGIN blend of *philosophical* and *pause,* on the pattern of *menopause.*

phone /fōn/
▸**verb** (**phone it in**) informal work or perform in a desultory fashion.

phys•i•cal the•a•ter /'fizikəl 'THēətər /
▸ **noun** a form of theater that emphasizes the use of physical movement, as in dance and mime, for expression.

phy•to•es•tro•gen /ˌfītō'estrəjən/
▸**noun** an estrogen occurring naturally in legumes, considered beneficial in some diets.

Pi•card /pi'kärd/, French
▸**noun 1** a native or inhabitant of Picardy.
2 the dialect of French spoken in Picardy.
▸**adjective** relating to Picardy, its inhabitants, or their dialect.

pico- /'pīkō/
▸**combining form** very small: *picornavirus.*

pic•ture /'pikCHər/
▸**noun** informal in the phrase (**the big picture**) the situation as a whole.

pic•ture-per•fect /'pikCHər 'pərfikt/
▸**adjective** completely lacking in defects or flaws; ideal: *a picture-perfect summer day.*

piece of work /'pēs əv 'wərk/
▸**phrase** informal a person of a specified kind, especially an unpleasant one: *he's a nasty piece of work.*

pig-root /'pig ˌro͞ot; -ˌro͝ot/ Austral./NZ informal
▸ **verb** [intrans.] (of a horse or other animal) kick upwards with the hind legs, keeping the head down and the forelegs firmly planted.
▸ **noun** the act of pig-rooting.

pike /pīk/
▸ **verb** [intrans.] Austral./NZ informal (**pike on**) let (someone) down.

pik•er /'pīkər/
▸ **noun** informal Austral./NZ a person who withdraws from a plan, commitment, etc.

Pi•la•tes /pi'lätēz/
▸ **noun** a system of exercises using special apparatus, designed to improve physical strength, flexibility, and posture, and enhance mental awareness: *this quest for better training has led many dancers to Pilates* | [as modifier] *the Pilates method.*
-ORIGIN 1960s: named after the German physical fitness specialist Joseph *Pilates* (1880–1967), who devised the system.

pill push•er /'pil ˌpo͝osʜər/
▸ **noun** informal a person, specifically a doctor, who resorts too readily to advocating the use of medication to cure illness rather than considering other treatments.
-DERIVATIVES **pill-push•ing** noun & adjective

Pimm's /pimz/
▸ **noun** trademark a gin-based alcoholic drink, served typically with lemonade or soda water and fresh mint.
-ORIGIN early 20th cent.: from the name of the proprietor of the restaurant where the drink was created.

pinch point /ˈpinCH ˌpoint/
▸ **noun** Brit. a place or point where congestion occurs or is likely to occur, especially on a road: *the planners have suggestions to ease traffic jams at ninety-two pinch points.*

pink /piNGk/
▸ **verb** [intrans.] become pink: *Cheryl's cheeks pinked with sudden excitement.*

pi•o•neer /ˌpīəˈnir/
▸ **noun** (in Ireland) a member of the Pioneer Total Abstinence Association, a Catholic temperance society.

pipe /pīp/
▸ **noun** Computing a command which causes the output from one routine to be the input for another.
–ORIGIN short for *pipeline.*

pit /pit/
▸ **noun** informal a person's armpit.

pk
▸ **abbreviation** pack.

plant•er /ˈplæntər/
▸ **noun** (in Irish history) an English or Scottish settler on confiscated land during the 17th century.

plas•ti•ciz•er /ˈplæstəˌsīzər/ (also Brit. **plas•ti•cis•er**)
▸ **noun** a substance (typically a solvent) added to a synthetic resin to produce or promote plasticity and flexibility and to reduce brittleness.

pla•toon /pləˈto͞on/
▸ **noun** [as modifier] Baseball playing in rotation with one or more teammates at the same position: *a platoon player.*

play•book /'plā,bŏŏk/
> ▸ **noun** a book containing a sports team's strategies and plays, especially in football.

play date /'plā ,dāt/
> ▸ **noun** a date and time set by parents for children to play together: *she has play dates with two other childen on Wednesdays and Saturdays.*

play•scape /'plā,skāp/
> ▸ **noun** a designed and integrated set of playground equipment, often made of wood.

pleath•er /'plethər/
> ▸ **noun** imitation leather made from polyurethane.
> –ORIGIN 1980s: blend of *polyurethane* and *leather*.

pluck /plək/
> ▸ **verb** Geology (of glacier ice) break off (pieces of rock) by mechanical force.

plunge saw /'plənj ,sô/
> ▸ **noun** an electric saw with a projecting blade that can make precision cuts by plunging into dense materials.

plus-size /'pləs ,sīz/
> ▸ **adjective** (of a woman or women's clothing) of a larger size than average (usually of sizes greater than size 14, 16, or 18): *a new line of plus-size bathing suits.*

Poin•dex•ter /'poin,dekstər/
> ▸ **noun** informal a boringly studious or socially inept person.
> –ORIGIN 1980s: apparently from the name of one of the main characters in the comedy film *Revenge of the Nerds* (1984).

Po•ke•mon /ˈpōkiˌmän/

▸ **noun** trademark a video game, card game or other toy featuring certain Japanese cartoon characters.

■ a colorful toy model of certain Japanese cartoon characters.

–ORIGIN from the name of the Japanese video game *Pokemon,* itself from *pocket monster.*

pok•ie /ˈpōkē/

▸ **noun** (pl. **pok•ies**) Austral. a slot machine.

–ORIGIN 1960s: from *poker machine,* a type of slot machine that pays out according to the combination of playing-card symbols that appear when the lever is pulled.

po•lar•i•ty ther•a•py /pəˈleritē ˌTHerəpē; pō-/

▸ **noun** a system of treatment used in alternative medicine, intended to restore a balanced distribution of the body's energy, and incorporating manipulation, exercise, and dietary restrictions.

pol•y•am•o•ry /ˌpälēˈæmərē/

▸ **noun** the philosophy or state of being in love or romantically involved with more than one person at the same time: *practicing polyamory can be complicated unless you have a firm grasp of your own limits.*

–DERIVATIVES **pol•y•am•o•rous** adjective; **pol•y•am•o•rist** noun

–ORIGIN on the pattern of *polygamy* and *polyandry.*

po•lyg•a•my /pəˈligəmē/

▸ **noun** Botany the condition of bearing some flowers with stamens only, some with pistils only, and some with both, on the same or different plants.

po•lym•er•ase chain re•ac•tion /pəˈliməˌrās ˈCHān rēˌæk-sHən; pəˈliməˌrāz/

▸ **noun** Biochemistry a method of making multiple copies of a DNA sequence, involving repeated reactions with a polymerase.

pol•y•nos•ic /ˌpäliˈnäsik/
▶ **noun** a long-fiber rayon-and-polyester blend with a soft finish, used mainly in clothing.

poor mouth /ˈpo͝or ˌmowTH; ˈpôr/ N. Amer. & Irish informal
▶ **noun** a person who claims to be poor in order to benefit from others.

Poo•ter•ish /ˈpo͞otəriSH/
▶ **adjective** self-important and mundane or narrow-minded: *a Pooterish, inhibited man.*
-ORIGIN 1960s: from the name of Charles *Pooter*, the central character of *Diary of a Nobody* (1892) by George and Weedon Grossmith.

pop /päp/
▶ **verb** (**popped, pop•ping**) [trans.] release, open, or engage (something) quickly or suddenly: *he pulled a can of beer from the refrigerator and popped its tab.*

pop quiz /ˈpäp ˈkwiz/
▶ **noun** a short test given to students without any prior warning.

pop-un•der /ˈpäp ˌəndər/
▶ **adjective** Computing. of, relating to, or denoting an additional window, usually an advertisement, that is under a Web browser's main or current window and appears when a user tries to exit: *a plague of flashing pop-under ads.*

porn /pôrn/ (also **por•no** /ˈpôrnō/) informal
▶ **noun** television programs, books, etc., regarded as catering to a voyeuristic or obsessive interest in a specified subject: *food porn.*

por•tal /ˈpôrtl/
▸ **noun** Computing an Internet site providing a directory of links to other sites.

port•fo•li•o /pôrtˈfōlēō/
▸ **noun** (pl. **port•fo•li•os**) [as modifier] relating to, denoting, or engaged in an employment pattern which involves a succession of short-term contracts and part-time work, rather than the more traditional model of a single job for life: *portfolio careers allow women to balance work with family.*

pos•i•tive /ˈpäzitiv; ˈpäztiv/
▸ **adjective** [in combination] (of a person or their blood) having a specified substance or condition: *HIV-positive.*

pos•sie /ˈpäzē/ (also **poz•zy**)
▸ **noun** Austral./NZ informal a place or position: *the bridge will provide a good fishing possie.*
■ a job.
–ORIGIN early 20th cent.: from *position* + *-ie.*

pos•ter boy /ˈpōstər ˌboi/ (or **pos•ter girl** /ˈpōstər ˌgərl/ or **pos•ter child** /ˈpōstər ˌCHīld/)
▸ **noun** a person or thing that epitomizes or represents a specified quality, cause, etc.: *the ever-grinning poster boy for the coastal good life.*
–ORIGIN from the use in print advertisements of good-looking young people and appealing children.

post•ing /ˌpōstiNG/
▸ **noun** a message sent to an Internet bulletin board or newsgroup.
■ the action of sending a message to an Internet bulletin board or newsgroup.

Post•Script /'pōst,skript/
> ▸ **noun** Computing, trademark a language used as a standard for describing pages of text.

pot /pät/
> ▸ **noun** a shot aimed at someone or something; a potshot.

POTUS /'pōt̬əs/
> ▸ **abbreviation** President of the United States.

pou•na•mu /pow'nämo͞o/
> ▸ **noun** NZ a variety of jade; greenstone.
-ORIGIN mid 19th cent.: from Maori.

pow•er•beads /'pow(ə)r,bēdz/
> ▸ **noun** a bracelet or necklace of round beads that are purported to enhance the spiritual well-being of the wearer in different ways depending on the color or material of the beads.

pow•er rat•ing /'pow(ə)r ,rātiNG/
> ▸ **noun** **1** the amount of electrical power required for a particular device: *a continuous power rating of 150 watts.* **2** a numerical representation of a sports team's strength for betting purposes: *a 99 power rating and a home field edge of four points.*

pow•er us•er /'pow(ə)r ,yo͞ozər/
> ▸ **noun** Computing an accomplished computer user who needs products having the most features and the fastest performance.

pow•er walk•ing /'pow(ə)r ,wôkiNG/
> ▸ **noun** a form of cardiopulmonary exercise consisting of fast walking with rhythmic swinging of the arms.

PQ
▸ **abbreviation 1** Parti Québécois.
2 Province of Quebec.

prai•rie-dog•ging /ˈprerē ˌdôgiNG/ (also **prai•rie dog•ging**)
▸ **noun** the practice of looking over the wall of an office cubicle to observe coworkers: *stop prairie-dogging and get back to work.*

pre•ad•ap•ta•tion /ˌprēædəpˈtāSHən/
▸ **noun** Biology an adaptation that serves a different purpose from the one for which it evolved.

pre-Böt•zing•er com•plex /prē ˈbœtsiNGər ˌkämpleks/
▸ **noun** a structure in the mammalian brain stem that controls respiration.

pre•but•tal /prēˈbətl/
▸ **noun** (in politics) a response formulated in anticipation of a criticism; a preemptive rebuttal.
–ORIGIN 1990s: blend of *pre-* and *(re)buttal.*

pre•dawn /prēˈdôn/
▸ **adjective** relating to or taking place before dawn: *in a predawn raid, troops stormed the university campus.*

pre•ex•ist•ing con•di•tion /ˈprēigˈzistiNG kənˈdiSHən/
▸ **noun** a medical condition existing at a time when new insurance is applied for. Typically the cost of its treatment is not covered by the insurance.

pre•kin•der•gar•ten /prēˈkindərˌgärtn; -ˌgärdn/
▸ **noun** daycare with some educational content for children younger than five, provided by elementary schools or preschools.

pre•launch /prēˈlônCH; -ˈlänCH/
▸ **adjective** concerning activities or conditions before the launch of a spacecraft, campaign, product, etc.

pre•loved /prēˈləvd/ (also **pre-loved**)
▸ **adjective** informal previously owned; secondhand: *preloved toys are just as appealing.*

pre•match /prēˈmæCH/
▸ **adjective** in or relating to the period before a sports match: *his prematch press conference.*

pre•mod•ern /prēˈmädərn/
▸ **adjective** anticipating the modern phase or period of something while not actually belonging to it: *our nostalgia for premodern times when natural bonds to kith and kin were unshakable continues to surface.*

pres•en•ta•tion graph•ics /ˌprezənˈtāSHən ˌgræfiks; ˌprēzen-/
▸ **noun** another term for PRESENTATION SOFTWARE.

pres•en•ta•tion soft•ware /ˌprezənˈtāSHən ˌsôftwer; ˌprēzen-/ (also **pres•en•ta•tion graph•ics** /ˌprezənˈtāSHən ˌgræfiks; ˌprēzen-/)
▸ **noun** a type of software used to create a sequence of text and graphics, and often audio and video, to accompany a speech or public presentation: *presentation software is easy to use, and even easier to abuse.*

pre•soak /prēˈsōk/
▸ **verb** [trans.] soak (something) as a preliminary process or treatment.

pre•test
▸ **noun** /ˈprēˌtest/ a preliminary test or trial.
▸ **verb** /prēˈtest/ [trans.] carry out a preliminary test or trial of: *prior to its use, the questionnaire was pretested on two groups of trainees.*

pre•text•ing /ˈprēˌtekstiNG/
▸ **noun** the practice of using a pretext to obtain personal

information from someone, usually over the telephone: *she used a combination of surveillance and pretexting to find both his work and home addresses and phone numbers.*

pre•tri•al /prē'trīəl/
▸ **adjective** in or relating to the period before a judicial trial: *a pretrial hearing.*

print queue /'print ,kyōō/
▸ **noun** Computing a series of print jobs waiting to use a printer.

pri•vate key /'prīvit 'kē/
▸ **noun** SEE PUBLIC KEY.

pro•bi•ot•ic /,prōbī'ätik/
▸ **adjective** denoting a substance that stimulates the growth of microorganisms, especially those with beneficial properties (such as those of the intestinal flora).
▸ **noun** a probiotic substance or preparation.
■ a microorganism introduced into the body for its beneficial qualities.

pro•gres•sive lens /prə'gresiv 'lenz/
▸ **noun** (usually **progressive lenses**) an eyeglass lens having a smooth transition between parts with different focal lengths, correcting for vision at all distances: *my doctor gave me a prescription for progressive lenses.*

pro•gres•sives /prə'gresivz/
▸ **plural noun** a pair of eyeglasses having progressive lenses: *progressives for use when driving, reading, or using a computer.*

PROM /präm/
▸ **noun** Computing a memory chip that can be programmed only once by the manufacturer or user.
-ORIGIN from *p(rogrammable) r(ead-)o(nly) m(emory).*

proof-of-pur•chase /ˈpro͞of əv ˈpərCHəs/
▸ **adjective** designating a feature or symbol on a product that can be removed by the buyer to prove that the product was purchased, in order to claim a rebate or refund.

pro•pel•ler-head /prəˈpelər ˌhed/
▸ **noun** informal a person who has an obsessive interest in computers or technology.

pro•sum•er /prōˈso͞omər/
▸ **noun 1** an amateur who purchases equipment with quality or features suitable for professional use: *the magazine is aimed at the prosumer who uses a $10,000 camera to make home movies of his dog.*
2 a prospective consumer who is involved in the design, manufacture, or development of a product or service: *a panel of prosumers weighed in on the plans for the new shampoo.*
■ a person who designs or produces a product for personal use or for sale: *she's a driven prosumer with one idea: to make a better-smelling toothpaste.* ■ a well-informed and proactive consumer: *prosumers read labels, sometimes obsessively.* .
–ORIGIN blend of *professional* or *producer* or *proactive* and *consumer*

pro•te•ase in•hib•i•tor /ˈprōtēˌās inˌhibitər/
▸ **noun** a substance that breaks down protease, thereby inhibiting the replication of certain cells and viruses, including HIV.

pro•te•ome /ˈprōtēˌōm/
▸ **noun** Genetics the entire complement of proteins that is or can be expressed by a cell, tissue, or organism.
–ORIGIN 1990s: a blend of *protein* and *genome*.

pro•te•om•ics /ˌprōtēˈämiks/
▶ **plural noun** [treated as sing.] the branch of molecular biology concerned with determining the proteome.
–DERIVATIVES **pro•te•om•ic** adjective

psych /sīk/ (also **psyche**)
▶ **verb** [as adj.] (**psyched**) excited and full of anticipation: *we've told him you were coming—he's really psyched.*

P2P /ˈpētəˈpē/
▶ **abbreviation** peer-to-peer, an Internet network that enables a group of users to access and copy files from each other's hard drives.

pub•cast•er /ˈpəbˌkæstər/
▶ **noun** a publically owned broadcaster: *a reality show developed for Norwegian pubcaster NRK.*

pub•lic key /ˈpəblik ˈkē/
▶ **noun** a cryptographic key that can be obtained and used by anyone to encrypt messages intended for a particular recipient, such that the encrypted messages can be deciphered only by using a second key that is known only to the recipient (called the **private key**).

puck•er•oo /ˌpəkəˈrōō/ NZ
▶ **adjective** broken; useless.
▶ **verb** [trans.] [often as adj]] (**puckerooed**) ruin or break.
–ORIGIN late 19th cent. (as a verb): from Maori *pakaru* 'broken.'

Puf•fa /ˈpəfə/ (in full **Puf•fa jack•et** /ˈpəfə ˌjækit/)
▶ **noun** Brit. trademark a type of thick padded jacket.
–ORIGIN 1990s: origin uncertain; perhaps respelling of *puffer.*

puf•ta•loon /ˌpəftə'lōōn/
> ▸ **noun** Austral. a small fried cake, spread with jam, sugar, or honey, and usually eaten hot.
> –ORIGIN late 19th cent.: origin uncertain; perhaps related to *puff*.

pull-quote /'pŏŏl ˌkwōt/
> ▸ **noun** a brief, attention-getting quotation, typically in a distinctive typeface, taken from the main text of an article and used as a subheading or as a design element.

pump /pəmp/
> ▸ **verb** [trans.] **1 (pump something out)** produce or emit something in large quantities or amounts: *carnival bands pumping out music.*
> **2 (pump something up)** informal turn up the volume of music.

purse net /'pərs ˌnet/
> ▸ **noun** a bag-shaped net with a mouth that can be drawn together with cords, for catching fish or rabbits.

push poll /'pŏŏSH ˌpōl/
> ▸ **noun** an ostensible opinion poll in which the true objective is to sway voters using loaded questions.
> –DERIVATIVES **push-poll•ing noun**

put•ta•nes•ca /ˌpŏŏtə'neskə/
> ▸ **adjective** [usually postpositive] denoting a pasta sauce typically including tomatoes, garlic, olives, and anchovies: *pasta puttanesca.*
> –ORIGIN Italian, from *puttana* 'prostitute' (the sauce is said to have been devised by prostitutes as one that could be cooked quickly between clients' visits).

PVR
> ▸ **abbreviation** personal video recorder.

Q

qaw•wal /kə'wäl/
▸ **noun** a performer of qawwali.

qaw•wa•li /kə'välē/
▸ **noun** a style of Muslim devotional music now associated particularly with Sufis in Pakistan.
-ORIGIN from Arabic *qawwāli*, from *qawwāl* 'loquacious,' also 'singer.'

Quaa•lude /'kwā,lōōd/
▸ **noun** trademark for methaqualone, a hypnotic drug used as a sedative and sleeping aid.
-ORIGIN 1960s: an invented name.

quak•ing bog /'kwākiNG 'bäg/
▸ **noun** a bog formed over water or soft mud, which shakes underfoot.

quan•tum com•put•er /'kwäntəm kəm,pyōōtər/
▸ **noun** a computer that makes use of the quantum states of subatomic particles to store information.
-DERIVATIVES **quan•tum com•put•ing noun**

quan•tum med•i•cine /'kwäntəm 'medisən/
▸ **noun** a branch of complementary medicine that uses uses low-dosage electromagnetic radiation in the treatment, diagnosis, and prevention of disease.

quoit /kwoit/
▸ **noun** Austral. informal a person's buttocks.

R

rac•er•back /'rāsər,bæk/
  ▸ **noun** [as adj.] denoting an article of clothing with a T-shaped back behind the shoulder blades to allow ease of movement in sporting activities.

ra•cial pro•fil•ing /'rāsHəl 'prōfiliNG/
  ▸ **noun** the practice of attributing criminal motives or intentions to people on the basis of their race.

Ra•el•i•an /rä'ēlēən/
  ▸ **noun** a member of an atheistic cult based on the belief that humans originated from alien scientists who came to earth in UFOs.
  ▸ **adjective** relating to the Raelians or their beliefs.
  –ORIGIN 1990s: from *Rael*, assumed name of Claude Vorilhon, French singer and journalist, author of *The Message Given to Me by Extraterrestrials* (1974).

rage /rāj/
  ▸ [with adj] **noun** an instance of aggressive behavior or violent anger caused by a stressful or frustrating situation: *desk rage* | *sports rage* | *PC rage.*

rag•ged•y-ass /'rægidē ,æs/ (also **rag•gedy-assed**)
  ▸ **adjective** [attrib.] informal shabby; miserably inadequate: *a raggedy-ass house.*
  ■ (of a person) new and inexperienced.

ram•kie /'ræmkē/
  ▸ **noun** S. African a stringed instrument resembling a guitar, formerly played by the Khoikhoi people of southern Africa.
  –ORIGIN early 19th cent.: from Afrikaans, from Nama

rangi-b, perhaps from Portuguese *rabequinha,* diminutive of *rabeca* 'fiddle.'

ranch /rænCH/ (also **ranch dress•ing** /'rænCH ˌdresiNG/)
▸ **noun** a type of thick white salad dressing made with sour cream.

ran•che•ra /rän'CHerə/
▸ **noun** a type of Mexican country music typically played with guitars and horns.
■ a ranchera tune or song.
–ORIGIN 1980s: from Spanish *cancion ranchera* 'farmers' songs.'

Rap•id Ther•mal Ex•change /'ræpid THərməl iks'CHānj/ (abbreviation: **RTX**)
▸ **noun** a system or device for cooling overheated muscles and organs by cooling blood in the palm of the hand, which then circulates throughout the body.

Ra•zor scoot•er /'rāzər ˌskōōt̲ər/
▸ **noun** trademark a type of lightweight aluminum collapsible scooter ridden by both adults and children.

RBE (also **rbe**)
▸ **abbreviation** relative biological effectiveness.

re•al•i•ty TV /rē'ælitē ˌtē'vē/
▸ **noun** television programs about real people and situations, designed to be entertaining rather than informative.

rear pro•jec•tion /'rir prə'jeksHən/ (also **rear-pro•jec•tion**)
▸ **noun** the projection of a picture onto the back of a translucent screen for viewing or for use as a background in filming.

■ an image projected in this way.
-DERIVATIVES **rear-pro•ject•ed** adjective

rea•son•a•ble wom•an stand•ard /'rēz(ə)nəbəl 'wŏŏmən ,stændərd/
▸ **noun** a guideline for determining what constitutes sexual harassment, based on suppositions about what a reasonable woman would find objectionable.

re•bal•ance /rē'bæləns/
▸ **verb** [trans.] balance again or restore the correct balance to.

re•board /rē'bôrd/
▸ **verb** [trans.] (of a passenger) board (a ship or vehicle) again.

re•book /rē'bŏŏk/
▸ **verb** [intrans.] book accommodations or a seat or ticket, etc., again: *a third of the tourists had rebooked for next year.*

re•com•bi•nase /ri'kämbi,nās; -,nāz/
▸ **noun** Biochemistry an enzyme that promotes genetic recombination.

re•com•pile /,rēkəm'pīl/
▸ **verb** [trans.] Computing compile (a program) again or differently.
-DERIVATIVES **re•com•pi•la•tion** /,rēkəmpə'lāsHən/ **noun**

re•cork /rē'kôrk/
▸ **verb** [trans.] put back or replace the cork in (a bottle of wine).

re•count /ri'kownt/
▸ **noun** an act or instance of giving an account of an event or experience.

re•cut /rē'kət/
▸ verb [trans.] remove further or different material from (a film or screenplay): *director Tony Scott is recutting several key scenes.*

re•de•pos•it /ˌrēdi'päzit/
▸ verb [trans.] deposit (something) again.

re•dis•play /ˌrēdis'plā/
▸ verb [trans.] display again or differently.

red top /'red ˌtäp/
▸ noun Brit. a tabloid newspaper.
-ORIGIN 1990s: from the red background on which the titles of certain British newspapers are printed.

re•fas•ten /rē'fæsən/
▸ verb [trans.] fasten again: *Norman stooped to refasten the padlock.*

re•fix /rē'fiks/
▸ verb [trans.] fix in position again or differently.

re•flect•ed glo•ry /ri'flektid 'glôrē/
▸ noun fame or approval achieved through association with someone else rather than through one's own efforts.

re•fold /rē'fōld/
▸ verb [trans.] fold (something) up again: *she refolded the newspaper and placed it back on the counter.*

re•found /rē'fownd/
▸ verb [trans.] found (a city or institution) again; re-establish: *Westminster was refounded as a Benedictine monastery under Mary Tudor.*
-DERIVATIVES **re•foun•da•tion** /ˌrē,fown'dāsHən/ noun

re•frame /rē'frām/
▸ **verb** [trans.] **1** place (a picture or photograph) in a new frame.
2 frame or express (words or a concept or plan) differently: *I reframed my question.*

re•gen•er•a•tive brak•ing /ri'jenərətiv 'brākiNG; ri'jenə ˌrātiv/
▸ **noun** a method of braking in which energy is extracted from the parts braked, to be stored and reused.

re•gift /rē'gift/
▸ **verb** [trans.] give (a gift one has received) to someone else: *do you think she'll regift that horrendous vase?* | [intrans.] *the survey showed that 53% of consumers plan to regift this holiday.*
▸ **noun** a gift that has been regifted: *most of my regifts are more meaningful than the usual bouquet of flowers.*
-DERIVATIVES **re•gift•er noun**

re•gime change /ri'zHēm ˌcHānj/
▸ **noun** a usually forcible change in leadership or management, as in a government or organization: *they were calling for a regime change, with or without all-out war.*

re•hire /rē'hīr/
▸ **verb** [trans.] hire (a former employee) again: *the company dismissed its workers and rehired them on a lower rate.*

re•in•flate /ˌrē-in'flāt/
▸ **verb** [trans.] inflate again.
-DERIVATIVES **re•in•flat•a•ble adjective**

re•in•hab•it /ˌrē-in'hæbit/
▸ **verb** [trans.] inhabit (a place) again.

re•in•stall /ˌrē-in'stôl/
▸ **verb** (**re•in•stalled, re•in•stall•ing**) [trans.] install again.
-DERIVATIVES **re•in•stal•la•tion** /ˌrē-instə'lāsHən/ **noun**

re•in•vade /ˌrē-in'vād/
› verb [trans.] invade again.

re•li•cense /rē'līsəns/
› verb [trans.] license again.

re•list /rē'list/
› verb [trans.] list again.

re•lock /rē'läk/
› verb [trans.] lock again.

re•pet•i•tive-mo•tion dis•or•der /ri'petətiv 'mōsHən dis ˌôrdər/
› **noun** work-related physical symptoms caused by excessive and repeated use of the upper extremities, especially when typing on a computer keyboard. Also called **repetitive injury**.

re•plas•ter /rē'plæstər/
› verb [trans.] plaster (a surface) again.

rep•li•cant /'replikənt/
› **noun** (in science fiction) a genetically engineered or artifical being created as an exact replica of a particular human being.
–ORIGIN from *replica* + *-ant*: first used in the movie *Blade Runner* (1982).

re•port /ri'pôrt/
› **noun** an employee who reports to another employee.

re•po•sa•do /ˌrepə'sädō/
› **noun** (pl. **re•po•sa•dos**) a type of tequila that has been aged in oak for between two months and a year.
–ORIGIN Spanish, literally 'rested.'

Re•pub•li•crat /ri'pəbli,kræt/ (also **re•pub•li•crat** or **Re• pub•lo•crat**)
▸ **noun** a Republican or Democrat whose political philosophy is a blend of policies and principles from both parties: *Republicrats are blurring the differences between our two parties* | [as modifier] *Republicrat senators.* ■ a member of a political faction that includes both Republicans and Democrats. ■ a conservative Democrat with Republican sympathies.
–DERIVATIVES **Re•pub•li•crat•ic** adjective
–ORIGIN blend of *Republican* and *Democrat*.

re•pur•pose /rē'pərpəs/
▸ **verb** [trans.] adapt for use in a different purpose: *they've taken a product that was originally designed for a CD-ROM and repurposed it for the Microsoft Network.*

re•qual•i•fy /rē'kwälə,fī/
▸ **verb** (**re•qual•i•fies, re•qual•i•fied, re•qual•i•fy•ing**) [intrans.] qualify again.
–DERIVATIVES **re•qual•i•fi•ca•tion** /rē,kwäləfi'kāsHən/ noun

re•rate /rē'rāt/
▸ **verb** [trans.] [often as noun] (**rerating**) rate or assess (something, especially shares or a company) again.

re•scale /rē'skāl/
▸ **verb** [trans.] change the scale of (something).

re•score /rē'skôr/
▸ **verb** [trans.] revise the score of (a piece of music).

re•sharp•en /rē'sHärpən/
▸ **verb** [trans.] sharpen (a blade or implement) again.

re•shoot /rēˈsHo͞ot/
 ▸ **verb** (past and past participle **re•shot** /rēˈsHät/) [trans.] shoot (a scene of a film) again or differently: *they had to reshoot the whole thing with another actor* | [intrans.] *the insurance was enough to allow them to reshoot or finish with a double.*
 ▸ **noun** an act of reshooting a scene of a film: *the reshoot is scheduled for Thursday.*

re•sole /rēˈsōl/
 ▸ **verb** [trans.] provide (a boot, shoe, etc.) with a new sole.

re•spec•i•fy /rēˈspesəˌfī/
 ▸ **verb** (**re•spec•i•fies, re•spec•i•fied, re•spec•i•fy•ing**) [trans.] specify again.

rest area /ˈrest ˌerēə/
 ▸ **noun** an area at the side of a road where vehicles may pull off the road and stop.

re•strain•ing or•der /riˈstrāniNG ˌôrdər/
 ▸ **noun** a temporary court order issued to prohibit an individual from carrying out a particular action, especially approaching or contacting a specified person.

re•sus•pend /ˌrēsəˈspend/
 ▸ **verb** [trans.] place (cells or particles) in suspension in a fluid again.
 –DERIVATIVES **re•sus•pen•sion** /ˌrēsəˈspensHən/ **noun**

re•tail park /ˈrētāl ˌpärk/
 ▸ **noun** a shopping development situated outside a town or city, typically containing a number of large chain stores.

re•tail ther•a•py /ˈrētāl ˌTHerəpē/
 ▸ **noun** humorous the practice of shopping in order to make oneself feel happier.

re•test /rē'test/
> **verb** [trans.] test (someone or something) again.
> **noun** an act of retesting someone or something.

re•thatch /rē'THæCH/
> **verb** [trans.] thatch (a roof or building) again.

re•tight•en /re'tītn/
> **verb** [trans.] tighten again.

Ret•in-A /'retn 'ā/
> **noun** Trademark a brand of tretinoin, used in the topical treatment of acne and to reduce wrinkles.

ret•i•no•ic ac•id /'retn'ō-ik 'æsid/
> **noun** a carboxylic acid, $C_{19}H_{27}COOH$, obtained from retinol by oxidation and used in ointments to treat acne.
-ORIGIN 1970s: from *retina*.

re•verse split /ri'vərs 'split/
> **noun** reduction in the number of a company's traded shares that results in an increase in the par value or earnings per share.

rhyth•mic gym•nas•tics /'riTHmik jim'næstiks/
> **plural noun** [usually treated as sing.] a form of gymnastics emphasizing dancelike rhythmic routines, typically accentuated by the use of ribbons or hoops.
-DERIVATIVES **rhyth•mic gym•nast** /'riTHmik 'jim,næst; -nəst/ **noun**

RICE
> **acronym** rest, ice, compression, and elevation (treatment method for bruises, strains, and sprains).

rice burn•er /'rīs ,bərnər/
> **noun** informal, derogatory a Japanese motorcycle.

rid•er /ˈrīdər/
▸ **noun** a supplementary clause in a performer's contract specifying such things as the provision of food and drink.

rid•gy-didge /ˈrijē ˌdij/
▸ **adjective** Austral. informal genuine, original, or good: *a true-blue ridgy-didge Aussie.*
-ORIGIN 1950s: from *ridge*, an old slang term meaning 'gold' or 'gold coin.'

right-click /ˈrīt ˈklik/
▸ **verb** [intrans.] Computing depress the right-hand button on a mouse. ◼ [trans.] click on a link or other screen object in this way: *right-click a graphic and choose Resize.*
-DERIVATIVES **right-click noun; adjective:** *right-click features.*

right stuff /ˈrīt ˈstəf/
▸ **phrase** (in full **the right stuff**) the necessary qualities for a given task or job: *he had the right stuff to enter this business.*

right-to-know /ˈrīt tə ˈnō/
▸ **adjective** of or pertaining to laws or policies that make certain government or company records available to any individual who can demonstrate a right or need to know their contents.

rip /rip/
▸ **verb** (**ripped, rip•ping**) [trans.] Computing use a program to copy (a sound sequence on a compact disc) on to a computer's hard drive.

rip•per /ˈripər/
▸ **adjective** informal, chiefly Austral. particularly good; excellent: *everyone had a ripper time | this record still sounds ripper.*

road war•ri•or /'rōd ˌwôrēər/
▸ **noun** informal a person who travels often as part of their job and does work at the same time.

roam•ing /'rōmiNG/
▸ **noun** [usually as modifier] the use of a cell phone outside of its local area: *the roaming charges were too high.*

rock /räk/
▸ see LIKE A SHAG ON A ROCK.

roll•ing /'rōliNG/
▸ **adjective** steady and continuous: *a rolling program of reforms* | *a rolling news service.*

Rom /rōm/
▸ **noun** (pl. **Ro•ma** /'rōmə/) a gypsy, especially a man.
■ [as plural noun] (**Roma**) gypsy people collectively.
-ORIGIN mid 19th cent.: abbreviation of *Romany*, the gypsy language.

rom•com /'rämˌkäm/
▸ **noun** informal (in movies or television) a romantic comedy.

ROM•ve•lope /'rämvəˌlōp/ (also **rom•ve•lope**)
▸ **noun** Computing a protective envelope or sleeve, usually made of cardboard, used to package or mail a compact disc: *you can have one of these ROMvelopes to protect your CD.*
-ORIGIN blend of *(CD-)ROM* and *(en)velope.*

rort /rôrt/
▸ **noun** informal Austral. dated a wild party.
▸ **verb** [trans.] manipulate (a ballot or records) fraudulently; rig. ■ work (a system) to obtain the greatest benefit while remaining within the letter of the law.

rose cam•pion /'rōz ˌkæmpēən/
▸ **noun** a Eurasian herbaceous plant of the pink family (genus *Lychnis* or *Agrostemma*) with a woolly stem and leaves and pink flowers.

rösti /'rästē/
▸ **noun** (pl. same) a Swiss dish of grated potatoes formed into a small flat cake and fried.
■ a flat cake of grated potato: *place four of the rösti in the pan.*
–ORIGIN 1950s: from Swiss German.

Roth IRA /'rôTH ˌī-är'ā; 'īrə/
▸ **noun** an individual retirement account on which taxes are paid at the time of deposit, yielding tax-free withdrawals.

rough as bags /'rəf əz 'bægz/
▸ **phrase** Austral./NZ informal lacking refinement; coarse.

rough•ie /'rəfē/
▸ **noun** Austral./NZ **1** an unfair or unreasonable act.
2 an outsider in a horse race.

rout•ing code /'rōōtiNG ˌkōd; 'rowtiNG/
▸ **noun** any of various codes used to direct data, documents, or merchandise, including:
■ the magnetically encoded numbers on a check. ■ a numeric code that directs telephone calls or Internet traffic.

rpt
▸ **abbreviation** report.

RTFM
▸ **abbreviation** Computing informal, coarse read the fucking manual (used especially in e-mail in reply to a question whose answer is patently obvious).

RTX
▸ **abbreviation** Rapid Thermal Exchange.

rub•ber john•ny /'rəbər 'jänē/
▸ **noun** another term for JOHNNY.

Rube Gold•berg /'rōob 'gōldbərg/
▸ **adjective** ingeniously or unnecessarily complicated in design or construction: *a Rube Goldberg machine.*
-ORIGIN 1950s: from the name of *Reuben Goldberg* (1883–1970), an American cartoonist whose illustrations often depicted devices with humorously complicated designs.

run a mile /'rən ə 'mīl/
▸ **verb phrase** informal used to show that one is frightened by or averse to something: *if someone proposed to me, I'd probably run a mile.*

run-time /'rən ˌtīm/ Computing
▸ **noun** the length of time a program takes to run.
■ the time at which the program is run. ■ a cut-down version of a program that can be run but not changed: *you can distribute the run-time to your colleagues.*
▸ **adjective** (of software) in a reduced version that can be run but not changed.

RVer /'är'vēər/
▸ **noun** a user of a recreational vehicle.

S

safe haven /'sāf 'hāvən/
▸ **noun 1** temporary refuge given to asylum seekers. ■ a country in which this is provided.
2 another term for safe room.

safe house /'sāf 'hows/
▸ **noun** a temporary refuge for victims of domestic abuse: *all contact with residents of the safe house is through this office; no one is given the direct phone number.*

safe room /'sāf 'ro͞om; 'ro͝om/
▸ **noun** a room in a house or other building that is invulnerable to attack or intrusion, from which security operations can be directed.

sa•hu•kar /ˌsəho͞o'kär/
▸ **noun** Indian a moneylender.
■ a banker.
–ORIGIN late 18th cent.: Hindi *sāhūkār* 'great merchant.'

sa•lade ni•çoise /ˌsæläd nē'swäz/
▸ **noun** (pl. **sa•lades ni•çoises** pronounced same.) a salad made typically from hard-boiled eggs, tuna, black olives, and tomatoes.
–ORIGIN French, 'salad from Nice.'

sa•lute the judge /sə'lo͞ot T͟Hə 'jəj/
▸ **phrase** Australian informal (of a horse) win a race.

same-store sales /'sām 'stôr ˌsālz/
▸ **noun** a figure used to determine what amount of sales growth is attributable to new store openings, based on sales made by stores that have been open more than one year.

sa•mi•ti /'sæmitē/
▸ noun (pl. **sa•mi•tis**) Indian a committee, society, or association.
-ORIGIN 1930s: Sanskrit, 'meeting, committee.'

sam•mie /'sæmē/
▸ noun Australian/NZ informal a sandwich.
-ORIGIN 1970s: representing a pronunciation of the first syllable of *sandwich*, modified by the following *w*, + *-ie*.

sao•la /'sowlə/
▸ noun a small two-horned mammal discovered in Vietnam in 1992, with similarities to both antelopes and oxen.
•*Pseudoryx nghetinhensis*.
-ORIGIN 1990s: a local name, literally 'spindle horn.'

sat•el•lite tel•e•vi•sion /'sætl̩,īt 'telə,viZHən/
▸ noun television broadcasting using a satellite to relay signals to appropriately equipped customers in a particular area.

save /sāv/
▸ noun Computing an act of saving data to a storage location, usually the hard drive.

sca•mor•za /skə'môrtsə/
▸ noun a mild white Italian cheese made from cow's or buffalo's milk, produced in small gourd-shaped balls.
-ORIGIN 1930s: Italian, from *scamozzare* 'cut off.'

scan•ty /'skæntē/
▸ plural noun (**scanties**) informal women's skimpy underwear.

Scheng•en a•gree•ment /'SHeNGən ə,grēmənt/
▸ an intergovernmental agreement on the relaxation of

border controls between participating European countries, the first version of which was signed in Schengen, Luxembourg, in June 1985 by France, West Germany, Belgium, the Netherlands, and Luxembourg, and ratified (in a revised form) in 1995. The ratified agreement was incorporated into the European Union in 1999 and the agreement was widened to include non-EU members of a similar Nordic union. Member countries now comprise Austria, Belgium, Denmark, France, Finland, Germany, Greece, Iceland, Italy, Luxembourg, the Netherlands, Norway, Portugal, Spain, and Sweden.

schiz•an•dra /skit'sændrə/
  ▸ **noun** a Chinese herb whose berries are credited with various stimulant or medicinal properties.
  •*Schisandra chinensis.*
  -ORIGIN mid 19th cent.: modern Latin *Schisandra,* formed as *schizo-* + Greek *andr-, anēr* man, on account of the divided stamens.

schli•ma•zel /sHlə'mäzəl/ (also **schle•ma•zel**)
  ▸ **noun** informal a consistently unlucky or accident-prone person.
  -ORIGIN Yiddish, from Middle High German *slim* 'crooked' + Hebrew *mazzāl* 'luck.'

schmo /sHmō/ (also **shmo**)
  ▸ **noun** (pl. **schmoes**) informal (also **Joe Schmo** /'jō 'sHmō/) a hypothetical ordinary man: *hanging with the schmoes at the corner bar | a lot of Joe Schmoes make it to the big leagues.*
  -ORIGIN 1940s: alteration of *schmuck.*

scis•sor•bill /'sizər,bil/
  ▸ **noun** informal an incompetent or objectionable person.

scoosh /skōōsH/ (also **skoosh**) Scottish
  ▸ **verb** [trans.] squirt or splash (liquid).

▸**noun** a splash or squirt of liquid.
■ a carbonated drink.
–ORIGIN imitative.

scrap•book /'skræp,bŏŏk/
▸**verb** [intrans.] [usually as noun] (**scrapbooking**) to create scrapbooks as a hobby: *that site has all the supplies you need for scrapbooking.*
–DERIVATIVES **scrap•book•er** noun

scrat•chi•ti /skræ'chētē/
▸**plural noun** [treated as sing. or pl.] graffiti that is scratched or etched onto a surface, usually glass: *names immortalized with scratchiti on the subway car window.*
–ORIGIN blend of *scratch* and *graffiti.*

scream•er /'skrēmər/
▸see TWO-POT SCREAMER.

screen•ag•er /'skrēn,ājər/
▸**noun** informal a person in their teens or twenties who has an aptitude for computers and the Internet.
–ORIGIN 1990s: blend of *screen* and *teenager.*

script kid•die /'skript ,kidē/
▸**noun** informal, derogatory a person who uses existing computer scripts or codes to hack into computers, lacking the expertise to write their own.

scunge /skənj/
▸**noun** Australian/NZ informal dirt; scum: *this glass has scunge on it.*
■ a person who is stingy with money; a scrounger.

sec•ond growth /'sekənd 'grōTH/
▸ **noun 1** woodland growth that replaces harvested or burned virgin forest.

2 a wine considered to be the second-best in quality compared to the first growth.

sec•ond•hand speech /'sekən(d),hænd 'spēCH/
▸ **noun** conversation on a cell phone that is overheard by people nearby: *I was alternately amused and annoyed by the secondhand speech in the waiting room.*

se•cret shop•per /'sēkrit 'SHäpər/
▸ **noun** a person employed by a manufacturer or retailer to pose as a shopper in order to evaluate the quality of customer service.

sec•tion /'sekSHən/
▸ **noun** NZ a building plot.

se•cure serv•er /si'kyo͝or 'sərvər/
▸ **noun** an Internet server that encrypts confidential information supplied by visitors to Web pages.

Seg•way /'seg,wā/
▸ **noun** trademark a two-wheeled motorized personal vehicle consisting of a platform for the feet mounted above an axle and an upright post surmounted by handles.

se•lec•tion /sə'lekSHən/
▸ **noun** Australian/NZ historical the action of choosing and acquiring plots of land for small farming on terms favorable to the buyer.

self-de•struc•tive /'self də'strəktiv/
▸ **adjective** destroying or causing harm to oneself.
–DERIVATIVES **self-de•struc•tive•ly** adverb

self-stick /'self 'stik/
▸ **adjective** coated with an adhesive on one side for ready application to a surface: *peel off the self-stick backing and attach to either side.*

sell•down /'sel,down/
▸ noun Australian/NZ the widespread selling of shares, resulting in falling prices.

sen•si•tiv•i•ty train•ing /sensi'tivitē ,trāniNG/
▸ noun training intended to sensitize people to their attitudes and behaviors that may unwittingly cause offense to others, especially members of various minorities.

se•quence /'sēkwəns/
▸ verb play or record (music) with a sequencer.

se•ri•al port /'sirēəl 'pôrt/
▸ noun a connector for a device that sends one bit at a time.

serv•ice e•con•o•my /'sərvis i,känəmē/
▸ noun an economy or the sector of an economy that is based on trade in services.

set /set/
▸ verb [trans.] (**set•ted, set•ting**) Brit. group (pupils or students) in sets according to ability.

set play /'set ,plā/
▸ noun Sports a prearranged maneuver carried out from a restart or after a time out by the team who has the advantage.

set•ting /'setiNG/
▸ noun the scenery and stage furniture used in a play or film.

sex in•dus•try /'seks ,indəstrē/
▸ noun (**the sex industry**) used euphemistically to refer to prostitution.

sex work•er /'sɛks 'wərkər/
▸ **noun** used euphemistically to refer to a prostitute or stripper.

shad•ow e•con•o•my /'ʃædō iˌkänəmē/
▸ **noun** illicit economic activity existing alongside a country's official economy, e.g., black market transactions and undeclared work.

shag /ʃæg/
▸ see LIKE A SHAG ON A ROCK.

shah•toosh /ʃä'tōōʃ/
▸ **noun** high-quality wool from the neck hair of the Himalayan ibex. ■ a shawl made from this.

shake /ʃāk/
▸ **noun** a kind of rough wooden shingle, used especially on rustic buildings: *cedar shakes.*

shak•en ba•by syn•drome /'ʃākən 'bābē ˌsindrōm/
▸ **noun** injury to a baby caused by being shaken violently and repeatedly. Shaking can cause swelling of the brain, internal bleeding, detached retinas leading to blindness, mental retardation, and death.

shape-mem•o•ry /'ʃāp ˌmem(ə)rē/
▸ **noun** the ability of a material to be deformed and then returned to its original shape when stimulated, as by heat.

shed•load /'ʃedˌlōd/
▸ **noun** Brit. informal a large amount or number: *he bought a shedload of toys for the kids at Christmas.*
  -ORIGIN 1990s: from *shed* + *load*; perhaps euphemistic after *shitload.*

shelf /ʃelf/ Australian/NZ informal
▸ **noun** (pl. **shelfs**) an informer.

▸**verb** [trans.] inform on (someone).

-ORIGIN early 20th cent. (as a noun): probably from the phrase *on the shelf* 'out of the way.'

shelf-sta•ble /'SHelf ˌstābəl/
▸**adjective** able to survive long periods on store or home shelves without spoiling: *a growing number of dairy-based beverages are shelf-stable and can be stored in the pantry rather than the refrigerator.*

shel•tered work•shop /'SHeltərd 'wərkˌSHäp/
▸ **noun** a supervised workplace for physically disabled or mentally handicapped adults.

she's ap•ples /ˌSHēz 'æpəlz/
▸ **phrase** Australian/NZ informal used to indicate that everything is in good order and there is nothing to worry about: *'Is the fire safe?' 'Yeah, she's apples.'*

-ORIGIN from *apples and spice* or *apples and rice*, rhyming slang for 'nice.'

Shin•ner /'SHinər/
▸ **noun** Irish informal, chiefly derogatory a member or supporter of Sinn Fein.

shi•so /'SHēsō/
▸ **noun** the Japanese name for perilla, a culinary herb.

shit /SHit/ vulgar slang
▸ **verb** (past and past participle **shit•ted** or **shit** or **shat**; **shit•ting**) [trans.] tease or try to deceive (someone).
▸ **noun** (**the shits**) diarrhea.

shit•can /'SHitˌkæn/
▸ **verb** (**shit•canned, shit•can•ning**) vulgar slang [trans.] throw (something) away: *rip up those pictures and shitcan the negatives.*

■ discard or reject (someone or something): *it's hard to shitcan someone who keeps winning writing awards.*

shit•load /'sHit,lōd/
▸ **noun** vulgar slang a large amount or number: *I have a shit-load of work to do this week.*
-ORIGIN 1990s: from *shit* + *load.*

shock cord /'sHäk ,kôrd/
▸ **noun** a bungee cord or other elastic cord with hooks at either end.

shoog•ly /'sHōōglē/
▸ **adjective** Scottish unsteady; wobbly.
-ORIGIN Middle English: probably of imitative origin.

shoot•ist /'sHōōtist/
▸ **noun** informal a person who shoots, especially a marksman.
-ORIGIN mid 19th cent.: from *shoot* + *-ist.*

shop•grift•ing /'sHäp,griftiNG/
▸ **noun** the practice of buying an item, using it, and then returning it for a full refund.

short-hand•ed /'sHôrt ,hændid/
▸ **adjective** Ice Hockey (of a goal) scored by a team playing with fewer players on the ice than their opponent. ■ (of a situation) occurring while or because a team has fewer than six players on the ice.
▸ **adverb** with fewer staff, crew, or players than usual: *because two cashiers were out with the flu, we worked short-handed.*

show time /'sHō ,tīm/
▸ **noun** used to signal the beginning of an event or process that is expected to be dramatic, decisive, or otherwise significant: *It's show time! Let's go!*

shrap•nel /'sHræpnəl/
> **noun** informal small change: *"What say we pick up a couple of beers?" "Sure. Want some shrapnel?"*

shrug /sHrəg/
> **noun** a woman's close-fitting cardigan or jacket, cut short at the front and back so that only the arms and shoulders are covered.

shu•mai /'sHOO,mī/
> **noun** small steamed dumplings, typically stuffed with seafood and vegetables.

sick /sik/
> **adjective** informal excellent: *I'm listening to a sick new remix.*

sight•hound /'sīt,hownd/
> **noun** a hound originally bred to hunt independently from humans, such as a greyhound or a whippet.

SIM /sim/ (also **SIM card**)
> **noun** a smart card inside a cell phone, carrying an identification number unique to the owner, storing personal data, and preventing operation if removed.
> -ORIGIN 1980s: acronym from *subscriber identification module*.

si•mul•se•quel•ing /'sīməl,sēkwəliNG/
> **noun** the practice of writing or filming two or more sequels simultaneously: *the simulsequeling of popular movies usually pays off because of reduced production costs.*
> -ORIGIN blend of *simultaneous* and *sequel*.

sin•gle cur•ren•cy /'siNGgəl 'kərənsē/
> **noun** a currency used by all the members of an economic federation.

■ (also **single European currency**) the currency (the euro) that replaced the national currencies of twelve member states of the European Union in 2002.

sin•gle nu•cle•o•tide pol•y•mor•phism /ˈsiNGgəl ˈn(y)o͞o-klēə,tīd ,pälēˈmôrfizəm/
▸ **noun** a variation in a single base pair in a DNA sequence.

sit•u•a•tion•ism /,siCHo͞oˈāSHə,nizəm/
▸ **noun** a revolutionary political theory that regards modern industrial society as being inevitably oppressive and exploitative.
–DERIVATIVES **sit•u•a•tion•ist** noun & adjective

size•ism /ˈsīzizəm/
▸ **noun** prejudice or discrimination on the grounds of a person's size: *requiring large passengers to buy two seats is pure sizeism.*
–DERIVATIVES **size•ist** adjective

skank /skæNGk/
▸ **verb** [trans.] informal swindle or deceive: *they made a tidy sum skanking the tourists.*
■ obtain by deception or theft: *I skanked the poster off some wall.*

skell /skel/
▸ **noun** informal (in New York) a tramp or homeless person.
–ORIGIN 1980s: perhaps a shortening of *skeleton.*

skim•mel /ˈskiməl/ (also **schim•mel** /ˈskiməl/)
▸ **noun** S. African a roan or dapple-grey horse.
–ORIGIN mid 19th cent.: Afrikaans, from Dutch *schimmel* 'mildew, mottled, grey horse.'

skim•ming /ˈskimiNG/
▸ **noun** the fraudulent copying of credit or debit card details with a card swipe or other device.

skin /skin/
▸ **noun** Computing a customized graphic user interface for an application or operating system.

skin•ner /ˈskinər/
▸ **noun** Horse Racing, Australian/NZ informal a horse that wins a race at very long odds.

skof /skäf/
▸ **noun** S. African **1** a period of work; a shift.
2 a stage of a journey.
-ORIGIN late 18th cent. (in sense 2): from Afrikaans, from Dutch *schoft*.

skoosh /sko͞osh/
▸ **verb** variant spelling of SCOOSH.

SKU /skyo͞o/
▸ **abbreviation** stock-keeping unit; a bar-encoded number that uniquely identifies a retail product.

slam /slæm/
▸ **verb** (**slammed, slam•ming**) [trans.] **1** short for SLAM-DANCE.
2 [usually as noun **slamming**] (of a telephone company) take over the account of (a telephone customer) without their permission.

sling /sliNG/ Australian/NZ informal
▸ **noun** a bribe or gratuity.
▸ **verb** (past and past participle **slung**) [intrans.] pay a bribe or gratuity.

SLV
▸ **abbreviation** standard launch vehicle.

small screen /ˈsmôl ˈskrēn/
▸ **noun** (in full **the small screen**) television as a medium:

*he's a wonderful actor; his career certainly won't be limited
to the small screen.*

small•goods /'smôl,gŏŏdz/
▸ **plural noun** Australian/NZ cooked meats and meat products.

smart card /'smärt ,kärd/
▸ **noun** a plastic card with a built-in microprocessor, used
typically to perform financial transactions: *you can use
your smart card at any store on campus.*

smart dust /'smärt ,dəst/
▸ **noun** collection of microelectromechanical systems
forming a simple computer in a container light enough
to remain suspended in air, used mainly for information gathering in environments that are hostile to life.

smart mob /'smärt ,mäb/
▸ **noun** a group of people who assemble, move, or act collectively by using cell phones or other wireless devices
to communicate: *smart mobs, moving from party to party
with each new reported celebrity sighting.*

smart su•ture /'smärt ,sŏŏcHər/
▸ **noun** a surgical suture made of biodegradable plastic
that ties itself into a knot on the basis of its shape-
memory.

smash-mouth /'smæsH ,mowTH/
▸ **adjective** Sports (of a style of play) aggressive and con-
frontational.

SME
▸ **abbreviation** small to medium-sized enterprise, a company with no more than 500 employees.

smoke•eas•y /ˈsmōkˌēzē/ (also **smoke-eas•y**)
▸ **noun** (plural **smoke•eas•ies**) a private club, bar, or other place where smokers gather to avoid anti-smoking laws: *after work we sometimes light up at a smokeeasy in the neighborhood.*
-ORIGIN on the pattern of *speakeasy*.

smok•ing /ˈsmōkiNG/
▸ **adjective** (often **smok•in'** /ˈsmōkin/) informal lively and exciting: *he claimed the band would be smokin' but they were lame.*

SMPTE
▸ **abbreviation** Society of Television and Motion Picture Engineers (used to denote a time coding system for synchronizing video and audiotapes).

SMS
▸ **abbreviation** Short Message (or Messaging) Service, a system that enables cell phone users to send and receive text messages.

snack•ette /snæˈket/
▸ **noun** a very small amount of food.

snag /snæg/
▸ **noun** Australian/NZ informal a sausage.

snake•board /ˈsnākˌbôrd/
▸ **noun** trademark a type of skateboard consisting of two footplates joined by a bar, allowing for greater speed and maneuverability than with a standard skateboard.
-DERIVATIVES **snake•board•er** noun; **snake•board•ing** noun
-ORIGIN 1990s: blend of *snake* and *skateboard*.

snake•head /'snāk,hed/
> ▸ **noun** a member of a Chinese criminal network chiefly engaged in smuggling illegal immigrants.
> -ORIGIN translation of Chinese *shetou*.

snak•y /'snākē/ (also **snak•ey**)
> ▸ **adjective** (**snak•i•er, snak•i•est**) Australian/NZ informal angry; irritable: *what are you snaky about?*
> -DERIVATIVES **snak•i•ly** adverb; **snak•i•ness** noun

snert /snərt/
> ▸ **noun** Computing informal a participant in an Internet chat room who acts in a rude, annoying, or juvenile manner: *I could tell he was a snert from his sarcastic comments.* ◾ a person whose online posts or e-mails are annoying to others: *do you ever get unsolicited messages from snerts?*
> -ORIGIN of uncertain origin, possibly an acronym from *snot-nosed egotistical rude twit* (or *teenager*).

snip /snip/
> ▸ **noun** a single nucleotide polymorphism.

SNP
> ▸ **abbreviation** single nucleotide polymorphism.

so /sō/
> ▸ **adverb** informal used to emphasize a clause or negative statement: *that's so not fair | you are so going to regret this.*

so•ba /'sōbə/
> ▸ **noun** thin buckwheat noodles, used in Japanese cooking.

soc•cer mom /'säkər ,mäm/
> ▸ **noun** informal a middle-class suburban housewife, typically having children who play soccer.

so•cial pro•mo•tion /'sōSHəl prə'mōSHən/
▸ **noun** the practice of promoting a child to the next grade level regardless of skill mastery in the belief that it will encourage self-esteem.

soft land•ing /'sôft 'lændiNG/
▸ **noun** the slowing down of economic growth at an acceptable degree relative to inflation and unemployment.

so•go•sho•sha /ˌsōgə'sōSHə/
▸ **noun** (in Japan) a general trading company involved in import and export.

SOHO /'sō,hō/
▸ **adjective** relating to a market for relatively inexpensive consumer electronics used by individuals and small companies.
–ORIGIN 1990s: acronym from *small office home office*.

son•of•a•bitch /'sənəvə,biCH/
▸ **noun** non-standard spelling of **son of a bitch**, used in representing informal speech.

sor•ta•tion /sôr'tāSHən/
▸ **noun** the process of sorting or its result.

soy•milk /'soi,milk/
▸ **noun** a beverage with the approximate color and consistency of milk, made from cooked soybeans and used as a nondairy milk substitute.

spade /spād/
▸ **noun** [as modifier] shaped like a spade: *a spade bit*.

spa•gy•ric /spə'jirik/ (archaic or literary)
▸ **adjective** relating to alchemy.
▸ **noun** an alchemist.

-ORIGIN late 16th cent.: modern Latin *spagiricus*, used and probably invented by Paracelsus.

speech rec•og•ni•tion /'spēCH ,rekəg,nisHən/
▸ **noun** the process of enabling a computer to identify and respond to the sounds produced in human speech.

speed bag /'spēd ,bæg/
▸ **noun** a small punching bag used by boxers for practicing quick punches.

speed di•al /'spēd ,dī(ə)l/
▸ **noun** a function on some telephones that allows numbers to be entered into a memory and dialed with the push of a single button.
▸**verb** (**speed-dial**) [trans.] dial (a telephone number) by pressing a single button that recalls the number from a memory.

spi•der /'spīdər/
▸ **noun 1** a long-legged rest for a billiard cue that can be placed over a ball without touching it.
2 Computing a crawler; a program that searches the Internet, typically in order to create an index of data.

spin•mei•ster /'spin,mīster/
▸ **noun** informal an accomplished or politically powerful spin doctor.
-ORIGIN 1990s: from *spin* + *-meister*.

spokes•mod•el /'spōks,mädl/
▸ **noun** informal an attractive, elegant, and stylishly dressed person who appears in advertising.

spoon /spo͞on/
▸ **verb** (of two people) lie close together sideways and front to back with bent knees, so as to fit together like spoons.

SSL
▸ **abbreviation** Secure Sockets Layer, a computing protocol that ensures the security of data sent via the Internet by using encryption.

stab•bing /'stæbiNG/
▸ **noun** an act or instance of wounding or killing someone with a knife: *the fatal stabbings of four women.*

stage-div•ing /'stāj ˌdīviNG/
▸ **noun** the practice (typically among audience members) of jumping from the stage at a rock concert or other event to be caught and carried aloft by the crowd below.
–DERIVATIVES **stage-dive** verb; **stage-div•er** noun

stained-glass ceil•ing /'stānd ˌglæs 'sēliNG/
▸ **noun** [usually in sing] **1** an unofficially acknowledged barrier faced by women who want to enter or be promoted within the clergy: *a stained-glass ceiling prevents more women from becoming rabbis.*
2 a discriminatory barrier that prevents a person from advancing in any field because of religious beliefs: *Roman-Catholic candidates are often at a disadvantage because of a stained-glass ceiling.*
–ORIGIN on the pattern of *glass ceiling.*

stair•climb•er /'ster,klīmər/
▸ **noun** an exercise machine on which the user simulates the action of climbing a staircase.

stake•hold•er pen•sion /'stāk,hōldər ˌpensHən/
▸ **noun** (in the UK) a pension plan, intended primarily for those who do not belong to a company pension scheme or who are self-employed, which invests the money a person saves and uses the fund on retirement to buy a pension from a pension provider.

stalk•er•az•zi /ˌstôkəˈrätsē/
▸ **plural noun** photojournalists who follow celebrities closely and persistently with the intention of obtaining sensational pictures.

stand•by /ˈstæn(d)ˌbī/
▸ **noun** (pl. **stand•bys**) an operational mode of an electrical appliance in which the power is switched on but the appliance is not actually functioning.

stat•in /ˈstætn̩/
▸ **noun** Medicine any of a group of drugs that act to reduce levels of cholesterol in the blood.
–ORIGIN 1980s: from *stat-* + *in*.

sta•tion hand /ˈstāSHən ˌhænd/
▸ **noun** Australian/NZ a worker on a large sheep or cattle farm.

sta•tus bar /ˈstætəs ˌbär; ˈstātəs/
▸ **noun** Computing a horizontal bar, typically at the bottom of the screen or window, showing information about a document being edited or the currently active program.

St Clem•ents /ˈsānt ˈklemənts/
▸ **noun** a non-alcoholic cocktail of orange juice mixed with lemonade or bitter lemon.
–ORIGIN 1980s: the name of a London church, with reference to the first line of the children's song *Oranges and lemons, say the bells of St Clements*.

stench war•fare /ˈstenCH ˌwôrfer/
▸ **noun** the use of highly offensive odors to sicken, immobilize, or drive away an enemy: *they are hoping to win a big contract for their innovations in stench warfare.*

stick•y /ˈstikē/
▸ **adjective** (**stick•i•er**, **stick•i•est**) informal (of a Web site)

attracting a long visit or repeat visits from users: *experts measure the attractiveness of pages by how sticky they are.*

sting•a•ree /ˌstiNGə'rē/
▸ **noun** US & Australian/NZ informal any stingray.

sto•cious /'stōSHəs/
▸ **adjective** Irish informal drunk; intoxicated.
–ORIGIN 1930s: of unknown origin.

stock•feed /'stäk,fēd/
▸ **noun** food for livestock.

stock swap /'stäk ,swäp/
▸ **noun 1** acquisition of a company in which payment consists of stock in the buying company.
2 a means of exercising stock options in which shares already owned are traded for a greater number of shares at the exercise price.

sto•len gen•er•a•tion /'stōlən ,jenə'rāSHən/
▸ **noun** Australian the Aboriginal people forcibly removed from their families as children between the 1900s and the 1960s, to be brought up by white foster families or in institutions.

stom•pie /'stämpē/
▸ **noun** (pl. **stom•pies**) S. African informal a cigarette butt.

stoo•shie /'sto͞oSHē/ (also **stu•shie**)
▸ **noun** Scottish informal a row or fracas.
–ORIGIN early 19th cent.: of unknown origin.

storm•ing /'stôrmiNG/
▸ **adjective** excellent: *I think this is a storming book—I don't know why she didn't like it.*

sto•ry /'stôrē/
▶ noun (pl. **sto•ries**) 1 (**the story**) informal the state of affairs; the facts about the present situation: *What's the story on this man? Is he from around here?*
2 the commercial prospects or circumstances of a particular company: *profitable businesses with solid stories.*

strange /strānj/
▶ adjective Physics having a non-zero value for strangeness, one of the six values of quark.

stream•ing /'strēmiNG/
▶ noun a method of relaying data (especially video and audio material) over a computer network as a steady continuous stream.

street-leg•al /'strēt ,lēgəl/
▶ adjective (of a vehicle) meeting all legal requirements for use on ordinary roads.

strep throat /'strep 'THrōt/
▶ noun a sore throat with fever caused by streptococcal infection.

strife /strīf/
▶ noun Australian/NZ trouble or difficulty of any kind.

string•er /'striNGər/
▶ noun 1 [in combination] a reserve sports player holding a specified position in an order of preference: *six of the team's 24 first-stringers are Canadian.*
2 a chain with hooks on which caught fish are strung.

stub•by /'stəbē/
▶ noun (pl. **stub•bies**) Australian/NZ informal (**Stubbies**) trademark a pair of brief men's shorts.

stud•muf•fin /'stəd,məfin/
▸ **noun** informal a man perceived as sexually attractive, typically one with well-developed muscles.

sub•sense /'səb ,sens/
▸ **noun** a subsidiary sense of a word defined in a dictionary.

sub•type /'səb,tīp/
▸ **noun** a secondary or subordinate type.
■ a subdivision of a type of microorganism.

su•i•cide gene /'sōoisīd ,jēn/
▸ **noun** an introduced gene that causes a tumor cell to produce an enzyme that will attract a lethal drug.

su•ma•trip•tan /'sōomə,triptən/
▸ **noun** a serotonin-agonist drug used for the acute treatment of migraine.

sun•down•er /'sən,downər/
▸ **noun** Australian/NZ informal, dated a tramp arriving at a sheep station in the evening under the pretense of seeking work, so as to obtain food and shelter.

sun•nies /'sənēz/
▸ **plural noun** Australian/NZ informal sunglasses.

su•per•fund /'sōopər,fənd/
▸ **noun** a fund established to finance a long-term, expensive project.
■ **(Superfund)** a US federal government program designed to fund the cleanup of toxic wastes: *billions have been spent on Superfund since 1980.*

su•pe•ri•or plan•et /sə'pirēər ,plænit/
▸ **noun** Astronomy any of the planets Mars, Jupiter, Saturn, Uranus, Neptune, and Pluto, whose orbits are further from the sun than the earth's.

su•per•size /'so͞opər,sīz/
▸ **verb** [trans.] produce or serve something in a larger size: *click here to supersize the picture.*
▸ **adjective** larger than normal: *this supersize clock has black 2-inch numbers on white face in a simple lightweight black frame.*

su•per•soap /'so͞opər ,sōp/
▸ **noun** a soap that contains a bactericide.

su•per•sta•tion /'so͞opər,stāsHən/
▸ **noun** a television station using satellite technology to broadcast over a very large area, especially an entire continent.

sup•port /sə'pôrt/
▸ **noun** evidence that serves to corroborate something: *the study provides support for both theories.*

sup•port sys•tem /sə'pôrt ,sistəm/
▸ **noun** a group of people who are available to support one another emotionally, socially, and sometimes financially: *a support system for gay teens.*

swag /swæg/
▸ **noun** Australian/NZ informal a large number or amount: *Howard has promised me a swag of goodies.*

swap•file /'swäp,fīl/
▸ **noun** Computing a file on a hard disk used to provide space for programs that have been transferred from the processor's memory.

swarm /swôrm/
▸ **verb** [often as n oun] [intrans] (**swarming**) to assemble, move, or act collectively, using cell phones or othe wireless devices to communicate: *the bartenders know t watch out for swarming when Leo walks in.*

SWAT team /'swät ˌtēm/
▸ **noun** a group of elite police marksmen who specialize in high-risk tasks such as hostage rescue.
■ any group of specialists brought in to solve a difficult or urgent problem.
-ORIGIN 1980s: acronym from *Special Weapons and Tactics*.

SWF
▸ **abbreviation** single white female (used in personal ads).

swing•man /'swiNGmən/
▸ **noun** (pl. **swing•men**) Basketball a player who can play both guard and forward.

SWM
▸ **abbreviation** single white male (used in personal ads).

sym•pa•thet•ic smok•er /'simpə,THetik 'smōkər/
▸ **noun** a person who smokes only in the company of another smoker: *sympathetic smokers are tempted the most in bars and at parties.*

symp•tom•ize /'simptə,mīz/ (also **symp•tom•ise**)
▸ **verb** [trans.] be a symptom or sign of: *hypothermia is symptomized by confusion, slurred speech, and stiff muscles.*

syn•tax /'sin,tæks/
▸ **noun** the structure of statements in a computer language.

syn•the•siz•er /'sinTHə,sīzər/ (also **syn•the•sis•er**)
▸ **noun** an electronic musical instrument, typically operated by a keyboard, producing a wide variety of sounds by generating and combining signals of different frequencies.

syn•thes•pi•an /sinˈTHespēən/

> ▸ **noun** trademark (in the US) a computer-generated actor appearing in a film with human actors and interacting with them or in a wholly animated film.

T

T-1 /'tē 'wən/ (also **T-3** /'tē 'THrē/)
▸ **noun** Computing a high-speed data line.

tab /tæb/
▸ **noun** Brit. & informal a cigarette.

tab•let PC /'tæblit ˌpē,sē/
▸ **noun** a type of notebook computer that, in addition to having a keyboard, allows a user to input drawings or handwriting directly onto an LCD screen by means of a stylus and either save the text as an image of the handwriting or convert it to an editable text document through handwriting recognition software: *I used my tablet PC to e-mail my handwritten notes to people attending the meeting.*

tab•loid•i•za•tion /'tæbˌloidi'zāSHən/
▸ **noun** a change in emphasis from the factual to the sensational, especially in television news: *the tabloidization of the nightly news during sweeps week.*

tack•ie /'tækē/ (also **tak•kie**)
▸ **noun** (pl. **tack•ies, tak•kies**) S. African informal **1** a rubber-soled canvas sneaker.
2 a tire.
-PHRASES **a piece of old tackie** an easy task.
-ORIGIN perhaps from *tacky* (sticky), with reference to the adhesion of the rubber, or *tacky* (of poor quality), with reference to their cheapness.

Tac•tel /'tæktel/
▸ **noun** trademark a polyamide fabric or fiber with a soft, silky feel.

tae-bo /'tī 'bō/
▸ **noun** trademark an exercise system combining elements of aerobics and kick-boxing.
–ORIGIN 1990s: from Korean *tae* 'leg' + *bo*, short for *boxing*).

tag wres•tling /'tæg ˌresliNG/
▸ **noun** a form of wrestling involving tag teams.

tail•gate /'tāl,gāt/
▸ **verb** [trans.] gain unauthorized entry to a secured area by following on the heels of someone with authority to enter: *a Toyota pickup that tailgated the delivery vehicle into the prison.*
–DERIVATIVES **tail•gat•ing** noun

tak•kie /'tækē/
▸ **noun** variant spelling of TACKIE.

talk time /'tôk ˌtīm/
▸ **noun** the time during which a cell phone is in use to handle calls, especially as a measure of the duration of the telephone's battery.

tal•war /'təlwär/ (also **tul•war**)
▸ **noun** Indian a sword, especially a type of saber.
–ORIGIN early 19th cent.: Hindi *talvār* from Sanskrit *taravāri*.

tank /tæNGk/
▸ **verb** informal, chiefly Scottish defeat heavily: *Rangers tanked the local side 8–0.*

tank•i•ni /tæNG'kēnē/
▸ **noun** a two-piece bathing suit consisting of a tank top and a bikini bottom.

tap•i•o•ca milk tea /ˌtæpēˈōkə ˌmilk ˈtē/
▸ **noun** another term for BUBBLE TEA.

Tar•dis /ˈtärdis/
▸ **noun 1** a time machine.
2 a building or container that is larger inside than it appears to be from outside.
−ORIGIN the name (said to be an acronym of *time and relative dimensions in space*) of a time machine that had the exterior of a police telephone box in the British TV science-fiction series *Doctor Who*, first broadcast in 1963.

tart /tärt/
▸ **verb** informal, chiefly Brit. [trans.] (**tart about** (or **around**)) (especially of a girl or woman) behave in a provocative or flamboyant way: *she tarted around the room in one of Mandy's dresses.*

tat•ter•de•mal•ion /ˌtætərdəˈmālyən/
▸ **adjective** tattered or dilapidated.
▸**noun** a person in tattered clothing.
−ORIGIN early 17th cent.: from *tatters* or *tattered*: ending unexplained.

tax-and-spend /ˈtæks ən ˈspend/
▸ **noun** a policy, usually associated with the political left, of increasing taxes in order to fund an increase in government spending, especially for social services.
■ [as adjective] relating to, denoting, or advocating a policy of tax-and-spend.
−DERIVATIVES **tax-and-spend•er noun**

tech•ni•cal sup•port /ˈteknikəl səˈpôrt/ (also **tech sup•port** /ˈtek səˈpôrt/)
▸ **noun** Computing a service provided by a hardware or soft-

ware company that provides registered users with help
and advice about their products.

■ a department within an organization that maintains
and repairs computers and computer networks.

tech•no-thril•ler /'teknō ˌTHrilər/
▸ **noun** a novel or movie in which the excitement of the
plot depends in large part upon the descriptions of
computers, weapons, software, military vehicles, or
other machines: *Tom Clancy's best-selling techno-thriller.*

teen•tail•er /'tēnˌtālər/
▸ **noun** a retail store that caters to teenagers, especially
teenage girls: *teentailers have been pleasing girls and exas-
perating parents in malls everywhere for several years.*
–ORIGIN blend of *teenager* and *retailer.*

Tef•lon /'teflän/
▸ **noun** [as modifier] having an undamaged reputation, in
spite of involvement in scandal or evidence of misjudg-
ment.

tel•e-im•mer•sion /ˌtelə iˈmərzHən/
▸ **noun** two-way remote communication in which each
party gets an audio and three-dimensional visual representation of the other, via high-speed data exchange.

tel•e•no•vel•a /ˌtelənōˈvelə/
▸ **noun** (in Latin America) a televised soap opera: *like all
the characters in the telenovelas, she was rich and beautiful.*

tel•e•pic /'teləˌpik/
▸ **noun** a movie made for television: *a series based on telepic
about kids who walk with dinosaurs.*

tel•e•scam /'teləˌskæm/
▸ **noun** a fraud conducted via telephone, especially one
using telemarketing: *they're cracking down on telescams
that target the elderly.*

tel•e•sur•ger•y /'telə,sərjərē/
▸ **noun** surgery performed by a doctor considerably distant from the patient, using medical robotics and multimedia image communication.
–DERIVATIVES **tel•e•sur•geon** /'telə,sərjən/ **noun**

tel•o•mer•ase /'teləmir,ās; -,āz/
▸ **noun** a reverse transcriptase enzyme that, when functioning normally, synthesizes telomeres and prevents their erosion.

ter•roir /ter'wär/, French
▸ **noun** the complete natural environment in which a particular wine is produced, including factors such as the soil, topography, and climate
■ (also **goût de ter•roir** /,go͞o də ter'wär/, French) the characteristic taste and flavor imparted to a wine by the environment in which it is produced.
–ORIGIN 1970s: French, from medieval Latin *terratorium*.

text mes•sage /'tekst ,mesij/
▸ **noun** an electronic communication sent and received by cell phone.
–DERIVATIVES **text mes•sag•ing noun**

text•phone /'tekst,fōn/
▸ **noun** a telephone developed for use by the deaf or hard of hearing, having a small screen on which a message can be received and a keyboard on which a message may be typed to be received by another textphone.

the•ke•dar /'tākə,där/ (also **thi•ka•dar** /'tēkə,där/)
▸ **noun** Indian a person who undertakes to provide labor or materials to do a job; a contractor.
–ORIGIN early 20th cent.: Hindi *thikadar*.

the•o•ter•ror•ism /ˌTHēō'terə,rizəm/
▸ **noun** terrorism that has a religious motive or purpose: *realistic worry about theoterrorism has caused a decline in tourism.*
–ORIGIN from *theo-* 'relating to God' + *terrorism.*

ther•mal im•ag•ing /'THərməl 'iməjiNG/
▸ **noun** the formation of images based on heat in the objects represented, using infrared and other technologies.

thi•a•zine /'THīə,zēn/
▸ **noun** any of a class of dyes whose molecules contain a ring of one nitrogen, one sulphur, and four carbon atoms.
–ORIGIN late 19th cent.: from *thio-* + *azine.*

thought lead•er /'THôt ,lēdər/
▸ **noun** one whose views on a subject are taken to be authoritative and influential: *these thought leaders are independent experts who keep our thinking both broad and deep.*

thread•ing /'THrediNG/
▸ **noun** a process in which unwanted facial hair is removed by using twisted cotton thread to pull the hair from the follicle.

TIFF /tif/
▸ **abbreviation** Computing tagged image file format, widely used in desktop publishing.

tight•y-whit•ies /'tītē '(h)wītēz/
▸ **noun** informal men's white cotton briefs.

time tri•al /'tīm ,trīəl/
▸ **noun** an exercise designed to test the time needed for a task or activity.

tin•ny /ˈtinē/ (also **tin•nie**)
▸ noun (pl. **tin•nies**) Australian/NZ informal a small boat with an aluminium hull.

tip•ping point /ˈtipiNG ˌpoint/
▸ noun the point at which a series of small ineffective changes acquires enough pressure or importance to cause a larger, more significant change.
■ the point at which the build-up of minor incidents reaches an unbearable level, causing someone to act in a way that they had formerly resisted.

TLA
▸ abbreviation three-letter acronym.

TMJ
▸ abbreviation temporomandibular joint.

tog /tôg/ informal
▸ noun Australian/NZ & Irish a bathing suit.

ton /tən/
▸ adverb (**tons**) informal much; a lot: *I feel tons better.*

tonk /täNGk/
▸ verb [trans.] informal hit (someone or something) hard.
■ defeat heavily; trounce.
–ORIGIN early 20th cent.: imitative of the sound of a powerful blow reaching its target.

top of the morn•ing /ˈtäp əv THə ˈmôrniNG; ˈtäp ə THə ˈmôrnin/
▸ phrase Irish used as a friendly morning greeting.

top•ple /ˈtäpəl/
▸ verb [trans.] remove (a government or person in authority) from power; overthrow: *disagreement had threatened to topple the government.*

tot•siens /tät'sēns/
▸ **exclamation** S. African until we meet again; goodbye.
–ORIGIN 1930s: from Afrikaans *tot (weer)siens*, from Dutch *tot* 'until' + *zien* 'see.'

touch•point /'təCH,point/
▸ **noun 1** any point of contact between a buyer and a seller.
2 a device like a miniature joystick with a rubber tip, manipulated with a finger to move the screen pointer on some laptop computers.

tow•el•head /'tow(ə)l ,hed/
▸ **noun** informal, offensive a person who wears a turban.

trac•tor beam /'træktər ,bēm/
▸ **noun** (in science fiction) a hypothetical beam of energy that can be used to control the movement of objects such as space ships or hold them stationary.

trail•er trash /'trālər ,træSH/
▸ **noun** offensive poor, lower-class white people, typified as living in mobile homes.

train•ing ta•ble /'trāniNG ,tābəl/
▸ **noun** a table in a dining hall where athletes in training are served specially prepared meals.

trans•gen•der /trænz'jendər; træns-/ (also **trans•gen•dered**)
▸ **adjective** transsexual.

tran•si•ent is•che•mic at•tack /'trænSHənt is'kēmik ə,tæk; 'trænzHənt / (abbreviation: **TIA**)
▸ **noun** technical term for MINISTROKE.

tran•si•tion /træn'ziSHən/
▸ **verb** [intrans.] undergo or cause to undergo a process or period of transition: *he transitioned into filmmaking easily.*

tran•si•tion se•ries /trænˈzɪʃən ˌsɪrēz/
▸ **noun** Chemistry the set of transition metals.

trans•par•ent /trænˈsperənt; -ˈspær-/
▸ **adjective** (of an organization or its activities) open to public scrutiny: *if you had transparent government procurement, corruption would go away.*

tre•tin•o•in /trəˈtinō-in/
▸ **noun** a drug related to retinol (Vitamin A), used as a topical ointment in the treatment of acne and other disorders of the skin.

tri•fold /ˈtrīˌfōld/
▸ **adjective** triple; threefold: *a trifold partnership between government, employers, and students.*

trip-hop /ˈtrip ˌhäp/
▸ **noun** a style of dance music, usually slow in tempo, that combines elements of hip-hop and dub reggae with softer, more ambient sounds.

trol•ley dol•ly /ˈträlē ˌdälē/
▸ **noun** Brit. informal an air stewardess.

tromp /trämp/
▸ **verb** informal [intrans.; with adjective of direction] walk heavily; trudge: *she tromped across the yard.*
■ (**tromp on**) tread or stamp on: *Larry took a step forward and tromped on Jack's wrist.*
–ORIGIN late 19th cent: alteration of *tramp.*

tro•phy child /ˈtrōfē ˌCHīld/
▸ **noun** a child whose achievements are paraded to enhance the parents' status: *I was a trophy child, a virtuoso pianist in the making from age 5 to 15.*

Trust•a•far•i•an /ˌtrəstəˈferēən/
‣ **noun** informal a rich young person who adopts an ethnic lifestyle and lives in a college town or a non-affluent urban area.
–ORIGIN 1990s: blend of *trust fund* and *Rastafarian*.

T-top /ˈtē ˌtäp/
‣ **noun** a car roof with removable panels.
▪ a car with removable panels in its roof.

TTS
‣ **abbreviation** text-to-speech, a form of speech synthesis used to create a spoken version of the text in an electronic document.

tune in /ˈt(y)o͞on ˈin/
‣ **phrasal verb** watch or listen to a television or radio broadcast.

tu•ri•sta /to͞oˈrēstə/
‣ **noun** informal a tourist.

Tus•sock moth /ˈtəsək ˌmôTH/
‣ **noun** a woodland moth whose adults and brightly colored caterpillars both bear tufts of irritant hairs. The caterpillars can be a pest of trees, damaging fruit and stripping leaves.
•Family Lymantriidae: many genera.

tween /twēn/ (also **tween•ie** /ˈtwēnē/)
‣ **noun** short for TWEENAGER.

tween•ag•er /ˈtwēnˌājər/
‣ **noun** informal a child between the ages of about 10 and 14.

twelve-step /ˈtwelv ˈstep/
‣ **adjective** [attrib] denoting or relating to a process of recovery from an addiction by following a twelve-stage

program, especially one devised or similar to that devised by Alcoholics Anonymous.

▸**verb** [intrans.] [often as noun **twelve-stepping**] (of an addict) undergo such a program.

-DERIVATIVES **twelve-step•per** noun

24-7 /'twentē,fôr 'sevən/ (also **24/7**)

▸ **adverb** informal twenty-four hours a day, seven days a week; all the time.

twig fur•ni•ture /'twig ,fərniCHər/

▸ **noun** a rustic style of furniture in which the natural state of the wood is retained as an aesthetic feature.

twist•ed pair /'twistid 'per/

▸ **noun** Electronics a cable consisting of two wires twisted around each other, used especially for telephone or computer applications.

two-pot scream•er /'tōō ,pät 'skrēmər/

▸ **phrase** Australian a person who shows the effects of alcohol after drinking comparatively little.

U

u•ber- /ˈo͞obər/ (also **über-** /ˈ ʏbər/)
  ▸ **prefix** denoting an outstanding or supreme example of a particular kind of person or thing: *an uberbabe* | *the uberregulator.*

u•biq•ui•tin /yoōˈbikwit̬(i)n/
  ▸ **noun** a single-chain polypeptide found in living cells that plays a role in the degradation of defective and superfluous proteins.

u•don /ˈo͞odän/
  ▸ **noun** wide, flat wheat noodles used in Japanese cooking.

Ugg boot /ˈəg ˌbo͞ot/ (also **Ugh boot**)
  ▸ **noun** Australian trademark a type of soft sheepskin boot.
  -ORIGIN 1960s: probably named after *Ugh*, a series of cartoon characters.

u•ma•mi /oōˈmämē/
  ▸ **noun** a category of taste in food (besides sweet, sour, salt, and bitter), corresponding to the flavor of glutamates, especially monosodium glutamate.
  -ORIGIN Japanese, literally 'deliciousness.'

um•bil•i•co•plas•ty /ˌəmˈbilikōˌplæstē/
  ▸ **noun** plastic surgery performed on the navel: *umbilicoplasty is what's next for the lifted-and-tucked set.*
  -ORIGIN *umbilicus* + *-plasty* 'the molding of a part of the body.'

um•fun•di•si /oōmˈfo͝ondisē; ˌo͞omfo͝onˈdēzē/,
  ▸ **noun** (pl. **ba•fun•di•si** /bäˈfo͝ondisē/ or same) S. African

(among speakers of Xhosa and Zulu) a teacher, priest, or missionary.
-ORIGIN early 19th cent.: from Xhosa and Zulu.

um•rah /'ŏŏmrä/
▸ **noun** the nonmandatory lesser pilgrimage made by Muslims to Mecca, which may be performed at any time of the year.
-ORIGIN Arabic 'umra.

UMTS
▸ **abbreviation** Universal Mobile Telephone System.

U•na•bomb•er /'yŏŏnə,bämər/
▸ the name given by the FBI to Ted Kaczynski, the elusive perpetrator of a series of bombings (1975–1995) in the United States that killed three and wounded 23. The victims were mainly academics in technological disciplines, airline executives, and executives in businesses thought to affect the environment.

un•aired /,ən'erd/
▸ **adjective** not aired.

un•a•mend•ed /,ənə'mendid/
▸ **adjective** not amended.

un•baked /,ən'bākt/
▸ **adjective** not baked.

un•braid /,ən'brād/
▸ **verb** [trans.] untie (something braided).

un•branched /,ən'brænCHt/
▸ **adjective** chiefly technical not divided into or having branches.

un•cas•trat•ed /ˌənˈkæsˌtrātid/
▸ **adjective** (of a male animal) not castrated.

un•clamp /ˌənˈklæmp/
▸ **verb** [trans.] remove the clamp from.

un•clip /ˌənˈklip/
▸ **verb** (**un•clipped, un•clip•ping**) [trans.] release from be-ing fastened or held with a clip.

un•clothe /ˌənˈklōTH/
▸ **verb** [as adj.] (**unclothed**) not wearing clothes: *her un-clothed body.*

un•cov•er /ˌənˈkəvər/
▸ **verb** [trans.] [as adj.] (**uncovered**) not covered: *uncovered stone floors.*

un•crate /ˌənˈkrāt/
▸ **verb** [trans.] remove (something) from a crate.

un•crease /ˌənˈkrēs/
▸ **verb** [trans.] [usually as adj.] (**uncreased**) remove the creases from.

un•crum•ple /ˌənˈkrəmpəl/
▸ **verb** [trans.] remove the crumples from; straighten.

un•der•cling /ˈəndərˌkliNG/ Climbing
▸ **noun** a handhold that faces down the rock face.
▸ **verb** [intrans.] climb using such handholds.

un•der•stored /ˈəndərˈstôrd/
▸ **adjective** supplied with fewer retail stores than the mar-ket demands: *there are specific market niches in which Chicago is understored compared to Los Angeles and New York.*

un•der•tip /'əndər'tip/ (**un•der•tipped, un•der•tip•ping**)
▸ verb [trans.] give (someone) an excessively small tip: *I wa so mad I undertipped the waiter.*

un•der•vote /'əndər,vōt/
▸ noun a ballot not counted because of unclear marking by the voter.

un•dimmed /,ən'dimd/
▸ adjective not dimmed.

un•en•riched /,ənen'riCHt/
▸ adjective (especially of uranium) not enriched.

un•fired /,ən'fīrd/
▸ adjective 1 (of clay or pottery) not fired.
2 (of a gun) not discharged.

un•fused /,ən'fyoōzd/
▸ adjective not fused or joined.

un•grad•ed /,ən'grādid/
▸ adjective not graded.

un•greased /,ən'grēst; -grēzd/
▸ adjective not greased.

un•ground /,ən'grownd/
▸ adjective not reduced to fine particles by grinding.

un•hemmed /,ən'hemd/
▸ adjective (of a garment or piece of fabric) not having a hem: *unhemmed jeans.*

un•hip /,ən'hip/
▸ adjective (**un•hip•per, un•hip•pest**) informal unaware of current fashions or trends.

un·hol·ster /ˌənˈhōlstər/
▸ verb [trans.] remove (a gun) from a holster.

u·ni·form re·source lo·ca·tor /ˈyo͞onəˌfôrm ˈrēsôrs ˌlōkā-tər/ (abbreviation: **URL**)
▸ noun a location or address identifying where documents can be found on the Internet.

un·in·stall /ˌəninˈstôl/
▸ verb (**un·in·stalled, un·in·stall·ing**) [trans.] remove (an application or file) from a computer.
-DERIVATIVES **un·in·stall·er noun**

un·i·ron·ic /ˌənīˈränik/
▸ adjective not ironic.
-DERIVATIVES **un·i·ron·i·cal·ly adverb**

un·liv·ing /ˌənˈliviNG/
▸ adjective not living.

un·marred /ˌənˈmärd/
▸ adjective not marred.

un·me·tered /ˌənˈmētərd/
▸ adjective not measured by means of a meter.

un·pack·aged /ˌənˈpækijd/
▸ adjective (of goods) not enclosed in a package.
■ (of a vacation) not organized as an inclusive package.

un·pad·ded /ˌənˈpædid/
▸ adjective not padded.

un·played /ˌənˈplād/
▸ adjective **1** (of a game, point, card, etc.) not played.
2 (of a musical instrument or recording) not played on or played back.

un•pruned /ˌənˈpro͞ond/
▸ **adjective** not pruned.

un•re•ac•tive /ˌənrēˈæktiv/
▸ **adjective** having little tendency to react chemically.

un•shack•le /ˌənˈsʜækəl/
▸ **verb** [as adj.] (**unshackled**) not chained or shackled: *he had handcuffs on his wrists but his feet were unshackled.*

un•sheathe /ˌənˈsʜēTʜ/
▸ **verb** [as adj.] (**unsheathed**) not placed in or protected by a sheath or covering: *all unsheathed wires must be enclosed in a noncombustible housing.*

un•shriv•en /ˌənˈsʜrivən/
▸ **adjective** not shriven.

un•staffed /ˌənˈstæft/
▸ **adjective** not provided with staff.

un•stayed /ənˈstād/
▸ **adjective** (especially of a mast) not provided with stays; unsupported.

un•ster•i•lized /ˌənˈsterəˌlīzd/ (also **un•ster•i•lised**)
▸ **adjective** (especially of medical instruments) not sterilized.

un•sub•scribe /ˌənsəbˈskrīb/
▸ **verb** [intrans.] cancel a subscription to an Internet newsletter, e-mail list, or discussion group: *she accidentally unsubscribed when she was trying to post a message.*

un•vent•ed /ˌənˈventid/
▸ **adjective** [attrib.] without a vent or outlet.

un•wired /ˌən'wīrd/
▸ **adjective** not wired.

up•side /'əp,sīd/
▸ **preposition** informal against; on: *if her mother saw her drinkin' that stuff she'd slap her upside her head.*

up•size /'əp,sīz/
▸ **verb** [trans.] [intrans.] undergo an increase in size, extent, or complexity: *the economy kept on upsizing.*

up•skirt /'əp,skərt/
▸ **adjective** having a point of view up a woman's skirt: *more upskirt streaming video than you've ever imagined.*

U•ra•ni•an[1] /yo͞o'rānēən/
▸ **adjective** relating to the planet Uranus.
▸ **noun** (in science fiction) an imagined inhabitant of Uranus.

U•ra•ni•an[2] /yo͞o'rānēən/ literary
▸ **adjective** 1 relating to heaven; celestial.
2 homosexual. [ORIGIN: late 19th cent.: with allusion to a reference to Aphrodite in Plato's *Symposium*.]
▸ **noun** a homosexual.
–ORIGIN early 17th cent.: from *urania* + *-an.*

USB /'yo͞o,es'bē /
▸ **noun** Universal Serial Bus, an external peripheral interface standard for communication between a computer and add-on devices such as audio players, joysticks, keyboards, telephones, scanners, and printers.

us•er in•ter•face /'yo͞ozər 'intər,fās/
▸ **noun** Computing the means by which the user and a computer system interact, in particular the use of input devices and software: *a graphical user interface allows a user*

to open programs or issue commands within programs by clicking on icons with a mouse.

Ut•tar•an•chal /ˌoͻtəˈrənCHəl/ a state in northern India, formed in 2000 from the northern part of Uttar Pradesh; capital, Dehra Dun.

V

vac•u•um-pack /ˈvækyo͞o(ə)m ˌpæk/ (also **vac•u•um pack**)
▸ **noun** a pack or wrapping in which the air surrounding the product has been removed so that the pack or wrapping is tight and firm.

vag•i•no•plas•ty /ˈvæjənōˌplæstē/
▸ **noun** Medicine plastic surgery performed to create or repair a vagina.
–ORIGIN late 19th cent.: from *vagina* + *-plasty*.

vamp /væmp/ informal
▸ **verb** [trans.] to turn (someone) into a vampire: *his lover is the one who vamped him.*

van•pool /ˈvænˌpo͞ol/
▸ **noun** an arrangement whereby commuters travel together in a van.
–ORIGIN on the pattern of *carpool.*

va•por•iz•er /ˈvāpəˌrīzər/ (also **vaporiser**)
▸ **noun** a device that generates a particular substance in the form of vapor, especially for medicinal inhalation.

vari- /ˈverē; ˈveri/
▸ **combining form** various: *variform.*
–ORIGIN from Latin *varius.*

vCJD
▸ **abbreviation** variant Creutzfeld–Jakob disease.

veg•e•tal /ˈvejətl/
▸ **adjective 1** formal of or relating to plants: *a vegetal aroma.*
2 [attrib.] Embryology of or relating to that pole of the ovum

or embryo that contains the less active cytoplasm, and frequently most of the yolk, in the early stages of development: *vegetal cells | the vegetal region.*

-ORIGIN late Middle English: from medieval Latin *vegetalis,* from Latin *vegetare* 'animate.' Sense 2 dates from the early 20th cent.

ver•mic•u•la•tion /vər,mikyə'lāsHən/
  ▸ **noun** Architecture wavy lines cut into the surface of stone, used for decoration.

ver•sion con•trol /'vərzHən kən,trōl/
  ▸ **noun** Computing the task of keeping a software system that consists of many versions and configurations well organized.

ver•tic•al•ly chal•lenged /'vərṯik(ə)lē 'CHælənjd/
  ▸ **adjective** jocular not tall in height; short.

ver•ti•cal sta•bi•liz•er /'vərṯikəl 'stābə,līzər/
  ▸ **noun** Aeronautics a small, flattened projecting surface or attachment on an aircraft or rocket for providing aerodynamic stability.

ver•ti•cal un•ion /'vərtikəl 'yōōnyən/
  ▸ **noun** a union whose members all work in various capacities in a single industry.

Ver•y Large Ar•ray /'verē 'lärj ə'rā/ (abbreviation: **VLA**)
  ▸ **noun** the world's largest radio telescope, consisting of 27 dish antennas in Socorro, New Mexico.

Vi•ag•ra /vī'ægrə/
  ▸ **noun** trademark a synthetic compound used to enhance male potency.

-ORIGIN 1990s: apparently a blend of *virility* and *Niagara.*

vi•bra•tion white fin•ger /vī'brāsHən '(h)wīt 'fiNGgər/
▸ **noun** Raynaud's disease caused by prolonged use of vibrating hand tools or machinery.

vic•tim /'viktəm/
▸ **noun** a person who has come to feel helpless and passive in the face of misfortune or ill-treatment: *I saw myself as a victim* | [as modifier] *a victim mentality.*

vid•e•o mail /'vidēō ‚māl/
▸ **noun** an e-mail message with a video clip attached.

vid•e•o pill /'vidēō ‚pil/
▸ **noun** a capsule containing a tiny camera that, when swallowed, transmits photographs of the stomach and intestines to a recording device: *video pills can be used to diagnose ulcers.*

vid•e•o•scope /'vidēō,skōp/
▸ **noun** a fiberoptic rod, attached to a camera, that transmits images from within the body to a television monitor, used in diagnosis and surgery.

vid•e•o•sur•ger•y /'vidēō,sərjərē/
▸ **noun** a minimally invasive approach to surgery using from one to five small incisions, each between $1/4$ inch and 1 inch in length, through which specially designed instruments are inserted into the body. One of these is a tiny fiberoptic rod attached to a camera, enabling the surgeon to see on a television monitor what is happening inside the body.

vi•nyl /'vīnl/
▸ **noun** generic term for phonograph records: *fans had to wait almost a year before the song eventually appeared* **on vinyl**.

-ORIGIN in reference to vinyl as the standard material used to make phonograph records.

vi•pas•sa•na /ˌvēpäˈsänä/
▸ **noun** Buddhist name for insight meditation.

vi•ral mar•ket•ing /ˈvīrəl ˈmärkətiNG/
▸ **noun** a marketing technique whereby information about a company's goods or services is passed electronically from one Internet user to another.
-ORIGIN 1980s: from the idea of the information being passed on like a computer virus.

vir•tu•al com•mun•i•ty /ˈvərCHo͞oəl kəˈmyo͞onitē/
▸ **noun** a community of people sharing common interests, ideas, and feelings over the Internet.

vir•tu•al en•gi•neer•ed com•pos•ite ˈvərCHo͞oəl ˌenjə ˈnird kəmˈpäzit
▸ **noun** a digitally controlled chemical molding system that uses water pressure to retain the shape of easily manufactured, nonrigid molds.

vir•tu•al•ize /ˈvərCHo͞oəˌlīz/
▸ **verb** [trans.] convert (something) to a computer-generated simulation of reality: *traditional universities have begun to virtualize parts of their curricula* | [intrans.] *our method makes it easy to virtualize.*
-DERIVATIVES **vir•tu•al•i•za•tion** noun; **vir•tu•a•li•zer** noun

vir•tu•al of•fice /ˈvərCHo͞oəl ˈôfis; ˈäfis/
▸ **noun** the operational domain of any business or organization whose work force includes a significant proportion of workers using technology to perform their work at home.

vir•tu•al pet /'vərCHŌŌəl 'pet/
▸ **noun** see CYBERPET.

vis•it•a•bil•i•ty /ˌvizitə'bilitē/
▸ **noun** a measure of a building's ease of access to people with disabilities: *we endeavor to create a community that is not only accessible to disabled persons, but is also a model of visitability.*
–DERIVATIVES **vis•it•a•ble** adjective

VLA
▸ **abbreviation** Very Large Array (radio telescope).

vogue /vōg/
▸ **verb** [intrans.] (**vogued, vogue•ing** or **vogu•ing**) dance to music in such a way as to imitate the characteristic poses struck by a model on a catwalk. [ORIGIN: 1980s: from the name of the fashion magazine *Vogue*.]

voice rec•og•ni•tion /'vois rekəgˌniSHən/
▸ **noun** computer analysis of the human voice, especially for the purposes of interpreting words and phrases or identifying an individual voice.

vol•u•met•ric sen•sor ˌvälyə'metrik 'sensər
▸ **noun** a security device that detects the movement of people or objects by sensing their shapes.

vor•tal /'vôrtl/
▸ **noun** an Internet site that provides a directory of links to information related to a particular industry.
–ORIGIN 1990s: blend of *v(ertical)* (as in *vertical industry*, an industry specializing in a narrow range of goods and services), and *(p)ortal*.

W

wag /wæg/
> ▸ **verb** [trans.] (**wagged, wag•ging**) Australian/NZ informal play truant from (school).

wake•board /'wāk,bôrd/
> ▸ **noun** a board towed behind a motor boat, shaped like a broad waterski and ridden like a surfboard.
> ▸ **verb** ride a wakeboard: *I have wakeboarded for three years.*
> –DERIVATIVES **wake•board•ing noun**

wal•la•by /'wäləbē/
> ▸ **adjective** Australian/NZ dated, informal usually (**on the wallaby**) (**track**) (of a person) unemployed and having no fixed address.

wall•ing /'wôliNG/
> ▸ **noun** the material from which a wall is built.

wan•ky /'wäNGkē; 'wæNG-/ mainly British
> ▸ **adjective** vulgar slang contemptible, worthless, or stupid: *I was determined not to end up as some Nigel doing wanky beer ads.*

WAP
> ▸ **abbreviation** Wireless Application Protocol, a set of protocols for connecting cellular phones and other radio devices to the Internet.

war•by /'wôrbē/
> ▸ **adjective** Australian informal shabby or decrepit: *a warby unshaven young man.*
> –ORIGIN 1920s: probably from *warb* 'larva of the warble fly' + '-y.'

war•chalk•ing /'wôr,CHôkiNG/ (**war chalk•ing**)
▸ noun Computing the practice of marking chalk symbols on sidewalks and other outdoor surfaces to indicate the location of unsecured wireless network connections: *savvy IT managers check their buildings' facades for signs of warchalking.*

wat /wät/
▸ noun (in Thailand, Cambodia, and Laos) a Buddhist monastery or temple.
–ORIGIN Thai, from Sanskrit *vāṭa* 'enclosure.'

Wat•su 'wätsoō
▸ noun trademark a form of shiatsu massage that takes place in water.
–ORIGIN 1980s: blend of *water* and *shiatsu.*

wear•a•ble /'werəbəl/ (also **wear•a•ble com•put•er**)
▸ noun a computer that is small or portable enough to be worn or carried on one's body: *wearable computers are the height of geek chic.*

web•cam /'web,kæm/
▸ noun trademark a video camera that inputs to a computer connected to the Internet, so that its images can be viewed by Internet users.
–ORIGIN 1990s: blend of *web* in the sense 'World Wide Web' and *cam(era).*

web•cast /'web,kæst/ (also **Web•cast**)
▸ noun a live video broadcast transmitted across the Internet: *an estimated 1.5 million to 2 million surfers clicked on to the live Webcast of the Victoria's Secret annual fashion show.*
–DERIVATIVES **web•cast•ing** noun

web host•ing /'web ˌhōstiNG/
‣ **noun** the activity or business of providing storage space and access for Web sites.

web•log /'web¸lôg; -¸läg/
‣ **noun** a Web site on which an individual or group of users produce an ongoing narrative.
-DERIVATIVES **web•log•ger** noun
-ORIGIN 1990s: from *web* in the sense 'World Wide Web' and *log* in the sense 'regular record of incidents.'

web•zine /'web¸zēn/
‣ **noun** a magazine published electronically on the World Wide Web.
-ORIGIN 1990s: from *web* in the sense 'World Wide Web' and *(maga)zine.*

wed•ding plan•ner /'wediNG ¸plænər/ noun
‣ someone whose job is to plan and organize weddings.

wedge is•sue /'wej ¸isHoo/
‣ **noun** a divisive political issue, especially one that is raised by a candidate for public office in hopes of attracting supporters to their campaign or in order to alienate an opponent's supporters from their candidate: *will the California Civil Rights Initiative be a wedge issue?*

wedg•ie /'wejē/
‣ **noun** informal an act of pulling up the material of someone's underwear tightly between their buttocks as a practical joke: *he was back there grabbing the waistband of their skivvies, preparing to give them the wedgie of a lifetime.*

weed whack•er /'wēd ¸(h)wækər/
‣ **noun** an electrically powered grass trimmer with a nylon cutting cord that rotates rapidly on a spindle.

weep•er /'wēpər/
▸ **noun** (**weepers**) dated long side whiskers worn without a beard.

wel•wit•schi•a /wel'wiCHēə/
▸ **noun** a gymnospermous plant of desert regions in SW Africa that has a dwarf, massive trunk, two long strap-shaped leaves, and male and female flowers in the scales of scarlet cones.
•Genus *Welwitschia*, family Welwitschiaceae: one species, *W. mirabilis*.
-ORIGIN mid 19th cent.: modern Latin, named after Friedrich *Welwitsch* (1806–72), Austrian botanist.

West Brit•on /'west 'britn/
▸ **noun** Irish, derogatory an Irish person who greatly admires England or Britain.

West Nile Vi•rus /'west 'nīl ‚vīrəs/
▸ **noun** a flavivirus of African origin that can be spread to humans and other mammals via mosquitoes, causing encephalitis and flu-like symptoms, with some fatalities.

what•ev•er /(h)wät'evər/
▸ **exclamation** informal said as a response indicating a reluctance to discuss something, often implying indifference: *if someone came running to say he'd just seen Jesus preaching, most New Yorkers would reply, 'Whatever.'*

white•list•ing /'(h)wīt‚listiNG/
▸ **noun** Computing the use of antispam filtering software to allow only specified e-mail addresses to get through: *whitelisting sometimes backfires because it filters e-mail from people or companies you might be interested in.*
-ORIGIN on the pattern of *blacklisting*.

white-van man /ˈ(h)wīt ˈvæn ˌmæn/
▶ **noun** British informal an aggressive male driver of a delivery or contractor's van: *sales reps and the infamous white-van man have to be targeted.*

Wi-Fi /ˈwīˈfī/
▶ **abbreviation** Wireless Fidelity, a group of technical standards enabling the transmission of data over wireless networks.

wig•ger informal /ˈwigər/
▶ **noun 1** a white person who emulates or acquires African-American behavior and tastes: *Whites who pal around with Blacks are called "wannabes" or "wiggers."*
2 an unreliable or flaky person: *the '80s wigger is the same as the '50s greaser, the '60s hippie, or the '70s burnout.*

wild /wīld/
▶ **adjective** produced from wild animals or plants without cultivation: *wild honey.*

wild•craft /ˈwīld,kræft/
▶ **verb** gather herbs, plants, and fungi from the wild, usually for some commercial purpose: *concentrates with wildcrafted goldenseal root.*
▶ **noun** the action or practice of wildcrafting.

word•robe /ˈwərdrōb/ **noun**
▶ a person's vocabulary: *once a period is established the appropriate wordrobe for the characters is extensively researched and developed.*

work•book /ˈwərk,bʊk/
▶ **noun** Computing a single file containing several different types of related information as separate worksheets.

work·ing mem·o·ry /ˈwərkiNG ˈmem(ə)rē/

▸ **noun** Psychology the part of short-term memory that is concerned with immediate conscious perceptual and linguistic processing.

■ Computing an area of high-speed memory used to store programs or data currently in use.

world beat /ˈwərld ˌbēt/

▸ **noun** Western music incorporating elements of traditional music from any part of the world, especially from developing nations: *the booming sounds of world beat in the background.*

world cit·y /ˈwərld ˈsitē/

▸ **noun** a cosmopolitan city, with foreigners visiting and residing: *the book charts Hong Kong's path to world city status.*

wran·gler /ˈræNGglər/

▸ **noun** a person who trains and takes care of animals on a movie set.

wrap·a·round mort·gage /ˈræpəˌrownd ˌmôrgij/ **noun**

▸ a second mortgage held by a lender who collects payments on it and the first mortgage from the borrower; the lender makes the payments to the original mortgage holder.

wrecked /rekt/

▸ **adjective** informal **1** very intoxicated on alcohol or drugs: *I'd like to get really wrecked and then go out and find some girls.*
2 exhausted.

Wy·o·tan·a /ˌwī-ōˈtænə/ **noun**

▸ a region consisting largely of mountain wilderness lying partly in southern Montana and partly in northern Wyoming.

X

Xen•i•cal /'zeni,kæl/
▸ **noun** trademark a synthetic drug that blocks pancreatic enzymes used in the digestion of fats, used to treat obesity.

xen•ol•o•gy /zə'näləjē/
▸ **noun** (chiefly in science fiction) the scientific study of alien biology, cultures, etc.
–DERIVATIVES **xen•ol•o•gist noun**
–ORIGIN 1950s: from Greek *xenos* 'stranger, foreigner,' (adjective) 'strange.'

Y

yad·da yad·da yad·da /'yädə 'yädə 'yädə/ (also **ya·da ya·da ya·da**) informal
▸ used as a substitute in written and spoken contexts for actual words where they are too lengthy or tedious to recite in full: *boy meets girl, boy loses girl, yadda yadda yadda.*

yah /yä/
▸ **noun** British informal an upper-class person: *the cafe is full of yahs whose daddies own chateaux in France.*

yet·tie /'yetē/ (also **Yet·tie**)
▸ **noun** informal a young person who earns money from a business or activity that involves the Internet: *he has all the electronic devices that characterize a yettie.*
-ORIGIN acronym from *young entrepreneurial technocrat* (or *tech-based*), on the pattern of *yuppie.*

yield man·age·ment /'yēld ˌmænijmənt/
▸ **noun** the process of making frequent adjustments in the price of a product in response to market factors such as demand or competition.

yo·gic fly·ing /'yōgik 'flī-iNG/
▸ **noun** a technique practiced chiefly by adherents of Transcendental Meditation that involves thrusting oneself off the ground while in the lotus position.

yoke /yōk/
▸ **noun** Irish informal a thing whose name one cannot recall, does not know, or does not wish to specify: *when everything quietened down, yer man, the gobdaw, asks me to get the yoke. 'What yoke?' says I. 'The hammer!' he says as if I should have known.*
-ORIGIN early 20th cent.: of unknown origin.

Z

zam•buk /ˈzæmˌbək/
▸ **noun** Australian/NZ informal a first-aid technician, especially a member of the St. John Ambulance.
–ORIGIN early 20th cent.: the proprietary name of a type of antiseptic ointment.

za•min•dar /zəˈmēndär/ (also **ze•min•dar**)
▸ **noun** Indian a landowner, especially one who leases his land to tenant farmers.
–ORIGIN via Urdu from Persian *zamīndār*, from *zamīn* 'land' + *-dār* 'holder.'

Zel•ig /ˈzelig/
▸ **noun** a person who is able to change his or her appearance, behavior, or attitudes, so as to be comfortable in any situation.
–ORIGIN 1980s: from the name of Leonard *Zelig*, central character in the film *Zelig* (1983).

ze•min•dar /zəˈmēndär/
▸ **noun** variant spelling of ZAMINDAR.

zi•kr /ˈzēkər/
▸ **noun** a variant spelling of DHIKR.

Zi•on /ˈzīən/ (also **Si•on** /ˈsīən/)
▸ **noun** a land of future promise or return from exile.
■ (among Jews) Israel. ■ (among Rastafarians) Africa.

zo•o•phile /ˈzōəˌfīl/,
▸ **noun** 1 a person who loves animals; an opponent of cruelty to animals.
2 a person who is sexually attracted to animals.

-DERIVATIVES **zo•o•phil•i•a** /ˌzōə'filēə/ **noun; zo•o•phil• ic adjective**

-ORIGIN late 19th cent. (originally in the botanical sense 'a plant pollinated by animals'): from *zoo* + *-phile*. The current senses date from the early 20th cent.

zorb•ing /'zôrbɪNG/

▸ **noun** a sport in which a participant is secured inside an inner capsule in a large, transparent ball that is then rolled along the ground or down hills.

-ORIGIN 1990s: invented word from *zorb* (the name of the ball used in this activity) + *-ing*.

Zy•ban /'zī,bæn/

▸ **noun** trademark the antidepressant bupropion, used to relieve nicotine withdrawal symptoms in people giving up smoking.

-ORIGIN 1990s: an invented name, probably from *ban* or *banish*.

New Words by Subject Area

Arts & Music

airdate
alt.country
am-dram
amp
autography
autopathography
bachata
back catalog
backstory
barkitecture
benga
bokeh
breakbeat
cathedral ceiling
cavaquinho
ceroc
chromakey
conjunto
construction paper
countrypolitan
crowd-surf
crown molding
crush space
cusping
dead white European male
death metal
djembe
dry mounting
ear candy
electronic music
electronica
emo

ETV
faience
failte
fascia
feis
fingerpick
flanger
foot-tapping
gablet
gangsta rap
hard core
headshot
high-concept
hysterical realism
illustrative
Jacobean
jasper
jazz funk
Krautrock
loungecore
mash-up
meta
mockumentary
montuno
multiculti
noodle
novela
OST
pattress
physical theater
qawwal
ramkie
ranchera

recut
rescore
reshoot
sequence
setting
simulsequeling
small screen
synthesizer
synthespian
techno-thriller
telenovela
telepic
trip-hop
unplayed
vermiculation
vinyl
vogue
world beat
wrangler

Business

accordion scheduling
advergame
automated clearinghouse
backdoor selling
blamestorming
blipvert
BOGOF
bootstrap
bracero
brand train
brand extension
brown goods
B2B
B2C
bullet point
bunce
burn rate
CAFE
call center
cap

carveout
cash machine
category killer
CFO
Chapter 13
Chapter 7
chargeback
clicks and mortar
codeshare
community bank
consignment shop
coopetition
core asset
core competency
corporatize
cost center
cramming
CRM
C2C
cube farm
cybercash
cybermall
cybershop
cybersquatting
day trading
demutualize
destination charge
direct debit
display ad
dot-bomb
dot-com
drop box
drop-ship
dumbsize
dynamic pricing
e
e-business
ecoconsumer
e-commerce
econobox
economic migrant

EEA
EEO
elevator talk
emerging market
e-tailer
fair-trade agreement
Federal Open Market
    Committee
feebate
feel-good factor
flexecutive
flip
footfall
forward contract
FTA
futures contract
gainsharing
geocode
gray goods
greentailing
hawala
holiday
hotelling
HR
hryvna
hyperflier
infomediary
insourcing
intrapraneur
job spill
karoshi
keiretsu
knowledge management
knowledge worker
kopiyka
LSE
M
m-commerce
management information system
maturity
merchant account

microcredit
mindshare
nakfa
new economy
nibble
non-net
open enrollment
optionaire
outgross
overstored
pad site
parachute
parasite store
permalancer
permatemp
portfolio
prairie-dogging
presentation graphics
presentation software
proof-of-purchase
prosumer
report
rerate
retail park
reverse split
road warrior
Roth IRA
routing code
same-store sales
secret shopper
selldown
service economy
sex industry
sex worker
shadow economy
sheltered workshop
single currency
SKU
slam
SME
soft landing

sogoshosha
stakeholder pension
stock swap
story
teentailer
touchpoint
understored
vertical union
viral marketing
virtual office
wraparound mortgage
yield management

Computing
@
access charge
ADSL
agent
aggregator
aliasing
a-life
antialiasing
archive
ASP
at sign
attachment
autodial
AYT
biocomputing
bloatware
BLOB
blog
Bluetooth
bookmark
bricks and mortar
brochureware
cgi
cgi-bin
character code
chat group
chatterbot

click rate
click-through
clickstream
computerese
content
cyberattack
cybernaut
cyberslacker
cyberstalking
cybersurfer
cyberterrorism
cybrarian
cyclic redundancy check
data set
data smog
datapoint
DDoS
decompile
deep magic
defrag
deinstall
dequeue
DES
DHTML
dictionary attack
digital locker
digital signature
disconnect
distribute
DLL
DNS
DOI
domain name
DoS
drag-and-drop
drill
DSL
dub-dub-dub
dynamic link library
E-fit
egosurf

endian
enqueue
extension
extranet
failover
filter
frame
gator
gender bender
glurge
google
grab
gray
grid
help desk
hit
iconize
ICT
IM
IMAP
in-box
information scent
instant messaging
IP address
ISP
ISV
joypad
jumpstation
keypal
knowledge
knowledge base
language engineering
Linux
loveware
lurker
malware
massively parallel
meta
meta key
metadata
middleware

microbrowser
microchip
microsite
misconfigure
mousetrap
mouthfeel
MP3
multicast
nagware
nastygram
navigate
network appliance
neural computer
neurocomputer
ohnosecond
Palm Pilot
parallel port
pipe
pop-under
portal
posting
PostScript
power user
print queue
PROM
P2P
public key
quantum computer
recompile
right-click
rip
ROMvelope
RTFM
run-time
save
script kiddie
secure server
serial port
skin
snert
SOHO

spider
SSL
status bar
sticky
streaming
swapfile
syntax
tablet PC
technical support
tele-immersion
text message
TIFF
T-1
uniform resource locator
uninstall
unsubscribe
USB
user interface
version control
virtualize
vortal
warchalking
wearable
web hosting
webcam
webcast
weblog
webzine
whitelisting
Wi-Fi
workbook
working memory

Encyclopedic
Antisthenes
Aoraki-Mount Cook
Astana
Baka
Banja Luka
chamise
Chattisgarh

coqui
damiana
dentex
Disneyland
Dixie Cup
Fitzroy
Godzilla
Goliath
Group of Eight
Hades
Ismail Samani Peak
Jharkand
Jordanesque
Klingon
Kolkata
leopard lily
margosa
Megaloceros
Mudville
Ned Kelly
Nihang
osteospermum
Poindexter
Pokemon
Pooterish
quaking bog
rose campion
Rube Goldberg
saola
Tardis
Tussock moth
Unabomber
Uttaranchal
welwitschia
Zelig

Food and Clothing
activewear
adobo
ahi
airpot

ajowan
asiago
baguette
ballotin
ballotine
bammy
bandeau
barista
barrique
Bellini
bento
besuited
bhuna
black bottom pie
boat neck
boba tea
bollito misto
boot-cut
Brazilian
bresaola
bridge mix
broast
brocciflower
broccoli rabe
bronzer
bubble tea
bucket hat
bunting
burqa
bushmeat
butcher's block
cachaca
caipirinha
cannoli
capellini
cargo pants
carpenter pants
catenaccio
chalupa
chef
chinois

choccy
chowhound
cigarette pants
clafoutis
clamdiggers
CoolMax
covert couture
crevette
Cullen skink
cupro
dashi
deep-pan
dehull
dehusk
designer stubble
desk dining
devoré
dirty rice
do-rag
dolphin-safe
dulce de leche
edamame
enoki
fake bake
farinaceous
farmers' market
fashionista
fatoush
flavor enhancer
foundation garment
Frankenfood
French-cut
fro-yo
funnel cake
fusion
gastropub
glügg
golden raisin
gosht
guayabera
gyoza

hairweaving
halloumi
hoodie
huevos rancheros
jalfrezi
jerk
juice box
kitten heel
Médoc
macchiato
maki
malfatti
Marsanne
Mary Jane
mezzaluna
mochaccino
mojo
monkfish
monobrow
mullet
nail wrap
nigiri zushi
overshirt
overwear
oyster bar
oyster sauce
palampore
panino
pearl tea
Pimm's
pleather
plus-size
powerbeads
Puffa
puftaloon
puttanesca
rösti
racerback
ranch
reposado
resole

salade niçoise
scamorza
scanty
second growth
shahtoosh
shelf-stable
shiso
shrug
shumai
soba
soymilk
St Clements
tankini
tapioca milk tea
terroir
threading
tighty-whities
udon
Ugg boot
umami

Language
anacronym
andro-
arrividerci
auto-
city
cued speech
da
effing
ELT
feh
gender-neutral
hand-waving
hunting
ka-ching
laniard
lateish
lemma
like
loan word

marker
meanwhile
moi
nano-
noughties
nu-
Pakhtun
patter of tiny feet
p-book
pico-
porn
positive
rage
run a mile
so
sonofabitch
subsense
TLA
uber-
vari-
whatever
wordrobe

Law, Politics, and Government
actionable
administrative law
affected class
al-Nakba
al Qaeda
AMBER Alert
asymmetrical warfare
Auschwitz Lie
bamboo curtain
Beige Book
Beltway bandit
big tent
bio-
blue dog Democrat
bottle bill
Brady Bill
child support

civic center
civil union
cold warrior
collateral damage
compliance
contingency fee
copyleft
county clerk
cross-party
cybercrime
cyberlaw
daisy-cutter
defund
delicense
delink
DfES
dissent
distant early warning
entitlement program
equal time
eurocreep
Euroland
Euro-sceptic
Eurozone
excusal
extension
fair use
fairness doctrine
Federal Register
go-team
Ground Zero
hired gun
intel
issue
Jane Doe
joined-up
just war
killing field
learnfare
logistics
mission creep

motor voter law
multi-utility
noncustodial
NU
nuclear threshold
number one
overfund
POTUS
PQ
prebuttal
pretrial
push poll
reasonable woman standard
regime change
Republicrat
restraining order
rider
right-to-know
safe haven
Schengen agreement
September 11th
situationism
snakehead
spinmeister
stench warfare
superfund
SWAT team
tailgate
tax-and-spend
Teflon
topple
transparent
undervote
wedge issue
world city
Wyotana

Lifestyle

adultescent
A-list
all-nighter

arm candy
army brat
ashtanga
assisted living
astanga
babymother
bach
Barcalounger
Barcelona chair
barebacking
barhop
beard
Belfast sink
bicoastal
Birkenstock
bling-bling
blonde moment
blunt
bogart
bomb
boomerang kid
booty call
bootylicious
Botox party
boutique hotel
boy band
brewski
bridezilla
bubbie
buckle bunny
bunny hugger
bunny-boiler
button man
buzzy
camgirl
care worker
carnapper
carriage house
casita
casual Friday
celebreality

cell yell
celly
channel-hop
chase the dragon
chick flick
chick lit
childminder
chimenea
close encounter
closure
club-sandwich generation
coked
combover
control freak
conversion van
co-sleeping
cringeworthy
crowd-pleaser
cuddle puddle
cup-holder cuisine
cyberpet
cyberphobia
cyberporn
dagga
date rape
Depression glass
designated driver
dickwad
dirtbag
dirty
dishpan hands
docusoap
doggy style
dress-down Friday
drink
drug mule
dryer sheet
dumpster diving
Dungeons and Dragons
Dustbuster
duvet day

early adopter
e-book
eco-warrior
eldercare
electronic organizer
event creation
express lane
Extropy
family hour
feed
FOAF
foam party
four-by-four
friend of Dorothy
ganzfeld
gap year
gastroporn
gateway drug
gaydar
Generation D
glamazon
go commando
G-ride
grrrl
hardbody
Harrington
head shop
headspace
head-trip
heightism
high-maintenance
hottie
huff
it girl
Jedi
jiggy
jissom
jockey shorts
jocks
johnny
jump the shark

kidult
life coach
lifestyle drug
loft
low-maintenance
lunch box
lush
manny
marriage of convenience
McMansion
meatspace
microcinema
microscooter
middlescent
mile-high club
miserabilism
mobe
mommy track
monster truck
morning after
multislacking
nanny cam
office park
office-park dad
OPD
overconnectedness
panic room
pepper spray
pester power
philosopause
play date
playscape
polyamory
preloved
premodern
propeller-head
Razor scooter
reality TV
regift
retail therapy
rice burner

romcom
rubber johnny
RVer
scrapbook
scratchiti
screenager
secondhand speech
Segway
sensitivity training
sequencing
shrapnel
sick
sizeism
skell
skinner
smokeeasy
smoking
snackette
soccer mom
spokesmodel
spoon
stage-diving
stairclimber
stalkerazzi
storming
street-legal
studmuffin
supersize
support system
swarm
SWF
SWM
sympathetic smoker
trailer trash
transgender
trophy child
Trustafarian
turista
tween
tweenager
twelve-step

24-7
twig furniture
turista
upskirt
vanpool
vertically challenged
victim
virtual community
visitability
wedding planner
wedgie
wigger
wildcraft
wrecked
yadda yadda yadda
yettie
yogic flying
zoophile

Medicine and Health
acid reflux
ACMOS
acupoint
adrenalized
aeromedical
aeromedicine
Ampakine
anatomically correct
andropause
androstenedione
aneuploid
angiostatin
antimalarial
aqua
auriculotherapy
autoerotic asphyxia
bag
bariatric surgery
bariatrics
Barnum effect
bed-blocking

beta-adrenergic
bigorexia
biopsy
biosurgery
biotherapy
biotransformation
birthing center
birthing room
BMI
body dysmorphic disorder
body image
body mass index
body mechanics
Botox
brachytherapy
bupropion
Buteyko method
cancer cluster
capsule endoscope
carcinomatosis
CCU
Celebra
chronotherapy
color therapy
combination therapy
comorbidity
conjoined twins
cord blood
cosmeceutical
cougher
cryptosporidiosis
crystal healing
cupping
cyberchondriac
date-rape drug
de Clerambault's syndrome
deconditioning
deep brain stimulation
deep-vein thrombosis
developmental delay
DI

dihydroepiandrosterone
disease management
DNR
dong quai
DOT
doula
dysmorphia
economy-class syndrome
efferent
EFM
embryectomy
embryopathy
enneagram
erotomania
euploid
evidence-based
extern
fenfluramine
fen-phen
fibromyalgia
fragile x syndrome
functional medicine
gelcap
gluteal
golden hour
guaifenesin
guarana
health care
heartsink patient
heartworm
hypericin
intradermal
kangaroo care
keratomileusis
LASIK
left-brained
lipectomy
lipodystrophy syndrome
LRD
LURD
MAOI

McTimoney
ME
medical examiner
methaqualone
milieu therapy
ministroke
muscle dysmorphia
nad
nandrolone
neutropenia
nocebo
Norovirus
Norwalk virus
NSAID
nutrigenomics
nvCJD
ob-gyn
off-label
orthokeratology
orthorexia
oxazolidinone
OxyContin
oxygen bar
panchakarma
panic disorder
pharmacogenomics
phytoestrogen
pill pusher
polarity therapy
pre-Bötzinger complex
preexisting condition
probiotic
progressive lens
progressives
protease inhibitor
proteome
Quaalude
quantum medicine
repetitive-motion disorder
Retin-A
retinoic acid

RICE
schizandra
shaken baby syndrome
statin
strep throat
sumatriptan
supersoap
symptomize
telesurgery
telomerase
TMJ
transient ischemic attack
tretinoin
umbilicoplasty
vaginoplasty
vaporizer
vCJD
Viagra
vibration white finger
video pill
videoscope
videosurgery
Watsu
West Nile Virus
working memory
Xenical
Zyban

People and Society

advanced placement
affluential
affluenza
Affrilachian
amakhosi
angry white male
Anytown
battered child syndrome
battered woman syndrome
battering parent syndrome
Bobo
borgata

bottom feeder
Carolinian
commentariat
consigliere
culturati
culture war
deep throat
Delphi technique
denazify
digital divide
downwinder
enviro
fedayeen
fidayeen
First Nation
flannel panel
food bank
gomer
goober
goofus
greenwash
ham-and-egger
hate crime
Holocaust denial
home study
homeroom
honeytrap
identity politics
informavore
Islamophobia
Ivorian
juneteenth
Kentucky colonel
kleptocrat
lactivist
ladette
literacy hour
lookism
media studies
men in black
men's movement

multiculti
need-blind
news peg
no-kill
nowheresville
open classroom
open marriage
Palookaville
partial-birth abortion
PETA
Picard
pinch point
prekindergarten
pretexting
pubcaster
racial profiling
Rom
safe house
safe room
shopgrifting
skimming
social promotion
stolen generation
superstation
tabloidization
telescam
thought leader
tipping point

Religion
acharya
age of reason
altar girl
amen corner
angelology
areligious
baldhead
bardo
bashert
biblicist
breatharian

croning
dhikr
discernment
faith-based
Falun Gong
hijab
ichthus
insight meditation
intelligent design
jihadi
multiverse
Raelian
stained-glass ceiling
theoterrorism
umrah
vipassana
wat
Zion

Science and Technology
AAVE
acoustic shock
active barrier
aerodyne
African Eve hypothesis
agglutinogen
alert
Allen wrench
ambulocetus
Andrewsarchus
animal
antiroll
aramid
areology
argan
astrobiology
bacterize
basilosaurus
BEV
BGH
big crunch

bioacoustics
bioastronautics
biochemical
bioclimatology
bioconversion
bioelectronics
biofilm
bioinformatics
biologic
biomaterial
biometeorology
biometric reader
biometric signature
biometrics
biopiracy
biosatellite
biotech
biotelemetry
bioterrorism
biowarfare
bleeding edge
boride
bottle jack
bovine growth hormone
brain fingerprinting
brane
brane world
brontothere
bunker buster
burn
burner
carbon sink
CDM
CDMA
chemical
chyron
circular polarization
clean room
climate change
climate jump
clipper

closed caption
cobot
coltan
combiner
compress
condensed tannin
consilience
coordination compound
cross-contamination
DAB
dark biology
dark energy
DARPA
deep ecology
demine
dendrimer
derecho
dial-around
digicam
digital camera
digital compact cassette
digital compression
digital television
Dobson unit
DOHC
donate
dopaminergic
downburst
DTV
DU
dumper
dwell time
e
early warning system
ecolodge
ecophysiology
EGD
egest
ELSS
enable
end use

environmental audit
EQ
ESV
Eve hypothesis
evolute
exoplanet
extrasolar
fabless
faceprint
faceprinting
facial profiling
Fermi-Dirac statistics
flexwing
flight simulator
foo fighter
fragment retention film
free-to-air
frozen smoke
fruit acid
Fujita scale
galactosamine
GAPA
gastornis
genetic blueprint
genetic pollution
genetically modified
genlock
genomics
genotype
geomatics
geospatial
geothermal
GHz
GLA
GM
golden rice
GPRS
grab
granular
granularity
grid

hands-free
high-band
homogeneous
homogeny
HSGT
hybrid car
hydrofluorocarbon
hypocenter
hypospray
ICANN
immunoblotting
i-Mode
impression
interoperability
isobutylene
ITV
junk science
killer app
knockout
Ku-band
Kuiper belt
La Niña
lane
laser gun
laser pointer
laser tweezers
lava tube
leucite
limescale
linguistic profiling
lookup
LW
lyocell
lysimeter
magnetar
MAT
mediascape
medium
megapixel
microarray
microelectromechanical

moeritherium
molecular electronics
moletronics
multipurpose device
nanobacterium
nanobe
nanowire
net metering
nondigital
no-tillage
old-growth
oleochemical
opera window
optical turnstile
overbreed
Paramotor
particle beam
Passface
patera
pharmacophore
Pilates
plasticizer
pluck
plunge saw
polygamy
polymerase chain reaction
polynosic
power rating
preadaptation
prelaunch
proteomics
purse net
PVR
Rapid Thermal Exchange
RBE
rear projection
recombinase
regenerative braking
replicant
resuspend
roaming

RTX
satellite television
second growth
shape-memory
SIM
single nucleotide polymorphism
SLV
smart dust
smart mob
smart suture
SMPTE
SMS
snip
SNP
speech recognition
speed dial
standby
strange
subtype
suicide gene
superior planet
Tactel
talk time
textphone
thermal imaging
thiazine
touchpoint
tractor beam
transition series
TTS
twisted pair
ubiquitin
UMTS
Uranian
vacuum-pack
vertical stabilizer
Very Large Array
video mail
virtual engineered composite
VLA
voice recognition

volumetric sensor
WAP
xenology

Sports
artificial climbing
air ball
b–ball
big air
blade
bokken
Bosman ruling
broomball
canyoning
catenaccio
coasteering
complete game
dead-ball line
drop
expansion team
game face
geocaching
goalhanger
green jersey
grommet
grudge match
hardgainer
jeet kune do
juke
kitesurfing
Krav Maga
lane
leg-rope
low post
March Madness
minicamp
Nassau
old-time
outhit
outpunch
outsprint

overhit
overspin
platoon
playbook
power walking
prematch
rhythmic gymnastics
set play
smash-mouth
snakeboard
speed bag
stringer
swingman
tae-bo
tag wrestling
training table
undercling
unplayed
wakeboard
zorbing

World English
ackers
act the maggot
bandobast
bibi
bladdered
blooter
bodgie
boerbull
bolter
bombora
bot
bulldust
bundobust
BYOG
cane
caned
cark
chib
chokidar

chowkidar
chuddies
chuddy
chuff
chuffing
clearskin
coacher
cod
codology
corker
corporator
cot-case
croweater
crubeen
cushty
cut lunch
dag
desperate
DETR
dinkum
doobry
doorknock
dosser
drum
durwan
dutchie
Dutchman
early doors
exclude
faujdar
feck
financial
finisher
fooster
footy
front bottom
gansey
geas
gey
good oil
gopura

gora
graunch
great
grind
gub
gutkha
handphone
highveld
history-sheeter
hokey-pokey
hot press
innit
in one's pelt
jack something up
kapai
kark
keech
khabar
kiasu
kisan
kloof
konfyt
kop
ladyboy
lairy
lamp
lank
large
lashed
like a shag on a rock
lost property
mag
maggot
maggoty
mahal
Manchester
marra
marrer
marrow
mash
minger

minging
mitch
mompara
monty
moulvi
muppet
murri
muti
nanny
ned
nippy
no-mark
no worries
numpty
oil
pants
pech
pelt
pig-root
pike
piker
pioneer
planter
pokie
possie
pounamu
praise singer
puckeroo
quietly
quoit
red top
ridgy-didge
ripper
rort
rough as bags
roughie
sahukar
salute the judge
samiti
sammie
scunge

section
selection
shedload
shelf
she's apples
shift
Shinner
shoogly
skimmel
skof
sling
smallgoods
snag
snaky
station hand
stingaree
stocious
stompie
stooshie
strife
stubby
sundowner
sunnies
swag
tab
tackie
takkie
talwar
tank
tart
thekedar
tinny
tog
tonk
top of the morning
totsiens
trolley dolly
two-pot screamer
umfundisi
wag
wallaby

wanky	ITV
warby	LSE
West Briton	LTR
white-van man	LW
yah	M
yoke	ME
zambuk	nad
zamindar	NSAID
zemindar	NU
zikr	nvCJD
	ob-gyn
Abbreviations	OPD
AAVE	OST
CAFE	PETA
CCU	pk
CDM	POTUS
CDMA	PQ
CFO	P2P
cgi	PVR
CRM	RBE
C2C	RICE
DETR	rpt
DfES	RTFM
DI	RTX
DNR	SKU
DNS	SLV
FOAF	SME
FTA	SMPTE
GAPA	SMS
GHz	SNP
GLA	SSL
GM	SWF
GPRS	SWM
HR	TIFF
HSGT	TLA
ICANN	TMJ
ICC	TTS
ICT	UMTS
IM	vCJD
IMAP	VLA
ISP	WAP
ISV	Wi-Fi

Quick Syllabification Guide

a•ban•don•a•ble	adjective	buc•ci•na•to•ry	adjective
a•bound•ing•ly	adverb	bug•gi•ness	noun
a•bridg•a•ble	adjective	butch•er•li•ness	noun
ab•sol•vent	adjective	but•ton•y	adjective
ac•ced•ence	noun	cae•su•ric	adjective
a•dapt•ed•ness	noun	ca•lam•i•toid	adjective
ad•mi•ra•ble•ness	noun	cap•i•ta•tive	adjective
ad•ren•al•ize	verb	cask•like	adjective
al•ien•a•tor	noun	cau•da•tion	noun
a•mor•al•ly	adverb	ceil•o•met•ric	adjective
an•a•chron•i•cal•ly	adverb	cen•sor•a•ble	adjective
An•glo•cen•tri•cal•ly	adverb	chair•per•son•ship	noun
a•pe•ri•od•i•cal•ly	adverb	chees•i•ly	adverb
ar•a•bil•i•ty	noun	chin•less•ness	noun
ar•ith•met•i•cal•ly	adverb	chris•mal	adjective
as•cend•a•ble	adjective	cla•dis•ti•cal•ly	adverb
a•tem•po•ral•ly	adverb	cloak•less	adjective
a•ton•a•ble	adjective	cod•i•fi•a•bil•i•ty	noun
a•veng•ing•ly	adverb	cog•niz•er	noun
a•ze•ot•ro•py	noun	com•men•su•rate•ness	noun
ba•boon•ish	adjective	con•cat•e•na•tor	noun
balk•i•ness	noun	con•fed•er•al•ist	noun
bar•ba•rous•ness	noun	co•nic•i•ty	noun
ba•sid•i•o•my•ce•tous	adjective	con•ta•gi•os•i•ty	noun
be•com•ing•ness	noun	cool•ing•ly	adverb
be•mire•ment	noun	cop•ro•la•li•ac	adjective
be•troth•ment	noun	cop•y•right•a•ble	adjective
bi•ax•i•al•ly	adverb	cos•mog•o•nal	adjective
blath•er•er	noun	crag•ged•ness	noun
block•head•ed•ness	noun	cru•ci•ate•ly	adverb
bo•lo•met•ri•cal•ly	adverb	cul•ti•va•bil•i•ty	noun
bot•a•niz•er	noun	cu•ta•ne•ous•ly	adverb
bo•vin•i•ty	noun	cut-rat•er	noun
bride•like	adjective	Dal•las•ite	noun

dat•a•ble•ness	noun	fu•gac•i•ty	noun
de•fea•si•ble•ness	noun	fu•si•bly	adverb
de•fin•i•tive•ness	noun	ga•len•ic	adjective
de•i•fi•er	noun	gauge•a•bly	adverb
dem•a•gog•i•cal•ly	adverb	ge•lat•i•nous•ness	noun
de•ter•ment	noun	germ•less	adjective
di•gest•ed•ness	noun	glee•some•ly	adverb
dis•bur•den•ment	noun	god•dess•hood	noun
dis•con•tin•u•er	noun	gor•get•ed	adjective
do•cent•ship	noun	gran•di•ose•ness	noun
dol•er•it•ic	adjective	groom•ish	adjective
dor•mered	adjective	grow•ing•ly	adverb
dot•like	adjective	guer•don•less	adjective
drach•mal	adjective	hack•ney•ism	noun
du•al•i•za•tion	noun	hal•lowed•ness	noun
dull--wit•ted•ness	noun	has•ten•er	noun
du•ti•a•bil•i•ty	noun	haw•thorn•y	adjective
ease•ful•ly	adverb	he•gem•o•nis•tic	adjective
ef•fem•i•na•tion	noun	hid•den•ly	adverb
e•jac•u•la•tive	adjective	hob•by•less	adjective
e•lec•tion•eer•er	noun	ho•log•ra•pher	noun
em•a•na•to•ry	noun	hot--blood•ed•ness	noun
en•ceph•a•lo•my•e•lit•ic	adjective	hov•er•ing•ly	adverb
ep•ar•chi•al	adjective	hug•ga•ble•ness	noun
e•ter•ni•za•tion	noun	i•am•bi•cal•ly	adverb
ex•ag•ger•at•ing•ly	adverb	i•co•nol•o•gist	noun
ex•haust•less	adjective	i•dol•a•trous•ness	noun
fab•ri•ca•tive	adjective	in•an•i•ma•tion	noun
fe•cun•da•to•ry	adjective	in•can•ta•tion•al	adjective
fe•lic•i•ta•tor	noun	in•ef•face•a•bly	adverb
fer•ment•a•bil•i•ty	noun	in•fun•dib•u•late	adjective
feuil•le•ton•ism	noun	in•no•cu•i•ty	noun
fi•bril•la•tive	adjective	in•quis•i•to•ri•al•ly	adverb
fis•sion•a•bil•i•ty	noun	in•tran•si•tive•ness	noun
flap•per•dom	noun	in•un•da•tor	noun
flaunt•ing•ly	adverb	in•var•i•ant•ly	adverb
fol•low•a•ble	adjective	Jac•o•bit•ic	adjective
for•giv•ing•ness	noun	jeop•ard•i•za•tion	noun
frag•men•tar•i•ness	noun	jolt•ing•ly	adverb
friz•zi•ly	adverb	kan•ga•roo•like	adjective
fruc•tu•ous•ness	noun	kid•dish•ness	noun

ky•an•i•za•tion	noun
la•bi•al•i•za•tion	noun
la•men•ta•ble•ness	noun
laud•a•to•ri•ly	adverb
leer•i•ly	adverb
lep•rous•ness	noun
li•ba•tion•al	adjective
lim•it•ed•ly	adverb
log•gish	adjective
los•ing•ly	adverb
lov•er•like	adjective
lu•bri•ca•tive	adjective
mac•ad•am•i•za•tion	noun
mal•ab•sorp•tive	adjective
mam•mal•i•ty	noun
mar•ca•sit•i•cal	adjective
maze•like	adjective
me•an•der•ing•ly	adverb
meg•a•lo•pol•i•tan•ism	noun
mer•chant•a• bil•i•ty	noun
mi•cro•cli•ma•tol•o•gist	noun
min•er•al•iz•er	noun
mith•ri•da•tism	noun
mod•er•a•to•ri•al	adjective
mop•ish•ness	noun
mul•ti•chan•neled	adjective
mu•si•cal•i•za•tion	noun
nap•pi•ness	noun
ne•ces•si•ta•tive	adjective
nick•nam•er	noun
nin•com•poop•er•y	noun
no•men•cla•to•ri•al	adjective
nul•li•fi•ca•tion	noun
ob•ject•less•ness	noun
ol•fac•to•ri•ly	adverb
on•co•ge•net•ic	adjective
op•er•et•tist	noun
os•se•ous•ly	adverb
out•put•a•ble	adjective
o•ver•crowd•ed•ness	noun
o•ver•qual•i•fi•ca•tion	noun
ox•i•met•ric	adjective
pach•y•der•moid	adjective
pal•an•quin•er	noun
pa•pa•bil•i•ty	noun
patch•work•y	adjective
pea•cock•er•y	noun
pel•let•i•za•tion	noun
pes•ter•some	adjective
phal•li•cism	noun
Pi•a•get•ian	adjective
pic•to•ri•al•ize	verb
piv•ot•al•ly	adverb
plan•u•lar	adjective
ple•be•ian•ism	noun
plumb•a•ble	adjective
po•et•as•ter•y	noun
po•ten•ti•a•tor	noun
praise•ful•ly	adverb
pre•op•er•a•tion•al	adjective
pris•moi•dal	adjective
pro•ba•tive•ly	adverb
prop•a•ga•tion•al	adjective
pro•ven•tric•u•lar	adjective
pug•na•cious•ness	noun
pu•pil•less	adjective
quad•ri•par•tite•ly	adverb
quar•ter•mas•ter•ship	noun
quit•ta•ble	adjective
rag•time•y	adjective
rasp•ish	adjective
re•cip•ro•cal•ness	noun
re•cum•bence	noun
re•jec•tion•ism	noun
re•mand•ment	noun
ren•o•va•tive	adjective
re•nun•ci•a•tive	adjective
rhi•zo•mor•phous	adjective
rhom•boi•dal•ly	adverb
rite•less	adjective
rol•lick•some	adjective
row•dy•ish	adjective

ru•in•a•ble	adjective	swol•len•ness	noun
rus•tic•ness	noun	syc•o•phant•ish	adjective
sac•cha•rim•e•try	noun	tag•ger	noun
sal•u•ta•tion•less	adjective	teach•er•less	adjective
sa•tia•bil•i•ty	noun	tel•e•vi•sion•al	adjective
sav•ior•hood	noun	ter•mi•na•tive	adjective
sce•nog•raph•er	noun	thaw•less	adjective
scratch•a•ble	adjective	think•ing•ly	adverb
se•cret•ness	noun	thwart•ed•ly	adverb
se•mes•tral	adjective	tim•breled	adjective
sep•ten•ni•al•ly	adverb	tol•er•a•tive	adjective
shale•like	adjective	torch•a•ble	adjective
shift•ing•ly	adverb	track•a•bil•i•ty	noun
Shi•va•ism	noun	tri•ax•i•al•i•ty	noun
si•de•re•al•ly	adverb	tuft•i•ness	noun
sim•u•la•tive•ly	adverb	tu•mor•al	adjective
sin•ning•ly	adverb	ug•li•fy	verb
slob•ber•er	noun	um•bel•late•ly	adverb
smile•less	adjective	un•know•a•ble•ness	noun
snub•by	adjective	un•well•ness	noun
sol•dier•li•ness	noun	u•re•al	adjective
so•vi•et•dom	noun	val•i•da•to•ry	adjective
sper•ma•to•ge•net•ic	adjective	ve•lar•i•za•tion	noun
spi•ral•i•ty	noun	vil•lage•y	adjective
spool•like	adjective	vo•cif•er•ance	noun
spur•tive	adjective	vul•ture•like	adjective
sta•tion•ar•i•ness	noun	wage•less	adjective
stig•ma•tiz•er	noun	wet•ta•bil•i•ty	noun
stran•gu•la•to•ry	adjective	whelp•less	adjective
strain•less•ly	adverb	wil•der•ment	noun
sty•lo•lit•ic	adjective	wolf•ish•ness	noun
sub•con•tract•a•ble	adjective	wool•grow•ing	adjective
suf•fo•ca•tive	adjective	xen•o•phil•i•a	noun
sup•plan•ta•tion	noun	yachts•man•ship	noun
swain•ish	adjective	Zi•on•is•tic	adjective
sweat•less	adjective		

A Select Bibliography of Oxford Dictionaries and Reference Works

Dictionaries

The Oxford English Dictionary. 2nd Ed. 20 vols. 1989.
   Also available online by subscription at http://www.oed.com
The New Shorter Oxford English Dictionary. Fifth Ed 2 vols. 2002.
   Not just an abridgement of the twenty-volume *OED*, the Shorter has its own independent research program. With more than 83,000 quotations, this has the *OED's* literary approach in a more manageable format. Also available on CD-ROM.
The New Oxford American Dictionary. 2001.
   A completely new dictionary of American English from Oxford, with an innovative arrangement of definitions in which the more prominent core senses are given first, with related senses arranged in blocks underneath. This allows for a nice overview of constellations of meaning not possible with other dictionaries. Also available on CD-ROM.
The Oxford American Dictionary and Thesaurus (with Language Guide.) 2003.
   A very good general dictionary with a complete thesaurus and a great deal of extra usage and language information, plus a 62-page Language Guide reference supplement.
The Concise Oxford Dictionary. 10th Ed. 1999.
   The classic desk-size dictionary for British English, including the most current words and phrases and scientific and technical vocabulary. Word Formation features identify complex word groups such as *-phobias, -cultures,* and *-ariums.*

Dictionaries of Usage

Burchfield, R.W. *The New Fowler's Modern English Usage.* 3rd Ed. 1996.
   A completely revised and expanded version of the beloved *Modern English Usage* with examples from modern authors such as Tom Wolfe, Saul Bellow, and Iris Murdoch.
Fowler, H.W. *A Dictionary of Modern English Usage.* 2nd Ed. 1983
   The most-beloved language reference book and the one by which all others are judged.
Garner, Bryan. *A Dictionary of Modern American Usage.* 1998.

The new authority for American usage and guidance not only for the grammar-impaired but for anyone who would like to write gracefully and precisely.

Other Reference Books

Ayto, John. *Twentieth Century Words.* 1999.
An overview of 5,000 words and meanings of the twentieth century, including *flapper, flower power,* and *road rage.*

Chantrell, Glynnis. *The Oxford Dictionary of Word Histories.* 2002.
This book describes the origins and sense development of over 11,000 words in the English language, with dates of the first recorded evidence from ongoing research for the OED.

Delahunty, Andrew; Sheila Dignan and Penelope Stock. *The Oxford Dictionary of Allusions.* 2001.
A guide to allusions most frequently found in literature both modern and canonical. It covers classical myths and modern culture and ranges from "Ahab" to "Teflon," "Eve" to "Darth Vader." Many entries include a quotation illustrating the allusion in use.

Greenbaum, Sidney. *The Oxford English Grammar.* 1996.
A complete overview of the subject, including a review of modern approaches to grammar and the interdependence of grammar and discourse, word-formation, punctuation, pronunciation, and spelling.

Knowles, Elizabeth, ed. *The Oxford Dictionary of Phrase and Fable.* 2000.
Drawn from folklore, history, mythology, philosophy, popular culture, religion, science, and technology, these alphabetically arranged entries include ancient gods and goddesses, biblical allusions, proverbial sayings, common phrases, fictional characters, geographical entities, and real people and events.

Lindberg, Christine. *The Oxford American Thesaurus of Current English.* 1999.
A great general thesaurus with an exclusive Writer's Toolkit and more than 350,000 synonyms.

Quinion, Michael, *Ologies and Isms: Word Beginnings and Endings.* 2003. A book about the building blocks of the English language—the beginnings and endings, and sometimes the middles—that help form or adapt many of the words we use.

Onions, C. T. *The Oxford Dictionary of English Etymology.* 1966.
The standard reference for scholars, this dictionary delves into the origins of more than 38,000 words.

Finding New Words

You're reading your favorite magazine, or a new novel, or your local paper, and you come across this sentence: "It was an eerie, crebadative feeling, as if she were being watched." *Crebadative?* you wonder. You check a dictionary (or two, or three) and you don't find it. What you have found is a new word. A classic new word, one that has a completely different arrangement of letters from any other existing word. You understand roughly what it means, from context, but you're not sure, and you file it away in your head as new and unusual. You probably won't write it or speak it yourself, unless you're very playful or adventurous—you don't have firm grasp on it, and there are plenty of other words in your storehouse that you feel more comfortable with. A little later, perhaps, you read this sentence: "Scientists in Melbourne have discovered a new enzyme responsible for fat digestion, lipafazil." *Lipafazil?* You probably don't check that one at all, slotting it instead into a neat compartment in your brain labeled "science stuff." And you don't use it (unless you yourself are an enzyme-research scientist) because you simply have no need for it.

This kind of new-word-finding experience is what most people think of when they (or if they) think about new words: the unique word appearing out of the blue, especially the unique science and technology word. This kind of new word is often called "coined," and in some cases a particular person can be credited with the invention of the word (as with the word *cyberspace*, which was coined by William Gibson in 1982). Even coined words, though, aren't usually completely original combinations of letters; a combination like *phygrttle* is certainly original, but it looks hard to pronounce and doesn't give readers any clue as to what it means, unlike the word *infomercial*, which is a readily recognizable "blend" of "information" and "commercial." Many coined words are blended from two already accepted words. One completely original coined words is *googol* ("ten raised to the hundredth power (10^{100})"), which was invented by the nine-year-old nephew of a mathematician.

However, from the lexicographer's point of view, most new words aren't the careful coinage of a single person, or even the simultaneous independent coinages of several people (which happens more often than you might think, to the frustration of all involved). Many new words are stolen by English from other languages; words like *keiretsu* from Japanese, or *chicano*, from Spanish. English is very likely to swipe words for food: *chianti, sauerkraut, tandoori*. Sometimes English, instead of taking the word, just transmutes the foreign word into English. German *Übermensch*, for example, became English *superman*. This is called a *calque* (from the French for 'copy') or a *loan translation*. Occasionally, people will hear foreign or unfamiliar words and reanalyze them to fit them into a more familiar form, making new words. This process is called folk etymology, and made words like *cockroach*, from Spanish *cucaracha*, and *woodchuck*, from an American Indian word often spelled *otchek*. Occasionally this process is more involved, as with *alligator pear*, "avocado"—given this name because they were supposed to grow where alligators were common.

New acronyms are very common, and occasionally become words whose acronymic origins are all but forgotten by users (words like *scuba* 'self-contained underwater breathing apparatus' and *snafu* 'situation normal, all fouled up' rarely come across as acronyms today, and the origin of a word like *gigaflops*, where the *–flops* is from 'floating operations per second' is not blatantly acronymic). There is even a recent trend towards making *bacronyms*, words that are made acronymically but for which the most important consideration is that the acronym make an appropriate (usually already existing) word or words, such as MADD, "Mothers Against Drunk Driving," or the recent USA-PATRIOT Act, in which USA-PATRIOT stands for "Uniting and Strengthening America by Providing Appropriate Tools Required to Intercept and Obstruct Terrorism."

Although entirely new words are exciting to the lexicographer and the layperson alike, changes to existing words can thrill as well. The meanings of words are no more fixed than any other aspect of human culture, and despite well-meaning efforts by many to make them stand still, they continue to change. Spotting these new meanings takes a more sophisticated approach to language, and one that is more sensitized to shades of definition instead of just knee-jerkishly categorizing a new meaning as 'wrong.'

A favorite kind of lexical change is metaphorical extension: the computer meanings of *mouse* and *virus* are good examples of this, as is the basketball meaning of *dunk*. An unfavorite, though frequent, kind of lexical change is change in grammatical function: the verbing of nouns. Why one kind of change is welcomed and thought clever by logophiles while the other kind is deplored and thought degrading is unclear, but *impact, contact, script, conference,* and other verbs-from-nouns are in very frequent use.

Words' meanings can get worse, a process called *pejoration*. This has happened in a big way to words like *barefaced*, which originally meant just "open, unconcealed," and then became "shameless," and in a small way to words like *poetess* and *actress*, which now seem like lightweights compared to *poet* and *actor*. Words can also improve their meanings, or *ameliorate*. The word *luxury* originally mean "lust," but gradually changed to mean "something desirable but not indispensable."

Besides getting better or worse, meanings can become more or less inclusive. Becoming less inclusive is called *specialization*, as when *amputate* went from meaning "to cut off" to meaning "to cut off a limb or other part of the body." Becoming more inclusive is called *generalization*, as when the word *pants* went from meaning specifically "pantaloons" to meaning almost any kind of lower-body covering.

Some new words are just shorter versions of old words. These are made either through clipping (*fax* from *facsimile* and *exam* from *examination* are standard examples) or from back-formation (*burgle* from *burglar*, *bus* from *busboy*, *edit* from *editor*). This is so common that most people don't register these words as "new" or are astonished to learn the longer word is older, and the shorter word is newer. This is probably because many other new words are formed by *derivation*, that is, by adding affixes to existing words, lengthening them. (Affixes are prefixes and suffixes, and, in facetious use only, infixes, which are parts inserted in the middle of words. These are usually only used with obscenities: "abso-damn-lutely.") Words like *ascertainable* and *finalization* are derivatives. Many of the new words are added to dictionaries are new derivatives, added to the end of existing entries. (Some additional new derivatives are listed in this book in a special section.)

Of course, some words are made from proper names, and are then called *eponyms*: *sequoia* and *silhouette* are two well-known examples. Using a proper name to stand for something having an attribute associated with that name is called *antonomasia*, and calling someone especially perspicacious a *Sherlock* is one example. When proper names are treated in this way they are very often added to dictionaries and thus count, for lexicographical purposes, as new words. The genericization of trademarks (like *thermos* and *aspirin*) also falls under antonomasia.

One last method of forming new words is echoing, or onomatopoeia, in which new words are made to resemble real-world sounds, like *bleep*, *bloop*, and *boing*! This might be the most entertaining way to make new words, but it is also less likely to create words that give off that "new" feel, especially if the sound is familiar.

With this field guide to word formation processes you should now be able to find new words everywhere you look—and possibly create a few yourself.

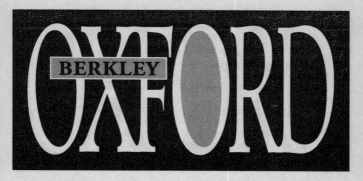

Hana-Kimi

For You in Full Blossom

11

story and art by
HISAYA NAKAJO

HANA-KIMI
For You in Full Blossom
VOLUME 11

STORY & ART BY HISAYA NAKAJO

Translation & English Adaptation/David Ury
Touch-Up Art & Lettering/Susan Daigle-Leach
Design/Andrea Rice
Editor/Gary Leach

Managing Editor/Annette Roman
Director of Production/Noboru Watanabe
Vice President of Publishing/Alvin Lu
Sr. Director of Acquisitions/Rika Inouye
Vice President of Sales & Marketing/Liza Coppola
Publisher/Hyoe Narita

Published by VIZ Media, LLC, P.O. Box 77010, San Francisco, CA 94107

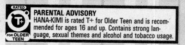

Shôjo Edition
10 9 8 7 6 5 4 3 2 1

First printing, April 2006

VIZ
MEDIA

www.viz.com
store.viz.com

CONTENTS

Hana-Kimi Chapter 56 3

Hana-Kimi Chapter 57 43

Hana-Kimi Chapter 58 75

Hana-Kimi Chapter 59 105

Hana-Kimi Chapter 60 135

Hana-Kimi Chapter 61 166

...I CAME OVER BECAUSE I HEARD YOU, BUT...

...I DON'T WANNA FREAK YOU OUT, BUT...

...I...

...DIDN'T HEAR ANYONE ELSE...JUST YOU.

FWAH

FAR AS I CAN TELL, YOU'VE BEEN ALONE THIS WHOLE TIME.

AND THERE'S NOTHING BEHIND THIS MANSION BUT A CLIFF OVERLOOKING THE LAKE. THERE'S NO WAY ANYONE LIVES THERE.

SHIVER

BUT...

WHAT ABOUT THAT KID?

I WISH I WAS IN A DOUBLE ROOM LIKE NAKATSU AND KAYASHIMA.

STILL THINKING ABOUT WHAT HAPPENED.

NO WAY I'M GONNA FALL ASLEEP TONIGHT.

MIZUKI... I LOVE YOU...

Umm...

MI...

BWINK

FW
UP

MIZUKI.

MIZUKI.

CR
E
A
K

14

SQUEEK

CREAK

MIZUKI.

FINALLY...

...I'VE FINALLY FOUND YOU.

15

NAKATSU?

...

YOU LITTLE—

WAIT.

SOMETHING'S NOT RIGHT HERE.

KAYASHIMA...

SHH...

∘∘∘**GIANT KING OF THE MOUNTAIN!**

ZIP IT.

Ah...

ASHIYA...

I KNOW IT'S NOT WHAT WE PLANNED, BUT LET'S JUST GET OUR BAGS PACKED AND THEN HIT THE SACK.

WE'LL JUST HAVE TO LEAVE FIRST THING IN THE MORNING.

WELL, NOTHING TO DO ABOUT IT TODAY.

...WHY NAKATSU WAS POSSESSED.

THAT PROBABLY HAS SOMETHING TO DO WITH...

HUH?

GOOD NIGHT.

CREAK

I'M SURE YOU'LL BE FINE, BUT WHY DON'T YOU HOLD ONTO ONE OF THESE TOO?

Just in case...

HE SEEMS TO HAVE MISTAKEN YOU FOR SOMEONE ELSE.

SO...

...
HIS
MIZUKI.

...HE
THINKS
I'M...

SHIVER

RUSTLE

RUSTLE

RUSTLE

HIS
FRIEND'S
NAME
AND
MINE...
ARE THE
SAME.

AHH! THIS IS TOO SCARY!

SHI VER SHI VER

SHI VER

CLACK

CLACK

CLACK

CLACK

WHA-WHAT? WHAT'S WRONG?

Hey, scoot over.

YOU'RE SUCH A SCAREDY CAT, I FIGURED YOU WOULDN'T BE ABLE TO SLEEP.

BWOINK

Sa—

SANO?

I KNEW IT.

CLICK

KNOCK KNOCK KNOCK

SHOCK

FWUP

WAH!

27

And how the heck are we supposed to do that?

HEY.

...TO GET RID OF WHATEVER'S LEFT OF THE GHOST'S SPIRIT, SO HE CAN MOVE ON TO THE NEXT WORLD.

WELL, OUR ONLY CHOICE IS...

WELL, WHAT THE HECK ARE WE SUPPOSED TO DO? WE CAN'T JUST LEAVE HIM LIKE THIS.

IT MIGHT BE IMPORTANT. MAYBE IT'LL GIVE US SOME CLUES.

I FOUND THIS IN THE STUDY BACK THERE, HIDDEN IN THE VERY BACK OF THE BOOKSHELF.

Look...

IT'S GOT AN "M" ON THE COVER. COULD STAND FOR MIZUKI.

M.

Huh...

LOOKS OLD. MAYBE IT'S A DIARY.

31

32

DAY
ND I
HT
MY
N, I
NOT
E MY
O
SE I
...

THE
REASON I
REFUSED
HIS
OFFER
WAS NOT
THAT I
HATED
YOU.

I AM VERY
GRATEFUL THAT
YOUR FATHER
WAS KIND
ENOUGH TO
ALLOW A
HUMBLE
SERVANT LIKE
MYSELF TO
ATTEND SCHOOL
ALONG WITH
YOU.

YOU LEFT
BEFORE
WE COULD
MAKE UP.

I'M SURE
YOU'RE
STILL MAD
AT ME.

AND NOW
I WILL
FINALLY BE
PUNISHED
FOR MY
BETRAYAL.

ONLY THROUGH THIS DIARY CAN I ESCAPE THE CHAINS OF THIS FORBIDDEN TABOO...

BACK IN THOSE DAYS...

...IT WASN'T JUST THE NATURE OF THEIR RELATIONSHIP THAT WAS TABOO, BUT THE DIFFERENCE IN CLASS AS WELL.

...AND LET YOU KNOW HOW I TRULY FEEL ABOUT YOU, SATORU.

...EVEN IN DEATH, THEY REMAIN APART.

SWIPE

THEY LOVED EACH OTHER, BUT...

HE'S BEEN ALONE FOR ALL THESE YEARS.

SATORU...

MIZUKI.

FWUH

SATORU?
MEDIUM — ONE WHO COMMUNICATES WITH SPIRITS.
SATORU, THE ONE YOU'RE...
...LOOKING FOR IS...
ASHIYA...
...AN AMATEUR SHOULDN'T TRY TO ACT AS A MEDIUM.
YOU'D BETTER STOP.
BESIDES...
...HE DOESN'T NEED US TO TELL HIM. HE ALREADY KNOWS.

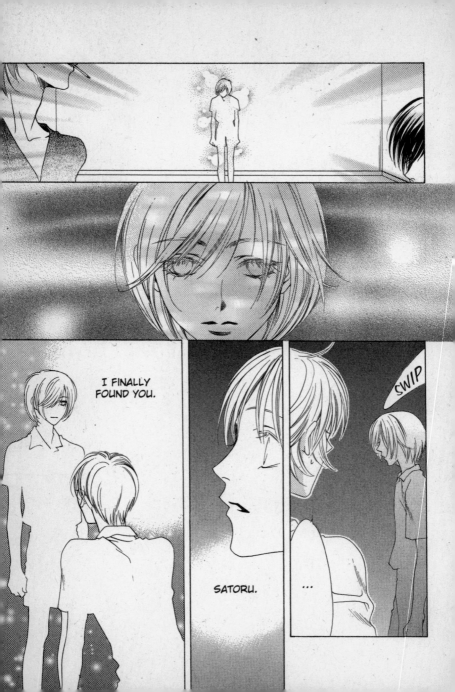

THAT'S
OKAY.

AND
THEN...

...THE
TWO
SPIRITS
FADED
AWAY
TOGETHER.

...

RAHH!
I'M
STAR-
VING.

FW
UP

AH...
NAKATSU'S
AWAKE.

HURRY
UP, OR WE'LL
LEAVE YOU
BEHIND.

I HOPE
THEY
FINALLY
FOUND
PEACE.

...BUT WHEN I TURN AROUND...

THEY'RE GONE...

...I CAN ALMOST SEE THEM STANDING IN THE SHADOWS...

...SURROUNDED BY THEIR BEAUTIFUL MEMORIES...

HANA-KIMI CHAPTER 56: END

THE TIME HAS FINALLY COME! THAT'S RIGHT, IT'S THE EVENT WE'VE ALL BEEN WAITING FOR... THE TRIENNIAL OSAKA HIGH/BLOSSOM GIRLS' HIGH SCHOOL CO-ED CHRISTMAS DANCE PARTY!

GET READY FOR SOME BIG NEWS, FELLAS!

MUSIC "Ringo Shiina"

I'VE ALWAYS LOVED LISTENING TO MUSIC, AND RIGHT NOW I'M REALLY INTO RINGO'S STUFF. SHE'S SO GREAT! SHE'S ONLY ABOUT 20 YEARS OLD, BUT HER VOICE AND THE POWER OF HER PERFORMANCES ARE ALREADY A CUT ABOVE THE REST. I HATE THE WAY THE MEDIA TREATED HER LIKE A TOTAL NOBODY BEFORE SHE GOT FAMOUS AND THEN SUDDENLY THEY STARTED TREATING HER LIKE A DIVA. I THINK OF HER AS A SORT OF JAPANESE BJORK. I LOVE HER SO MUCH I CAN'T EVEN COMPARE HER WITH OTHER PERFORMERS FROM HER GENERATION. OBVIOUSLY, I LIKE HER WAY MORE THAN HIKII.

49

WHAT'S WRONG, NAKAO?

Why are you sighing?

THAT MEANS IT ONLY HAPPENS ONCE DURING OUR THREE YEARS OF HIGH SCHOOL.

That's pretty special.

IT'S ONLY ONCE EVERY THREE YEARS, SO...

IF ONLY...

...I'D GONE TO SAINT BLOSSOM.

Then I'd get to dance with Nanba.

SIGH

WITH A FACE LIKE MINE, I COULD'VE BLENDED IN. IT'S ONLY THREE YEARS.

I mean it!

SHE'S THE ONE INFILTRATING AN ALL-BOY'S SCHOOL.

...WO BBLE

GROSS

STAB

PERVERT

AH-HEM.

HE KNOWS.

AW MAN! THAT'S SO GROSS! WHAT ARE YOU, A PERVERT?

WAIT A MINUTE! I HAVE TO DANCE WITH THEM TOO!

Hold on...

DRIP DRIP

HMM.. DANCING WITH GIRLS.

50

Whispered Secrets "The way of manga"

SOME OF YOU HAVE PROBABLY NOTICED, BUT LATELY MY ASSISTANTS HAVE BEEN DRAWING THE BACKGROUNDS. THAT'S RIGHT, UNTIL NOW, I'D BEEN DRAWING THEM ALL BY MYSELF BECAUSE I ACTUALLY LIKED DRAWING BACK- GROUNDS. BUT I JUST DON'T HAVE TIME TO DO IT ANYMORE. HEH, HEH, HEH. AND THIS WORKS OUT MUCH BETTER THAN HAVING TO RACE AGAINST TIME, AND ENDING UP WITH REALLY LAME-LOOKING BACKGROUNDS. UNTIL NOW, I'D ALWAYS THOUGHT THAT "IF THE AUTHOR ONLY DRAWS THE CHARACTERS, THEN YOU CAN'T CALL IT 'HER' MANGA." I THOUGHT YOU COULD ONLY CALL IT YOUR OWN WORK IF YOU'D DONE IT ALL BY YOURSELF.

Apparently, that's what most manga artists do.

Oh, heh, heh. I see... so every-body has their assistants do it.

A CHRISTMAS DANCE PARTY...

WHAT'S WRONG? WHY'RE YOU ALL SWEATY?

Huh?

UH...NO REASON.

Ha ha ha ha

I WISH I COULD DANCE WITH SANO.

If only...

FIRST YOU'LL BE DIVIDED INTO DIFFERENT GROUPS WITH DIFFERENT ROLES.

...WITH THE REST OF YOU GOING INTO THE COSTUME GROUP, THE LIGHTING GROUP, THE PROP GROUP, THE SETTING GROUP, THE SOUND GROUP, ETC.

DON'T WORRY...

THE THREE RESIDENCE ADVISORS WILL BE THE MAIN ORGANIZERS...

IT'S ALMOST LIKE AN AMERICAN GRADUATION PARTY.

THE BLOSSOM GIRLS WILL BE SIMILARLY DIVIDED, WITH EVERYONE WORKING TOGETHER.

Hmm...

Hmm...

...YOU'LL HAVE LOTS OF CHANCES TO MEET THE GIRLS.

IF SHE SAYS YES, THEN YOU'RE ALL SET. IF SHE SAYS NO, MOVE ON TO THE NEXT GIRL.

THE GUYS ALWAYS DO THE ASKING.

AS FOR PAIRING UP, JUST PICK YOUR PARTNER AND ASK HER SOMETIME BEFORE THE DANCE.

GULP!

A GIRLFRIEND FROM BLOSSOM?

Ha ha ha!

A LOT OF GUYS END UP FINDING GIRLFRIENDS THIS WAY, SO GO GET 'EM, FELLAS!

WHAT'S THE BIG DEAL?

Huh?

THEY SAY DANCE PARTY, BUT IT'S A FORMAL DANCE.

Yeah!

SO KNOCK 'EM DEAD!

YOU'RE FREE TO ASK A GIRL FROM ANY GROUP, NOT JUST YOUR OWN.

HA HAHA

YOU FREAK IN' IDIOT!

WHAT THE HECK'S WITH YOU?

Both of you?

SHIVER

GIRLFRIENDS! WE CAN FIND GIRLFRIENDS!

CRICK

I WONDER..

Ah...

I'M STARVING.

YAWNN...

Uh-oh... I bet Nakatsu's gonna come over here. I'll look away.

sorry.

OH, RIGHT... YOU'RE GAY.

Mizuki is...

SHUT UP!

...my one love.

GRRR!

54

THIS YEAR I'M GETTING HIM SOMETHING REALLY SPECIAL!

YEAH

CRINCH

ALL RIGHT!

I WAS SO INVOLVED IN OTHER STUFF LAST YEAR...

...I DIDN'T GET TO GIVE HIM A PRESENT.

FSSS

WILL THAT BE ENOUGH?

I'D BETTER FIND A PART TIME JOB.

FSSS

...PLUS WHAT MY FOLKS SENT ME.

I'LL USE THE MONEY I EARNED AT THAT HAUNTED MANSION...

MAN, ARE THE GUYS IN OUR CLASS EASILY EXCITED OR WHAT?

WHAT SHOULD I GET HIM?

YEAH, THEY GOT PRETTY WORKED UP.

Ha ha ha...

IDIOTS. MINAMI DANGLES THAT CARROT IN FRONT OF THEM, AND THEY GO HARING AFTER IT.

EVERYBODY'S REALLY RARIN' TO GO.

...

CARROT!?

!

SO... UHH...

...WHAT'S YOUR IDEAL TYPE OF GIRL?

I'm curious.

HMM...

HMM...

...

...

HRRMMM

HMM...

60

NUNNA YER BUSINESS! HIT THE RACK, DODO!

UMPH!

SLAP

IDIOT!

YOU...

...IT'S YOU!

ANSWER ME, SANO!

WHAT? WHAT'S HE MEAN? IS THERE SOMEONE OR NOT?

WOBBLE

WOBBLE

64

Old man Konaki

DING DING

DING DONG

How beautiful!

WHOA...

Dynamite!

NOW...

...

PLUNK

CLOP

CLOP

Ah...

YOU MUST BE THE BOYS FROM OSAKA HIGH.

KNOCK KNOCK

COME IN.

I BROUGHT THE BOYS FROM OSAKA HIGH.

YES, I SEE. THANK YOU.

You may go.

I'M HIBARI HANAYASHIKI...

...PRESIDENT OF THE SAINT BLOSSOM STUDENT BODY.

THIS IS OUR FIRST MEETING.

CLANK

68

WOW... SHE LOOKS JUST LIKE A PRINCESS.

I'M GOING...

HIBARI HANAYASHIKI?

SHE'S THE REAL THING!

MASAO.

HOW DO YOU DO?

Oh, my...

A ho ho ho

UNLIKE A CERTAIN SOMEONE, I EXCEL AT WHAT I DO. NATURALLY I'D BECOME PRESIDENT.

...

I KNEW YOU ATTENDED SAINT BLOSSOM, BUT NOT THAT YOU WERE THE PRESIDENT.

71

END OF HANA-KIMI CHAPTER 57

Hana-Kimi

For You in Full Blossom

CHAPTER 58

...THAT INCLUDES YOU TWO HUMMING-BIRDS ♡

Of course...

...WHY DON'T WE HAVE SOME BOYS FROM OSAKA HIGH FILL IN?

WHAT I SAID WAS, ENROLLMENT'S DOWN AT OUR SCHOOL THIS YEAR, SO...

UH...

STUDENT CONFERENCE ROOM

WHAT DID YOU JUST SAY?

NO WAY...

DRIP DRIP

I'm a real novice about music... ♪

MUSIC "Eccentric Opera"

I FIRST BECAME AWARE OF EO WHEN I HEARD SOME MUSIC THEY'D DONE FOR A TV COMMERCIAL. PROBABLY MOST OF YOU WOULD RECOGNIZE THEIR SONGS EVEN IF YOU HAVEN'T HEARD OF THEM. EO MIXES OPERA STYLE VOCALS WITH MODERN MUSIC. IT'S A REFRESHINGLY NEW, YET NOSTALGIC SOUNDING FEMALE DUO. (LIKE A JAPANESE VERSION OF ENIGMA.) THE VOCALS STILL HAVE A REAL OPERA FEEL, BUT THE OVERALL SOUND IS VERY ORIGINAL. I GUESS THEY'RE A BIT LIKE BULGARIAN VOICE. ANYWAY, IT REALLY STRUCK A CHORD WITH ME.

I FEEL THE SAME WAY ABOUT YOKO KANNO.

77

78

OSAKA HIGH SCHOOL
DORMITORY

BLAH CAFETERIA *BLAH*

ARE YOU REALLY SURE...

...YOU WANNA DO THIS?

YEAH, NO PROBLEM.

CHOMP

I MEAN, I'LL BE SO BUSY GETTING READY FOR THE DANCE PARTY...

...I WON'T HAVE TIME TO GET A JOB ANYWHERE ELSE.

PROBABLY ...

HA HA

HA HA HA

I JUST DRESS UP LIKE A GIRL AND GET PAID FOR IT, RIGHT?

PIECE OF CAKE!

Yay!

STOP CRYING ON YOUR FOOD. IT'S GROSS.

Uh-huh...

IT'S GOOD TO BE ALIVE!

HOLD ON... IF WE'RE DANCING, THAT MEANS...

...OUR BODIES WILL BE PUSHED UP AGAINST EACH OTHER.

WHY THE LONG FACE, MY PRECIOUS LITTLE KITTY?

SH

OCK

PLOP

Na! willkommen!
(COME TO ME.)

WHAT
THE HELL
ARE YOU
DOING
HERE?

You're in dorm
three.

Wah!

Heh...

LOVE
HAS
NO
BORDERS.

I WILL
COMFORT
YOU.

AMBIGUOUS
MEANING

Why is
he
here?

...

WARN
US?

HE'S JUST
TRYING TO
STAND OUT,
SO WE DON'T
CONFUSE
HIM WITH A
CERTAIN
SOMEONE.

WHY
DO YOU
HAVE TO
POSE LIKE
THAT?

You
idiot.

Never
mind...

BEWARE
OF HIBARI
HANAYASHIKI.

CHOMP
CHOMP
CHOMP
CHOMP

ACTUALLY,
I NEED TO
WARN YOU
GUYS ABOUT
SOMETHING.

83

IN JUNIOR HIGH WE COMPETED IN ALL KINDS OF EVENTS.

WE WON EVERY SINGLE CONTEST. THEY CALLED US "THE TROPHY HUNTERS."

COME ON, YOU TWO. YOU'RE BOTH EQUALLY GOOD.

NO!

WAH!

WE DID NOT GET ALONG AT ALL.

I AM... I AM...

...THE BEST!

WE'VE BEEN COMPETING AS LONG AS I CAN REMEMBER.

KIDS' SINGING CONTEST

HMPH!

THEY'RE ALWAYS SO CUTE.

IT'S THE HIMEJIMA BOY AND THE HANAYASHIKI GIRL.

HE'S BEING TORMENTED BY OLD MEMORIES.

There was that one time...

Pant Pant

IN SHORT, YOU PLAGUE EACH OTHER.

MUMBLE MUMBLE

...and then that time...

AKIHA! YOU'RE BACK!

I JUST ARRIVED TODAY.

Yeah.

OH, YEAH...

I'm home!

AH...

I'll sit down.

MEDICAL CENTER

WELL, I STARTED OUT IN ITALY, THEN STOPPED IN SPAIN ON THE WAY BACK.

CRAZY DOLL...

UH... WHERE DID YOU SAY YOU WENT, AKIHA?

Thanks.

Oh, yeah!

It's a rare Spanish Barbie.

Handmade clothes, sold only in street stalls.

HERE! THIS IS FOR YOU ♡

TA-DAH

DR. UMEDA?

Huh?

He's awfully quiet...

PLO INK

U-UMEDA...

PAT
PAT

HUH?

YOU'RE GONNA FILL IN AT SAINT BLOSSOM HIGH?

YOU'RE TOO YOUNG TO UNDERSTAND, ASHIYA.

Heh, heh, heh...

I'M SAVING UP FOR SANO'S BIRTHDAY PRESENT.

PAYING YOU? WHY SHOULD THAT MATTER?

Do you have stingy parents?

GRIN

I GUESS NOT! AND THEY'RE PAYING ME.

GEEZ...YOU JUST CAN'T STAY OUT OF TROUBLE, CAN YOU!

Ever try to say no?

88

I WAS TOO BUSY TO GET HIM ANYTHING LAST YEAR, SO...

AND I WANNA DO IT WITH MONEY I EARNED ON MY OWN.

...I'VE GOTTA MAKE UP FOR IT!

...

SHE'S GOT TRUE LOVE WRITTEN ALL OVER HER FACE...

Huh?

NO.

DO YOU KNOW HOW THAT DANCE PARTY ORIGINALLY GOT STARTED?

Whispered Secrets "I'm not just your average princess."

TO BE HONEST, I LIKE HIBARI. IN THE BEGINNING, THIS CHARACTER WAS GOING TO BE A STUDENT LIVING IN DORM NUMBER THREE. I ORIGINALLY NAMED THIS CHARACTER MANA TAKARAZUKA. SINCE I BASED HIMEJIMA'S CHARACTER ON GACKT (EXCUSE ME), I THOUGHT I'D CREATE A CHARACTER BASED ON MANA TOO! [NOTE: GACKT AND MANA USED TO BE MEMBERS OF THE BAND MALICE MIZER.] I APOLOGIZE TO ALL THEIR FANS OUT THERE! HER CHARACTER WAS ORIGINALLY BASED ON MANA, BUT SHE LOOKS MORE LIKE MEGUMI MATSUMOTO! ← SHE'S MY TYPE. (UNFORTUNATELY, SHE QUIT THE ENTERTAINMENT BUSINESS. WHY, MEGUMI? ARE THERE ANY COLLECTIONS OF HER PINUP PHOTOS FOR SALE OUT THERE?) BY THE WAY, I KNOW THIS IS ANCIENT HISTORY, BUT THERE'S A MISTAKE IN ONE OF THE BEAUTY CONTEST SCENES IN BOOK FIVE. KADOMA MENTIONS HE LOOKS LIKE "ANJU SUZUKI," BUT THAT WAS SUPPOSED TO BE "AN SUZUKI!" THE PRINTING COMPANY DIDN'T KNOW ABOUT HER, SO THEY CHANGED IT WITHOUT PERMISSION. I'M SO SAD. ↑
HE DOESN'T LOOK LIKE ANJU SUZUKI. ANJU HAS A REALLY LONG FACE!

He was originally a gorgeous boy with black hair, not a girl with curly hair.

She played Ayumi Himekawa in the TV drama "Garasu no Kamen." She also played the lead's sister in "Seikonetora Eiji." I used to be a huge fan.

...THAT THE PAIR WHO WINS THE BEST COUPLE AWARD...

...WILL STAY TOGETHER...

...AND LIVE HAPPILY EVER AFTER.

97

WHOA...

THANK YOU. THAT WAS WONDERFUL!

WOW!

LOVELY!

BEAUTI-FUL!

YEAH... OUR RESIDENCE ADVISORS ARE ALL GREAT DANCERS.

WASN'T THAT AMAZING, KUJO?

AMAZ-ING, NANBA

But she stinks...

Wow!

CLAP CLAP

CLAP

100

ONE STEP BACK WITH YOUR RIGHT, THEN LEFT WITH YOUR LEFT...

TIME FOR THE REST OF YOU TO GIVE IT A TRY♡

It's okay...

WHAT?

SHOCK

...THEN MOVE YOUR RIGHT SO YOUR LEGS COME TO-GETHER!

1, 2, 3...

1, 2, 3...

Oh, I yeah... HEARD HE CAN ARRANGE FLOWERS WHILE HE DANCES.

HISASHI KAWACHI-MORI. HE'S RELATED TO A TOP KATANO-STYLE FLOWER ARRANGE-MENT MASTER.

THAT GUY'S NOT BAD.

Who is he?

He's got the moves

You're very good.

DANCE MASTER

...

THEY'RE OFF TO A PRETTY ROCKY START.

101

102

END OF HANA-KIMI CHAPTER 58

Hana-Kimi
For You in Full Blossom

CHAPTER
59

HUH? NO WAY!

YOU WANT ME TO PUT IT ON RIGHT NOW?

MUSIC "Yasuaki Shimizu"

I HAPPENED TO HEAR HIS MUSIC ON A TV COMMERCIAL, AND I TOTALLY GOT INTO IT. (I ALWAYS HAVE MY TV ON EVEN THOUGH I NEVER ACTUALLY WATCH IT.) HE'S A SAX PLAYER, AND I REALLY LIKE HIS RECORDINGS OF BACH'S "UNACCOMPANIED CELLO SUITES 1, 2, 3!" APPARENTLY, HE WAS THE FIRST ONE EVER TO RECORD THEM.) ← HE RECORDED THESE SONGS IN AN UNDER-GROUND QUARRY AND AN EMPTY CONCERT HALL! HE'S SO COOL! I ALSO LOVE LIS-TENING TO THE CELLO (ESPECIALLY YO YO MA), THE GUITAR (I LOVE GONTITI) AND THE VIOLIN. LISTENING TO THE SAX IS VERY SOOTHING, AND I REALLY ENJOY IT! WHENEVER I LISTEN TO SUITE 1, I IMAGINE THAT I'M FLOATING IN THE TRANQUIL DEPTHS OF THE SEA...

107

YOU'VE SEEN IT, HAVEN'T YOU?

HAIR-LESS?

HIS WHOLE BODY?

WAAH! YOU'RE SO EVIL!

Little liar.

BYOING

WHAT ARE YOU TALKING ABOUT? I BET YOUR WHOLE BODY IS COMPLETELY *HAIRLESS.*

...

HOW ABOUT THEY WEAR THE UNIFORMS NEXT TIME?

Ahem...

WHY DON'T WE CALL IT A DAY...

...SINCE IT SEEMS THE IDEA OF WEARING GIRLS' GYM OUTFITS HAS CAUGHT EVERYONE OFF GUARD.

Y...

YAY!

OKAY, I GUESS YOU'RE RIGHT.

I THINK THEY NEED TO GET USED TO THE IDEA.

Whispered Secrets "The Umeda Family"

YAY! PAPA AND MAMA UMEDA FINALLY MADE THEIR LONG-AWAITED FIRST APPEARANCES! [LAUGHS] SINCE MY FRIEND M INSISTED, I BASED PAPA UMEDA ON SUGIZO FROM THE BAND LUNASEA. M IS ACTUALLY THE ONE RIO'S CHARACTER WAS BASED ON. BUT I LATER REALIZED THAT PAPA UMEDA DOESN'T LOOK LIKE SUGIZO AT ALL. (HE ENDED UP LOOKING LIKE DR. UMEDA.) MAMA UMEDA WEARS A LOT OF CLOTHES FROM PINK HOUSE. THE CLOTHES THAT MIZUKI BORROWED FROM RIO IN BOOK TWO PROBABLY BELONGED TO MOM BEFORE. BY THE WAY, MANY READERS HAVE ASKED ME ABOUT UMEDA'S HAIR COLOR. ACTUALLY, HE HAS RED HAIR. IT'S KIND OF LIKE A MIX OF ORANGE AND BROWN. IO HAS BLACK HAIR, AND RIO HAS BROWN HAIR. MINAMI'S HAIR IS DARK BROWN.

The outdoor concert during the summer of '99 was awesome! (I saw the video.) I loved his violin. He's got cool skeleton designs on it.

109

HUH?

BUT...

HO HO HO HO HO

...THERE'S NO TELLING WHAT I MIGHT DO! IS THAT CLEAR, EVERYBODY?

IF I HEAR ANYONE COMPLAIN ABOUT WEARING GIRLS' OUTFITS AT OUR NEXT PRACTICE...

HUJJUSH

M-Miss Hibari's scary...

111

112

TA-DAH

IS THAT UMEDA'S BROTHER?

UH... W-WE'RE FRIENDS OF RIO'S, AND...

HIS... BROTHER?

HEY, AZUMA.

CLOP CLOP

HUH?

UH... UM...

CAN I HELP YOU?

SHOCK

KYA.

Huh?

DOES RIO HAVE A TWIN SISTER?

SHOCK

JUST HOW BIG *IS* THIS FAMILY?

CHOP CHOP CHOP

STOP TRYING TO SCARE RIO'S FRIENDS.

PLEASE, COME RIGHT IN ♡

THANK YOU.

I HAVEN'T THE SLIGHTEST IDEA.

Now I've seen every-thing...

MUMBLE

Hey!

WHAT'S THE DEAL WITH THESE PEOPLE, MIZUKI?

118

JUST GREETING YOUR GUESTS.

...they shouldn't be left alone.

D... Daddy?

I mean...

WHAT?!

Yiii!

—DADDY! WHAT'RE YOU DOING HERE?

GASP

WAIT... THAT MEANS THEY'RE UMEDA'S PARENTS...

Right?

MUMBLE

MY GOD... HE'S RIGHT!

I'M RIO'S MOTHER ♡

Age 51 →

I'M RIO'S FATHER.

SORRY IF HE FREAKED YOU GUYS OUT. THIS IS...

Age 54 →

HEH

SHOCK

PLEASED TO MEET YOU...

GOOD GRIEF...

SO THAT MEANS THEY'RE ALSO NANBA'S GRANDPARENTS...

Right?

OKAY, NOW...

HEH

HOKUTO.

HA HA HA HA

THEIR LOVE CHILD

BELIEVE IT OR NOT, UMEDA WAS THEIR BABY BOY!

The mysteries of DNA...

FEH!

But...we'd like to get to know your friends better.

TIME FOR YOU TWO TO GO.

FWUSH

GLARE

TOUGH AS HER BROTHER AND SISTER...

Wow!

NO, I'M NOT!

Me neither. I couldn't bear it.

ARE YOU IN A REBELLIOUS PHASE AGAIN?

SHIVER

120

BLUSH

Remembers →
yesterday.

Can't
look at
him...

OKAY,
LET'S GET
STARTED.

GOD,
I'M SO
EMBARRASSED!
I CAN'T
BELIEVE I'M
WEARING
THIS!

1, 2, 3...

1, 2, 3...

1, 2...

STEP!

OKAY.

RIO! WOULD YOU MIND DANCING WITH THESE GUYS OVER HERE?

ALL RIGHT.

I Dunno... HEARD THEY'RE SORTA RELATED, BUT...

WHY'S HE CALLING HER BY HER FIRST NAME?

I'M NOT LYING.

HE'S TERRIBLE!

RUMBLE

TUMBLE

GLARE

KYAAA!

Won't give up...!

YOU'RE NEXT, SANO!

Idiot! ALL YOU DID WAS MAKE YOUR PARTNER DIZZY.

Whatta you mean?

I'M A PRO!

TWIRL

125

I'M KANNA AMAGASAKI.

Ah...

THANK YOU.

UM...

HERE.

PHEW... I'M WIPED OUT...

KANNA, EH? SEEMS LIKE A SWEET GIRL.

SMILE

THANKS, KANNA.

YOU'RE WELCOME.

My pleasure.

Like me?

SO... YOU'RE A SOPHOMORE?

WE'RE ON THE STUDENT COUNCIL, AND THE NUMBER OF LINES TELLS WHAT GRADE WE'RE IN.

...YOU AND MISS HANAYASHIKI WEAR RIBBONS WITH LINES. WHY IS THAT?

UH... I WAS WONDERING...

YES?

YEAH.

130

WARM AND FUZZY

SHE MAKES ME FEEL SO RELAXED...

HEY!

G A S P !

AGH!

MUMBLE

WHAT'RE YOU DOING HITTING ON MY GIRLFRIEND?

YOU SAID... SHE'S YOUR GIRLFRIEND!?

Wait...

DID I, NOW?

YOU STARTLED ME, KUJO!

SO...

I'M NOT TELLING.

Geez...

...SEEMS IT'S ALL WORKING OUT AS I EXPECTED.

Ho ho ho ho

HA HA HA

WILL WE HAVE TO WEAR DRESSES ON THE BIG DAY?

NOW THESE GUYS SHOW UP AND...

OF COURSE WE WILL!

WE'RE GIRLS, Y'KNOW!

...I'M SUPPOSED TO COMPETE WITH THEM TOO?

YOU BOYS ARE NOT GETTING IN MY WAY!

END OF HANA-KIMI CHAPTER 59

It's December..

Hey! We gotta get set decorations!

The Christmas dance party is coming up fast...

We'll walk you to the station.

Thanks for coming, girls.

You're welcome.

ACTIVITY ROOM

CLOP CLOP CLOP CLOP CLOP

...And students from both schools have been busy with dance practice and stuff (like finding perfect partners).

Sorry!

Hey, wardrobe guys! Don't drop needles on the floor!

Ack! We're over budget!

OSAKA PRIVATE HIGH SCHOOL

SIGH...

Everybody looks so happy.

Can we use the other room?

MUSIC "Bulgarian Voice"

I FINALLY GOT IT! I'M SO EXCITED! I WANT TO THANK ALL THE FANS WHO SENT IN TAPES AND CDS. I SWEAR I'D LOOKED ALL OVER THE PLACE, AND STILL COULDN'T FIND IT. I WAS GETTING REALLY DESPERATE. I WAS SO MOVED BY YOUR KINDNESS. SNIFF. PLEASE LET ME TAKE THIS OPPORTUNITY TO THANK YOU ALL AGAIN. ACCORDING TO THE INFO THAT PEOPLE SENT IN, "BULGARIAN VOICE" IS A CHORUS GROUP THAT PERFORMS BULGARIAN FOLK SONGS, AND THE MEMBERS ARE ALL AMATEUR MUSICIANS. (SOME OF THEM ARE FARMERS' WIVES WHO'VE WON NATIONAL CONTESTS.) THEY NEED AT LEAST THREE PEOPLE TO PERFORM THE SONGS PROPERLY, AND THEY'RE NOT ALLOWED TO PERFORM UNLESS THEY'RE WITH A CONDUCTOR OR A GROUP THAT'S APPROVED BY THE COUNTRY. THEY'RE A REALLY PRESTIGIOUS CHORAL GROUP. WHOA. I HEARD THEY EVEN INFLUENCED "GEINO YAMASHIROGUMI."

By the way, ever since I mentioned I was looking for the opening song for "Hiei," you guys have sent in lots of tapes and LPs (Whoa). Thank you so much! I listen to them in my office. ❤

137

I'D LOVE TO DANCE WITH SANO.

JUST ONE DANCE WITH HIM...

...AND I'D FINALLY FEEL LIKE A GIRL AGAIN.

JUST FOR ONE MOMENT...

...I'D LIKE TO BE IN HIS ARMS...

...AND BE MYSELF AGAIN.

IS THAT TOO MUCH TO ASK?

Guess so...

ALMOST EVERYBODY'S GOT A PARTNER EXCEPT ME!

I'm so jealous!

HUH? BUT WHAT ABOUT MINAMI?

SIGH

FWUMP

Hi, Rio.

Hi.

"Ah...

SIGH...

Ha ha ha...

DON'T BE SO PICKY, RIO!

THERE'S NO WAY I'M DANCING WITH MY NEPHEW, OKAY?

145

YAHOO! I GET TO BE MIZUKI'S PARTNER!

MY PATENTED "LAST MINUTE AMBUSH" STRATEGY IS A SUCCESS!

ARE YOU SURE YOU'RE READY TO LEAD, NAKATSU?

You made your last partner dizzy!

I'VE GOT EVERY- THING UNDER CONTROL!

Missed his chance

Grr

...

SNAP

T HU D

Kansai tempo

SEE WHAT I MEAN?

ONE, TWO, THREE!

ONE, TWO, THREE!

YAAH!

After all that practice, he'd better be.

HE AND ASHIYA MAKE A GOOD PAIR.

WELL, HE'S NOT PERFECT, BUT HE'S NOT BAD EITHER.

FW OOSH

I NEVER MAKE THE SAME MISTAKE TWICE!

147

THAT TAKES CARE OF NAKATSU AND ASHIYA.

Okay.

NEXT.

...NOPE, NO ONE ELSE.

NAKAO.

Wah!

I WANNA DANCE WITH YOU ♡

GUESS THAT'S HOW IT IS...

Back at Saint Blossom.

WELL... UMM...I'M FLATTERED, BUT I'M AFRAID I'M ALREADY SPOKEN FOR.

WHAT? SHOCK

Whispered Secrets "Cosplay"

I GOT A BUNCH OF PICTURES FROM FANS DOING HANA-KIMI COSPLAY! THEY MADE ME SO HAPPY! APPARENTLY, THE FANS DRESSED UP AT SCHOOL FESTIVALS AND COMIC CONVENTIONS. THANK YOU. EVERYBODY WORKED SO HARD ON THEIR COSTUMES, AND THEY ALL LOOKED SO GOOD. ONE GIRL, WHO LOOKS LIKE HYDE, DRESSED AS MINAMI, AND SOME PEOPLE EVEN USED THEIR CHARACTERS' IMAGE FLOWERS. I WAS SO TOUCHED! ONE READER WROTE SAYING, "I DIDN'T GET TO TAKE PICTURES, BUT I SAW PEOPLE DOING HIMEJIMA & HIBARI COSPLAY!" AND ANOTHER READER WROTE "I SAW SOMEBODY DOING UMEDA COSPLAY!" (I'D LOVE TO SEE THEM!) SEEMS LIKE HANA-KIMI COSPLAY IS KIND OF POPULAR OUT THERE. ONE BOY WROTE TO ME SAYING, "MY SISTER DRESSES UP IN UMEDA COSPLAY, AND SHE GETS A LOT OF ATTENTION." PLEASE SEND ME HER PICTURE!

151

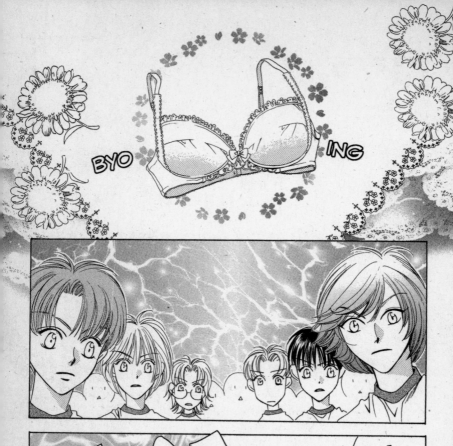

BYO—ING

WHAT...
WHAT...

WHA—

WHA—

...THE HECK IS THAT THING?

SPEECHLESS

I PICKED BRAS WITH A SIMPLE DESIGN SINCE YOU'LL BE WEARING THEM UNDER YOUR DRESSES.

I HAD MY GIRLS MEASURE YOUR BUST SIZES, SO THEY SHOULD FIT EACH OF YOU PERFECTLY.

157

158

160

THAT'S MY BEST FRIEND WOULD TELL ME ANYWAY.

BELIEVE ME, IF YOU ONLY FOCUS ON YOUR NEGATIVE QUALITIES, YOU'LL NEVER GET ANYWHERE.

But... YOU CAN'T LET YOURSELF GET SUCKED INTO SELF-HATRED!

I REALLY KNOW HOW YOU FEEL, KANNA!

WHEN I WAS GROWING UP IN THE STATES, KIDS ALWAYS MADE FUN OF MY FLAT FACE.

IT GAVE ME A TERRIBLE COMPLEX FOR YEARS.

MAYBE YOU'RE RIGHT! I CAN'T KEEP BEATING MYSELF UP LIKE THIS.

I'm gonna make him want me!

HUH?

THAT'S THE SPIRIT!

SLAP

THE GUYS FROM MY GROUP ARE ALL CRAZY ABOUT YOU. EVERYBODY SAYS YOU'RE SO SWEET!

EVERY-BODY'S SPECIAL IN THEIR OWN WAY.

You're wonderful, Kanna ♡

I heard 'em.

Heh heh

OH...

Are you okay?

T H U D

YAAH!

T-THAT NASTY LITTLE~!

Hee hee

...DON'T LET YOUR-SELF SPACE OUT DURING PRACTICE...

...OR YOU MIGHT GET HURT!

END OF HANA-KIMI CHAPTER 60

Hana-Kimi

For You in Full Blossom

CHAPTER 61

MERRY
CHRISTMAS!

....
....
....
....
....
....

WHAT...
A...
BITCH!

YAAH!

Hee
hee
hee

GRAA

RR RH

DON'T
LET
YOURSELF
SPACE OUT
DURING
PRACTICE OR
YOU MIGHT
GET HURT!

SHE
TOTALLY
DID
THAT ON
PURPOSE!

ARR...

My Exercise Equipment Collection Relaxation products, that is.

PORTABLE MASSAGE MACHINE— THIS WAS THE MOST EXPENSIVE ONE.

LOW FREQUENCY PAD (FOR NECK, SHOULDERS, LOWER BACK AND THIGHS)

SQUEEK
SQUEEK

LOW FREQUENCY ADJUSTER.

IT ROLLS UP AND DOWN YOUR BODY.

AIR WALKER— SINCE I DON'T GET ENOUGH EXERCISE.

DA-DUM DA-DUM
DA-DUM

L SHAPED SHOULDER MASSAGER—

Work can be murder on the body.

BLAST IT! THAT STUPID LITTLE—!

GRR

SLAP

WHAT DID I EVER DO TO HER?

ACTIVITY ROOM

SOMETHING WRONG, NAKAO?

...WHAT'S GOING ON?

UH...

NO UNAUTHORIZED ADMITTANCE

Eats when he's stressed out

PAUSE

CHOMP CHOMP CHOMP

Hi, Ashiya.

Ah...

HEY, GUYS!

SURE... SURE...!

YOICKS! WHAT'D I START?

SOMETHING WRONG?! JUST LISTEN TO THIS!

JURI KISHINOSATO, THAT'S WHO!

UH... WHO IS THIS "BITCH"?

THAT BITCH!

SHE KEPT CRITICIZING MY DANCE TECHNIQUE RIGHT IN FRONT OF MINAMI. SHE WAS ALL, "LOOK AT YOU! YOU'VE GOT THE STEPS ALL WRONG. CAN'T YOU DO ANYTHING RIGHT?" JUST IMAGINING HER DANCING WITH MINAMI MAKES ME SICK!

Stay out of range...

You bet...

Crumbs →

KADOMA, SHE WAS PICKING ON YOU LAST WEEK, WASN'T SHE?

YOU SHOULD GO TELL HER OFF!

!!

SHOCK

SMACK

HUH?

I WAS STANDING RIGHT THERE. I SAW THE WHOLE THING.

WHAT? SHE WAS PICKING ON KADOMA?

Whispered Secrets "Ballroom dancing"

WHILE I WAS WORKING ON THE DANCE PARTY EPISODE, I WAS LUCKY ENOUGH TO SEE CELEBRITIES BALLROOM DANCING ON THE COMEDY SHOW "URI NARI." I WATCHED IT RELIGIOUSLY SO I COULD LEARN ALL THE STEPS AND MOVES. THEN I STARTED THINKING "HEY, THE BROTHER CHARACTER (PLAYED BY AYA SUGIMOTO) IS JUST LIKE IO." [LAUGHS] (DON'T YOU THINK SO? I MEAN, THEY BOTH ACT SO TOUGH ALL THE TIME...) I ALSO LIKE THE CHARACTER KOME-CHAN. WHEN DANCING IN REAL LIFE, IT'S NOT EXACTLY A GOOD IDEA FOR PAIRS TO HAVE SUCH A VAST DIFFERENCE IN HEIGHT. FOR EXAMPLE, PAIRS LIKE SANO & IO AND KUJO & KADOMA WOULD BE TOUGH, BUT I'VE COMPLETELY IGNORED THAT FACT IN THIS MANGA. SEE YOU ALL IN BOOK 12. ♥

HISAYA NAKAJO, FEBRUARY 2002

...I'M NOT GIVING UP! NO MATTER WHAT!

UNTIL I EARN ENOUGH FOR SANO'S PRESENT...

THAT'S RIGHT!

MORNING!

Works in medical center two.

I HAVE SOME BUSINESS AT THE MAIN MEDICAL CENTER.

Yeah...

You scared me!

AH... UMEDA!

I'VE NEVER SEEN YOU IN THE MAIN BUILDING BEFORE.

175

THEY'LL FORM A PACK, THEN GANG UP ON ONE PERSON. THE WORST PART IS THEY DON'T EVEN FEEL "GUILTY" ABOUT IT.

WOMEN ARE SCARY.

It's so sick.

Win or lose, I just...

...don't like it.

YOU SAY BEING PICKED ON BY JUST ONE GIRL IS NO BIG DEAL?

WE'RE READY TO FIGHT BACK AND ALL, BUT...

Maybe we are...

Sigh

DEPOSIT EMPTY CANS IN TRASH.

SO...

...THIS GIRL'S PICKING ON YOU, EH?

WHY DON'T YOU JUST LET IT GO?

IT DOESN'T SOUND LIKE SHE'S DONE ANYTHING THAT BAD. MAYBE YOU'RE MAKING TOO BIG A DEAL OUT OF IT.

Oh well...

Yeah.

I CAN SEE WHY THEY MIGHT GO A LITTLE HAYWIRE.

I BET THOSE SAINT BLOSSOM GIRLS ARE OBSESSED WITH BECOMING QUEEN. THAT'S A LOT OF PRESSURE.

176

181

187

190

GASP

Phew!

I TOTALLY FREAKED OUT.

...

SQUEEK
SQUEEK
SQUEEK
SQUEEK

Th...

THANKS!

I'D BETTER HIT THE SACK. GOOD NIGHT!

CHOP
CHOP
CHOP

SLIDE

...!

THAT DRESS LOOKS NICE ON YOU.

I-I just remembered.

BLUSH

OH MY GOD! SANO LOOKS SOOO GORGEOUS!

HEY!

FWOOSH

OLP!

MIZUKI! YOU LOOK SO CUTE!

I SURE HOPE THEY DO!

HA HA...

You shoulda stuck with cute!

Sano smacked him.

EVEN YOUR BOOBS LOOK REAL.

YOU REALLY DO LOOK GREAT IN THAT DRESS.

!

YOU LOOK GREAT TOO, NAKATSU!

...?!

END OF HANA-KIMI CHAPTER 61

LOVE SHOJO? LET US KNOW!

☐ Please do NOT send me information about VIZ Media products, news and events, special offers, or other information.

☐ Please do NOT send me information from VIZ' trusted business partners.

Name: _____

Address: _____

City: _____ **State:** _____ **Zip:** _____

E-mail: _____

☐ **Male** ☐ **Female** **Date of Birth** (mm/dd/yyyy): ___ / ___ / ___ (**Under 13? Parental consent required**)

What race/ethnicity do you consider yourself? (check all that apply)

☐ White/Caucasian ☐ Black/African American ☐ Hispanic/Latino

☐ Asian/Pacific Islander ☐ Native American/Alaskan Native ☐ Other: _____

What VIZ shojo title(s) did you purchase? (indicate title(s) purchased)

_____

What other shojo titles from other publishers do you own? _____

_____

Reason for purchase: (check all that apply)

☐ Special offer ☐ Favorite title / author / artist / genre

☐ Gift ☐ Recommendation ☐ Collection

☐ Read excerpt in VIZ manga sampler ☐ Other _____

Where did you make your purchase? (please check one)

☐ Comic store ☐ Bookstore ☐ Mass/Grocery Store

☐ Newsstand ☐ Video/Video Game Store

☐ Online (site:_____) ☐ Other _____

How many shojo titles have you purch... (please check one from each column)

SHOJO MANGA
- [ ] None
- [ ] 1 – 4
- [ ] 5 – 10
- [ ] 11+

VIZ...
- [ ]
- [ ]
- [ ] 5 – 10
- [ ] 11+

What do you like most about shojo graphic novels? (check all that apply)

- [ ] Romance
- [ ] Comedy
- [ ] Other _____

- [ ] Drama / conflict
- [ ] Real-life storylines

- [ ] Fantasy
- [ ] Relatable characters

Do you purchase every volume of your favorite shojo series?

- [ ] Yes! Gotta have 'em as my own
- [ ] No. Please explain: _____

Who are your favorite shojo authors / artists? _____

_____

What shojo titles would like you translated and sold in English? _____

_____

THANK YOU! Please send the completed form

VIZ **MEDIA**

NJW Research
ATTN: VIZ Media Shojo Survey
42 Catharine Street
Poughkeepsie, NY 12601